SOCIAL PROBLEMS
and the quality of life

reviewer acknowledgments

David Nickell
West Kentucky Community & Technical College

Dennis D. Engbrecht
Bethel College

Franklin (Buddy) Renahan
Faulkner University

Shawna Huggins
University of Idaho

Bethaney Ferguson
Cape Fear Community College

Kimberly Lancaster
Coastal Carolina Community College

Tami Dale
South Dakota State University

SOCIAL PROBLEMS
and the quality of life

Fourteenth Edition

Robert H. Lauer
Alliant International University

Jeanette C. Lauer
Alliant International University

Mc
Graw
Hill
Education

To Jon, Kathy, Julie, Donna, Jeffrey, Kate, Jeff, Nina, Krista, Benjamin, David, John Robert, and Addie

". . . the greatest of these is love."

SOCIAL PROBLEMS AND THE QUALITY OF LIFE, FOURTEENTH EDITION

Published by McGraw-Hill Education, 2 Penn Plaza, New York, NY 10121. Copyright © 2019 by McGraw-Hill Education. All rights reserved. Printed in the United States of America. Previous editions © 2014, 2011, and 2008. No part of this publication may be reproduced or distributed in any form or by any means, or stored in a database or retrieval system, without the prior written consent of McGraw-Hill Education, including, but not limited to, in any network or other electronic storage or transmission, or broadcast for distance learning.

Some ancillaries, including electronic and print components, may not be available to customers outside the United States.

This book is printed on acid-free paper.

1 2 3 4 5 6 7 8 9 LWI 21 20 19 18

ISBN 978-1-259-91430-0
MHID 1-259-91430-5

Portfolio Manager: *Jamie Laferrera*
Product Developer: *Alexander Preiss*
Marketing Manager: *Kaitlyn Lombardo*
Content Project Manager: *Maria McGreal*
Buyer: *Laura Fuller*
Design: *MPS Limited*
Content Licensing Specialist: *Melisa Seegmiller*
Cover Image: *@McGraw-Hill Education*
Compositor: *MPS Limited*

All credits appearing on page or at the end of the book are considered to be an extension of the copyright page.

Library of Congress Cataloging-in-Publication Data

Lauer, Robert H., author.
    Social problems and the quality of life / Robert H. Lauer, Alliant International University, Jeanette
        C. Lauer, Alliant International University.
    Fourteenth Edition. | New York : McGraw-Hill Education, [2018]
    LCCN 2017047912| ISBN 9781259914300 (acid-free paper) | ISBN 1259914305 (acid-free paper)
    LCSH: United States—Social conditions. | Quality of life—United States. | Social problems—United States.
    LCC HN57 .L39 2018 | DDC 306.0973—dc23 LC record available at https://lccn.loc.gov/2017047912

The Internet addresses listed in the text were accurate at the time of publication. The inclusion of a website does not indicate an endorsement by the authors or McGraw-Hill Education, and McGraw-Hill Education does not guarantee the accuracy of the information presented at these sites.

mheducation.com/highered

brief contents

contents

©Purestock/Getty Images

PART **3** **Problems of Inequality 159**

©Plush Studios/Blend Images LLC

©Photodisc Collection/Getty Images

PART 5 Global Social Problems 415

14 War and Terrorism 416

15 The Environment 448

©Steve Allen/Brand X
Pictures

list of figures

list of tables

People everywhere want to maximize the quality of their lives. There is widespread agreement that a high quality of life requires such things as a good education, freedom from fear of crime, good housing, meaningful work, and good health. A high quality of life, then, can only be attained if people deal with the social problems that detract from that quality. As we point out in the first chapter of this text, a social problem is, by definition, a condition or pattern of behavior that is incompatible with people's desired quality of life.

To deal with a problem, you must understand it—how it affects one's quality of life, what causes it, what tends to maintain it. Sociologists have used three theoretical perspectives to answer these questions in order to analyze and deal with social problems. We discuss the three major perspectives in Chapter 1 and show how we use elements from each to analyze individual problems and talk about how the problem can be attacked.

We do not mean to give the impression here that either understanding a problem or attacking it is a simple matter. Even experts disagree on such things. The factors that combine to cause and perpetuate any particular problem are many and complex. We have seen students feel overwhelmed as they study these factors. As one said: "I don't see how society can ever deal with some of these problems. The more I understand about what causes them, the more hopeless I feel."

It is interesting to note, therefore, that some problems are less serious than they were when this book was in its first edition. Among other things, poverty among the aged has declined, many crime rates have dropped, divorce rates have declined, the cold war and the accompanying arms race between the superpowers have come to an end, and air and water pollution levels have decreased significantly. Other problems, however, are still as serious—or even more so. For instance, addictions continue to ruin lives and traumatize families; domestic and international terrorism are of the highest concern to citizens and the government; war remains a vexing problem; white-collar crime is more widespread and more of a threat to the economy than previously recognized; health problems afflict great numbers of people, many of whom have no health insurance; racial minorities have lost some of the gains made in previous years; poverty has increased among some groups; increasing numbers of single parents mean increasing problems for children; equitable opportunities remain elusive for homosexuals; and the threats posed by such things as global warming and toxic wastes are more serious than previously thought. These advances and setbacks are all discussed in the text.

Changes in the Fourteenth Edition

A social problem is a product of social definition. That is, something becomes a problem, and becomes a more or less serious problem, as it is so defined by the people of a society. People's definitions of problems and the problems themselves continually change.

Each new edition of a social problems text, therefore, strives to capture the current status of an ever-changing phenomenon. To achieve this goal, we have updated all materials in this edition with hundreds of new references as well as the most recent data available from the government and other sources.

There are changing concerns among the public as well as changing emphases among researchers. To reflect current interests and concerns more adequately, we have included new or expanded materials on such topics as e-cigarettes, the misuse of opioids, the difference between decriminalization and legalization of prostitution, the issue of transgender rights, efforts to keep minorities from voting, the Tea Party in politics, bullying in schools, the debt incurred in getting a college education, how technological change affects health, the use of torture and drones by the military, and the Flint, Michigan, drinking water crisis.

Organization

We have divided the book into 5 parts and 15 chapters. Part 1 introduces students to social problems. Chapter 1 discusses the various tools needed, including the difference between social problems and personal problems, sociological theories and methods, and fallacious ways of thinking.

In Part 2, we look at a cluster of problems that involve behavior that deviates from social norms. Chapters 2 through 5 cover the problems of alcohol and other drugs, crime and delinquency, violence (including rape), and sexual deviance (prostitution and pornography).

Part 3 examines problems that involve social inequality. Poverty (Chapter 6) is inequality in income and wealth. Gender and sexual orientation comprise another area of inequality (Chapter 7), as women and homosexuals strive to gain equal rights. Racial and ethnic inequality (Chapter 8) include the multiple ways in which there is disparity in valued things between the various racial and ethnic groups in the nation.

Part 4 focuses on problems of social institutions. Chapters 9 through 13 cover the institutions of government and politics, work and the economy, education, family, and health care. These institutions are factors in other kinds of social problems but are also problematic in themselves.

Finally, Part 5 covers two global social problems: war and terrorism (Chapter 14) and the environment (Chapter 15). These problems pose a threat to civilization itself and cannot be understood apart from their global context.

Learning Aids

We use a variety of learning aids to facilitate understanding of the materials:

- Chapter-opening vignettes personalize the various problems. They make each problem not just a set of facts, but a social reality that disrupts and diminishes the quality of people's lives in concrete, understandable ways.
- Chapter objectives and marginal key terms keep students on track as they work through the chapters.
- Global Comparison boxes add dimension to students' understanding of social problems by seeing how they work out in another nation or nations.

- Dealing with the problems is as important as knowing what causes them. Each chapter, therefore, contains a section, called Public Policy and Private Action, that suggests ways to ameliorate each problem. We have found that most students are like the one quoted near the beginning of this preface—they don't simply want to know about problems; they also want to know what can be done to address those problems. We do not claim that the suggestions will eliminate the problems. But they do demonstrate that problems have solutions, and the solutions are always, to some extent, up to each individual.

- Marginal icons identify places in the text where we show how people use the fallacies of thinking discussed in Chapter 1 to draw erroneous conclusions about social problems.

- End-of-chapter summaries, key terms lists, study questions, and Internet resources and exercises provide students with ample review, study materials, and self-learning projects.

Supplements Package

As a full-service publisher of quality educational products, McGraw-Hill does much more than sell textbooks. The company creates and publishes an extensive array of print, video, and digital supplements for students and instructors. This edition of *Social Problems* is accompanied by an extensive, comprehensive supplements package.

For the Student

- McGraw-Hill Connect™ provides students with an eBook, personalized study path, and assignments that help them conceptualize what they learn through application and critical thinking. Access this title at www.mheducation.com /connect.

For the Instructor

The fourteenth edition of *Social Problems and the Quality of Life* is now available online with Connect, McGraw-Hill Education's integrated assignment and assessment platform. Connect also offers SmartBook for the new edition, which is the first adaptive reading experience proven to improve grades and help students study more effectively. All of the title's website and ancillary content is also available through Connect, including:

- Instructor's Manual/Testbank—chapter outlines, key terms, overviews, lecture notes, discussion questions, a complete testbank, and more.

- PowerPoint Slides—complete, chapter-by-chapter slide shows featuring text, tables, and visuals.

- Create—a unique database publishing system that allows instructors to create their own custom text from material in *Social Problems* or elsewhere and deliver that text to students electronically as an e-book or in print format via the bookstore.

Acknowledgments

Many people are important in producing a book. The staff at McGraw-Hill Publishers have been most helpful and supportive. Time and again, we have been impressed with the quality of work done by the various editors with whom we have worked. We appreciate each of them, and particularly Alexander Preiss, who worked with us on this latest edition. We would also like to thank the academic reviewers who are listed facing the title page; their suggestions have, we believe, enhanced this book.

Robert H. Lauer

Jeanette C. Lauer

connect®

McGraw-Hill Connect® is a highly reliable, easy-to-use homework and learning management solution that utilizes learning science and award-winning adaptive tools to improve student results.

Homework and Adaptive Learning

- Connect's assignments help students contextualize what they've learned through application, so they can better understand the material and think critically.
- Connect will create a personalized study path customized to individual student needs through SmartBook®.
- SmartBook helps students study more efficiently by delivering an interactive reading experience through adaptive highlighting and review.

Over **7 billion questions** have been answered, making McGraw-Hill Education products more intelligent, reliable, and precise.

Connect's Impact on Retention Rates, Pass Rates, and Average Exam Scores

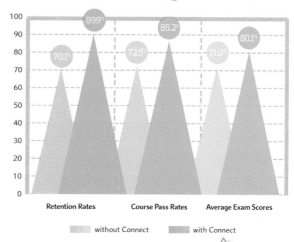

without Connect   with Connect

Using **Connect** improves retention rates by **19.8** percentage points, passing rates by **12.7** percentage points, and exam scores by **9.1** percentage points.

73% of instructors who use **Connect** require it; instructor satisfaction **increases** by 28% when **Connect** is required.

Quality Content and Learning Resources

- Connect content is authored by the world's best subject matter experts, and is available to your class through a simple and intuitive interface.
- The Connect eBook makes it easy for students to access their reading material on smartphones and tablets. They can study on the go and don't need internet access to use the eBook as a reference, with full functionality.
- Multimedia content such as videos, simulations, and games drive student engagement and critical thinking skills.

Robust Analytics and Reporting

- Connect Insight® generates easy-to-read reports on individual students, the class as a whole, and on specific assignments.

- The Connect Insight dashboard delivers data on performance, study behavior, and effort. Instructors can quickly identify students who struggle and focus on material that the class has yet to master.

- Connect automatically grades assignments and quizzes, providing easy-to-read reports on individual and class performance.

©Hero Images/Getty Images

Impact on Final Course Grade Distribution

without Connect		with Connect
22.9%	A	31.0%
27.4%	B	34.3%
22.9%	C	18.7%
11.5%	D	6.1%
15.4%	F	9.9%

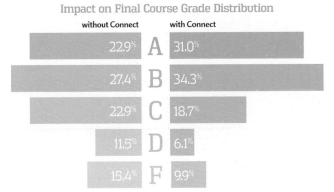

More students earn **As** and **Bs** when they use **Connect**.

Trusted Service and Support

- Connect integrates with your LMS to provide single sign-on and automatic syncing of grades. Integration with Blackboard®, D2L®, and Canvas also provides automatic syncing of the course calendar and assignment-level linking.

- Connect offers comprehensive service, support, and training throughout every phase of your implementation.

- If you're looking for some guidance on how to use Connect, or want to learn tips and tricks from super users, you can find tutorials as you work. Our Digital Faculty Consultants and Student Ambassadors offer insight into how to achieve the results you want with Connect.

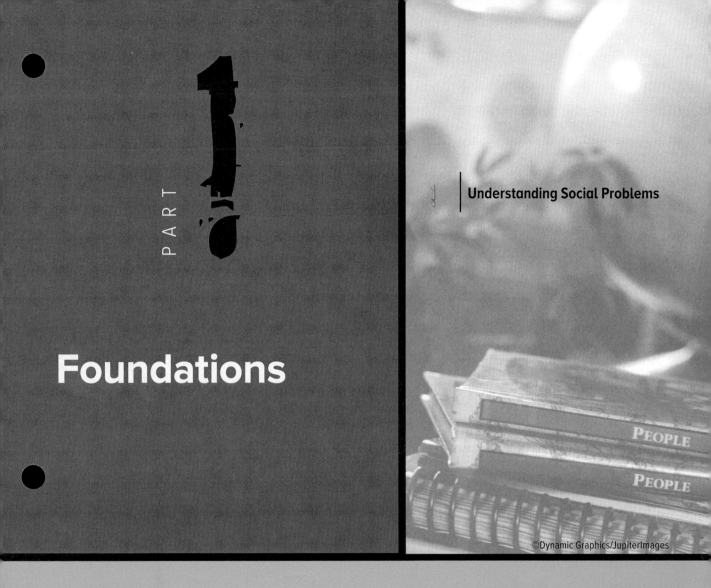

Foundations

Understanding Social Problems

A Chinese philosopher remarked that one should not attempt to open clams with a crowbar. In other words, any task demands the proper tools. Part 1 of this book is about the proper tools for the study of social problems. What kind of perspective should you bring to the study? What kind of information do you need, and what are the proper ways to gather it? Unless you answer such questions appropriately, you cannot answer the vexing question of how to deal with social problems. This part, then, prepares you to delve into particular problems. It shows you how to use the proper tools to open the "clams."

CHAPTER

Understanding
Social Problems

OBJECTIVES

1 Explain the difference between personal and social problems.

2 Understand the model used to explain social problems.

3 Discuss the fallacies of thinking, including how they have been used to explain social problems.

4 Explain the meaning of social research.

5 Give examples of different kinds of social research and describe how they have been used to study social problems.

©Beathan/Corbis

"Why Is It My Fault?"

Marie, her husband Jim, and their two children had a good life until he lost his job. Stress built up, their marriage fell apart, and he moved to another state. Marie's life has never been the same:

I've never gotten any financial help from Jim since we were divorced. I went to work. It was really hard, raising two kids by myself and working full-time. But we were making it. And I enjoyed working—having people tell me I was doing a good job. Then the company downsized and I was laid off. It's been awful since then.

For the first time in my life, I know what it's like to be poor. I know what it's like to try to get help from the government. And you know one of the worst things? It's feeling ashamed. It's feeling like for some reason it's my fault, like there's something I could have done to avoid it. Why is this my fault? I keep telling myself I shouldn't feel that way, but I can't help it.

Introduction

Who is at fault if you are poor? Are you responsible because you are lazy and unwilling to work or because you are a spendthrift and refuse to properly manage your finances? If so, you have a personal problem. Or are there other factors such as the state of the economy that are responsible for your situation? If so, you are caught up in a social problem. Later in this chapter we define social problems precisely. As a preliminary definition, however, think of social problems as behaviors or conditions that are caused by factors external to individuals and that detract from the quality of life.

Actually, "we are all part of some social problem" (Lopata 1984:249). In fact, we are all part of the biggest social problem of all—the race to save the planet (Brown 2000). These assertions will become increasingly clear in subsequent chapters. In addition, many individuals are wrestling with several problems at once. For example, the stress of poverty may lead to health problems, both mental and physical. If the impoverished individual is a woman or a minority, the stress may be intensified. The individual also may have to deal with unemployment or underemployment, poor performance at school by a child, and the threat of victimization by criminals. Indeed, social workers deal with families who are coping simultaneously with the majority of problems discussed in this book.

But what exactly is a social problem? How do sociologists decide what is or isn't a social problem? And once you identify something as a social problem, how do you go about analyzing it so that you can understand it? The first part of this chapter answers these questions. We begin by looking at the difference between personal problems and social problems because Americans tend to make all problems personal. That is, they believe that the problem is in some way *the fault of the individual who is struggling with it.* As you shall see, however, to say that a problem is social means that its causes, its consequences, and the way to deal with it all involve the social structure in which individuals live.

Social scientists do not arbitrarily decide which problems are social. Rather, they focus on those conditions that arise from contradictions in the society and that diminish people's quality of life. There is considerable consensus throughout the world on the kinds of things important to the quality of life, so the same kinds of problems tend to be identified in all societies.

Once a problem is identified, because large numbers of people agree that it detracts from their quality of life, we analyze and understand it by looking at the numerous social factors involved in creating and maintaining the problem. Only then can we realistically discuss ways to address the problem. The model we provide later in this chapter shows the kinds of factors that sociologists have found to be important.

Finally, we discuss two important tools of analysis for social problems—critical thinking skills and methods of research. These tools enable us to get valid information about the social factors involved in the problems—information that is crucial to making a realistic and useful analysis from which we can deduce effective ways to address the problem.

personal problem
a problem that can be explained in terms of the qualities of the individual

social problem
a condition or pattern of behavior that contradicts some other condition or pattern of behavior; is defined as incompatible with the desired quality of life; is caused, facilitated, or prolonged by social factors; involves intergroup conflict; and requires social action for resolution

Personal versus Social Problems

We define a **personal problem** as one whose causes and solutions lie within the individual and his or her immediate environment. A **social problem,** on the other hand, is one whose causes and solutions lie outside the individual and the immediate environment. This distinction is not based on the individual's experience of suffering because a certain amount of suffering may occur in either case.

C. Wright Mills (1959:8-9) made a similar distinction, calling personal problems the "personal troubles of milieu" and social problems the "public issues of social structure." He offered many illustrations of the difference between the two. If one individual in a city is unemployed, that individual has a personal trouble. The person may have personality problems, may lack skills, or may have family difficulties that consume all of his or her energy. But if there are 100 million jobs in a society and 150 million people are available for work, this is a public issue. Even without personal problems, a third of the people will be unemployed. Such a problem cannot be resolved solely by dealing with individual personalities or motivations.

Similarly, a man and woman may have personal troubles in their marriage. They may agonize over their troubles and ultimately separate or divorce. If theirs is one of few marriages that experience such problems, you may conclude that they have personal problems and their marriage broke up because of some flaw in their personalities or in their relationship. But when the divorce rate soars and millions of families are broken up, you must look for causes and solutions beyond the personalities of individuals. The question is no longer "What is wrong with those people?" but "What has happened to the **institution** of marriage and the family in our society?"

Whether you define a problem as social or as personal is crucial. The distinction determines how you perceive the causes of the problem, the consequences of the problem, and *appropriate ways* to cope with the problem.

institution
a collective pattern of dealing with a basic social function; typical institutions identified by sociologists are the government, economy, education, family and marriage, religion, and the media

The Causes of Problems

When asked why there is poverty in affluent America, a 31-year-old female bank teller said the poor themselves are to blame because most of them "are lazy and unreliable . . . and the little money they do make is spent on liquor and nonnecessities rather than for their economic advancement." This is a common approach, namely, that problems are personal. *The victim is blamed as both the source and the solution of the problem.*

Similarly, African Americans are said to have problems because they don't work to advance themselves. If you accept such an individualistic explanation, you are not likely to support government programs designed to raise the status of African Americans. National polls found that 81 percent of whites but only 45 percent of African Americans believe that the latter have as good a chance as whites to get any kind of job for which they are qualified (Polling Report 2016). When people believe that we already have equal opportunity, they will not support new laws or programs. This is well illustrated by the fact that a majority of African Americans (76 percent) but a minority of whites (48 percent) believe that the nation needs voting rights legislation to address the issue of state laws in recent years that tended to suppress the vote of minorities. Thus, the way problems are defined—as social or personal—has important consequences for identifying causes. In turn, the kind of causes identified affects the way problems are handled.

A word of caution is in order here. We are not arguing that *all* problems are social problems, nor that personal problems have no social factors, nor that social problems are free of any personal elements. There are certainly psychological and, in some cases, physiological factors at work. The point is that if you do not look beyond such factors, you will have a distorted view about the causes of problems.

The Consequences of Problems

Viewing a problem as either personal or social leads you to identify very different consequences as well as different causes. Consider, for example, a father who can obtain only occasional work and whose family, therefore, lives in poverty. If the man defines his problem as the result of his own inadequacies, he likely will despise himself and passively accept his poverty. Sennett and Cobb (1972:96) told of a nearly illiterate garbage collector who placed the blame for his lowly position entirely on himself: "Look, I know it's nobody's fault but mine that I got stuck here where I am, I mean . . . if I wasn't such a dumb— . . . no, it ain't that neither . . . if I'd applied myself, I know I got it in me to be different, can't say anyone did it to me." This man defined his problem as personal and, consequently, viewed himself as inadequate.

The *sense of inadequacy*—blaming or downgrading oneself—is not uncommon among those victimized by social problems. Some children who grow up in impoverished homes view themselves unfavorably, believing that their impoverishment is proof of their inferiority. Some women who are beaten by their husbands feel they have done something to deserve the abuse. Some people who lose their jobs during an economic crunch believe they are failures even though they had no control over what happened.

If a problem is defined as personal, *individual strategies* are employed to cope with the problem. Thus, the individual looks inward for a solution. Sometimes that solution is found in an *escape mechanism,* such as neurosis, physical illness, heavy drinking, or self-destructive behavior. At other times a solution is sought from specialists such as psychotherapists or religious advisors who help the person to change. These specialists may facilitate adjustment to the problem but not ultimately resolve it. If America's troubled families sought the help of counselors, they might learn to cope with or endure their troubles. But troubled families would continue to appear just as frequently.

Identifying something as a social problem presents it from a much different perspective and leads to far different conclusions and actions. Thus, if a man defines his poverty as the result of a declining economy, he may join in collective action such as a social movement, a rent strike group, or an organization set up to relieve the plight of the poor. Rather than blame himself for his poverty, he sees it as a *social* problem and takes action to redress it.

Or consider the problem of rape. Whether rape is defined as a social or personal problem makes a great deal of difference (Figure 1.1). Defining it as a personal problem either *blames the victim* or *castigates the offender.* Defining it as a social problem recognizes the need for *collective action* that attacks factors outside the individual.

FIGURE 1.1
Some Possible Differences When a Problem—Rape in This Case—Is Defined as Social or Personal.

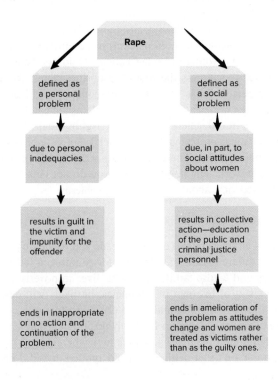

Several cases of rape (as reported in the news media) illustrate the need to consider it a social rather than a purely personal problem. A physician, 39 years old, married, and the father of two children, confessed to raping 22 women and sexually attacking at least 10 other women, one of whom was a nun. The doctor was a respected member of his community by day but an attacker of women by night. A teenage girl who decided to follow others and cool off in a park fountain on a hot July day was raped by two young men while at least three adults ignored her screams for help. Another young woman met a man at a New Year's Eve party. The man's sister, whom the young woman knew, introduced them. The man drove the two women home, dropped his sister off first, then asked if he could come up to the young woman's apartment for coffee. He was a genial, polite man, and since she had no reason to suspect him, she agreed. Once in her apartment, however, the man forced her to participate in various sex acts. When she prosecuted, she discovered that the man was on parole for a prior rape conviction. Yet people who had been at the party testified on the man's behalf, claiming that they had seen the couple talking and that the woman had been drinking. The man was acquitted. Subsequently he was brought to trial again for the alleged rape of a 13-year-old girl.

How can we account for these rapes? Were the victims at fault in these cases? Did they bring it on themselves by luring their attackers? A female student told us, "My father always said that if a woman was raped, it was her fault, that she somehow provoked the guy to do it." Or can the rapes be attributed to mentally ill or evil males? Are the rapists "sick" individuals who need therapy? Or are they evil men who ought to be castrated? You can blame the victims and say that they have personal problems—their wayward behavior. Or you can accuse the rapists of having personal problems—disturbed or evil natures. Neither will resolve the problem. Women who fight, scream, and risk their physical well-being (and even their lives) to ward off an attacker can hardly be said to be luring the man—and there was no evidence that the attackers were mentally ill.

Nor would castration solve the problem. Contrary to popular belief, castration does not prevent a man from having sexual relations. Castration has been used in a number of European countries to punish sex offenders (Incrocci et al. 2002); but of 39 offenders in West Germany who had voluntarily agreed to castration, 11 could still have sexual relations a number of years afterward, and 4 of the men had sex one to three times a week (Heim 1981).

Rape, in sum, is not a personal problem that can be solved by individual efforts. Like other social problems, rape requires collective action to attack such things as the social attitudes that legitimate exploiting women and a legal system that may treat the victim as harshly as the rapist does. Important differences, thus, result from defining a problem as social rather than personal. Unless problems like rape are defined as social, causes may not be identified nor solutions found.

A Model for Understanding

Given that problems are social and not merely personal, how do we go about understanding them? First let's define precisely what we mean by a *social problem:* It is *a condition or pattern of behavior that (1) contradicts some other condition or pattern of behavior and is defined as incompatible with the desired quality of life; (2) is caused, facilitated, or prolonged by factors that operate at multiple levels of social life; (3) involves intergroup conflict; and (4) requires social action to be resolved.* We explain this definition in the following pages. It uses major insights of sociological theories and is the basis for the model we use in discussing each of the problems in this book.

structural functionalism
a sociological theory that
focuses on social systems and
how their interdependent parts
maintain order

conflict theory
a theory that focuses on
contradictory interests,
inequalities between social
groups, and the resulting
conflict and change

symbolic interactionism
a sociological theory that
focuses on the interaction
between individuals, the
individual's perception of
situations, and the ways in
which social life is constructed
through interaction

interaction
reciprocally influenced
behavior on the part of two or
more people

contradiction
opposing phenomena within
the same social system

norm
shared expectations about
behavior

role
the behavior associated with a
particular position in the social
structure

values
things preferred because they
are defined as having worth

stratification system
arrangement of society into
groups that are unequal
with regard to such valued
resources as wealth, power,
and prestige

A Theory-Based Model

There are three major theoretical perspectives in sociology: **structural functionalism, conflict theory,** and **symbolic interactionism.** Each theory has distinctive emphases that are useful for understanding social phenomena. Structural functionalism focuses on social systems and the way in which their interdependent parts maintain order. Conflict theory focuses on contradictory interests of groups, inequalities in society, and the resulting conflict and change. Symbolic interactionism focuses on the **interaction** between individuals, the importance of knowing individuals' perspectives to understand their behavior, and the ways in which social life is constructed through interaction.

To illustrate these three approaches, consider the problem of crime. A structural-functional approach would point out the way that rapid change has weakened social solidarity and social institutions like the family, so that insufficient order is maintained. A conflict approach would note that the powerful groups in society define the kind of behavior that is crime (resulting in higher rates among the poor), and that much crime results from the lack of opportunities for the poor and for racial or ethnic minorities. A symbolic interactionist approach would stress the fact that people learn criminal behavior by interacting with, and accepting for themselves the perspective of, others who approve of such behavior. Figure 1.2 briefly summarizes the theories, how they are used to understand social problems, and how they can be applied to another problem—poverty.

Some sociologists use only one of the theoretical approaches to analyze social problems. We believe that all three approaches are necessary. Each of the theoretical approaches to crime is valid. Our model, therefore, incorporates emphases of each perspective (Figure 1.3). In essence, the model posits mutual influence between social structural factors, social psychological/cognitive factors, and social interaction. Social problems arise when people define **contradictions** among these various elements as incompatible with their quality of life.

Each of the three theories contributes to this model. In structural functionalism, a problem involves a system of interdependent parts, including institutions (collective means of dealing with basic social functions such as government, the family, the mass media, and the economy), **norms** (shared expectations about behavior), **roles** (behavior associated with particular positions in the social structure), and **values** (things preferred because they are defined as having worth). The parts are interrelated and exert pressure to maintain the system.

According to conflict theory, however, contradictions and inequalities exist between the parts of the system that generate conflict between groups. This is manifest in the **stratification system,** the pattern of inequality of wealth, power, and prestige that exists in all societies.

And according to symbolic interactionism, social interaction and the perspectives of individuals, including their **attitudes** (predispositions of individuals toward something) and **ideologies** (sets of ideas that explain or justify some aspect of social life), are important components of the system. Only as you understand how an individual perceives his or her social world can you understand that individual's behavior.

The pairs of arrows in the model indicate *mutual influence.* For example, social structural factors affect the way people interact. Norms and roles may lead a white person and a black person to treat each other as equals at the factory but not in other settings. The influence can go both ways: patterns of social interaction can alter the social structural factors. In recent years, for instance, women have interacted with men in ways that have altered the female role. Similarly, African Americans have persisted in interacting with whites in ways that have changed traditional roles. An ideology of white

	Structural Functionalism	Conflict Theory	Symbolic Interaction
Assumptions of the theory	Society is an integrated system of interdependent parts, bound together by shared values and norms.	Society is a system of diverse groups, with conflicting values and interests, vying with each other for power, wealth, and other valued resources.	Society is an arena of interacting individuals who behave in accord with their definitions of situations and who create shared meanings as they interact.
How the theory might explain social problems generally	Problems arise out of social disorganization, a state in which consensus about norms has broken down.	Problems are the result of dominance over, and exploitation of, some groups by others.	A situation or form of behavior becomes a problem when people define it as such.
How the theory might explain poverty	Political, economic, and educational institutions are not functioning adequately (often because of rapid social change), so that old arrangements are obsolete before new arrangements are in place.	The upper and middle classes oppress and exploit the poor through such things as using political and economic institutions for their own benefit and creating ideologies that blame the poor and justify their poverty.	Poverty became a social problem in the United States when people accepted the influential media's definition of it as such; people remain poor when they define their poverty as the result of their own deficiencies.
Illustration of the explanation	Schools train increasing numbers of students for jobs that are diminishing in number as firms adjust to the changing global economy and "outsource" many of those jobs.	Upper- and middle-class lawmakers regularly support corporate welfare (e.g., subsidies and tax breaks) but reject such welfare ideas for the poor as a guaranteed minimum annual income.	The public did not consider poverty as a social problem until the publication of Michael Harrington's influential book *The Other America* in 1962.

FIGURE 1.2   Theoretical Explanations of Poverty.

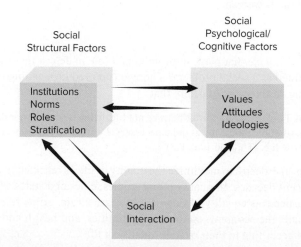

FIGURE 1.3
A Model for the Analysis of Social Problems.

attitude
a predisposition about something in one's environment

ideology
a set of ideas that explain or justify some aspect of social reality

supremacy can help to create and maintain blacks in a subservient role, but as minorities refuse to accept the role and assume instead the same kinds of roles as whites, the ideology will be rejected by increasing numbers of people.

By the very nature of social life, there are numerous *contradictions* among the elements in Figure 1.3. This means that opposing phenomena exist within the same social system. The phenomena are opposed in the sense that both cannot be true or operative. When the contradictions are defined as incompatible with the *desired quality of life,* you have a social problem. For example, the limited opportunities available in the economy are a contradiction to the ideology that all people should support themselves by working. The contradiction, as we shall see in Chapter 6, is incompatible with the desired quality of life of the poor.

By our definition, not all societal contradictions signal social problems, only those defined as detracting from the quality of life. In other words, objective data alone do not compose a problem. In accord with symbolic interactionism, only when people define a situation as problematic and persuade others to view it in the same way is there a social problem (Fine 2000). For instance, religion tends to be a unifying force, proclaiming a duty to love, make peace, and establish brotherhood. Recent terrorist acts by Islamic extremists and religious conflict in various nations contradict this peaceful role. Still, religion generally is not considered a social problem by most observers.

Whether people generally define something as detracting from their quality of life depends upon such things as how the problem is presented in the media (including the increasingly influential Internet blogs), how the problem squares with people's experiences, how readily people can understand the various facets of the problem, and how political leaders shape public opinion on issues (Hawdon 2001; Sacco 2003; Maratea 2008).

Finally, consider gender equality as another example of the usefulness of the model. Among the opposing phenomena involved in the problem are:

1. The *ideology* of equal opportunity versus the *reality* of limited opportunities for female participation in the economy.
2. The *value* of the pursuit of happiness versus the *narrowness* of the traditional female *role.*
3. The *value* of human dignity versus male-female *interaction* in which females are treated as intellectual inferiors.

Each of these oppositions has consequences that are incompatible with the desired quality of life of many women.

Quality of Life

What is this *quality of life* that plays so prominent a role in determining whether a contradiction is defined as a social problem? Thoreau captured its meaning in his desire to avoid discovering, at the point of death, that

> I had not lived. I did not wish to live what was not life, living is so dear; nor did I wish to practise resignation, unless it was quite necessary. I wanted to live deep and suck out all the marrow of life. (Thoreau 1968:113)

The desire to "live deep," to maximize the quality of life, is reflected in a proliferation of studies in recent decades. In quality-of-life studies, cities and states are evaluated in terms of such aspects as equality of opportunity, agriculture, crime rates, technology, education, climate, the economy, cultural opportunities, and health and welfare. They are then ranked according to their overall "quality of life."

After decades of these studies, there is considerable agreement about what Americans define as important to the quality of their lives (Ferriss 2000). In essence, they evaluate their quality of life according to how well they are doing financially, physically, emotionally, socially, and culturally. Americans want well-paying and meaningful work and financial security. They want good health, access to good health care facilities, opportunity for a good education, opportunity to participate in cultural activities, and opportunity to live and work in areas with minimal crime. Americans also want respect from others, self-respect, and a sense of personal worth. Finally, they want to live without fear and with reasonable freedom from stress.

One effort to categorize and quantify quality of life in nations is the Social Progress Index (2016). The Index uses three broad categories: basic human needs (such as nutrition, medical care, and sanitation); foundations of well-being (health, environmental quality, access to basic knowledge and information); and opportunity (personal rights and freedom, tolerance, access to advanced education). When the Index was used to rate and rank 133 nations, comprising 94 percent of the world's population, Finland had the highest quality of life, with a score of 90.1. The worst score, 30.0, was the Central African Republic. The United States ranked 19th with a score of 84.6, lower than Japan, Canada, and most European countries.

When people are asked about their quality of life, they indicate a lowered quality when they lack the kinds of things in the Index. Thus, researchers have found a reduced quality of life reported because of such things as personal health problems (Alonso et al. 2004; La Grow et al. 2011), work demands that interfere with nonworking time (Rice, Frone, and McFarlin 1992), environmental problems (Tickell 1992), and the experience of financial problems and status inequality (Coverdill, Lopez, and Petrie 2011).

Americans are not unique in their view of what constitutes a high quality of life. Studies of other nations show that people everywhere value many of the same things that Americans do (Ventegodt et al. 2005; Liu 2006; Headey, Muffels, and Wooden 2008). Quality of life, then, involves far more than income. You may be able to purchase security devices for your home, but you can't buy total peace of mind when the newspapers regularly remind you of the pervasiveness of crime. You may be able to afford the best seats in the house, but that's meaningless if your community lacks cultural opportunities. You may live in the most expensive area available, but you can't shut out the polluted air that engulfs your property.

Moreover, undesirable conditions that diminish the quality of life affect you both directly and indirectly. For example, some people are the direct victims of criminal activity: assaults, muggings, robberies, rapes, swindles, and so forth. But everyone has some *fear of criminal victimization,* even people who have never been directly victimized. This fear may put limits on where they go or what they do or how secure they feel—limits that reduce the quality of their lives.

In sum, there are numerous contradictions in society that create conditions incompatible with the desired quality of life. Everyone is affected, though some suffer far more than others. Because of the diminished quality of life, we define these contradictions and the conditions they create as *social problems.*

Multiple Levels of Social Problems

Social problems are manifested at *multiple levels of social life.* The factors that cause, facilitate, and help to perpetuate social problems are found at the individual level (e.g., attitudes), group levels (e.g., ideologies of terrorist groups), societal levels (e.g., the government), and in some cases, global levels (e.g., globalization of the economy).

Explaining social problems requires many factors rather than a single cause.

©Con Tanasiuk/Design Pics

Think, for example, about the problem of racial and ethnic relations (for brevity's sake, we shall refer to this problem by the commonly used phrase "race problem," though the "problem" is not race per se, but the relation between people of diverse racial and ethnic backgrounds). We could analyze the problem in terms of a stratification system in which racial minorities are disadvantaged, kept in inferior roles, and systematically subjected to discrimination. Such arrangements restrict interaction between the races and justify prejudice and claims that the disadvantaged group is naturally inferior.

Or we could analyze the problem in terms of attitudes of prejudice combined with a value of individualism (meaning that the government should not force people to interact with other races). Add to this an ideology that defines the oppressed race as inferior and therefore deserving of an inferior position. These values, attitudes, and ideology explain and perpetuate a structure in which the oppressed race remains in the least desirable roles, institutional positions, and socioeconomic stratum. Furthermore, interaction between the races is restricted, permitting little opportunity for reevaluation and change.

The point is, as our model indicates, *mutual influence* exists among the various factors at differing levels of social life. Prejudice restricts interaction and restricted interaction fosters prejudice. The two feed on each other. Similarly, education can be structured in such a way as to deprive minorities of adequate learning, thereby justifying an ideology of racial inferiority; but the ideology can also justify inaction in securing adequate education for minorities.

The multiple-level factors, in sum, work together to maintain the problem. Meantime, inequalities in the system lead people to act in their own behalf to bring about change; and interaction is never so confined as to prevent the development of new values, attitudes, and ideologies. Eventually, there may be changes in interaction patterns and in the social structure.

The pressure to change may arise as members of the oppressed race react to the contradiction between an ideology of the free pursuit of happiness and the realities of their situation. They may use the ideology and the contradiction to shape new attitudes and values among the oppressed and the oppressors. They may create new ideologies, such as a myth of their own superiority. They may strive to alter patterns of interaction and elements of the social structure. They may try to change the content of education, the power structure of government, and the practices and policies of the economy.

Thus, understanding and dealing with a social problem is never a simple matter. A social problem cannot be reduced to one thing, such as the race problem's being due merely to prejudice or poverty's being due merely to people's failure to work. All the factors in our model enter into each problem.

Social Action for Resolution

Social problems often give rise to *protest groups* and intergroup conflict as expressions of social action. Protest groups arise because not everyone in the society defines a particular situation the same way. For example, the contradiction between the ideals of American life and the reality of life for most African Americans is not defined by all Americans as incompatible with the quality of life. Some deny that African Americans have less access than whites to the desirable aspects of American life. In other words, they deny the existence of a contradiction.

If all Americans denied the contradiction, there would be no racial problem in this country (even though a foreign observer might see the contradiction). On the other hand, if all Americans affirmed the contradiction and demanded change, the problem might be quickly resolved. Because the contradiction is defined differently by different collectivities, intergroup conflict plays a part in resolving social problems.

We use the term *collectivity* here in reference to members of opposing groups in the conflict who agree on particular issues. The race problem, for example, is not simply a matter of white versus minority. The abortion problem is not just a case of Catholics versus Protestants. Gender inequality is not simply men versus women. Poverty is not merely rich versus poor. In each case there are members of both groups on either side of the issue.

All social problems are characterized by opposing groups with differing ideologies and contrary definitions of the contradiction. One side will argue that the contradiction is incompatible with the desired quality of their lives, while the other side will argue that there is no contradiction, that the contradiction is necessary, or that the contradiction exists but is not rooted in the social system (in other words, the victims of the contradictions are blamed for their plight). Such conflict is the context in which efforts to resolve problems take place.

In subsequent chapters we discuss the ways in which problems may be attacked by social action (both public policy and private action). There are many reasons resolution of most social problems through social action are slow and agonizing: problems are manifested at multiple levels of social reality; numerous factors are involved in causing and maintaining problems; intergroup conflict surrounds most problems; and efforts to resolve a problem may ameliorate one problem but create new problems (Fine 2006).

The Changing Nature of Social Problems

One additional factor adds to the difficulty of resolving social problems—both the definition and the objective aspects of a particular problem change over time. Sometimes the change may be so rapid that an issue barely has time to be a problem. Until the exceptionally hot and dry summer of 1988, the public did not respond much to the warnings of scientists about global warming (Ungar 1992). That summer brought the problem to the public's attention. When the summer passed, the problem's importance waned in the public mind as other issues rose to the fore. Although virtually all scientists agree that global warming is occurring, there is still dispute in the nation as to whether it is a social problem.

Thus, problems may *rise and decline in perceived importance,* as illustrated by the problem of poverty. Views of poverty have changed over time. A 1952 edition of a social problems text omitted the two chapters on poverty that had appeared in the original 1942 edition (Reinhardt, Meadows, and Gillette 1952). The omission reflected the belief in the 1950s that poverty was largely a problem of the past. (Even the 1942 edition reflected more the opinion of sociologists than that of the public.) Gallup opinion polls about the most important problems facing the nation, taken since November 1935, show that the public did not consider poverty an important problem until 1965 (Lauer 1976). Concerns about poverty peaked in the 1960s and 1970s then tended to diminish. In a national poll in late 2016 that asked about the nation's most important problem, poverty was mentioned by only 3 percent of Americans (Polling Report 2016). The economy and jobs, terrorism, immigration, and race relations were all identified by more people than was poverty.

The objective conditions of poverty also have changed over time: the amount of poverty has changed (as measured by some standard such as family income); the composition of the poor has changed (such as the relative proportions of racial, ethnic, and age groups); and the organization of antipoverty efforts has changed (such as the vigor and focus of protest groups and official attitudes and programs).

Recognizing such changes in problems is important for both understanding and action. For example, many people continue to identify poverty as essentially a problem of work—the poor are unemployed. As you will see, the problem of poverty would be little changed even if every able-bodied person in America had a job. It is true that during the depression of the 1930s a considerable number of the impoverished were unemployed. Many people who lived through that period continue to associate poverty with unemployment, failing to recognize the changed nature of the problem. Today, a large number of poor people are working but still live in poverty. Therefore, to continue associating the two concepts is to misunderstand the contemporary problem and thereby fail to take appropriate action.

As you study the various problems, you will see fluctuations in all of them. Some appear to be getting better, and some appear to be getting worse. It is important to remember that improvement does not mean that the problem is resolved (gains can be quickly lost in the ongoing struggle for justice and equality), nor does deterioration mean that the problem is hopeless (lost ground may be regained and new ground may be gained dramatically when appropriate social action is taken).

Analyzing Social Problems

The definition of the term "social problems" that we presented earlier in this chapter shapes our approach to each problem considered in this book. First, we "get the feel" of the problem by seeing how it affects people's lives and examining how the problem involves a contradiction and is defined as incompatible with the desired quality of life. Second, we analyze the multiple-level factors involved in the problem. We do not relate every factor identified in Figure 1.3 to each problem: Research has not yet identified the components of every problem. Yet in each we see the multiple-level components that show how the problem arises and is perpetuated. Third, we consider various ways to attack the problem. Our examination is sketchy (any adequate treatment would require a book in itself), but we do discuss some kinds of both public policy and private action that can ameliorate each problem.

Before we turn to specific problems, we need to address an additional issue. Seemingly reasonable statements are made about every social problem. For example, following the series of highly publicized killings by preteens and teenagers in the 1990s, explanations ranged from the pampering of criminals by the legal system to violence in video games and movies to mental illness. How do you know which of these explanations, if any, are correct? Or to put it another way, how do you distinguish opinion from valid analysis?

critical thinking
the analysis and evaluation of
information

First, you need to *develop critical thinking skills.* **Critical thinking** is the process of carefully attending to spoken or written information in order to evaluate its validity.

Make sure you understand the information; then evaluate it by asking such questions as whether it is logical and reasonable. One important way to evaluate information is to look for any *fallacies of thinking.* These fallacies are commonly used when people analyze social problems. You will find illustrations throughout this book on how fallacies lead to misunderstandings.

Second, you need to examine how sociologists research social problems by gathering data to test various explanations. The data may lead you to revise your explanations. Remember, the study of social problems is not an exercise in speculation; it needs explanations that are supported by evidence. Let's look, then, at fallacious ways of thinking and at methods of social research.

Critical Thinking: Recognizing Fallacies

Nine different fallacies have been used to analyze social problems. An important aspect of critical thinking is the ability to recognize these fallacies. This ability enables you not only to assess the validity of information and arguments presented by others but also to make your own analyses with logic and clarity.

Fallacy of Dramatic Instance

The **fallacy of dramatic instance** refers to the tendency to *overgeneralize,* to use one, two, or three cases to support an entire argument. This mistake is common among people who discuss social problems. It may be difficult to counter because the limited number of cases often are a part of an *individual's personal experience.* For example, in discussing the racial problem in the United States, a man said to us: "Blacks in this country can make it just as much as whites. I know a black businessman who is making a million. In fact, he has a better house and a better car than I have." We pointed out that this successful businessperson is an exception. The man dismissed the point: "If one guy can make it, they all can." The fallacy of dramatic instance mistakes a few cases for a general situation.

This fallacy is difficult to deal with because the argument is based partly on fact. There are, after all, African Americans who are millionaires. Does this mean there is no discrimination and that any black person can attain success? To use another example, many Americans believe that welfare recipients are "ripping off" the rest of us, that we are subsidizing their unwillingness to work and supporting them at a higher standard of living than we ourselves enjoy. Is this true? Yes, in a few cases. Occasionally, newspapers report instances of individuals making fraudulent use of welfare. But does this mean that most welfare recipients are doing the same? Do people on welfare really live better than people who work for a living?

The point is, in studying social problems, you must recognize that exceptions exist. To use such cases in support of your argument is to fall into the trap of the fallacy of dramatic instance because social problems deal with general situations rather than with individual exceptions.

As this fallacy suggests, the fact that you hear about a lazy poor person or a rich African American or a corrupt politician does not mean that such cases represent the typical situation. Millions of people are involved in the problems of poverty, race, and government. *Systematic studies* are needed to determine whether the one or two cases you know about represent the norm or the exception. For instance, the fact that there

fallacy of dramatic instance
overgeneralizing

are black and Hispanic millionaires is less important than the government report show-ing that in 2014 the median annual household income for non-Hispanic whites was $60,256, whereas that for Hispanics was $42,491 and that for African Americans was $35,398 (DeNavas-Walt and Proctor 2015). That same year, 10.1 percent of non-Hispanic whites, 23.6 percent of Hispanics, and 26.2 percent of African Americans lived in poverty. Such figures are more pertinent to the race problem than are cases that represent exceptions to the general pattern.

We are not saying that individual examples or cases are unimportant or unusable. At various points throughout this book (including the chapter opening vignettes) we use examples of people's experiences. These examples are not given as proof or even as evi-dence. Rather, we use them to *illustrate the impact of social problems on people's quality of life.* These examples may dramatize better than statistics the ways in which people's lives are adversely affected by social problems.

Fallacy of Retrospective Determinism

fallacy of retrospective determinism
the argument that things could not have worked out any other way than they did

The **fallacy of retrospective determinism** is the argument that things could not have worked out any other way than the way they did. It is a *deterministic* position, but the de-terminism is aimed at the past rather than the future. The fallacy asserts that what hap-pened historically *had* to happen, and it *had* to happen just the way it did. If you accept this fallacy, the present social problems are inevitable. Whether the issue is racial dis-crimination, poverty, war, or the well-being of the family, the fallacy of retrospective determinism makes it unavoidable.

This fallacy is unfortunate for a number of reasons. History is more than a tale of *inevitable tragedies.* History is important for understanding social problems. You can-not fully understand the tensions between America's minority groups and the white majority unless you know about the decades of exploitation and humiliation preceding

Those who are born poor are likely to remain poor. Their poverty, however, is caused by social conditions, not fate.
©Denis Tangney Jr./Getty Images

the emergence of the modern civil rights movement. Your understanding will remain clouded if you regard those events as nothing more than an inevitable process. Similarly, you cannot fully understand the tension between the People's Republic of China and the West if you view it only as a battle of economic ideologies. It is vital to know that the tension is based in the pillage and humiliation to which China was subjected by the West. Yet your understanding will not be enhanced by the study of history if you regard the Western oppression of China in the 19th century as inevitable.

If you view the past in terms of determinism, you have little reason to study it and are deprived of an important source of understanding. Furthermore, the fallacy of retrospective determinism is but a small step from the stoic *acceptance of the inevitable.* That is, if things are the way they have to be, why worry about them? Assuming that the future also is determined by forces beyond your control, you are left in a position of apathy: There is little point in trying to contest the inevitable.

This fallacy is probably less common in discussions about social problems than the fallacy of dramatic instance, but it does appear in everyday discussions. For example, in responding to the question about the causes of poverty in America, a 64-year-old service station owner told us: "Go back through history, it's traditional; there's no special reason, no cause for it. We can't get away from it. It has just always been this way." A businessman expressed a similar fatalism: "I don't actually know the cause of poverty, but it's here to stay and we must learn to live with it. We have to take the good with the bad."

An individual might view social problems in deterministic terms for reasons other than intellectual conviction. Determinism can relieve you of responsibility and can legitimate a lack of concern with efforts to effect changes you do not want. Whatever the basis for affirming determinism, the outcome is the same: You may as well accept the problem and learn to live with it, because it is inevitably and inextricably with you.

Fallacy of Misplaced Concreteness

Some people have a tendency to explain some social problems by resorting to **reification**—making what is abstract into something concrete. "Society," for example, is an abstraction. It is not like a person, an animal, or an object that can be touched. It is an idea, a way of thinking about a particular collectivity of people. Yet we often hear people assert that something is the fault of "society" or that "society" caused a certain problem. This is the **fallacy of misplaced concreteness.** In what sense can society "make" or "cause" or "do" anything? To say that society caused a problem leaves you helpless to correct the situation because you haven't the faintest notion where to begin. If, for example, society is the cause of juvenile delinquency, how do you tackle the problem? Must you change society? If so, how?

The point is that "society" is an abstraction, a concept that refers to a group of people who interact in particular ways. To *attribute social problems to an abstraction* like "society" does not help resolve the problems. Sometimes people who attribute the cause of a particular problem to society intend to *deny individual responsibility.* To say that society causes delinquency may be a way of saying that the delinquent child is not responsible for his or her behavior.

You can recognize the social causes of problems without either attributing them to an abstraction like society or relieving the individual of responsibility for his or her behavior. For instance, you could talk about the family's role in delinquency. A family is a concrete phenomenon. Furthermore, you could say that the family itself is a victim of some kind of societal arrangement, such as government regulations that tend to

reification
defining what is abstract as something concrete

fallacy of misplaced concreteness
making something abstract into something concrete

perpetuate poverty, cause stress, and create disruption in many families. You could say that families can be helped by changing the government regulations that keep some of them in poverty and, thereby, facilitate delinquent behavior.

Society, in short, does not cause anything. Rather, problems are caused by that which the concept of society represents—people acting in accord with certain social arrangements and within a particular cultural system.

Fallacy of Personal Attack

fallacy of personal attack
argument by attacking the opponent personally rather than dealing with the issue

A tactic among debaters is to attack the opponent *personally* when they can't support their position by reason, logic, or facts. This tactic diverts attention from the issue and focuses it on personality. We call this the **fallacy of personal attack** (philosophers call it *ad hominem*). It is remarkably effective in avoiding the use of reason or the consideration of evidence in discussing a social problem. In analyzing social problems, this fallacy can be used either to attack an opponent in a debate about a problem or to *attack the people who are the victims of the problem.* Ryan (1971) called this "blaming the victim" and said it involves nearly every problem in America.

Historically, the poor have suffered from this approach. Instead of offering sympathy or being concerned for the poor, people may label the poor as disreputable and, consequently, deserving of or responsible for their plight. People who are not poor are relieved of any responsibility. In fact, government efforts to alleviate poverty are even thought to contribute to the problem by taking away any incentive of the poor to help themselves, and leading them instead to become sexually promiscuous, irresponsible, and dependent on others (Somers and Block 2005). Attitudes have been changing. Increasing numbers of Americans agree that the poor are victims of circumstances beyond their control. Still, by 2014 a national poll reported that 44 percent of Americans believed that the poor were not doing enough to help themselves (O'Connor 2014).

The meaning and seriousness of any social problem may be sidestepped by attacking the intelligence or character of the victims or of those who call attention to the problem. Name-calling and labeling, thereby, change the social problem into a personal problem.

Fallacy of Appeal to Prejudice

fallacy of appeal to prejudice
argument by appealing to popular prejudices or passions

In addition to attacking the opponent, a debater may try to support an unreasonable position by using another technique: **fallacy of appeal to prejudice.** (Philosophers call it argument *ad populum*.) With this fallacy, debaters use popular prejudices or passions to convince others of the correctness of their position. When the topic is social problems, debaters use *popular slogans* or *popular myths* to sway people emotionally rather than using reasoning from systematic studies.

Some slogans or phrases persist for decades and are employed to oppose efforts to resolve social problems. "Creeping socialism" has been used to describe many government programs designed to aid the underdogs of society. The term is not used when the programs are designed to help business or industry, or when the affluent benefit from the programs. As someone remarked, "What the government does for me is progress; what it does for you is socialism."

In some cases, the slogans use general terms that reflect *traditional values.* Thus, the various advances made in civil rights legislation—voting, public accommodations, open housing—have been resisted in the name of the "rights of the individual." These slogans help to perpetuate the myth that legislation that benefits African Americans infringes on the constitutional rights of the white majority. More recently, those who oppose same-sex marriage argue that they are simply acting in *defense of marriage and the family*. They claim that making same-sex marriage legal will further damage or even destroy the traditional family life that is the bedrock of a stable society.

Unfortunately, in the absence of other information or evidence, people tend to rely on myths to assess situations. Thus, some Americans continue to assume that rape is often the woman's fault because she has sexually provoked the man. These Americans either have seen no evidence to the contrary or have dismissed the evidence as invalid. Unfortunately, myths tend to become so deeply rooted in people's thinking that when people are confronted by new evidence, they have difficulty accepting it.

Myths are hard to break down, but if you want to understand social problems, you must abandon popular ideas and assumptions and resist popular slogans and prejudices that cloud your thinking. Instead, you must make judgments based on evidence.

Fallacy of Circular Reasoning

The ancient Greek physician Galen praised the healing qualities of a certain clay by pointing out that all who drink the remedy recover quickly—except those whom it does not help. The latter die and are not helped by any medicine. Obviously, according to Galen, the clay fails only in incurable cases. This is an example of the **fallacy of circular reasoning:** using conclusions to support the assumptions that were necessary to draw the conclusions.

fallacy of circular reasoning using conclusions to support the assumptions that were necessary to make the conclusions

Circular reasoning creeps into analyses of social problems. Someone might argue that Hispanics are inherently inferior and assert that their inferiority is evident because they hold only menial jobs and do not do intellectual work. In reply, you might point out that Hispanics are not doing more intellectual work because of discriminatory hiring practices. The person might then counter that Hispanics could not be hired for such jobs anyway because they are inferior.

Similarly, you might argue that homosexuals are sex perverts because they commonly have remained secretive about their sexual preference. But, we counter, the secrecy is due to the general disapproval of homosexuality. No, you reply, homosexuality is kept secret because it is a perversion. Thus, in circular reasoning people bounce *back and forth between assumptions and conclusions*. Circular reasoning leads nowhere in the search for an understanding of social problems.

Fallacy of Authority

Virtually everything you know is based on some authority. You know comparatively little from personal experience or personal research. The authority you necessarily rely on is someone else's experience, research, or belief. You accept notions of everything from the nature of the universe to the structure of the atom, from the state of international relationships to the doctrines of religion—all on the basis of some authority. Most people accept a war as legitimate on the authority of their political leaders. Many accept the validity of capital punishment on the authority of law enforcement officers. Some accept that use of contraceptives is morally wrong on religious authority. Most rely on the authority of the news media about the extent and severity of various problems.

The knowledge that you acquire through authority can be inaccurate and can exacerbate rather than resolve or ameliorate social problems. The **fallacy of authority** means an *illegitimate appeal to authority*. Such an appeal obtrudes into thinking about social problems in at least four ways.

fallacy of authority argument by an illegitimate appeal to authority

First, the *authority may be ambiguous.* Thus, appeal is made to the Bible by both those who support and those who oppose capital punishment. Supporters of capital punishment point out that the Bible, particularly the Old Testament, decreed death for certain offenses. Opponents counter that the death penalty contradicts New Testament notions of Christian love. An appeal to this kind of authority, then, is really an appeal to a particular interpretation of the authority. Because the interpretations are contradictory, people must find other bases for making judgments.

Second, the *authority may be irrelevant to the problem.* The fact that a man is a first-rate physicist does not mean he can speak with legitimate authority about race relations. Most of us are impressed by people who have significant accomplishments in some area, but their accomplishments should not overwhelm us if those people speak about a problem outside their area of expertise.

We rely on authorities for information, but authorities are not always right.

©Masterfile Royalty-Free

Third, the *authority may be pursuing a bias* rather than studying a problem. To say that someone is pursuing a bias is not necessarily to disparage that person because pursuing it may be part of a job. For example, military officers are likely to analyze the problem of war from a military rather than a moral, political, or economic perspective. This is their job—and this is why decisions about armaments, defense, and war should not be left solely to the military. From a military point of view, one way to prevent war is to be prepared to counter an enemy attack. The nation must be militarily strong, according to this argument, so that other nations will hesitate to attack—and military strength requires the most sophisticated technology, a stockpile of weaponry, and a large, standing military force.

The shortcomings of this line of reasoning were dramatically illustrated by the incidents of September 11, 2001, when terrorists seized jetliners and crashed them into the World Trade Center towers in New York City and the Pentagon in Washington, D.C. At the time, the United States was clearly the strongest military power in the world. Nevertheless, the terrorists struck and they struck effectively. As we discuss in Chapter 14, the notion of defending against enemies must now be reexamined in light of a new face of war in the world.

Although some people pursue a bias as a normal part of their work, others pursue it because of *vested interests.* That is, the authority may deliberately or unconsciously allow biases to affect what he or she says because it is personally advantageous. The head of a corporation that builds private prisons and argues that the private sector can deal with prisoners more effectively than can the government will obviously benefit from public policy that privatizes state and federal prisons. The corporate executive who talks about federal overregulation would clearly benefit if the government withdrew from consumer protection programs. Political leaders credit their own policies when crime rates fall and point to uncontrollable circumstances when crime rates rise. Their policies may have no effect on crime rates, but they benefit if they can persuade people that their actions have lowered the rate or will do so in the future.

Finally, *the authority may simply be wrong.* This problem often occurs when one authority cites another. For example, in 2003, the Census Bureau issued a report on the foreign-born population of the United States (Schmidley 2003). The report showed the years of entry of the 32.5 million foreign-born people now living in the nation: 4.1 million came before 1970, 4.6 million came during the 1970s, 7.96 million came during the 1980s, and 15.8 million came after 1990. Suppose we wanted information about immigration patterns, and we consulted newspapers instead of the Census Bureau. We examined three respectable sources and found the following interpretations of the report. A national financial paper said that the number of immigrants continued to grow at "a blistering pace." An urban newspaper reported that immigration continued at a steady pace during "the past two years." And a national newspaper claimed that the Census Bureau report stated that the number of foreign-born coming to live in the United States has "slowed considerably"! Clearly, when one authority cites another, it is best to check out the initial authority before drawing any conclusions.

Fallacy of Composition

That the whole is equal to the sum of its parts appears obvious. That what is true of the part is also true of the whole likewise seems to be a reasonable statement, but the former is debatable, and the latter is the **fallacy of composition.** As economists have illustrated, the notion that *what is valid for the part is also valid for the whole* is not necessarily true. Consider, for example, the relationship between work and income. If a farmer works hard and the weather is not adverse, the farmer's income may rise; but if every farmer works hard and the weather is favorable, and a bumper crop results, the total farm income may fall. The latter case is based on supply and demand, whereas the former assumes that a particular farmer outperforms other farmers.

fallacy of composition
the assertion that what is true of the part is necessarily true of the whole

In thinking about social problems, *you cannot assume that what is true for the individual is also true for the group.* An individual may be able to resolve a problem insofar as it affects him or her, but that resolution is not available to all members of the group. For example, a man who is unemployed and living in poverty may find work that enables him to escape poverty. The work may require him to move or to work for less money than someone else, but still he is able to rise above poverty. As you will see in our discussion of poverty, however, that solution is not possible for most of the nation's poor. Thus, something may be true for a particular individual or even a few individuals and yet be inapplicable or counterproductive for the entire group of which the individuals are members.

Fallacy of Non Sequitur

A number of the fallacies already discussed involve non sequitur, but we look at this way of thinking separately because of its importance. Literally, non sequitur means *"it does not follow."* This **fallacy of non sequitur** is commonly found when people interpret statistical data.

fallacy of non sequitur
something that does not follow logically from what has preceded it

For example, data may show that the amount of welfare payments by state governments has increased dramatically over the past few decades. What is the meaning of such data? You might conclude that the number of people unwilling to work has

"Use it or lose it" is a common saying. We might paraphrase that and say "Use it and learn it." That is, one of the best ways to learn something is to use it and not simply to memorize it. For this involvement, therefore, we are asking you to learn the fallacies by using them.

Select any social problem in which you are interested. Show how people could use each of the fallacies to "explain" that problem. Construct nine different explanations that are one or two sentences long. Try to make your explanations sound reasonable. Test them by sharing them with someone and seeing how many you can get the other person to accept. If the entire class participates in this project, gather in small groups and have each member share his or her explanations. Group members should then try to identify the fallacy in each of the explanations. Be sure not to present the fallacies in the order in which they appear in the book.

As an alternative, use simple observation to test the accuracy of common (or your own) notions about people involved in particular social problems. For instance, visit a gay bar. Or attend a meeting of gay activists, a feminist group, Alcoholics Anonymous, or an environmental group. Ask a number of people to describe the typical member of the group you visit, and compare their responses (and your own preconceptions) with your observations.

increased and that more and more "freeloaders" are living off the public treasury, but there are other explanations. The increase may reflect adjustments due to inflation, better efforts to get welfare money to eligible recipients, or a rise in unemployment due to government action to control inflation.

Daniel Bell (1960) showed how statistics on crime can be misleading. In New York one year, reported assaults were up 200 percent, robberies were up 400 percent, and burglaries were up 1,300 percent! Those were the "facts," but what did they mean? A crime wave? Actually, the larger figures reflected a new method of crime reporting that was more effective in determining the total amount of crime. An increase in reported crime rates can mean different things, but it does not necessarily signify an actual increase in the amount of crime.

One other example involves studies of women who work. Some employers believe that women are not desirable workers because they are less committed to the job than men, as indicated by their higher turnover rate. Women do indeed have a higher rate of turnover than men. But what does this mean? Are women truly less committed to their jobs?

When you look at the situation more closely, you find that the real problem is that women tend to be concentrated in lower-level jobs. Also, women who quit a job tend to find another one quickly. Thus, women may be uncommitted to a particular low-level job but strongly committed to work. Furthermore, if you look at jobs with the same status, the turnover rate is no higher for women than men.

These illustrations are not meant to discourage you from drawing conclusions. Instead, they are reminders of the need for thorough study and the need to avoid quick conclusions, even when those conclusions seem logical on the surface. Contrary to popular opinion, *"facts" do not necessarily speak for themselves.* They must be interpreted in light of the complexities of social life and with the awareness that a number of different conclusions can usually be drawn from any set of data.

Fallacies and Mass Media

In subsequent chapters, we discuss how mass media contribute to particular social problems. Here we want to point out how the media contribute to misunderstandings by committing or facilitating the various fallacies.

In some cases, the media may inadvertently create fallacious thinking by the way something is reported. For instance, a newspaper story about someone who is guilty of welfare fraud, which omits the fact that such fraud represents only a tiny minority of recipients, can lead readers to commit the fallacy of the dramatic instance: The story proves that those on welfare are cheats who want handouts rather than responsibility. Or a story in a religious magazine about a formerly gay man who is now married to a woman, which omits any mention of the numerous gays who have tried and failed to change their sexual orientation, can lead readers to commit the fallacy of non sequitur: If one man can do it, they all can.

Because the media represent authority in the matter of information, they are particularly prone to the fallacy of authority. That is, they might provide information that is misleading or wrong. It may be a case of bias on the part of those gathering and/or presenting the information. It may be a case of misunderstanding the original source of the information. Or it may be a case of the original source itself being wrong. For example, in 2006 a survey commissioned by the American Medical Association found a startlingly high rate of binge drinking and unprotected sex on the part of female college students while on spring break (Rosenthal 2006). The study, reported widely on TV and in newspapers, was based on a "random sample." It turned out, however, that the sample was not random. Those who participated were volunteers, and only one-fourth of them had actually been on a spring break trip. In essence, then, no conclusions about college women in general could be drawn from the survey.

We do not intend to commit the fallacy of dramatic instance ourselves by suggesting that such incidents are typical or even very common. Rather, they illustrate the need to be alert, thoughtful, and cautious about the things you read and hear about social problems.

The Sources of Data: Social Research

The various "intellectual blind alleys" we have described create and help to perpetuate myths about social problems. *Social research* is designed to gain information about social problems so that you can have a valid understanding of them and employ realistic efforts in resolving them.

Not everything called research is scientifically valid. Therefore, you need to use critical thinking skills as well as information and arguments to evaluate research. Some so-called social research aims to shape rather than gain information. For example, we once received a letter from a U.S. congressman inquiring about our attitudes toward labor unions. Actually, the letter attempted to shape information, and the questionnaire that accompanied it was designed to enlist support for the congressman's antiunion stance. The letter began by saying, "What will happen to your state and local taxes—your family's safety—and our American way of life, if the czars of organized labor have their way in the new Congress?" It used such phrases as "henchmen," "power hungry union professionals," "rip-offs which enrich the union fat cats at your expense," and "freedom from union tyranny." The questionnaire itself requested yes-or-no responses to questions such as "Do you feel that anyone should be forced to pay a union boss for permission to earn a living?" Clearly, this inquiry resorted to *the fallacies of personal attack and appeal to prejudice.* A critical-thinking approach would treat the results as little else than an illustration of people with biases against labor unions.

If you want to gain information and discover the nature of social reality, you must use scientific social research. Scientific research is both rational and *empirical.* That is, it is logical and comes to conclusions based on evidence rather than speculation or feelings. The stages of such research typically include a clear statement of the problem or issue to be researched; formulation of *hypotheses* so that the problem or issue is in researchable form; selection of the appropriate method, including the sample; collection of the data; analysis of the data; and interpretation and report of the conclusions. A guiding principle throughout the foregoing stages is the desire to discover evidence, not to confirm preconceptions.

Many different methods are used in social research. We look at four methods that have yielded important information about social problems: survey research, statistical analysis of official records (particularly of government data), experiments, and participant observation.

Survey Research

survey
a method of research in which a sample of people are interviewed or given questionnaires in order to get data on some phenomenon

socioeconomic status
position in the social system based on economic resources, power, education, prestige, and lifestyle

variable
any trait or characteristic that varies in value or magnitude

The **survey** uses interviews and/or questionnaires to gain data about some phenomenon. The people from whom the information is gathered are normally a *sample* (a small number of people selected by various methods from a larger population) of a *population* (a group that is the focus of the study). The data include everything from attitudes about various matters to information such as gender, age, and **socioeconomic status.** You can learn two important aspects of social reality from surveys. First, you can discover the *distribution of people along some dimension.* For example, you can learn the proportion of people who say they will vote Republican or Democratic in an election; the proportion of people who favor, oppose, or are neutral about capital punishment; or the proportion of people who believe that homosexuals should be allowed to marry. Second, you can discover *relationships among* **variables.** (A *variable* is any trait or characteristic that varies in value or magnitude.) For instance, you can investigate the relationship between people's positions in the stratification system (socioeconomic status) and their attitudes toward the race problem, gender inequality, or the plight of the poor.

Survey research is probably the most common method used in sociology. Let's examine one piece of such research that deals with the problem of wife rape. The example illustrates both the technique of survey research and the kind of information that survey research can yield about a social problem.

Can a man rape his wife? In our experience, students have diverse opinions. Some believe that wife rape is as serious an offense against a woman as rape by a stranger. Others believe that rape makes no sense in the context of marriage, that sex in marriage is "his right" and "her duty" (Durán, Moya, and Megias 2011), a view that is supported by a long legal tradition. The so-called marital rape exemption goes back to 17th-century England, when Chief Justice Matthew Hale declared that a husband cannot be guilty of raping his wife "for by their mutual matrimonial consent and contract the wife hath given up herself in this kind unto the husband which she cannot retract" (quoted in Russell 1982:17). This decision was based on the idea that wives are property and that sex is a wife's duty. It was the prevailing legal guideline in the United States until the 1970s. In 1977, Oregon deleted the spouse-immunity clause from the rape statute, and a man was tried (though not convicted) for wife rape the next year. Marital rape is now a crime in all 50 states, and it is estimated that 10 to 14 percent of all married women and 40 to 50 percent of battered women will experience it (Martin, Taft, and Resick 2007).

Apart from public and legal opinions, is it reasonable to speak of wife rape? Does the wife suffer the same kinds of trauma as other rape victims? Diana Russell (1982) investigated the question of wife rape by surveying a random sample of 930 women in the San Francisco Bay area. ("Random" does not mean they were chosen at random, but that they were carefully selected using a method that gave every woman in the area an equal chance of being chosen.) She interviewed the 644 women who were or had been married. About 14 percent, or one in seven, told about "sexual assaults" by their husbands that could be classified as rape. The wives were raped by force, by the threat of force, and by their inability to consent to sexual intercourse because of being drugged, asleep, or somehow helpless. The forced sex included oral and anal sex as well as sexual intercourse.

Some of the women said their husbands threatened to beat them if they did not submit. Others said they were held down forcibly. In a few cases, weapons were used to intimidate them or they were beaten with fists or objects. Overall, 84 percent of the wives indicated that some kind of force was used. Pushing and pinning down were the most common kinds of force employed by the husbands, but 16 percent of the women said that their husbands hit, kicked, or slapped them, and 19 percent said they were beaten or slugged. About 1 out of 10 of the women pointed out, without being asked, that they had been injured during the attack, ranging from bruises to broken bones and concussions.

The husbands also made verbal threats and even used weapons: 13 percent of the husbands had guns and 1 percent had knives. Twenty-one percent threatened to kill their wives. These wives were obviously and understandably intimidated.

What about the argument that forced sex with one's husband cannot possibly be as traumatic as forced sex with a stranger? Russell compared the responses of her sample with those of women who had been raped by strangers; acquaintances; authority figures; and friends, dates, or lovers. In terms of the proportion of women who reported being "extremely upset" by the incident, the proportions were 65 percent of those raped by a relative other than the husband (usually a childhood rape), 61 percent of those raped by a stranger, 59 percent of those raped by a husband, 42 percent of those raped by an acquaintance, 41 percent of those raped by an authority figure, and 33 percent of those raped by a friend, date, or lover (Russell 1982). Further, the same percentage— 52 percent—of women who were raped by their husbands and women who were raped by a relative other than the husband indicated "great long-term effects" on their lives, compared to 39 percent of those raped by a stranger, and smaller percentages of those involved in the other kinds of rape.

Clearly, wife rape is no less traumatic than other kinds of rape and is more traumatic than many kinds. Women who had been raped by their husbands suffered, among other effects, increased negative feelings toward their husbands and men generally; deterioration of the marriage (including divorce); changed behavior patterns (drinking more, or never remarrying if a divorce resulted); increased fear, anxiety, anger, or depression; and increased negative feelings about sex. Two of the raped women tried to commit suicide.

Russell's research has clear implications for dealing with the problem. Many states still have various forms of the marital rape exemption on their statute books. In some cases, a distinction is made between rape by a husband and rape by someone else, with the former being a less serious offense; but Russell's research shows that rape by a husband is a serious offense from the victim's point of view. Such research not only provides insight but also suggests realistic ways of resolving a problem.

Statistical Analysis of Official Records

Suppose you want to see how *self-esteem* enters into various social problems. For instance, you might want to see whether prejudice and discrimination affect the self-esteem of minorities, whether negative attitudes about growing old affect the self-esteem

mean
the average

of the aged, or whether rapists or other offenders have low self-esteem. You could use a questionnaire to measure self-esteem, then compute the **mean** (average) scores of your respondents.

Let's say that the mean score of a random sample of offenders was 8.9 and the mean score of a random sample of average citizens of the same age, gender, and socioeconomic status was 10.2. The offenders have lower self-esteem. But is the difference between 8.9 and 10.2 a significant one? If not, how much difference would be required before you could say that it was significant—that is, before you could say with some confidence that the two groups differ in level of self-esteem?

test of significance
a statistical method for determining the probability that research findings occurred by chance

The question can be answered by using a **test of significance,** which is a technical way of determining the probability that your findings occurred by chance. That is, if the difference is not significant statistically, then you cannot say that offenders have a lower self-esteem than nonoffenders. A different set of samples might yield scores of 9.4 for both groups, or a slightly higher mean for offenders than for nonoffenders. If the difference is statistically significant, however, you can say with some confidence that offenders generally have lower self-esteem than nonoffenders.

We will not examine details of tests of significance; they require greater knowledge of statistics. Note, however, that many of the findings about social problems discussed in this book—whether gathered through survey research, experiment, or official records—have been subjected to statistical tests. This gives you confidence that the results reflect significant differences between the groups and, if the samples were adequate, that the results apply to more groups than the ones tested. Thus, you can make general statements about, say, women in America without having surveyed the majority of American women.

Some other questions can be asked about data gathered in research. For example, you might want to know how many of the offenders scored high, medium, and low in self-esteem. To get this information, you need a **frequency distribution,** which we use in subsequent chapters. The frequency distribution provides information not available in the mean.

frequency distribution
the organization of data to show the number of times each item occurs

As Table 1.1 shows, you can have different frequency distributions with the same number of cases and the same mean. If the scores in the table represented thousands of income dollars of women in an organization, you would draw different conclusions about the women's economic well-being in the two cases even though the means were the same.

median
the score below which are half of the scores and above which are the other half

Another question that can be asked is, "What is the **median** score?" The median is the score below which half the scores fall and above which the other half fall. This

TABLE 1.1
Frequency Distribution of Two Sets of Hypothetical Data

Score	Number In: Set A	Set B
1	10	3
2	2	10
3	2	7
4	6	0
Mean score	2.2	2.2

	Number of Families	
Income Level	Set A	Set B
$ 1,000	2	1
2,000	1	2
3,000	1	1
4,000	1	0
5,000	2	1
10,000	0	2
Mean	$3,000	$4,714
Median	3,000	3,000

TABLE 1.2
Frequency Distribution, Mean, and Median of Two Sets of Hypothetical Income Data

furnishes important information for dealing with things such as income distribution. For instance, if A and B represent two communities in Table 1.2, the mean incomes of the two are quite different. You might conclude that the people in community B are better off than those in community A. Actually, the median income is the same for both A and B, and the higher mean for B is due to the two families with very high incomes. Thus, *extreme figures* will affect the mean but not the median. When you find a big difference between the mean and the median, you know extremes are involved.

Statistical analysis is useful for several types of research. Suppose you want to see whether women are discriminated against with respect to income. You will need a frequency distribution of male and female incomes as well as mean and median income for the two groups. This information can be obtained from government census data: The analysis has already been made, and you need only interpret it. You do not need to make a test of significance because census data involve the entire population; tests of significance are used only when you want to know the probability that your findings about a sample are true for the population.

Not all official records are analyzed statistically, and not all are as complete as census data. Yet many data are available that you can use to improve your understanding of social problems. An example of the utility of the statistical analysis of official records is provided by Jacobs and Carmichael's (2002) study of the death penalty. The researchers raised the question of why the death penalty exists in some states but not others. Is it simply a matter that some people believe the penalty is an effective crime deterrent while others do not? Or are other factors at work as well?

Using various theoretical considerations, the researchers set up hypotheses about the impact of economic, political, and racial factors on the death penalty. They tested the hypotheses by using official records, including whether a state had the death penalty, the extent of economic inequality in the state, the unemployment rate, the proportion of African Americans and Hispanics, the proportion of families headed by a woman, the extent of public conservatism (measured by the ideologies of the state's elected congresspeople), and the strength of the Republican Party (measured by whether the governor was Republican and the proportion of Republicans in the state legislature).

In accord with their hypotheses, the researchers found that states with the largest black populations, the greatest economic inequality, Republican dominance in the state legislature, and stronger conservative values were more likely to have the death penalty. In accord with our model, the researchers identified multiple social factors associated with the death penalty—institutions, stratification, values, and ideologies—and they showed that whether a state has the death penalty is not simply a matter of believing in its value as a deterrent to crime. Economic threats, racial divisions, and ideologies all enter into the matter.

Experiments

In essence, the *experimental method* involves manipulation of one or more variables, control of other variables, and measurement of the consequences in still other variables. The manipulated variables are called the **independent variables,** while those that are measured to see the ways they have been affected are called the **dependent variables.** To see whether the independent variables cause change in the dependent variables, the experimenter uses *both an experimental group and a control group.* Measurements are taken in both groups, but the control group is not exposed to the treatment (the independent variable).

independent variable
the variable in an experiment that is manipulated to see how it affects changes in the dependent variable

dependent variable
the variable in an experiment that is influenced by an independent variable

Suppose you want to set up an experiment to test the hypothesis that prejudice is increased by negative interpersonal encounters with people of other races. You get a group of white volunteers, test them on their level of prejudice, and select 20 who score about the same (that is, you control for level of prejudice). You then divide them into two groups and give each group the same brief lecture by an African American. One group is treated kindly by the lecturer, while the other group is treated in an abusive manner. Following the lecture, you again test the 20 subjects for their level of prejudice.

If the 10 who hear the abusive lecturer increase their level of prejudice while the 10 who listen to the kindly lecturer show no increase, the hypothesis is clearly supported. In practice, experiments never come out this neatly. Some people who listen to the abusive speaker will not increase their level of prejudice, and some who listen to the kindly speaker will show more prejudice afterward. In other words, factors other than just the interpersonal contact are at work. The experimenter tries to control the setting and the subjects in order to minimize the effect of these other factors.

The utility of experiments is illustrated in a study of how using a cell phone while driving affects other drivers (McGarva, Ramsey, and Shear 2006). One-third or more of all drivers use cell phones while driving, and cell phone users are more likely than others to be involved in collisions. Is it possible that using cell phones increases the amount of hostility and road rage in others when users are seen driving in ways that are frustrating or hazardous? If so, then cell phone usage while driving may be a factor in the total amount of violence in our society.

How could we find out? McGarva, Ramsey, and Shear (2006) set up two experiments to observe reactions to drivers on cell phones. In the first experiment, one of the researchers drove an older car on some two-lane roads within the city limits of a Midwestern town. The car was equipped with a hidden camera that recorded drivers behind the researcher's car. When a car approached from the rear, the researcher slowed down to 10 miles per hour less than the posted speed limit. In some cases, the researcher appeared to talk on a cell phone while driving slowly (the experimental group); in other cases, the researcher drove with both hands on the wheel (the control group).

In the second experiment, when the researcher's car was at a red light and another car was waiting behind it, the researcher's car paused approximately 15 seconds after the light had turned green. Again, in some cases the researcher appeared to be talking

Drivers on cell phones increase the amount of roadway aggression.
©David Buffington/Getty Images

on a cell phone (the experimental group) while in other cases the researcher simply sat in the car with both hands on the wheel.

In both experiments the researchers found that when the driver appeared to be talking on a cell phone, men in other cars honked their horns more quickly and frequently than when the driver was not on a cell phone. Women in other cars tended to use their horns less, but judgments of their facial expressions concluded that they were more angry when the researcher was on a cell phone than when the researcher had both hands on the wheel.

The researchers concluded that the use of cell phones by drivers adds to the growing problem of roadway aggression. It would be useful to know whether those frustrated drivers with elevated levels of hostility act more aggressively or violently afterward. Such a question illustrates why researchers invariably point out that additional research is necessary.

Participant Observation

Participant observation, the last method we consider, involves a number of elements, including interaction with subjects, participation in and observation of pertinent activities of the subjects, interviews, and use of documents and artifacts. In participant observation, the researcher directly participates in and observes the social reality being studied. The researcher is both a part of and detached from the social reality being studied.

However, there are differences in the extent to which the researcher is involved in the social reality being studied. The relative emphasis on participation versus observation, and whether the researcher reveals his or her identity to participants, are decisions that must be made (and are matters of ethical debate). For instance, if a researcher uses observation to study poverty, he or she might live in an impoverished community

participant observation
a method of research in which one directly participates and observes the social reality being studied

and pretend to be a poor person. Or the researcher might acknowledge that research is being conducted while he or she participates in community activities. The researcher might decide to participate only in selective community activities that he or she specifically wants to observe. Or the researcher could choose to be primarily an observer, watching poor children in a schoolroom behind a one-way mirror. Which will yield the best information? Which, if any, would be considered unethical? Researchers must answer such questions.

As an example of participant observation research, we looked at Gwendolyn Dordick's (2002) research into a transitional housing program for the homeless. Numerous programs exist to deal with the problem of homeless people. How effective are these programs? This question needs to be addressed in order to frame public policy and provide guidelines for private efforts to attack the problems.

Dordick pointed out that the initial emphasis on setting up emergency shelters and giving monetary assistance for housing has given way to programs that combine temporary shelter with a variety of social services. The services are designed to address the basic causes of homelessness, such as substance abuse, mental illness, and chronic unemployment. Homeless individuals or families are given temporary shelter while they take advantage of the services to deal with the cause of their homelessness. The goal is to make the homeless "housing-ready."

Dordick spent 18 months as a participant observer in On the Way, a transitional program for homeless, single, substance-abusing men. Her goals were to determine the meaning of "becoming housing-ready" and to see how effective the program was in making people housing-ready.

Dordick did not live in the home where the program was run, but she visited it nearly 100 times, spending two to six hours there each time. She joined in staff and community meetings, observed group therapeutic activities, and hung out with people in the home and in the residents' rooms. She also conducted interviews with current and past staff members and residents.

The services provided by On the Way included mental health counseling, education, job training, and training in independent living skills. Basic questions Dordick tried to answer were: How does one know when a resident is housing-ready, prepared to live on his or her own? How do the staff know when to tell a resident that he or she is ready to move on? The ability to pay rent or the eligibility for government subsidy were not among the criteria used. Rather, the staff used very subjective means such as the "quality of sobriety." A staff member found it very difficult to define precisely what he meant by quality of sobriety. He just had a sense of it from his own experience.

So how well did the program work? While Dordick was there, and during the year following her research, seven residents and two resident managers left On the Way. One secured his own apartment and another moved to a permanent subsidized housing facility. The others moved in with relatives or girlfriends. As Dordick summed it up, there was no transition to independent living for most of them. It was just a matter of substituting "one set of dependencies for another" (Dordick 2002:27).

By the use of participant observation, then, Dordick was able to evaluate the effectiveness of one program designed to help the homeless. The minimal success of this program does not mean that the homeless are hopeless. It means that we must keep searching for effective ways to help.

Summary

You need to distinguish between personal and social problems. For the former, the causes and solutions lie within the individual and his or her immediate environment. For the latter, the causes and solutions lie outside the individual and his or her immediate environment. Defining a particular problem as personal or social is important because the definition determines the causes you identify, the consequences of the problem, and how you cope with the problem.

The model we use to analyze social problems treats them as contradictions. It emphasizes that multiple-level factors cause and help perpetuate problems. You must understand social problems in terms of the mutual influence between social structural factors, social psychological or cognitive factors, and social interaction.

In addition to attending to the multiple factors involved, two additional tools are necessary for an adequate understanding of social problems. One is to use critical thinking skills to identify fallacious ways of thinking that have been used to analyze social problems and that create and perpetuate myths about those problems. The other is to understand the methods of social research. An adequate understanding of social problems is based on research and not merely on what seems to be reasonable.

Nine different fallacies have been used to analyze social problems. The fallacy of dramatic instance refers to the tendency to overgeneralize, to use a single case or a few cases to support an entire argument. The fallacy of retrospective determinism is the argument that things could not have worked out differently. The fallacy of misplaced concreteness is the tendency to resort to reification, to make something abstract into something concrete. The fallacy of personal attack is a form of debate or argument in which an attack is made on the opponent rather than on the issues. Appeal to prejudice is the exploitation of popular prejudices or passions. Circular reasoning involves the use of conclusions supporting assumptions necessary to make those conclusions. The fallacy of authority is an illegitimate appeal to authority. The fallacy of composition is the idea that what is true of the part is also true of the whole. Finally, non sequitur is drawing the wrong conclusions from premises even though the premises themselves are valid.

Four methods of social research that are useful for understanding social problems are survey research, statistical analysis of official records, experiment, and participant observation. Survey research employs interviews and questionnaires on a sample of people in order to get data. Statistical analysis of official records may be simple (computing means, medians, and frequency distributions) or relatively complex (computing tests of significance). Experiment involves manipulation of one or more variables, control of other variables, and measurement of consequences in still other variables. Experiments frequently take place in a laboratory setting, where the researcher has a high degree of control over what happens. Finally, participant observation involves both participation and observation on the part of the researcher; the researcher is both a part of and detached from the social reality being studied.

Key Terms

Attitude	Ideology
Conflict Theory	Independent Variable
Contradiction	Institution
Critical Thinking	Interaction
Dependent Variable	Mean
Fallacy of Appeal to Prejudice	Median
	Norm
Fallacy of Authority	Participant Observation
Fallacy of Circular Reasoning	Personal Problem
	Reification
Fallacy of Composition	Role
Fallacy of Dramatic Instance	Social Problem
	Socioeconomic Status
Fallacy of Misplaced Concreteness	Stratification System
	Structural Functionalism
Fallacy of Non Sequitur	Survey
Fallacy of Personal Attack	Symbolic Interactionism
Fallacy of Retrospective Determinism	Test of Significance
	Values
Frequency Distribution	Variables

Study Questions

1. Using rape or some other problem as an example, how would you distinguish between a personal and a social problem?

chapter 1 review

2. What difference does the distinction between personal and social problems make in understanding the causes and consequences of problems?

3. Define each of the concepts in the authors' model and illustrate how each can enhance understanding of social problems.

4. What is meant by "quality of life," and in what way is it a part of social problems?

5. Illustrate each of the nine fallacies of thinking by showing how each can be used to "explain" a social problem.

6. How is survey research used to study social problems?

7. In what ways are official records useful for the study of social problems?

8. How do you set up a scientific experiment to research a social problem?

9. What did participant observation teach you about a program designed to help the homeless, and how did the researcher go about being a participant observer?

Internet Resources/ Exercises

1. Explore some of the ideas in this chapter on the following sites:

http://www.asanet.org   The official site of the American Sociological Association. Includes press releases and other information of value to students of social problems.

http://www.sssp1.org Official site of the Society for the Study of Social Problems, with access to the *SSSP Newsletter.* Links to other sites relevant to social problems.

www.davidcoon.com/soc.htm   A list of sociology sites on the Internet, including links to many sites useful in dealing with social problems.

2. The journal *Social Problems* is published by Oxford. Go to its site: http://www.socprooxfordjournals.org. Find the journal and examine the table of contents over the past year. Compare the kinds of problems dealt with in the articles with those explored in this text, with those you think are of concern to most Americans, and with those of most concern to you personally. Is the journal dealing with the issues of most concern?

3. Input the term "fallacies" into your search engine. Select a number of sites and compare their materials with those in the text. Are there other fallacies that should be included in the text? Are there fallacies that seem more appropriate than some of those described in the text for understanding social problems? In addition to those dealt with in the text, what other fallacies do you find helpful for understanding patterns of thinking?

For Further Reading

Best, Joel. *Damned Lies and Statistics: Uncovering Numbers from the Media, Politicians, and Activists.* Berkeley: University of California Press, 2001. Discusses the various ways people use and misuse statistics as they think about and report on social problems.

Black, Beth, ed. *An A to Z of Critical Thinking.* New York: Continuum, 2012. Gives definitions and examples of more than 130 terms and concepts employed in critical thinking. Helps you to better understand the differences between such things as facts, fallacies, arguments, logic, and opinions.

Diestler, Sherry. *Becoming a Critical Thinker: A User Friendly Manual.* 4th ed. New York: Prentice-Hall, 2004. A comprehensive but accessible survey of critical thinking on controversial issues, including exercises to hone your skills.

Gilbert, Nigel, ed. *Researching Social Life.* 3rd ed. Thousand Oaks, CA: Sage, 2008. Shows how qualitative and quantitative methods can be used to research social phenomena.

Huff, Darrell. *How to Lie with Statistics.* New York: W. W. Norton, 1993. A readable, fascinating exposition of proper and improper use of statistical data. Shows how statistics as well as myths can impart incorrect information.

Rapley, Mark. *Quality of Life Research: A Critical Introduction.* Thousand Oaks, CA: Sage, 2003. A critical introduction to the concept of quality of life and the ways in which people research it. Uses an interdisciplinary approach in its analysis.

Sribnick, Ethan G., ed. *A Legacy of Innovation: Governors and Public Policy.* Philadelphia: University of Pennsylvania Press, 2008. Explores the role of state governors vis-à-vis the federal government in addressing a number of social problems.

Problems of Behavioral Deviance

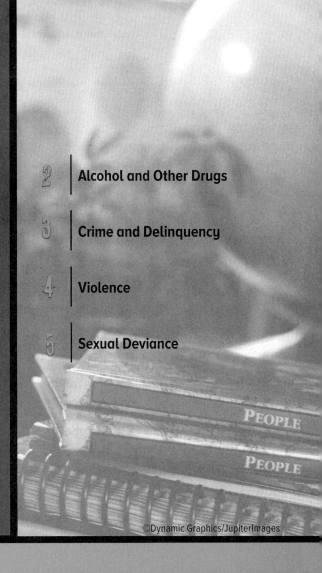

2 | Alcohol and Other Drugs

3 | Crime and Delinquency

4 | Violence

5 | Sexual Deviance

©Dynamic Graphics/JupiterImages

What do such actions as prostitution, drug addiction, and arson have in common? They all involve behavior that deviates from social norms. As such, most Americans view the behavior as within the individual's control and responsibility. That is, if a person engages in prostitution, uses drugs, or robs a store, it is a matter of his or her free choice. Further, because it is a choice that violates social norms, the person who engages in any kind of behavioral variance is likely to be (1) condemned and punished, (2) defined as "sick" and given therapy, or (3) both.

As you will see, the matter is not as simple as this view suggests. If, for example, you define crime as any infraction of the law—including such activities as speeding or failing to report income on tax returns—few if any Americans are innocent of crime. Like all problems discussed in this book, problems of behavioral deviance are complex issues that involve social contradictions, are defined as having adverse effects on the quality of life, and have multilevel causes.

CHAPTER

2

Alcohol and Other Drugs

Despair and Hope

Two voices illustrate the trauma of drug abuse. The first is a cocaine addict, a man mired in despair. The second is the parent of an alcoholic, a mother who has hope after years of despair.

• Mark, the cocaine addict, grew up in a small southern town. After two years of college, he found a good-paying job in a large city. For a while, his life seemed to be on a fast, upward track:

But I lost it all because I got hooked on crack. I wanted to hang out with the fast people. But crack is a double-edged sword. It makes you feel great, but it tears your life apart. I was always able to meet every challenge of my life. But I can't beat this drug thing. My company paid tens of thousands of dollars to send me through two rehabilitation programs. I didn't get any better, so they fired me.

©Scott T. Baxter/Getty Images

I've had a heart operation, but I'm still smoking. Coke is a cruel mistress, man. She don't care who she takes from. And she doesn't give anything back.

Mark, now homeless, is resigned to a dismal existence. In his own mind, he will never be anything other than a cocaine addict.

• Betty, the mother of an alcoholic, is also a victim of the drug problem. Her years of pain underscore the fact that it is not only the abusers who suffer destructive consequences. Her son, Curt, is sober at the present time. But Betty vividly remembers the years of abuse:

He was only 14 when he started drinking. I don't know why. But he began avoiding us, and skipping school. He spent a lot of time alone in his room when he was at home. For years I cried for my boy. But I refused to admit that he had a drinking problem. My husband told me that Curt was getting drunk, but I insisted it was just his allergies.

When he was 18, he left home. You can't imagine the pain I felt. But three months later, he suddenly appeared at the kitchen door. He was dirty, hungry, and thin. I gave him some food. He stayed home, but a year later he came home drunk again and was foul-mouthed. My husband told him to go to bed, and when he sobered up he should leave our house. He did, but three months later he called. He was desperate. We got him into a short-term treatment center, then brought him home again. My husband died shortly after that. I was afraid Curt would go off on another binge, but he's stayed with me and is working now and helping support me.

Betty is hopeful but also apprehensive about Curt's long-term prospects. Like everyone connected with a person who abuses alcohol, she can only live day by day. The grimness on her face as she tells her story powerfully expresses her uncertainty.

Introduction

Americans have had ambivalent feelings about alcohol and other drugs throughout their history. In general, the colonists regarded alcoholic beverages as one of God's gifts to mankind. As Furnas (1965:18) noted, our forebears "clung long to the late medieval notion that alcohol deserved its splendid name, *aqua vitae*, water of life." Drunkenness was punished, but drinking was generally considered one of life's pleasures. Yet by the 19th century a growing temperance movement began urging its members to abstain from all alcoholic beverages (Furnas 1965:67).

addiction
repeated use of a drug or alcohol to the point of periodic or chronic intoxication that is detrimental to the user or society

Until the beginning of the 19th century, the use of opium and its derivatives was less offensive to Americans than smoking cigarettes or drinking. After the Civil War, however, some Americans began to warn about the dangers of **addiction.** Eventually these warnings became part of national policy, as seen in the war on drugs that began in the 1980s.

abuse
improper use of drugs or alcohol to the degree that the consequences are defined as detrimental to the user or society

This ambivalence about drugs is based partly on the distinctions among use, **abuse,** and addiction. The abuse of alcohol and other drugs, not the use, creates the problem. We define *abuse* as the *improper use of alcohol and other drugs to the degree that the consequences are defined as detrimental to the user or to society.* Addiction is a form of abuse. Addiction has been called a "brain disease" because continued abuse of a drug causes changes in brain function that drive the addict to compulsively seek and use the drug (Leshner 1998).

Not every case of abuse involves addiction. A man may not be an alcoholic, but he may get drunk and kill someone while driving his car. A woman may not be hooked on any drugs, but she may be persuaded to try LSD, have a "bad trip," and commit suicide.

Our focus in this chapter is on abuse, including addiction. We look at alcohol and other drugs, discussing their effects on users, patterns of use, effects on the quality of life, multilevel factors that create and perpetuate the problems, and ways people have attempted to cope.

Alcohol

The use and abuse of alcohol is the nation's most serious health problem. We examine first the effects of this troublesome drug.

Effects

All alcoholic beverages contain the same drug, ethyl alcohol or ethanol, but the proportion varies in different beverages. An individual can consume about the same amount of alcohol by drinking a pint of beer, a glass of wine, or a shot (1.5 ounces) of whiskey. What happens when that alcohol is ingested? The alcohol is burned and broken down in the body at a relatively constant rate. If an individual drinks slowly, there is little or no accumulation of alcohol in the blood; but if an individual consumes alcohol more quickly than it can be burned in the body, the *concentration of alcohol in the blood increases.*

A small amount of alcohol can result in changes in an individual's mood and behavior, and the effects become more serious as the concentration of alcohol in the blood increases (National Institute on Alcohol Abuse and Alcoholism 2001). A blood alcohol level of about 0.05 percent (one part alcohol to 2,000 parts blood) can make the individual feel a sense of release from tensions and inhibitions. This mild euphoria is the aim of many people who drink moderately. As the alcohol level increases, however, there is an increasing loss of control because alcohol acts as a depressant on brain functions. At the 0.10 percent level, the individual's motor control is affected—hands, arms, and legs become clumsy. At 0.20 percent, both the motor and the emotional functions of the brain are impaired, and the individual staggers and becomes intensely emotional. This is the level at which someone is defined as drunk.

At 0.30 percent, an individual is incapable of adequately perceiving and responding to the environment and may go into a stupor. At 0.40 or a higher percent, the individual lapses into a coma and may die.

What do these numbers mean in actual drinks? Suppose you are a 150-pound individual who drinks on an empty stomach. After drinking two bottles of beer or the equivalent (11 ounces of wine, 2 highballs, or 2 cocktails), you will feel warm and relaxed. After three bottles of beer or the equivalent, you will start experiencing more intense emotions and are likely to become talkative, noisy, or morose. Four bottles of beer or its equivalent produces clumsiness and unsteady walking and standing. At this point, you are legally drunk in most states. If you drink four bottles of beer or the equivalent on an empty stomach, it takes about eight hours for all the alcohol to leave your body.

The damaging effects of alcohol abuse are most obvious in the *alcoholic*—the individual who is addicted to alcohol. Alcoholism is defined in terms of four symptoms (National Institute on Alcohol Abuse and Alcoholism 2001): (1) a craving or compulsion to drink; (2) loss of control to limit drinking on any particular occasion; (3) physical dependence, so that withdrawal symptoms (nausea, sweating, shakiness, anxiety) are experienced if alcohol use ceases; and (4) tolerance, the need to drink increasingly greater amounts in order to get "high." Because the effects can be so deleterious and the use of alcohol is so widespread, many experts consider alcohol abuse the major drug problem in the United States today.

Patterns of Use

binge drinking
having five or more drinks on the same occasion

A majority of adult Americans are drinkers. A national survey of those aged 12 or older found that 52.7 percent were current drinkers, 23.0 percent had participated in **binge drinking** (5 or more drinks on the same occasion), and 6.2 percent were heavy drinkers (5 or more drinks on the same occasion on each of 5 or more days in the past 30 days) (National Center for Health Statistics 2016). Alcohol use varied by age, of course, from 2.1 percent of those aged 12–13 to 66.0 percent of those aged 26–34. The 18- to 25-year-olds had the highest rates of binge drinking and heavy use. Another national survey found that alcohol use and impairment affects 15 percent of the workforce (Frone 2006). Some drink before work and some during work. Millions work while under the influence of alcohol, and millions more work with a hangover. By their own admission, then, tens of millions of Americans have a problem with alcohol abuse.

Drinking patterns vary across different groups, though all groups are affected to some extent. American Indians probably have the highest rates of use and abuse of alcohol. Compared to the general population, they begin drinking at an earlier age, drink more frequently and in greater amounts, and have a higher alcohol-related death rate (Mitchell, Beals, and Whitesell 2008; Friese et al. 2011; Landen et al. 2013). Alcohol is involved in about one of every six American Indian deaths.

Among other racial/ethnic groups, whites have the highest rate of current use (57.7 percent) and of heavy drinking (7.1 percent). Hispanics have the highest rate of binge drinking (24.7 percent). Asian Americans have the lowest rates of current use (38.7 percent), binge drinking (14.5 percent), and heavy drinking (2.0 percent)

Alcohol use and abuse are more likely to take place in groups.
©Image Source/Getty Images

(National Center for Health Statistics 2016). Interestingly, the rate of drinking varies considerably among the various subgroups of Hispanics, with Mexican Americans and Puerto Ricans having much higher rates than other Hispanics and than the general population (Caetano, Ramisetty-Mikler, and Rodriguez 2008). Across all racial and ethnic groups, men drink more than women. Gender differences are decreasing, but *alcohol abuse and alcoholism are primarily male problems*.

Alcohol abuse is also more common among the young. A survey of college students reported that on an average day during a one-year period, 2,179 full-time college students took their first drink of alcohol (Lipari and Jean-Francois 2016). And more than a third of the students engaged in binge drinking in the past month. Binge drinkers are far more likely than others to have unprotected sex, to drive after drinking, to fall behind in school, to be aggressive, and to be involved in property damage. Interestingly, going to a four-year college is associated with higher rates of heavy drinking for whites, but with lower rates for African Americans and Hispanics (Paschall, Bersamin, and Flewelling 2005).

A substantial proportion of children and young adolescents also drink. In the national survey, 11.5 percent of 12- to 17-year-olds were current drinkers (National Center for Health Statistics 2016). The proportion who are binge drinkers has declined since 1980, but in 2015 about 5 percent of 8th graders, 11 percent of 10th graders, and 17 percent of 12th graders reported binge drinking (Forum on Child and Family Statistics 2016). The importance of such figures is seen in the fact that excessive drinking results in thousands of deaths a year among underage youth in the United States and in the fact that the earlier a child begins drinking the more likely that child is to become dependent on alcohol or other drugs and to have alcohol-related behavior problems (Roeber 2007; Hingson, Heeren, and Edwards 2008; Cheadle and Whitbeck 2011).

Thus, the skid-row image of the alcohol abuser is false. Those most likely to drink frequently and to consume higher quantities of alcohol per drinking session are young, white, male, and comparatively well-to-do (Moore et al. 2005).

Alcohol and the Quality of Life

Alcohol, like other drugs, has some medical benefits when used in moderation. In fact, there is evidence that moderate drinkers, compared to both abstainers and heavy drinkers, have a lower rate of coronary heart disease and are less likely to have a heart attack (Mukamal and Rimm 2001). Alcohol abuse, on the other hand, is highly deleterious to the quality of life.

Physical Health.   The physical consequences of alcohol abuse contradict the American *value of physical well-being*. As mentioned earlier, the immediate effects of intoxicating levels of alcohol include impaired motor performance. The long-range effects of abuse include more than 30 medical problems such as cirrhosis of the liver, infectious diseases, cancer, diabetes, mental health problems, cardiovascular disease, liver and pancreas disease, brain damage, gastrointestinal problems, and early death (Rehm 2011). It is estimated that alcohol abuse is responsible for 3.2 to 3.7 percent of all cancer deaths (Nelson et al. 2013). Brain damage is also common, affecting the cognitive functioning of the individual (Cairney, Clough, Jaragba, and Maruff 2007; Mukherjee, Vaidyanathan, and Vasudevan 2008). At any given time, the neuropsychological functioning of the alcoholic—as measured by such things as eye-hand coordination and spatial ability—will be equivalent to that of someone about 10 years older. In *terms of cognitive ability*, in other words, alcoholism costs the user about 10 years of life.

Heavy drinking also may result in muscle diseases and tremors. Heart functioning and the gastrointestinal and respiratory systems may be impaired by prolonged heavy drinking. Whereas moderate alcohol consumption protects the heart, heavy consumption increases the risk of strokes. The ills of the gastrointestinal system range from nausea, vomiting, and diarrhea to gastritis, ulcers, and pancreatitis. Problems of the respiratory system include lowered resistance to pneumonia and other infectious diseases. Among women, alcohol abuse can result in menstrual cycle irregularity, inability to conceive, and early onset of menopause (Gavaler 1991). Among men, alcohol can lead to impotence and sterility (Wright, Gavaler, and Van Thiel 1991).

Alcohol abuse can lead to early death (Costello 2006). A study of male veterans found that the death rate among alcoholics was 2.5 times higher than that of nonalcoholics, and that alcoholics in the 35- to 44-year-old age group were 5.5 times as likely to die as were nonalcoholics of the same age (Liskow et al. 2000).

Alcohol plays a role in various kinds of physical trauma. Consider the following (Rivara et al. 1997; Greenfield 1998; Males 2010; Fierro, Morales, and Alvarez 2011; Terry-McElrath, O'Malley, and Johnson 2014):

Alcohol use is associated with an increased risk of injury and violent death (suicide or homicide) in the home.

About 35 percent of violent victimizations involve an offender who had been drinking.

Two-thirds of the victims of intimate violence report that alcohol was a factor in the attack.

Intoxicated drivers are more prone to road rage, are involved in nearly a third of all fatal accidents, and are the sixth leading cause of death for teenagers.

Alcohol also affects the unborn children of women who drink. The most severe cases are those of *fetal alcohol syndrome* (Burd, Cotsonas-Hassler, Marsolf, and Kerbeshian 2003). The health problems of children born with fetal alcohol syndrome are head and face deformities; major organ problems that result in heart defects, ear infections, hearing loss, poor eyesight, and bad teeth; and problems with the central nervous system, leading to such problems as mental retardation, hyperactivity, stunted growth, learning disorders, epilepsy, and cerebral palsy (Streissguth 1992; Aronson and Hagberg 1998; Burd et al. 2003).

Alcohol abuse generally, and the fetal alcohol syndrome in particular, illustrate an important point—social problems have consequences at the community level as well as the individual level. In a real sense, a community can become the victim of a problem, for social problems can strain the community's resources and deprive it of the positive contributions that could otherwise be made by people caught up in the problems.

This point is dramatized in American Indian communities (Parker et al. 2010). Alcohol is a factor in about one out of every six American Indian deaths. A study of the fetal alcohol syndrome among American Indians pointed out some of the consequences, including an overload on community institutions (such as sheltered care), dramatic increases in health care costs, and problems of adoption and foster home placement (May 1991). Add to those costs the loss to the community of positive contributions that could be made by those who are abusing alcohol or those suffering from fetal alcohol syndrome. Thus, the community at large, as well as individuals, suffers.

Psychological Health.   The *desire for psychological well-being* is contradicted by the various degrees of impairment that result from alcohol abuse. Even a small amount of alcohol can reduce the individual's sensitivity to taste, smell, and pain. Vision can be affected by large amounts of alcohol (one factor in the dangers of driving while drinking). Continued heavy use of alcohol is associated with major depression and with impaired cognitive functions such as memory and visuospatial ability (Schuckit, Smith, and

ALCOHOLISM IN EASTERN EUROPE

In the 10th century, a Slavic prince noted that drink was the joy of the people. "We cannot live without it," he asserted. Time appears to have borne out his observation. Slavs and other Eastern European people drink, on average, far more than Americans and have high rates of alcoholism. The problem worsened considerably after the breakup of communism began in 1989.

A World Health Organization survey found that worldwide the consumption of alcohol was about 6.13 liters per person aged 15 years and older. The amount for the United States was 9.44 liters. But in Eastern Europe, consumption levels ranged from a low of 12.4 liters for Bulgaria to 15.8 liters for Russia. In other words, Eastern European people drink double or more the worldwide average. Russians purchase 250 million cases of vodka a year. This is three times the amount sold in all the rest of the world and more than the total amount of hard liquor sold in the United States.

It is not surprising, then, that the average life span for Russian men is only 58. Nor that Russia has about 8 million alcoholics; the rate is more than double that of the United States.

Other Eastern European nations face similar problems with alcoholism and consequent health problems and premature death. In Poland, the annual per capita consumption of pure alcohol is around 3 gallons, a figure twice as high as the 1987 rate. In Hungary, cirrhosis of the liver is the leading cause of death of men aged 36 to 60. The number of alcoholics in Hungary doubled from 1989 to 1992.

Why do the Eastern Europeans drink so heavily? There is no simple answer. During the communist era, it was popular to blame alcoholism on the repressiveness of the regimes. But as we just noted, alcoholism increased rapidly after the breakdown of communism.

A number of factors seem to be at work. In the new market economies, alcohol is much cheaper than it was under communism. In the mid-1980s, the average Polish worker's monthly salary could buy 11 liters of vodka. By the mid-1990s, it could buy 35 liters! In the transition to capitalism, Eastern Europeans have also faced high rates of unemployment and considerable insecurity about the future, conditions that tend to breed higher rates of alcohol abuse. Finally, the Eastern Europeans have a long tradition—stretching back hundreds of years—of heavy drinking. The combination of all these factors has created the highest rates of alcoholism in the world.

SOURCES
Chicago Tribune, April 23, 1995; U.S. News & World Report, April 15, 1996; McKee and Shkolnikov 2001; Mackenbach et al. 2008; World Health Organization 2011b.

Kalmijn 2013; Nguyen-Louie et al. 2015). Such problems occur because alcohol adversely affects the brain. In the alcoholic, the adverse effects are severe (National Institute on Alcohol Abuse and Alcoholism 2001; Vanheusden et al. 2008). At least half of all alcoholics have difficulty with problem solving, abstract thinking, memory tasks, and psychomotor performance. Severe alcoholics may succumb to *alcohol amnestic disorder* (short-term memory impairments) or *dementia* (general loss of intellectual abilities, impaired memory, and possible personality change). Some alcohol abusers take the final solution to their despair: Alcohol abuse is associated with a substantial proportion of suicides (Roy 2003; Mann et al. 2006).

One popular belief is that alcohol "releases inhibitions," so that the person who drinks "loosens up" and may, for example, be more motivated toward sexual activity. Actually, heavy drinking inhibits sexual performance, and alcoholics report a deficient sex life or even impotence (Peugh and Belenko 2001). Another belief is that a drink in the evening helps the individual to relax and thereby to sleep better. Whatever the value of one drink, having several drinks before going to sleep decreases the amount of dreaming, which can impair concentration and memory and increase anxiety, irritability, and a sense of tiredness.

Interpersonal Problems. Alcohol abuse leads to *problems of interaction* both within and outside the family. Pregnant women who drink put their unborn children at risk even if they

"I'D KILL BEFORE I'D DRINK"

We once attended a meeting of Alcoholics Anonymous with a friend who had been "dry" for a short time. As we drove through the countryside to the small town where the group met, the friend kept commenting on the beauty of the scenery. He was enchanted by what we thought was a fairly common view on a warm spring evening. But his years as an alcoholic had been a living hell, and in the course of rediscovering what life can be like when you are free of addiction, he was finding beauty in the commonplace. "I really think," he told us, "that if someone tried to force me to take a drink I

would kill them." The thought of ever returning to alcohol terrified him.

One of the best ways to understand the impact of addiction on an individual is to talk with an ex-addict. If you do not know an ex-alcoholic, contact Alcoholics Anonymous and attend one of their open meetings. Ask one or two members if they would be willing to discuss their understanding of why they became addicted, what their life was like when they were addicted, and what finally led them to seek the help of AA.

List the adverse effects on the quality of life discussed in this chapter that apply to your informants. Based on your interviews, make a report, oral or written, of your recommendations for dealing with the problem of alcoholism.

do not drink heavily enough to induce fetal alcohol syndrome. In a small study, children aged 10–18 who were exposed prenatally to alcohol had lower levels of moral maturity and higher rates of delinquency than those not exposed (Schonfeld, Mattson, and Riley 2005).

Early use of alcohol by children is associated with an increased risk of violence in young adulthood (Green, Doherty, Zebrak, and Ensminger 2011). It is also associated with early sexual activity, with all its potential hazards, including pregnancy and disease (Phillips-Howard et al. 2010). Alcoholic husbands are more likely to have an extramarital affair and to engage in risky sexual behavior (not using condoms) than are nonalcoholic husbands (Hall, Fals-Stewart, and Fincham 2008). Marriages in which one spouse has alcohol abuse disorder are more prone to break up (Cranford 2014). Adult alcoholics have poorer relationships generally with friends, coworkers, spouses, and children (McFarlin, Fals-Stewart, Major, and Justice 2001). Alcohol is associated with aggressive behavior, which leads to ill will and conflict with others (Harford, Wechsler, and Muthen 2003; Graham, Osgood, Wells, and Stockwell 2006; Duke et al. 2011). This aggression may result in a severe form of violence against acquaintances or dates or family members (Xue, Zimmerman, and Cunningham 2009; Rothman et al. 2011). Homes in which one or both spouses abuse alcohol have higher rates of both verbal and physical abuse (Stuart, Moore, Ramsey, and Kahler 2003, 2004; Snow et al. 2006). A comparative study of alcohol and homicide in Russia and the United States concluded that 73 percent of the homicides in Russia and 57 percent of those in the United States involve the use of alcohol (Landberg and Norstrom 2011).

Even if an alcoholic does not become abusive, his or her behavior is certain to cause stress within the family. Mates and children of alcoholics tend to develop physical and psychological problems of their own (Tempier et al. 2006; Keller et al. 2011). Children tend to develop behavior disorders (Haber et al. 2010). And compared to those from nonalcoholic homes, the children of alcohol abusers are more likely to have poorer self-concepts, higher rates of drug use, and higher rates of anxiety, depression, alcoholism, and other disorders when they become adults, as well as lower rates of marriage and of marital quality when they do marry (Obot, Wagner, and Anthony 2001; Watt 2002; Osborne and Berger 2009). The intensity of the stress in an alcoholic home is illustrated by the widow who declared herself to be the happiest person alive because her husband had finally drunk himself to death and thereby set her and her children free.

Economic Costs.   Alcohol abuse is costly to the nation. A study of underage drinking alone put the cost higher than the price of the drink (Miller, Levy, Spicer, and Taylor 2006). In one year, underage drinking resulted in 3,170 deaths and 2.6 million other harmful events, costing around $61.9 billion in medical expenses, work loss, and lost quality of life.

The costs for adult abuse also run into tens of billions of dollars. The costs include the expenses of the arrest, trial, and imprisonment of people who are drunk (in some cities, more than half of all arrests are for drunkenness). They include business losses: People with drinking problems are absent from work about two and a half times as often as others. Moreover, when they are on the job, they may have problems of interaction. Costs to industry are as much as $10 billion a year because of lost work time and lowered productivity of alcoholic employees. All these costs represent resources that could be channeled into activities and programs to enhance the nation's quality of life.

Contributing Factors

The factors that contribute to the alcohol problem both maintain demand and guarantee supply. The problem is embedded in the American way of life.

Social Structural Factors.   Being a part of a *group whose norms and behavior condone drinking* is the most powerful predictor of an individual's drinking (DuRant et al. 2008; Simons-Morton et al. 2016). Males, in fact, use alcohol to bond with each other and to enhance their sense of importance and power (Liu and Kaplan 1996). Some groups establish a tradition of periodic heavy drinking. For example, about half of those people who drink and attend fraternity or sorority parties engage in heavy drinking in those settings (Harford, Wechsler, and Seibring 2002). Off-campus parties and bars are also settings in which heavy drinking takes place among college students. The hazards of such drinking go beyond any immediate effects. A national study of college and university students found that those who were drunk prior to the age of 19 were significantly more likely than others to become alcohol dependent and frequent heavy drinkers, to report that they drove after drinking, and to sustain injuries requiring medical attention after drinking (Hingson et al. 2003).

Integration into a group in which the use of alcohol is approved does not mean the individual will abuse it. Many people use alcohol without becoming addicted. A lower rate of alcoholism is correlated with the following characteristics (National Institute on Alcohol Abuse and Alcoholism 2001):

1. Children are given alcohol early in life in the context of strong family life or religious orientation.
2. Low-alcohol-content beverages—wines and beers—are most commonly used.
3. The alcoholic beverage is ordinarily consumed at meals.
4. Parents typically provide an example of moderation in drinking.
5. Drinking is not a moral question, merely one of custom.
6. Drinking is not defined as a symbol of manhood or adulthood.
7. Abstinence is as acceptable as drinking.
8. Drunkenness is not socially acceptable.
9. Alcohol is not a central element in activities (like a cocktail party).
10. There is general agreement on what is proper and what is improper in drinking.

Under such conditions, a group or an entire society could have high per capita rates of alcohol consumption and relatively low rates of alcoholism. Group norms are an important factor in alcohol use and abuse, but they need not demand abstinence to prevent abuse. Both Jews and Italians in the United States use alcohol as part of a traditional way of life, but alcoholism in those groups is extremely low. The norms of many religious groups also make abuse less likely. Thus, active participation in religion is associated with lower levels of drinking (Bjarnason et al. 2005; Jessor, Costa, Krueger, and Turbin 2006).

Role problems that generate emotional distress can lead to alcohol abuse (Holahan et al. 2001; Lemke, Brennan, Schutte, and Moos 2007). People trying to cope with role conflict may resort to alcohol for relief. Those under stress at school or work and those who believe that alcohol relieves stress are more likely to drink (Park, Armeli, and Tennen 2004; Crosnoe 2006). Undesirable role changes also may lead to alcohol abuse. A major loss (for example, divorce or death of a spouse) or separation can result in alcohol abuse, particularly for men (Horwitz and Davies 1994). The stress resulting from financial strain, from poverty, or from unfair treatment because one is a member of a minority group can also lead to alcohol abuse (Mulia, Ye, Zemore, and Greenfield 2008; Shaw, Agahi, and Krause 2011). Whether from poverty or racial/ethnic identity or both, those who are severely disadvantaged have a two to six times greater risk of having alcohol problems.

Three kinds of *family experiences* are involved in alcohol abuse. First, abuse is more likely when the individual grows up in a family where there is a history of alcoholism or where there is poor marital quality or violence between the parents (Warner, White, and Johnson 2007; Bossarte and Swahn 2008; Hair et al. 2009). Second, alcohol abusers are more likely to come from *broken homes* (Wolfinger 1998; Bjarnason et al. 2003). Third, alcohol abuse is associated with various *problematic relationships within the family,* including dysfunctional marriages and troubled parent-child relationships (Silberg, Rutter, D'Onofrio, and Eaves 2003; Whisman, Uebelacker, and Bruce 2006; Hoffmann and Bahr 2014). Problem drinking among adolescents is associated with homes in which the parents express hostility to the adolescents or in which there is severe family conflict (Conger et al. 1991; Smith, Rivers, and Stahl 1992).

The *mass media also contribute to alcohol abuse.* Researchers who examined 601 popular movies found that 92 percent depicted drinking (Sargent et al. 2006). The researchers surveyed thousands of adolescents to determine the relationship between watching movies and drinking. There was an association between higher exposure to movie alcohol use and drinking by the adolescents. The researchers concluded that exposure to movie alcohol use is a risk factor for early-onset teen drinking. Similarly, television programs show a great deal of drinking with no negative consequences; adolescent viewers of such drinking are more likely to drink themselves (Pinkleton, Fujioka, and Austin 2000). A survey of alcohol advertising on radio showed that nearly half of the ads were placed in programs for which the local audience was disproportionately underage youth, thus adding yet another influence of the media on underage drinking (Centers for Disease Control 2006b). Additionally, a study of problem drinking among black women found higher rates of abuse among women who lived in an area where they were exposed to outdoor alcohol advertising (Kwate and Meyer 2009). And a survey of middle-school youth reported an average of two to four ads a day on their handheld computers, putting the students at risk for earlier or more frequent drinking (Collins et al. 2016).

Finally, any social structural factors that increase stress levels are likely to increase the prevalence of alcohol abuse (Young-Wolff, Kendler, and Prescott 2012; Jones-Webb et al. 2016). In the United States, a *rapidly changing structure* has been associated with increased alcoholism. Both the high rate around 1830 and the increased consumption in the 1960s and 1970s have been associated with stresses induced by a rapidly changing society (Rorabaugh 1979). Another source of stress is a sense of *powerlessness*. You are not comfortable when you feel powerless. Yet the world situation, national problems, your work, and other organizations with which you are involved may induce a sense of powerlessness. If you feel powerless, you are more likely to drink heavily and to have a drinking problem (Seeman, Seeman, and Budros 1988).

Social Psychological Factors. *Attitudes* toward drinking and drunkenness tend to be different from attitudes toward use and abuse of other drugs. Although alcoholism is a major factor in death and disease, there is little public outcry. Parents who would be horrified to find their children smoking marijuana have allowed them to drink spiked punch or other alcoholic beverages at parties.

The importance of attitudes is underscored by the fact that heavy drinkers have more positive and more indulgent attitudes about the use of alcohol. They are likely to believe that their drinking is no different from that of others in the groups to which they belong and that their own drinking is not enough to be called a problem (Wild 2002). For example, a large proportion of college students overestimate the amount of drinking by their peers (Pedersen and LaBrie 2008; Lewis et al. 2011). And their misperceptions are strongly related to the amount of alcohol they consume: They drink as heavily as they believe that others are drinking. In addition, some male college students associate heavy drinking with masculinity (Wells et al. 2014). In other words, the masculine image they want for themselves is affirmed when they engage in heavy drinking.

The problem of alcoholism is further complicated by ideologies—by *the ideology that transforms it into a personal rather than a social problem, and the campus ideology that heavy drinking at parties is both acceptable and the way to maximize one's fun.* Many Americans believe that the alcoholic can recover if he or she "really wants to change"—that alcoholism is basically a problem of individual self-control. And many students believe that heavy drinking, drinking contests, and hangovers are all legitimate ways to maximize their pleasure and prove their mettle.

Public Policy and Private Action

Instead of asking what can be done for an alcoholic, you need to ask first what kind of alcoholic you are dealing with. Experts are attempting to sort out the special needs of the alcoholic with psychiatric problems, the chronically relapsing alcoholic, the alcoholic's family members who may be both victims of and contributors to the problem, and addicted adolescents and women. Special programs are being developed for these special needs.

Whatever the special needs may be, of course, the alcoholic is likely to need one or more of the following: *individual therapy, drug therapy, behavior therapy,* or *group therapy.* Drug therapies involve administration of either a nausea-producing agent along with an alcoholic beverage or a "deterrent agent" that causes intense headaches and nausea when alcohol is consumed. Obviously, drug therapy requires close supervision by a physician.

In group therapy, the alcoholic is in a group with other alcoholics and with a therapist as facilitator. The task of the group members is to attain insight into their individual reasons for drinking and to get control over drinking. A form of group therapy that is quite successful and does not utilize a professional therapist is Alcoholics Anonymous (AA), which was started by alcoholics. Members gather regularly in small groups to share their experiences and to sustain each other in sobriety. Each member is available to every other member at any time help is needed—when, for example, a member needs to talk to someone in order to resist the urge to drink. Those who join AA begin by admitting they are powerless over alcohol and lack control of their own lives. This admission is significant because it opposes the ideology discussed earlier (an ideology, incidentally, held by alcoholics as well as by others). New members also agree to surrender to a Higher Power (as they understand it), to make amends to those harmed by their drinking, and to help other alcoholics become sober.

Millions of alcoholics have sought help through AA, which is still one of the most effective ways to deal with alcoholism (Connors, Tonigan, and Miller 2001; McKellar, Stewart, and Humphreys 2003; Moos and Moos 2004). Of course, not everyone who comes to AA will break the habit; no form of help can claim a 100 percent success rate. The extent to which a particular form of help will succeed depends on, among other things, factors in the social background of the individual seeking help. For instance, a study of adolescent problem drinkers found that those with a background of religious participation found it easier to integrate into the AA program than did those with little or no religiosity (Kelly, Pagano, Stout, and Johnson 2011).

Two spin-offs of AA that are designed to help family members of the alcoholic are Al-Anon and Alateen. Al-Anon is for the alcoholic's spouse or significant other. It helps the person both to deal with the problems caused by the alcoholic and to see his or her own contribution to the interpersonal problems that may be a factor in the alcoholism. Members of Al-Anon learn to take care of their own needs and to stop focusing their lives around the alcoholic's problems. Alateen uses the same principles to help the teenaged children of alcoholics. Frequently, the sponsor of an Alateen group is a member of Al-Anon.

Behavior therapy is based on the principle of rewarding desired behavior in order to reinforce behavior. The reward can be quite simple, such as the pins given at Alcoholics Anonymous meetings to recognize extended periods of sobriety. Or the rewards can be more substantial, such as the vouchers or tokens given by some therapists for each week or month of sobriety; these vouchers or tokens can be exchanged for various kinds of retail goods or entertainment (gift certificates for stores, restaurants, etc.). The use of vouchers or tokens is a form of behavior contracting (also called contingency contracting or contingency management), which is more effective than methods designed to educate, confront, or shock the alcoholic (Miller and Wilbourne 2002).

A somewhat recent trend is so-called brief therapy. Rather than attending therapy sessions over an extended period of time, the alcohol abuser has only a few sessions with a therapist. At a minimum, brief therapy with alcohol abusers involves a 15-minute initial contact and at least one follow-up. A survey of research studies done of brief behavioral interventions for risky and harmful alcohol use reported that 12 months after the counseling, the clients had reduced their average number of drinks per week 13 to 34 percent more than those who did not have the therapy (Whitlock et al. 2004). During counseling, the patient receives an assessment of his or her health status, advice, help in goal setting, a motivational message, and other kinds of help.

The problem of alcoholism also has been attacked through various other programs and facilities. Among these are community care programs, which allow alcoholics to remain in their homes and communities while undergoing treatment. Other programs remove alcoholics from their environments. Throughout the nation, there are hundreds of *halfway* houses for alcoholics, places where they can function in a relatively normal way while receiving therapy. Most of these locations have Alcoholics Anonymous groups, counseling, and other services available to the alcoholics. Alcoholics who are acutely ill may have to be hospitalized for a period of time before going to a halfway house or returning to their homes.

Ultimately, to resolve the problem, the social bases of alcoholism must be attacked through public policy. As with other drugs, *enforcement as well as prevention and education programs* are needed. Research has shown that raising the minimum legal drinking age to 21, increasing alcohol taxes, and intensifying the enforcement of drinking-and-driving laws all reduce the number of alcohol problems (Hollingworth et al. 2006; Fell et al. 2016).

Prevention and education programs face difficulty because group norms and alternative means of coping with stress are involved. Nevertheless, there is evidence that educational programs can help reduce the negative effects of alcohol (Flynn and Brown 1991).

Educational programs must help people understand not only the dangers of alcohol but also ways they can deal with the pressure to drink. For instance, adolescents, who are most likely to give in to peer pressure, can resist drinking even in high-pressure situations by using a number of cognitive and behavioral techniques. These techniques include defining themselves as nondrinkers and defining drinkers in negative terms (e.g., drinkers are weak), developing strong refusal skills, finding alternative activities (such as volunteering or religious activities), and limiting direct exposure to high-risk situations (such as not going to a party at which heavy drinking will occur and may even be expected) (Weitzman and Kawachi 2000; Brown, Parks, Zimmerman, and Phillips 2001; Guo, Hawkins, Hill, and Abbott 2001; Grekin, Sher, and Krull 2007; Wallace et al. 2007).

Finally, both informal and formal measures can be taken to help those victimized by alcohol-impaired driving and to ameliorate or prevent further victimization. At an informal level, peer intervention—trying to stop a friend or acquaintance from driving drunk—has been shown to be effective in the bulk of cases (Collins and Frey 1992).

At a formal level, campaigns against alcohol-impaired drivers began in the 1980s when a California woman founded Mothers Against Drunk Drivers (MADD). She took action after her teenaged daughter was killed by a man who was not only drunk but out on bail from a hit-and-run arrest for drunken driving just two days prior to the accident. Within two years, the group had chapters in more than 20 states. Other groups formed as well—Students Against Driving Drunk (SADD) and Remove Intoxicated Drivers (RID). As a result of the work of these organizations, a number of states have taken measures to reduce the risks to citizens from alcohol-impaired drivers, including raising the drinking age, using roadside sobriety tests, and suspending licenses of offenders. In some states, a driver with a blood alcohol content of more than 0.10 automatically loses his or her license for 90 days, regardless of the outcome of the court case. As a result of these varied formal and informal measures, the proportion of fatal crashes that were alcohol-related declined from 60 percent of all fatal crashes in 1982 to 41 percent in 2006 (Maguire 2012).

Follow-Up. Has anyone close to you—a family member or friend—ever had a problem with alcohol? How did it affect the person's behavior and relationship with you? Describe any efforts or programs that didn't help, and any that did.

Other Drugs

Although alcohol abuse is the major drug problem, the use and abuse of other drugs affect nearly all Americans directly or indirectly. We begin our examination of the problem by looking at the different kinds of drugs and their effects.

Types and Effects

Seven main types of nonalcoholic drugs and some of their possible effects are summarized in Figure 2.1. We should note that these do not include all drugs, only some of

Category and Name	Commercial and Street Names	Intoxication Effects/ Potential Health Consequences
Cannabinoids		*Euphoria; slowed thinking and reaction time; confusion; impaired balance and coordination/ cough, frequent respiratory infections; impaired memory and learning; increased heart rate, anxiety; panic attacks; addiction.*
Hashish	Boom, chronic, hash, hemp, gangster	
Marijuana	Dope, grass, joints, pot, weed, blunt, ganja, mary jane	
Depressants		*Reduced anxiety; feeling of well-being; lowered inhibitions; slowed pulse and breathing; lowered blood pressure; poor concentration/ fatigue; confusion; impaired coordination, memory, judgment; addiction; respiratory depression and arrest; death.*
Barbiturates	Amytal, Seconal, Phenobarbital; barbs, reds, yellows, yellow jackets	
Benzodiazepines	Ativan, Librium, Valium, Xanax; candy, downers, tranks	*Also, for barbiturates— sedation, drowsiness/ depression; unusual excitement; fever; irritability; slurred speech; dizziness; life-threatening withdrawal.*
Flunitrazepam*	Rohypnol; Mexican valium, R2, roofies, rope	*For benzodiazepines— sedation, drowsiness/ dizziness.* *For flunitrazepam—visual and gastrointestinal disturbances; urinary retention; memory loss for the time under the drug's effects.*

Category and Name	Commercial and Street Names	Intoxication Effects/ Potential Health Consequences
Hallucinogens		*Altered states of perception and feeling; nausea/persisting perception disorder (flashbacks).*
LSD	Lysergic acid diethylamide; acid, boomers, cubes, yellow sunshines, blue heaven	*Also, for LSD and mescaline—increased body temperature, heart rate, blood pressure; loss of appetite; sleeplessness; numbness; weakness; tremors.*
Mescaline	Buttons, cactus, mesc, peyote	
		For LSD—persistent mental disorders.
Psilocybin	Magic mushroom, purple passion, shrooms	*For psilocybin— nervousness; paranoia.*
Opioids and Morphine Derivatives		*Pain relief; euphoria; drowsiness/constipation; confusion; sedation; respiratory depression and arrest; addiction; unconsciousness; coma; death.*
Codeine	Empirin with Codeine, Robitussin A-C; Cody, schoolboy	
Heroin	Diacetylmorphine; brown sugar, dope, H, smack, skunk	
Morphine	Rosanol; M, miss emma, monkey	*Also, for heroin— staggering gait.*
Oxycodone HCl	Oxy, O.C., killer	
Hydrocodone bitartrate	Vicodin; vike	
Stimulants		*Increased heart rate, blood pressure, metabolism; feelings of exhilaration, energy,*

FIGURE 2.1
Continued

(continued)

FIGURE 2.1
Continued

Category and Name	Commercial and Street Names	Intoxication Effects/ Potential Health Consequences
Amphetamine	Dexedrine; bennies, black beauties, speed, uppers, crosses, hearts	*increased mental alertness*/rapid or irregular heart beat; reduced appetite; weight loss; heart failure; nervousness; insomnia.
Cocaine	Cocaine hydrochloride; blow, bump, C, candy, coke, crack, snow, charlie, rock	*Also, for amphetamine— rapid breathing*/tremor; loss of coordination; irritability; anxiousness; restlessness; delirium; panic; paranoia; impulsive behavior; aggressiveness; addiction; psychosis.
MDMA (methylenedioxy-methamphetamine)	Adam, clarity, ecstasy, Eve, lover's speed, molly, X, XTC	
Methamphetamine	Desoxyn; chalk, crank, crystal, glass, ice, speed	*For cocaine—increased temperature*/chest pain; respiratory failure; nausea; abdominal pain; strokes; seizures; headaches; malnutrition; panic attacks.
Methylphenidate	Ritalin; JIF, R-ball, skippy, the smart drug	*For MDMA—mild hallucinogenic effects; increased tactile sensitivity; empathic feelings*/ impaired memory and learning; hyperthermia; cardiac toxicity; renal failure; liver toxicity.
Nicotine	Cigarettes, cigars, smoke-less tobacco, snuff, chew	*For methamphetamine— aggression, violence, psychotic behavior*/ memory loss; cardiac and neurological damage; impaired memory and learning; addiction.
		For nicotine—adverse pregnancy outcomes; chronic lung disease; cardiovascular disease; stroke; cancer; addiction.

Category and Name	Commercial and Street Names	Intoxication Effects/ Potential Health Consequences
Other Compounds		*For anabolic steroids—no intoxication effects/* hypertension; blood clotting and cholesterol changes; liver and kidney cancer; hostility and aggression; in males, prostate cancer, reduced sperm production, shrunken testicles, breast enlargement; in females, menstrual irregularities, development of masculine characteristics (e.g., a beard).
Anabolic steroids	Anadrol, Oxandrin, Equipoise; roids, juice	
Inhalants	Solvents (paint thinners, gasoline, glues), gases (butane, propane, aerosol propellants); laughing gas, poppers, snappers	*For inhalants—stimulation; loss of inhibition/*headache; nausea or vomiting; slurred speech; loss of motor coordination; wheezing; unconsciousness; cramps; weight loss; muscle weakness; depression; memory impairment; damage to cardiovascular and nervous systems; sudden death.

*A rape drug, associated with sexual assaults.
SOURCE: National Institute on Drug Abuse, "Commonly Abused Drugs," NIDA Website, 2006 and 2012.

FIGURE 2.1
Continued

those that are more commonly abused. New *designer drugs* continue to appear, some of which are performance-enhancing drugs for athletes. In addition, **psychotherapeutic drugs** have become an important source of abuse. Psychotherapeutic drugs are prescription drugs—pain relievers, tranquilizers, stimulants, and sedatives—that are used for their intoxication effects rather than for medical purposes.

For some drugs, the intoxication effects vary depending on the chemical composition, the amount taken, the method of administration, and the social situation in which the drug is administered. In other words, you need to know more than the physiological effects of a drug to understand the experience of the individual taking it.

There are no intrinsic and automatic effects of a particular drug on every individual who takes it. Rather, the *effects vary according to how they are defined* (Becker 1953). A famous experiment by Schachter and Singer (1962) found that individuals who have a physiological experience for which there is no immediate explanation (e.g., you find your heart racing but don't know why) will *label the experience* with

psychotherapeutic drugs prescription drugs, including pain relievers, tranquilizers, stimulants, and sedatives, that are used for intoxication effects rather than medical purposes whatever information is available. Thus, one person may label a sensation as joy, while another labels the same sensation as anger or fear.

In this experiment, some students received an injection of the hormone epinephrine, and others received a **placebo.** Among the physiological effects of epinephrine are palpitation, tremor, and sometimes accelerated breathing and the feeling of being flushed. All the students were told they had received the drug in order to determine its effects on their vision. Some were given no information on any side effects, some were correctly informed of those effects, and others were misinformed about the effects. While waiting for the effects, each student was sent to a room where a student who was an accomplice of the experimenter created a situation of euphoria for some of the students and of anger for others. Students who had been injected with epinephrine and who had received either no information or misinformation about side effects "gave behavioral and self-report indications that they had been readily manipulable into the disparate feeling states of euphoria and anger" (Schachter and Singer 1962:395).

Similarly, based on 50 interviews, Becker (1953) found that *defining the effects of marijuana as pleasurable is a learning process.* First, the person must learn the technique of smoking marijuana. Then he or she must learn what the effects of the drug are and learn to associate those effects with its use. For example, if intense hunger is an effect, the user must learn to define that hunger as a sign of being high. Finally, the person must learn to define the effects as pleasurable rather than undesirable. Effects such as dizziness, thirst, and tingling of the scalp can be defined as undesirable or as symptoms of illness. Yet by interacting with others who define those effects as desirable, the user can learn to define them as desirable.

Legal drugs can harm or kill you just as effectively as illicit ones. In addition to alcohol, tobacco is one of the deadliest drugs in American society. In 1997 the Liggett Group, the maker of Chesterfield cigarettes, openly acknowledged that smoking is both addictive and deadly (Vedantam, Epstine, and Geiger 1997). Being legal does not mean that a drug is harmless. Sometimes it is difficult, however, to determine how harmful the drug is, as illustrated by the recent (2004) advent of electronic cigarettes (also called e-cigarettes).

E-cigarettes are smoked by vaporizing a liquid composed of nicotine, flavorings, and other chemicals. They are touted as a healthful alternative to regular tobacco products, a way to reduce tobacco-related deaths as smokers switch to them (Levy et al. 2016). However, it appears that smokers who use e-cigarettes do not stop smoking tobacco, and those who begin with e-cigarettes tend to move on to tobacco products (Leventhal et al. 2015; Sutfin et al. 2015). We don't know how many users there are, but a study of middle- and high-school students in California found that one in four had tried e-cigarettes and 13 percent were current users (Bostean, Trinidad, and McCarthy 2015). Some adverse effects of using e-cigarettes are already known (Higham et al. 2016). More, including effects of second-hand inhalation, may be known in the future.

Finally, increasing attention is being paid to the *abuse of psychotherapeutic drugs.* Of course, such drugs have enormously increased our physical and mental well-being. Countless numbers of people would have been unable to function as well or at all and would have died sooner without the use of prescription drugs. Nevertheless, those drugs can be abused to one's detriment as well as used to one's enhanced health.

In some cases, the abuse is the unintended by-product of attempts at self-medication. A national survey of Americans aged 57 through 85 concluded that nearly 1 in 25 were at risk for a major drug–drug interaction with the potential for adverse health consequences (Qato et al. 2008). Another study looked at death certificates and found that the proportion of deaths due to mixing prescription with nonprescription drugs (including alcohol) increased nearly 3,200 percent over a two-decade period (Phillips, Barker, and Eguchi 2008).

placebo
any substance having no physiological effect that is given to a subject who believes it to be a drug that does have an effect

More commonly, however, psychotherapeutic drugs are taken for their intoxication effects, and they rank second, after marijuana, as the drug of choice for Americans. In recent years, the concern has grown about the misuse of opioid painkillers (Percocet, Vicodin, OxyContin, and illegal heroin). A dramatic rise in the number of prescriptions and the number of nonmedical uses of the drugs led some experts to call the problem an "epidemic" (Binswanger and Gordon 2016). A survey in Maine, for example, reported that in 2014 opioids were dispensed to 22.4 percent of the residents, enough to give every person in Maine a 16-day supply (Piper et al. 2016). Nationally, in 2014 more than 28,000 Americans died from an overdose of one of the opioids.

Patterns of Use

It is difficult to know the number of drug users in the United States. Not all users are addicts, and not all addicts are known to the authorities. There is wide variation in use, depending on such factors as the type of drug and the age, sex, race/ethnicity, and social class of the user. Alcohol is the most widely used drug, followed by tobacco and marijuana. Among Americans aged 12 or older, 25.2 percent used tobacco in 2014 (National Center for Health Statistics 2016). This was down from 30.4 percent in 2002, part of a continuing decline in tobacco use. Marijuana usage in 2014 was reported by 8.4 percent of the population, which was up from 6.2 percent in 2002. A later poll by the Pew Research Center put the proportion at 13 percent for 2016 (McCarthy 2016).

Illicit drug use varies by a number of demographic factors (National Center for Health Statistics 2016). The proportion of current users is higher for males (12.8 percent) than for females (9.1 percent). The proportion is higher among the young, particularly the 18- to 25-year-olds (22.0 percent). And the second highest proportion (16.5 percent) occurs in the 16- to 17-year-olds.

Use also varies by race/ethnicity. The proportion of users of illicit drugs in 2014, was, from highest to lowest: Native Americans, 14.9 percent; African Americans, 12.4 percent; whites, 10.4 percent; Hispanics, 8.9 percent; and Asian Americans, 4.1 percent (National Center for Health Statistics 2016). Finally, drug use is higher in the lower than in the middle or upper social classes (Barbeau, Krieger, and Soobader 2004). In general, then, *the highest rates of drug use and abuse occur among those who are male, young, and poor.*

Table 2.1 shows the proportion of current users of various drugs by age group. These proportions are, of course, smaller than the proportion of those who have ever used the drugs. For example, compared to the proportion who are current users, the

TABLE 2.1
Use of Selected Drugs (percent who used in last 30 days)

Substance	Total	Age Group		
		12–17 Years	18–25 Years	26–34 Years
Any Illicit Drug	10.2	9.4	22.0	15.1
Marijuana	8.4	7.4	19.6	12.7
Psychotherapeutics	2.5	2.6	4.4	4.1
Alcohol	52.7	11.5	59.6	66.0
Tobacco	25.2	7.0	35.0	34.8

SOURCE: National Center for Health Statistics 2016.

proportion who have ever tried an illicit drug is close to half the adult population (Maguire 2012).

Trends.   Drug use rose rapidly after 1960 and peaked in 1979 (U.S. Department of Health and Human Services 1995). During the 1980s, the upward trend stopped and even reversed for most drugs. Since then, drug use has fluctuated. For example, the proportion of high school seniors who are current users of any illicit drug was 16.4 percent in 1991, reached a high of 26.2 percent in 1997, and stood at 23.6 percent in 2015 (Miech et al. 2016).

Multiple use of drugs is common.

©Ingram Publishing

To some extent, the variation in rates of usage may reflect changing definitions of the effects. For instance, when cocaine became popular during the 1980s, one of the appealing aspects was the claim that it gave users a great "high" without undesirable physical effects. However, most people now seem to realize that cocaine and crack (an especially dangerous form of cocaine that can be smoked) may lead to both physical and mental health problems, including chronic sore throat, hoarseness, chronic coughing, shortness of breath, depression, hallucinations, psychosis, and death from overdose (Smart 1991).

Multiple Use.   A question often raised is whether the use of one drug leads to the use of others. A number of studies have investigated the question, and in general they support the conclusion that there is a *tendency for multiple use* (Martin, Clifford, and Clapper 1992; National Center on Addiction and Substance Abuse at Columbia University 1998). Smokers are likely to drink alcohol (Costello, Dierker, Jones, and Rose 2008). Those who use alcohol and/or tobacco may move on to abuse prescription drugs or to use marijuana and then hard drugs (White et al. 2007; Sintov et al. 2009). And youth who abuse prescription drugs also have higher rates of tobacco use, heavy drinking, and the use of illicit drugs like marijuana and cocaine (National Institute on Drug Abuse 2014).

Nevertheless, we cannot say that the use of one drug causes the individual to experiment with another drug. To do so would be the *fallacy of non sequitur*. At this point, we can only say that whatever leads an individual to experiment with one substance may lead that individual to experiment with others.

Age of Initiation. Drug use is beginning at an increasingly earlier age (Johnson and Gerstein 1998). Among those born in the 1930s, for example, only alcohol, cigarettes, and marijuana were used by more than 1 percent of people before the age of 35. For those born between 1951 and 1955, 10 drugs were used by more than 5 percent of people before the age of 35.

In both rural and urban areas, children begin experimenting with drugs as early as the third grade (McBroom 1992). Inhalants are more likely the first drugs with which children experiment (Fritz 2003). As many as 6 percent of American children have tried an inhalant by the fourth grade. Young children also experiment with smoking and drinking alcohol (Miech et al. 2016). In 2015, 7 percent of 8th graders said they had started smoking in grade 6 or earlier. And 26 percent had tried alcohol and 10.9 percent said they had been drunk one or more times.

In their teen years, young people have increasing exposure to, and opportunities for, drug use. Few users begin experimenting as adults. Adults who smoke, for example, typically become daily smokers before the age of 20 (Centers for Disease Control 1995b). Similarly, adults who use other kinds of drugs, including heroin, typically begin at an early age (Epstein and Groerer 1997).

Drugs and the Quality of Life

It is clear that drug abuse is a widespread problem in America and affects both abusers and nonabusers. Residents in drug-trafficking neighborhoods are often terrorized by and fearful of dealers and users. As we discuss the effects of *abuse on the quality of life of individuals*, keep in mind how whole communities are affected.

Physical Health. Drug abuse contradicts the American *value of physical well-being*. A person may experiment with drugs because they seem to hold the promise of fulfillment, but the fulfillment is elusive; greater and greater quantities are consumed, and ultimately the person suffers physical and psychological deterioration.

The *physical harm resulting from the use of illegal drugs includes* (U.S. Department of Justice 1992:10):

1. Death.
2. Medical emergencies from acute reactions to drugs or toxic adulterants.
3. Exposure to HIV infection, hepatitis, and other diseases resulting from intravenous drug use.
4. Injury from accidents caused by drug-related impairment.
5. Injuries from violence while obtaining drugs in the drug distribution network.
6. Dependence or addiction.
7. Chronic physical problems.

This list is greatly abbreviated, of course. For example, consider the *multiple consequences of using a drug such as methamphetamine* (National Institute on Drug Abuse 2005). Even small amounts can result in increased wakefulness, decreased appetite, increased respiration, hyperthermia, irritability, insomnia, confusion, tremors, convulsions, anxiety, paranoia, and aggressiveness. Methamphetamine also can cause irreversible damage to blood vessels in the brain, producing strokes, irregular heartbeat, and, ultimately, cardiovascular collapse and death. The point is, drug use involves a long list of physical, psychological, and social consequences that are destructive.

Drug abuse is now the main preventable cause of illness and premature death in the United States. Each year hundreds of thousands of Americans die from smoking, alcohol abuse, and the use of illicit drugs. Early death from illegal drugs is often associated with an overdose of the drug. Heroin slows the vital functions of the body, and if a sufficient amount of the drug is ingested, those vital functions will completely stop. The addict can never be sure how much of the drug constitutes an overdose, nor can he or she be sure about the purity of the drug. Also, the *addict's tolerance level can vary* from one day to another, depending on how much of the drug has been used. If the addict manages to avoid death by overdose, he or she still may die from infections carried by the needle. Thus, the user *is at risk not merely from the drug itself but from other factors associated with drug use.*

The health consequences go beyond the addict herself in the case of a pregnant woman. Cocaine and tobacco use are both associated with a significant risk of spontaneous abortion (Ness et al. 1999). Children who survive the risk and are born to addicted mothers have a significant number of perinatal medical problems, behavioral problems in early infancy, and developmental deficiencies in their cognitive and psychomotor skills (Singer et al. 2002). Children of mothers who smoked during pregnancy are also more likely to be born with heart defects (Malik et al. 2008).

Tobacco Use Is a Global Problem.   In the United States, tobacco use causes more physiological damage than any nonalcoholic drug and is the leading cause of preventable death—mortality among smokers is two to three times as high as that among those who never smoked (Carter et al. 2015). Globally, tobacco causes about 6 million deaths each year (World Health Organization 2016). About 600,000 of those deaths are due to secondhand inhalation.

The consequences of tobacco use are well established. Among the known consequences of smoking are increased probability of lung cancer and other respiratory diseases, increased risk of heart disease, increased risk of colorectal cancer, and increased probability of complications during childbirth (LaCroix et al. 1991; Botteri et al. 2008; Kabir et al. 2008). The risks are dramatized by the fact that a 29 percent decline in smoking prevalence in Massachusetts over a 10-year period was associated with a 31 percent decline in deaths due to coronary heart disease (Kabir et al. 2008). There are, of course, people who smoke regularly and live to a "ripe old age," but using them to counter the systematic evidence is the *fallacy of dramatic instance.* What matters is not the few exceptions, but the great numbers who support the conclusions.

Moreover, nonsmokers who are exposed to a smoking environment also may suffer. Nonsmokers who live or work in a smoking environment are more likely than those not in such an environment to develop coronary heart disease or lung cancer (U.S. Department of Health and Human Services 2006). Thus, thousands of nonsmokers die each year as a result of inhaling secondhand smoke. Pregnant women exposed to secondhand smoke have increased odds of giving birth before full term or of low birth weight for a full-term baby (Ghosh, Wilhelm, and Ritz 2013). Researchers also have found that babies are more likely to develop a respiratory tract infection and to die of sudden infant death syndrome when they are exposed to smoke (Pollack 2001; Blizzard et al. 2003). Smoking parents also increase the chances of their children developing asthma and, in later life, lung cancer (Scott 1990b; Sturm, Yeatts, and Loomis 2004). As a result of such findings, smoke-free environments at work and in public places are becoming common.

Some consequences of other drugs were briefly noted in Figure 2.1. We need to examine in more detail, however, the effects of marijuana, which have been a matter of controversy.

Marijuana.   Early in the controversy over the use of marijuana, some people insisted that it causes nothing more than slight physiological changes in the user and that it is not as dangerous a drug as alcohol, but numerous studies underscore the fact that marijuana has undesirable consequences that are both acute (brief and severe) and chronic, and both physiological and psychological (National Institute on Drug Abuse 1998; Office of National Drug Control Policy 2003b). In brief, those consequences are

1. Acute effects of marijuana intoxication:
   a. Impaired memory, thinking, speaking, and problem solving.
   b. Impaired time perception.
   c. Increased heart rate (as high as 160 beats per minute).
   d. Reddening of the eyes.
   e. Impaired psychomotor performance (resulting in automobile accidents and deaths).
2. Chronic effects:
   a. Adverse effects on the respiratory system, similar to those of cigarettes.
   b. Reduced sperm count in males.
   c. Possible adverse effects on children when the mother uses the drug, including lowered birth weight and more fetal abnormalities.
   d. Interference with the normal pattern of sex hormones, impairing their release from the brain.

Although it appears that marijuana poses a greater threat to well-being than was once believed, it also may have more medical uses than previously thought—including treating glaucoma patients, relieving the pain of cancer patients, ameliorating the side effects of chemotherapy, and relieving the suffering of asthmatics. Undoubtedly, research on the effects of marijuana will continue.

Psychological Health.   Americans value psychological as well as physical health. The search for "happiness," "peace of mind," or "contentment" is common. The short-range euphoria that follows drug use is misleading because the long-range effects of drug abuse contradict the *quest for psychological well-being.* In essence, drug use leads to poorer mental health, and multiple use intensifies the detrimental effects (Booth et al. 2010). For example, the high that is produced by a drug such as crack can be followed by severe depression. You need only listen to the stories of addicts or ex-addicts to realize the devastation to psychological health that results from drug abuse (Engel 1989). You also should note that, in contrast to the common belief that people turn to drugs for relief from distress, a study of adolescents found that users did not start drugs because of preexisting psychological distress; rather, the drug use led to both physical and psychological impairments (Hansell and White 1991).

The greater the use, the more intense the problems. A study of 161 adolescents reported that increased drug use was associated with increased depression, decreased self-esteem, and a deterioration of purpose in life (Kinnier, Metha, Okey, and Keim

1994). Even smoking is associated with psychological problems. Nicotine-dependent individuals are more likely to have problems with depression, anxiety, and lower self-esteem (Croghan et al. 2006; Hu, Davies, and Kandel 2006; McCaffery et al. 2008). By midlife, heavy smoking can lead to cognitive impairment and decline (Richards, Jarvis, Thompson, and Wadsworth 2003; Nooyens, van Gelder, and Verschuren 2008). And a mother who smokes while pregnant can decrease her baby's IQ (Olds, Henderson, and Tatelbaum 1994).

Similarly, marijuana use poses serious mental health problems (Office of National Drug Control Policy 2003b). Regular use by adolescents impairs memory, attentional ability, learning, and psychomotor performance (Solowij et al. 2002). Adolescents who seek relief from depression through marijuana may actually intensify their depression (Office of National Drug Control Policy 2008; Womack et al. 2016). An English study found that marijuana users increase their chances of developing a psychotic disorder later in life by about 40 percent (Moore et al. 2007). And a study of Italian men who used only marijuana found that 83 percent were dependent on the drug, 46 percent abused it, and 29 percent of occasional users had at least one emotional disorder (Troisi, Pasini, Saracco, and Spalletta 1998).

The dangers of marijuana have increased because the drug is stronger than it used to be (Office of National Drug Control Policy 2003b). Marijuana with 2 percent tetrahydrocannabinol (THC) can result in severe psychological damage, including paranoia and psychosis. Currently, however, average levels are 6 percent THC, or three times the amount that can cause serious damage to the user.

Interpersonal Difficulties.   In addition to a sense of physical and psychological well-being, the desired quality of life for Americans demands harmonious relationships. This value is contradicted by relationship problems that tend to result from drug abuse.

A variety of interpersonal problems are associated with drug use and abuse (U.S. Department of Justice 1992; Office of National Drug Control Policy 2003b). They include arguing with family and friends, feeling suspicious and distrustful of people, encountering troubles at school or work, and getting into trouble with the police. Drug users are three to four times more likely than nonusers to engage in criminal behavior (Bennett, Holloway, and Farrington 2008). Marijuana users experience less cohesion and harmony in their relationships and have more relationship conflict than nonusers (Brook, Pahl, and Cohen 2008). Inhalant users have higher rates of both childhood and adult antisocial behavior than nonusers, including bullying, starting fights, using weapons, and being physically cruel toward others (Howard et al. 2010). Children whose parents abuse drugs are almost three times more likely to be abused and more than four times more likely to be neglected than are children of nonabusing parents, and they are also likely to have emotional, academic, and interpersonal problems (Reid, Macchetto, and Foster 1999; Wilens et al. 2002).

Interpersonal problems may continue for addicts even after they no longer abuse drugs. The ex-addict may attempt to compensate for past failures and assume a role of leadership. The outcome may be a power struggle between the ex-addict and his or her mate. In other cases, there may be unrealistic expectations about the outcome of treatment. The mate of an ex-addict may expect immediate and dramatic changes, and when such changes do not appear, the result can be disillusionment or bitterness. Also, the ex-addict may find that long-term or permanent damage has been done to his or her relationships.

Economic Costs.   All social problems involve certain *economic costs,* and these affect the quality of life. The more money required to deal with a social problem, the less money there is for other desired services and programs.

Determining the exact dollar cost of any social problem is difficult. The costs of the drug problem include some that can be measured and some that can only be estimated. There is, of course, a cost to the user: the expense of maintaining the habit (for some, hundreds of dollars a week or more) and the loss of earnings over their life span.

The measurable costs to the nation are staggering. Federal funding for various drug control programs was more than $26 billion in 2012 (Maguire 2012). State and local expenditures and other costs cannot be easily estimated. They include (U.S. Department of Justice 1992:127):

Criminal justice expenditures on drug-related crime.

Health care costs of injuries from drug-related child abuse and accidents.

The cost of lost productivity due to absenteeism and inefficiency and errors of users at the workplace.

Loss of property values due to drug-related neighborhood crime.

Property damage from drug-related activities.

Loss of agricultural resources, which are used for cultivation of illegal drugs.

Toxins introduced into public air and water supplies by drug production.

Emotional and physical damage to users as well as their families, friends, and co-workers.

Overall, the Office of National Drug Control Policy (2011) put the cost to the nation at more than $193 billion for 2007. And the cost continues to rise each year.

Contributing Factors

The various contributing factors have a double-barreled effect: They maintain demand by encouraging use of drugs, and they guarantee a supply.

Social Structural Factors.   As with alcohol, *group norms* are one of the most important factors in the problem of other drugs, creating *peer pressure* that leads individuals to drug use. For the most part, young people do not take drugs to relieve emotional distress but to be accepted by their peers—and the pressure begins in elementary school.

Group Norms.   Group norms are important for adults as well. Being *integrated into a group in which drug use is approved* is one of the strongest factors associated with drug use at all ages (Leatherdale, McDonald, Cameron, and Brown 2005; Kilmer et al. 2006). The "group" may be your family, your friends, or your peers at school or work. A survey of 1,802 fourth- and fifth-grade pupils found perceived family use to be the strongest influence on the children's drug use (Bush, Weinfurt, and Iannotti 1994). A study of employees who abused drugs reported that they tended to come from families with substance abuse problems and that they, in turn, associated with substance-abusing friends (Lehman, Farabee, Holcom, and Simpson 1995).

Some Americans who regard themselves as respectable citizens find it difficult to imagine following group norms when those norms are illegal. They need to realize that people all follow the norms of their groups and follow them for basically the same reasons. The respectable citizen who abides by the norm that the appearance of one's house and yard should be neat and clean derives satisfaction and a sense of acceptance from that normative behavior. Similarly, the youth who uses drugs finds certain *rewards*—including admiration, respect, and acceptance—in that usage when it is the norm of his or her group.

Role Problems.   Role problems are a second social structural factor in the drug prob-lem. *Role problems create stress* in the individual, who may then use drugs to deal with the problems and their consequent stress (Goeders 2003). Indeed, when you consider that the first use of a drug like tobacco is likely to be a highly unpleasant experience, it is reasonable that strong forces are at work to develop the habit. Once a youth tries a cigarette, either peer pressure or stress can lead to subsequent tries, but stress seems to lead the individual more quickly to develop the habit (Hirschman, Leventhal, and Glynn 1984). Of course, the student role is inherently stressful for most people. For some, the stress is sufficiently severe to search for relief in drugs. A study of college stu-dents found that students who experience academic strain have higher levels of depres-sion, and some try to relieve the depression with the nonmedical use of prescription stimulants (Ford and Schroeder 2009).

What kinds of role problems create such stress? One is the socially devalued role. That is, certain roles rank low in terms of such things as social acceptance. Those in such roles may become victims of prejudice and discrimination. The role of immigrant is one such role. Thus, an investigation of adult immigrants in the Midwest found a higher rate of drug use among those who had experienced discrimination (Tran, Lee, and Burgess 2010).

A second stress-generating role problem is **role conflict.** Two or more roles may be contradictory—as, for example, when a woman experiences a contradiction between her role as a physician and her role as a wife because she does not have time to meet the expectations of both her patients and her husband. Contradictory expectations may impinge upon a single role, as when a physician's patients demand the right of abortion and his or her peers and friends define abortion as illegal and immoral. An individual may define the expectations of a role as somehow unacceptable or excessive, as when a physician feels overwhelmed by the multiple demands made upon his or her time and professional skills.

Physicians have been deliberately used in the examples here because of the high rate of drug addiction among doctors. The actual cause of addiction is not known, but it probably is rooted in a combination of easy access to drugs and the stresses of the role. Drug abuse is a symptom of stress, and role problems do generate stress in the individual. To the extent that particular roles are especially likely to create problems, people who occupy those roles will be particularly vulnerable to stress and perhaps to using drugs to deal with stress.

An important point here is that role conflict is a social phenomenon, not an indi-vidual phenomenon. It is not a particular doctor who is oppressed by the demands of the role; rather, all doctors must come to terms with the role of a physician in American society. The expectations attached to the role tend to create the same problems for everyone who occupies the role.

Another role problem that can generate stress and increase the likelihood of drug abuse is a *role change that is defined as undesirable*. Such a role change occurs when a spouse dies. Suddenly a person is no longer a husband or a wife—that role has been lost.

After the loss (which may be the result of separation or divorce as well as death), the individual must work through the grief process. A person copes with a significant loss by passing through a series of emotional phases. The process may take as long as two or more years. Typically, the initial phase is shock, followed by a period of numbness, or lack of intense emotion. In the next phase, the individual wavers between fantasy and reality, overcomes fantasies, and then experiences the full impact of the loss. A period of increasing adjustment follows, punctuated sporadically by episodes of painful

role conflict
a person's perception that two or more of his or her roles are contradictory, or that the same role has contradictory expectations, or that the expectations of the role are unacceptable or excessive

memories. Finally, if the full grief process has been experienced, the individual accepts the loss and reaffirms his or her life. The grief process is painful, and some individuals may resort to drugs.

Family Experiences. Family experiences also are involved in the use and abuse of drugs. Families that are strong, healthy, and highly cohesive tend to inhibit the use and abuse of drugs (Wilens et al. 2002; Dorius, Bahr, Hoffman, and Harmon 2004). Family values and practices such as religious involvement and eating dinner together are associated with less likelihood of drug abuse (Hardesty and Kirby 1995; National Center on Addiction and Substance Abuse at Columbia University 1998).

However, the three kinds of family experiences that contribute to the alcohol problem also are involved in the abuse of other drugs. First, as noted earlier in this chapter, drug abusers are more likely to come from homes in which other family members are abusers (Petoskey, Van Stelle, and De Jong 1998; Kilpatrick et al. 2000).

Second, drug abusers are more likely to come from broken homes than are nonabusers. Adolescents who grow up in single-parent homes are more likely to use tobacco and illegal drugs than those who live with both parents (Flewelling and Bauman 1990). Looking at overall drug involvement (including alcohol), rates are higher among those whose homes are disrupted by divorce than those who grow up in intact homes (Wolfinger 1998).

Third, drug abuse is associated with various problematic relationships within the family. The problems may be severe, such as sexual abuse (Kang, Magura, and Shapiro 1994). Even parental conflict and *alienation between youth and their parents* can lead to both the use and abuse of drugs. In their study of adolescents, Simcha-Fagan, Gersten, and Langner (1986) looked at factors associated with the use of marijuana, of drugs other than marijuana, and of heroin. Youths in a home with a traditional marriage and a traditional, restrictive type of mother were less likely than others to use marijuana. Those who used drugs other than marijuana were more likely to come from a home with an unhappy marriage, to report parental coldness, and to have conflict with their parents. Another study reported that adolescents with authoritarian fathers (which typically results in parent-child conflict) are more likely to use drugs (Bronte-Tinkew, Moore, and Carrano 2006). Heroin users also reported an unhappy parental marriage, parental coldness, and conflict with parents. In addition, they were likely to have mothers with some kind of physical or emotional illness. Thus, the use and abuse of all kinds of drugs are likely to be associated with disturbed family relationships.

Of course, the sense of rejection and alienation from parents can follow from drug use rather than precede it. Even if it is true, for instance, that a young person first uses drugs because of his or her group's norms and then becomes alienated from his or her parents, this alienation is likely to perpetuate the drug use. Thus, even if alienation is not one of the causes of initial use, it is likely to be a cause of continuing use.

Government. A fourth structural factor is the government, and especially the *government's definition of drug use as illegal.* For some drugs, the illegal status is the consequence of social and political processes rather than of scientific evidence. Why, for example, is tobacco legal while other drugs are not? Once a drug is declared illegal, criminal elements enter the drug traffic in order to profit from black-market dealings. In essence, illegality raises the cost of maintaining the drug habit, deeply involves criminals in the drug traffic, strains the criminal justice system, and leads the addict

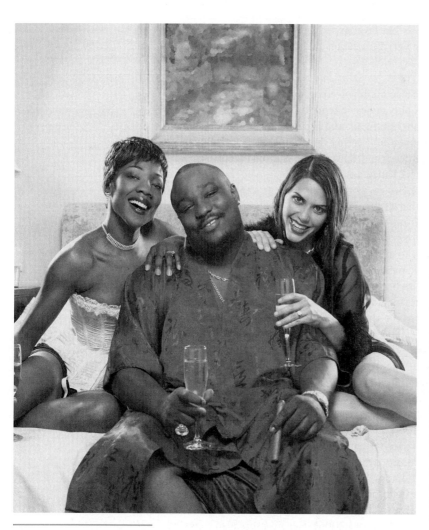

Ads portray drug users as leading happy glamorous lives.
©Plush Studios/Blend Images LLC

to undesirable behavior. Criminal involvement results from the potential for high profits. For example, the street value of heroin may be 50 times or more its wholesale cost and 10,000 times the amount paid to the farmer who supplies the opium! Similar profits are realized in the sale of other illicit drugs, which is one reason pushers risk prison to ply their trade.

Economy.   A fifth structural factor is the *economy*. The economy supports the drug problem in at least two ways. First, many people who get involved in the distribution, sale, and/or use and abuse of drugs come from the margins of the economy. That is, they are from the more impoverished families and have little hope of achieving any kind of financial success apart from that which drugs appear to offer them. Second, the legal drugs—alcohol and tobacco—are marketed freely and openly, and the industries are so profitable that they exert enormous pressure on the government to remain a legitimate part of the economy, including pressure to allow their products to be advertised in markets that will reach young people.

Mass Media.   The mass media can contribute to the drug problem by allowing celebrities to laughingly discuss their use of marijuana and their abuse of alcohol. Movies, TV programs, magazines, and the Internet provide outlets for those who send the message—a message likely to be particularly effective to the young—that people should not miss experiencing the use of illegal drugs and the abuse of legal drugs. Such a message turns the once-popular phrase about drug use, "just say no," on its head. The message now is: Just say yes, because it's an experience you won't want to miss.

Popular movies and music reinforce the message and increase the use of drugs (Chen, Miller, Grube, and Waiters 2006). A study of 200 popular movies and 2,000 popular songs reported that illicit drugs appeared in 22 percent and alcohol and tobacco appeared in more than 90 percent of the movies (Roberts, Henriksen, and Christenson 1999). A fourth of the movies that included illicit drugs had explicit information about the preparation and use of the drugs. Illicit drugs or alcohol was mentioned in 27 percent of the songs. References to drugs were particularly heavy in rap lyrics: 63 percent mentioned illicit drugs and almost half mentioned alcohol.

In essence, a part of the culture has become an advocate of drug usage and has thereby increased the number of people who are users and abusers. A study of adolescents who took up smoking reported that a third of the youth nominated a movie star who smoked on-screen as one of their favorites (Distefan, Pierce, and Gilpin 2004). And a study of fifth and eighth grade students found that those who saw actors and actresses smoking in movies were more likely than others to begin smoking themselves (Wills et al. 2007).

Finally, the mass media also affect usage through the advertising of legal drugs. Some studies have found that ads are more influential than peers on adolescents' decisions to start smoking (Evans et al. 1995). Research over a three-year period in California concluded that a third of all experimentation with smoking resulted from advertising (Pierce et al. 1998). Cigarette ads in the U.S. have declined considerably, but a study of sixth and eighth grade students in India reported that exposure to tobacco ads was significantly related to increased tobacco use (Arora, Reddy, Stigler, and Perry 2008).

Supply. Although the structural factors that create the *demand for drugs* are crucial, there is also a *powerful organization of supply*. Massive amounts of coca, marijuana, and opium, for example, are grown in Latin America, processed in refineries, and smuggled into the United States. Hundreds of tons of cocaine alone are produced and smuggled into the United States each year (Office of National Drug Control Policy 2003a). About three-fourths of the coca grown for processing the cocaine is from Colombia. Of all the cocaine that enters the nation, 72 percent passes through the Mexico/Central America corridor, 27 percent moves through the Caribbean, and the other 1 percent comes directly from South America. The main ports of entry are central Arizona, El Paso, Houston, Los Angeles, Miami, and Puerto Rico.

Some of the drug suppliers have their own armies and use terrorist activities to intimidate officials. In addition, smugglers exploit the massive corruption that exists at all layers of government (including law enforcement agencies) and among businesspeople (who may "launder" drug money) in the United States and Latin America.

The supply network in Latin America and elsewhere is so powerful and the potential profits are so enormous that efforts to cut off supplies have been fruitless. Cut off at one point, smugglers find alternatives. Efforts to stop the supply should not be abandoned, but many experts agree that as long as there is demand and profits are high, the suppliers will find a way to provide drugs.

Social Psychological Factors. People *who have positive attitudes* toward drug use are more likely to become users. Both adolescents and adults underestimate their risks from using legal or illegal drugs (Strecher, Kreuter, and Kobrin 1995; Ayanian and Cleary 1999). Abusers may not be unaware of risks, but the value to them of the psychic effects—euphoria, pleasure, and change of mood—exceeds any concern they have about risks. As reported in a study of psychotherapeutic drug abusers in Florida, the psychic effects are one of the most important motivations for using drugs (Rigg and Ibanez 2010). The two other most frequently named reasons were "to sleep" and "for anxiety/stress."

The quest for psychic effects also was noted in a study of people who had reached a physical and/or emotional crisis from their drug abuse (Table 2.2). Those who reach a crisis stage are also likely to recognize their dependence and to admit their suicidal intentions.

TABLE 2.2

Motivation for Drug Abuse by Age, Race, and Sex of Abuser and Selected Drugs (*percent of mentions*)

	Psychic Effects	Dependence	Self-Destruction	Other
All mentions	38	22	33	7
Age				
15 and under	60	7	22	10
16–19	57	17	20	6
20–29	36	28	30	7
30–39	23	24	46	9
40–49	16	21	53	10
50 and over	13	14	61	12
Race				
White	39	18	35	8
Black	33	35	24	7
Other	41	27	26	6
Sex				
Male	46	29	19	6
Female	31	15	45	9

SOURCE: U.S. Department of Justice, Drug Enforcement Administration, Drug Abuse Warning Network, Phase II Report, July 1973–March 1974 (Washington, DC: Government Printing Office).

Two other motivations we should note are *boredom and curiosity,* which are likely to be factors particularly among adolescents (De Micheli and Formigoni 2002; Adams et al. 2003). Adolescents with too few demands on their time may find themselves attracted to experimenting with drugs simply to relieve the boredom. Others may have a natural curiosity that spurs them to want to know what the drug experience is like. Unfortunately, if they define that first experience as highly gratifying, they may continue to use and ultimately abuse the drug.

Motivations may change over the years. A study of 60 clients of a clinic reported that most said they began drug use because of its popularity during their school years (Johnson and Friedman 1993). Once they reached the point of using heroin, however, the motivation became mainly physiological survival.

Finally, *ideology* is a factor in the drug problem. In fact, positive attitudes, group norms, and ideologies about drug use reinforce each other. Friedenberg (1972) identified the following ideology about marijuana:

1. People who are enjoying themselves without harming others have an inalienable right to privacy.

2. A drug whose effect is to turn its users inward upon their own experience, enriching their fantasy life at the expense of their sense of need to achieve or relate to others, is as moral as alcohol, which encourages a false gregariousness and increasingly pugnacious or competitive behavior.

3. Much of the solicitude of the older generation for the welfare of the young merely expresses a desire to dominate and control them for the sake of adult interests and the preservation of adult status and authority.

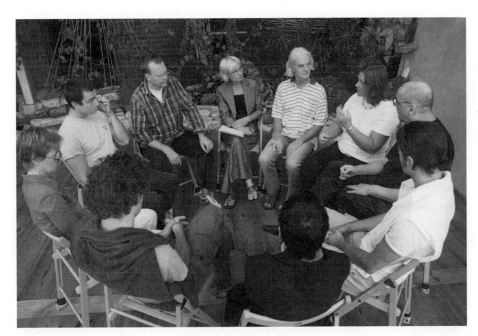

Group therapy can be effective
in the treatment of some
addicts.
©Getty Images

This ideology, like all ideologies, serves the purpose of explaining and validating certain behavior, thereby reinforcing the behavior.

Public Policy and Private Action

Is it possible to eliminate the drug problem? No society we know of has completely solved the problem. Even China, which seemed to have eradicated the problem, has experienced renewed problems of drug abuse (Lu and Wang 2008).

Still, progress can be made, and the severity of the problem can be lessened. For that to happen, programs must attack the social bases as well as treat individual addicts and also focus on *reducing demand rather than stopping the supply*. For example, as noted in this chapter, demand and use are highest in the lower social classes. Public policy that enables those in the lower strata to better their lot will also reduce the demand for illegal drugs. We are not saying that enforcement is useless but only that treatment as well as programs of education and prevention must be given at least as much, and perhaps more, attention and support. Demand for some drugs may be reduced through legislation. A study of 10 years of tobacco control in New York City found that such measures as high excise taxes and smoke-free air laws resulted in a decline of 28 percent in adult smoking and 52 percent in youth smoking (Kilgore et al. 2014). For the nation overall, researchers estimate that the decline in smoking from 1964 through 2012 resulted in 8 million fewer premature deaths and an extended life span of 19 to 20 years for those who quit (Holford et al. 2014).

Enforcement Programs. Enforcement programs involve efforts to prevent drugs from entering the country or from being produced within the country. It also includes the capture, prosecution, and imprisonment of users, dealers, and pushers. A controversial form of enforcement is mandatory testing of employees at the workplace.

Some people feel that such testing is a violation of an individual's civil liberties. Yet federal law now requires railroads, airlines, and trucking companies to develop and administer drug-testing programs, and many other firms are setting up programs on their own. Federal law also bans smoking on all domestic airplane flights. Many states have passed laws restricting smoking in restaurants and regulating smoking in private workplaces. These regulations have reduced the risk of heart attacks and heart disease associated with breathing secondhand smoke (National Academy of Sciences 2009).

Some local-level strategies are enforcing the laws on drugs other than tobacco (Mazerolle, Kadleck, and Roehl 2004). In street enforcement programs, police watch the hot spots for drug sales and arrest both the seller and the buyer. In some cases, police will seize the assets of a buyer, such as the buyer's car. They also may use a *reverse sting.* Undercover police pose as dealers and arrest users who ask to buy drugs.

Community policing by citizens offers another means of enforcement (Xu, Fiedler, and Flaming 2005). In the case of drugs, citizens organize to eliminate the conditions that facilitate drug sales. Among other things, they may set up a drug hotline, lobby for new laws and jail space, and set up neighborhood cleanup projects.

Treating Addicts.   The purpose of treating an addict is to reduce or eliminate his or her dependence on the drug. Because there is no single cause for all addictions, however, there is no single treatment that will work for everyone (Rodgers 1994). One method that has claimed some success with cocaine addicts is a form of behavioral therapy—contingency contracting (Petry and Martin 2002). In contingency contracting, the addicts make an agreement with the therapist to pay a severe penalty if urine tests reveal that they have ingested any of the drug during the week. For instance, a nurse signed a contract in which she agreed that she would write a letter to her parents confessing her drug habit and asking that they no longer give her any financial support. She would write a second letter to the state board of nursing in which she would confess her habit and turn in her license.

detoxification
supervised withdrawal from dependence on a drug

With heroin addicts, a first step is **detoxification,** *the elimination of dependence* through supervised withdrawal. One of the more common methods of treating heroin addiction is *methadone maintenance.* In methadone maintenance, the addict orally ingests the drug methadone, which is considered less dangerous than heroin and has a number of properties that allow the addict to lead a more normal life than is possible with heroin. Methadone may also be used in the detoxification program, but detoxification involves the elimination of all drug use—including the methadone after it helps mitigate withdrawal symptoms.

Although there is some disagreement as to whether methadone maintenance is more effective than drug-free treatment programs, it is clear that the methadone program reduces the use of heroin (Marsch 1998). Unfortunately, methadone cannot be prescribed by a physician but must be dispensed at a licensed clinic (Wren 1997). In addition, methadone is itself a drug that is abused (Belluck 2003). And even when it succeeds in enabling users to overcome their heroin addiction, it may cause them, as found in a Danish study, to feel inferior and vulnerable (Järvinen and Miller 2010).

A more recent form of treatment is *brief intervention therapy* (Rodgers 1994). In a relatively few sessions, the therapist seeks to establish a warm and supportive relationship with the addict, while giving advice, exploring various ways to deal with the addiction, and helping the addict see that he or she must take responsibility for getting free of the addiction. The therapist also instills a sense of empowerment in the addict—not only "I *have* to do this," but "I *can* do this."

Addiction is more than physiological, of course. Relationships are involved. Consequently, successful treatment must enable the individual to cope with the conditions that led to the addiction. For many people, this treatment involves group therapy.

One type of group therapy is *family therapy*. Because, for example, adolescent drug abuse is a symptom of family problems in many cases, family therapy may be the most effective mode of treatment (Reilly 1984). For adults, small-group therapy may be helpful. Cocaine Anonymous emerged in the 1980s (Cohen 1984). It is run by former addicts and provides group support to the addict as a means of breaking the habit.

Another variation of group therapy that may be combined with individual therapy is the *drug treatment center*. The efficacy of the centers is a matter of debate. However, one study showed that 80 percent of the treated addicts were off hard drugs after completing a program at an inpatient or an outpatient center (Biden 1990).

A form of group therapy that is effective for some people involves *religious or religious-type experiences*. A religious orientation enables many people to abstain from experimenting with drugs or to stop using drugs. Adolescents who are high in religiosity are less likely to use drugs (Bahr, Maughan, Marcos, and Li 1998; National Survey on Drug Use and Health 2004). In a nationwide survey, the National Center on Addiction and Substance Abuse at Columbia University (1998) found that teenagers who attend services at least four times a month are less likely to use tobacco or marijuana than those attending less than once a month.

Finally, a more recent form of group therapy involves the use of peer support (Levy, Gallmeier, and Wiebel 1995). Peer support is not new, of course, but the program— "outreach-assisted peer support"—is unique in that it targets active addicts who are not in treatment and who may decide to continue drug use while in the group. Whether they opt for total abstinence or for reduced or controlled usage, addicts may join the group.

Education and Prevention Programs. Most of the money allocated to the drug problem goes into enforcement, but many people believe that education and prevention are as important—if not more so—because they reduce the demand. Thus, a nationally representative sample of high school seniors found that those who said they would not use marijuana in the coming year gave a number of reasons for their decision that showed they had been well educated about the effects of drugs (Terry-McElrath, O'Malley, and Johnston 2008). The most frequent reasons were the psychological and physical harm involved and the fact that they did not want to get high.

The value of prevention and education programs is also evident in the significant decline of tobacco use in cities and states that have implemented such programs, which include an increase in the tax on cigarettes, requiring smoke-free work sites, and placing antismoking ads in the mass media (Bauer et al. 2005; Frieden et al. 2005; Netemeyer, Andrews, and Burton 2005; Sung et al. 2005). Programs in schools, of course, must begin early because drugs are available even in elementary schools. In fact, the National Institute on Drug Abuse (2004) recommends that prevention programs begin in preschool. It recommends that programs from first grade through high school increase the academic and social competence of students so that they gain the skills needed to resist drug use.

Much of what young people learn, of course, occurs outside the schools. Antidrug advertising has helped make youth attitudes less favorable toward drugs and less likely to use them. Pressure can be exerted on the media to portray drug use, if at all, negatively. For example, smoking shown in movies declined from 1950 to the early 1980s, but in 2002 it was at the same level it was in 1950 (Glantz, Kacirk, and McCulloch 2004).

Parental behavior is also a factor in prevention. Miller-Day (2008) studied the ways parents express their expectations about alcohol or other drug use to their children. She found seven different strategies: let the children use their own judgment; give hints that the children shouldn't use drugs; have a "no tolerance" rule; give information about drug use; threaten punishment; reward nonuse; and ignore the issue. The only strategy to have a significant effect on usage was the "no tolerance" rule. As one subject explained it: The parents said "they would not put up with me doing it and that was that."

Finally, *decriminalization of drug use* is a possible way to attack the social bases of the problem. Although decriminalization would reduce the demand for illegal drugs, it is a controversial issue (Cussen and Block 2000; Sher 2003). Advocates claim that it would resolve many aspects of the problem. It would help safeguard our civil liberties (people would have the option to choose whether to use drugs and could choose usage with legal impunity). Drug traffic would no longer be profitable (making it useless for organized crime). The courts would not be overwhelmed with cases of drug violators. Addicts would not be required to engage in criminal activity to support their habits. The reduction of crime would improve the quality of life in the inner cities. Taxes could be lowered, or the money and other resources now spent on enforcement could be used for better purposes.

Opponents argue that decriminalization would only exacerbate the problem. People would get a wrong and destructive message, namely that drug use is OK. Cheaper, readily available drugs would increase the rate of addiction. The health costs of dealing with abusers would skyrocket. Families would be harmed when an addicted member could no longer provide monetary or emotional support. Children would be harmed when an addicted parent or parents abuse and neglect them. Children born to a mother who used drugs during pregnancy would face various and permanent physical, emotional, and social disabilities. And both the individual abuser and the society would suffer the loss of a meaningful and productive life.

Whatever stance one takes on decriminalization, therefore, should be taken with caution. There are strong arguments both for and against legalization. Recently, a number of states have legalized marijuana, and this might eventually provide data that will guide future action. We say "might" because in other nations such as Great Britain, the Netherlands, and Switzerland where some drugs have been legalized, there is disagreement about the effectiveness of the move. The issue is likely to be controversial for the foreseeable future.

Follow-Up.   Do you favor the decriminalization of drugs as a way to ease the problem? Why or why not?

Summary

The problem of alcohol and other drugs is one of abuse and not merely of use. Various drugs have various effects, and the effects depend on the method of administration, the amount taken, and the social situation as well as the chemical composition of the drug. Alcohol is the most widely used drug, and its effects can be extremely deleterious. Many experts consider alcohol abuse much more serious than abuse of other drugs.

Around 1980, drug use of all kinds began to decline for the first time in two decades. In the 1990s, patterns of use fluctuated. Although less than in the peak years, use and abuse are still quite high. A majority of Americans drink, and a substantial number say that drinking has been a source of trouble in their families. Millions of Americans indicate that they are current users of marijuana. Many users tend toward multiple drug use. Most alcohol abusers are young and male but not poor, whereas other drug addicts tend to be young, male, and poor.

The meaning of the drug problem for the quality of life is seen in the consequences for physical health, psychological health, interpersonal relationships, and economic costs. Abusers suffer various undesirable effects in all areas, and they inflict suffering on others. The nation as a whole also suffers great economic cost because billions of dollars per year are involved in lost services and in efforts to combat the deleterious effects of abuse.

Various structural factors contribute to the problem. An important one is group norms. Integration into a group that approves drug use is one of the most reliable predictors of use. Role problems, including being in a socially devalued role, role conflict, and undesirable role change, create stress in the individual and that stress can lead to abuse. Abusers are more likely to come from homes in which family members are abusers, from broken homes, or from homes with problematic relationships. The government's definition of many drugs as illegal has several implications: more people are classified as criminal; previously classified criminals become deeply involved in the drug traffic; the criminal justice system is strained; and users and abusers are led into various kinds of undesirable behavior. Finally, the suppliers of illegal drugs are organized effectively and take advantage of corruption, so that a supply will always be available when there is a demand and profits are high.

Among social psychological factors is the alienation of users from the larger society. Many people believe drug use produces desirable psychic effects. These positive attitudes toward drug use combine with group norms and various ideologies that develop in groups. The ideologies explain and validate drug use.

In treating the problem, efforts to help the individual abuser or reduce the supply available to users have far exceeded efforts to get at the social roots of the problem. If it is to be dealt with effectively, both approaches are needed—attacks on the social factors as well as treatment of individual abusers.

Key Terms

Abuse	Placebo
Addiction	Psychotherapeutic Drugs
Binge Drinking	Role Conflict
Detoxification	

Study Questions

1. What is meant by the statement that Americans have had ambivalent feelings about alcohol and other drugs throughout their history?
2. Identify the various types of drugs and briefly note their effects on people.
3. Who are the most likely users and abusers of alcohol and other drugs?
4. How do the use and abuse of alcohol and other drugs affect physical health?
5. What are the consequences of alcohol and other drugs for psychological health?
6. How does alcohol affect interpersonal relationships?
7. Indicate the economic costs of drug use and abuse.
8. In what ways do group norms affect patterns of drug use?
9. What kind of role problems enter into drug use and abuse?
10. How do social institutions contribute to the problem?
11. What are the attitudes and ideologies that are important in understanding the drug problem?
12. Name some steps that can be taken to alleviate the problem of alcohol and other drugs.

chapter 2 review

Internet Resources/Exercises

1. Explore some of the ideas in this chapter on the following sites:

http://www.nida.nih.gov The National Institute on Drug Abuse site contains news, publications, and links to other sources.

http://www.casacolumbia.org Site of the National Center on Addiction and Substance Abuse at Columbia University, with a focus on studying and combating substance abuse. Has publications and links to other resources.

http://ash.org The Action on Smoking and Health home page provides information on nonsmokers' rights, smoking statistics and information, and help for stopping.

2. Look at Figure 2.1 in the text. Select five drugs and get detailed information on them from the National Institute on Drug Abuse site. If everyone had this information, how many people would still experiment with the drugs? Give arguments both for maintaining that nobody would be a user and for asserting that some would still be users.

3. Search the Internet for "drug use" and "tobacco." Find sites that defend people's right to be users. List the reasons, and respond to them with materials in the text.

For Further Reading

Brandt, Allan. *The Cigarette Century: The Rise, Fall, and Deadly Persistence of the Product That Defined America.* New York: Basic Books, 2009. An account by a medical professor of how cigarettes affect us culturally, biologically, and healthwise as well as a discussion about the deception of the public by the tobacco industry.

Cheever, Susan, John Hoffman, Susan Froemke, and Sheila Nevins. *Addiction: Why Can't They Just Stop?*
New York: Rodale Books, 2007. Uses personal narratives, experts, and statistical data to show the difficulty of breaking an addiction and the impact that addiction has on other people, the social order, and the economy.

Dodes, Lance M. *The Heart of Addiction: A New Approach to Understanding and Managing Alcoholism and Other Addictive Behaviors.* New York: Harper Collins, 2002. Identifies myths about addiction and discusses the common elements in addictions of all types. Includes addiction problems of particular groups and ways to get help.

Gahlinger, Paul M. *Illegal Drugs: A Complete Guide to Their History, Chemistry, Use, and Abuse.* Las Vegas, NV: Sagebrush Press, 2001. A professor of medicine provides a comprehensive account of all aspects of drug use and abuse for the nonspecialist general reader.

Hepola, Sara. *Blackout: Remembering the Things I Drank to Forget.* New York: Grand Central Publishing, 2016. A writer shares the story of her addiction to alcohol, including the blackouts, loss of memory, sex with strangers, loss of friends, and finally the painful process of getting sober.

Jersild, Devon. *Happy Hours: Alcohol in a Woman's Life.* New York: HarperCollins, 2001. Both statistics and personal stories highlight the increasingly serious problem of women's abuse of alcohol, including the unique challenges women face as they try to overcome their addiction.

Kuhn, Cynthia, Scott Swartzwelder, and Wilkie Wilson. *Buzzed: The Straight Facts About the Most Used and Abused Drugs from Alcohol to Ecstasy.* 3rd ed. New York: Norton, 2008. Three professors from the Duke University Medical Center discuss the history, effects, and hazards of 12 kinds of drugs, then probe such topics as the role of the brain, the nature of addiction, and legal issues.

Crime and Delinquency

©Laurent Hamels/Photoalto/PictureQuest

A Victim Recovers

Marcia, in her 20s, is one of the few survivors of an attack by a serial killer and rapist. After her assailant was sentenced to die for the murder of five young women and the rape of two others, Marcia told her story publicly. Like others, she felt a kind of double victimization:

I was only 22 when he appeared in my bedroom doorway, a bandanna covering his features, a knife raised high as he leaped toward my bed. A week before, he had been a visitor in my home, passing the time during the week he stayed as the houseguest of a neighbor.

Nothing could have prepared me for the viciousness I would experience in the following hours, reduced from a human being to an "it" in the mind and actions of this man. He dragged me around my house by the neck for several hours, forced me to do unspeakable things and twice strangled me into unconsciousness.

I fully expected to die before the night passed, hoping only to die with some dignity. He is 14 inches taller than me and twice my weight. I began to fight him with my mind. It became critical that I showed no fear because when I showed fear, he fed on it. I told him excuses for his behavior. Each time he hurt me, I chastised him almost cheerfully as though I was his friend. Four and a half hours after it started, he walked away of his own accord. I had managed to convince him that he had nothing to fear from me.

Just as nothing could have prepared me for him, nothing prepared me for the seven years ahead, in which I would keep alive these hideous memories for the appeasement of an overburdened and overindulgent criminal defense system. I remember being disheveled and in shock in my living room and the policeman asking me how committed I was to prosecuting my assailant. I told him that I would do whatever I had to do. I could not have known that it would take seven years and three trials. I had to describe to three juries in painful detail the kind of agony he meted out to his victims. Despite my anger that the families of the victims and myself have been further victimized to this extent by a system that gave him every reasonable—and unreasonable—concession and delay over the years, I do not regret my decision to testify.

In the end, I can only mourn at the tragic waste he represents, not only in his victims—and I am no longer one of them—but in himself. However, I'm not so noble as to keep back some satisfaction that this random killer should find that the blood on his hands is also his own.

Introduction

Americans frequently get upset or angry about the problem of crime. A small child is killed, a mother is strangled by her estranged husband, or a businessman cheats people out of their retirement. Such crimes enrage people and can lead to an increased demand for law and order.

Is there reason for such concern? After all, crime rates have generally been falling since about 1990, and some have fallen dramatically (see Table 3.2). For example, the murder rate was 9.4 per 100,000 in 1990, but down to 4.5 in 2014. The victimization rate for all other violent crimes fell from 31.3 per 1,000 people aged 12 and above in 1991 to 20.1 in 2014 (Truman and Langton 2015). Property crime rates have also declined. Such figures are encouraging, but they take on a different cast when you realize that in 2014 there were still 5.4 million Americans victimized by violent crime and 10.4 million victimized by property crime (burglary and theft). Or think of it this way: it is doubtful if any American can reach adulthood without being the victim of a crime or having a family member or acquaintance who has been a victim. In short, despite the declining rates, crime remains a serious social problem.

Major crimes like murder, robbery, and theft capture people's attention and generate concern. But historian Herbert Butterfield suggested that a society can be destroyed by crimes involving "petty breaches of faith" of "very nice people" (Butterfield 1949:54). These two contrasting points of view form the theme of this chapter: Crime is a social problem that pervades American society, and it *includes both respectable and nonrespectable citizens.*

First, we look at the varieties of crime and define crime and delinquency. We then examine the extent of crime in the United States, the effects that crime and delinquency have on the quality of life, and the kinds of sociocultural factors that contribute to the problem. Finally, we discuss measures that can be taken and have been taken to resolve the problem.

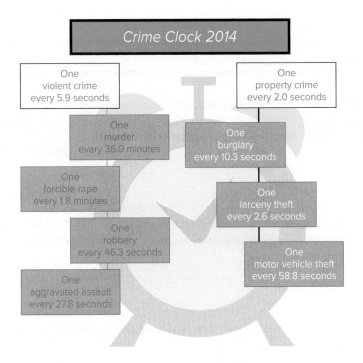

Crime Clock 2014

One violent crime every 5.9 seconds
One property crime every 2.0 seconds
One murder every 36.0 minutes
One burglary every 10.3 seconds
One forcible rape every 1.8 minutes
One larceny theft every 2.6 seconds
One robbery every 46.3 seconds
One motor vehicle theft every 58.8 seconds
One aggravated assault every 27.8 seconds

FIGURE 3.1
The Crime Clock Dramatizes the Extensiveness of Crime in the United States.
Source: Truman and Langton 2015.

The Varieties of Crime

Technically, crime is any violation of the criminal law. However, as you will see when we examine white-collar crime, this definition is inadequate. Nevertheless, we begin with a discussion of the kinds of acts embodied in the criminal law—acts that are defined as threatening to the state or to citizens whom the state is obligated to protect.

Predatory Crime

When the word *crime* is mentioned, people generally think of **predatory crimes**—*acts that have victims who suffer loss of property or some kind of physical harm.* Property crimes are more common, but the public generally defines crimes against persons as more serious. Less than 10 percent of all crime involves acts such as murder and rape, but these violent acts are the ones that arouse the greatest public apprehension.

A commonly used measure of *crime rates*—the *Federal Bureau of Investigation Crime Index*—covers eight major felonies, all serious violations of the criminal law, and all predatory crimes. The FBI defines them as follows (Federal Bureau of Investigation 2002): (1) *Murder and nonnegligent manslaughter* are willful killing of a person. Not included are deaths by negligence, suicide, accident, and justifiable homicide. (2) *Aggravated assault,* "an unlawful attack by one person upon another for the purpose of inflicting severe bodily injury," usually involves a weapon. (3) *Forcible rape* is defined as actual or attempted sexual intercourse "through the use of force or the threat of force." (4) *Robbery* is the use of force or threat of force to take something of value from a person. (5) *Burglary*—by definition the "unlawful entry of a structure to commit a felony or theft"—does not necessarily mean force was used to gain entry. (6) *Larceny-theft* is the "unlawful taking or stealing of property or articles without the use of force, violence, or

predatory crimes
acts that have victims who suffer loss of property or some kind of physical harm

fraud." It includes shoplifting, picking pockets, purse snatching, and the like. (7) *Motor vehicle theft* includes both actual and attempted theft of any motor vehicle. (8) Finally, *arson* is any "willful or malicious burning or attempt to burn, with or without intent to defraud, a dwelling house, public building, motor vehicle or aircraft, personal property of another, etc."

Because not all predatory crimes are included in the FBI Index, the Index cannot be used as an indication of the total amount of crime in the society. Fraud, for example, is not counted, nor are many of the white-collar crimes that we discuss.

Illegal Service Crimes

Illegal service crimes do not involve a definite victim but rather *a relationship between a criminal and his customer.* The illegal service rendered might be drugs, gambling, prostitution, or high-interest loans. Although these relationships violate the law, they are not likely to be reported because the criminal and the customer probably prefer to have the service available.

Public Disorder Crimes

Public disorder crimes also have no definite victim. They involve behavior that *is treated as criminal only when it occurs before some audience that will be offended.* These crimes include behavior such as disorderly conduct, drunkenness, and indecent exposure. Public disorder crimes are more common than predatory or illegal service crimes, according to arrest figures.

Crimes of Negligence

Crimes of negligence involve an *unintended victim or potential victim.* They include actions such as reckless driving and other infractions of the law by automobile drivers. The "criminal" in this case is not deemed to be deliberately trying to harm anyone. Rather, the behavior is a threat or a nuisance from which the public should be protected. Negligence crimes and public disorder crimes compose the bulk of police work in the United States.

Cybercrime

Cybercrime is the use of the computer to engage in criminal activity. Victims include individuals, organizations, and, potentially, an entire nation (Shawn 2011). A nation can be attacked by terrorist groups that hack into government records or disrupt the financial or military system in some way. Organizations such as businesses and corporations are victimized when hackers steal information that can be used to gain a competitive advantage. One company, for example, reported a loss of years' worth of research and development valued at $1 billion. And the loss occurred almost overnight!

Organized crime is increasingly operating over computer networks (Shawn 2011). Rather than robbing banks at gunpoint, they break into the computer systems of financial institutions and steal a wealth of data that can then be sold or used for financial gain.

As for individual victims, the FBI has identified a multitude of scams and frauds (Federal Bureau of Investigation 2010). Two of these are newer versions of "phishing" (you get an e-mail that claims to be from your bank or credit card company asking you to update your information and password). The newer versions are "smishing" (which combines texting and phishing) and "vishing" (which combines voice and phishing).

The criminals set up an automated dialing system that calls people in a particular area or that uses telephone numbers stolen from banks or credit unions. Victims get a message telling them there's a problem with their account or that their ATM card needs to be reactivated. The victims also receive a telephone number or a Web site they must contact to address the problem. Victims are then asked for personal information that enables the criminal to steal the victim's money from bank accounts, use the victim's charge cards for purchases, create a false ATM card, and so on.

Cybercrime has become such a serious matter that the FBI and the National White Collar Crime Center established the Internet Crime Complaint Center in 2000. According to the FBI Web site, the center received 25,000 complaints a month in 2010. Two common complaints are from people who did not receive a promised payment or merchandise for which they had paid or from victims of identity theft. In 2014, an estimated 17.6 million Americans, 7 percent of all those aged 16 and older, were victims of identity theft (Harrell 2015). Eighty percent of the cases involved the misuse of a bank account or credit card.

White-Collar Crime

White-collar crime is the crime of "respectable" people. The term was coined by Edwin Sutherland (Sutherland and Cressey 1955), who said that white-collar crimes are *committed by respectable people in the course of their work.* White-collar crimes include consumer fraud, which may be the most widespread of all the crimes (Rosoff, Pontell, and Tillman 2002); environmental offenses; insider trading in stocks; securities fraud; government corruption; cybercrime; and misleading advertising.

white-collar crime crimes committed by respectable citizens in the course of their work

In an effort to categorize the various kinds of white-collar crime, Edelhertz (1983) suggests four types. First are "personal," or "ad hoc," crimes. The individual in this case generally does not have a face-to-face confrontation with the victim. Cheating on federal and state income taxes is one example of such a crime.

A second type of white-collar crime involves "abuses of trust," which are crimes committed by people who have custody of someone else's wealth (e.g., embezzlement) or who have the power to make decisions (e.g., accepting a bribe to make a favorable decision).

Third are crimes that are "incidental to and in furtherance of organizational operations," though they are not part of the purpose of the organization. Violations of antitrust laws and the federal Corrupt Practices Act fit in here. Or on a smaller scale, Edelhertz says that this "most troublesome" of the four categories involves such issues as fraudulent Medicare or Medicaid claims and the false weight on purchases at the grocery store. Edelhertz calls this third category the most troublesome because the offenders do not think of themselves as criminals and generally have high status in their communities. Nevertheless, the outcome is victimization of people. Consider, for instance, the problem of deceptive advertising. The advertising agency and the corporate executives who pay for ads do not think of themselves as engaging in criminal activity. Yet millions of Americans buy products based on this deceptive advertising.

The fourth category is white-collar crime carried on as a business by full-time con artists. This category includes actions from stock swindles to street games in which people are cheated out of their money.

White-collar crime abounds at all levels: individuals, small businesses, large corporations, and governmental agencies. Examples of individuals include cyber criminals, some of whom work out of their homes to defraud companies. At the small business level, numerous cases of fraud emerged in the first decade of this century in financial

White-collar criminals are usually high-status individuals who appear to be successful and respectable.

©UpperCut Images/Alamy Stock Photo

schemes. For example, two men who had gained a reputation for making shrewd, profitable investments in the stock market bilked hundreds of millions of dollars from investments made by public pension funds and universities (Kouwe 2009). The investors were unable to recover their losses because the men had spent it on a lavish lifestyle.

Large corporations also get involved in white-collar crime, including, in recent years, a brokerage firm that committed 2,000 felonies, a health care organization that paid bribes and kickbacks to doctors, a health maintenance organization that defrauded government health programs, an accounting firm that set up fraudulent shelters to help rich clients evade billions of dollars in taxes, and the Enron Corporation's "creative" accounting practices and manipulation of energy markets (Eichenwald 2002; McClam 2005). The Enron case illustrates how far-reaching the effects of corporate crime can be. Among other things, the actions of the Enron executives resulted in California energy costs that soared when markets were manipulated, hurting countless individuals and businesses that could not afford the higher rates; investors lost huge sums of money and many, including Enron employees, lost their life savings and retirement when the corporation collapsed; and many Enron employees lost their jobs.

Although some Enron officials received prison sentences, in many cases of corporate crime the only punishment meted out is a fine. In fact, some of the "crimes" are not defined as illegal by the law. Corporate lawyers are skilled at advising business executives on ways to avoid breaking the law while engaging in questionable practices. Sometimes their advice may be counterproductive: Many of the Enron accounting practices and trading strategies were approved by law firms advising the corporation (France 2004). In other situations, such as a tax shelter that the Internal Revenue Service declares illegal, the fact that the individual or company was advised by a lawyer that the shelter was legal often means no criminal prosecution and lower civil liability (France 2004).

Because of such abuses, Sutherland argued that many practices of respectable people that are not defined by the law as crimes should be treated as crimes. He asserted, in fact, that businesspeople were more criminalistic than people of the ghettoes. A major difference is that criminal law distinguishes between the two groups, so that some acts that logically could be defined as crime are not in the criminal law. Further, some acts involving businesses and corporations are handled by government commissions rather than the criminal justice system. You can reasonably argue that when a company advertises a 6 percent interest rate on installment payments and actually collects 11.5 percent, it is committing fraud. The executives of the company will not be charged with fraud; the company will merely be ordered by the Federal Trade Commission (FTC) to stop advertising the false rate.

Even when the offense is covered by the criminal law, white-collar criminals may receive less severe punishment or escape punishment altogether. For one thing, the number of white-collar crimes prosecuted declined 28 percent in the early 2000s as concern shifted to homeland security and prosecution of illegal immigration (Marks 2006). For another thing, when fines are levied against companies, they may have their fines reduced later or the fines may go unpaid (Mendoza and Sullivan 2006). Still, the courts have sentenced a number of executives to prison terms in recent years, ranging from 1 to 150 years. Experts applaud such convictions, arguing that white-collar crime is at least as serious as, or even more serious than, the violent acts of street criminals. Street criminals tax the patience and resources of society, but white-collar criminals are like an insidious corrosion that slowly but surely destroys.

Organized Crime

The term "organized crime" brings up images of Al Capone, machine guns, the Mafia, the Mob, La Cosa Nostra, the Syndicate, and films like *The Untouchables* and *The Godfather.* Is organized crime such a phenomenon in the United States? Are there groups that control the criminal activities of cities, regions, or even the entire nation? Criminologists themselves do not agree on the exact nature of organized crime, but there is some consensus on five characteristics of **organized crime:** the determination of a group of people to make money by any means necessary; the provision of illegal goods and services to people who want them or can be coerced into taking them; the use of political corruption to maintain and extend the activities; the persistence of the activities by the same organizations over successive generations of people; and a code of conduct for members (see, e.g., Berger 1999). There is also likely to be some involvement in legitimate business, which is used to launder illegal funds or stolen merchandise. For instance, profits from drug sales may be claimed as legitimate profits of a legitimate business by manipulating its accounting records.

organized crime
an ongoing organization of people who provide illegal services and goods and who maintain their activities by the aid of political corruption

The activities of organized crime include gambling, prostitution, drugs, extortion, loan-sharking, and various legitimate enterprises (such as restaurants) that are used to launder money received from the illegal activities (Motivans 2003). There is, however, no single organization that controls all organized crime at the international or national level. Rather, there are numerous and diverse groups.

Although the Mafia and La Cosa Nostra are the most well-known organized crime groups, the Federal Bureau of Investigation (2009b) points out that the face of organized crime has changed over time. The current concerns of the Bureau are with: Russian mobsters who fled to the U.S. in the wake of the Soviet Union's collapse; groups from African countries like Nigeria that engage in drug trafficking and financial scams;

Chinese tongs, Japanese Boryokudan, and other Asian crime rings; and enterprises based in Eastern European nations like Hungary and Romania. These groups engage in various illegal activities, including drug trafficking, extortion, murder, kidnapping, home invasions, prostitution, illegal gambling, loan sharking, insurance/credit card fraud, stock fraud, and the theft of high-tech components. They also engage in human trafficking, particularly in bringing Chinese migrants and selling them into sex or sweatshop slavery.

Organized crime is no longer the province of any particular racial or ethnic group. Rather, it involves diverse groups who use it to gain economic and social mobility.

Juvenile Delinquency

The concept of juvenile delinquency is a modern one. Until the late 19th century, juvenile offenders were regarded as incapable of certain crimes or were treated as adults in the criminal justice system. This concept changed in the 19th century when a group of reformers set out to redeem the nation's wayward youth (Platt 1969). These "child savers" helped establish the juvenile court system in the United States. As a result, juveniles were treated differently from adults, and certain behavior that was once ignored or handled in an informal way came under the jurisdiction of a government agency. Thus, the *concept of delinquency* was "invented" in America in the 19th century.

The nation's first *juvenile court* was established in 1899 in Illinois. All states now have juvenile court systems. The court's primary responsibility is to protect the welfare of youth, and its secondary task is to safeguard the community from youthful offenders. This orientation has given juvenile judges considerable discretion to make whatever decisions they deem necessary for the juveniles' protection and rehabilitation.

Three types of juveniles come under the court's jurisdiction. (A *juvenile* is typically defined as someone between the ages of 7 and 17.) *Youthful offenders* are those who engage in behavior for which adults can be tried in a criminal court. All predatory crimes are included here. Further, in the mid-1990s most states overhauled their laws so that more youths can be tried as adults in a criminal court and offenders are no longer protected by the confidentiality of juvenile court proceedings. The second type of juvenile handled by the juvenile court is the *status offenders,* those who violate the juvenile court code rather than the criminal code. Behavior such as truancy, running away from home, and breaking the curfew is included in this category. Finally, the court deals with *minors in need of care*—those who are neglected or abused and in need of the court's care. They do not fall into the category of delinquent, but they are the responsibility of the juvenile court.

The range of behavior defined as delinquent tends to be broad. Perhaps as many as 90 percent of all young people have engaged in behavior that would fall under the jurisdiction of juvenile court, including activities such as fighting, truancy, and running away from home. In some states, statutes define delinquency so broadly that virtually all juveniles could be categorized as delinquent. Delinquency, then, includes a much greater range of behavior than does crime.

Juvenile Violence and Juvenile Gangs

Perhaps "delinquency" is a term that does not sufficiently capture the *severity of the problem of youth crime.* Youths under the age of 18 account for 13.7 percent of all arrests for violent crime and 22 percent of all arrests for property crime (Maguire 2012).

Youths join gangs for a variety of reasons, among them being the desire to gain status and escape poverty.
©Patrick Sheandell/Photo Alto

Part, but not all, of the problem of juvenile violence stems from juvenile gangs. *The proliferation of gangs, along with involvement in drugs and the ready availability of guns, has exacerbated the problem of violent crime by youths.* Gang members account for a disproportionate number of arrests for serious offenses (Thornberry, Huizinga, and Loeber 2004; Harrell 2005).

Juvenile gangs are now pervasive, appearing everywhere from large metropolitan to rural areas of the nation. A national survey reported an estimated 30,700 gangs and 850,000 gang members (Egley, Howell, and Harris 2014). The gangs exist in all 50 states. An increasing number of females are joining gangs. One study found that in high-risk, high-crime neighborhoods, 29.4 percent of girls and 32.4 percent of boys said they were members of a gang. The girls join because of such problems as family abuse and the appeal of being an integral part of a group (Miller 2001).

One reason for the increasing number of gangs is that the conditions that spawn the gangs—poverty, discrimination, and lack of legitimate opportunities—continue to exist throughout the nation. Once gangs appear in an area, they *tend to perpetuate themselves by setting models for each succeeding generation.* They also are perpetuated by a small number of members who stay in the gangs into adulthood and even parenthood.

Youths who enter gangs may be *socialized quickly into violence* (Sanchez-Jankowski 1991). Entry into the gang itself may require the new member to be beaten by the others. Fighting among members is common and may be even more frequent than fighting with outsiders. Such violence has a number of purposes, including disciplining, demonstrating courage and toughness, establishing individual status within the group, and gaining the skills necessary to defend the gang's "turf" (Sanchez-Jankowski 1991; Kennedy and Baron 1993).

Youths join gangs for various reasons. One of the more important is that the gang enables them to gain status (Alleyne and Wood 2010). They also, of course, gain income from the illegal activities of the gang. In impoverished areas, there are few opportunities for the young to gain either money or status, so gang membership can be very appealing.

Gangs engage in various kinds of crime, including smuggling, armed robbery, assault, auto theft, drug trafficking, extortion, fraud, identity theft, murder, and weapons trafficking. They are also involved in about 16 percent of all homicides in the nation (Egley, Howell, and Harris 2014). In many communities, gangs commit as much as 80 percent of the crime. Selling drugs is the major means for gangs to maintain their operations and the lifestyles of their members. Some gangs use such fronts as clothing stores, hair salons, and music recording and production companies to launder the money they get from selling drugs.

The Extent of Crime and Delinquency

How widespread are crime and delinquency? The question is difficult to answer because of certain problems with official statistics. Here we examine ways to gather data, look at problems with official records, and then draw conclusions about the extent of crime and delinquency.

Sources of Data

The three basic sources of data on crime are *official records, victimization studies,* and *self-reports.* A frequently used official record are the data published annually by the FBI. As noted previously, the FBI's Crime Index includes only eight major felonies. A great deal of crime—indeed, most crime—does not appear in this annual report. Other official sources include municipal police records and the records of juvenile courts. Because juvenile courts have no uniform system of reporting, we can only estimate the number of delinquency cases processed annually.

Victimization studies secure information from the victims of crime rather than from officials or official records. A victimization study usually involves interviews at a representative sample of homes. People in those homes are asked whether they or members of their families have been the victims of a crime or crimes during the previous year. The major source of victimization data is the National Crime Victimization Survey conducted annually by the Department of Justice.

In contrast to the *FBI data,* which are based on statistics gathered from thousands (but not all) of law enforcement authorities in America's cities and towns, the National Crime Victimization Survey includes both a greater range of crimes and crimes never *officially reported.* Because of nonreporting, the Victimization Survey data are sometimes twice as high as those of the *FBI.*

Self-reports are usually used with youths. The youths are asked whether they engaged in any of a number of different kinds of criminal activity. Various techniques are used to try to ensure honesty and accuracy, and there is evidence that self-reported crime by young people is fairly accurate.

Problems with Official Records

If you attempt to estimate the crime rate from official records, you encounter a number of problems. First, quite a number of crimes are *undetected*. There are two ways to get an estimate of the amount of undetected crime. One is by asking people whether they have ever committed various crimes. When allowed to respond anonymously, people will often admit to a number of felonies for which they were never convicted as a criminal. The other way is to ask people whether they have been victims of the various crimes and then compare their responses with official records.

Second, *a substantial number of crimes are never reported to the police.* The rate of reporting varies with the type of crime (Figure 3.2), and the reasons for not reporting also vary (Table 3.1). Official figures underreport nearly every kind of crime.

A third problem with official records is that *definitions of crime change* and the *methods of reporting crime change*. Because a crime is a violation of the criminal law, any change in the law changes the amount of crime. In the early 1930s a considerable number of inmates in federal prisons were there for crimes that would not have been crimes a few years earlier. They were serving time for violating laws related to the Eighteenth Amendment to the Constitution—the amendment that established Prohibition.

Changes in the method of reporting crime can result in an apparent crime wave that may really be a "crime reporting" wave. For example, some years ago the FBI discovered that police were reporting only about half the number of property crimes that insurance companies were reporting. A new system was implemented, and during the next year there was an enormous increase in the police-reported rate of assaults, robberies, and burglaries. The rates reflected the new reporting methods but not necessarily any increase in the actual rate of crime.

FIGURE 3.2 Reporting Victimizations to the Police.
Source: Truman and Langton, 2015.

Reason	All Crimes, Total	Crimes of Violence		Property Crimes		
		Robbery	Assault	Burglary	Auto Theft	Theft
Reported to another official	13.0	5.4	14.2	5.2	3.4	8.3
Personal/private	20.7	12.2	21.8	7.0	7.9	5.3
Object recovered, offender unsuccessful	17.3	11.2	18.5	21.4	16.3	26.7
Not important enough	6.2	1.9	7.1	6.2	0.0	4.4
Lack of proof	3.4	10.2	2.1	12.1	13.1	9.9
Police wouldn't want to be bothered	6.3	11.4	5.8	10.9	3.1	10.5
Police ineffective or biased	4.6	17.8	3.1	6.9	15.3	3.8
Fear of reprisal	7.3	5.8	7.3	1.0	1.3	0.5
Inconvenient	4.7	7.5	4.2	3.5	6.4	4.1
Other reasons	15.7	13.8	15.6	10.3	24.2	10.4

TABLE 3.1

Reasons for Not Reporting Crimes to the Police (in percent not reported)

SOURCE: U.S. Department of Justice 2008:110.

A fourth problem with official records involves *police procedures*. Whether some behavior is defined officially by the police as criminal depends on factors other than the behavior itself. For instance, the police may be caught in political cross-pressures when they decide whether to report offenses (Selke and Pepinsky 1982). If they report offenses, they may be blamed for failing to stem the rising tide of crime. If they fail to report them, they may be blamed for being unresponsive. There also may be pressure to keep reported offenses low in order to make areas more attractive to business, residents, and tourists.

A final problem with official records relates to *changing expectations* in society. At one time in U.S. history, many crimes in slum areas and sections of cities populated by minority groups were unreported. Indeed, the police were not necessarily even notified when criminal offenses occurred. In recent decades, the poor and minority groups expect and demand adequate protection. Although a great many crimes are never reported, there is evidence that more are now being reported than in the past, thus making the rate of crime appear to be increasing.

These qualifications to the reliability of official records suggest that the amount of crime in the nation is considerably greater than official records indicate. They also suggest that caution must be exercised when comparing rates across time and drawing a quick conclusion that a "crime wave" is in process. However, when official records are used in conjunction with victimization studies and other evidence, the conclusions are more reliable.

The Amount of Crime and Delinquency

What do the data reveal about the amount of crime and delinquency in America? The amount differs depending on whether you look at FBI or victimization data. According to FBI data, rates of serious crime fluctuate over time. However, there has been a general downward trend in rates over the past few decades. Still, the rates were far higher by the end of 2014 than they were in 1960 (Table 3.2).

Year	Violent Crime				Property Crime		
	Murder	Forcible Rape	Robbery	Aggravated Assault	Burglary	Larceny/ Theft	Auto Theft
Number (1,000)							
1960	9.1	17.2	108	154	912	1,855	328
1970	16.0	38.0	350	335	2,205	4,226	928
1980	23.0	82.1	549	655	3,759	7,113	1,115
1990	23.4	102.6	639	1,055	3,074	7,946	1,636
2000	16.0	90.0	408	912	2,051	6,972	1,160
2014	14.3	84.0	326	741	1,730	5,858	690
Rate (per 100,000)							
1960	5.1	9.6	60	86	509	1,035	183
1970	7.9	18.7	172	165	1,085	2,079	457
1980	10.2	36.4	244	291	1,668	3,156	495
1990	9.4	41.2	257	424	1,236	3,195	658
2000	5.5	32.0	145	324	729	2,477	412
2014	4.5	26.4	102	232	542	1,837	216

TABLE 3.2
Crime and Crime Rates by Type, 1960 to 2014

SOURCE: U.S. Census Bureau 1975:153; Federal Bureau of Investigation Web site 2016.

Victimization data also show fluctuating rates over time. Table 3.3 gives the rates for 2014. Overall, there were 20 violent victimizations for every 1,000 people aged 12 or older and 118 property crimes for every 1,000 households. About one out of every eight households, therefore, experienced some kind of property crime in 2014.

Obtaining information about white-collar crime is difficult. The FBI has some information on specific kinds of white-collar crime but acknowledges that it is impossible to give an accurate, overall portrait. Still, it is clear that unethical and illegal behaviors abound in business and industry. Much of the business crime, however, involves insiders,

TABLE 3.3
Victimization Rates, Personal and Household Crimes, 2014 (per 1,000 persons aged 12 or older or per 1,000 households)

SOURCE: Truman and Langton 2015.

Type of Crime	Number (1,000s)	Rate
Crimes of violence	5,360	20.1
Rape/sexual assault	284	1.1
Robbery	664	2.5
Assault	4,411	16.5
Aggravated assault	1,092	4.1
Simple assault	3,319	12.4
Property crimes	15,288	118.1
Household burglary	2,993	23.1
Motor vehicle theft	534	4.1
Theft	11,760	90.8

including businesspeople at the higher levels of the organization. The loss caused by owners and executives is far greater than that caused by rank-and-file employees. Bank employees steal more from banks than do robbers. And businesses are offenders as well as victims, engaging in criminal activity against consumers and customers. Indictments for criminal activity and fines for serious misbehavior occur regularly among both small businesses and the nation's largest corporations.

Finally, this nation has an enormous amount of delinquency. Keep in mind, however, that delinquency by definition includes some relatively trivial kinds of behavior. Juveniles may be arrested for conduct that would not be defined as criminal on the part of an adult (e.g., violation of curfew, running away from home, and possession of an alcoholic beverage). But juveniles also are involved in serious crimes. In 2014, 2.6 percent of all arrests involved those 14 years old or under (Federal Bureau of Investigation 2015). And 13.9 percent of those arrested were 15 to 19 years of age. That represents more than double their proportion in the population.

The Distribution of Crime

Crime is unequally distributed in the United States. There are variations by region, by state, and by population size. For example, the murder rate for the nation as a whole in 2014 was 4.5 per 100,000 inhabitants (Federal Bureau of Investigation 2015). The highest rate, however, was in cities with populations between 1/2 and 1 million inhabitants—11.3, or more than double the overall rate. Cities of that size also had a rate of auto theft that was more than double the rate for the nation as a whole.

Group variations also exist. In general, males, young people, racial/ethnic minorities, and the poor have higher rates of victimization than others. For example, the 2014 murder rates varied by race/ethnicity (45 percent of the victims were white, 51 percent were African American, and 15.6 percent were Hispanic) and by gender (77 percent were male) (Federal Bureau of Investigation 2015).

The Criminal Justice Process

To understand the problem of crime in the nation, it is important to know about the criminal justice process. What happens when you report a crime to the police? The path from the reporting to the final settlement is long and complex. Here we can only give you a sketch of the process to illustrate its complexity.

After a crime is reported and law enforcement officers verify that it has indeed been committed (a proportion of incidents reported to the police are not defined by them as crimes), a suspect must be identified and apprehended. Frequently, extensive investigation is required to properly identify the suspect. After an arrest is made, information about the suspect and the case is given to the prosecutor, who will decide whether to file formal charges with the court. If charges are not filed, the suspect is released.

A suspect who is charged is brought before a judge or magistrate without any unnecessary delay. The judge or magistrate informs the accused of the charges and decides whether there is probable cause to detain the suspect. If the offense is a minor one, a decision about guilt and penalty can be made at this point. If the offense is serious, the process continues. In many jurisdictions, the next step is a preliminary hearing, which is an effort to decide whether there is probable cause to believe that the accused committed a crime within the jurisdiction of the court. If the judge does not find probable cause, the case is dismissed. If the judge finds probable cause, or if the accused waives the preliminary hearing, the case can be turned over to a grand jury. The grand jury hears the evidence and decides whether there is enough to justify a trial. If so, the grand jury issues an *indictment,* which gives the basic facts of the offense charged against the accused.

Once the indictment is filed, the accused is scheduled for *arraignment,* at which time the accused is informed of the charges, advised of his or her rights, and asked to enter a plea to the charges. In most cases, the accused will plead guilty in order to take advantage of *plea bargaining.* Generally, plea bargaining means that the prosecution and defense agree to a lesser offense or to only one of the original charges. Plea bargaining allows the offender to get a lighter sentence, assures the prosecutor that the offender will not be totally acquitted, and saves everyone the time and expense of a court trial. If the plea is "Not guilty," or if the plea is "Guilty" but is refused by the judge (the judge may believe that the accused was coerced into the plea), the case proceeds to trial. The trial can be by jury, or the accused may request that the case be decided by a judge.

If the trial results in conviction, the defendant may appeal to a higher court. If no appeal is made, or if the appeals are rejected, the offender must submit to the sentence imposed by the judge or jury. Sometimes a sentence is handed down only after a sentencing hearing in which the defense presents mitigating circumstances to help minimize the severity of the sentence.

This process is not followed exactly in every jurisdiction, and the juvenile justice system differs in a number of important ways. Yet this explanation outlines the basic process and shows how decisions are made at a number of points in the process. Decision at each point may result in the release of the accused. The system reflects the American belief that the accused is presumed innocent until proven guilty. The result is, as Figure 3.3 shows for federal cases, that half or fewer of those arrested for crimes are ever convicted and incarcerated.

FIGURE 3.3
Federal Criminal Case Processing, 2004.
Source: U.S. Department of Justice 2006:1.

Crime, Delinquency, and the Quality of Life

Widespread crime contradicts American values of freedom from fear, of well-being, and of the right to keep personal property. Crime, by definition, often involves exploitive or violent relationships and thereby contradicts both the *values and ideology* about America being a land of opportunity for all. The "land of opportunity" notion loses some of its appeal for those who fear that their success can make them victims if it attracts criminal activity. Thus, crime diminishes the quality of life by exacting high physical, psychological, and economic costs.

Physical and Psychological Costs of Crime

Crime causes physical and psychological suffering. Although it is difficult to measure, there is evidence that this suffering is considerable. Crime affects physical and emotional health, increases fear, and fosters alienation.

trauma
physical or emotional injury

Physical and Mental Health.   The victim of a crime experiences **trauma.** The victim may be temporarily or permanently injured (either physically or emotionally) or even killed. A fourth of all violent crime victims, and half of rape victims, are injured (Simon, Mercy, and Perkins 2001). Emotional trauma such as anxiety, depression, shame, humiliation, or despair is also likely (Hochstetler et al. 2014). A substantial number of crime victims get mental health counseling or therapy, or join a support group every year.

White-collar crime also takes its toll on Americans' physical and mental health. Some people have lost their businesses or life savings because of fraud. Identity theft can cause severe stress because victims may be denied loans, housing, education, or job opportunities and can even be arrested for crimes they did not commit (Morton 2004). Consumers have suffered financial and health losses because of corporate practices. For example, the suppression of negative information about the defects and dangers of silicone breast implants resulted in health problems and emotional trauma for many women who had implants (Chapple 1997).

Fear and Its Consequences.   Widespread crime can produce pervasive fear in a society. With the falling crime rates since the early 1990s, the fear of crime also diminished. Still, a 2016 Gallup poll found that 53 percent worry a "great deal" about crime (Davis 2016). And a third or more of all Americans admit they are afraid to walk alone at night. The fear generated by crime means that everyone loses—victims, people who are afraid they might be victims, and residents and businesspeople in high-crime areas.

alienation
a sense of estrangement from one's social environment, typically measured by one's feelings of powerlessness, normlessness, isolation, meaninglessness, and self-estrangement

Alienation.   Sutherland (1968) argued that white-collar crime has a psychological impact that cannot be measured in monetary terms alone. He pointed out that such crimes create an atmosphere of distrust in a society, lowering social morale and creating widespread social disorganization. People not only become cynical about social institutions (illustrated by the common belief that all politicians are crooked), but they also have a tendency to develop a social Darwinist approach to life ("It's a dog-eat-dog world and you have to look out for yourself above all else"). In a sense, then, white-collar crime may be more damaging to a society than predatory crime. It indicates that the whole society is corrupt—that fraud, theft, and exploitation pervade the paneled offices of professionals as well as the littered streets of the slums. White-collar crime, thus, produces a pervasive sense of distrust and **alienation** and suggests that the society is sick.

Economic Costs of Crime

A great many factors must be taken into account when we try to assess the economic losses due to crime. These factors include the personal loss of property; expense of insurance; cost of loan sharks, false advertising, and shoddy workmanship on consumer goods; work absences and lost wages resulting from physical and emotional trauma; medical cost for treating injuries; cost of maintaining security systems and other crime prevention measures; and cost of maintaining the criminal justice system. The criminal justice system alone (including local, state, and federal levels of government) costs hundreds of billions of dollars each year. An analysis of cybercrime estimated the global cost at nearly $400 billion each year, involving more than a million victims every day (Shawn 2011). And white-collar crime results in hundreds of billions of dollars every year, more than the losses from property crimes and bank robberies combined (Morreale 2015).

Some costs cannot even be measured. Consumers pay higher prices because of organized crime's involvement in legitimate business and because of business losses from crimes (including employee theft). Shoplifting adds to the cost of retail items. Many crimes of fraud, embezzlement, and arson-for-profit are never detected. Some crimes go unreported because the victims are afraid (blackmail or retaliation), embarrassed (con games), or involved in illegal activity (gambling).

When the costs are added, including direct losses due to personal and household crime and the cost of maintaining the criminal justice system, crime costs Americans hundreds of billions of dollars every year.

Contributing Factors

Like crime itself, the factors that generate and sustain crime involve both respectable and nonrespectable elements of society.

Social Structural Factors

Age Structure of the Population. As we noted earlier in this chapter, a disproportionate amount of crime is committed by young males. Males account for nearly three out of four of all arrests and eight out of ten arrests for violent crime (Federal Bureau of Investigation 2015). Thus, a partial explanation for the decreasing crime rates of the 1990s and early 2000s is the decline in the number of young males (Phillips 2006).

As the age structure of the nation shifts, with smaller or larger proportions falling into the lower age categories, crime rates should vary accordingly; but we must be cautious about predictions because no single factor is involved in the amount of crime. Although the current younger generation is more violent than previous ones, the homicide rates have fallen for them also, in part because of the shrinking urban market for crack cocaine (much of the increased killing in the late 1980s and early 1990s occurred in urban crack markets) (Rosenfeld 2002).

Hot Spots. Cohen and Felson (1979) developed a "routine activities" approach to crime. They focused on circumstances rather than the characteristics of offenders. In particular, they emphasized the importance of *likely offenders, suitable targets,* and *a lack of capable guardians* occurring at a particular place and time. "Capable guardians" can include anything from the presence of police to alarm systems. The convergence, or lack of convergence, of these three factors can explain changing crime rates, and why certain areas become "hot spots," or locales of high crime rates (Weisburd and Mazerolle 2000).

Van Koppen and Jansen (1999) used this approach to explain daily, weekly, and seasonal variations in robbery rates. Robbers' expectations of the amount of money available at a particular time and place constitute the suitable target, whereas the increased number of dark hours during the winter mean less adequate guardianship. Bryjak (1999) explained the drop in burglary rates in the 1990s in terms of increased guardianship of suitable targets; namely, the fact that more people are spending time in their homes because of personal computers, cable television, VCRs, and video games. This approach also helps explain fraud (Holtfreter, Reisig, and Pratt 2008), cybercrime victimization (Holt and Bossler 2009), juvenile crime (Weisburd, Groff, and Morris 2011), and using the cell phone for sexting (sending sexually explicit photos or videos) (Wolfe et al. 2016). The juvenile crime study focused on Seattle, Washington, where the researchers discovered that half of all juvenile crime occurred in less than 1 percent of street segments, concentrating in public and commercial areas where youth gathered rather than in residential areas.

Other research, covering 52 nations over a 25-year period, suggests that this approach may apply more to property crime than to personal crime (Bennett 1991). At any rate, the convergence of offenders, suitable targets, and inadequate guardianship helps explain a certain amount of crime (Hipp Bauer, Curran, and Bollen 2004). It follows that changing any one of the three factors may alter crime rates. For example, convenience stores are targets for robbery. Some local governments have passed ordinances requiring convenience stores to have at least two clerks on duty at all times. These additional clerks may reduce the amount of armed robbery by increasing the number of capable guardians.

Norms.   The **differential association theory** of crime and delinquency emphasizes the importance of *norms*. The theory states that potential or actual criminals or delinquents have their significant interactions with people whose norms violate the criminal law. Consistent with the theory, researchers have found that delinquents tend to spend more time with friends who are delinquent than with those who are nondelinquent (Haynie 2002). Delinquents who grow up in impoverished areas are also likely to live with one parent, to be unemployed, and to be school dropouts.

differential association theory
the theory that illegal behavior is due to a preponderance of definitions favorable to such behavior

Thus, the lower-class delinquent has few or no experiences with people who would lead him or her to accept the norms of the larger society (Paternoster and Mazerolle 1994). The delinquent is drawn to a group because of the need for companionship, and the group develops norms that violate the law. Because *group membership* is more meaningful to this youth than anything else he or she has experienced, those norms are accepted and followed. Those youths, on the other hand, who have their significant interactions with people who affirm the norms of the larger society—family, religious groups, and so on—are much less likely to engage in delinquent behavior (Johnson, Jang, Larson, and De Li 2001; Pearce and Haynie 2004).

Norms are involved in white-collar crime also. Certain practices in business and industry may be justified on the basis that everyone does them, that they are necessary for continuing one's enterprise, or that they are acceptable to those in authority. News accounts have reported corporate executives justifying illegal behavior on the grounds that their competitors engaged in the behavior; so if they did not, they would lose business and profits. American businessmen have paid off influential foreigners in order to secure contracts for business, and then shrugged off the practice by pointing out that the alternative was to not do business in those foreign countries. Such practices are learned early. A study of 133 MBA students found them likely to decide to further market and produce a hypothetical drug that was about to be recalled by the Food and Drug Administration when coworkers and the board of directors agreed with that decision (Piquero, Tibbetts, and Blankenship 2006).

The Politics of Control: The Prison. The United States has a higher proportion of its population incarcerated than does any other Western nation. While the proportion has gone down some since 2009, 1.56 million Americans (612 per 100,000 residents age 18 or older) were in state and federal prisons in 2014 (Carson 2015). Both the number and the rate are far higher than past decades. For example, in 1990 the number was 738,894, a rate of 294.15 per 100,000. In addition to those in prisons, there are hundreds of thousands more in jails (a jail is a locally administered institution that has authority to retain adults for 48 hours or longer; a prison is a state or federally administered facility for correction only). As a result, the incarceration rate in the U.S. is about seven times the rate in Europe (Ferguson 2014). The prison population is so large that one in nine government employees works in corrections, and many states spend more money each year on prisons than they do on education.

The high rate of incarceration is a political decision. There are alternative ways of dealing with criminals (see Global Comparison). Some people believe that **rehabilitation** should be the focus of the criminal justice system, whereas others believe criminals should be put into prisons for *punishment* and *isolation from society.* Still others believe that rehabilitation should be combined with the punishment of imprisonment. To address the issue, we examine what happens in the nation's prisons and jails. A basic problem is that, as Petersilia (2011) put it, "we have a corrections system that does not correct." Rehabilitation programs can be effective in reducing **recidivism** (repeated criminal activity and incarceration), but not all prisoners have access to rehabilitation programs, particularly the kind that are effective (such as high-school equivalency diploma programs, vocational training, and drug treatment). This is the case in the nation's jails, where only a fraction of the total jail population has access to any programs other than religious services (Freudenberg et al. 2005). The need for programs of support and rehabilitation is underscored by the fact that *people in jails have high rates of infectious and chronic diseases, substance abuse, mental health problems, and suicide rates that are far higher than those in prisons and in the larger society* (Freudenberg et al. 2005; Mumola 2005). On average, a prisoner stays in jail about 17 days, though some may remain for a year or more because of the shortage of prison space. The prisoner, who may be frightened, confused, or emotionally disturbed, has no one to talk with except other prisoners.

Among those jails that do have rehabilitation programs, basic adult education is the most common, followed by vocational training. Only the larger jails (those with 250 or more inmates) are likely to have such programs.

Even if rehabilitation programs are available, the *nature of prison life reduces the probability that rehabilitation will occur.* In addition, the longer the time spent in prison, the more the likelihood of recidivism. For one thing, jails and prisons are seriously overcrowded (Welsh 2002). Because there are too many prisoners for the amount of space available, nearly two-thirds of prison inmates are confined to units with less than 60 square feet of space, and a third spend 10 or more hours a day in that space. Such conditions are stressful and make any efforts at rehabilitation difficult. In addition, the stress is sufficiently severe that it makes many prisoners—particularly those with a history of incarceration—more vulnerable to infectious diseases and other physical and emotional illnesses that arise out of stress (Massoglia 2008). A national survey of jails and prisons reported that about four out of ten prisoners suffer from a chronic medical condition (Wilper et al.

rehabilitation
resocializing a criminal and returning him or her to full participation in society

recidivism
repeated criminal activity and incarceration

ALTERNATIVES TO IMPRISONMENT: GERMANY AND ISRAEL

The fact that the United States has a higher proportion of its population in jails and prisons than any other country in the world does not mean that the nation also has higher crime rates or more effective policing (which would catch greater numbers of criminals). The high incarceration rate reflects the societal attitude that criminals should be removed from society and punished. Would alternatives to imprisonment be beneficial for both the criminal and society? Evidence from Germany and Israel suggest that they would.

German courts make use of suspensions, probation, fines, and community service. Judges have lifetime appointments and sole authority to sentence offenders who are 18 to 20 years old. Hard-line judges continue to use imprisonment, whereas liberal judges try to use alternatives. The alternatives are common. In one year, for example, 634,735 adults were sentenced under the criminal law. The most frequent sentence, meted out to 80 percent of the offenders, was a fine. Of those sentenced to prison, two-thirds received a suspended sentence with probation. Only 6 percent actually went to prison.

Researchers have found that those imprisoned had higher rates of recidivism than did those given alternative sanctions. Even if the imprisonment included job training, offenders had a harder time getting a job after release than did those who had an alternative sanction. A study of regions reported that the proportion of offenders increased over a period of four years by 7 percent where imprisonment was the norm, and fell by 13 percent where alternative sanctions were the norm.

In Israel, the Kibbutz Resocialization Program is an effort to put offenders into a close-knit society that will change them into respectable citizens. The offenders are placed with an adoptive family, put into a cohesive work group, and expected to become productive members of the kibbutz.

A study of 27 long-term offenders assigned to a kibbutz found that, three years after being assigned, three-fourths of them had no additional criminal activity: nine were working full-time, five served in the army, five were engaged or married, and eight remained in the kibbutz as members.

Thus, programs in both nations offer evidence that alternatives to imprisonment may be a more effective way to deal with some kinds of criminals. If the goal is to rehabilitate, alternatives may work better than imprisonment.

SOURCES

National Institute of Justice 1996a; Fischer and Geiger 1996; Jehle 2005.

2009a). In addition, two-thirds of those in federal and state prisons and nearly half of those in jails were on a psychiatric medication.

Far from serving as a deterrent to further crime or as a place of rehabilitation, the jail or prison at best keeps criminals away from the public for a period of time. At worst, the prison becomes a *training ground* for making criminals more competent and more committed to a life of crime. If the abnormal circumstances of the prison, including extended, close association with hardened offenders, does not ensure continued criminal behavior, the stigma of having been in prison probably will. The prison itself is a *dehumanizing institution,* and people who enter it are unlikely to escape being brutalized, hardened, and better trained in criminal behavior. The same kind of threats to well-being found in the larger society must be faced by those in prison. Homicides, sexual assault, and gang formation and violence characterize prison life (Allender and Marcell 2003; Beck and Harrison 2006). It is estimated that about 4 percent of prisoners experience sexual assault by a fellow inmate or a prison staff person that ranges from unwanted touching to rape (Beck et al. 2013). Sexual violence also occurs in juvenile facilities, both youth-on-youth and staff-on-youth (Beck, Harrison, and Guerino 2010).

CODDLING CRIMINALS

Many Americans believe that one way to deal with the problem of crime is to stop "coddling" criminals. Actually, it is true that some criminals are coddled. Consider, for example, the following cases from the American system of justice:

> *Item:* The portfolio manager of two mutual funds cheated investors out of almost $10 million. He was sentenced to six months in prison and put on five years' probation.
>
> *Item:* The manufacturer of drugs watered down an antidote for poisoned children with a useless substance. He was given one year's probation and a $10,000 fine.
>
> *Item:* A judge in a state supreme court was involved in receiving and transporting $800,000 in stolen U.S. Treasury bills. He was fined $10,000 and sentenced to one year in prison.

These cases are just a few examples of the numerous white-collar crimes in which the offenders received very light punishment.

In this chapter we have stressed the seriousness of white-collar crime. How aware are the people in your area of the extent and corrosiveness of this crime? For one week, note any articles in your local newspaper that talk about crime. Assuming that the newspaper gave an accurate picture of the problem of crime in your area, how much and what kind of a crime problem exist? Do you think your paper is sensitive to the significance of white-collar crime? Make a list of various crimes, including street crimes and white-collar crimes. Ask some people in your community to rank them by seriousness, and ask them why they ranked them as they did. How do they feel about the different kinds of crime?

involvement

About 12 percent of youth in juvenile facilities report experiencing one or more incidents of sexual assault, with assaults by staff far more common than assaults by other youth. All of this takes place in a setting that almost seems designed to create degradation and humiliation (Tregea and Larmour 2009). It is not surprising, then, that self-injurious behaviors, including attempts at suicide, occur in correctional facilities (Smith and Kaminski 2011).

Normal behavior and feelings are impossible in prison. The prison is a **total institution,** a place where the totality of the individual's existence is controlled by various external forces. Offenders who enter the maximum security prison are immediately deprived of valuable things: liberty, goods and services, heterosexual relationships, autonomy, and security (from attacks of other prisoners). Moreover, they are in a place with a high proportion of disturbed individuals. Over half of those in state prisons, 45 percent of those in federal prisons, and 64 percent of those in local jails have or have had some kind of mental health problem, including serious mental illness, breakdowns, and brain damage (James and Glaze 2006; Lovell 2008). The constraints of prison life are so severe that an individual must focus on survival rather than personal development or change.

The combination of the inmate code and the demands of the authorities virtually eliminates any possibility of individual growth or personal lifestyle. There is a popular notion that "stone walls do not a prison make" and that even in a cell the individual's mind is free to roam and explore, but only a rare individual can transcend the forces that impinge on him or her and thereby avoid the dehumanization of the prison.

The *inmate code* contributes to the **dehumanization.** The code requires that an inmate must never report infractions of rules by another inmate and must never notice anything. For example, an inmate walking down a prison corridor saw a fellow inmate lying on the floor, bleeding. He had an impulse to help the man on the floor but went to his cell instead. Other inmates who discussed the incident with the prison psychiatrist agreed with the behavior. They pointed out that if the man had called a guard, the guard would have suspected him of having struck the man on the floor or would have

total institution
a place in which the totality of the individual's existence is controlled by external forces

dehumanization
the process by which an individual is deprived of the qualities or traits of a human being

93

intensely questioned him. Further, any other inmate who saw him call the guard would have accused him of "snitching." Had he stopped to help the fallen man, he might have been beaten by the man's attacker. Also, to personally help would suggest a homosexual relationship between the two inmates.

Finally, to survive in such an inhuman context, inmates practice and hone the same skills they used in their criminal careers. The most likely outcome of a prison sentence, then, is an improvement of criminal skills and thus the high probability of a continued criminal career and an eventual return to prison.

The Family Background of Offenders.   Because the *family plays a significant role in the socialization of children,* much attention is focused on family background to discover why young people become delinquents. Many family factors have been associated with delinquency, but the most important is the *quality of the relationships between parents and children.*

In essence, there is less delinquency among those youths whose parents value, love, accept, and spend time with them (Brody et al. 2001; Milkie, Nomaguchi, and Denny 2015). In contrast, rates of delinquency are higher among youths in abusive, troubled, or disrupted families (Thornberry et al. 2004; Fagan 2005; Wu et al. 2014; Shukla and Wiesner 2016). Rates of homicide are higher in cohorts of youth with a higher percentage born to unwed mothers, suggesting again the importance of the family in crime rates (O'Brien, Stockard, and Isaacson 1999).

When there are poor relationships in the family, parental moral and emotional authority is weakened. The diminished authority tends to weaken children's bonds to the social order and increases the likelihood of delinquency (Browning and Loeber 1999). Don't commit the *fallacy of retrospective determinism* here. Not all children from such families are delinquents. Family background helps you *understand* why some youths become delinquent, but it does not condone delinquency or absolve delinquents of responsibility for their behavior.

Adult criminals are also likely to have had troubled family relationships (Raine, Brennan, and Mednick 1994; Grogan-Kaylor and Otis 2003). We are not saying that the criminal behavior began in adulthood, of course. In fact, virtually all criminal careers (other than white-collar crime) begin before the age of 18. A large number of youths who engage in serious delinquent behavior will continue their criminal activities as adults.

Social Stratification and Crime.   Crime and delinquency are related to the social stratification system in three ways: (1) The kind of behavior considered criminal is defined by those who have power within the system. (2) Different kinds of crime tend to be committed within different strata of the system. (3) Disproportionate numbers of criminals come from different socioeconomic levels.

A good deal of the behavior of relatively powerless people is defined as criminal whereas similar behavior among more powerful people is not defined as criminal. This finding is true especially when the behavior involves monetary exploitation. A corporate executive might support the definition of employee theft as criminal but would not define false advertising and exploitation of consumers as theft or crime. A physician might deplore abuses of the welfare system, labeling them criminal fraud, but think little about prescribing expensive brand-name drugs rather than less expensive generic counterparts because, in part, his or her retirement plan rests on investments in the pharmaceutical industry. In both cases, the people who influence the defining process are the *holders or wielders of power in society,* and they *do not define their own behavior as criminal.*

fallacy

Prison life is dehumanizing.
©Design Pics / Kristy-Anne Glubish

The second way in which social stratification intersects with crime and delinquency involves the kinds of crime committed. Those in the lower socioeconomic strata are more likely to be both the offenders and the victims of delinquency, property crime, and violent crime, including murder of a family member (Markowitz 2003; Diem and Pizarro 2010). In contrast, white-collar criminals are more likely to come from the middle and upper strata.

Delinquency, violence, and property crime are more characteristic of those people struggling to survive the deprivations of a seriously unequal society. Thus, there is more delinquency among those who face ongoing and severe economic problems (Agnew et al. 2008). Unable to buy their needed goods and services, deprived youth resort to various kinds of delinquent and criminal behavior. Basically, the more impoverished an area and the fewer opportunities it offers for dealing with economic deprivation, the higher the rates of crime (Lee and Ousey 2001; Weiss and Reid 2005).

The third way the stratification system is related to crime is in the disproportionate number of criminals who come from the lower socioeconomic strata (Western, Kleykamp, and Rosenfeld 2006). As suggested earlier, part of the reason is that the powerless and deprived are more likely to be defined as criminals. Several studies over the last few decades have revealed many consistencies in the characteristics of people *labeled as criminals.* Their general *powerlessness* and their location in the stratification system are clear. Criminals are more likely to (1) lack *social anchorage* in the sense of growing up in a stable family that is integrated into the community, (2) come from a lower-income family, (3) be young, (4) be male, and (5) come disproportionately from a minority group.

In sum, *the powerless are more likely to be defined as criminals throughout the criminal justice system.* They are more likely to be suspects and more likely to be arrested. In some states, judges have the option of withholding **adjudication** of guilt from people placed on probation. The judge's decision, then, determines whether *the individual will*

adjudication
making a judgment; settling a judicial matter

carry the stigma of being a convicted felon. Those people most likely to carry that stigma are the powerless—the poor and minorities. We are not saying that these people are innocent; rather, we are pointing out the unequal treatment received by those in the lower strata.

Social Psychological Factors

Respectable people define crime as reprehensible—but how do criminals define it? In a classic and creative analysis, Katz (1988) pointed out that a part of the explanation of crime is found in the fact that criminal acts possess certain "sensual dynamics." Each kind of crime has a certain appeal, one that results in the criminal's feeling good or even exhilarated. In line with this, Lopez (2008) found a number of different reasons why adolescents commit property crimes. They included the usual reasons of stress and economic gain, but also included the "thrills" the offender experienced when successful. Katz also discussed the property crime of robbery, which typically involves considerable risk and minimal gain. What makes robbery attractive, according to Katz, is not just the money gained, but the excitement, adventure, and sense of conquest in the act. "In virtually all robberies, the offender discovers, fantasizes, or manufactures *an angle of moral superiority* over the intended victim" and makes "a fool of his victim" (Katz 1988:169, 174).

Other kinds of crimes have their own emotional rewards. The murderer may gain a sense of righteous revenge. Youths in street gangs may gain a sense of triumph over a destructive and dehumanizing environment. The point is that crime has *both emotional and material rewards for people* (Meadows and Anklin 2002). In part, motivation to continue a criminal career may lie in the emotional rewards.

Attitudes as well as emotions are important in crime. We noted earlier that the attitudes that prison conditions generate in inmates help to perpetuate crime. *Attitudes of respectable people* also contribute to the problem by providing necessary support for much officially defined crime, even though they don't view themselves as culpable or as contributors to crime. The assertion has been made that prostitution could not continue without official support. Certainly it could not continue without the support of the respectable clientele it serves or without the overt or covert support of the police.

Automobile theft is another example of crime supported by respectable people. Upwardly mobile young men in business and the professions sometimes buy stolen luxury cars for a fraction of their retail cost. They may know, or at least suspect, that they are buying a stolen car. Such crimes would have no payoff without these respectable customers ("After all," they reason, "if I don't buy it, someone else will").

Attitudes of respectable people that stigmatize criminals contribute to continuation of the criminal careers (Pager 2003; Davies and Tanner 2003). Often, the very people who decry crime resist providing any help to the criminal. They get mired in the *fallacy of circular reasoning.* They believe that criminals can't be trusted in respectable jobs, then condemn criminals for not becoming respectable people. The ex-criminal who sincerely wants to become respectable becomes the victim of the process.

Attitudes toward white-collar criminals are ambivalent. Generally, unless the acts are flagrant and overt violations, white-collar criminals may not be prosecuted as criminals. However, white-collar criminals are not as invulnerable to the criminal justice system as they once were, in part because of a reaction to the Watergate scandal of the Nixon administration. Some white-collar criminals receive stiff penalties and sentences for their offenses. Nevertheless, their chances for leniency are far greater than are those for other criminals. In addition, white-collar criminals do not face the same

fallacy

kinds of hurdles when they try to reenter society following imprisonment (Kerley and Copes 2004). Unless such criminals have multiple arrests or are arrested and imprisoned before the age of 24, they are able to secure stable employment much easier than are other offenders.

Finally, in looking at the social psychology of *committed criminals or delinquents,* you find a distinctive set of attitudes, values, and other attributes. For these individuals, delinquency or crime has become a way of life. They have a *"subterranean" set of values*—hedonism, a focus on immediate gratification, and the ability to outwit and con others. They appear to be untouched by punishment, continue their deviant ways, and account for much of the crime in the nation. For them, deviance is a way of life. This finding is illustrated by studies that have examined the *self-concepts of delinquents.* Typically, the studies reveal congruence between attitudes toward the self and behavior. Low self-esteem fosters delinquent behavior, and the behavior, in turn, may raise the individual's self-esteem (Mason 2001). The delinquent behavior is a protection of the self as well as a rejection of law-abiding society.

Public Policy and Private Action

Our discussion of the causes of crime suggests the kinds of actions that will reduce the amount of crime. For example, whatever ameliorates economic deprivation reduces crime rates (Hannon and Defronzo 1998; Rosenfeld 2002). Intensive police patrolling of "hot spots" reduces crime rates (Rosenfeld 2002; Zimring 2011). Reducing drug use brings a decline in crime (Blumstein and Rosenfeld 1998). Youth curfew laws cut down on the number of offenders in hot spots and reduce burglary, larceny, and simple assault (McDowall, Loftin, and Wiersema 2000). Finding employment for older offenders reduces recidivism (Uggen 2000; Duwe 2015). Prevention programs that help youths by fostering a healthy family life, making communities safe, encouraging the young to stay in school, and developing skills and healthy lifestyle choices can reduce the number who begin a life of crime (Coolbaugh and Hansel 2000). Stronger laws can aid the fight against white-collar crime (Goldsmith 2004). Setting up a neighborhood watch program tends to reduce the amount of crime in the area (Bennett, Holloway, and Farrington 2006). And being in a stable relationship with a law-abiding woman reduces a man's likelihood of continued criminal activity (Forrest 2014; Andersen, Andersen, and Skov 2015). Various other programs hold promise, but first we must look at the issue of punishment versus rehabilitation.

Punishment or Rehabilitation?

Will crime be reduced by punishing or by rehabilitating criminals? Should criminals be required to reimburse their victims? Are criminals themselves victims, people who can be rehabilitated with the proper methods, or are their offenses unjustified acts that demand punishment? Can you trust a criminal to become a law-abiding citizen again? Such questions are behind the various solutions proposed for the problem of crime.

For many centuries the societal reaction to crime was simply one of punishment in order to deter others who might consider the same acts. Now more people advocate *rehabilitation instead of punishment.* In this view, the criminal has the potential to become a law-abiding citizen and should be given the opportunity to do so. Even if this view is true, some people would argue that *criminals should make restitution* to their victims, and in recent years some courts have required offenders to do so. Usually, the restitution is a cash payment large enough to offset the loss, and the payment may be reduced to fit the earning capacity of the offender. But what kind of payment can be made to compensate for emotional trauma? Sometimes services that benefit the victim directly or indirectly also may be required or substituted for the cash payment.

Experts who advocate rehabilitation face the problem of the offender's *reintegration* into the community. How can offenders be reintegrated into society? Because many offenders got in trouble because of the environment in which they lived, reintegration requires community resources such as vocational counseling and employment to restructure the offender's life. The goal is to help the offender find a legitimate role in the community.

That goal will not be easy. As Talbot (2003) notes, about 1,600 people leave state and federal prisons each day. Most come out with nothing more than a small amount of money ($20 to $200) and a one-way bus ticket. Some are drug abusers who received no treatment. Some are sex offenders who received no counseling. Some are high school dropouts who took no classes and received no training in job skills. Many are sick (HIV, tuberculosis, and hepatitis C). And only about one in eight received any kind of prerelease program to prepare them for life outside the prison.

Clearly, the task of reentry is massive. Nevertheless, rehabilitation is possible; recidivism rates can be reduced. In particular, recidivism is less likely when the offender is able to secure housing and employment and complete treatment programs (community-based programs tend to be more effective than those based in prisons) (Makarios, Steiner, and Travis 2010; Clement, Schwarzfeld, and Thompson 2011).

Capital Punishment

Some people advocate a *get-tough* policy on crime, including the use of *capital punishment*. Twenty states and the District of Columbia do not allow the death penalty, even though it was reinstated as constitutional by the Supreme Court in 1976. From 1977 through 2015, 1,422 prisoners have been executed, 37.8 percent of them in Texas (Death Penalty Information Center 2016). Forty-four and a half percent of those executed were racial/ethnic minorities. At the end of 2015, 2,943 prisoners were under a death sentence.

Although a 2015 Gallup poll found that 60 percent of Americans say the death penalty is morally okay (Swift 2015), capital punishment is controversial from both a moral and a criminal justice point of view. From a moral point of view, the question is whether the state has the right to kill someone as punishment for murder. Opponents of capital punishment view it as extreme and inhumane—an official form of the same heinous crime committed by the individual. Furthermore, they argue, keeping an individual on death row is a form of torture, as underscored by the fact that suicide and natural causes, rather than execution, are the leading cause of deaths of prisoners on death row (Locke 1996). The appeals process can take so long that some prisoners literally die of natural causes, and the process of waiting is so agonizing that many commit suicide or become mentally ill.

In addition, critics point out the danger of executing people who are innocent. Using DNA tests and discovering other evidence has led to the exoneration and release of hundreds of prisoners sentenced to death, some of whom were on death row for a decade or more (Westervelt and Cook 2008).

Religious groups take varying positions on the moral issue (Falsani 1996). Protestants and Jews are divided. The official Roman Catholic position, as defined in a 1995 encyclical by Pope John Paul II, is one of opposition. The Pope argued for nonlethal means of combating crime.

From the criminal justice point of view, is capital punishment an effective deterrent for murder? Experts disagree. Stack (1990) found a 17.5 percent drop in homicide rates in South Carolina in months with publicized executions. In contrast, Bailey (1990) examined national monthly rates over a 12-year period. He found no drop in homicide rates in months with nationally publicized executions. Sorenson, Wrinkle, Brewer, and Marquart (1999) found no evidence of deterrence in Texas (the most active execution state in recent times) from 1984 through 1997. Finally, states without capital punishment tend to have lower homicide rates than states with it (Death Penalty Information Center 2016).

Arguments about the effectiveness of punishment versus rehabilitation go on. Advocates of punishment and isolation are correct when they contend that prisons do not rehabilitate. But rehabilitation programs can be effective. In fact, rehabilitative efforts may need to be combined with punishment. There is strong evidence that punishment is a deterrent to crime. However, the *certainty of punishment* is as important as the severity of punishment for purposes of deterrence (Matthews and Agnew 2008; Zhang, Smith, and McDowell 2009). To the extent that people are convinced that, if caught, they will be punished (rather than avoiding punishment through legal maneuvers), crime rates fall.

Thus, the criminal justice system in the United States should be revamped in two ways: First, punishment for crime must be made more certain. Second, efforts must be made, through reform of prisons or through innovative alternatives, to establish effective rehabilitation programs. Certainty of punishment will act as a deterrent for some criminals and will remove others from society, whereas more effective rehabilitation programs will effect change in others and help them live socially useful lives.

Innovative Alternatives

Some innovative alternatives to the present system, including some that are popular with citizens and law enforcement officials, are ineffective in reducing crime. In a comprehensive study of crime prevention programs, researchers concluded that the following are among the programs that do not lower crime: gun buyback programs, drug prevention classes that focus on fear or on building self-esteem, increased arrests or raids on drug market locations, correctional boot camps using military basic training, "Scared Straight" programs in which juvenile offenders visit adult prisons, intensive supervision on parole or probation, and community mobilization against crime in high-crime poverty areas (Sherman et al. 1998).

In contrast, the researchers identified about 30 programs that show promise for dealing with crime, including community policing with meetings to set priorities, greater respect by the police for arrested offenders (may reduce repeat offending), higher numbers of police officers in cities, monitoring of gangs by community workers and law enforcement officials, mentoring programs for youths, prison-based vocational education programs for adult inmates, enterprise zones to reduce unemployment, drug treatment in jails followed by urine testing in the community, and intensive supervision and aftercare of juvenile offenders.

Community programs can reduce crime.

©S. Meltzer/PhotoLink/Getty Images

Private prisons (that is, prisons privately owned and operated under contract with a state) are an alternative that may be no better, or even worse, than the prisons operated by the government. Advocates claim that private prisons can lower costs and reduce recidivism. However, an early study found that private prisons are *not* more cost-effective (Pratt and Maahs 1999). And an Oklahoma study concluded that recidivism was actually higher among those who had been in a private prison (Spivak and Sharp 2008). The failure of private prisons is underscored by the fact that in 2016 the Justice Department announced it was going to phase out the use of private prisons for federal prisoners because the private facilities are less safe and less effective at providing correctional services (Zapotosky and Harlan 2016). Other nations have experimented with private prisons also. A study of one in Scotland found that, compared to the government prisons, the private prison had lower morale and greater risks to both the inmates and the prison staff (Taylor and Cooper 2008).

Community Action and Involvement

Crime prevention is not just a matter of official action. A number of community programs can reduce crime (Loeber and Farrington 1998; Sherman et al. 1998). Parents, neighborhood groups, and school personnel can work together to teach children values and to encourage and reward law-abiding behavior. Community-based after-school recreational programs may help reduce local juvenile crime. Organized community projects and employment opportunities diminish problems with juvenile gangs (Spergen and Curry 1990).

Even the physical arrangements in a community affect crime. Greener surroundings in the inner city and increased lighting reduce both the fear of crime and the amount of actual crime (Kuo and Sullivan 2001; Clarke 2008). Always having two workers in convenience stores at night lessens the likelihood of robbery, and neighborhood parks and recreational facilities can provide alternatives to gang activity.

Finally, whatever can be done to enhance cohesion in a community will deter crime. Three researchers who examined violent crime in urban neighborhoods concluded that the more that residents trust each other, share values, and are willing to intervene in the lives of children (e.g., to stop truancy and graffiti painting), the lower the rate of crime will be (Sampson, Raudenbush, and Earls 1997).

Aid to Victims

An important public policy effort involves *aid to the victims*. Aid to victims is provided by governments to prevent a double victimization—once by the offender and again by the criminal justice system. Some problems faced by the victim of a crime include a lack of transportation to court, difficulty in retrieving stolen property from the police, threats by defendants if the victim testifies, and the amount of time consumed by the various procedures in the criminal justice system. An aid program can compensate for some of these losses incurred by the victims.

Most states now have compensation programs to help the victims of violent crime. Awards vary from small amounts to tens of thousands of dollars. Some states require the victim to show financial need, and most require that the crime be reported to police and the claim filed within a specified time period (ranging from a few days to a number of months).

The compensation programs provide for the recovery of medical expenses and lost earnings. In a number of states, money to aid victims is accumulated through penalties assessed against offenders or by expropriating the money earned by offenders resulting from their crimes (e.g., by writing a book).

Follow-Up. Do you think prisons should primarily punish or primarily rehabilitate inmates? Based on your answer, design the "perfect" prison to achieve your goals.

Summary

Crime is one of the problems about which Americans are most concerned. Technically, crime is any violation of the criminal law. Therefore, the acts defined by law as crime vary over time. We classify crime into four broad types: (1) Predatory crime, which includes white-collar crime, is an act that causes a victim to suffer physical harm or loss of property. (2) Illegal service crimes involve offenses such as drugs or prostitution. (3) Public disorder crimes have no definite victim but are acts that offend the public. (4) Crimes of negligence involve an unintended victim or potential victim. Cybercrime may be either predatory or illegal service, whereas white-collar crime is primarily predatory. Organized crime involves groups of people in an ongoing organization who provide illegal goods and services and who use predatory crime and political corruption to maintain their activities. The term "juvenile delinquency" covers a broad range of behavior, frequently including fighting, truancy, and running away from home. Juvenile gangs may get involved in a range of criminal activities, from predatory crime to illegal goods and services.

Crime and delinquency are widespread, as measured by various indexes—official records, victimization studies, or self-reports. Crime is not uniformly distributed, however; the likelihood of being a victim depends on the kind of crime; where the person lives; and his or her sex, race, age, education, and income.

Crime diminishes the quality of life and exacts physical, psychological, and economic costs. Crime threatens physical and mental health. It generates fear, which restricts the activities of people. White-collar crime can lead to pervasive cynicism and alienation. Crime costs the nation billions of dollars yearly, and the costs are increasing.

Norms are an important sociocultural factor contributing to the problem of crime and delinquency because they encourage members of certain groups to engage in criminal behavior. In particular, norms that are counter to the law have developed among lower-class youths and groups of businesspeople and professionals.

The political aspects of crime control contribute to the problem, especially through the nation's prison system. Prisons make rehabilitation unlikely because they tend to dehumanize offenders, remove them further from noncriminal social control, and make them more competent in criminal activity.

The family may be a factor in crime. A disproportionate number of delinquents come from families with poor relationships between parents and children or from broken homes. Adult offenders are likely to have had troubled family backgrounds.

The stratification system also relates to crime. Monetary exploitation of others is more likely to be defined as crime among lower-class people than among middle- and upper-class people. The lower class has a greater proportion of violent crime and delinquency, whereas middle and upper classes have more white-collar crime. A lower-class individual is more likely to be defined as a criminal by the processes of the criminal justice system.

Emotionally, crime may provide a certain thrill or reward to offenders. Many attitudes tend to perpetuate crime. Crimes are facilitated by the attitudes of respectable people about their own behavior—especially their use of the services offered by criminals. Stigmatizing criminals tends to keep them in criminal careers. Minimizing the seriousness of white-collar crime also encourages it. Finally, the attitudes, values, and other social psychological characteristics of some criminals and delinquents form a consistent set that makes for a way of life. Having deviant values and attitudes and thinking of themselves as people who engage in criminal or delinquent behavior, they tend to maintain their way of life even when they are punished.

Key Terms

Adjudication	Predatory Crimes
Alienation	Recidivism
Dehumanization	Rehabilitation
Differential Association Theory	Total Institution
	Trauma
Organized Crime	White-collar Crime

Study Questions

1. Define and illustrate the various types of crime.
2. What are the problems in obtaining accurate data on the amount of crime?
3. How much crime is there in the United States, and where is a person most likely to be a victim?
4. How does crime affect physical and psychological well-being?
5. What is the cost of crime in economic terms?
6. How is the amount of crime affected by the age structure of the population?
7. What is the role of norms in criminal activity?

8. How do prisons help or worsen the problem of crime?

9. In what ways do the family and the social stratification system contribute to the problem of crime?

10. How do the attitudes of respectable people bear on the amount of crime in the nation?

11. What can be done to reduce crime?

Internet Resources/Exercises

1. Explore some of the ideas in this chapter on the following sites:

http://www.fbi.gov   The FBI site offers current crime news, information about the most wanted criminals, and crime data.

http://www.usdoj.gov   The Department of Justice site gives information about all kinds of crime and crime prevention, and includes a link to the Bureau of Justice Statistics.

http://journals.sagepub.com/loi/ijo   This is the site for the International Journal of Offender Therapy and Comparative Criminology. You can read the abstracts of articles published in the journal from 1966 to the present.

2. Log on to the international journal site. Find and read the abstract of an article that focuses on a topic in criminology that interests you and that involves a country other than the United States. Search the internet to see if additional materials on the topic are available. How do your findings compare with information in the text? What conclusions would you draw about the effectiveness of the criminal justice system in different countries?

3. Investigate how victimization rates have varied over time. The Department of Justice site has the data. Chart the data for various crimes over a period of three decades. How do the patterns of the crimes compare with each other? How do they compare with the FBI data in Table 3.2? What are some possible explanations for the patterns?

For Further Reading

Bedau, Hugo, and Paul Cassell. *Debating the Death Penalty: Should America Have Capital Punishment?* New York: Oxford University Press, 2003. Gives the pro and con arguments for the death penalty, including the perspectives of judges, lawyers, philosophers, and a state governor who put a moratorium on the death penalty in Illinois.

Duran, Robert J. *Gang Life in Two Cities: An Insider's Journey.* New York: Columbia University Press, 2013. A Latino and former gang member, Duran shows why belonging to a gang is not primarily a way to participate in crime but a way to adapt to oppressive social environments.

Elliott, A. Larry, and Richard J. Schroth. *How Companies Lie: Why Enron Is Just the Tip of the Iceberg.* New York: Crown Business, 2002. Two corporate consultants argue that a new business culture has arisen that justifies any means used to increase profits, including those that are illegal or unethical. The notorious Enron case is but one example.

Hassine, Victor. *Life Without Parole.* 4th ed. New York: Oxford University Press, 2008. Law school graduate Victor Hassine, convicted of a capital offense in 1981 and sentenced to life in prison without parole, describes what it is like to be confined to prison amidst such things as rape, gangs, violence, and prison politics.

Ross, Jeffrey Ian, ed. *Varieties of State Crime and Its Control.* Monsey, NY: Criminal Justice Press, 2000. Case studies of government crimes in the United States and other nations, including political corruption and various kinds of violence and repression by governments against their citizens.

Roth, R. *American Homicide.* Cambridge, MA: Belknap Harvard, 2009. A history professor explores the process of America's shift from being one of the least homicidal Western nations in the mid-18th and early 19th centuries to one of the most homicidal societies in the world today.

Simpson, Sally, and Carole Gibbs, eds. *Corporate Crime.* Burlington, VT: Ashgate, 2007. A collection of classic and contemporary articles that examine every aspect of the problem of corporate crime in the United States and other nations.

Whitman, James Q. *Harsh Justice: Criminal Punishment and the Widening Gap between America and Europe.* Oxford, England: Oxford University Press, 2003. Shows the many different ways in which American justice is harsher than that of Europe, including the U.S. prison system, the number of punishable kinds of behavior, and the length of sentences.

CHAPTER 4

Violence

©Purestock/Getty Images

"I Felt Guilty"

The trauma of rape is described by Tammi, a 20-year-old woman who was raped while walking to the parking lot of a college:

It happened about 10 p.m. I had been doing some research at the library and I was in a hurry to get home because I wanted to see a movie on TV. I was standing next to my car, looking in my purse for my keys. I didn't see the man or hear him until all of a sudden he grabbed me from behind and had me on the ground before I knew what had happened. He held a knife to my throat and told me to do what he said and I wouldn't get hurt. I was too scared to move anyway because I could feel the knife pressing against my neck. He was disgusted that I had on jeans and made a derogatory remark about the way girls dress today. He made me take off my pants and perform oral sex on him. Then he raped me. He kept asking me if I liked it, but I was too scared to answer him. He got angry because I wouldn't answer him and he hit me in the breast with his fist. I started crying and he got off of me and let me get dressed. He told me if I told anyone he would come back and rape me again. He said that he knew who I was and where I lived. I started crying harder and shaking all over. He patted me and told me to grow up, that he'd done me a favor and that I was old enough to enjoy sex with a man. He finally left and I got into my car and went home.

I felt so dirty I took a shower and scrubbed myself all over and got into bed. At 12:30 my roommate came home and I told her what had happened. She insisted I call the police, so I did. Two policemen came to our apartment. They asked such things as where did it happen, and what did he look like, and what time did it happen. They acted like I made it up when they found out it happened two hours ago. The young cop asked me if I had an orgasm and if he had ejaculated. I didn't know what to say as I didn't know, since this was my first encounter with sex. I don't think they believed that either. They told me to come down to the station the next day if I wanted to press charges, but that since I had taken a shower and waited so long I probably didn't have a case. No one told me to go to the hospital to be treated for V.D. or that they could give me something to prevent pregnancy until I talked to a friend the next day. She went with me to the emergency room of a hospital and they told me they didn't treat rape victims. I started crying and she took me home. I was pretty shook up. For three or four days I stayed in bed. I cut all my classes. Finally, I went back to school and everything seemed to be fine until I saw a story about rape on TV. I got so upset my roommate called the Rape Crisis Center and had me talk to them about my feelings. I called them eight or nine times in all.

I felt guilty. I thought it was my fault because my mother had been against my leaving home to go to college and against my having an apartment. She had also warned me never to go out alone at night. I didn't tell her I had been raped because I was afraid she'd make me leave school and come back home. So instead of blaming the guy, I blamed myself for being so dumb and naive. It took about three months to get my head together. I feel I have now, but I still am uneasy if a guy comes on too strong, or stops to talk to me in an isolated place, or even if he gets too close in an elevator. I haven't dated since it happened. I guess I shut everyone out and went on my own head trip, but I've started going places with my girlfriends lately and I think I have it together now.

Introduction

In April 1999, two teenage boys shot and killed 12 students and a teacher and wounded a number of other students at Columbine High School in Littleton, Colorado. The boys then committed suicide. During a three-week period in October 2002, two snipers randomly shot people in the region around Washington, D.C., killing 10 and wounding three others. In October 2006, a man went into an Amish school in Pennsylvania and shot 10 girls before killing himself. Five of the girls died. In April 2007, a student went on a violent rampage at Virginia Tech University. He killed 32 people, wounded numerous others, and then killed himself. In October 2011, a man walked into a hair salon in Seal Beach, California, and shot and killed his ex-wife (with whom he was in a custody dispute over their son) and seven other people in the salon. In late February 2012, a high school student in Chardon, Ohio, shot five students, killing three of them, in the school's cafeteria. In June, 2016, a heavily armed man walked into a gay nightclub in Orlando, Florida, killed 50 and wounded another 53. These incidents are just a sampling of what one of our students called "the horror stories that keep popping up in the news." In addition to such dramatic and terrifying incidents, Americans are confronted by stories of violence daily in the news media.

Because social problems involve *intergroup conflict,* violence enters into nearly every social problem at some point. The conflict often becomes violent, as illustrated by gangs of straight youths who beat up homosexuals, by race riots, by murders when a drug dealer tries to move in on someone else's market, and so on.

In this chapter we deal with various kinds of interpersonal and intergroup violence, all of which concern Americans and all of which are widely believed to detract from the quality of life. We begin by discussing the meaning, the kinds, and the amount of violence in the nation. We show the ways that violence detracts from the quality of life and identify the various sociocultural factors that contribute to the problem. We discuss ways in which violence can be minimized or eliminated from human life.

We then discuss rape. Although some people have thought of rape as a form of sexual deviance, it is essentially an act of violence. The victim may be further victimized by the reactions of family, friends, police officers, and male jurors.

What Is Violence?

In general, **violence** implies *use of force to kill, injure, or abuse others.* It occurs between two or more individuals as *interpersonal violence,* or it involves identifiable groups in the society and erupts as *intergroup violence* between two or more different races, religions, or political groups. In intergroup situations the violence ultimately means confrontation between individuals whose actions are legitimated by their group affiliation. Interpersonal violence often occurs between people who knew each other prior to the violent confrontation. Intergroup violence, however, is likely to involve people who were strangers prior to the confrontation.

violence
the use of force to kill, injure, or abuse others

How Much Violence Is There?

It is difficult to estimate the amount of violent behavior in the United States. Much is never reported, and for some kinds of violence—riots, gang beatings, violent demonstrations, and terrorist activities—there is no systematic effort to record all incidents. But evidence indicates that there is and always has been a considerable amount of violence in the United States.

For example, the following incidents were reported over a period of a couple of months in a western city:

A distraught man walked into the emergency room of a hospital and began shooting randomly, killing two people and wounding two others.

Militant antiabortion protestors tried to shut down an abortion clinic, resulting in a violent confrontation that required police intervention and numerous arrests.

A confrontation between two rival youth gangs resulted in a number of injuries, including knife wounds.

Several women who were out jogging were caught and raped by a man who may be a serial rapist.

A brawl erupted between police and members of a religious sect after a police officer attempted to arrest a member of the sect for a routine traffic violation.

A university decided to cancel an annual festival that had taken place for more than 50 years because a weekend of rioting caused more than 100 injuries.

Violence comes in numberless forms and occurs in all settings. Violence is no respecter of age. Both children and the elderly are victims of abuse and murder. In 2014, the age group with the highest rate of violent victimization was those between 12 and 17 years (Truman and Langton 2015). A national study of elder abuse reported that 4.6 percent suffered emotional abuse, 1.6 percent endured physical abuse, 0.6 percent had been sexually abused, and 5.1 percent suffered from neglect (Acierno et al. 2010).

There is no safe haven from violence. Workplace violence has decreased considerably over the past two decades but is still about one-third the rate that occurs in nonworkplace situations (Harrell 2011). The police, security guards, and bartenders have the highest rates of nonfatal workplace violence. Similarly, violence in the family setting has declined, but the family is one of the most violent institutions in society (see Chapter 12).

Violence occurs in all societies, but the United States is one of the most violent nations in the Western world. Violence is so common and so pervasive that about 61 percent of American children are victims of, or witnesses to, some kind of violence at one or more points in their childhood (Finkelhor et al. 2009).

Interpersonal Violence

As noted earlier, violence afflicts people of all ages and in all situations. For example, although rates of violence (other than rape and sexual assault) on college campuses are lower than those in noncollege situations, a good many studies report that dating violence is a serious and widespread problem among college students (Shorey, Stuart, and Cornelius 2011). A study of 1,530 undergraduates reported that one in four had been involved in a physically abusive dating relationship that included at least two acts of physically violent behavior (Miller 2011). Another study found that students who had hearing disabilities, were homosexual, or were part of a racial/ethnic minority had even higher rates of victimization than did white, heterosexual students (Porter and Williams 2011).

In general, the young are more likely to be victims of, or witnesses to, interpersonal violence. Adolescents aged 18–20 years have the highest rates of assault victimization, and those aged 12–14 years have the second highest rates (U.S. Department of Justice 2011). In 2014, the highest rate of victimization for serious violent crimes (including sexual assault, aggravated assault, and robbery) occurred in the 18- to 24-year-old bracket (Truman and Langton 2015). A survey of 104 fourth- and fifth-grade children in an impoverished inner-city area found that 89 percent had heard the sound of gunfire; 65 percent had been slapped, punched, or hit by someone; 65 percent had seen someone beaten up or mugged; 16 percent had seen someone killed; and 11 percent had been shot at (Ceballo, Dahl, Aretakis, and Ramirez 2001). Bullying is not included in the crime data. But we identify it as a form of violent behavior, A survey of 66 studies of bullying found that one in three children is involved in some form of bullying and one in five is involved in cyberbullying (Zych, Ortega-Ruiz, and Del Rey 2015). Much of the violence experienced by children occurs in the school setting (see Chapter 11).

Violence occurs in intimate relationships (dating, cohabitation, marriage) at every age. A national survey reported that in the course of their lifetime nearly one in five women have been raped (a current or former intimate partner was the perpetrator in more than half the cases); nearly a third have been physically abused; a fourth have been severely abused physically by an intimate partner; and nearly half have been verbally abused by an intimate partner (Black et al. 2011). For men, the lifetime rates are: 1.4 percent have been raped; a fourth have been physically abused; one out of seven have been severely abused physically by an intimate partner; and nearly half have been verbally abused by an intimate partner.

Rates of intimate partner violence are higher among dating teens than they are among adults (Office of Juvenile Justice and Delinquency Prevention 2006). A national survey reported that about 20 percent of boys and girls experience physical and/or sexual abuse when dating, and more than 60 percent were involved in psychological abuse (Mumford and Taylor 2014). Rates of victimization are similar for males and females, although girls are more likely than boys to claim self-defense as one of their motivations (Mulford and Giordano 2008). Girls are also more likely to suffer negative long-term consequences such as depression, attempted suicide, and drug use. Violent males, on the other hand, injure their dates more severely and more often. About one in five female high school students reports having been physically and/or sexually abused by a dating partner. Overall, women in the 16- to 24-year-old age group have rates of victimization by an intimate partner that are nearly three times the national average.

Violence claims victims of both sexes, all racial and ethnic groups, and all ages.

©Laurent Hamels/Photoalto/ PictureQuest

Rates of victimization for females and males are also similar among adults. A national survey found that violence occurred in nearly a fourth of the relationships of those aged 18–28 years, and both partners were violent in about half of them (Whitaker, Haileyesus, Swahn, and Saltzman 2007). Although the rates are about the same, there is a difference between the violence of men and that of women (Hamberger and Larsen 2015). Women's physical violence tends to be a response to an abusive partner. And in emotional abuse, women tend to use yelling and shouting, while men are more likely to use threats of various kinds. As a result, abused women are likely to be more severely traumatized than are abused men.

The rates of abuse do vary by race/ethnicity, with black women having the highest rates of victimization. A small survey of Chinese American women reported that 8 percent had experienced severe intimate partner violence in their lifetime (Hicks 2006). Among those ever married, the rate was higher, and nearly a third of those abused had physical injuries that affected their work or education.

Intimate partner violence is a problem in other nations. A New Zealand study reported that domestic conflict (ranging from minor emotional abuse to severe assault) occurred in nearly 70 percent of intimate relationships, with men and women equally likely to be both the perpetrators and the victims of the violence (Fergusson, Horwood, and Ridder 2005).

Intergroup Violence

How much intergroup violence is there? Ted Gurr (1969:576) attempted to estimate the amount of civil strife in the United States from June 1963 through May 1968, a time of intense conflict. He identified more than 800 events that were either civil rights demonstrations, black riots and disturbances, or white terrorism against blacks and civil rights workers. There were more than 2 million participants and more than 9,400 casualties. The most common type of violence was interracial.

In 1995, antigovernment militants used a truck bomb to destroy a federal building in Oklahoma City, killing 168 and wounding more than 500. Americans became aware of the problem of **domestic terrorism** (we discuss international terrorism in Chapter 14). *Domestic terrorism* is the use, or threatened use, of violence by people operating entirely within the United States to intimidate or coerce the government and/or citizens in order to reach certain social or political aims.

The Oklahoma City incident was neither the first nor the last encounter between the federal government and right-wing militias. In 1983, a shootout resulted in the death of Gordon Kahl, a tax resister, militia member, and suspected killer of two U.S. marshals. In 2010, nine members of a Michigan militia were charged with seditious conspiracy and attempted use of weapons of mass destruction in a plot to attack law enforcement and start a general uprising against the government (Federal Bureau of Investigation 2011).

All the militias view the government as a tyrannical enemy (Pitcavage 2001). However, *the militias vary according to purpose* (Smolowe 1995). The Aryan nation is a white-supremacist group. The Survivalists are expecting, and preparing for, the breakdown of the economy and the government by preparing to defend and support themselves in the resulting chaos. The Patriots stress the rights of states and the people over the federal government. Posse Comitatus is a tax-resistance group that is also anti-Semitic. Various militias (more than a dozen scattered throughout the nation) accumulate weapons to promote and defend the kind of society they believe the Constitution was meant to create (Witt 2004). Other forms of domestic terrorism include extremist groups that engage in direct action (such as arson and destruction of property) to protect animals and the environment from what they regard as exploitation and destruction of the natural world.

As long as such groups operate, there is a strong potential for violence. Many groups not only have sophisticated weapons but also engage in regular training exercises in their use. Their members are deadly serious about what they see as their mission and are prepared to engage in violent measures to achieve it.

Violence and the Quality of Life

You can get a feel for how violence detracts from the quality of life by looking at both objective and subjective evidence. As will be evident, the negative impact of violence on the quality of life can be severe and long term.

domestic terrorism
the use, or threatened use, of violence by people operating entirely within the United States to intimidate or coerce the government and/or citizens in order to reach certain social or political aims

Human Injury and Destruction

Violence results in *human destruction* and is, therefore, a *contradiction* to American values of well-being and freedom from fear. Violent crime, riots, and other forms of interpersonal and intergroup violence can lead to both injury and death. Labor-management and interracial confrontations are the kinds of intergroup conflict most likely to result in deaths and serious injuries. One of the worst riots in modern U.S. history occurred in Los Angeles in 1992 following the acquittal of white police officers who had severely beaten a black man who had resisted arrest (Pringle 1997). Three days of rioting left 55 people dead, 2,300 injured, and 1,093 buildings damaged or destroyed. The injured or killed in such situations include spectators or people who are traveling through the area.

People who are injured as the result of violence may suffer various kinds of long-term health problems. Abused children have a higher rate of health problems in adulthood than do nonabused children (Thompson, Kingree, and Desai 2004; Corso, Edwards, Fang, and Mercy 2008). A substantial number of battered women sustain brain injuries (Valera and Berenbaum 2003). Women abused during pregnancy are at greater risk of miscarriage (Morland et al. 2008). A substantial number of homeless women have fled from violent husbands (Jasinski, Wesely, Wright, and Mustaine 2010), choosing to face the health-debilitating life of the streets rather than the domestic violence. Long-term victims of violence are far more likely than others to rate their health as poor and may develop a *stress-related somatic disorder,* which involves pain, fatigue, negative moods, problematic cognitive functioning, and sleep disturbance (Crofford 2007; Boynton-Jarrett, Ryan, Berkman, and Wright 2008).

Psychological Disruption and Dehumanization

Victims of violence endure various kinds of *psychological trauma.* Sexual and/or physical abuse at the hands of a parent, other close relative, or an intimate partner is especially traumatic. Adolescent experiences of violence in intimate relationships can result in depression, running away from home, thoughts of suicide, dropping out of school, teenage pregnancy, and becoming a perpetrator as well as a victim of violence (Hagan and Foster 2001; Spano, Rivera, and Bolland 2010). Similarly, adult victims of intimate partner violence are more likely than others to suffer depression, impaired ability to function normally at home and work, thoughts of suicide, problems of drug abuse, lower self-esteem, lower life satisfaction, and thoughts of suicide (Zlotnick, Johnson, and Kohn 2006; Calder, McVean, and Yang 2010; Smith, Elwyn, Ireland, and Thornberry 2010; Randle and Graham 2011; Crowne et al. 2011).

Depending on the relationship between victim and abuser, *the victim may come to see himself or herself as a bad person who somehow deserves the abuse.* For example, you—like the rest of us—want to believe that your parents are good, loving people, so if they abuse you, you may feel that it is because you deserve it. The outcome of the abuse, then, can include such problems as low self-esteem or even self-hatred, emotional instability, behavior problems, and disturbed relationships with an inability to trust or relate in a healthy way to others (Litrownik et al. 2003; McMullin, Wirth, and White 2007). Even if parents do not abuse their children, the *children may be harmed by witnessing violence between the parents.* Being exposed to such violence raises the probability that the child will engage in delinquent behavior and develop a depressive or anxiety disorder, a substance abuse problem, or other kinds of mental health impairment (Herrenkohl et al. 2013; Huang et al., 2015).

posttraumatic stress disorder
an anxiety disorder associated with serious traumatic events, involving such symptoms as nightmares, recurring thoughts about the trauma, a lack of involvement with life, and guilt

Moreover, *the consequences can be long term, enduring even after the individual is no longer in the abusive situation.* Both adolescents abused by parents or peers and women abused by husbands or boyfriends may develop **posttraumatic stress disorder** (Dutton et al. 2005; Lawyer et al. 2006). This disorder involves emotional and physical difficulties after a traumatic experience. The difficulties can last for years—even a lifetime. They include such symptoms as nightmares, recurring thoughts about the traumatic experience, a lack of involvement with life, and feelings of guilt.

Both violent victimization and exposure to violence can produce posttraumatic stress disorder and other emotional problems (Ceballo et al. 2001; Scarpa 2004). For example, the Oklahoma City bombing resulted in the disorder among some people who were exposed to, though not directly involved in, the violence (Sprang 1999). Although Oklahoma City residents were most likely to be adversely affected, even people who lived hundreds of miles away reported emotional problems six months afterward. Similarly, a study of Palestinian adolescents, who regularly are exposed to violence, found that they had significantly high levels of aggression, mental health symptoms, and problems of family and social functioning (Al-Krenawi and Graham 2012).

Interpersonal violence not only traumatizes the victim, it also perpetuates the violence. Parents who abuse their children typically were beaten as children. Thus, the *dehumanization process* continues. In addition, as a study of women who were sexually assaulted as children showed, childhood sexual abuse means that the victims are more likely to be revictimized in adulthood, engage in unhealthy or no sexual activity, and experience little or no gratification from sexual activity (Lemieux and Byers 2008). They also have higher rates of disrupted marriage.

Intergroup violence is no less disruptive and dehumanizing than interpersonal violence. For example, adolescents exposed to the ongoing violence between Catholics and Protestants in Northern Ireland have more mental health problems and lower self-esteem than youths more insulated from the conflict (Muldoon and Wilson 2001).

Violence as Seductive Self-Destruction

Throughout American history, groups have resorted to violence either to bring about certain changes or to try and maintain the status quo. In either case, violence often has been defined as the "only way" to reach the desired goals but instead has facilitated the victory of the opposition. Because expectations and outcome often have been contradictory, violence has frequently been a kind of *seductive self-destruction.*

A survey of violence associated with the labor movement concluded that when laborers resorted to violence, it was almost always harmful to the union (Taft and Ross 1969). In general, violence did not bring the advantages the workers had wanted. Historian Richard Hofstadter (Hofstadter and Wallace 1970) agreed with this conclusion, pointing out that one of the more effective tactics of labor was the series of sitdown strikes in the 1930s. These strikes were designed to avoid rather than instigate violence.

Hofstadter also made the point that violence has seemed more effective in maintaining the status quo than in bringing about change, at least in the short run. The long history of violence by whites against blacks to maintain blacks in a subordinate status was seductively self-destructive. Whites did not keep blacks subjugated; nor did management, which employed violence far more than workers did, prevent unionization of workers.

Violence, in sum, can appeal to people as a means either to bring about or to resist certain changes, but violence typically turns out to be counterproductive. Not only does the group using violence fail to achieve its goals, but it also may ensure victory for its opponents. Nonviolence, in contrast, not only avoids the destructiveness of violent protest but, as Chenoweth and Stephan (2011) document in their study of civil resistance movements in many nations, is more than twice as effective as violence in bringing about the desired change.

Economic Costs

Violence carries a high price tag. The costs of interpersonal violence include maintaining the criminal justice system and family service agencies, obtaining needed medical care, and lost productivity. A study by the Centers for Disease Control estimated the total costs at $70 billion, which was more than the total federal aid to education for the year (University of Georgia 2007).

Intergroup violence involves not only medical costs but also the cost of repairing damaged property. The 1992 Los Angeles riot resulted in an estimated loss of $1 billion from the damages (Pringle 1997). In addition, businesses lose considerable sums of money while damaged stores are closed.

Contributing Factors

Violence has been linked with a *human need to be aggressive.* Many psychologists argue that **aggression** is related to *frustration.* Certainly, the frustrations produced by firings and other stressors in businesses have contributed to a rise in the level of violence in the workplace (Johnson and Indvik 1994).

aggression
forceful, offensive, or hostile behavior toward another person or society

But frustration-generated aggression does not adequately explain violence, for aggression can be channeled into such outlets as competitive sports, hobbies, or hard physical labor. To fully explain violence, let's look at various sociocultural factors that contribute to the problem.

Social Structural Factors

Norms. Group norms legitimate various kinds of violent behavior (Reitzel-Jaffe and Wolfe 2001). If you have abusive friends, you are more likely to be abusive in your own relationships. In some families, children observe their parents using violence to settle disagreements or they are taught to employ violence in defending themselves or asserting their rights. This may be based on the *fallacy of non sequitur:* "If I hit you, you will stop doing the things I dislike." It does not follow that violence stops further violence. In fact, the violence is likely to elicit more violence.

fallacy

This tendency for the norms that justify violence to perpetuate rather than stop further violence is seen in urban ghettoes. A study of black youth living in impoverished areas found support for the existence and impact of a "code of the street" (first formulated by Elijah Anderson) that develops among poor youth (Stewart and Simons 2009). The "code" is a set of norms that governs behavior on the streets, including the norm of using violence to deal with any perceived lack of respect. Those who do not respond appropriately (namely, violently) to any instance of disrespect lose face with their peers. Because lack of respect can involve even such apparently minor acts as eye contact that lasts too long, there are frequent occasions where violence is justified.

The point is underscored by another norm that involves children—*the norm of physical punishment.* In the short term, physical punishment may lead children to conform to adult expectations. But what happens subsequently? Studies using national samples have concluded that over time, *the use of physical punishment increases the likelihood of aggressive behavior, delinquency, and antisocial behavior by children and is also associated with violent crime in adulthood* (Straus, Sugarman, and Giles-Sims 1997; Straus 2001; Sheehan and Watson 2008). The more severe the abuse, the more severe the adult crimes are likely to be. A study of juvenile child molesters reported that the molesters, compared to other kinds of offenders, were more likely to have been physically and sexually abused themselves as children (Ford and Linney 1995).

Historically, American norms have legitimated official violence—against radicals and striking laborers, for instance. This official violence is supported by attitudes that approve the use of violence for social control. Throughout the nation's history, groups defined as radical or as a threat to social order also have been defined as legitimate objects of suppression by violence.

An example is the violence of the Chicago police against young antiwar demonstrators during the Democratic Convention of 1968. The committee that investigated the situation called it a "police riot." The police injured many innocent bystanders, including some reporters and news photographers (Hofstadter and Wallace 1970:382). One witness said the police acted like "mad dogs" looking for something to attack. Many people were horrified by the brutality of the police, but public opinion polls showed that the majority of people supported the police. This support came not only because some of the young people had baited the police by taunting them with obscenities, but also because Americans tend to expect and approve violence in the name of social order.

Political Arrangements. Certain political factors affect the level of violence in American society. United States history is characterized by the *exclusion of minorities from the core benefits of and participation in American life.* (*Exclusion* here means both lack of access to economic opportunities and denial of access to the political power by which grievances can be redressed.) This exclusion was maintained and continues to exist to some extent because of political action or inaction. The exclusion has been an important factor in race riots and other interracial violence.

Riots are one form of violence that erupts periodically in the United States.
©McGraw-Hill Education./Jill Braaten, Photographer

In more recent years, the antiabortion movement has been associated with violence. In 1998, Dr. Barnett Slepian, a physician who performed abortions, became the seventh person killed in the United States by antiabortionists (Gegax and Clemetson 1998). In addition, arson and bombing of abortion clinics and violent confrontations between anti- and pro-abortion groups have characterized the struggle over abortion. Although there has been a decline in the violence in recent years, newspapers continue to report incidents of death threats, stalking, vandalism, protestors shouting at those entering abortion clinics, and arson (a clinic in Florida was burned to the ground on January 1, 2012). Those who support abortion believe their rights of choice are threatened and that women's health is jeopardized by the antiabortion movement. Those who oppose abortion feel that the rights of the unborn have been legislated away by court decisions and that politicians seem to ignore their cause. Thus, they resort to militant and even violent actions to influence the political process and bring about new laws that restrict a woman's right to have an abortion.

In essence, then, *political arrangements virtually guarantee a certain amount of violence* in a society that has groups with diverse and strong beliefs, interests, and demands, and in which violence is defined as a legitimate way to pursue group interests. If blacks make political gains, the Ku Klux Klan or other white-supremacist groups may become more militant and violent. Violence against Asian immigrants has occurred both from white supremacists and from people who feel economically threatened (such as the commercial fishermen in Texas who tried to stop Vietnamese immigrants from fishing). The government can never fully satisfy all the diverse interests of the people. Whatever decisions are made are likely to generate adverse reactions and even violence from people who feel cheated, deprived, or oppressed by these decisions.

The Politics of Gun Control.   Government policy on *gun control* bears on violence in the United States. Gun control is highly controversial, with strong arguments on both sides of the issue (including the debate about whether the Second Amendment guarantees citizens the right to own firearms). Let's begin with some data. Although the proportion of households with guns in the United States has declined in recent decades, Americans are still one of the *most heavily armed people on Earth*. In 2014, 31 percent of households had one or more guns (Smith and Son 2015). That's a considerable decline from the high of 50.4 percent in 1977. Yet with less than 5 percent of the world's population, Americans own almost half of all civilian-owned guns in the world (Lopez 2015). Because many owners have multiple guns rather than just one, there are nearly as many guns as people in the nation. And Americans have the highest rate of firearm deaths in the world—six times the rate in Canada and 15 times the rate in Germany.

The *government's ability to guarantee security* to the citizenry affects the number of handguns. The less confidence that citizens have in the federal government, the more likely they are to own firearms (Jiobu and Curry 2001). The important point here, incidentally, is not whether the government protects citizens well by some objective standard but whether the citizens perceive a secure social order.

The significance of the number of guns is underscored by their role in violence. As Table 4.1 shows, guns are the most common weapon used in violent crimes. Furthermore, contrary to the argument that a thoroughly armed citizenry would reduce the number of firearm deaths, numerous studies show a relationship between the number of guns and the amount of violence. A study of firearm deaths in all 50 states from 1981 to 2010 found that the more guns in an area, the more homicides and suicides there will be (Siegel, Ross, and King 2013). For each 1 percent increase in household gun

TABLE 4.1
Weapon Usage in Selected Crimes

Type of Weapon	Percent in Which Weapon Used			
	Violent Crime	Rape/Sexual Assault	Robbery	Assault
Firearm	9	7	29	6
Knife	5	2	10	4
Other	7	*	2	8

*Less than 0.5%
SOURCE: U.S. Department of Justice 2011.

ownership, the researchers found a 0.9 percent increase in the homicide rate. Another study reported that the murder rate of law enforcement officers was three times higher in states with high firearm ownership than in those with low ownership (Swedler et al. 2015). And the suicide rates of men are higher in those states with high rates of firearm ownership (Siegel and Rothman 2016).

Since 1960, more than a million Americans have died from gun-related homicides, suicides, and accidents. The rate of children killed by guns is higher in the United States than in any other industrialized nation. On an average day in the United States, 20 children and adolescents sustain firearm injuries that require hospitalization (Mitka 2014). Access to guns has also been shown to be an important factor in the killing of intimate partners, gang violence, and school rampage shootings (Braga 2003; Campbell et al. 2003; Newman et al. 2004). And don't overlook the large number of injuries. For every person killed, nearly three others are wounded by firearms (Annest, Mercy, Gibson, and Ryan 1995).

In addition to numbers, there is the sheer horror and senselessness of the incidents. A man goes to a school and wounds and kills children whom he does not know. A man and a boy are snipers who kill people they have selected at random. A man walks into his place of employment and starts shooting at everyone, including those who had no part in whatever grievances he has. The point is, the victims of the violence are frequently innocent adults and children who just happened to be where the assailant chose to carry out the attack or attacks.

In spite of tragic incidents like these and in spite of the relationship between the number of gun-involved crimes and gun-control legislation, the issue of gun control is hotly debated. Many people insist, in spite of the evidence presented above, that the widespread existence of guns does not contribute to the amount of violence in the nation. One argument is that it is people, not guns, that kill; if a gun is not available, a person will find a different weapon. Professionals dispute the relationship between the number of guns and the amount of violence. Some argue that this society is a violent one and that violence will not be reduced simply by controlling the sale and possession of guns. Many Americans agree that the effort at control would be frustrating at best and counterproductive at worst. As a popular slogan puts it, when guns are outlawed, only outlaws will have guns. This slogan illustrates the *fallacy of appeal to prejudice.* However, evidence, not emotional slogans, is needed to make a reasonable decision about the issue.

In the first place, guns are the weapon most frequently used in homicides. Contrary to the argument that killers would simply find alternative weapons, the gun is the deadliest of weapons; the fatality rate for shootings is about five times higher than the rate for stabbings. Moreover, murder frequently is an act of passion that the killer himself or herself might later regret. At least in some cases, without the gun there would be no murder.

fallacy

At one time, most of the states had laws prohibiting abortions except when necessary to protect the mother's life. Initially, physicians led the way in calling for a reform of abortion laws. Some lawyers also pressed for change. Abortion should be allowed, they argued, when the mother's mental health or life was jeopardized by the pregnancy or when the pregnancy resulted from rape or incest. Women's groups joined the movement, ultimately resulting in the 1973 Supreme Court decision to legalize abortion.

The Right-to-Life movement then began to work vigorously to reverse the effects of the 1973 decision. Members have pressed for such changes as a constitutional amendment to ban abortions and legislative action to stop funding welfare abortions. Some members became more aggressive, picketing abortion clinics or trying to block people from entering the clinics. Beginning in the 1980s, the efforts have included acts of violence. Arson, bombing of clinics, and even murders have occurred. Some members of the movement—probably a very small number—have resorted to violence to oppose what they define as violence against human life.

Arrange an interview with workers in one or more abortion clinics in your area. Ask them what effect the activities of the Right-to-Life movement have had on their work. Do they fear violence? How do they respond to the charge that they are violently ending human life?

Also interview some members of the Right-to-Life movement. Ask them if they approve of bombing clinics. Is violence against a clinic justifiable? Why? How far would they go in opposing abortions? What answer do they give to people who charge that they are trying to impose their morals on others?

Second, guns are the most frequent weapons used in armed robberies. A gun often seems essential for armed robbery, because without it the offender is unable to produce the necessary threat of force. The fatality rate in armed robberies involving guns is about four times as high as the rate involving other weapons.

Some citizens believe that firearms are necessary to defend their home. This argument has little substance. Many murders occur in homes, but seldom do they involve strangers. The most frequent kind of offender-victim relationship in homicide in homes is that of husband and wife. There is also the possibility of accidental injury or death because of a gun in the home. Children who live in homes with one or more guns are more likely than others to be both victims and perpetrators of violence (Ruback, Shaffer, and Clark 2011). A study of shootings in Philadelphia found that individuals who possessed a gun were 4.5 times more likely to be shot in an assault than those without a gun (Branas et al. 2009).

Finally, it may be true that people, rather than guns, do the killing; but it is also true that people with guns are more likely to kill than are people without guns. Berkowitz (1981) conducted research that suggests that the mere presence of a gun increases aggressiveness, so that although it is true that "the finger pulls the trigger," it also appears that "the trigger may be pulling the finger." In the research, each student was paired with a partner, ostensibly another student but actually a confederate of the researcher. The two were to come up with ideas to improve record sales and boost the image of a popular singer. Each student was to explain his or her ideas to the partner, who would then administer electric shocks—1 shock if the partner thought the ideas were good and up to 10 shocks if the partner thought the ideas were relatively poor. Some of the students became angry after being given seven shocks. Those students then evaluated their partners. They were taken to the room containing the electric-shock machine and a telegraph key that administered the shocks. Some saw nothing but the key lying on a table. Others saw a badminton racket and shuttlecocks, and a third group saw a shotgun and a revolver. Those students who saw the firearms gave their partners a greater number of shocks and administered each for a longer period of time.

The evidence suggests, then, that gun control could reduce some kinds of violence (murder and armed robbery) and minimize the destructiveness of other kinds (assaults and arguments). Public opinion polls show that most Americans favor the *registration of firearms.* There are two important reasons for the existence of political inaction in the face of the evidence and the will of the people. One is that the evidence is still ambiguous; legislators are not convinced of the value of control. The other reason is the strong *lobbying efforts* of the National Rifle Association (NRA). The NRA has a large, paid staff and thousands of local clubs in every state. It spends millions of dollars a year on direct lobbying efforts. Consequently, as of this writing, little has been done to reduce the number of guns in American society.

The Stratification System.   In an effort to put violence in the United States in historical perspective, Graham and Gurr (1969) identified certain *political and economic inequalities* between various groups that have been associated with violence. The early Anglo-Saxon settlers gained the political and economic leverage necessary to resist *efforts by subsequent groups of immigrants to share fully in the nation's opportunities.* Difficult economic times have been particularly fertile for fueling violence, as illustrated by the mob violence against African Americans in the South during inflationary shifts in the price of cotton (Beck and Tolnay 1990).

Inequalities also have been identified as factors in urban riots. In the 1992 riot in Los Angeles, inequality *formed the motivating basis for many of the participants.* Using interviews with 227 African Americans living and/or working in the area at the time of the riot, researchers compared participants with nonparticipants (Murty, Roebuck, and Armstrong 1994). Participants tended to be younger males with lower incomes and lower amounts of education. They also had more arrest records than nonparticipants. But *nonparticipants as well as participants indicated general acceptance of the rioting.* It wasn't that they approved of rioting as such but that they believed collective violence is the only way to get the larger society to address their grievances (poverty, discrimination, unemployment, and police brutality).

At an interpersonal level, boys whose fathers have a history of unemployment are more likely to engage in violent behavior than are sons of fully employed fathers. Violent behavior here refers to beating up or hurting someone on purpose (other than a brother or sister). Of course, unemployed fathers are more likely to be found in the lower socioeconomic strata. Unemployment generates strains in the family life of lower- and working-class youths. In turn, these strains seem to be conducive to greater violent behavior. Thus, both children and adults who live in economic deprivation are more prone to violent behavior and aggression, including murder (Benson, Fox, DeMaris, and Van Wyk 2003; Pollock, Mullings, and Crouch 2006; Schneider, Hacknett, and McLanahan 2016).

Clearly, then, *certain kinds of inequality are related to violence.* Inequality generates frustrations and rage in individuals when they find themselves powerless to resolve their situation, and the probability of violence goes up. Some people may engage in the collective violence of riots and public disorder. Others may vent their rage by fighting on their own. In any case, the violence is the consequence of a stratification system that leaves some Americans in the gutters of the economy.

Role of the Mass Media.   *The mass media expose Americans to an enormous amount of violence.* It would be interesting to record the number of violent incidents that impinge upon your life in a week of reading, listening to the radio, and watching television.

Concern about violence on television began in the 1950s when it became evident that there was a high degree of violence in everything from children's shows to late-night adult entertainment. From time to time, television executives have promised to scale back the amount of violence, but the level remains high.

Children who watch television regularly, play video games, or attend movies are likely to be exposed to thousands of violent deaths and a staggering number of violent incidents during their childhood. Even Disney films portray a great deal of violent behavior. A study of 45 animated feature films produced by Disney between 1937 and 2006 found 561 incidents of child maltreatment among the 1,369 child characters in the films (Hubka, Hovdestad, and Tommyr 2009). In addition, 62 percent of the main child characters in the films suffered maltreatment at least once.

What are the consequences of all this violence? Some observers argue that it results in an increase of violent behavior. Others argue that watching violence on television provides a kind of **catharsis,** *a discharging of aggressive emotions* through vicarious participation in violence. For example, a man who has become extremely hostile toward his wife can discharge his aggression and avoid violence against his wife by watching violent acts on television.

catharsis
discharge of socially
unacceptable emotions in a
socially acceptable way

But displacement of aggression and vicarious discharge of aggression are not the same thing. Contrary to the idea of catharsis, portrayal of violence in motion pictures and on television increases the level of violence in society. And there is evidence to support this conclusion. Those who watch violence on TV can be *socialized into the norms, attitudes, and values that support and foster violence.* In other words, the more that people—particularly children and adolescents—watch violent TV programs, the more likely they are both to approve of and to engage in violent behavior (American Academy of Pediatrics 2001; Huesmann, Moise-Titus, Podolski, and Eron 2003). Moreover, as a study of third- to fifth-grade children found, there is likely to be a decrease in prosocial behavior as well as an increase in violence, and the violent behavior includes both verbal and physical violence (Gentile, Coyne, and Walsh 2011). Researchers have also found that aggressive attitudes and behaviors increase from reading violent comic books, listening to songs with violent lyrics, and playing violent video games (Kirsh and Olczak 2002; Polman, de Castro, and van Aken 2008; Willoughby, Adachi, and Good 2012; Hummer 2015).

How much violence on TV does someone have to watch before being socialized into the violence? How long does it take for the violent shows to have their effect? In order to answer the questions, some researchers have looked for possible effects over a period of years. For example, Johnson et al. (2002) assessed 707 individuals over a 17-year period. The researchers found a significant association between the amount of time spent watching television as adolescents and young adults and subsequent aggressive behavior. But the effects can occur in a much shorter period of time. A study of youths 10–15 years of age who had used the Internet in the previous six months identified a portion of the youth who had engaged in seriously violent behavior (Ybarra et al. 2008). Of those who had been violent, 38 percent were exposed to violence online. Those who reported seeing violence between real people (rather than cartoon or computer-generated characters) were significantly more likely than others to engage in seriously violent behavior. Another study looked at the effects on both Japanese and American students of playing violent video games (Anderson et al. 2008). Among both the Japanese and the Americans, those who played the games habitually early in the school year became more physically aggressive later in the school year.

The consensus among researchers, then, is that viewing violence in the media socializes some individuals into a more violent way of life. As Murray (2008) states in his review of 50 years of research on the effect of TV violence on children, the conclusion is "inescapable" that the effects of media violence on children are both real and strong, increasing aggressive attitudes, values, and behavior.

Another consequence of media violence is that the viewer can develop a jaundiced view of the world. People may believe that there is even more violence than actually occurs, and may become distrustful and fearful of others. They may also become less concerned about the victims of violence. In an experiment with fourth- and fifth-grade students, Molitor and Hirsch (1994) found that those who watched violence were afterward less likely to be concerned about two other children who engaged in a violent confrontation. The subjects watched a TV monitor that supposedly showed two children in an adjacent room. The subjects were told to get help if anything happened. Those who had watched clips from a violent movie were less likely to, or slower to, get help when the children on the monitor became violent with each other.

Finally, note the possibility that even watching violent sports can increase aggression. Researchers who investigated the rate of violent assaults on women in the Washington, D.C. area reported an increase in admissions to hospital emergency rooms following victories by the Washington Redskins' football team (White, Katz, and Scarborough 1992). They speculate that viewing the success of violence—even in a sporting event—may give some fans a sense of license to try and dominate their own surroundings by the use of force.

Admittedly, even with all the research we have noted, it is difficult to state unequivocally that exposure to the mass media leads to specific effects because of the many other factors that operate within people's lives. However, the evidence is growing and overwhelmingly supports the position that mass media violence is associated with aggressive attitudes and behavior. The evidence suggests that mass media violence teaches people how to be violent and tends to create violent behavior in viewers.

Social Psychological Factors

Attitudes.   *Certain attitudes legitimate violence.* One is the attitude of approval of violence itself. To be sure, people have a tendency to be selective about what circumstances justify violence (Bethke and DeJoy 1993). Still, most Americans accept violence as a problem solver, and about "two-thirds think that the use of physical force is often justified" (Patterson and Kim 1991:132). In particular, many Americans accept intimate partner violence if the circumstances warrant it (Sacks et al. 2001). A study of high school students reported that 77 percent of the females and 67 percent of the males endorsed some form of sexual coercion, including unwanted kissing, genital contact, and sexual intercourse (Office of Juvenile Justice and Delinquency Prevention 2006:4).

relative deprivation
a sense of deprivation based on some standard used by the individual who feels deprived

One explanation of violence is **relative deprivation,** which means that people have a *sense of deprivation in relation to some standard.* Here, the attitudes people have toward their deprivation are more important than any objective assessment of that deprivation. This observation goes back at least as far as de Tocqueville (1955), who pointed out that the French were experiencing real economic gains prior to the Revolution. An observer could have told the French that, objectively, they were better off at the time of their revolt than they had been at other times in the past. Yet what if the people used a different standard than their past to measure their deprivation? They might then perceive themselves to be less well off than they *should* be and rebel, which is precisely the idea of relative deprivation.

Davies (1962) used the notion of relative deprivation to explain revolutions. He constructed a *"J-curve" theory of revolution.* In essence, the theory states that a *widening gap between what people want and what they get leads to a revolutionary situation.* People do not revolt when the society is generally impoverished. Rather, people develop a revolutionary state of mind when they sense a threat to their expectations of greater opportunities to satisfy needs.

You will always experience a gap between your expectations and the satisfaction of your needs. Some degree of gap is tolerable, and although over time both your satisfactions and your expectations tend to increase, something may happen to suddenly increase the gap. Expectations continue to rise while actual need satisfactions remain level or suddenly fall. The gap then becomes intolerable, and a revolutionary situation is created.

According to Davies' theory, the deprivation of people in a revolutionary situation is relative. Actual satisfaction of their needs may be higher at the time of a revolution than earlier, but their expectations are also higher. The people may be better off in terms of their past, but worse off in terms of their expectations. Their attitudes rather than their objective condition make the situation revolutionary.

Relative deprivation has been identified as a factor in racial militancy and the approval of violent protest by northern blacks. Interviews with 107 riot-area residents of Detroit in 1967 showed that those who were most militant in their attitudes and who believed the riots helped the black cause were those who felt relatively deprived rather than relatively satisfied (Crawford and Naditch 1970).

A survey of 6,074 young adults found that those who saw themselves as economically deprived compared to their friends, neighbors, and Americans generally were more likely to engage in violent behavior (Stiles, Liu, and Kaplan 2000). The sense of deprivation led to negative feelings about themselves, which motivated them to use violent means to cope with their situation.

Finally, *attitudes about firearms help maintain the large number of guns in American homes.* In a Pew Research Center survey, 52 percent of Americans said it is more important to control gun rights than it is to control gun ownership; in fact, support for

Television, including children's programs, exposes children to an enormous amount of violence.

©Daniel Pangbourne / Digital Vision / Getty Images

gun control laws has actually fallen since 1990 (Kohut 2015). Such attitudes support the continued proliferation of guns in the nation, and this means the continued problem of gun-related violence.

Values.   Attitudes that justify violence are often reinforced by certain values. In American society, people are likely to agree on the values of **retributiveness** and self-defense.

retributiveness
paying people back for their socially unacceptable behavior

Retributiveness, or retributive justice, is summarized by the notion of "an eye for an eye and a tooth for a tooth." It is a value of punishment, of paying people back for their antisocial behavior. This value comes into play when people insist on the death penalty and other harsh forms of punishment.

Self-defense as a value means an *affirmation of the right to violence, including killing, in order to defend yourself or your family.* Some people would extend the value to include the defense of your home as well. In part, these values are maintained through the mass media which, as we have seen, justify various kinds of violent behavior.

Public Policy and Private Action

We already have discussed some steps for reducing violence, because whatever effectively deals with the problem of crime also reduces the level of violence. In addition, the various norms, attitudes, and values that support violence need to be changed. Early intervention in the lives of children can teach them alternatives to violence and aggression in solving their problems and gaining their goals in life. In families, schools, and churches, children need to learn how to employ nonviolent methods to survive and to find fulfillment. For example, a violence prevention program called Peace Builders has been shown to decrease aggression and increase social competence in children in kindergarten through fifth grade (Vazsonyi, Belliston, and Flannery 2004). Such programs cost relatively little and reach children at an early age.

American norms and attitudes about when violence is legitimate also need to change. In particular, no one should be taught that he or she deserves violent treatment from another person. Many women abused by a male partner remain in the relationship for years in the belief that they somehow brought the violence on themselves. Or they are convinced that they will eventually change the partner into a nonviolent individual. Women who break away from such relationships have learned to reject the notion that they deserve abuse or that they are responsible for helping their partner to change (Rosen and Stith 1995).

Second, *gun-control measures* may reduce the violence in our society. Homicide is the leading cause of death in Colombia, South America; but when two cities—Cali and Bogotá—banned the carrying of firearms on weekends, holidays, and election days, the homicide rates went down (Villaveces et al. 2000). In another study, researchers found, in states that passed laws making gun owners responsible for storing firearms so that they were inaccessible to children, unintentional shooting deaths of children younger than 15 declined by 23 percent (Cummings, Grossman, Rivara, and Koepsell 1997). Similarly, the 1994 federal ban on assault weapons contributed to lower gun murder rates and murders of police officers by criminals armed with assault weapons (Roth and Koper 1999). A study of suicide rates in states reported that the rates went down when the states passed such gun-control laws as background checks, gun locks, and open carrying regulations (Anestis and Anestis 2015). Finally, there were 13 mass shootings in Australia between 1979 and 1996, leading that nation to pass new gun-control laws (Chapman, Alpers, and

Jones 2016). Since then (as of May, 2016), there have been no mass shootings and the mean rate of firearm deaths dropped from 3.6 to 1.2 per 100,000 population.

Third, violence in the mass media should be reduced. The reduction is needed in cartoons as well as other kinds of programming. An experiment with third- and fourth-grade children found that cutting back on the amount of time children spent watching television and playing video games reduced the amount of aggressive behavior (Robinson et al. 2001).

Not only should violence be reduced, but the programs should include a greater amount of modeling of desirable behavior. *Television could become a medium for promoting more prosocial behavior.* After all, if the depiction of violence leads some people to become more aggressive, it is reasonable to expect that the depiction of prosocial behavior will increase the amount of such behavior in the society. Indeed, one researcher found such an effect from the words of popular songs (Greitemeyer 2009). Three separate studies showed that listening to songs with prosocial lyrics led to more empathy for others and fostered helping behavior. Other research found that playing prosocial video games led people to be more likely to help someone after a mishap and to intervene in a harassment situation (Greitemeyer and Osswald 2010).

Finally, violence will lessen as we deal with some of the inequalities in our society. We discuss this further when we consider poverty and other problems in Part 3.

Follow-Up. Would you like to see a ban on corporal punishment of children become a matter of public policy? Why or why not?

The Violence of Rape

We know of no society that completely lacks rape or that fails to punish it. The definition of rape, however, varies. The American legal code distinguishes between two kinds of rape: forcible and statutory. **Forcible rape** is defined as the "carnal knowledge of a female forcibly and against her will" (Federal Bureau of Investigation 2002:454). The victim of forcible rape can be of any age, and attempts or assaults to rape are included. **Statutory rape** refers to sexual intercourse with a female who is under the legal age for consenting.

forcible rape
the carnal knowledge of a female forcibly and against her will

statutory rape
sexual intercourse with a female who is below the legal age for consenting

Rape is an extremely *traumatic experience* for victims. For the perpetrators, rape is typically an expression of violent aggression against women, not an act of sexual passion.

How prevalent is rape in the United States? It is difficult to say because an unknown number of rapes are *never reported*. In 2014, a third of women who said they had been raped did not report the crime to the police (Truman and Langton 2015). Adult victims are often reluctant to report a rape because of fear that the rapist will try to get even with them or will attack them again. They also fear publicity, embarrassment, and the way they may be treated by police and prosecutors (Monroe et al. 2005).

An increasing proportion of rape victims do report the crime to the police. Still, we get a more accurate picture of the amount of rape in the victimization studies. In 2014, there were 284,350 rapes (Truman and Langton 2015). In addition, there were perhaps that many attempts to rape that were successfully fought off.

Not everyone is equally likely to be a victim of rape or sexual assault (attacks, including verbal threats, that involve unwanted sexual contact between the victim and the offender). Table 4.2 shows how the rates vary by various demographic factors. Mixed-race and black women have the highest rates, followed by white, Hispanic, and Asian women. Rates also vary by age, with higher rates in younger age groups. These data do not include rapes of those under the age of 12, but one survey found that 21.6 percent of

TABLE 4.2
Demographics of Rape and
Sexual Assault Victims

Marital Status		Victimizations per 1,000 Females Age 12 or Older			
		Race/Hispanic origin		Age	
Never married	4.1	White	2.2	12–17	4.1
Married	0.6	Black	2.8	18–34	3.7
Widowed	0.8	Hispanic	1.4	35–64	1.5
Divorced/Separated	4.4	Asian	0.7	65 or older	0.2
		Two or more races	5.1		

SOURCE: Planty et al. 2016.

women who reported being raped said that their first experience of rape occurred before the age of 12 (Tjaden and Thoennes 2006).

Contrary to popular belief, there is little interracial rape, and most rapes *do not involve strangers.* Of those women who have been rape victims, 51.1 percent identified the perpetrator as a current or former intimate partner, 12.5 percent identified a family member, and 2.5 percent identified a "person of authority" such as a boss, teacher, coach, clergyman, doctor, or therapist (Black et al. 2011). Only 13.8 percent of rapists were strangers to the victim.

incest
exploitative sexual contact
between relatives in which the
victim is under the age of 18

Finally, there is the problem of sexual assault on children, including **incest,** which refers to exploitative sexual contact between relatives in which the victim is under 18 years of age. With regard to sexual assault on children generally, a national study reported that more than 285,000 children, 17 years old or younger, were sexually abused in one year (Finkelhor, Hammer, and Sedlak 2008). The bulk of them were female (89 percent) and between the ages of 12 and 17 (71 percent). About 4 percent were five years old or younger. Most of the victims were non-Hispanic whites (64 percent). Non-Hispanic African Americans accounted for another 18 percent. And 71 percent were assaulted by a relative or someone they knew.

With regard to incest, there is very little research. A pioneering study by Russell (1986) reported that 19 percent of the women interviewed had been victims of *incestuous abuse.* A survey of some university students in Turkey found that 6.3 percent reported incest (Aydin, Altindag, and Ozkan 2009). A study of young girls in Internet chat rooms reported that 38 percent had had sex with a relative (Atwood 2007). None of these studies had a random or representative sample, so it is not possible to say how many females are victimized by incest. It is clear, however, that incest is not rare.

According to the victims' reports, the most common type of incest is that between a father and his daughter; the incest is painful, often begins before the girl is 10 years old, and may continue for years on a regular basis. The victims' suffering does not end when the abuse stops, but results in the same kind of long-term, devastating psychological consequences as rape (Lorentzen, Nilsen, and Traeen 2008; Aydin et al. 2009).

Rape and the Quality of Life

Regardless of the background characteristics of the victim, the consequences for the quality of life are similar: Rape is a highly traumatic experience, and fear of rape probably causes uneasiness in most women at some time.

Emotional and Physical Trauma

Rape victims suffer *intense emotional trauma.* Rape contradicts the ideal of healthy, voluntary, and nonviolent relationships. The emotional trauma that results from rape is incompatible with the desired quality of life.

Children who are sexually abused are likely to experience both short-term and long-term negative consequences. They are at risk for anxiety disorders, stress disorder, and posttraumatic stress disorder (Maniglio 2013). Female victims, compared to those who are not sexually abused, have higher rates of bodily pain, poorer general health, and higher rates of depression (Coles et al. 2015).

Adult victims of rape experience what Burgess and Holmstrom (1974) delineated as the *rape trauma syndrome.* The syndrome involved two phases of reaction of the victim: *an initial, acute phase of disorganization and a long-term phase of reorganization.* The acute phase, which lasted for a few weeks after the incident, involved both physical and emotional reactions. The *physical reactions* included soreness and bruises resulting from the violence of the offender; tension headaches, fatigue, and disturbance of sleep; various gastrointestinal disturbances such as nausea, stomach pains, and lack of appetite; and genitourinary problems such as vaginal itching and pain. The *emotional reaction* during the acute phase ranged "from fear, humiliation, and embarrassment to anger, revenge, and self-blame. Fear of physical violence and death was the primary feeling described" (Burgess and Holmstrom 1974:983). Although it may seem surprising that victims should feel guilty or blame themselves, such feelings are common (see "I Felt Guilty," at the beginning of this chapter). A young woman reported strong guilt feelings in these terms:

> I'm single but I'm not a virgin and I was raised a Catholic. So I thought this might be some kind of punishment to warn me I was doing something against the Church or God.

Another victim remarked, "My father always said whatever a man did to a woman, she provoked it" (Burgess and Holmstrom 1974:983).

Rape is one of the most traumatic experiences a woman endures.
©Brand X Pictures

The long-term phase of reorganization included *motor and emotional consequences.* Common motor consequences included actions such as changing residence, changing telephone numbers, and visiting family and friends to gain support. Among the emotional consequences were nightmares; the development of various phobias, such as the fear of being indoors, outdoors, alone, in a crowd, or hearing but not seeing people walking behind one; and sexual fears. One victim reported that five months after the incident she could still get hysterical with her boyfriend: "I don't want him near me; I get panicked. Sex is OK, but I still feel like screaming" (Burgess and Holmstrom 1974:984).

In a follow-up study of 81 victims, reinterviewed from four to six years after they were raped, Burgess and Holmstrom (1979) found that less than a full recovery was reported by 71 percent of the victims who had never had sexual relations, 27 percent of those inactive at the time of the rape, and 35 percent of those sexually active when they were attacked. More than two-thirds of the victims said they had decreased sexual activity, and many of them said that they experienced pain and discomfort and had difficulty reaching an orgasm when they resumed sexual activity.

Subsequent studies confirm and extend the findings of Burgess and Holmstrom (M. B. Stein et al. 2004). Virtually every area of a woman's life is negatively affected by the experience of rape (Black et al. 2011). Among other things, victims are more likely than others to experience problems of physical and mental health, feelings of fear, anxiety about safety, sleep problems, activity limitations, missed days at work, and posttraumatic stress disorder. Although the number of male victims is considerably smaller and male rape has received less attention, a survey of nearly 60,000 men found similar consequences for male rape victims: poorer mental health and life satisfaction, activity limitations, and lower levels of emotional and social support (Choudhary, Coben, and Bossarte 2010).

Finally, most women experience at least some trauma because of the *fear of rape* (Mesch 2000). As one female student told us: "Every woman knows that she is a potential victim of a rapist." Such a fear takes a toll on free movement and peace of mind.

Physical Abuse

Although most female victims who report being injured have relatively minor kinds of physical injuries, rapists may use weapons, beat or choke the victim, and use strength or threats to subdue her (DiMaio 2000). Some victims require medical treatment for their physical injuries. The *force and brutality so commonly involved in rapes* lead us to conclude that rapes are acts of violence rather than sexual passion. The rapist is not someone with an overwhelming sex drive; he is, typically, a man who feels compelled to assault and humiliate women. He uses rape as a weapon to express his hatred of females. Physical abuse, therefore, is an inevitable consequence for the female victim.

Contributing Factors

Most of the factors that contribute to other kinds of violence also contribute to rape as a particular form of violence. Other factors distinctively associated with rape tend to *encourage offenders* and to *oppress the victims.*

Social Structural Factors

Norms.   Certain *traditional norms about sex roles* may be factors in rape. That is, in the traditional roles, males are aggressive and females are submissive. The more strongly that men adhere to traditional rather than egalitarian roles, the more likely they are to have victim-callous rape attitudes (Whatley 2005). For some men, it may be acceptable to rape an assertive woman so that she learns her "proper place."

In general, it seems *the more that men are integrated into a culture where the norms support male dominance and superiority,* the more likely they are to find rape acceptable (Locke and Mahalik 2005). The locker-room talk of athletes tends to treat women as objects, encourage sexist attitudes, and promote rape (McMahon 2007). Such talk seems to correlate with behavior, for *athletes are more likely than other men to be sexually aggressive* and to participate in gang rapes (Koss and Gaines 1993).

The *college norm of heavy drinking at parties* is also a factor in rape (Mohler-Kuo, Dowdall, Koss, and Wechsler 2004). A survey of thousands of women in 119 colleges and universities over a three-year period found that 1 in 20 (4.7 percent) reported being a victim of rape (Mohler-Kuo et al. 2004), and nearly three-fourths of them were raped while they were intoxicated. The researchers concluded that a female student's chances of being raped are far greater on campuses in which the student body as a whole has a high rate of binge drinking and in which individuals consume large amounts of alcohol. Nor is this true only for those who "can't hold" their liquor. As shown in the research of Testa and Hoffman (2012), heavy drinking in college is a significant risk factor for sexual victimization for both experienced and inexperienced drinkers.

Family.   *Negative family experiences can foster the development of a rapist.* Three researchers who compared a sample of rapists with a sample of child sexual abusers found such problems in the family of origin of both groups (Simons, Wurtele, and Durham 2008). Nine out of 10 men in each group reported inadequate bonding with their parents and frequent exposure to violence in the media when they were growing up. Among the child sexual abusers, 65 percent had been exposed to pornography before the age of 10, and 73 percent had been victims themselves of childhood sexual abuse. Among the rapists, 7 out of 10 reported having been physically and/or emotionally abused as children, and 78 percent witnessed parental violence.

The great majority of the sexual offenders, in short, had abusive experiences as children. As with other social problems, both the quality of family life and exposure to violent media are important variables in understanding sexual offenders.

Mass Media.   As with violence in general, the mass media also play a role in the problem of rape. As we shall see in the next chapter, violent pornography is a factor in the sexual aggression of men (Davis et al. 2006). This conclusion is supported by a series of pioneering experiments (Donnerstein 1980; Donnerstein and Linz 1984; Weisz and Earls 1995) that showed men who watch movies that portray sexual violence, including those shown in theaters around the country, are more likely to engage in bizarre or antisocial behavior. Even a few minutes of watching a sexually violent movie can lead to antisocial attitudes and behavior. The men in the experiments were more likely afterward to accept the myths about rape (that, for instance, a woman really wants to be raped; see the list in the following section), to indicate a willingness to commit rape, to engage in aggressive behavior against a woman in a laboratory situation, and to have less sensitivity to the trauma of rape for women. In another experiment, men who watched a film that was sexually degrading to women were more likely than other men to believe that

ATTITUDES OF TURKISH STUDENTS TOWARD RAPE

Is it rape if the woman lures him on? Is it rape if she agrees to go with him to his apartment? Is it rape if the woman is his wife? Should the rape be reported to the police regardless of the circumstances? Americans have had differing opinions about the appropriate answer to such questions. People in other nations also differ in their attitudes about rape.

Four researchers who investigated the attitudes of Turkish university students toward rape found a high degree of condemnation by both male and female students but also some interesting variations depending on gender and the circumstances. The sample consisted of 432 females and 368 males from a number of universities in Istanbul.

Each student was presented with three different rape scenarios. The first was of a young man and woman who knew each other for two years and had been dating for six months. On a date that involved drinking and dancing until 2 a.m., they went to his house for a cup of coffee. They kissed and stroked each other, but the woman didn't want to go any

further. She asked to go, but he ignored her and engaged in physically forced sex.

The second scenario was of a woman who was followed home by a stranger after shopping at the supermarket. She heard him as she was walking down the dark and empty street toward her house. She walked faster, but he caught up with her, put a knife to her throat, and raped her.

The third scenario also involved a stranger, but rape myth information was added. The young woman was returning home alone at 1 a.m. wearing a miniskirt, a low-cut blouse, and high boots. She was raped after getting off a bus and walking to her house.

The students were asked, for each of the scenarios, whether the rape should be reported to the police, whether a crime was committed, and what kind of punishment (if any) should be meted out to the offender. Figure 4.1 shows the proportion of students who agreed that the rape should be reported. Nearly all the students agreed that the rape by a stranger should be reported. The great majority agreed that the rape by a stranger of the woman wearing the provocative clothing should be reported, though slightly more women than men agreed. And a majority would report the date rape,

a rape victim found the experience pleasurable and "got what she wanted" (Milburn, Mather, and Conrad 2000). Finally, an experiment in which young men played a video game that included violence against women and depicted them as sex objects, raised the men's level of rape-supportive attitudes (Beck et al. 2012).

Social Psychological Factors

Attitudes.   Are the following statements true or false?

Rape tends to be an unplanned, impulsive act.
Women frequently bring false accusations of rape against men.
Most women fantasize about being raped and find erotic pleasure in the fantasy.
A woman who is raped is usually partly to blame for the act.
It is not possible for a man to rape a healthy woman unless she is—consciously or unconsciously—willing.

What are your answers? If you said that any of the previous statements is true, you have accepted one of the *myths about rape.* In point of fact, many people—even a minority of college women—accept one or more of these beliefs (Holcomb, Holcomb, Sondag, and Williams 1991; Carmody and Washington 2001). Overall, however, men are more likely to accept rape myths and to blame the victim than are women (Grubb and Harrower 2009). And men, older people, political conservatives, and people from the lower socioeconomic strata are more inclined to commit rape and are less likely to be sympathetic toward rape though significantly more of the women than the men agreed. More women than men also agreed that the date rape was a crime (22.6 percent of the men said "no"). And in all three scenarios, women would mete out greater punishment than would the men. Thus, in Turkey, as in most societies, men are less likely than women to view rape as a serious, violent crime when they can use circumstances to justify the rape.

SOURCE:
Golge, Yavuz, Muderrisoglu, and Yavuz 2003.

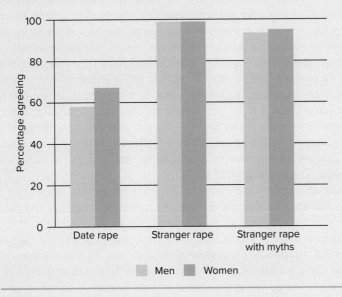

FIGURE 4.1   Proportion Agreeing Victim Should Report Rape to Police.

victims (Chiroro, Bohner, Viki, and Jarvis 2004). They thereby not only lend support to those who rape but also help perpetuate injustice in the efforts to prosecute rapists.

It is important, then, to deal with the attitudes expressed in the myths. In contrast to the notion that rape is impulsive, significant proportions of convicted rapists have admitted that they intended to find a victim prior to the rape and that they looked for women who they thought could not or would not resist the attack (Stevens 1994). As for the fantasy myth, only a small proportion of women report that they fantasize about being forced to have sex.

The myth that women frequently bring false charges of rape against men has no factual basis. There is a good deal of evidence that women frequently do not report rape to the authorities, but no evidence that they frequently make false accusations.

Let's look in more detail at the other two myths, for they are more difficult to answer definitively. First, the humiliating treatment to which a rape victim is often subjected during a trial follows from the *attitude that the victim was somehow to blame* for provoking the offender. This is the *fallacy of personal attack* at its worst. Instead of receiving help and support, the victim of violence becomes the defendant of her own integrity. The attitude that "the victim was asking for it" ignores three things. One, women are socialized to make themselves attractive to men by their dress and mannerisms. Two, provocative dress cannot be considered sufficient justification for inflicting the physical and emotional brutality of rape upon a woman. As Horos (1974:12) argued,

fallacy

Does a woman's dress or mannerisms give any man the right to rape her? Because you carry money in your pocket, does it mean that you're asking to be robbed? Perhaps this myth arose because rape is the only violent crime in which women are never the perpetrators, but always the victims.

Three, provocative dress is not even involved in all rapes. The victim may be an elderly woman in a long robe, a woman wearing a coat, or a young girl in modest school clothes. In any case, to focus on dress is simply another way of *blaming a victim for an injustice.*

fallacy

The attitude that a healthy woman can always prevent rape also may help acquit an offender and oppress the victim. This attitude may reflect the *fallacy of retrospective determinism.* In essence, people may be saying to the victim: "The situation could have had no other outcome. The man is not to blame because you allowed it to happen—and you allowed it to happen because of the kind of person you are."

This attitude ignores the *paralyzing fear* that can grip a woman. Perhaps a third or more of rape victims exhibit *tonic immobility,* which is an involuntary, reflexive response to a fearful situation, a response in which the victim "freezes" as though paralyzed (Galliano, Noble, Travis, and Puechl 1993).

This attitude also ignores the *amount of force* used by rapists. Recall that rape typically involves the use of a weapon. Furthermore, beating, choking, and the threat of death may be effective even though no weapon is visible.

We already have pointed out the lack of sympathy and help a victim may experience in encounters with the police. The *attitude of the police* may be that the woman provokes the attack and that a healthy woman cannot be raped. In addition, the police may suspect the woman is merely using the charge of rape to punish a man or get attention for herself. To be sure, there are rare cases in which a woman charges rape to retaliate against a man or fulfill some pathological need.

Furthermore, the police know that not all victims of rape are respectable citizens with backgrounds free of suspicious behavior. In part, then, the attitudes of the police reflect a genuine need for caution. Nevertheless, a past police record, provocative clothing, or minimal resistance do not give a man license to forcibly rape a woman.

Considerable improvement has occurred in recent decades in the treatment of rape victims. Yet it is still true that the police, along with legal and medical personnel, can fail to give victims needed services (Campbell et al. 2001). Victims who go to formal authorities for help receive more negative reactions than those who rely on informal sources such as friends and family (Ullman and Filipas 2001).

Justification and Values.   Finally, we raise the question of the social psychology of the offender. What kind of man is a rapist? When the rapists themselves were asked about their behavior, they either had no explanation at all or gave reasons that justified or minimized the negative significance of rape (Scully and Marolla 1984; Mann and Hollin 2007). Among the things they said are that it was an impulsive act; that the victims were seductive; that women say "no" but they really mean "yes"; that most women eventually relax and enjoy the experience; that women who are "nice" will not get raped; and that the act was at best a minor offense that did not merit the penalty the offender was now suffering. In other words, the men appeared to accept the rape myths. As we noted earlier, men who accept the myths are more likely to be sexually aggressive and to approve of rape.

Other offenders, however, admitted their guilt and viewed their behavior as morally wrong. They claimed that the rape was either the result of their use of alcohol or drugs, or the result of their emotional problems. They also tended to try to present an image of themselves as "nice" guys whose "true" self should not be judged on the basis of the rape.

Macho values also seem to be a factor in the tolerance of, and proneness to, rape. In one experiment, young men were asked to listen to the tape of a simulated rape and imagine themselves in the role of the rapist (Mosher and Anderson 1986). The tape described an encounter between a man and a woman stranded on a lonely road because of a flat tire. The man forced the woman to have sex with him. Some of the listeners found the tape repugnant, but others found it interesting and sexually arousing. In particular, those with macho values (real men engage in violence and find danger exciting) were more likely to have a positive reaction to the tape.

Finally, whatever else he may or may not be, the rapist and the man who accepts the myths about rape have a high level of hostility toward women (Marshall and Moulden 2001). Every rape involves aggression.

Public Policy and Private Action

Four lines of attack can be pursued in dealing with the rape problem. First, *programs of prevention* need to be established (Bryant-Davis 2004). We have noted the high rate of date rape. Many colleges and universities have established programs to make students aware of date and acquaintance rape. Research has shown that rape-education programs can change attitudes of both men and women (Fonow, Richardson, and Wemmerus 1992).

Some cities also have set up prevention programs. These programs include a variety of services such as self-defense training, public education activities, and support services to professionals in the sexual assault field. The programs may prepare and provide booklets on prevention and self-defense and work with the mass media to gain a wide audience for their educational materials.

The idea of self-defense presents women with a dilemma. On the one hand, the woman who does not struggle may find the police or some jury members unsympathetic to her case. On the other hand, the research on physical resistance has come up with mixed results in terms of recommendations (Ullman 1998). Some earlier researchers claimed that forceful fighting and screaming reduced the severity of the sexual abuse, but others argued that resistance only increased the likelihood of physical injury. A more recent evaluation, using a larger sample of victims, concluded that those who had been trained in self-defense were more likely than the untrained to say that resistance stopped the offender or lessened his aggression (Brecklin and Ullman 2005). A study of 300 college women who had self-defense training found that, compared to those untrained, the trained knew more self-protective behaviors, felt more able to resist potential attackers, and were less likely to suffer an attack (Orchowski, Gidycz, and Raffle 2008).

Second, *sex-role norms, legal processes, and attitudes* need to be changed. Some changes will occur only through a painfully slow process of education, for even knowledgeable and well-educated people can be deeply ignorant about rape. A male graduate psychology student told us, "There is a simple way for women to avoid the trauma of rape. They should just decide to relax and enjoy it." Such attitudes encourage offenders and oppress the victims. The fact that a graduate student could hold this kind of attitude illustrates the point that changing attitudes is going to be a painfully slow process. But changing such attitudes, including attitudes about the various rape myths, will reduce the amount of sexual assault (Lanier 2001).

Third, *rapists need treatment.* Rapists tend to be psychologically disturbed in some way. As such, they need therapy, some kind of rehabilitation, and not simply punishment. Punishment may remove the rapist from society for a period of time, but it will not deter him from future offenses.

The fourth line of attack is to *provide help for the victims* of rape (Kalmuss 2004). The victims clearly need a good deal of help, including emotional support. But a study of 103 women who had been victimized found that their romantic partners provided relatively little support and aid and often tended to blame the victim for the rape (Ahrens, Cabral, and Abeling 2009). Counselors and friends were more helpful than romantic partners.

An important source of help for rape victims are the *rape crisis centers* that have been established throughout the nation. The centers offer assistance in dealing with authorities, information about available legal and medical care, and counseling to facilitate recovery from the emotional trauma. The centers also frequently have prevention programs and offer courses in self-defense.

The centers may also offer the services of a rape victim advocate. A study of 81 rape victims in two urban hospitals reported that those who had the help of a rape victim advocate were more likely to have police reports taken and less likely to be treated negatively by police officers (Campbell 2006). They also reported less distress with the legal and medical systems, and they received more medical services such as emergency contraception and sexually transmitted disease prophylaxis. *Rape victim advocates should be available* in all areas.

The attitudes of authorities seem to be changing in the direction of greater sympathy for the victims of rape. A number of cities have established *rape squads* of male/female police teams with the specific responsibility of dealing with rape cases. The female member of the team interviews the victim while the male helps gather evidence. Various states have reformed their laws on rape, and hospitals are beginning to open rape reception centers instead of refusing to treat victims. Ultimately, the aim is prevention rather than sympathetic treatment of victims. Meanwhile, the new types of services for the victims and potential victims are a welcome help for women. They suggest that men finally may be realizing that the rape victim should be helped and not oppressed further by humiliating encounters with the authorities.

Follow-Up.   With volunteers from your class, explore, and then report back to the class, any programs you have on campus for educating students about date rape and for aiding victims when date rape occurs.

Summary

Violence is a problem that concerns most Americans. Generally, violence refers to the use of force to kill, injure, or abuse others. Interpersonal violence occurs between individuals or a number of individuals. Intergroup violence involves identifiable groups, such as different races or religions.

In estimating the amount of violence, we find an impressive amount based on self-reports, newspaper accounts, and police statistics. The United States has one of the highest homicide rates in the world. Virtually all Americans are exposed to a vast amount of violence in the mass media.

The meaning of violence can be summed up in terms of human destruction and injury, psychological disruption and dehumanization, economic costs, and "seductive self-destruction." These factors all diminish the quality of life, and their impact can be both severe and long term.

Violence has been linked with a human need for aggression, yet this explanation is not sufficient. Various sociocultural factors contribute to the problem. One structural factor is group and societal norms, which make violence more likely among members of those groups. An important factor in intergroup violence is exclusion from the political process. People who are unable to exert power through legitimate political means may resort to violence. An important factor in interpersonal violence is the lack of adequate gun control. Inequality is related to violence; political and economic inequalities between groups in a society increase the likelihood of violence.

Among the social psychological factors in violence are a number of attitudes that legitimate violence. The majority of Americans agree that physical force is sometimes justified, including the use of force in intimate relationships. A frequent explanation of violence involves the notion of relative deprivation, which means that attitudes toward deprivation rather than the objective condition are the critical factor.

Certain values support violence, including retributiveness and self-defense. Such values can be internalized, along with attitudes, through exposure to the mass media. The extent to which the mass media socialize people into violent attitudes and behavior is a matter of controversy. However, the bulk of the evidence indicates that violence portrayed and conveyed in the mass media is related to aggressive attitudes and behavior.

Rape is a form of interpersonal violence that afflicts tens of thousands each year. Fear of rape is one of the more common fears of women. All rapes involve both physical and emotional trauma. The rape trauma syndrome involves several weeks of acute symptoms and disorganization, and a long period of painful emotional readjustment.

The more men agree with traditional norms about sex roles, and the more they are integrated into a culture whose norms support male dominance and superiority, the more likely they are to be sexually aggressive and to minimize the harm of rape.

The mass media contribute to the problem of violence against women in general and rape in particular through portrayals of sexual violence. These portrayals increase the tendency of males to engage in antisocial attitudes and behavior. Studies of offenders show that they had negative family experiences and are psychologically disturbed. All have extremely high levels of aggression.

Key Terms

Aggression	Posttraumatic Stress
Catharsis	Disorder
Domestic Terrorism	Relative Deprivation
Forcible Rape	Retributiveness
Incest	Statutory Rape
	Violence

Study Questions

1. How would you define violence? How much violence is there in America?
2. What are the physical and emotional consequences of being a victim of violence?
3. What social structural factors contribute to the level of violence in America?
4. What role do the mass media play in violent behavior?
5. How common is rape?
6. Discuss the physical and emotional consequences of being a victim of rape or attempted rape.
7. Why do men rape?
8. What can be done about the violence, including rape, in American society?

chapter 4 review

Internet Resources/Exercises

1. Explore some of the ideas in this chapter on the following sites:

http://www.vpc.org   Site of the Violence Policy Center, with an emphasis on gun control in order to reduce violence in America.

http://www.ncadv.org   The National Coalition Against Domestic Violence offers surveys, discussions of public policy, and ways for victims to get help.

http://www.rapecrisis.com   Has information, services, and links for sexual assault victims and their families.

2. Investigate a group involved in domestic terrorism, such as a right-wing militia, the Earth Liberation Front, or the Animal Liberation Front. How does the group justify its stance? How do law enforcement officials and other observers define the activities of the group? What social structural and social psychological factors do you think contribute to the existence and work of the group?

3. Find stories of rape victims. Compare their accounts with the discussion in the text about the rape trauma syndrome. How does the text's description of the syndrome capture or fail to fully capture the victims' experiences?

For Further Reading

Bergen, Raquel Kennedy, Jeffrey L. Edleson, and Claire M. Renzetti, eds. *Violence Against Women.* Boston: Allyn & Bacon, 2004. Essays from a broad range of perspectives that address the issue of sexual and physical violence against women, including commentaries by the authors about their research and its impact.

Bourke, Joanna. *Rape: Sex, Violence, History.* Glebe, Australia: Counterpoint, 2007. A historian examines such issues as the history of sexual aggression, laws about sexual psychopathology in the United States and Britain, how military culture affects views of sexual assault, how rapists respond to their offense, and the ways in which popular culture informs our discussion of rape.

Gottesman, Ronald, ed. *Violence in America: An Encyclopedia.* New York: Charles Scribner's Sons, 1999. Covers every aspect of violence, summing up what researchers have found, including not only violence against people but also violence against animals and property.

Harding, Kate. *Asking For It: The Alarming Rise of Rape Culture—and What We Can Do About It.* New York: De Capo Lifelong Books, 2015. Argues that American culture is more supportive of the rapist than the victim, and offers various ideas on how to take a more realistic and helpful approach to sexual abuse and still honor the rights of the accused.

Kleck, Gary. *Point Blank: Guns and Violence in America.* New York: Aldine Transaction, 2005. A thorough look at the major issues involving guns, gun control, and violence, including suggestions for a national weapons policy.

Newman, Katherine, Cybelle Fox, David Harding, Jal Mehta, and Wendy Roth. *Rampage: The Social Roots of School Shootings.* New York: Basic Books, 2004. An extensive investigation of school shootings, including various factors that help explain why students resort to such violence.

Scheper-Hughes, Nancy, and Phillipe I. Bourgois, eds. *Violence in War and Peace: An Anthology.* Malden, MA: Blackwell, 2004. Two anthropologists put together a collection of essays that explore social, literary, and philosophical theories of violence, ranging from violence in everyday life to genocide to war.

CHAPTER 5

Sexual Deviance

OBJECTIVES

1 Learn the meaning and some of the types of sexual deviance.

2 Be able to discuss why cybersex is a problem.

3 Understand factors that make prostitution and pornography social problems.

4 Show how prostitution affects a woman's quality of life.

5 Know how pornography affects people's behavior.

6 Identify ways to address the problems of prostitution and pornography.

©McGraw-Hill Education/John Flournoy, photographer

"My Husband Is a Porn Addict"

Kathy is a 26-year-old woman who has been married for four years. She was quite happy in her marriage for the first two years. Then she happened to catch her husband viewing pornographic sites on his computer. The last two years have been a struggle for her:

When I accidentally caught Jake watching porn, I was shocked. I had no idea he was into that kind of thing. I knew he liked sex a lot. But so do I. Or at least, I did. Our sex life hasn't been much to talk about these past couple of years. It's really tough for me to feel aroused by him when I know how much time he's spending watching that stuff on his computer.

That's the thing that shocked me the most—the amount of time he spends at it. I didn't realize it at first because he would watch it late at night after I was asleep or when I was out of the house. However, one night I caught him watching porn when he thought I was in the shower. After a quick shower, I decided to sneak up on him before I dressed and invite him to go to bed, but I stopped dead in my tracks when I saw his computer screen. He tried to convince me that it was all harmless. That it only increased his desire for me and made our sex life better.

That didn't make sense to me. "You mean you have to watch other naked women to feel sexy toward me?" I asked him. He couldn't give me a satisfactory answer. Then I asked him how long and how often he had been watching the porn. He tried to weasel out of a direct answer, but he finally admitted that he had been into it for years—even before we were married. At that point, I realized that my husband is a porn addict!

Previously, I had thought that all porn addicts were perverts, but I've discovered that a lot of seemingly normal men are addicted to porn. And some of them are a lot worse than Jake. I've been attending a small support group for wives of porn addicts. One woman told us about how her husband was into the violent stuff and would act it out with her. She got tired of the above, and refuses to have sex with him any more. They'll probably get divorced soon. Another woman said that her husband convinced her to watch with him. He said it would spice up their sex life. She tried, but she couldn't take it. And when she refused to watch any more, he got verbally and emotionally abusive.

Jake hasn't gone that far. But to be honest about it, that doesn't make it any easier for me. I feel like he's having affairs. He's investing himself emotionally in other women. And I just can't feel the same way about him while he's doing it. At this point, I think I still love him. I certainly love the man I thought I married. But I'm not sure how much longer I can stay married to a porn addict.

Introduction

There's an old story about an expert who was scheduled to give an after-dinner speech on sex. At the appointed time, he arose and said: "Ladies and gentlemen. Sex. It gives me great pleasure." Then he sat down.

Clearly, sex is a source of great pleasure to humans. It is also a source of pain and controversy. Whether it is one or the other depends on whom you're talking to and what kind of sex you're talking about. In this chapter, we look at what is meant by sexual deviance. Then we expand on two kinds of sexual deviance that are regarded as social problems: prostitution and the use of pornography.

Examples of Sexual Deviance

What is sexual deviance? The answer depends on which society you are talking about. All societies regulate sex, but not all regulate it in the same way. Studies of sexual norms show that there are variations both within and between societies (Bolin and Whelehan 2003; Higgins and Browne 2008). In the United States, for example, lower-class women are more likely than middle-class women to believe that men's sex drive is a biological necessity, thereby limiting the lower-class women's prerogative to refuse sex. And in contrast to the United States, some other societies consider the behavior that Americans have historically regarded as deviant (such as homosexuality and extramarital sex) to be acceptable. Of course, people everywhere take their own norms seriously, but the point is that sexual behavior, like all other behavior, is social. No particular type of sexual behavior is "natural" or "normal" in contrast to other types.

Nevertheless, there are certain kinds of sexual behavior that are considered deviant in most societies. Some of these behaviors characterize only a very small proportion of the population. For example, it is likely that *exhibitionism* (exposing one's genitals to a stranger) and *voyeurism* (spying on people who are having sexual relations) are practiced by only a small proportion of people. We don't know the figures for America, but two Swedish researchers reported that 3.1 percent of a national sample admitted to exhibitionism and 7.7 percent had engaged in voyeurism (Langstrom and Seto 2006).

Another type of sexual behavior considered deviant in most societies is **promiscuity,** sex between an unmarried individual and an excessive number of partners. Both men and women say that they prefer sex to occur in the context of an intimate relationship and that the emotional satisfaction of sex is strongly associated with being in a committed, exclusive relationship (Waite and Joyner 2001). Although men are often portrayed as having sex whenever they can get it, a national survey reported that two-thirds of the single men said they didn't like a woman who was willing to make love on the first date (Arrington 1990). And an experiment that used college students as subjects reported that the students considered people who are promiscuous less desirable as potential dating or marriage partners (Perlini and Boychuk 2006).

> **promiscuity**
> undiscriminating, casual sexual relationships with many people

Extramarital sex also varies from American norms. From a list that included such events as divorce, gambling, having a baby outside of marriage, abortion, suicide, and cloning humans, the item that the fewest people regarded as morally accepted was an extramarital affair (Bowman 2004:48). Behavior doesn't always reflect attitudes, however, and in point of fact a substantial number of Americans engage in extramarital sex. We don't know exactly how many. A national survey reported that about 25 percent of married men and 15 percent of married women admit to ever having an affair (Laumann, Michael, Gagnon, and Michaels 1994). The proportion may be on the rise, particularly among older men and young couples (Parker-Pope 2008). Among young couples, the proportion of wives who cheat has risen and is equal to that of husbands. Nevertheless, most Americans practice fidelity, though not as many as say they disapprove of infidelity.

Still another form of deviant sex is **cybersex,** sexual activity conducted via the Internet. A forerunner of cybersex was telephone sex, which involved a per-minute charge to engage in a sexual conversation with someone (Ross 2005). Telephone sex never attracted as many customers, however, as has cybersex.

> **cybersex**
> sexual activity conducted via the Internet

Cybersex can be carried on in a number of ways. In one form, the individual uses online pornographic sites for sexual pleasure or for exhibitionism. Some people do this by posting nude pictures of themselves. A number of websites cater to people who want to expose their nude bodies on the Internet (Jones 2010). It is probably more common, however, to engage in **sexting,** sending erotic or nude photos or videos of oneself to a particular person or to a number of others via a cell phone or the Internet. The purpose of sexting is to enhance sexual desire and/or to ultimately have sexual intercourse.

> **sexting**
> sending erotic or nude photos or videos of oneself to a particular person or to a number of others via a cell phone or the Internet

Another way to use the Internet for sexual pleasure is to search for sexual partners. In a survey of 5,187 people who used a website for married people wanting partners for extramarital sex, the researchers found that males and females were equally likely to cheat but that females were more likely than males to engage in sexting (Wysocki and Childers 2011).

The Internet is also used to enhance sexual desire. A small number of people literally become addicted to Internet pornography (Weinstein and Lejoyeux 2010). Others, however, use it occasionally, either alone or with a partner, as a form of arousal. Some users report that they are more open to new sexual experiences and find it easier to talk about what they want sexually as a result of watching sex online. Others say that they have less sex with the partner who uses online sex sites or that they are less aroused by real sex after watching sexual acts online (Grov, Gillespie, Royce, and Lever 2011).

In a second form of cybersex, two or more people engage in sexual talk while online in order to gain sexual pleasure. A Swedish study found that those who engaged in this form of cybersex also tended to have more offline sexual partners (Daneback, Cooper, and Manisson 2005).

A third form of cybersex is the online game in which the participants can do such things as create their own characters (who can resemble themselves) and have those characters engage in whatever kinds of sexual behavior they desire (Biever 2006). In some of the games, people can go beyond the online sex and use the site to date those with whom their characters have had sex.

Is such online sex just harmless fun? In one study, 41 percent of a sample of people engaged in cybersex did not consider what they did to be cheating on a relationship partner at all (Ross 2005). But the story at the beginning of this chapter gives one woman's account of the harm done to her marriage by a husband involved in cybersex. And a survey of 91 women and 3 men whose partners had been heavily involved in cybersex found a good deal of hurt—feelings of betrayal and rejection, jealousy, and anger—as well as adverse effects on their children (Schneider 2003).

Finally, many Americans view *strip clubs* as a form of deviant sex. In both male and female strip clubs, patrons can watch people strip and engage in erotic dancing and, in some cases, chat with the strippers. For women, the shared experience of being at the club with friends and bonding with other women may be more important to them than the show itself (Montemurro, Bloom, and Madell 2003). For men, on the other hand, regular attendance at strip clubs is associated with their sexuality and masculinity. Katherine Frank (2003, 2005) found a variety of motivations among men for going to strip clubs, including a desire to express a masculine self free of obligations and commitments; experience adventure; feel desirable; and have a sexualized interaction with a woman that is without risk.

Let's look in greater detail at prostitution and pornography. Both have been strongly condemned and vigorously defended.

Prostitution

prostitution
having sexual relations for remuneration, usually to provide part or all of one's livelihood

Prostitution is a paid sexual relation between the prostitute and his or her client. Male prostitutes are often young boys—mostly from impoverished homes. They have run away or been thrown out of their homes and offer themselves as sexual partners to gay men. Many regard themselves as heterosexuals; in any case, they view what they do as a job that gives them a source of income (Bimbi 2007). Whatever their age, male prostitutes secure clients in a variety of ways: through agencies, personal ads, working on the streets, or via one of the websites throughout the nation that offer their services (Logan 2010). Because research on male prostitution is sparse, our focus here is on the female prostitute and her clientele.

fellatio
oral stimulation of the male genitalia

cunnilingus
oral stimulation of the female genitalia

Although not every prostitute agrees to perform every sexual act, prostitutes are available for a variety of sexual services. These include **fellatio** (oral stimulation of the male genitalia), **cunnilingus** (oral stimulation of the female genitalia), and various other sexual practices that an intimate partner may not want to engage in. In a survey of 1,342 men arrested for solicitation in four western cities, fewer than one in six said that vaginal sex is the most common type they have with a prostitute (Figure 5.1). While most prostitutes

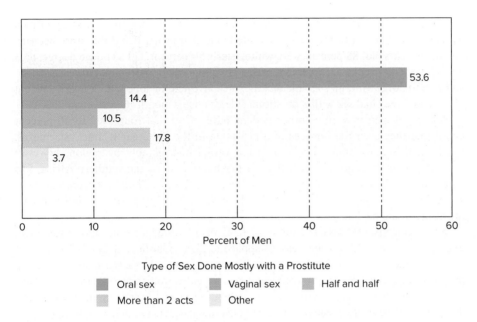

FIGURE 5.1
What Men Want from Prostitutes.
Source: Giusta, DiTommaso, Shima, and Strom 2009.

basically offer anonymous and impersonal sex acts, a few (not streetwalkers) specialize in a more intimate and emotional experience for the client (Bernstein 2007). Such a prostitute may function as a girlfriend for the time she spends with her client.

How much prostitution exists in the United States? Official records depend on arrests. The FBI website indicates 47,598 arrests for prostitution in 2014, but an unknown number of these were repeat offenders and not all prostitutes are arrested. Part of the problem of estimating is that there are *various kinds of female prostitutes,* from streetwalkers to high-paid call girls to brothel workers to prostitutes who use the Internet to solicit customers (Roane 1998). Some work full time, and others use prostitution to supplement their incomes. Some work for decades, and others quit after a short time. On average, it is estimated that the work life of American prostitutes is four to five years (Potterat, Woodhouse, Muth, and Muth 1990). Whatever the total number who have ever been a prostitute, it seems safe to say that at any one time hundreds of thousands of prostitutes are at work in the nation. Some of them are adolescents, usually runaways or "throwaways."

Hundreds of thousands is a reasonable figure in light of the amount of prostitution in other parts of the world. The proportions range from 0.7 percent to 4.3 percent among nations in sub-Saharan Africa, from 0.2 percent to 2.6 percent among nations in Asia, from 0.1 percent to 1.4 percent in western Europe, and from 0.2 percent to 7.4 percent among nations in South America (Vandepitte et al. 2006). If we assume there are 200,000 to 300,000 prostitutes in the United States, the comparable figure would be somewhere between 0.1 percent and 0.2 percent of the female population, which is comparable to that of other industrial nations.

Who uses the services of a prostitute? Again, it is impossible to give exact figures. Yet considering the number of prostitutes available and the number of times they can have sex each day, it is clear that a substantial portion of the male population has some experience with a prostitute. One researcher estimates that 16 percent of American men pay for sex at some point in their lives (Westerhoff 2009). Although men of any age may use a prostitute, the typical customer, or "john," is a married, middle-aged, well-educated white male (Giusta, Di Tommaso, Shima, and Strom 2007; Farley et al. 2011). Only a small proportion of the men limit their use of prostitutes to one time. A study of men who used the Internet to secure a prostitute found that nearly two-thirds were between 40 and 60 years old, 85 percent were white, nearly 80 percent had a college degree, 66.3 percent were married, and 27 percent used a prostitute one or more times a week (Milrod and Monto 2012). And in a sample of 1,342 men arrested for solicitation, nearly one out of eight said they had sex with a prostitute at least once a month (Giusta et al. 2007).

Surveys of men in various other nations have found that roughly 9 to 10 percent admit that they used the services of a prostitute in the past year (Carael, Slaymaker, Lyerla, and Sarkar 2006). The proportion varied considerably by region, however: 13 to 15 percent in central Africa, 10 to 11 percent in eastern and southern Africa, 5 to 7 percent in Asia and Latin America. Keep in mind that these numbers represent those who said they had sex with a prostitute in the past year; the proportion who ever used a prostitute would be considerably higher.

Why do men pay for sex? The survey of 1,342 men arrested for solicitation asked them to indicate which of 13 possible reasons applied to them (Giusta et al. 2007). They could agree with more than one of the reasons. The most frequently chosen reasons (and the proportion agreeing with them) were: wanting to be with a woman who "likes to get nasty" (52 percent); approaching a prostitute is exciting (43 percent); wanting to be in control during sex (42 percent); preferring a variety of sexual partners (41 percent); wanting a different kind of sex than he has with his regular partner (41 percent); and feeling awkward when trying to meet a woman (41 percent). In the study of men who used the Internet to find a prostitute, the top three motives with which they agreed strongly were: "I like to be with a woman who really likes sex (84.4 percent); "I like to be with a woman who likes to act very uninhibited and horny (71.7 percent); and "I like to have a variety of sexual partners (45.3 percent) (Milrod and Monto 2012). These reasons suggest that the men (most of whom are married or living with someone) desire some kinds of sexual experiences that they don't have with their regular partner.

Prostitution and the Quality of Life

Prostitutes typically prefer their profession to other perceived options. This preference is not so much evidence of the high quality of life for prostitutes as it is testimony to the *low quality of life endured by the women before they decided to become prostitutes.*

In Prince's (1986) interviews of 300 prostitutes, all of the streetwalkers named money as the major advantage of their work. Brothel workers and call girls were more likely to name such things as time flexibility, adventure, and learning about themselves and others. Whatever the advantages, however, there are serious problems with the quality of life.

Physical Problems.   In the first place, *prostitution contradicts our value of physical well-being.* Americans cherish good health and value the youthful physique. Most prostitutes, however, face certain occupational hazards that may lead to physical problems. In the past, *venereal disease* was a prominent problem. Today it is less frequent because many prostitutes get regular medical checkups and also carefully examine each customer for signs of venereal disease. Juvenile prostitutes, however, may be resistant to medical help because they fear attracting the attention of authorities.

Another common physical problem "is a chronic pelvic congestion characterized by a copious discharge from the cervix and vaginal lining, and a sensation of tenderness and fullness of the side walls of the pelvis" (Winick and Kinsie 1971:70). The congestion results from the prostitute's avoidance of orgasm. She may try to get relief through narcotic drugs.

Finally, prostitutes face the hazard of contracting acquired immune deficiency syndrome (AIDS) (Yuan et al. 2016). They run the risk both from their clients and from the tendency of some to become intravenous drug users. In the United States, prostitutes not only contract but help spread AIDS (Stine 1998). Rates of infection are particularly high among male prostitutes. A study of young male prostitutes in San Francisco reported that 12 percent of them were infected (Bacon et al. 2006). Fewer than half of the prostitutes required their clients to use condoms, and only 41 percent of those infected were even aware of their condition. Even higher rates have been found in other nations. A survey of Cambodian prostitutes reported an infection rate of 54 percent (Ohshige et al. 2000). A study of prostitutes in Vancouver, Canada, reported a 26 percent rate of infection (Shannon, Bright, Gibson, and Tyndall 2007). Rates are even higher in some African nations, and are particularly high among the street prostitutes who use drugs (Needle et al. 2008).

A different problem is the *physical abuse that threatens the prostitute* (Raphael and Shapiro 2004). The abuse is most likely to come from customers. A survey of 325 prostitutes in Miami reported that over 40 percent had experienced violence in the preceding year: 24.9 percent had been beaten, 12.9 percent had been raped, and 13.8 percent had been threatened with a weapon (Surratt, Inciardi, Kurtz, and Kiley 2004). A study of prostitutes in China found similar frequencies of verbal abuse, beatings, and rape (Zheng 2009).

There are different kinds of prostitution, with different consequences for the prostitute.
©Ingram Publishing/SuperStock

pimp
one who earns all or part of his or her living by acting as a manager or procurer for a prostitute

A prostitute may also suffer abuse at the hands of her husband or boyfriend and her **pimp** (one who earns all or part of his or her living by acting as a manager for the prostitute) (Dalla 2000). The highly paid call girl, who serves a more affluent clientele, is not likely to endure physical abuse, but the streetwalker must be constantly alert.

The constant threat of abuse is one reason a prostitute needs a pimp. Ironically, Norton-Hawk (2004) found that, among the 50 jailed prostitutes she interviewed, pimp-controlled prostitutes were more likely to be victims of customer violence than were those without pimps. The pressure to make extra money to support the pimp may lead these prostitutes to take more risks, exposing themselves to a greater chance of violence.

At the same time, the pimp himself inflicts physical abuse (Williamson and Cluse-Tolar 2002). Sometimes the pimp will beat a prostitute when he begins his relationship with her to establish his dominance and to ensure the woman's loyalty. If the prostitute does not behave in a way the pimp deems appropriate, he may continue to abuse her. One prostitute explained the pimp's behavior in terms of the master-slave relationship. The master seems to have total power but lives in fear because of the uncertainty of how the slave will react to his or her bondage. Like the master with his slave, the pimp fears the loss of his property.

We do not know how frequently prostitutes endure physical abuse from customers or their pimps, but the threat of abuse is constant. It is unlikely that any prostitute can ply her trade for many years without suffering abuse (Nixon et al. 2002). A study of 130 prostitutes in San Francisco reported that 82 percent had been physically assaulted; 83 percent had been threatened with a weapon; and 68 percent had been raped while working as a prostitute (Farley and Barkan 1998). It is estimated that street prostitutes are 60 to 100 times more likely to be murdered than are other women (Salfati, James, and Ferguson 2008). Such violence in their lives, along with the drug use that is common, is a major reason for the higher rate of mortality among prostitutes (Potterat et al. 2004). Compared with other women of their age, prostitutes are nearly twice as likely to die.

Psychological and Emotional Problems.   A psychological problem reported by prostitutes arises from the contradiction between the value of sexual fulfillment and the role of the prostitute. The problem is a psychological counterpart to the previously mentioned physical ailment that can result from the prostitute's avoidance of orgasm. Far from achieving sexual fulfillment, the prostitute often becomes *virtually asexual* with respect to her own sexual functioning (Dalla 2001). Again, however, we have to distinguish between different kinds of prostitutes. Prince (1986) found that two-thirds of the streetwalkers agreed that they should avoid orgasms, but only a little over a third of the brothel workers and 4 percent of the call girls agreed.

There is also a contradiction between the value of *human dignity* and the prostitute's role. The continual exposure to violence, along with other aspects of the prostitute's work, may lead to various kinds of emotional trauma (including depression and post-traumatic stress disorder), drug use and abuse, feelings of isolation and worthlessness, attempted suicide, and sexually transmitted diseases including AIDS (Norton-Hawk 2002; Burnette, Schneider, Timko, and Ilgen 2009; Krumel-Mancuso 2016). Emotional problems are intensified by the fact that prostitutes generally do not form a cohesive group among themselves because they are competing for customers. They mainly have contempt for their customers and do not establish bonds with them. They often cannot form close relationships with people not connected with "the life" because of the stigma attached to their role. Therefore, prostitutes are barred from a sense of community with anyone.

One way prostitutes cope with this problem is to seek *refuge in drugs* (Gunn et al. 1995; Dalla 2000; Degenhardt, Day, Conroy, and Gilmour 2006). A considerable number of prostitutes need help with addiction (Valera, Sawyer, and Schiraldi 2001). In many cases, the prostitutes were drug users before they began to engage in sex work (Bletzer 2005). Once they started working as prostitutes, however, their drug use tended to escalate.

When the drugs no longer are sufficient to make their existence bearable, prostitutes may try to end their lives. The rate of *attempted suicide* is quite high among prostitutes (Ling, Wong, Holroyd, and Gray 2007). In Prince's (1986) study, 68 percent of the streetwalkers, 25 percent of the call girls, and 19 percent of the brothel workers admitted trying to kill themselves.

There is, then, ample evidence of psychological and emotional problems among prostitutes. Moreover, these problems are built into the role of the prostitute, making escape

CHILD PROSTITUTES

In the United States, women may become prostitutes because, among other reasons, they come from impoverished backgrounds. In some other countries, the relationship between poverty and prostitution takes a different twist—children sell themselves, or are sold by their parents, into prostitution in order to survive. The United Nations estimates that 1.2 million children are trafficked across international borders every year, most of them destined for prostitution.

We should note that not all child prostitution comes out of impoverished settings. Cultural norms also play a role. For example, in Thailand girls sometimes go into prostitution because it appears to be the only choice they have in order to fulfill the norms of their culture. Those norms dictate that the young should repay their parents for the sacrifices the parents have made and should help improve their parents' financial standing. They have the obligation to do so even if the family is relatively well off. But females have little opportunity to make enough money to enhance the family's income and status. Consequently, some of them opt for prostitution as a "bearable" way to fulfill their cultural obligations.

Most child prostitution, however, is tied up with poverty and the need to survive. The close link between child prostitution and survival is illustrated by the account of a 17-year-old Chilean prostitute, who told how the first effort she and her brothers made to get food was to go out and beg, or pick up leftovers at the market. Then they started selling celery, but when they couldn't sell enough to get the food needed by the family,

"my mom almost beat us to death." After that, the girl began to sell herself. A Chilean sociologist has estimated that as many as 50,000 children in Chile engage in prostitution in order to survive.

Southeast Asia is another area with child prostitutes. No one knows just how many, but estimates run into the hundreds of thousands and as high as a million. One-fifth of prostitutes in Thailand begin their work between the ages of 13 and 15, and girls as young as 8 are in the brothels of Thailand, Cambodia, India, China, Taiwan, and the Philippines. Many of the girls were sold to the brothel owners by their parents in order to get money for food or other essentials for their families. Once sold, the girls are considered the property of the brothel owners and must work until they pay off their purchase price—or until they get AIDS.

In some cases, the family may run its own prostitution business. A mother with four daughters in Manila looked for clients for the two youngest daughters, ages 8 and 12. When the 12-year-old resisted, the mother held her down while the men raped her.

The clients of child prostitutes come from many different nations, including America. Why do they want children? No doubt they have various motivations, but one seems to be the fear of AIDS. The AIDS virus is spreading rapidly among prostitutes in Asia. The younger the prostitute, so the reasoning goes, the less likely she is to have AIDS. As a result, hundreds of thousands of Asian girls are living in sexual slavery.

SOURCES
Chicago Tribune, March 17, 1996; *New York Times,* April 14, 1996; Kuo 2000; Willis and Levy 2003; Bower 2005; Mathews 2006.

difficult. For some women, prostitution seems to be more desirable than other available options, but the psychological and emotional quality of the prostitute's life is low.

Exploitation. Quality of life is further diminished by the *contradiction between the roles of the prostitute and the people with whom she must deal and the ideal of "I-Thou" relationships* in which people relate to each other as person to person and not as person to thing. The role of prostitute involves exploitation. Pimps, madams, bellboys, taxi drivers, lawyers, disreputable medical examiners, abortionists, police officers receiving hush money—the prostitute must deal with them all, and they all treat her as a "thing" rather than as a person by using her to make or to supplement their own living. The women offer their sexual services to men, pay their fines to men, and return to the streets only to be arrested again by men—all to satisfy the public's sense of "decorum."

Arresting prostitutes satisfies the public because the appearance of police safeguarding morality is maintained. The prostitute is exploited by many different people, all of whom regard her as an object to serve their own interests.

Perhaps the most exploited of prostitutes are those who are "sex slaves," women forced unwittingly into prostitution by men who kidnap them or who lure them into another country with the promise of work or husbands (van Hook, Gjermeni, and Haxhiymeri 2006). In some cases, the women fled into another country trying to fend off extreme poverty and even starvation. Once there, however, they were forced into prostitution as the only way to survive.

There are probably hundreds of thousands of sex slaves throughout the world. Asian nations have particularly high rates of sex slaves, but there are tens of thousands of them in the United States (Field 2004). Federally funded human trafficking task forces found more than 2,000 incidents of sex trafficking between January 2008 and June 2010 (Banks and Kyckelhahn 2011). Although most sex slaves in the United States are from a Latin American or Southeast Asian background, the task forces reported that 83 percent of the victims in the incidents they identified were American citizens. Like sex slaves in other nations, those in the United States are typically deceived and forced into prostitution by those exploiting them for personal gain.

Contributing Factors

If the quality of life for the prostitute is so low, and if many Americans believe the very presence of prostitutes offends traditional morals, why does prostitution continue?

Social Structural Factors.   Social structural factors help explain both why men seek prostitutes and why women enter into the life. American society has traditionally held to the norm of sex only within marriage. In addition, sex has not been openly discussed through much of the nation's history. These two factors—*rejection of nonmarital sex and no open discussion of sex*—were set forth by Winick and Kinsie (1971) as crucial determinants of the amount of prostitution in a society. They pointed out that among the Tokopia of the Solomon Islands, both nonmarital sex and open discussion of sex are accepted, and there is practically no prostitution. They hypothesize that in societies in which social norms forbid either or both of these conditions, there will probably be prostitution. This line of reasoning is supported by the fact that open discussions about sex have become more acceptable, and nonmarital sex (especially premarital) has become more widely accepted in American society. At the same time, although roughly the same number of men appear to use the services of prostitutes, fewer are young men, and the number of visits by each man may have declined.

In addition to traditional norms about nonmarital sex and discussion of sex, the *institution of marriage* does not provide the kinds of sexual experiences that some men desire (Monto 2004). Nor, we would add, should it. A wife is a human partner, not a sex slave who must fulfill her husband's every fantasy regardless of her own needs. Of course, most married men are content with their experiences in marital sex. But some men go to prostitutes to experience variety, to compensate for a lack of gratification with their mates, or to avoid concern about pregnancy (Brents, Jackson, and Hausbeck 2010). Married men who give and receive oral sex report that they are happier with their sex lives and their marriages, but it appears that wives are less into oral sex than are their husbands. Consequently, as shown in Figure 5.1, the desire for fellatio is an important reason some men use prostitutes (Monto 2001).

Men may also go to prostitutes because their wives do not desire sexual relations as often as they do. The prostitute then provides a sexual outlet that does not require the time and emotion that would be involved in an extramarital affair.

The nature of the economy also facilitates male use of prostitution (Davis 1993). Workers such as male truck drivers and salesmen must spend a considerable amount of time away from home. Symanski (1974) reported that tourists, traveling salesmen, and truck drivers were among the major sources of business for the Nevada brothels. And a study of Chinese men who used prostitutes reported that one type of client was the man who was required to work far away from his wife or girlfriend (Pochagina 2006). To the extent that *the economy requires travel,* there will likely be clientele for the prostitute.

Structural factors help explain why women enter the life. They tend to come from a *low position in the stratification system.* They may have existed in a situation of poverty, abuse, and family instability in their early years (McCarthy, Benoit, and Jansson 2014). They usually have little education and few job skills, and resort to prostitution out of what they regard as economic necessity (Dalla 2000; Kramer and Berg 2003). A study of women working in Nevada brothels found that three-fourths were sex workers because of financial considerations (Brents et al. 2010). Young, homeless male and female prostitutes also resort to this way of life in order to survive (Tyler and Johnson 2006). Some of these youth view prostitution as nothing more than a desperate attempt to get the necessities of life. They see no other alternative. Pimps take advantage of their desperation by looking for runaway girls in bus stations, arcades, and malls (Albanese 2007). They act like concerned new friends, buying the girls food and clothing and eventually having sex with them. After that, they use the girls' emotional and financial dependence to force them into prostitution, using drugs and threats if necessary. The pimp is no longer a friend; he is the boss, the man who tells the prostitute how much money she must earn for him each day. An example of how pimps work is the man who recruited Canadian girls, took them to Hawaii, and then seized their passports so they could not leave (Albanese 2007). He drugged and handcuffed them, and told them to comply with his demands or he would send photos of them engaging in sex to magazines or to their families.

Studies of prostitutes in other nations reveal a similar pattern: Prostitutes tend to come from impoverished backgrounds and feel compelled to engage in prostitution in order to survive. Often, perhaps most of the time, it is not only a matter of the individual's survival but also that of her family (Wong, Holroyd, Gray, and Ling 2006). In some cases, it may not be a matter of sheer survival, but of the level of income available to women. In Tijuana, Mexico, sex workers can earn 5 times as much as average professionals and 10 times what most people earn (Kelly 2008).

In addition to their position in the socioeconomic system, prostitutes frequently come from backgrounds of *disturbed family experiences and participation in groups with norms that accept prostitution.* Prince (1986) reported that the prostitute's relationship with her father seems to be the most important family factor. In particular, the prostitutes tended to describe a father who abandoned the family, who lost contact after a divorce, or who treated the girl abusively or with indifference. About 9 out of 10 of the streetwalkers said that they did not have a close or happy relationship with either their mother or father while growing up. The call girls tended to have a good relationship with their mother, but fewer than half had one with their father. Among the brothel workers, the proportions reporting good relationships were 43 percent with their mother and 39 percent with their father.

Similarly, interviews with 33 parents of teenage prostitutes reported that the parents were stressed from a history of failed intimate relationships and financial hardships (Longres 1991). They also raised their daughters in neighborhoods conducive to easy entry into prostitution.

In many cases, the disturbed family experiences go beyond mere deprivation. Prostitutes come disproportionately from families involved in physical and/or sexual abuse, alcoholism, and use of other drugs (Dalla 2001; Nixon et al. 2002; Lung, Lin, Lu, and

Shu 2004). Prince (1986) found abuse, including incest, particularly common among the streetwalkers. A study of 72 Australian prostitutes found that all but one of them had traumatic experiences that typically began in early childhood, including child sexual abuse (Roxburgh et al. 2006). A study of Mexican brothel workers reported that a number of the women became prostitutes to support themselves so they could escape from an abusive, violent relationship with a husband or lover (Kelly 2008). Abuse, exploitation, and deprivation continue to lead many young women to run away from home. Faced with the urgency of getting food and shelter, and possessing little or no money, they are lured into prostitution in an effort to survive. Even if they do not run away, early sexual abuse increases the chances of their becoming prostitutes (Simons and Whitbeck 1991).

Social Psychological Factors.   Although "respectable" people are frequently thought to abhor prostitution, the bulk of the prostitute's clientele are so-called respectable people. Their psychological and social adjustment may be somewhat less than that of others. A study of 1,672 men arrested for trying to hire a street prostitute reported that they, compared to men generally, were less likely to be married, less likely to be happily married if they were married, and more likely to report being generally unhappy (Monto and McRee 2005). But, as the researchers pointed out, the differences tended to be small, suggesting that the customers differed from others by degree rather than by significant amounts.

A study of Chinese men found eight different motivations for using prostitutes (Pochagina 2006). First, some young men with no sexual experience or who have difficulty forming a lasting intimate relationship engage prostitutes. Second, because there are millions more men than women in China, some men gain sexual satisfaction through prostitutes. Third, some men who find it difficult to find sexual satisfaction with a wife or girlfriend use prostitutes. Fourth, others use prostitutes when age, appearance, or psychological makeup make them unable to form a meaningful sexual relationship. Fifth, some men engage prostitutes as a way to bolster their self-esteem. Sixth, others turn to prostitutes when they are required to work away from wives or girlfriends. Seventh, some use prostitutes to reduce tension in their lives. And finally, some are married but are looking for diversity while on a trip or a vacation.

Other social psychological factors that maintain prostitution include the tolerant attitudes of officials and public acceptance of the ideology that male sexuality needs the outlet. With regard to the former, it is often noted that prostitution could not continue if the authorities were determined to eliminate it. Although this is an overstatement, it is true that police seldom make a determined effort to stop all prostitution. Of course, as long as there is a demand for the services of prostitutes, it is unlikely that the police can eliminate the practice even if they wished to do so.

Tolerance about prostitution is partly rooted in the ideology about male sexuality. In Nevada towns where prostitution is legal, law enforcement people favor brothels because "they have fewer complaints of disorderly conduct from the houses than from other establishments which serve alcohol. . . . Brothels are not so much good in and of themselves as they are better than alternative institutions" (Symanski 1974:376). Parents say that prostitution kept their sons from marrying early and their daughters from getting into trouble. The Nevada brothels were credited with decreasing the amount of rape and other violent crime. Implicit in such statements is the ideology that male sexuality, in contrast to female sexuality, must find expression and that traditional values about marriage, the family, and the purity of women are contingent on men's having a sexual outlet. People who accept this ideology will tolerate prostitution.

Public Policy and Private Action

Prostitutes and civil rights activists argue that prostitution should be legalized, or at least decriminalized. To legalize it would make it a legitimate business like any other and would gain the maximum benefits for communities, for law enforcement, and for those involved in the business (Weitzer 2012). Decriminalization, on the other hand, would mean that while people could no longer be prosecuted as criminals, the trade could still be regarded as a misdemeanor subject to fines or as a practice requiring special permits.

There are a number of reasons for advocating legalization. The United States is one of relatively few nations in the world that define prostitution as illegal. In most nations, prostitution is either legal with restrictions (e.g., prostitutes must register and have regular health exams) or legal and regulated (e.g., age limits, no forced prostitution, registration, and regular health exams) (Westerhoff 2009).

In addition, advocates for legalization argue that prostitution should be neither a sin nor a crime. Rather, it falls into the realm of work, choice, and civil rights (Miller and Jayasundara 2001). Women who choose prostitution as their work have their civil rights violated because of existing laws. Moreover, as Weitzer (2007:31) points out, legalized prostitution "can be organized in a way that increases workers' health, safety, and job satisfaction." Indeed, in those Nevada counties where prostitution is legal, prostitutes are able to work without fear of arrest and are better able to protect their health (Brents and Hausbeck 2005). In general, compared to streetwalkers, indoor prostitutes (those who work in such places as bars and brothels or who work as call girls on their own or through an escort service) earn more money, are safer from violence, and are less likely to abuse drugs or to contract a sexually transmitted disease (Weitzer 2007). Nevertheless, the majority of Americans oppose legalization and regulation of prostitution, so it is unlikely that there will be a widespread change in public policy in the near future.

Even decriminalization will not completely solve the problem. If prostitution were decriminalized, there would still need to be regulation of the business (Kuo 2002). One reason for regulation is health. Current efforts to suppress prostitution are based in part on the effort to control the spread of venereal disease (Ness 2003). There is also the issue of the prostitute's own health—regular checkups are needed.

In addition, because of potential abuse from customers, prostitutes may still feel the need for pimps. If the prostitutes work in brothels, thereby avoiding the need for pimps, they will still be treated as objects rather than as people and will confront the various psychological and emotional problems inherent in the life.

The problem can also be attacked by lessening the demand rather than punishing the supply. In many cities the police have begun to arrest johns and even to publish their names. Some states have a First Offender Prostitution Program, which allows men arrested for solicitation to pay a fine and attend a class in which they hear a lecture about the law, watch slides that depict the effects of venereal disease, and listen to ex-prostitutes tell how much they despised their customers. In return, the arrest for soliciting sex is removed from their records. Although such programs may be effective, the fact is that most states and municipalities ignore laws that allow them to arrest pimps, traffickers, and customers and focus instead on the prostitutes themselves (Miller and Jayasundara 2001).

Finally, a good part of the problem of prostitution could be resolved if women from lower socioeconomic positions had opportunities to gain some measure of success in other kinds of work. The problem could also be alleviated if women with drug habits and/or women who come from abusive homes had other ways to support themselves and to get the help they need to deal with their problems.

Follow-Up.   Set up a debate in your class on the question "Should prostitution be decriminalized? Yes or no."

Pornography, Erotica, and Obscenity

One person's pornography is another person's literature. It is no surprise, then, that this subject generates strong feelings and great disagreement. What exactly are we talking about when we speak of pornography and how extensively does it penetrate society?

Nature and Extent of the Problem

What comes to mind when you see or hear the word *pornography?* What, if anything, do you think should be done about materials that you would personally label as pornographic? Read the following materials, then return to these questions and see whether your answers have changed in any way.

Definitions.   People tend to label as pornographic any kind of *sexual materials that they find personally offensive.* Researchers who asked a sample of over 2,000 people to rate 20 different samples from sexual media, found a range of responses from some who saw very little of what they would call pornography to those who labeled even the slightest hint of sexual content as pornographic (Willoughby and Busby 2016). Clearly, the definition of pornography cannot be left to individual tastes. Rather, we need to differentiate between pornography, erotica, and obscenity (Hyde and DeLamater 2007). Generally, social scientists define **pornography** as *literature, art, or films that are sexually arousing.* You can further distinguish between so-called soft-core pornography, which is suggestive but does not depict actual intercourse or genitals, and hard-core pornography, in which sexual acts and/or genitals are explicitly depicted.

Some people are aroused by sexual acts that others would consider degrading, such as forced sex or sex involving children. **Erotica** refers to *sexually arousing materials that are not degrading or demeaning to adults or children.* Erotica, for example, may involve a depiction of a husband and wife engaged in sex play and intercourse. To be sure, some people will find this erotica offensive and degrading. Yet for many, including scholars who research this area, there is an important distinction between erotica and pornography. A woman being raped is pornographic. Two mutually consenting adults engaged in sexual intercourse is erotica, not pornography.

Obscenity is the legal term for pornography that is defined as unacceptable. It refers to those materials that are *offensive by generally accepted standards of decency.* A 1957 Supreme Court decision, *Roth v. the United States,* attempted to establish precise guidelines for deciding when a book, movie, or magazine would be considered obscene (Francoeur 1991): The dominant theme of the material as a whole must appeal to a prurient (lewd) interest in sex; the material must be obviously offensive to existing community standards; and the materials must lack any serious literary, artistic, political, or scientific value. The 1973 *Miller v. California* decision reaffirmed the position that obscenity is not protected by the First Amendment.

However, the decisions did not resolve a number of vexing questions: Who decides what is a prurient interest? What is the "community" whose standards must be followed? Who decides whether something has literary, artistic, political, or scientific value? What about the Internet? Should the government regulate Internet content to protect children from pornographic materials? The struggle between opposing positions continues in both public forums and the courts.

pornography
literature, art, or films that are sexually arousing

erotica
sexually arousing materials that are not degrading or demeaning to adults or children

obscenity
materials that are offensive by generally accepted standards of decency

Extent of the Problem.   Erotica, pornography, and obscenity appear in many places—books, magazines, videos, telephone messages, and the Internet. It's difficult to know just how much is available overall. In one year, however, Americans spent $13.3 billion on X-rated magazines, videos, DVDs, live sex shows, strip clubs, adult cable shows, and computer pornography (Weitzer 2010). In addition, a good deal of pornography is available free in the more than 260 million pages of pornography on the Internet (Paul 2004). A large-scale survey of Internet users found that 75 percent of the men and 41 percent of the women had viewed or downloaded pornographic materials (Albright 2008). And 87 percent of the men and 31 percent of the women in a sample of students from six colleges admitted to using pornography (Carroll et al. 2008). As much as 20 percent of the pornographic Internet pages involve child pornography (Klein, Davies, and Hicks 2001). A study of 1,501 young users of the Internet reported that about one in five had gotten a sexual solicitation, and dozens said they had been asked to meet with or telephone the solicitor, or had received mail, money, or other gifts (Bowker and Gray 2005).

Free or easily accessible pornography on the Internet has led to a dramatic decline in the numbers of pornographic videos and DVDs that Americans rent each year (Richtel 2007). Still, hundreds of millions are rented. Pornographic magazines are also readily available. A study of magazines and videos available in a New York township reported that 25 percent of the magazines and 26.9 percent of the videos contained some kind of sexual violence (Barron and Kimmel 2000).

Moreover, as technology continues to advance, new outlets for pornography appear. The increasing capabilities of cell phones have opened the way for mobile porn (Tanner 2006). Sex magazines like *Playboy* and *Penthouse* now have mobile divisions in their organizations. And an estimated 20 percent of mobile Google searches involve pornography.

Lebeque (1991) reviewed the 3,050 magazine and book titles surveyed in the 1986 Attorney General's Commission on Pornography to see whether the titles themselves fulfilled the criteria for an act of **paraphilia** (the need for a socially unacceptable stimulus in order to be sexually aroused and satisfied). Paraphilia is a disorder listed and described by the American Psychiatric Association. Using their criteria, Lebeque found that 746 (one-fourth of all the titles) fit the definition of paraphilia. **Sadomasochism** is the most common kind of paraphilia. It includes such behavior as being tied up, gagged, whipped, or beaten and using verbal abuse as part of a sexual encounter.

We cannot say exactly how much of this type of material is consumed by Americans. Much child pornography used by **pedophiles** (adults who depend on children for sexual stimulation) is underground. We do know that Americans spend hundreds of millions of dollars every year to buy erotic and pornographic magazines and billions of dollars to rent or buy hundreds of millions of X-rated videos, and that a substantial number subscribe to porn television stations (Schlosser 1997; Paige 1998). Moreover, consumption has increased in recent decades. Comparing the 2000s with the 1970s, a national survey reported a 16 percent increase in consumption among young men and an 8 percent increase among young women (Price et al. 2016).

Like prostitution, pornography is a global problem, not merely an American one. For example, a study of a random sample of Norwegians found that 82 percent of those responding admitted that they had read pornographic magazines (Traeen, Nilsen, and Stigum 2006). A slightly higher proportion, 84 percent, had seen pornographic films, and 34 percent had looked at pornography on the Internet. Significantly more men than women made use of the pornography (this is also true in the United States).

paraphilia
the need for a socially unacceptable stimulus in order to be sexually aroused and satisfied

sadomasochism
the practice of deriving sexual pleasure from the infliction of pain

pedophile
an adult who depends on children for sexual stimulation

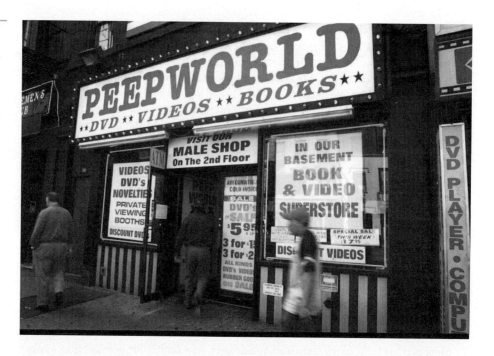

Pornography, Erotica, Obscenity, and the Quality of Life

With most social problems, there is some consensus about the ways in which a particular problem affects the quality of life. Researchers in the area of pornography, erotica, and obscenity, however, proceed from different premises (Francoeur 1991). Some assume that pornographic materials provide people with an outlet for sexual feelings and needs. The materials are like a safety valve, allowing people to reduce sexual tension without harming others. A different premise is that the materials do just the opposite: They offer models of behavior that lead people to act in sexually aggressive and offensive ways that are harmful to others. Thus, researchers, like the general population, are divided in their assumption about and approaches to the problem.

It is our position that pornography and obscenity do have adverse effects on the quality of life, including the quality of relationships. For example, the extensive use of pornography produces negative attitudes about the value of marriage, and wives who discover such use by their husbands struggle with the meaning of their marriage, their own worth and desirability, their sense of security in the relationship, and their satisfaction with lovemaking (Arkowitz and Lilienfeld 2010). The romantic partners and wives of men who consume pornography report lower sexual and relationship quality (Stewart and Szymanski 2012; Poulsen, Busby, and Galovan 2013; Perry 2016). A study of men who watched an X-rated movie in the past year found them more likely to be divorced, more likely to have an extramarital affair, and less likely to be happy (Doran and Price 2014). Young adults who use pornography are more likely to engage in risky sexual behavior and use drugs (Carroll et al. 2008). Women who watch online porn report such things as a lowered body image, partners who are critical of their bodies, and pressure to perform the kinds of acts seen in pornographic films (Albright 2008). Ironically, they also have less actual sex. In fact, there is evidence that pornography has contributed to the rise in various sexual issues of men—erectile dysfunction, delayed ejaculation, decreased sexual satisfaction, and lower sexual desire (Park et al. 2016).

There is also evidence of a relationship between pornography and abusive behavior. Research on rural women in Ohio identified pornography as a major factor in intimate abuse (DeKeseredy and Hall-Sanchez 2016). Another study found that physically abused wives are significantly more likely to be sexually abused when their husbands are into pornography (Shope 2004). There is a higher rate of recidivism among those child molesters who continue to consume pornography (Kingston et al. 2008). Finally, there is evidence that exposure to televised pornography has potential negative effects on children, including the modeling of the behavior; interference with normal sexual development; emotional problems such as anxiety, guilt, confusion, and shame; stimulation of premature sexual activity; and the development of harmful attitudes and beliefs about sex and sexual relationships (Benedek and Brown 1999). Consider a few other consequences.

Exploitation of Children. Although the use of pornography continues to be defended and cast in positive terms by some, on one point most agree—child pornography is exploitation. Films and pictures that depict sexual acts with children clearly victimize the children (Hyde and DeLamater 2007). Because of their developmental level, children are unable to give truly informed consent to engage in such activities. When persuaded or coerced into doing so, they run the risk of severe emotional trauma.

Such exploitation is a contradiction with the value of *a child's right to dignity and protection.* Unfortunately, those who are responsible for protecting children—parents and other adult relatives—are frequently the ones who are the exploiters. When a porn magazine ran an ad for young girl-child models, dozens of parents responded. An 11-year-old girl was accepted and told to have sex with a 40-year-old man. She ran to her mother and said she couldn't do it, but her mother told her she had to do it because they needed the money.

Degradation of Women. American ideology says that all people should be treated with dignity and respect, but much pornography contradicts that ideal. This degradation seems clear in obscenity or pornography that portrays, for example, rape or men urinating on women. Even if there is no violence, however, pornography generally is degrading to women because it depicts them as sex objects whose bodies can be used for male pleasure (Yao, Mahood, and Linz 2010).

Pornography also reinforces certain **stereotypes.** Mayall and Russell (1993) analyzed pornographic magazines, books, films, videos, games, and cards to see how women of various ethnic groups were portrayed. Generally, they found that Asian women were depicted as pliant dolls, Latin women as sexually voracious but also completely submissive, and African American women as dangerous sexual animals.

stereotype
an image of members of a group that standardizes them and exaggerates certain qualities

Degradation also occurs because most pornography and obscenity involve male dominance, female subjection, and, frequently, verbal and physical aggression against the women (Sun et al. 2008). And these characteristics are found in films made by both male and female directors. Even if no aggression is involved, most women are likely to react negatively to the porn because of the dominance-subjection relationship. Thus, when erotic and pornographic slides were shown to a group of female undergraduates, they reacted positively to the erotica (Senn and Radtke 1990) but disliked the pornography and strongly disliked the pornography that included violence. Measures of mood before and after watching the slides showed that the pornography led to significant mood disturbance.

Violence. One of the more controversial aspects of the problem is whether the use of pornographic and obscene materials leads to violent behavior. Some researchers find little or no relationship between the use of pornography and violent behavior (Ferguson and Hartley 2009). Far more, however, find a definite connection. Research supporting

SEXY OR DISGUSTING?

Looking at an erotic picture of a scantily clad young woman, a man responded: "That is the sexiest thing I've ever seen." A woman evaluated the same picture with: "I think it's disgusting." Do men and women always react so differently to erotic materials? Take a survey of a number of students at your school. Enlist the aid of at least one other student of the opposite sex, or make this a class project.

Interviewers should interview a minimum of 10 subjects of their own gender. Ask the following three questions:

1. Do you see any positive value to magazines like *Playboy?* What? (List as many as respondents can think of.)

2. Do you see any negative consequences from such magazines? What? (Again, list as many as possible.)

3. Have you ever looked at, or do you now look at, such magazines? Why or why not?

Analyze your results. What positive values do students see in such materials? What negative consequences? Do men and women differ in their opinions? If so, how? Did nonreaders have very strong opinions? Did nonreaders differ from readers? How? Finally, if the positive values and negative consequences identified by your respondents represented the thinking of all Americans, including researchers, what recommendations would you make about the availability of such materials?

the latter includes the work of Boeringer (1994), who distinguished between different types of pornography in his testing of 477 college men. Those who watched pornography that included violence and rape were more likely to be sexually aggressive. Those who watched soft-core pornography were less likely to approve of or engage in rape, but more likely to use sexual force and other kinds of coercion.

Boeringer's research is consistent with that of others who have found an association between pornography—both the violent and the nonviolent kind—and aggressive attitudes and behavior on the part of both male and female users of the pornography (Shope 2004; Kernsmith and Kernsmith 2009; Hald, Malamuth, and Yuen 2010; Mancini, Reckdenwald, and Beauregard 2012; Foubert and Bridges 2016). In fact, two researchers who gathered data from 100 female victims of sexual violence reported that 28 percent of the victims said the abuser used pornography and 12 percent said that the abuser imitated the pornography during the abusive incident (Bergen and Bogle 2000).

Violent pornography, then, *contradicts our value on human well-being as well as the norm that sexual behavior should be voluntary and not coerced.* Violent pornography affects not only the women who are directly involved. The existence of violent pornography is a threat to all women. Every time a woman sees a store that sells such materials, she is reminded that she is a potential victim.

Contributing Factors

Clearly one of the big factors in maintaining the supply of pornographic and obscene materials is the demand. By the nature of the industry, it is not easy to know who the customers are. An analysis of hundreds of users of Internet pornography reported that the strongest predictors were weak religious ties and an unhappy marriage (Stack, Wasserman, and Kern 2004). Some women are consumers of pornography, but the majority of consumers are men. Social structural and social psychological factors help guarantee a continuing supply of materials for those men.

Social Structural Factors. From an institutional perspective, *the economy and the legal system both work to maintain the supply of materials.* Economically, the porn business is extremely profitable. The profit margin on magazines is high; a store with a brisk business can bring in hundreds of thousands of dollars in gross sales a year. Overall, Americans spend billions of dollars on pornographic materials each year, and a considerable proportion of the money is spent on child pornography (Hyde and DeLamater 2007).

The legal system presents an extremely difficult issue: *Does any effort to suppress materials, to exercise censorship, violate First Amendment rights?* As we noted earlier, a continuing series of court cases following the 1957 case have attempted to define what is obscene. The reason for the ongoing cases is that the battle over pornography and obscenity involves a *conflict of values.* Some people value openness in sexual matters. They believe that the worst thing that could happen would be to pass any laws infringing on the constitutional right of free speech, and they point out some of the extremes to which people go as they try to guard their own version of morality—such as the removal of a copy of Goya's masterpiece *The Nude Maja* from a classroom wall at Pennsylvania State University on the grounds that it made some of the female students uncomfortable (Strossen 1995) or the order of Attorney General John Ashcroft in 2002 to cover the bare breast of the statue *Spirit of Justice* in the Justice Department's Great Hall.

Others contend that society must be responsible and responsive to the needs of people whose quality of life is depressed by the materials. They argue, for instance, that to protect the right of pornographers in the name of free speech is a violation of the more basic right of women to freedom from exploitation and inequality (Leidholdt and Raymond 1990).

Each side tends to use the *fallacies of dramatic instance and personal attack.* For example, those who argue for regulation may cite a newspaper article about sexual violence by someone who read pornographic magazines and call their opponents the destroyers of personal and social morality. Those who stand for openness, on the other hand, may offer Nazi Germany as an example of a repressive society and argue that Americans are heading in the same direction when they suppress materials simply because some people find them offensive. They may call their opponents prudes or narrow-minded people who are willing to sacrifice the basic rights of all Americans to alleviate their own fears.

In essence, *the legal system has helped both sides.* By its ongoing effort to specify what is obscene, the Supreme Court has made the production and distribution of some offensive materials a criminal matter. In the effort to maintain the right of free speech, on the other hand, the courts have allowed the continued production and distribution of materials that women find offensive and degrading, as well as some materials (violent pornography) that increase the aggressiveness of men against women.

Social Psychological Factors. *Americans are divided in their attitudes toward pornographic materials.* They are divided, among other things, along the lines of age and according to whether they are users or nonusers. In the survey of students from six colleges, 67 percent of the young men and 49 percent of the young women agreed that using pornography is acceptable behavior (Carroll et al. 2008). In a national survey of a larger age span, however, 41 percent said that magazines showing adults having sexual relations should be banned from their communities, 48 percent said it is appropriate for stores to remove magazines like *Playboy* and *Penthouse* from their newsstands, and 8 out of 10 Americans want Internet obscenity laws vigorously enforced (Pierce 2002). Perhaps this ambivalence reflects a conflict between the value of personal freedom and a particular ideology of sexual morality. Or perhaps it reflects the more tolerant attitude toward sexual openness among the young. In any case, because a substantial number of Americans have tolerant attitudes about the use of pornography, the supply is likely to remain large and available.

Public Policy and Private Action

A number of steps can be taken to reduce the flow of pornographic materials in general and violent pornography in particular. One is to provide *education at an early age about the ways in which pornography degrades women.* If boys understand how such materials affect females, they may be less prone to consume them.

A second step is the *mobilization of groups to picket, boycott, and protest in other ways the sale of materials they find offensive.* Boycotts against stores that sold materials offensive to people in a community have led to the removal of the materials. Economic pressure may be effective where other attempts at persuasion fall short.

Third, citizens can mobilize to press for *stricter enforcement of existing obscenity laws.* They can urge more stringent regulation or even a ban of porn cable programs and dial-a-porn telephone services. Such efforts, however, will likely be stymied unless people distinguish between erotica, pornography, and obscenity. Efforts at regulation should begin with those materials most clearly offensive—violent pornography.

Fourth, government at all levels can take action, including the passage of legislation. Local governments have engaged in a number of successful campaigns to reduce the amount of pornography in their communities. For example, New York City officials closed down an entire block of businesses in Manhattan, including porn movie houses, bookstores, and strip joints (Kirby 1996). The city helped bring in retail stores and more wholesome forms of entertainment to the area.

Congress enacted laws in the late 1990s to punish people who make obscene materials available to minors via the Internet. The laws ran into problems in the courts because they violated the First Amendment right of free speech. The challenge, therefore, is to enact laws that regulate obscenity without violating the First Amendment. Children, who have access to some of the worst pornography available, need protection. One such law was the 2000 Children's Internet Protection Act that required libraries receiving federal technology funds to install pornography-blocking software on their computers. The American Civil Liberties Union and a number of librarian groups challenged the law as a violation of free speech, but it was upheld by the Supreme Court in 2003.

Clearly, laws are needed that address the problem of pornography without raising allegations of First Amendment violations. Knee (2004) has suggested enacting laws that make illegal the giving or receiving of payment to perform sex acts. Such laws, he argues, would put some of the largest pornographers out of business because they could no longer pay people to perform in hard-core pornographic films.

Fifth, businesses and corporations can help by reducing the supply. Small businesses can refuse to stock and sell pornographic magazines. Video rental chains can refuse to stock and rent pornographic videos and DVDs. And large corporate enterprises such as cable companies can block offensive sites. A number of cable companies have already begun to purge Internet bulletin boards and websites that feature child pornography from their systems (Hakim 2008).

Finally, there is a need for *research on the customers of pornographic materials.* What needs do such materials fulfill? Why and how are they used? Answering such questions will point to ways for reducing the demand. This approach is crucial. For as long as there is demand, there will be a supply—whether legal or not.

Follow-Up.   Apart from legislation, what other effective ways can you think of to protect children from pornography on the Internet?

Summary

Sexual gratification is an important part of American life. Some kinds of sex are considered "deviant" rather than "normal." Deviant sex includes such things as exhibitionism, voyeurism, promiscuity, extramarital affairs, cybersex, and strip clubs. Prostitution and pornography are two additional ways of gaining sexual gratification that deviate from the norm. Both involve contradictions and incompatibility with the desired quality of life, and both are sustained by multilevel factors. At any one time, hundreds of thousands of prostitutes are at work in the nation. The prostitute's quality of life is diminished by physical problems inherent in "the life," as well as by psychological, emotional, and economic problems, including fear, alienation, isolation, and exploitation.

Prostitution is maintained because of (1) norms about nonmarital sex and open discussion of sex; (2) lack of sexual gratification in marriage; and (3) characteristics of the economy, such as jobs that require men to travel and discrimination against women in job opportunities and income. The tolerance of prostitution on the part of both the public and officials is rooted in American ideology about sexuality—the notion that male sexuality, in contrast to female sexuality, must find expression.

It is important to distinguish between pornography, erotica, and obscenity. Such materials are available in multiple forms and are widely consumed in America. Pornographic and obscene materials have a negative impact on the quality of life by exploiting children; degrading women; and in the case of violent pornography, increasing aggressive attitudes and behavior of men toward women.

The materials continue to be widely available for a number of reasons: They are extremely profitable; efforts to suppress them raise the issue of First Amendment rights; and public attitudes are divided, perhaps reflecting concern over censorship.

Key Terms

Cunnilingus	Pimp
Cybersex	Pornography
Erotica	Promiscuity
Fellatio	Prostitution
Obscenity	Sadomasochism
Paraphilia	Sexting
Pedophile	Stereotype

Study Questions

1. What is meant by sexual deviance?
2. Name and explain six kinds of sexual deviance.
3. What problems do prostitutes face?
4. Why do women and men become prostitutes?
5. What factors help maintain prostitution in American society?
6. How would you differentiate between pornography, erotica, and obscenity?
7. How do pornographic and obscene materials affect men? Women? Children?
8. Discuss the factors that contribute to the problem of pornography.

Internet Resources/Exercises

1. Explore some of the ideas in this chapter on the following sites:

http://www.prostitutionresearch.com   Has numerous materials on various aspects of prostitution; sponsored by the San Francisco Women's Centers.

http://www.asacp.org   Home page of the Association of Sites Advocating Child Protection, an organization devoted to eliminating child pornography from the Internet.

http://aclu.org   The American Civil Liberties Union site posts warnings on the abridgment of free speech.

2. Good arguments can be made both against and in defense of prostitution. Use the prostitution and ACLU sites listed above, along with a search engine to find additional materials on prostitution, and construct a list of arguments on both sides of the issue. The results can be used for a class debate.

3. Pornography, including child pornography, is a global problem. Search the Internet for materials that discuss the extent of the problem. Compare what you find with materials in the text on pornography in the United States.

For Further Reading

Albert, Alexa. *Brothel: Mustang Ranch and Its Women.* New York: Random House, 2001. Interviews with prostitutes at a legal house of prostitution in Nevada, telling how they came to be there and how they feel about what they do.

Hall, Ann C., and Mardia J. Bishop, eds. *Pop-Porn: Pornography in American Culture.* New York: Praeger, 2007. An examination of the way in which soft-core porn has spread throughout the culture, including the marketing of sexually arousing women's lingerie and clothing, reality television, and the statements and lifestyles of famous people.

Hardy, Kate, Sarah Kingston, and Teela Sanders, eds. *New Sociologies of Sex Work.* Burlington, VT: Ashgate, 2010. An examination of various facets of prostitution in nations throughout the world, including such topics as public policy, sexual tourism economies, and the organization of sex workers.

Jenkins, Philip. *Beyond Tolerance: Child Pornography Online.* New York: New York University Press, 2001. A study of the men who participate in online pornography that involves adolescent and prepubescent girls; includes the men's justifications for their behavior.

Moran, Rachel. *Paid For: My Journey Through Prostitution.* New York: W.W. Norton & Company, 2015. The experiences of a former prostitute, who left home at age 14 and entered prostitution in order to survive, including the emotional damage the trade caused her.

Raphael, Jody. *Listening to Olivia: Violence, Poverty, and Prostitution.* Boston: Northeastern University Press, 2004. Tells the life story of an American prostitute, from the time she first entered the life until she left it.

Wilson, Gary. *Your Brain on Porn: Internet Pornography and the Emerging Science of Addiction.* Richmond, VA: Commonwealth Publishing, 2015. Combines neuroscience with the experiences of porn consumers to portray the addictive nature of pornography.

chapter 5 review

PART

3

Problems of
Inequality

6 | **Poverty**

7 | **Gender and Sexual
Orientation**

8 | **Race, Ethnic Groups,
and Racism**

©Dynamic Graphics/JupiterImages

The next three chapters address inequalities in the distribution of things that Americans value. These inequalities are so significant that major segments of the population suffer from serious deprivations. We look first at the unequal distribution of wealth in the United States and discuss the problems of the poor in some detail. Then we examine inequalities experienced by three groups in the population: women, the gay/lesbian community, and racial/ethnic minorities.

The people we focus on in this part are largely victims of inequality because of the circumstances of their birth. That is, they did not choose the socioeconomic status of the family into which they were born, or their gender, or their sexual orientation, or their race or ethnicity. And in contrast to the problems discussed in Part 2, in which people were acting in ways that are contrary to and disapproved of by the vast majority of Americans, those who cope with the problems discussed in this part are more likely to face inequitable treatment by a society whose norms and values they affirm and strive to follow.

CHAPTER

6

Poverty

OBJECTIVES

1 Define and discuss the extent of poverty in the United States.

2 Identify the people most likely to be poor.

3 Show how poverty affects basic human rights and needs.

4 Discuss the way in which social institutions contribute to the problem of poverty.

5 Explain how both the attitudes toward the poor and the attitudes of the poor contribute to the perpetuation of poverty.

Source: USDA

Marlene is in her late 30s, married, the mother of two, and poor. Poverty is something new in her life. For some years, her married life resembled the middle-class home in which she was raised. Then an accident forced her to go on long-term disability leave, her husband's business failed, and for the past three years they have lived deep in poverty. Savings, credit, friends, and relatives helped for a while, but now they have reached "the year I lost 25 pounds without even trying":

We've hit bottom. We have no insurance. We are continually harassed by collection agents. They tell us we're deadbeats. Actually we feel like deadbeats. The first time I really got angry was a few months ago when I saw a guy with a toy attached to his car window. I knew that toy cost around $15, and I could feel the anger rising in me as I thought about how much food I could buy with $15.

I thought about my kids, who now are getting used to strange combinations of vegetables and rice or noodles, and how much they would enjoy the meal I could buy. And all of a sudden I was enraged at someone I didn't even know for spending so much money on a joke. Then it made me mad that $15 seemed like so much money. Then it made me mad that I had gotten mad.

I started watching the expensive cars go by when I was walking or taking a bus. It's like they were advertising the fact that they made it and I haven't. I've never had that kind of car, but it bothered me that other people did. Suddenly I began to take their arrogance personally. And when I read about a guy paying

$20,000 for a watch, I wondered if he was part of the human race. How could he do that when there were hungry kids living just a few miles away?

I've gotten to the point where I see that without money, a person just doesn't matter. I thought I was a pretty knowledgeable person, but I had no idea of the violent, demoralizing effect of poverty. I had no idea how it would feel to have no food in the house, no gas to drive to buy food, no money to buy gas, and no prospect of money. My husband and I believe we'll pull out of this. But I have a dread in my bones that the worst is not over yet, and that even when it is over, it will never be altogether in the past for any of us.

Introduction

A wealthy car dealer who was elected to Congress sought to lower taxes on the rich and retain tax breaks for corporations, and he questioned the value of unemployment checks for workers who lost their jobs (Whoriskey 2011). He explained his own wealth as the result of working hard all his life. No doubt the man did work hard. But he didn't mention all his initial advantages: the fact that his father had owned a car dealership, that he had attended an elite university, and that a few years after graduation he married an heiress to an oil fortune.

He sees himself as an example of the fulfillment of the American dream. But his attitudes about wealth and poverty are part of an American myth: that through persistent hard work anyone can succeed. The pursuit of the American dream is far more complex than the simple faith in persistent hard work suggests. In this chapter we examine that segment of the population for whom the American dream has been elusive and see how the difficulties of the poor are related to the behavior of the nonpoor. To understand why the poor are poor, it is important to understand why the rich are rich.

We discuss what is meant by poverty, identify who the poor are and how many there are, and examine how poverty affects the quality of life. After we identify the structural and social psychological factors that contribute to poverty, we consider what has been done and what might be done to address the problem.

What Is Poverty?

Poverty in the United States is old and new. It is old in the sense that it has always existed, and it is new in the sense that it was not *commonly defined* as a problem until more recently. As late as the 1950s, economists assumed that, economically, Americans were consistently improving. They were producing more and incomes were increasing. The question about poverty was not *whether* but *when* it would be eliminated. Although sociologists have always identified poverty as a problem, the Gallup poll showed that not until 1965 did the public begin to identify it as one of America's serious problems (Lauer 1976). An influential factor in creating an awareness of the problem was a book by Michael Harrington (1962), *The Other America*. Harrington portrayed the plight of millions of impoverished people in affluent America.

What, exactly, is poverty? **Poverty** is a state in which income is insufficient to provide basic necessities such as food, shelter, medical care, and clothing. *Absolute poverty* means that the insufficiency is so severe that it is life-threatening. *Relative poverty* means that the insufficiency is substantially greater than that of most others in the society.

Why did Americans generally fail to identify poverty as a social problem until the 1960s? One reason is that the poor were largely invisible to many Americans. Another reason is many people failed to make the distinction between absolute and relative poverty; they insisted that even the lowest-income groups in America were not really poor because they fared better than the starving people in other countries.

To be sure, many of America's poor have more food, more clothing, better shelter, and so on than the poor in other nations; but the standard for evaluating America's poor cannot be the starving people in other nations. Rather, poverty in the United States must be evaluated in terms of the *standard of living* attained by the majority of Americans. To tell a poor American whose family suffers from malnutrition that people in other nations are starving to death is not consoling, particularly when the poor person knows that millions of Americans throw away more food every day than that person's family consumes.

In discussing poverty in the United States, then, we are talking about people who are better off than some others in the world but who have much less than most Americans. But less of what? And how much less? The federal government answers these questions in terms of *income*. In the 1960s, the Department of Agriculture developed an "economy food plan" for temporary or emergency use when a family's financial resources were minimal. At the time, the poor spent an estimated one-third of their total budget on food. The government, therefore, simply multiplied the cost of the economy food plan by 3 and came up with the dividing line between "poor" and "nonpoor." In 1964, that meant a family of four with an income below $3,000 per year was officially classified as at the **poverty level.** By 2016, a family of four (two adults and two children) with an annual income less than $24,339 was officially poor.

This method of defining poverty is considered woefully inadequate by many social scientists. For one thing, it ignores the cost-of-living differences between various areas. For another, it puts millions of Americans above the poverty level even though they cannot afford what most of us would regard as a minimal standard of living.

Finally, the official poverty level uses a nutritionally inadequate food plan as a primary criterion, bases any increases on the **consumer price index,** and maintains the ratio of food to nonfood costs at one-third. But Americans now spend an average of about an eighth of their income on food (U.S. Census Bureau 2012). The relative costs of other items, such as housing, have increased considerably since the 1960s. Thus, you could argue that the poverty level should be eight times the cost of food, which would raise substantially the proportion of Americans who are poor.

Because of the clear inadequacies of the existing definition, the Census Bureau released a new Supplemental Poverty Measure in 2011 (Aguilera 2011). This measure takes into account such factors as regional differences in the cost of living, child care expenses for working parents, and government benefits such as food stamps. The Supplemental Poverty Measure changes the proportion of the poor in various groups (such as age groups, racial/ethnic groups), raising the rates in some groups and lowering them in others. But it tends to increase somewhat the rate for the nation as a whole.

For example, an analysis of the 2013 numbers found that the Supplemental rate was 0.9 percent higher than the official rate (Short 2014). But the Supplemental rate for those under 18 was lower than the official rate for that group, It was also lower for

poverty
a state in which income is insufficient to provide the basic necessities of food, shelter, clothing, and medical care

poverty level
the minimum income level that Americans should have to live on, based on the Department of Agriculture's calculations of the cost of a basic diet called "the economy food plan"

consumer price index
a measure of the average change in prices of all types of consumer goods and services purchased by urban wage earners and clerical workers

African Americans than was the official rate. For other groups, the Supplemental rate increased the proportion who were poor.

Many scholars would argue that even the Supplemental Poverty Measure underestimates the number of people who should be considered poor. For whether the official or the new measure is used, the definition *excludes many people who define themselves, and whom most of you would define, as poor.* It isn't known yet whether the Supplemental Poverty Measure will replace the official measure, but as of this writing government and scholarly writings use the official measure, so that is what we shall use in the remainder of this chapter.

Consider now three questions concerning the *extent of poverty* in the United States: How many poor are there? Who are the poor? Are the majority of the poor better off or worse off now than they were in the past?

Extent of Poverty

The proportion of Americans officially defined as poor has fluctuated over time. The rate declined substantially from 1960 through the 1970s, then rose again and has fluctuated ever since (Figure 6.1). By 2015, 43.1 million Americans were officially in poverty, representing 13.5 percent of the population. These figures are higher than they were during the War on Poverty in the 1960s and 1970s. In fact, the United States has one of the highest rates of poverty among the rich industrial nations of the world.

A caution—one dealt with in the previous section—is that the official figures minimize the number of poor. Many of you would probably consider yourselves poor if your income were just above the official poverty level. The Census Bureau defines "near" poverty as between 100 and 125 percent of the poverty threshold (Hokayem and

FIGURE 6.1   The Number and Proportion of the Poor, 1970–2015.

Source: Proctor, Semega, and Kollar 2016.

Heggeness 2014). People in that range will likely have an ongoing struggle with making ends meet and satisfying their basic needs. In 2012, there were nearly 15 million Americans living in "near" poverty.

One other caution: most of those in poverty are an ever-changing group. That is, there are people who are not now poor but will be and people who are not now poor but have been. In other words, there is always movement into and out of poverty, so the number of poor at any given time does not reveal the total number of people who will be affected by the problem during their lifetime. For example, during the 4-year period from 2009 to 2012, 34.5 percent of the population had at least one period of poverty that lasted two or more months (Proctor, Semega, and Kollar 2016). Only 2.7 percent of Americans lived in poverty for the entire 48 months. Such figures indicate that poverty will be a part of the experience of a majority of Americans at some point in their lives.

Who Are the Poor?

Wealth and poverty are *not distributed equally* among various social groups. Most Americans are neither wealthy nor impoverished, but the chances of being in one of these categories are greater for certain social groups. For example, the probability of being poor is greater for families headed by a female, for racial and ethnic minorities, and for those under 18 years of age (see Figure 6.2). Single-parent families headed by mothers are the most impoverished group in the nation. One survey of single mothers found that most had at least a high school education, were in their mid-thirties, and had an average of two children (National Coalition for the Homeless 2000).

Among those racial/ethnic minorities for whom the Census Bureau regularly collects and publishes data, African Americans have the highest poverty rate (24.1 percent). If we

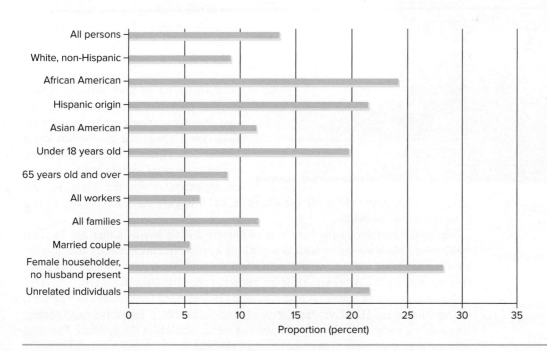

FIGURE 6.2 Proportion of Poverty for Different Kinds of People.

Source: Proctor, Semega, and Kollar 2016.

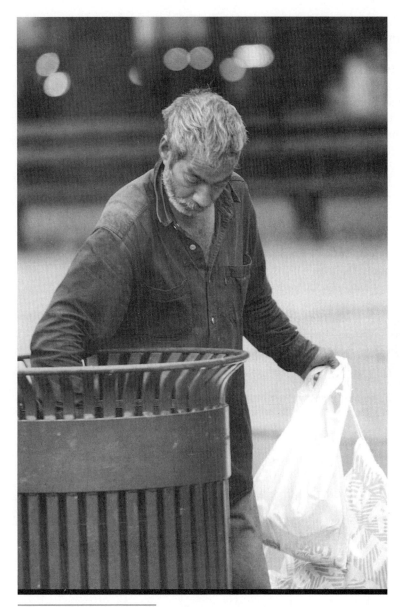

A homeless person digs through garbage in an attempt to survive.

©McGraw-Hill Education./Gary He, photographer

ghetto
an area in which a certain group is segregated from the rest of society; often used today to refer to the impoverished area of the inner city

look at absolute numbers rather than rates, the racial/ethnic group with the largest number of poor is non-Hispanic whites (because the white population is so much larger than that of other races). In 2015, for example, the numbers (and rates) of poverty were: non-Hispanic whites, 17.8 million (9.1 percent); African Americans, 10.0 million (24.1 percent); Asian Americans, 2.1 million (11.4 percent); Hispanics, 12.1 million (21.4 percent) (Proctor, Semega, and Kollar 2016).

Note that above we pointed out that African Americans have the highest poverty rate of any racial/ethnic minority for whom the Census Bureau regularly collects and publishes data. Not included in the annual tables are American Indians. A Facts for Features on the Census Bureau (2015) website, however, notes that the 5.4 million American Indians in 2014 had the highest poverty rate of any racial/ethnic group: 28.3 percent. American Indians have been the most impoverished group in any year for which we have data. Even the proliferation of tribal casinos has not sufficed to dramatically improve their lot (Davis, Roscigno, and Wilson 2016).

In short, the *number* of poor whites is substantially higher than the number of poor Hispanics or poor African Americans or poor Native Americans, but the *rate of poverty* among whites is substantially lower than that among the other groups (see Figure 6.2). These data are the basis for what sounds like a paradoxical statement: If you are white, you are less likely to be poor than if you are nonwhite, but if you are poor, you are more likely to be white than nonwhite.

Figure 6.2 also shows the high rate of poverty among youths under age 18. This *high rate of poverty among children* is something new in American history, and it is the highest rate among the industrial countries of the world (Duncan and Magnuson 2011). One out of every five American children below the age of 18 lives in poverty.

Finally, the rate of poverty is higher outside (16.5 percent) than inside (14.9 percent) metropolitan areas (DeNavas-Walt, Proctor, and Smith 2011). Extensive rural poverty is one reason many Americans are unaware of the seriousness of the problem. The rural poor are even less visible than those in urban **ghettoes.**

Although people move into and out of poverty, there is also a core of people who remain in poverty, an underclass that experiences unemployment, substandard housing, chronic hunger, and **malnutrition** (Hoefer and Curry 2012). Insufficient food increases depression and suicide attempts and it inhibits cognitive and psychological development (Alaimo, Olson, and Frongillo 2001, 2002). The underclass is only a minority of the poor, but it presents the nation with poverty's most serious challenge—how to deal with those who seem caught in the throes of poverty on a more or less permanent basis.

The Working Poor.   An additional fact about the identity of the poor is important. Contrary to popular opinion, people are not poor simply because of their *unwillingness to work*. A good many of the poor do not work, to be sure, but they include people who can't find a job, the disabled, the elderly, and single parents who would have to pay more for child care than they would earn in the jobs available to them. Many of those who are not working both want, and intend, to find a job at some point that will enable them to support themselves and their families. As a young single mother told us:

> I know the stereotype of a welfare mother. Well, that's not me. I don't sit around watching TV. I work 40 hours a week, go to college at night, and have worked and paid taxes since I was a teenager. I don't intend to be on welfare all my life, but I just don't have a choice right now.

Who are those Americans who are working but still poor? The Bureau of Labor Statistics (2016b) identifies the working poor as individuals who spend at least 27 weeks in the labor force during the year (working or looking for work) but whose incomes are still so low that they are in poverty. In 2014, there were 9.5 million such people, a substantial number of whom worked full-time. The working poor comprised more women (5.1 million) than men (4.4 million). African Americans and Hispanics were more than twice as likely as whites and Asians to be among the working poor. Finally, the working poor tended to have less education than the nonpoor and were more likely than other workers to be in a service occupation.

Even though they work, therefore, millions of Americans suffer all the usual consequences of poverty. For example, two-thirds of low-income Americans find it hard to pay for the food they need (Jacobe 2008). In some cases, they may forgo certain food purchases to pay for other necessities; the combination of work income and government assistance is insufficient for their needs, and they must make frequent trips to free food distribution organizations (Berner, Ozer, and Paynter 2008).

The Homeless.   The homeless are those who live in their cars or on the streets because they cannot afford any kind of housing. The very lack of a stable, identifiable residence makes it difficult to know exactly how many Americans are homeless. The National Alliance to End Homelessness (2016) estimates that there were 564,708 homeless people in 2015. This represents a decline from previous years. And most of the homeless stay in a shelter or in transitional housing; only a third are on the street or in abandoned buildings. A majority of the homeless are individuals, but 37 percent were families and 6.5 percent were youth or children on their own.

The chronically homeless will die on the streets. Those who are not chronically homeless may spend anywhere from months to a few years on the street. Those who are homeless for a shorter period of time are likely to be younger, earn income, have family support, and lack a history of arrest or addiction (Caton et al. 2005).

Many homeless women are on the streets because they fled from domestic violence. One study concluded that one out of four homeless women left her home because of the abuse she suffered (Jasinski et al. 2010). These women decided that living on the streets would be preferable to the ongoing violence in their homes. Tragically, many find that their lives on the streets offer no more safety from violence than did their lives in homes. A survey of homeless young people in Columbus, Ohio, reported that among

malnutrition
inadequate food, in amount or type

those who were in an intimate relationship, about a third experienced verbal and/or physical abuse (Siesnick et al. 2010).

High rates of mental illness and addictions exist among the homeless (National Coalition for the Homeless 2009). At least a fourth of the homeless struggle with some kind of serious mental illness: as many as 4 out of 10 homeless adults are addicted to alcohol, and a fourth or more have problems with other kinds of drugs. The homeless are also vulnerable to being victimized by hate crimes (National Coalition for the Homeless 2016). A number of homeless people are beaten or even killed each year. Most victims and perpetrators are male.

People are not homeless, then, simply because they prefer the streets to gainful employment. Some, like the children and the mentally ill, cannot support themselves. Others are victims of the economy. Home and rental costs have soared in recent decades. Millions of Americans now spend half or more of their income on housing. This means that the homeless, who often work for minimum or near-minimum wages, can't get any kind of housing even if they could spend half their income on it. People who work for the federal minimum wage would need two or three times that much just to rent a home in an urban area. Some states have minimum wage requirements higher than the federal level, but none are sufficient to cover housing costs. Thus, families throughout the nation are at risk of homelessness if they are supported by a single, low-wage worker. Any kind of unexpected, additional financial burden can result in eviction from rental property or the loss of a home (Desmond and Kimbro 2015; West and Mottola 2016).

The Changing Nature of Poverty

How has the lot of the poor changed over time in the United States? Certainly the proportion of Americans who are poor is lower than it was in the past—but are those who are poor now in better or worse condition than the poor of other generations? Although we have no systematic evidence on the question, it seems reasonable that poverty is more difficult when the proportion becomes smaller. It is one thing to be poor when the majority of people, or even a substantial minority, share your poverty. It is another thing to be poor when most people are living comfortably or in affluence.

Still, if the poor were making gains relative to the rich, poverty might be less stressful than in the past. Unfortunately, they are not. Table 6.1 shows the percentage of income received by people in various income brackets. In 2015, for example, those at the top 20 percent got 51.1 percent of the income, which is two and a half times the amount they would have gotten if there had been perfect equality (no "top" or "bottom"). Moreover, their share of the total income has increased since 1970. Note, in contrast, what has happened to the bottom 40 percent. Their share of income has dropped substantially. In other words, the poor have lost ground relative to the rest of the population for nearly four decades.

TABLE 6.1

Distribution of Money Income of Households, Ranked According to Income Received, 1929–2015 (percent of aggregate income)

	1929	1941	1950	1960	1970	1980	1990	2000	2015
Lowest 40%	12.5	13.6	16.4	17.0	17.6	16.7	15.4	14.1	11,3
Next 40%	33.1	37.6	40.8	41.8	41.4	41.8	40.4	38.3	37.5
Highest 20%	54.4	48.8	42.8	41.3	40.9	41.6	44.3	47.4	51.1
Top 5%	30.0	24.0	17.3	15.9	15.6	15.3	17.4	20.8	22.1

SOURCES: U.S. Census Bureau 1961, 1976, 2012; Proctor, Semega, and Kollar 2016.

Although, as Table 6.1 shows, the richest are getting a smaller proportion of income than they did before World War II, it is important to keep in mind that money income is only a part of the wealth of the rich, and for many it is not the most important part. Net wealth is all assets minus all liabilities. Assets include real estate, savings and checking accounts, investments, and retirement accounts. Liabilities include all indebtedness—mortgages, unpaid loans and bills, and so forth. Consider the following facts about the distribution of, and changes in, wealth (Allegretto 2011):

- The wealthiest 1 percent of Americans hold more than one-third of all the wealth.
- The bottom 80 percent of Americans have only 12.8 percent of all the wealth.
- Since 1962, the bottom 80 percent's share of wealth has decreased from 19.1 percent to 12.8 percent.
- In 2009, the bottom 20 percent had negative net worth; that is, owed more than they owned.
- Although the United States is one of the wealthiest nations in the world, the gap between the rich and the poor is greater than in any other industrial nation.

We should also note that the rich fare better than others both in a good economy and in a recession. During the severe recession from 2007 to 2009, the share of wealth of the top 20 percent increased by 2.2 percent, whereas that of the bottom 80 percent decreased by 2.2 percent.

In sum, in terms of income there has been a redistribution, but it has not benefitted the poor. Rather, the middle- and upper-middle groups are the beneficiaries of income redistribution. Since the late 1960s, the upper 20 percent have made gains in both income and total wealth at the expense of the lower 80 percent. Much of this gain is due to good luck rather than hard work, for "the majority of new wealth arises from short-term speculative investments, such as hedge funds" (Anderson 2009:72). The result is a dramatic accumulation and concentration of wealth at the top. Since 1980, there are hundreds of new billionaires and millions of new millionaires. And the pay for CEOs has jumped from roughly 30 to 40 times that of the average worker in past years to 331 times that of the average worker in 2015 (AFL-CIO 2016). When you try, therefore, to assess the meaning of poverty in the United States, you must recognize that although the proportion of the poor is less than it was in the twentieth century, the lot of the poor is worse when compared with the rest of society. Americans who are poor today may have more possessions than the poor of 1920, but they are worse off relative to others in the society than were their counterparts in 1920.

Poverty and the Quality of Life

Some sense of the trauma of living in poverty, even if you assume that it is only a temporary state, may be seen in the account of Marlene (see "We Feel Like Deadbeats," at the beginning of the chapter). In essence, the trauma arises from the fact that the poor get less of everything considered important and necessary for a decent life (less money, food, clothing, and shelter). The *deprivation of the poor is pervasive* (Corcoran 2000; Samaan 2000; Rank 2001). Compared to infants of the nonpoor, infants of the poor are more likely to die. Their children are more likely to fail in school even when they are intelligent. Their children are more likely to drop out of school. They are more likely to become mentally ill. They are more likely to lose their jobs and to drop out of the labor force. They are more likely to experience hostility and distrust rather than neighborliness with those around them. They are less likely to participate in meaningful groups and associations. They are more likely to get chronic illnesses. In the face of more health problems, they are less likely to own health insurance (a problem only partly relieved by Medicaid). In the ultimate deprivation, they are likely to die at a younger age. Thus, poverty diminishes the quality of a person's life in many ways.

The Right to Life and Happiness

The position of the poor in the economy contradicts the American value of the right to life and the pursuit of happiness. The inadequacy of their financial resources deprives the poor of freedom to pursue a full and happy life. Some people argue that lack of money should not be equated with lack of happiness, that many of the poor are carefree, spontaneous, and even better off without the worries that accompany possession of money. It's generally only people with money who use this argument. There is, in fact, a positive correlation between income and *perceived happiness.* Surveys of attitudes both in the United States and in 55 other nations show that the proportion of people who describe themselves as very happy is lower among those in the lower-income than those in the middle- and upper-income groups (Pew Research Center 2006; Ball and Chernova 2008; Alderson and Katz-Cerro 2016). Poverty brings *more despair than happiness and more fear than fullness of life.*

Discontent and Despair.   When deprivation was widespread during the Great Depression of the 1930s, unrest was also widespread. People marched and demonstrated, demanding food and expressing a willingness to fight rather than starve. In a 1932 Chicago demonstration there were "no bands" and "no quickstep," only "rank after rank of sodden men, their worn coat collars turned up, their caps . . . pulled down to give as much protection as possible" as they marched in driving rain (Hutchinson 1962:274).

The multitude of problems and frustrations of poverty—crowded, dilapidated housing in crime-ridden neighborhoods; inadequate health care; constant financial strain; poor-quality and inadequate food; lack of opportunities for betterment; and so on—are so overwhelming that the impoverished individual may suffer from chronic depression. Low-income mothers, for example, are likely to be depressed, which adversely affects the development of their children (Petterson and Albers 2001). The children are stressed not only by the negative emotions of their parents, but by high rates of family turmoil and disruption, violence, and the lack of order and routine in their lives (Evans, Brooks-Gunn, and Klebanov 2011).

Despair is not the lot of all the poor, but it is much more frequent among the poor than among the nonpoor. When the despair comes, it can be devastating, and it can strike even the young. Consider Elaine, a teenager whose mother is a chronic alcoholic. Elaine lives in poverty with her grandmother in an urban apartment. She watches television 10 or more hours a day, even though the television only increases her depression because it continually reminds her of how much she lacks. Despite her superior intelligence, Elaine has always felt extremely ashamed in school:

> "If I only had some clothes." Today Elaine . . . [is] dressed in neatly ironed jeans that are badly frayed at the cuffs and worn thin. On top she wears a stained cheerleader's sweater, out in one elbow, which she has had since she was thirteen. Despite its holes and stains, Elaine wears the sweater every day. It reminds her, she says, of a time when she was happy. (Williams and Kornblum 1985:8)

POVERTY IN THE WORLD SYSTEM

Gross inequalities exist not only within most nations but also between the nations of the world. There are various ways in which we could characterize the inequalities: average family income, average life span, expenditures for health care or education, and so on. Figure 6.3 shows one measure—the gross national income per capita. Keep in mind that a high figure does not mean that everyone in the society is rich, nor does a low figure mean that everyone is poor. Every society has inequality. And the extent of the inequality, as measured by the gap in income between the richest 10 percent and the poorest 10 percent, has increased in recent decades.

As Figure 6.3 illustrates, the inequality between nations is as dramatic as the inequality within nations. Switzerland's national income of $65,430 per capita is 198 times higher than the $330 figure for Ethiopia. People in richer nations have seven or more times as many physicians per 1,000 population as those in poorer nations. The infant mortality rates in the poorer nations range from 5 to 30 times higher than those in the richer nations. More than a billion people suffer from hunger and malnutrition in the poorer nations, and the life expectancy of people in the richer nations is generally 15 to 20 years higher than in the poorer nations. A child born in the United States in 2010 could expect to live to age 78; a child born in Afghanistan, Angola, or Mozambique could expect to live less than 45 years.

In other words, the people of poorer nations suffer the kinds of deprivations that afflict the very poorest people in the United States. The number of the poor throughout the world is staggering. Of the world's 6.7 billion people, more than 1 billion live on $1 a day or less, particularly in South Asia and sub-Saharan Africa. Those who earn $2 a day or more are in the top half of the income distribution! And the disparity between the rich and the poor nations is increasing. The richest 10 percent of people in the world now get over half of all the income, whereas the poorest 50 percent get less than 10 percent. Even though many of the poor live in agricultural societies, hundreds of millions have inadequate shelter, food, and medical care. They lack safe drinking water and educational opportunities for their children. And millions die every year simply because they are too poor to survive.

SOURCES:
Lauer 1991; Gardner and Halweil 2000; Bowles, Durlauf, and Hoff 2006; U.S. Census Bureau 2012.

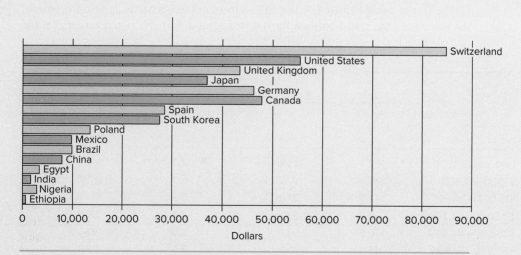

FIGURE 6.3 Gross National Income Per Capita for Selected Countries.
SOURCE: World Bank website, 2016.

The despair that always threatens to overcome the poor is manifested in what Rainwater (1967) called *survival strategies*—ways of living that enable the poor to adapt to their "punishing and depriving milieu." The *expressive strategy* involves manipulating others and making oneself appealing through means such as bettering someone in a rap session, gaining the affection of a female, wearing dramatic clothes, or winning a gambling bet. The *violent strategy* involves actions such as fighting, shoplifting, or making threats. It is a dangerous strategy for everyone, and not many of the poor adopt it. The *depressive strategy*, which involves withdrawal and isolation, characterizes a great number of the poor as they grow older. An individual may alternate among the strategies as he or she grows older, but all three strategies have the same purpose—to enable the individual to cope with a punitive situation. As such, they dramatize the despair that always hovers near the poor.

Freedom from Fear.   We mentioned in Chapter 5 that freedom from fear is a condition of the right to life and the pursuit of happiness. The poor live in a *capricious world*. The chronic uncertainty of their lives means they have much to fear. We discuss this topic further under the subheading "Dilemmas of Poverty" later in this chapter. Here we look at two kinds of fear that affect the poor more than others—the *fear of being the victim of a crime* and the *fear of being harassed by law enforcement officers*.

As Table 6.2 shows, the poor are more likely than other people to be victims of crime. The table shows rates for property crimes, but the poor are also more victimized more than others by violent crime (Harrell and Langton 2014). In fact, their rates of victimization by such crimes as assault, rape, and robbery are twice as high as the rates for those in high-income households. The poor are, of course, aware of the high crime rates in the areas where they live, and so they typically express a greater fear of walking alone at night than do the well-to-do.

The fear of being harassed by law enforcement officers is particularly a problem for the homeless (National Coalition for the Homeless 2006). We noted earlier that the

| Household Income Level | Victimizations per 1,000 Households | | | |
	Total	Burglary	Auto Theft	Theft
Less than $7,500	168.7	44.4	4.0	120.4
$7500—14,999	170.4	47.2	5.9	117.3
$15,000—24,999	144.9	32.8	8.3	103.7
$25,000—34,999	133.9	27.1	7.4	99.4
$35,000—49,999	120.5	21.6	5.9	93.1
$50,000—74,999	115.4	19.1	5.9	90.4
$75,000 or more	119.3	16.7	5.1	97.5

TABLE 6.2

Property Crime Victimizations, by Income

SOURCE: U.S. Department of Justice 2011.

number of homeless has been growing, and the number of shelter beds available for them is inadequate. Faced with the growing numbers, many cities have now criminalized the problem of the homeless by prohibiting such things as sleeping, camping, eating, sitting, or begging in public places and using the ordinances to punish the homeless. Some cities even use laws against loitering or having open containers against the homeless. Finally, there have been sweeps of areas where the homeless live. The homeless are driven out and their personal property may be destroyed.

The Right to Dignity as a Human Being

For the poor, the *right to dignity as human beings* is violated by the *contradiction between the American ideal of the worth of every individual and the pattern of interaction between the poor and the nonpoor.* At best, the poor tend to be treated paternalistically. At worst, they tend to be subjected to contempt and rejection, and blamed for their plight (Cozzarelli, Wilkinson, and Tagler 2001). The loss of dignity is manifested in a number of myths about the poor, myths that employ the *fallacy of personal attack* to discredit the poor and legitimate an unwillingness to support programs to help them.

fallacy

"The poor are lazy."   It's a myth that the poor are lazy; they are willing to work, and in fact, most male heads of poor families do work. To say that the poor are lazy justifies the nonpoor's contempt and disavowal of personal or societal responsibility for dealing with poverty. No evidence supports the myth, but it is still prevalent, and it robs the poor of human dignity.

"People on welfare have it good."   The expressive style of coping may have helped create the myth that people on welfare often live at higher standards than do people who work. A few "con artists" may manage to get a substantial living by *welfare fraud,* but the majority of people on welfare (and the majority of the poor in general) live in circumstances that would be repugnant to most Americans. What dignity is there, for instance, in not being able to buy adequate food for your children, or in living in a rat-infested apartment, or in huddling inside your apartment at night in fear of thieves and drug addicts?

And what kind of dignity is there in trying to survive on welfare payments that may mean an income far below the poverty level? Many nonpoor Americans have a distorted notion of how much help people receive from welfare. Actually, as one analysis put it (Johnson 2014), welfare recipients receive only the "barest minimum amount," an amount that enables them to do little more than survive. For example, the analyst pointed out, the Supplemental Nutrition Assistance Program (previously known as food stamps), gave an average benefit per person of $1.50 per meal! One could hardly say that people receiving such help "have it good."

"Welfare is draining us."   One myth by which the poor are humiliated is that they are social leeches. This myth asserts that the cost of maintaining the poor is depriving the nonpoor by raising taxes and reducing the standard of living. As we noted, however, the poor receive a lower share of national income now than they did in the early twentieth century. Historically, welfare payments have done little to reduce the inequity, and the standard of living for middle- and upper-class Americans is higher than ever. A large number of Americans now possess two or more automobiles and television sets, items that were luxuries in the not-too-distant past.

The poor, especially the homeless, lose their dignity as human beings.
©McGraw-Hill Education./Gary He, photographer

"Welfare turns people into lazy, dependent deadbeats."   "Welfare bums" is the term used by some Americans to show their contempt for people who rely on welfare rather than on their own earnings. Even with the change to "workfare" (discussed later in this chapter), people who receive government aid may still be regarded as lazy and unmotivated, preferring a "free ride" at the expense of Americans who work (Seccombe, Walters, and James 1999).

This myth ignores certain important facts. First, most of the people on welfare are not able-bodied workers. Well over half of welfare recipients are children, the aged, the disabled, or mothers of small children (some of whom work).

Second, as shown by a number of studies, the able-bodied workers generally prefer to work rather than to be on welfare. In-depth interviews with 47 recipients of Temporary Assistance to Needy Families (TANF), previously Aid to Families with Dependent Children (AFDC), found that the recipients were eager for welfare reform and were supportive of work requirements (Seccombe et al. 1999).

Third, there is very little long-term dependency among welfare recipients. In fact, as we pointed out earlier, there is a *good deal of movement in and out of poverty.* Only one of four children who spend most of their growing-up years in poverty is still poor at age 25 to 29 (Corcoran 2000).

Poverty and Health

The circumstances under which the poor are required to live cause higher rates of mental and physical illness among the poor than among the rest of the population (Jackson and Mustillo 2001; Chen, Matthews, and Boyce 2002). The *homeless are particularly prone to ill health.* A substantial proportion of the homeless suffer from various physical ailments, hunger, malnutrition, drug addiction, and mental illness (Stratigos and Katsambas 2003; Lee and Greif 2008). It isn't clear, however, whether addiction and mental illness are the *causes* or the *result* of homelessness (Wasserman and Clair 2010).

FROM RICHES TO RAGS

In a now-famous experiment, a reporter had his skin darkened and his hair shaved close, and then he began traveling through four southern states to see what it was like to be a black man. It was a revelation to him. Some nights, he reported, he was so upset by the way people treated him that he cried himself to sleep.

There are times when the only way to understand what a social problem means for the victims is to "walk a mile in their shoes." This project will involve you in a personal experience of poverty, but you will find it easier to do if you work with someone else.

First, try to live for two weeks on a poverty-level food budget. In the latest figures from the U.S. Census Bureau, find the current poverty-level income threshold. (Remember, this is the most you can have to be classified as living in poverty.) Use the figure given for a nonfarm family of two, and divide it by three to get a yearly food budget comparable to the way the poverty level was originally defined. Divide that figure by 26 to get the two-week budget. For example, in 2015 the poverty level for two people under the age of 65 was $15,871—about $5,290.33 for food. For the two weeks of the experiment, that amounts to $203.47 for food for you and your partner.

As a second part of your experiment, dress in some shabby clothing. Try to achieve a poor though clean look. Then, go to a public place and ask directions. Also go into a department store and ask for help in finding some relatively expensive clothes.

Record your experiences. Describe in detail your experiences and feelings about grocery shopping, cooking, and eating on a poverty budget. Discuss the reactions you received when asking for directions and when seeking to look at some expensive clothing. Compare the way people related to you with the way you normally experience relationships.

The problem of poverty has received less attention from the mass media in subsequent decades than it did in the 1960s. As a final part of your project, you might share your experience by writing an article that reminds people of the great numbers of poor in the United States. Submit it to the features editor of a local newspaper or a general magazine.

In either case, the health needs of the homeless are unlikely to be met. A national study found that 73 percent of homeless respondents reported at least one unmet health need, including medical and surgical care, medications, mental health care, and dental care (Baggett, O'Connell, Singer, and Rigotti 2010).

Even the poor who are not homeless suffer a disproportionate amount of ill health. Compared to those of the nonpoor, the health problems of the poor are manifested in higher rates of physical illness, infant mortality, clinical depression and other problems with mental health, and difficulty with such daily living tasks as cooking, shopping, managing money, walking, eating, and dressing (Belle 2003; Wheaton and Clarke 2003; Okechukwu et al. 2012; Stewart et al. 2016). Even a short time in poverty damages people's health, and getting out of poverty does not repair all the damage done (McDonough and Berglund 2003). There can be long-term negative consequences for both adults and children. Thus, those who were poor from birth through age 5 are nearly three times as likely as those who were well-to-do to report poor health as adults (Duncan and Magnuson 2011). An Australian study found that children who spent time in poverty in their early years had a greater risk of problems with anxiety and depression when they were examined at age 14 and again at age 21 (Najman et al. 2010).

One possible reason for the long-range consequences may be that people develop poor health habits while they are in poverty (skipping medical checkups and eating cheap but unhealthy food) that tend to persist even if their income rises above the poverty level. Another reason is the higher proportion of the poor who lack health insurance. In 2015, about one in seven households (14.8 percent) of those in the lowest (under $25,000) income bracket was uninsured, compared to 4.5 percent of those in the highest bracket ($100,000 or more) (Barnett and Vornovitsky 2016). The uninsured rate for children under age 19 who lived in poverty was 7.5 percent, compared to the 4.8 percent of children not living in poverty. The lack of insurance, combined with insufficient medical care facilities in poor areas, means that many of the poor get no medical help until their situation becomes critical or unbearable (Kirby and Kaneda 2005).

Some of the health problems of the poor result from poor nutrition, which, in turn, is related to inadequate income. In 2015, 12.7 percent of American households were food insecure (i.e., they did not have adequate food because of lack of money or other resources) (Coleman-Jensen et al. 2016). In 5 percent of the households, there was "very low" food security: the food intake of some household members was reduced and normal eating patterns were disrupted. And children were food insecure at times during the year in 7.8 percent (3 million) households. In contrast, only 7 percent of Canadians are food insecure, and compared to the United States, a much smaller proportion of the Canadian food insecure are children (Nord and Hopwood 2008).

The consequences of inadequate food or of malnutrition are serious (Alaimo, Olson, Frongillo, and Briefel 2001). Food-insecure adults tend to suffer from depression as well as various physical problems (Wu and Schimmele 2005). Food-insecure children are vulnerable to a variety of physical and mental problems. In recent decades, American children have suffered from pellagra, scurvy, rickets, parasitic worms, and mental retardation as a result of prolonged malnutrition. Children who receive an inadequate amount of protein can suffer a variety of maladies, including an inability to concentrate and to learn in school (Kar, Rao, and Chandramouli 2008). Even mild undernutrition can have long-term adverse effects on children's development. Opponents of the welfare system sometimes ask how many children have starved to death in America. The answer is few, if any; but this is little solace to the mother who watches her child grow up with mental or physical deficiencies because of inadequate diet.

Clearly, poverty contradicts the value of good health. The relationship between poverty and health, in fact, is another of the *vicious circles* that often characterize social problems. Because health problems put additional strains on a family's meager financial resources, illness can be perpetuated. Poverty can generate stress that leads to illness that intensifies the stress, and the circle continues.

Dilemmas of Poverty

autonomy
the ability or opportunity to govern oneself

Americans *value **autonomy** and equal opportunity.* They want to control their own destinies and they want opportunities for advancement. These values are *contradicted* by the realities of poverty. People at the lower end of the stratification system have little control over their lives and have few, if any, opportunities compared to people at the upper end. Poverty is an ongoing series of *dilemmas.* Even when a poor person can choose between options, all the options may have undesirable aspects.

Consider the problems of existing on a poverty budget. Even Americans with incomes that are low but somewhat above the poverty level have to deal with frustrating dilemmas. Matters that would be an inconvenience to people with higher incomes—car problems, illness, appliance breakdowns—can become a crisis for low-income families (Shipler 2004). In fact, anything that adds to the expense of living presents a dilemma to the poor. An unexpected spell of cold weather that raises heating bills means less food for poor parents and their children (Bhattacharya, DeLeire, Haider, and Currie 2003).

Even if a poor family is able to spend the full third of its income on food, how adequate would the food be? What kind of a diet would you have if you existed on the food budget allocated to the poor? The exercise in the Involvement box challenges you to try eating on a poverty-level food budget for two weeks. If you conduct this experiment by yourself rather than with a partner, the 2015 poverty-level figure of $12,331 for one person under the age of 65 will allot you $11.26 per day for food. Keep in mind that this figure is for people who are at the top of the poverty scale. Since most of the poor are not at the top, most have less money for food. How much of what you like to eat now would you be able to have? Another way to look at it is that the poor person's food budget for a whole day could be spent at one meal at a fast-food hamburger restaurant. For some of the poor, the choice may be between adequate nutrition and clothes, or between adequate nutrition and medical care. Most students do not face such limited choices.

One of the key dilemmas of the poor is the *choice between security and change.* Should poor individuals maintain whatever security they have or take some risks in order to change their lot? For instance, the ghetto child may be told that the only way to escape poverty is to stay in school and use the education to get a good job, but the only security the child's family may have against utter deprivation is for the child to drop out of school and earn money to add to the family income. At the same time, perhaps the only way the child can be *psychologically secure* is to accept the negative judgments of his or her peers about school. The low value that many of the poor place on intellectual achievement threatens ostracism to any young person who is serious about education. Furthermore, the child has grown up in an unpredictable world and has felt the powerlessness of the individual to change his or her lot in life. Why should the child risk years of schooling (which involves a loss of income) when the payoff is vague and uncertain?

Adults also face dilemmas and the *frustrations of powerlessness.* Consider, for example, the single mother living in poverty who wants to better her lot and that of her children, but who neither has a car nor the resources to get one. In essence, her problem with transportation means that she has restricted access to opportunities for education or work that could lift her and her children out of poverty (Blumenberg and Agrawal 2014). Or consider the incident shared with us by a woman who grew up in poverty in a ghetto area: "When I was a girl, I was given a part in the school play. I was as happy as I could be, and proud to think of my parents watching me perform. But on the night of the play my father got drunk instead of coming to school. I was terribly upset at the time, but later on I realized why he had gotten drunk. He was ashamed to come to the play in the clothes he had, and he didn't have enough money to buy anything new. He didn't know what to do; so he got drunk."

It is easy enough to condemn the man, but remember, the poor live with an agonizing mixture of ambition and powerlessness, of the need for security and the need for change. The security is meager, but the risk of change may appear to be great.

Contributing Factors

It is true that there always have been poor people. It is also true that poverty is a global problem and that the poor of other nations are worse off in absolute terms than are the poor of America. But why is there any poverty at all in affluent America? In part, this is because a number of structural and social psychological factors that operate to create poverty also tend to perpetuate it.

Social Structural Factors

The structural factors that bear upon the problem of poverty include the institutional arrangements of government, the economy, the family, and education. We examine each in turn.

Political Decision Making.   Poverty continues in America, in large part, because of the *distribution of power.* The people who control the wealth are among the most powerful, whereas the poor are among the most powerless in America. As a result, governmental decisions typically reflect the interests of the well-to-do rather than of the poor. Thus, Hacker and Pierson (2010) pointed out that the dramatically disproportionate increase since the 1970s in income received, and wealth accumulated, by the wealthiest of Americans can be explained by a number of government actions: lowered business and corporate taxes, deregulation of financial markets and executive pay, and the weakening of groups such as labor unions that work for the middle class and the poor. All of these actions clearly reflect the interests and enhance the power of the wealthy.

Another problem relates to the location of governmental and nongovernmental agencies that help the poor. These agencies are not always found in the areas where the need is greatest (Allard 2008). It is much more difficult for the poor who live in the more impoverished areas or in areas where racial/ethnic minorities are the majority to get help than it is for those who live in more affluent or white areas.

In addition, the political structure is detrimental to the poor because of the *multiple decision-making centers.* The term *"multiple decision-making centers"* refers to the federal, state, and local governmental levels and also to the multiple branches—executive, legislative, and judicial—at each level. All these facets of government have certain decision-making powers, and all have different constituencies. Most categories or organizations of citizens can exercise influence at some point, but there are also many points at which a program or a policy initiative can be stopped. However, some categories of the population have little influence at any point in this complex, and one such category is the poor.

The political arrangements, therefore, mean that programs designed to help the poor are particularly vulnerable to variation, veto, sabotage, or atrophy through neglect. One such example is the 1967 Medicaid program that was intended to ensure adequate health care for the poor. The program was to be operated by the states, which would set up their own schedules of benefits and definitions of eligibility. The federal government would pay half or more of the costs of the program. States could choose not to participate or to provide fewer benefits than other states. Some states were unwilling to assume any financial responsibility for health care of the poor, so they did not participate. Others set up programs with limited benefits. The majority of the poor are still not covered by Medicaid.

Many other programs have been set up to help the poor. Unfortunately, the failure of these programs to sufficiently reduce or eliminate poverty led to a backlash in the 1990s. The largest assistance program for poor families with children—Aid to Families with Dependent Children—was replaced in 1996 with Temporary Assistance to Needy Families (TANF), which included limited help and work requirements. The exact requirements for receiving help were left to the various states. The amount of help was, and continues to be, so small in many cases that the combined value of TANF benefits and food stamps leave the family far below the poverty level. In fact, since TANF was created in 1996, the benefits have tended to decline. By the middle of 2016, TANF benefits in every state of the union for a family of three with no other cash income were below 50 percent of the poverty line (Stanley, Floyd, and Hill 2016)!

Hundreds of thousands of the poor received even less help when government at all levels faced budget crises because of the severe recession that began in 2007. Many states made deep cuts in TANF benefits (Schott and Pavetti 2012). The cuts affected more than a million children who were already living far below the poverty level, and included eliminating the assistance that had been given to families with physical or mental health problems. Some states also cut assistance for child care, making it difficult for poor parents who had jobs to keep them.

Class Composition of Government.   Regardless of the intentions of the various programs and policies, the work of interest groups and the middle-class composition of government make it unlikely that the poor will greatly benefit or that the middle strata will be greatly hurt by government action. Consider housing. The federal government loses more in revenue by allowing people to deduct mortgage interest from income taxes than it spends on housing programs for low-income Americans. In other words, in the area of housing the well-to-do benefit far more from government programs than do the poor.

Another fact that underscores the *class composition of the government* is that the non-poor generally benefit as much from the programs designed to help the poor as the poor themselves do. Programs that would help the poor at the expense of other groups are unlikely to be implemented or even proposed. Medicaid helps some of the poor, but it also makes a number of physicians wealthy. Job-training programs help some of the poor, but they also provide high-salaried positions for a number of middle-class administrators.

Who Benefits from Government?   Given the multiple decision-making centers and the class composition of government, it is not surprising that the middle and upper classes benefit far more from government programs than do the lower class generally and the poor in particular. Some of the poor do not even benefit from programs that were created specifically to help them. One reason is the cumbersome and often bewildering application process. Similarly, other kinds of programs never reach the intended recipients because of inadequate staffing of government offices, complex application processes, and inadequate communication of the availability of the programs. In a survey of low-income parents in Los Angeles County, 51 percent said they were never informed about child care services for which they were eligible, and 52 percent said that the lack of child care caused them to lose a job (National Coalition for the Homeless 2000).

Some benefits do filter down to the poor, but the primary beneficiaries of government decisions and programs are (and always have been) the well-to-do. Two researchers who analyzed the rapidly growing income of the super-rich over the past few decades identified the crucial role of government action (or inaction) in the economy: an increasingly conservative Congress; declining union membership; lower tax rates for those in the higher income brackets; more open trade policies; and asset bubbles in the stock and real estate markets (Volscho and Kelly 2012). In the light of this, it is ironic that the people on welfare are castigated as "freeloaders," whereas the well-to-do have used their power since the beginning of the Republic to secure handouts from the federal government; but the handouts that the well-to-do secure are referred to as **subsidies,** or tax benefits to stimulate business. From extensive gifts of land to the railroads, to guaranteed prices for various farm products, to tax concessions and research money for industry,

subsidy
a government grant to a private person or company to assist an enterprise deemed advantageous to the public

the federal government has been engaged in a long history of acts that have benefited the well-to-do. In many cases the benefits received by the well-to-do are not as obvious as those given to the poor, even though they are greater.

Consumer advocate Ralph Nader (1990) identified four areas of abuse in the American "corporate welfare state." The first area of abuse is *bailouts,* the federal government's guaranteed loans or guaranteed restitution for corporate mismanagement. In the 1970s, the government guaranteed loans to Lockheed Corporation and Chrysler Corporation to prevent bankruptcy. In the 1990s, hundreds of billions of dollars were needed to deal with the ravages of fraud and speculation in the savings and loan industry and cleanup costs for nuclear weapons plants managed by private firms. And in 2007, the economy was rocked by the consequences of making massive numbers of loans to unqualified home buyers (VanDenburgh and Harmelink 2008). The irresponsible brokers, bankers, and others involved created a financial crisis that threatened to wreck the nation's economy. The federal government again had to step in with hundreds of billions of dollars of aid.

Resource depletion is a second area of abuse. The government has leased at "bargain-basement prices" the rights to minerals and timber. In Alaska, taxpayers paid to build the roads into some timberland that would reap huge profits for those companies that had been given the low-cost lease.

A third area of abuse is *taxpayer-funded research and development.* The government has funded research, including studies in government labs, and then given patent rights to private business. The National Cancer Institute developed the application of the drug AZT to the problem of AIDS. A private drug firm then secured an exclusive patent to market AZT without paying royalties to the government and without agreeing to any price restraints on the drug.

Finally, *subsidies to profit-making businesses* is the fourth area of abuse. The federal government has subsidized everything from private golf clubs to farm crops to giant corporations. **Corporate welfare** refers to government benefits given to corporations that are not available to individuals or to other groups. Federal, state, and local governments all contribute to the welfare, which takes the form of such benefits as tax exemptions and tax reduction, training grants, investment credits, infrastructure (roads, water and sewer lines, etc.) improvements, and low-rate loans. Corporate welfare has been on the increase in recent decades. Thus, in the 1950s, corporate taxes were 28 percent of all federal taxes collected, whereas by 2010 they were only 9 percent (Tax Policy Center 2011).

Why is it immoral to feed the hungry and moral to pay for private golf clubs? Is the president of an airline, whose high salary is possible partly because of government subsidies, more moral than the child who has no father and receives paltry sums of money through welfare? If the government can pay millions of dollars to rescue a corporation from bankruptcy, why is it wrong to rescue people from poverty? The answer is that the poor are powerless to secure what the well-to-do secure with relatively little difficulty. Ironically, through the structure and functioning of government, the well-to-do and powerful give to each other that which they say is immoral to give to the poor.

Probably few people in the middle class are aware of how many benefits they receive from government programs. For example, a young man attends a public school, rides on a free school bus, and eats a free or subsidized (and therefore cheap) lunch. If he later spends time in the armed forces, he may pursue a subsidized college education. He then may buy a farm or a home with a loan that is subsidized and guaranteed by the federal government. He may go into business for himself with a low-interest loan from the Small Business Administration (SBA). The young man may marry and have children who are born in a hospital that was built in part with federal funds. His aged parents may have

corporate welfare governmental benefits given to corporations that are unavailable to other groups or to individuals serious and expensive health problems, which are largely covered by the federal Medicare program. This program enables him to save his own money, which he banks in an institution protected and insured by the federal government. His community may benefit economically from an industrial project underwritten by the government, and his children may be able to go to a college because of financial assistance from the government. Then the man, like many good Americans, may rebel against federal programs and high taxes and assert that this country was built on rugged individualism, unaware that his whole existence is enriched and subsidized by various government programs.

The interests of the middle and upper strata are also reflected in the *tax structure.* Presumably, the tax structure is an equalizing mechanism that takes disproportionately from the rich in order to benefit the poor. This equalization has not happened. Both wealthy individuals and corporations continue to be adept at finding loopholes in federal tax laws that reduce their tax burden. For example, a study of 280 corporations found that from 2008 through 2010, 30 of them paid no federal taxes at all (McIntyre et al. 2011). And the average tax rate paid by all 280 corporations on their more than $1.35 trillion profit during the three years was 18.5 percent.

For individuals, the wealthy tend to pay higher rates of federal income tax than do the middle class and the poor. However, most state and local tax systems severely penalize the poor (Institute on Taxation and Economic Policy 2015; Newman and O'Brien 2011). This is particularly true for states that rely for their revenue more on sales tax than on progressive property and income taxes. Nationwide, the richest Americans pay 5.4 percent of their income in state and local taxes, compared to about 9 percent for middle-income families and 10.9 percent for the poor. Even when federal taxes are added in, the proportion of income paid in taxes declines consistently from the poorest to the wealthiest.

Although the wealthy do enjoy advantages, we do not mean to imply that they pay no taxes. Most do, in fact, pay a considerable amount in taxes. The question is whether they have paid a proportionately larger amount of their income than the nonwealthy. The answer depends on whether only federal taxes or the total taxes paid—federal, state, and local taxes—are included. When all taxes are considered, the poor have paid a higher proportion of their income than have the nonpoor.

Poverty and the Economy.   The American economy works for the rich and against the poor in various ways. A capitalist economy, which is supported by government policies, allows *concentration of wealth.* The fact that the share of income of the richest Americans has declined during this century (see Table 6.1) is misleading unless you recognize that a large part of the wealth of the very rich does not come from personal income. *Stocks, bonds, and real estate are important sources of wealth* for those at the top of the socioeconomic ladder. This is why it is important to consider wealth and not merely income when assessing the amount of inequality.

A second way the economy works against the poor is by *entrapping them in a vicious circle.* Consider, for example, a woman whose job pays her only poverty-level wages. She cannot get a better-paying job because she lacks education or skills. She cannot afford to quit to gain the skills or advance her education because she has a family to support. There is no union, and she is unwilling to risk her job and perhaps her physical well-being to try and organize her fellow workers or even to support a move to unionization. Meanwhile, her debts mount, she may accumulate medical bills, and the rate of inflation may far surpass any wage increase she gets. As she sinks more deeply into debt, she is less and less able to risk the loss of the income she has. Ultimately, she may reach the point of despair that we described earlier. Perhaps she will cling to the hope that at least some of her children can escape the poverty that has wrung the vigor out of her own life.

A third way the economy hurts the poor is by *guaranteeing that a certain proportion of the population will be unable to find employment or unable to find jobs that pay more than poverty-level wages* (Rank, Yoon, and Hirschl 2003). Although most of the poor are not unemployed, a substantial number of families are poor because the family head is either squeezed out of the job market or can find only low-paying jobs. This "squeezing out" can occur when companies close down or downsize, recessions occur, and technological changes make jobs obsolete. Some of these people will spend time on welfare as they struggle against economic forces that are beyond their control.

The low-paying jobs that keep the working poor impoverished are most likely to be found in the service industry, particularly in food preparation and service jobs (Bureau of Labor Statistics 2016b). A disproportionate number of those who fill such jobs are young (under the age of 25), female, and work part-time. In 2015, 870,000 workers earned the minimum wage—$7.25 per hour. But federal regulations do not cover all workers. An additional 1.7 million Americans worked for less than the minimum. To understand the impact of working at such jobs, consider the following: if an individual worked full-time (40 hours per week) year-round (52 weeks), that individual's income would put him or her a little above the poverty line; but if that individual were responsible for one or more other people, the family would be in poverty. Clearly, no one can be an adequate breadwinner for a family and work for the federal minimum wage.

Immigrants are prime targets for companies that pay low wages. A New York reporter went into a Brooklyn garment factory that had a sign posted in Chinese: "Earnestly, urgently looking for workers" (Lii 1995). Because the reporter spoke Chinese, the owner assumed that she was an immigrant seeking her fortune in America. She accepted the job and took her place in a long line of Chinese women bending over sewing machines and working diligently in silence. At the end of seven days and 84 hours of work, she was told that in three weeks she would be paid $54.24—which came to 65 cents an hour! She walked away "from the lint-filled factory with aching shoulders, a stiff back, a dry cough and a burning sore throat."

Similar stories could be told of Asians and Hispanics in various parts of the country. Both legal and illegal immigrants are exploited. Lacking language skills and/or legal status and desperate for income, they may fall prey to managers who pay only the minimum wage or less.

One way to deal with low-paying jobs is to *unionize* the workers. Unfortunately, as we point out in Chapter 10, unions have had their own problems in recent years in organizing the workforce. The problem of low-paying jobs is likely to continue for some time.

The same economy that allows low-paying labor furthers the disadvantage of the poor in regard to the purchase of consumer goods and services, including everything from groceries to health care (Brookings Institution Metropolitan Policy Program 2005; Talukdar 2008). Thus, one study showed that low-income families in Philadelphia paid at least $500 more than other families for the same kind of car and $400 more per year for insurance for the car. Similarly, a study of the cost of being poor in Gary, Indiana, reported that stores

Immigrants are prime targets for low-paying jobs.

©C. Zachariasen / PhotoAlto

in the poor neighborhoods charged more for food and clothes than did stores in other areas (Barnes 2005). Why don't the poor simply go to the other stores, then? They may have neither the time nor the resources to travel to cheaper but distant stores. And some who did found themselves being watched with suspicion in grocery stores when they used food stamps or treated discourteously when shopping for clothes.

To be sure, it is more costly to do business in ghetto neighborhoods than elsewhere because of greater losses through theft and higher insurance premiums. Although higher prices may be legitimate from a business perspective, they do contribute to keeping the poor impoverished.

Patterns of Family Life.   One aspect of family life that tends to perpetuate poverty is the size of the family. The rate of poverty among large families is two to three times that of two-person families.

Even in small families, however, the family is likely to perpetuate its own poverty because of *certain social-class differences in family life* (Heymann 2000; Pittman and Chase-Lansdale 2001; Lareau 2003). Family life among the poor can discourage intellectual achievement (and, therefore, the higher levels of education that are vital for upward mobility). Among the factors that are important for a child's intellectual growth are parents' willingness to give time to the child, parental guidance, parental aspirations for the child's achievement, provision of intellectual stimulation, and the use of external resources such as nursery schools and advice from experts. Children who live in poverty for a period of time are less likely to receive this kind of family help than are those who are not poor (Evans 2004; Evans et al. 2011).

The advantages that accrue to the children of the well-to-do are underscored in a long-term study of a sample of schoolchildren in Baltimore (Alexander, Entwisle, and Olson 2007). The children were monitored from the time they were in first grade until they were 22 years old. Those from the middle and upper social strata had varied kinds of summer learning experiences that gave them an advantage in academic progress over their peers from poorer families. The experiences were not only summer classes or programs, but also the parents working with their children to enhance their knowledge and skills. The additional learning in the summer led to higher academic achievement, which, in turn, led to a greater likelihood of being in a college preparatory track and actually attending a four-year college. The poorer children, by contrast, had lower test scores and were therefore less likely to be in a college-preparatory program. They were also less likely to complete high school. Nationally, dropout rates from high school in 2014 were 11.6 percent for those in the lowest income bracket compared to 4.7 percent of those in the high-middle bracket and 2.8 percent for those in the highest bracket (Kena et al. 2016).

Why? Can't poor parents provide the same kind of motivation and help as the nonpoor? In theory, yes. But consider the circumstances of living in poverty. The atmosphere of the impoverished home is unlikely to be conducive to learning. In a poor family, *interaction of children with adults generally, and parents in particular, tends to be minimal* (Heymann 2000). The home of the poor child is likely to be crowded, busy, and noisy. There are likely to be many people, including a number of children, living in the home, though it is less likely that there are two parents. No single child gets much attention. The children watch television, listen to music, and see movies, but do little reading. Moreover, they have little sustained interaction with adult members of their families.

Evidence also shows that consistent mothering by one person facilitates development of children's ability to express themselves verbally. Children in poor families are less likely to have such a relationship in their early years. Instead, responsibility for child care tends to be assumed by a number of people, including adults and other children. TANF policy, which requires single mothers to find work and become self-supporting, exacerbates the problem.

The interaction that does occur may hinder rather than facilitate intellectual growth because there is a *greater proportion of nonverbal compared to verbal interaction* among the poor. The emphasis on the nonverbal rather than the verbal and on the physical rather than the mental is why children from poor homes tend to move their lips while reading and to use their fingers while counting.

Because the verbal ability of poor adults is generally low, increasing the amount of verbal interaction between adults and children would not resolve the problem. Many language differences have been found between the lower and the middle and upper socioeconomic strata. These language differences involve grammatical distinctions; pronunciation, stress, and intonation; range of vocabulary; and style and taste in the selection and use of words and phrases. Differences in these linguistic features mean differences in how the world is experienced and communicated. In general, poor parents are equipped with neither the financial resources nor the intellectual tools necessary to maximize the intellectual growth of their children. The parents' own opportunities to acquire these resources and tools are minimal, and hence the family environment they provide will tend to perpetuate the limitations in their children.

Another aspect of family life that bears crucially on the problem of poverty is the *high rate of divorce*. Recall that persons in female-headed families have the highest rates of poverty in the nation (see Figure 6.2). Divorce is likely to have negative economic consequences for women and may be particularly severe for women with children. One study, for example, found that the financial status of mothers and their children fell by 37 percent, compared to a drop of 16 percent for the nonresident fathers (Stirling and Aldrich 2008). Among those with low incomes, the poverty rate for fathers was 28 percent, while that for mothers was 73 percent! Indeed, nearly half the increase in child poverty in recent years is due to changing family structure (more children born to single women and greater numbers of single-parent families because of separation, death, or divorce).

The Education of the Poor.   In general, the lower the income, the lower the educational achievement of children (Kena et al. 2016). As noted previously, family patterns contribute significantly to this pattern. In addition to the way parents interact with their children at home, parental involvement in the school is less among the lower- than the higher-income families. Among other things, parents in the highest income bracket are twice as likely to attend a class event and volunteer at school as those in the lowest income bracket. Even the educational expectations of both poor children and their parents tend to be lower than those in the middle and upper classes (Goyette 2008). These expectations are reflected in lower levels of educational achievement. This educational disadvantage in turn exacerbates the worst aspects of poverty, depressing well-being and shutting people out of many economic opportunities.

Unfortunately, the educational environment itself contributes in a number of ways to the low academic achievement of the poor. Chapter 11 considers the problem of the inequitable distribution of quality education and shows that schools in poor neighborhoods tend to have meager facilities and inexperienced or inadequate teachers. Here we focus on the ways *school personnel affect poverty-level students* at the interpersonal level.

Children of poor families may experience **discrimination** when they attend school with children of nonpoor families. Teachers come primarily from middle-class backgrounds. They may find it difficult to understand and relate in a helpful way to children from poor homes. They may also *have different expectations for students from different socioeconomic backgrounds,* and the expectations of teachers can significantly retard or stimulate intellectual growth and performance (Sparks 2010). Hence, when middle-class teachers expect students from poor families not to perform well, this expectation can lead the children to perform below their capabilities.

discrimination
arbitrary, unfavorable treatment of the members of some social group

In essence, the poor are less likely than the nonpoor to have gratifying and encouraging experiences in school. They are, therefore, more likely to drop out. Children from lower socioeconomic levels, compared to those from the middle and upper strata, also tend to be more dissatisfied with school, report more interpersonal problems (such as not being popular), feel more difficulty in expressing themselves well, and are more likely to express difficulties concentrating and studying. It is not surprising, then, that the majority of school dropouts are from the lower strata.

In sum, the poor are less likely than the nonpoor to perform well in school or to seek more than minimal education—not necessarily because of innate ability, but because of sociocultural factors. Even when ability levels of poor and nonpoor are equated, the poor are less likely to pursue higher education.

Social Psychological Factors

Some attitudes and values held by both the nonpoor and the poor help perpetuate poverty (Rogers-Dillon 1995). For example, many nonpoor accept the *fallacy of retrospective determinism* with regard to poverty: They believe that poverty is inevitable—"There have always been poor people, and there always will be poor people." This kind of attitude

fallacy

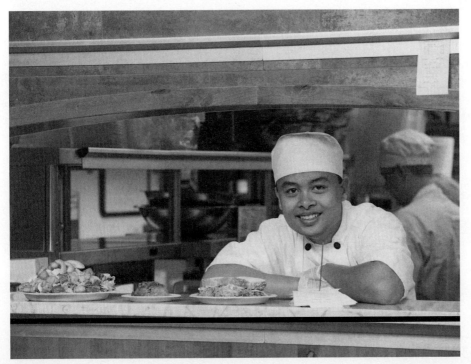

People with menial jobs may be poor even though they work full-time.

©Tetra Images/Alamy Stock Photo

may manifest itself as opposition to government antipoverty programs, pitting the non-poor against the poor as various interest groups vie for funds.

Disparagement and Discrimination.   As we pointed out earlier, *the nonpoor tend to disparage the poor.* Throughout history, and in virtually all societies, the poor have been considered disreputable in some sense. Such attitudes seriously undermine self-respect among the poor and at the same time perpetuate the political and economic processes that maintain poverty. You might think that people's disparagement of the poor would lessen during times of more general hardship, but there is no evidence that beliefs about the causes of poverty and attitudes toward the poor or toward welfare change even when the entire society is in an economic recession.

Negative attitudes toward the poor may become **self-fulfilling prophecies.** If a man is poor because he is out of work, he may find that when he secures work, hostility is directed toward him because he comes from an impoverished background. We once lived in a community in which a manufacturing company placed a full-page advertisement in the local newspaper, pointing out that a program to bus inner-city workers to the plant had failed. The ad asked what was wrong with the workers. Why were the jobs still open? The company implied that what many people think is actually true: The poor are too lazy to work and will not accept an opportunity even if it is offered to them. A subsequent investigation showed that the chronically unemployed, who were all black, were unwilling to work because of pressures, hostility, and racial bias.

self-fulfilling prophecy
a belief that has consequences (and may become true) simply because it is believed

The tendency to disparage the poor is also at the root of opposition to government programs designed to alleviate poverty. A national poll that asked whether government should do more to help needy Americans, even if that meant going deeper in debt, reported that 57 percent of those with income of less than $20,000 per year said "yes," the government should do more (Krogstad and Parker 2014). Less than half of all other income groups, and only 38 percent of the highest income group, agreed with the statement.

The Ideology of Wealth and Poverty.   Many Americans *believe strongly in an ideology of individualism, attributing both wealth and poverty to the qualities of individuals rather than to the social system.* A *New York Times* survey reported that 80 percent of the respondents believed that people can start out poor, work hard, and become rich (Scott and Leonhardt 2005). This is in accord with an individualist ideology of wealth and poverty, which argues that each individual is responsible for his or her own status because the system itself allows opportunities to all. Clearly, such an ideology allows no basis for political action that would alleviate poverty. It is understandable, therefore, that Americans, compared to those in some European nations, are less concerned about establishing a minimum income level for all citizens (Osberg and Smeeding 2006).

Public Policy and Private Action

There have, of course, been attempts to resolve the problem of poverty. The so-called War on Poverty initiated in the 1960s was a multifaceted attack on the problem. The Economic Opportunity Act of 1964 set up several programs intended to benefit the poor, including the Job Corps (to train young people who have little education or skills), the College Work Study Program (to help college students from low-income families), and the Community Action Program.

The failure of the War on Poverty to eliminate the problem is used by some Americans to disparage any government efforts and to insist that, ultimately, the poor themselves must take advantage of the opportunities in the land to lift themselves from poverty. This argument not only ignores the fact that the war was often more rhetoric than support but also ignores the genuine gains that were made. The poverty rate fell from more than 22 percent in 1959 to a low of 11 to 12 percent in the 1970s. The subsequent rise occurred with the cutback in government programs. Without the programs that exist now, the rate would be much higher than it is. You must also realize that some programs will fail; the study of human behavior is not sufficiently scientific to be able to put together an infallible solution to a problem. Some programs have worked well. Head Start and other early childhood education programs have provided impoverished children with skills that have enabled them to reach higher levels of academic achievement and success (West et al. 2010). Kenworthy (1999) examined the effects of social welfare programs in 15 affluent nations, including the United States, and found that the programs have reduced poverty rates in all of them.

To eliminate poverty, some attitudes and ideologies among people generally, and political leaders in particular, must be altered. Typically, the more information people have and the more they are exposed to impoverished individuals, the more positive their attitudes are likely to be toward the poor (and, therefore, the more likely they are to support programs that help the poor). Three researchers who studied attitudes toward the homeless found that people who were most exposed to homelessness—including everything from television shows and articles to having been in or worked in a homeless shelter—had the most favorable attitudes (Lee, Farrell, and Link 2004). Whatever governments and community organizations can do to increase exposure is likely to increase support for programs that help.

The attitudes and ideologies of political leaders are also crucial, and the commitment of the federal government is essential. Unfortunately, federal commitment varies enormously from one administration to another. New policies and programs are needed, but the emphasis in the early 2000s was on cutting back old programs.

Because single mothers have the highest rate of poverty in the nation, strategies to help them must have priority. The welfare reform of 1996 assumed that if single mothers were deprived of long-term support they would marry and their husbands' income would lift them out of poverty. Unfortunately, unmarried women with children are not appealing as mates for men who could support them (Graefe and Lichter 2007). One way to help the mothers who work but are still in poverty would be to create a system of fringe benefits for low-wage workers. The benefits could include an increase in the Earned Income Tax Credit, tax credits for child care expenses, and a tax credit for housing expenses.

Some of the poor also could be helped by raising the minimum wage. An individual worker cannot support a family above the poverty level by working full time at the minimum wage level.

Another important step is *to continue to search for antipoverty programs, including welfare programs,* that work. It appears that workfare, introduced in the 1980s, is going to be the policy for the foreseeable future. Under the TANF program, the federal government does not provide long-term aid to the poor. Instead, states are given block grants to run their own programs. Each state has considerable flexibility, but certain guidelines must be followed. Generally, the guidelines are that no family will be given welfare payments for more than five years, and if the head of a family does not find work within two years, the family will lose benefits.

How effective has workfare been so far? First, the program has greatly reduced welfare rolls and moved many former recipients into work (Grogger and Karoly 2005). Second, however, *the reduction in welfare benefits has been far greater than the reduction of poverty*. The earnings from the kinds of jobs available to those moving out of welfare (who are likely to have minimal skills) are frequently no more than the benefits they were receiving from welfare. Thus, they are working, but they are no better off financially than they were while on welfare. Some are even worse off because the jobs they secure offer no benefits such as health care, assistance in child care, and leave for maternity or even for family or personal illness (Collins and Mayer 2010).

Most disturbing is the fact that, for whatever reasons, the TANF average caseload fell from 4.4 million families in 1996 to 1.6 million in 2014, at the same time that the number of people living in poverty (including the number of families with children who have incomes below half of the poverty level) has risen significantly (Center On Budget and Policy Priorities 2016). In essence, then, TANF is helping far fewer families than previous programs. At the beginning, TANF helped 68 out of every 100 families in poverty, but by 2014 only 23 of every 100 families received help. It is not surprising, then, that studies of workers who have participated in TANF programs show that *the majority are not able to escape from poverty* even though they follow through to the end of the process that is supposed to rescue them (Cancian et al. 2003; Blalock, Tiller, and Monroe 2004). Moreover, there are some recipients, particularly those with less than a high-school education and a poor work history, who are unable to secure a job within the time limits set by the state (Taylor, Barusch, and Vogel-Ferguson 2006). They are left with nothing.

In addition, another problem has plagued the poor under workfare. Although one of the goals was to strengthen family life by encouraging parents to be responsible breadwinners, workfare has had no effect on the living arrangements of poor white children, has increased the proportion of Hispanic children living with a married parent, but has actually decreased the proportion of black children living with any parent (Bitler, Gelbach, and Hoynes 2004). And a study of low-income single mothers who moved from welfare to work found that the conditions of employment (long hours, erratic work schedules, lengthy commutes, etc.) resulted in a variety of emotional and interpersonal problems among the children (Dunifon, Kalil, and Bajracharya 2005).

In short, workfare may not even be a solution for all the able-bodied workers who have been on welfare, much less for those who are not able to work. A writer who tried to survive by working for a month at low-paying jobs put it this way:

> I lost almost four pounds in four weeks, on a diet weighted heavily toward burgers and fries. How former welfare recipients and single mothers will (and do) survive in the low-wage workforce, I cannot imagine. . . . I couldn't hold two jobs and I couldn't make enough money to live on with one. (Ehrenreich 1999:52)

What, then, is to be done at the level of public policy? A number of steps need to be taken at both the federal and state levels of government, including:

- Provide benefits for as long as it takes (rather than the current limits) to enable families to escape poverty.
- Spend all unused TANF money (billions of unspent dollars are available to the states), or replace TANF with more effective programs.
- Simplify the process of getting available benefits such as food stamps, child care, health care, and transportation so that the poor are both aware of and able to get the help they need.
- Set a federal minimum wage that enables workers to be self-supporting and able to afford housing.

- Expand educational and training programs so that workers can secure better-paying jobs.
- Provide more supportive services for low-income families.

Finally, various forms of private action can help the poor. One example is Habitat for Humanity, which has built more than 100,000 homes for poor people in the United States and other countries. Interested Americans can volunteer to help in the construction or can donate money to support others who do the work. Other programs include the work of various civic and religious groups in repairing and renovating homes, providing food for the hungry, offering health care to the poor, and giving scholarships to poor children. Such programs reach a portion of the poor, but they cannot replace the broader public policies that are needed to help the millions of poor Americans.

Follow Up. Think about actions that you as a private citizen have taken to help alleviate the problem of poverty. What more could you do in the future?

Summary

Poverty may not be as bad in America as it is in some parts of the world, but America's poverty must be evaluated in terms of the standard of living attained by the majority of Americans. The government's definition of poverty is based on the cost of a basic diet called the "economy food plan." It is revised to account for inflation and varies according to location (farm or nonfarm), size of the family, and sex and age of the head of the family. In 2015, a family of two adults and two children with an annual income or $24,036 or less was officially poor. This official definition is challenged as inadequate or unrealistic because it sets the poverty level quite low.

The proportion of people who are poor varies over time. Poverty is not equally distributed among the population, however. Your chances of being poor are greater if you are in a female-headed family, are a member of a minority group, are under 18 years of age, and are living in a rural area. Contrary to popular opinion, poverty is not basically a problem of unemployment. Many of the poor work, and some work full time. Some of the poor are homeless. Homelessness is associated with many other problems, such as mental and physical health.

The quality of life for the poor can be characterized as pervasive deprivation: The poor get less of everything that is valued in American society, including rights to life and the pursuit of happiness. Poverty brings despair and fear, including the fear of being victimized by crime. Various myths that disparage the poor diminish their dignity as human beings. Their health is poorer than that of most Americans, and their poverty and ill health can become a vicious circle. The individual living in poverty is forced to choose between limited, undesirable alternatives.

Among the structural factors that contribute to poverty, the distribution of power is of prime importance. People who control the wealth are the most powerful, and their interests are typically reflected in governmental decisions. Both the structure and the functioning of American government tend to work to the detriment of the poor. Multiple decision-making centers, the middle-class composition of the bureaucracy, and the complexities of getting aid all work to the detriment of the poor. Ironically, the well-to-do and powerful give to each other through government actions what they say is immoral to give to the poor. The economy works against the poor in three ways: by allowing the concentration of wealth, by entrapping the poor in a vicious circle, and by guaranteeing that a certain proportion of the population will be unable to find employment or jobs that pay more than poverty-level wages.

The family environment tends to perpetuate poverty when there are many children in the family. Even when there are few children, poor families tend to transmit poverty by anti-intellectual attitudes and patterns of interaction that inhibit intellectual development. Disrupted families are also an important source of poverty, and many widows and divorced women spend a part of the time after disruption in poverty. Educational arrangements themselves contribute to the problem because quality education is much less likely to be available to poor children than to nonpoor children. Also, poor children tend not to have gratifying and encouraging experiences in school or to pursue higher education even when they have the ability to do so.

Attitudes and values of both the poor and the nonpoor contribute to the poverty problem. The attitudes and values of the nonpoor legitimate their disparagement of and discrimination against the poor. The American value of individualism and ideology of equal opportunity combine to justify negative attitudes toward the poor and programs designed to help them.

Key Terms

Autonomy	Poverty
Consumer Price Index	Poverty Level
Corporate Welfare	Self-Fulfilling Prophecy
Discrimination	Subsidy
Ghetto	
Malnutrition	

Study Questions

1. What do we mean by "poverty"? How many Americans are poor?
2. Who is most likely to be poor in America?
3. How have the problems of poverty and the lot of the poor changed over time in our country?
4. Explain the various ways in which poverty affects the basic rights and needs of people.
5. What is meant by the "dilemmas of poverty"?

6. How do social institutions contribute to the problem of poverty?

7. How do attitudes and ideologies help perpetuate poverty?

8. What are some steps that could be taken to eliminate or at least minimize poverty?

Internet Resources/Exercises

1. Explore some of the ideas in this chapter on the following sites:

http://www.census.gov   The U.S. Census Bureau offers regular reports and the latest data on poverty in the United States.

http://ssc.wisc.edu/irp   The University of Wisconsin's Institute for Research on Poverty offers a wealth of information, including a newsletter with reports from their researchers.

http://www.northwestern.edu/ipr/research/respoverty1.html   The Institute for Policy Research offers a variety of publications on poverty that can be downloaded free.

2. TANF requirements vary from state to state. Choose four states and get information on their TANF programs. Also gather, if possible, any data on the effectiveness of the programs (numbers of people moved off welfare, numbers of those out of poverty, etc.). Which of the programs do you think is most effective? In which state or states would a poor person get the most help?

3. European nations tend to have lower rates of poverty than the United States. Investigate what various European nations are doing to alleviate poverty and ensure at least a minimally adequate income for all citizens.

For Further Reading

Danziger, Sheldon H., and Robert H. Haveman, eds. *Understanding Poverty.* Cambridge, MA: Harvard University Press, 2002. Various experts address the causes and consequences of poverty, antipoverty policies, and efforts by local communities and neighborhoods to ameliorate the problem.

Desmond, Matthew. *Evicted: Poverty and Profit in the American City.* New York: Crown, 2016. Puts a face on one kind of experience of poor-the loss of housing–with stories of landlords and tenants in impoverished areas of Milwaukee. Shows through both stories and data the traumatic effects on individuals, families, and the entire community.

Edwards, John, Marion Crain, and Arne L. Kalleberg, eds. *Ending Poverty in America: How to Restore the American Dream.* New York: The New Press, 2007. A collection of articles by a diverse group of social scientists, business people, and community organizers on varied facets of the problem of poverty. Includes suggestions on the kinds of public policies that could solve the problem.

Jensen, Eric. *Teaching with Poverty in Mind: What Being Poor Does to Kids' Brains and What Schools Can Do about It.* Alexandria, VA: Association for Supervision & Curriculum Development, 2009. Discusses the nature of poverty, how poverty affects the behavior of children, including academic behavior, and what can be done in schools and in the classroom to foster academic success among the children of the poor.

Lareau, Annette. *Unequal Childhoods: Class, Race, and Family Life.* Berkeley, CA: University of California Press, 2003. A participant observation study of 12 families in which there were children who were 9 or 10 years old. Shows how parenting and daily routines differ between the middle-class families and those that are working-class or poor.

Rank, Mark Robert. *One Nation, Underprivileged: Why American Poverty Affects Us All.* New York: Oxford University Press, 2004. A leading poverty researcher explores the basic causes of poverty, the extent of poverty, and the reasons poverty is an issue of vital concern to the nation.

Shipler, David K. *The Working Poor: Invisible in America.* New York: Alfred A. Knopf, 2004. A thorough study of people who are working but still poor or nearly poor by the official poverty level. The author spent as many as seven years working with some of his subjects; he well understands their struggles.

chapter 6 review

CHAPTER

7

Gender and Sexual Orientation

OBJECTIVES

1 Discuss the issue of biological versus social bases for gender differences.

2 Show how inequalities between the sexes affect women's lives.

3 Explain the social structural and social psychological factors that contribute to gender inequality.

4 Learn various explanations of homosexuality.

5 Identify how homophobia affects the quality of life of homosexuals and how to address the problem of homophobia.

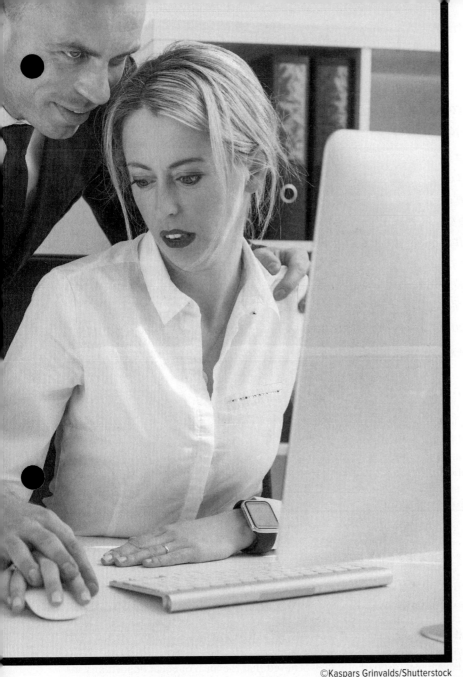

©Kaspars Grinvalds/Shutterstock

"I Didn't Need the Extra Hassles"

Sandra, a high-ranking university administrator in her 50s, started her graduate work when the youngest of her two children began school. In a sense she has it all—family and a successful career—but, as she notes, it has at times been a "journey of outrage":

When I had the chance to go to graduate school, I was deliriously happy. Most of the other students were younger, but I could tell they accepted me and enjoyed having me around. I'm sure part of it was my enthusiasm for the program. I soon discovered, however, that I was embarking on a journey of outrage as well as one of a new career. My first inkling was when one of my fellow students hit on me one day in the library. He wanted to take me out somewhere. I must admit that I was rather flattered, since I was 10 years older than he was. So I just smiled and reminded him that I was married. He smiled back and said, "I don't mind." I told him that I did mind and that I had to get on with my studying.

I could have easily shrugged it off. But every time I tried to study in the library, he would sit at a table nearby and stare at me. I complained to the librarian, but he said that the student had broken no rules. I reminded him that this was really threatening to a woman. How could I be sure that the guy wouldn't try to do something crazy? The librarian looked sympathetic but helpless. I did the only thing I could. I stopped studying at the library and studied at home whenever I could find a quiet moment. Shortly after that, one of the faculty members started making overtures to me. This was really threatening, because I knew he could blackball me. I had to do a dance around him for three years. He did a good job of quenching a lot of my enthusiasm for school.

I could tell countless stories, but one more will illustrate why I call all this a journey of outrage. I came up for tenure in my first academic position. They turned me down. I hadn't published a whole lot, but I had published as much as a male colleague who got tenure. A friend told me that they rejected me because they thought my productivity would decline because of my family commitments. So all the way along, I faced one outrage after another. And just because I'm a woman. It was hard enough to do graduate work and start a career while raising a family. I didn't need the extra hassles. And what makes them so outrageous is that if I were a man they wouldn't have happened.

Introduction

What does it take for a group to suffer from inequality in the United States? It isn't size, because while one of the groups we examine in this chapter is comparatively small (homosexuals), the other represents a majority (women comprise nearly 51 percent of the population). In other ways, the two groups are similar in the extent to which biological versus social factors affect their behavior. Moreover, both have a long history of suffering from both discrimination and oppression.

Gender Inequality

Do you believe there are more advantages to being a man or a woman in American society today? In a national poll some years ago, 32 percent of men and 48 percent of women agreed that men have more advantages, while 9 percent of men and 4 percent of women said that women have more advantages. Most of the rest stated that neither has more advantages. Why would nearly half of all women and a third of men agree that men have more advantages? Apparently they believed that the ideal of equal opportunity for all Americans has been elusive for women. And, as we shall see in this chapter, they were correct. Gender inequality is not as great as it was in the past, but it continues to vex the lives of many women.

innate
existing in a person from birth

sex
an individual's biological identity as male or female

gender
the meaning of being male or female in a particular society

gender role
the attitudes and behavior that are expected of men and women in a society

Because women suffer from inequality as a result of an **innate** characteristic (their sex), women are called the *largest minority* in America even though they are a slight majority of the population. As we discuss gender inequality, we use a number of important terms. **Sex** refers to an individual's biological identity as male or female. **Gender** is the meaning of being male or female in a particular society, and **gender role** refers to the attitudes and behavior that are expected of men and women in a society.

The terminology indicates that *some aspects of men and women are determined by social rather than biological factors.* This social aspect is the first issue we examine. Contrary to the argument that gender inequalities are the necessary outcome of biological differences, we show that the problems are sociocultural in origin and how they affect the quality of life for women. Finally, we look at structural and social psychological factors that contribute to gender inequality and suggest some ways to address the problems.

Biology or Society?

There are numerous differences in the attitudes, behavior, and personalities of the sexes (Marano and Strand 2003; Goldman et al. 2004; Schmitt, Realo, Voracek, and Allik 2008). Among other aspects, men and women differ in their attention span, their aspirations, the strategies they use in competitive games, the amount they smile, their vulnerability to particular diseases and to addictions, the structure and functioning of their brains, their sexual interests, and the extent to which they are agreeable and conscientious. The question we want to examine here is, what accounts for those differences? Are they rooted in biology or in society? The questions are important because people who hold to a strong biological position are likely to fall into the *fallacy of retrospective determinism,* arguing that whatever has happened to women in American society is inevitable because people are determined by their own biological makeup to behave and function in certain ways.

fallacy

Gender and Biology. The "damsel in distress" and "white knight" of folklore illustrate the longstanding notion that men are the independent and women the dependent creatures. An empirical basis for asserting the natural subservience of women is claimed by people who draw on research in the areas of sociobiology (the use of biological factors to explain social phenomena), the brain, and human hormones (Wilson 2000; Pfaff 2002). These researchers claim, on the basis of various kinds of evidence, that human behavior must be understood in terms of *innate biological differences between the sexes.* Some stress humans' continuity with other animals and argue that male and female behavior reflect the imperatives of the evolutionary process—the struggle to survive and to perpetuate one's kind.

People who draw on research on the brain and hormones also stress the biological differences but do not necessarily talk about them in terms of evolutionary imperatives. Rather, the differences are used to explain such factors as the higher levels of aggression among males, the greater verbal abilities of females, and the tendency of women to be more stressed than men by emotional conflict (Brizendine 2006).

Clearly, there are differences between males and females in both the structure and functioning of the brain (Kreeger 2002), but the implications of these differences are controversial. First, many of the differences are relatively small or even trivial (Hyde 2005). Second, research continues to modify some of the conclusions about differences. For example, it is not true, as many have believed, that boys are inherently better at math than are girls. An analysis of hundreds of studies comparing how males and females perform in math concluded that there are no differences (Lindberg, Hyde, Petersen, and Linn 2010). The two sexes have equal capacity for doing math and science.

Thus, the implications for behavior of the differing brain and hormonal structures of males and females are uncertain and controversial. It is best, we believe, to accept the conclusion of a biologist that social interaction affects biological processes as well as vice versa, so that mind, body, and culture interact with each other (Fausto-Sterling 1992). Behavior is always a function of multiple factors, and no one can say with certainty how much of any particular behavior is biologically driven and how much is socially formed.

Men's Issues. In the late 1980s, a *men's movement rapidly gained momentum.* In the University of California reference system, the number of books related to men and masculinity

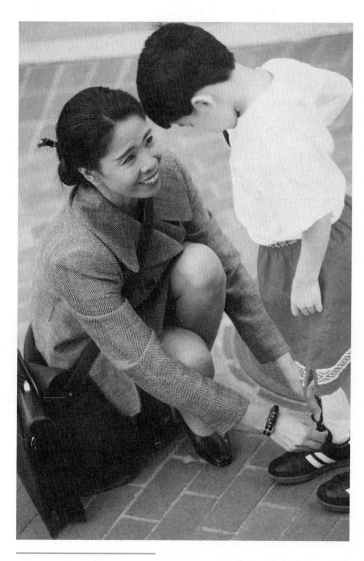

Nurturing is a significant part of the traditional role of women.

©EyeWire Collection / Getty Images

increased sevenfold between 1989 and 1995 (Newton 1998). During the period, the number of scholarly essays in the area tripled and the number of popular magazine articles increased tenfold.

We look briefly at this movement for two reasons. First, we don't want to give the impression that men have all the advantages and none of the problems. Men's issues are as legitimate as women's. Second, the men's movement illustrates our point that gender behavior is sociocultural and not merely biological.

Issues of concern to men include (Throop 1997; Newton 1998; Blais and Dupuis-Deri 2012):

- The meaning of masculinity in a time of changing gender roles.
- The meaning of being a father and a husband in the face of feminist assertions and cultural expectations.
- The rights of divorced and single fathers.
- Perceived discriminatory treatment by lawyers and the courts in divorce and child custody hearings.
- Reverse bias in hiring and promotions when women are chosen over men who are more qualified.

Some segments of the men's movement take the position that men, not women, are the truly oppressed group today (Ferber 2000). They argue that men have been "demasculinized," that women and the women's movement are responsible, and that men must reclaim their masculinity and their rightful authority.

Others in the movement are concerned with more specific issues such as fatherhood (Ranson 2001). In the past, fathers were thought of as breadwinners who had limited time to spend with their children. Today fathers are expected to be much more involved in their children's lives, but they are also expected to be successful in the workplace. How can they meet the competing demands? What do they do when parenting and work requirements contradict each other? What is the role of the wife and mother in all this?

Clearly, such questions arise not out of biology but out of the social milieu. Men's issues, like women's, are a reflection of the sociocultural context—or, to put it another way, gender roles result from sociocultural, not merely biological, factors.

Gender Inequality and the Quality of Life

Although men as well as women have problems and complaints, our focus is on the inequality faced by women. Epstein (2007) pointed out that the world is "made up of great divides" such as nationality, wealth, race, and class. Where you stand in such categories has a profound effect on your life. But the "most fundamental social divide," she argued, is sex. Your life is significantly affected and shaped by whether you are male or female. In this section we will see the basis for such a claim as we examine *the contradictions between the ideology of equal opportunities and the reality of life for women.* Keep in mind that the gender inequalities we discuss are not merely an American problem, but are pervasive in the world. The United States is neither the best nor the worst when it comes to gender equality. Rather, it ranked 28th out of 146 countries studied in terms of their degree of gender equality in the areas of economic participation and opportunity, educational attainment, health and survival, and political empowerment (World Economic Forum 2015). The three countries with the greatest equality were Iceland, Norway, and Finland; the three with the greatest inequality were Syria, Pakistan, and Yemen.

Career Inequality. After World War II, the ideal pattern for women was to marry and become a homemaker and stay-at-home mother. Both the ideal and the reality have changed. The proportion of married women in the labor force rose from 23.8 percent in 1950 to 57.3 percent in 2014; the proportion of women who were in the labor force and had children under 6 years of age increased even more dramatically, from 11.9 percent in 1950 to 64.3 percent in 2014 (Bureau of Labor Statistics 2015). It might appear that this means increasing equality in the labor market. Such a conclusion would be further buttressed by unemployment rates (Table 7.1), which measure the number of people who desire employment but are out of work. Until the 1990s, the rates were nearly always higher for women than for men, a contradiction of the *ideology of equal opportunity.* Since 1990, however, the rates have tended to be roughly equal or to be higher for men than for women.

Yet equal economic opportunities only begin at the point of employment. What about women's opportunities for advancement? What about their income? Are they also equal to those of men?

Unfortunately, the ideology of equal opportunity is *contradicted by the discriminatory treatment of women in various occupations.* Women experience discrimination in hiring, in on-the-job training, in promotions, and in the way they are treated by supervisors and coworkers (Knoke and Ishio 1998; Yoder and Berendsen 2001; Gorman and Kmec 2009). And this is not only an American problem. A study of 22 industrialized

TABLE 7.1
Unemployment Rates, by Sex, 1948 to 2014
(persons 16 years and over)

Year	Male	Female
1948	3.6	4.1
1950	5.1	5.7
1960	5.4	5.9
1970	4.4	5.9
1980	6.9	7.4
1990	5.6	5.4
2000	3.9	4.1
2010	10.6	8.6
2015	5.3	5.2

SOURCES: U.S. Census Bureau, *Statistical Abstract of the United States,* various editions, and Bureau of Labor Statistics website.

nations reported that while developed welfare states (such as Sweden) have a high proportion of women in the labor force, those women tend to be concentrated in female-
typed occupations and are less likely to be in managerial occupations (Mandel and
Semyonov 2006). The consequences of discrimination in pursuing a meaningful career
include increased physical and emotional health problems (Pavalko, Mossakowski,
and Hamilton 2003).

Consider the following facts about the amount and kind of discrimination women
encounter. In many occupational categories, women are found disproportionately in
the lower-echelon jobs. Although far more women than men are teachers, the proportion of women in top administrative jobs in education (superintendents, assistant superintendents, principals, and assistant principals) is low (Wrushen and Sherman 2008).
Increasing proportions of admissions to medical schools are female, but women may be
encouraged to pursue the traditional "female" specialties such as pediatrics, psychiatry,
and preventive medicine. Moreover, although women compose nearly half of all medical students, only 35 percent of full-time medical faculty, 19 percent of full professors
in medical schools, and 13 percent of medical department chairs and deans are women
(Association of American Medical Colleges 2011).

Table 7.2 illustrates the fact that many occupations continue to be male or female
dominated, what social scientists call a *segregated labor market*. Such segregation has
detrimental consequences for women. The occupations that have a high proportion of
women tend to be lower in status and lower in pay (Cohen and Huffman 2003). In some
cases, the occupations are also less desirable from the point of view of meaningful work.

In other words, in a segregated labor market, people tend to evaluate jobs and careers in terms of the predominant gender of the workers as well as the education and
skills required. An apparently obvious solution would be for women to choose male-
dominated occupations if they want to maximize their status and their income. Unfortunately, women do not gain the same prestige as men when they enter predominantly
male occupations. Many women in male-dominated careers feel that they not only must
prove their competence but must do so by performing their job even better than a man
would. Yet when men enter predominantly female occupations, their competence is
more likely assumed (Williams 1995). Ironically, a study of 404 medical technologists,
a female-dominated occupation, found that the women reported more gender discrimination than did the men (Blau and Tatum 2000).

Finally, women face career discrimination because they are more likely than men to
experience conflict between their work and their home responsibilities, a conflict that
is intensified if the woman has more responsibility for child care (Hill, Hawkins, Maartinson, and Ferris 2003). Women continue to find childbearing costly to their careers,
and those in a male-dominated occupation where long hours are the norm for workers
may drop out of the labor force entirely (Cha 2013; Kahn, Garcia-Manglano, and Bianchi
2014). Although it is true that wives work and fathers are more involved with their children than in past eras, fathers are still less likely than mothers to miss or cut back on work
to care for their children's needs (Maume 2008). Moreover, there is an income penalty for
working mothers at all income levels, and the largest penalty occurs for low-wage workers
(Budig and Hodges 2010). Finally, when a man works long hours, the wife's likelihood
of quitting her work increases significantly, particularly when the couple has children,
whereas the same is not true for the husband when the wife works long hours (Cha 2010).

Income Inequality.   Slower advancement means that women tend to cluster in the
lower levels of virtually all occupational categories and are, therefore, accorded less

Occupation	Percent Female	Occupation	Percent Female
Total	46.8		
Managerial and Professional		*Service*	
Chief executives	27.9	Dental assistants	94.1
Managers, medicine/health	73.7	Firefighters	5.9
Architects	25.7	Chefs and head cooks	19.6
Civil engineers	12.6	Waiters and waitresses	70.1
Computer programmers	21.0	Child care workers	94.9
Physicians and surgeons	37.9	Pest control workers	4.7
College/university teachers	46.5	Police officers/sheriffs	13.6
Elementary school teachers	80.7	*Natural Resources and Construction*	
Librarians	83.0	Farming, fishing, forestry	24.2
Lawyers	34.5	Carpenters	1.8
Writers and authors	59.4	Electricians	2.3
Social workers	83.8	Highway maintenance	2.0
Sales and Office		*Production and Transportation*	
Cashiers	72.5	Bakers	60.8
Secretaries	94.5	Machinists	6.7
Receptionists	90.6	Laundry/dry cleaning	60.8
Postal clerks	46.0	Painting workers	12.9
Bank tellers	87.3	Pilots/flight engineers	9.4
Wholesale sales reps	27.9	Taxi drivers/chauffeurs	14.6

SOURCE: Bureau of Labor Statistics website.

TABLE 7.2
Employed Persons by Sex and Selected Occupation, 2015

prestige and lower salaries than men. The demand of the women's movement for *equal pay for work of equivalent value* reflects the fact that women are not rewarded equally with men even when they are equally prepared, equally qualified, and equally competent. There is a "glass ceiling," a term used to refer to the arbitrary and often invisible barriers that limit women's advancement. The glass ceiling on income exists in all occupational categories (Cotter, Hermsen, Ovadia, and Vanneman 2001).

Overall, from the 1950s until the late 1970s, women received about 60 percent of the income men received. Then the gap began to close, although the disparity is still large: by 2014, the median earnings of women who worked full-time year-round was 82.5 percent of that for men (Bureau of Labor Statistics 2015). As Figure 7.1 shows, the disparity holds for all races.

Even when taking into account such factors as education, occupational category, hours worked, experience, and performance ratings, there is still a substantial wage gap that is not explained (Dey and Hill 2007; Castilla 2008; Fernandez-Mateo 2009). For example, Roth (2003) examined a group of Wall Street securities professionals who were similar to each other in terms of such factors as education and ability. She found significant gender differences in earnings that could not be explained by anything other than discrimination. Similarly, a study of University of Michigan law school graduates reported that 15 years after graduation the men earned 52 percent more than the women, 17

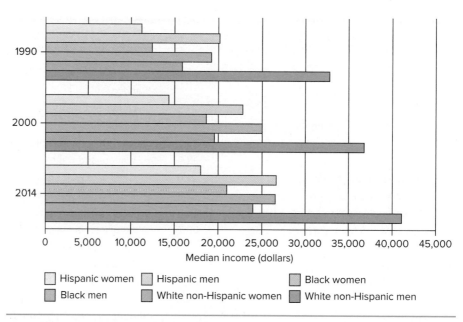

FIGURE 7.1   Median Income of Persons, 1990–2014.
Source: U.S. Census Bureau website.

percent more than women with similar characteristics, and 11 percent more than women with similar characteristics in the same job settings (Noonan, Corcoran, and Courant 2005). In the medical field, female registered nurses far outnumber male nurses, but the males are paid more and the income gap has persisted for decades (Muench et al. 2015). And a study of physicians who teach at medical schools reported an average gender gap of $20,000 a year even after controlling for age, experience, specialty, faculty rank, and productivity (Jena, Olenski, Blumenthal 2016).

The Beauty Myth.   The "beauty myth" involves a *contradiction between the belief in the dignity of all humans,* on one hand, and the *ideology about a particular group,* on the other hand. According to the beauty myth, a woman must be beautiful to be acceptable and attractive (Sullivan 2001). It's a destructive myth. Women spend billions of dollars a year on cosmetics and cosmetic surgery in an effort to appear more beautiful. Teenage girls use a variety of surgical procedures to enhance their beauty, including breast augmentation, eyelid surgery, liposuction (to remove fat), reshaping of the nose, and the "tummy tuck" to tighten the abdomen (Gross 1998). Beauty is a trap. Women who feel homely cannot enjoy their accomplishments because they are haunted by their failure to be beautiful, and women who are beautiful and successful may attribute their success to their beauty rather than to their abilities.

A particularly destructive aspect of the beauty myth is the current ideal of a slender figure for women. Bombarded by media depictions of thinness as the ideal, many women develop *a problem of body image.* They become dissatisfied with the shape and size of their bodies. White and Hispanic women are slightly more likely than black women to experience body dissatisfaction, but the problem occurs among all races (Grabe and Hyde 2006; Boroughs, Krawczyk, and Thompson 2010). It develops quite early in girls' lives. A study of 55 preschool girls concluded that girls may become emotionally invested in the thin ideal as early as 3 years of age (Harriger, Calogero, Witherington, and Smith 2010).

Body dissatisfaction can result in a variety of negative consequences for well-being. It can lead to lowered self-esteem, problematic sexual functioning (including risky sexual behavior), depression, and anxiety (Davison and McCabe 2005; Gillen, Lefkowitz, and Shearer 2006). It also leads some women, in an effort to get thinner, to succumb to eating disorders, such as *anorexia nervosa (a form of self-starvation)* and *bulimia (repeated binge eating followed by vomiting or laxatives)* (Hesse-Biber 1996). The disorders are associated with a variety of physical and emotional health problems. For example, anorexia nervosa is associated with the loss of the menstrual period, anemia, loss of hair and bone density, and kidney failure (Torpy and Glass 2006). Eating disorders are also associated with depression (Stice and Bearman 2001).

In extreme cases, some young women have died from these eating disorders. A woman can go to such an extreme because the disorders involve a disturbed body image (Miyake et al. 2010). That is, the woman does not see herself as thin even when others see her as emaciated.

Body image is an issue for men also (Grogan and Richards 2002). For men, a well-toned, muscular body provides confidence and a sense of power in social situations. Like women, men may engage in unhealthy dieting behaviors in an effort to realize their ideal (Markey and Markey 2005). But the problem of body image is more severe among women, who expressed more dissatisfaction than did men about their body shape (Demarest and Allen 2000).

Harassment and Violence. A different form of assault on dignity is the **sexual harassment** to which so many women have been subjected. Sexual harassment refers to unwelcome sexual advances, requests for sexual favors, and other verbal or physical conduct of a sexual nature that results in some kind of punishment when the victim resists or that creates a hostile environment. Although both men and women may be sexually harassed, the proportion of women who experience it is higher. For example, a survey of sexual harassment and assault experienced by reservists during military service found that 60 percent of females (compared to 27.1 percent of males) reported being victims of sexual harassment, and 13.1 percent of the females (compared to 1.6 percent of the males) reported a sexual assault (Street et al. 2008). A national survey of college students found that 35 percent of females and 29 percent of males had been physically harassed (touched, grabbed, pinched in a sexual way), while 57 percent of females and 48 percent of males had been verbally harassed (American Association of University Women 2006). A national study of middle school and high school students found that 56 percent of the girls and 40 percent of the boys had been sexually harassed (American Association of University Women 2012). Nearly a third experienced electronic harassment by such means as texting, e-mail, and Facebook, and many of them were also harassed in person.

Sexual harassment, then, occurs in all kinds of settings, among all ages, and both personally and electronically. It happens to female graduate students (Rosenthal, Smidt, and Freyd 2016). It happens to women in positions of authority as well as those in subordinate positions (McLaughlin, Uggen, and Blackstone 2012). And it happens to workers in all occupations from professionals (e.g., lawyers, professors, scientists) to blue-collar workers (e.g., autoworkers) who report experiences of sexual harassment (Bronner, Peretz, and Ehrenfeld 2003; Menard, Phung, Ghebrial, and Martin 2003; Hinze 2004; Settles, Cortina, Malley, and Stewart 2006). Overall, estimates are that at least half of all women will be harassed at some point during their academic or working lives, resulting in such things as lowered job satisfaction, negative mental health, and

sexual harassment
unwelcome sexual advances, requests for sexual favors, and other sexual behavior that either results in punishment when the victim resists or creates a hostile environment or both

OCCUPATIONAL SEX SEGREGATION IN DEVELOPING COUNTRIES

As noted in the text, occupational sex segregation is detrimental to the interests of women in the job market. In a highly segregated job market, women's income and status, compared to those of men, both tend to be depressed. Although researchers have found such segregation not only in the United States but also in other industrial nations, little has been done to examine it in developing countries. Chang's (2004) recent work, however, not only examined the patterns and extent of sex segregation in a number of developing nations but also identified the effects of government policies on the segregation.

Occupational sex segregation exists in all countries, though the extent of the segregation varies considerably (Figure 7.2). Interestingly, Chang found that government policies were the strongest predictor of variations in the extent of segregation. In particular, the lower levels of segregation occurred in nations that have maternity leave legislation. When women must be given maternity leave, increased numbers of them are able to enter the otherwise male-dominated managerial and production occupations.

On the other hand, a surprising finding was that those nations whose governments had enacted antidiscrimination legislation had the highest levels of segregation! Because Chang did not have data both before and after the legislation, it is possible that the legislation did reduce the amount of segregation. But because the levels were so high prior to the legislation, those nations still had higher levels of segregation than the others. It is also possible that antidiscrimination legislation is less effective because it is difficult to enforce and may not be enforced because of cultural restrictions on male-female interaction.

Finally, Chang found that the levels of occupational sex segregation in the developing nations that she studied were higher than the levels found by other researchers in the developed nations. With increasing development, the amount of segregation—and, consequently, the detrimental consequences for women—may diminish. But no nation yet has achieved sexual equality in the job market.

even posttraumatic stress symptoms (Street, Gradus, Stafford, and Kelly 2007; Chan, Lam, Chow, and Cheung 2008; Woods, Buchanan, and Settles 2009).

The perpetrator of harassment is most likely to be someone in a position of authority over the victim (Uggen and Blackstone 2004). In fact, perhaps the most destructive harassment occurs in the *sexual exploitation of women by men of authority in the helping professions.* Such male power figures include psychiatrists and other therapists, physicians, lawyers, clergymen, and teachers or mentors. Women are particularly vulnerable to sexual pressures in dealing with such power figures. A therapist, for example, may convince a woman that he can provide her with the kind of sexual experience she needs to work through her problems. A clergyman may convince a woman that there is some kind of divine sanction to their relationship. Although we don't know the number of women exploited in this way, increasing attention is being paid to the problem. Indeed, some professional organizations have explicitly condemned such behavior in their codes of ethics.

Finally, violence is the ultimate assault on the dignity of women. Hundreds of thousands of violent acts are committed against women every year, and about a fifth of all violence against women comes from an intimate partner. The problem is worldwide. A United Nations global survey found that during their lifetime, 67.2 percent of women reported physical or sexual violence and 81.6 percent reported psychological violence by their current husband (Fokir 2011). And a fourth of women reported such violence by someone other than their husband.

FIGURE 7.2 Occupational Sex Segregation.
Source: Chang 2004.

Contributing Factors

As with all social problems, many factors contribute to gender inequality. As we examine these factors, it will be clear that the problem is not simply one of men versus women but of a plexus of factors that together create and maintain this inequality.

Social Structural Factors. The *normative role of the female* is an important factor in gender inequality because *gender roles specify certain kinds of behavior as appropriate, and other kinds as inappropriate, for men and women.* What, then, is the *traditional role for the American female,* and how does this role contribute to inequality?

In essence, Americans have advocated the *traditional homemaker role of females and the parallel traditional breadwinner role of males.* Certainly, not all females conform to the traditional role. Working-class and African American women, in particular, have been likely to work outside the home. For the bulk of middle- and upper-class whites, however, the wife has been expected to provide a home for her husband and children and to find her fulfillment in caring for her family. The role assumes, then, that a woman will marry and have children and will focus on pleasing her husband and caring for her children.

In the 1960s and 1970s women's attitudes toward this traditional role changed considerably. Yet the traditional view still receives considerable support, particularly with respect to the woman's responsibility for the home. When the Southern Baptist

The beauty myth can result in a body image problem.
©Brand X Pictures / Punchstock

Convention, speaking for the nation's largest Protestant denomination, declared in 1998 that wives should "graciously" submit to the "servant leadership" of their husbands, Fox News polled a national sample of voters, asking whether they agreed or disagreed with the statement. Overall, a third agreed, including 34 percent of men and 32 percent of women (Polling Report 2012).

The traditional role obviously discourages women from pursuing higher education or a career. In a social context in which being female means taking care of a home and family and submitting to one's husband, it may be difficult to secure an advanced degree or to commit oneself to a career.

The research on women's aspirations suggests that if females are treated the same as males, if parents hold similar expectations for their girls and boys and encourage them equally, women will achieve the same levels of education and probably the same levels of work and careers. A great many women would like to work or pursue a career but do not because it conflicts with other role obligations. Only a minority of women prefer either a career without marriage or marriage and children without a career.

The ability to opt for multiple roles is crucial because a *restrictive role for women can lead to illness.* For both men and women, both marriage and employment increase well-being (Burke 1995). Multiple roles not only promote well-being, including physical health, but also tend to lengthen a woman's life (Moen, Dempster-McClain, and Williams 1992; Rose et al. 2004). To be a wife, a mother, and also have a career, then, tends to enhance the emotional and physical well-being of women.

Even though women who go to work have better physical and mental health, working does not solve all their problems. Such women are still likely to have more health

problems than their male counterparts. A number of factors bear on the question of how much married women
with children will benefit by working outside the home or
pursuing a career, including the nature of the work and the
division of labor in the home. As far as the nature of the
work is concerned, mothers are healthier when they have
high-quality jobs, and when they prefer to work rather
than to be a stay-at-home mother (Usdansky, Gordon,
Wang, and Gluzman 2011). During the preschool years of
their children, mothers may benefit more from part-time
than full-time work (Buehler and O'Brien 2011). Indeed,
a study of women in 28 countries found that homemak-
ers are slightly happier than those who work full-time, but
not happier than those who work part-time (Treas, van der
Lippe, and Tai 2011).

With regard to the division of labor in the home, the
likelihood is that having a job outside the house means "in
addition" rather than "instead of" taking care of the home.
There has been a trend toward greater sharing of household responsibilities, but employed women still spend
substantially more hours than their husbands doing housework (Kulik 2011). Surveys of how Americans spend their
time show that by 2013, the average amount of time spent
on household activities (housework, meal preparation and
cleanup, and lawn and garden care) each day was 1.89
hours for mothers working full-time and 1.18 hours for
fathers working full-time (Bureau of Labor Statistics web-
site). On an average day, 87.6 percent of the mothers but only 65.8 percent of the fathers
engaged in such tasks. Caring for the children's needs consumed an additional 1.29
hours for the mothers and .87 hours for the fathers. On an average day, 73.5 percent of
the mothers but only 55.2 percent of the fathers engaged in child care activities. The
result of this inequity in the household division of labor is a higher level of stress and
a greater likelihood of depression for the woman (Frisco and Williams 2003). Mothers
are also stressed by their greater likelihood of sleep deprivation as they care for the
needs of their family (Maume, Sebastian, and Bardo 2010). In short, working outside
the home may have positive health benefits for mothers, but the benefit would increase
measurably if fathers would assume an equitable share of housework and child care.

A second important social structural factor in gender inequality is the *socialization
that occurs at home, in school, and through the mass media.* In the home, parents tend
to treat their sons and daughters differently from the beginning, with the result that
children become aware of gender-role differences by as early as 2 years of age (Witt
1997). The differential treatment continues in the kinds of toys and play activities parents, probably unaware of the effects, provide for their children (Campenni 1999). For
example, a Barbie doll can create the desire in young girls for a thinner body (Dittmar,
Halliwell, and Ive 2006). And girls who played with Barbie dolls also believed they had
fewer future career options than boys did (Sherman and Zurbriggen 2014). By the early
school years, children already have a sense of which occupations are "feminine" and
which are "masculine," as well as the relative status of the various occupations (Teig
and Susskind 2008). Some girls who otherwise might have pursued a career in science,

Many children are reared in accord with gender stereotypes.
©Ryan McVay/Getty Images

engineering, or math may already have their interest in such a career undermined by stereotypes of what is feminine and what is masculine in the world of work (Shapiro and Williams 2012).

Parents also react differently to sons and daughters in the emotional realm. Fathers reward girls but punish boys for expressing sadness and fear (Bayrakdar-Garside and Klimes-Dougan 2002). When children misbehave in ways that could lead to injury, mothers are angry with their sons but disappointed with their daughters, whereas once an injury occurs, mothers attribute their sons' risky misbehavior to factors beyond their control and daughters' risky misbehavior to factors they can influence (Morrongiello and Hogg 2004).

The school may reinforce the parental pattern. Girls get higher scores than boys on most academic and cognitive tests (Francis and Skelton 2005). Nevertheless, teachers can, like parents, treat boys and girls in terms of traditional gender roles. For example, various studies have found that teachers expect girls to behave better, that they treat boy underachievers as bright but bored and overlook girl underachievers (perhaps they don't consider it as important for girls to achieve academically), and that in physical education boys get more attention and feedback (praise, criticism, technical information) than do girls (Jones and Myhill 2004; Myhill and Jones 2006; Nicaise, Cogerino, Bois, and Amorose 2006).

The *mass media are an important source of gender-role socialization.* Children's books (including picture books for the very young, elementary reading books, the Sunday comics in newspapers, TV ads, Halloween costumes, and Valentine cards all still tend to portray males and females in traditional dominant-submissive roles (Diekman and Murnen 2004; Kahlenberg and Hein 2010; McCabe, Brewster, and Tillman 2011; Mager and Helgeson 2011; Mumem et al. 2016). An analysis of music videos found that they reinforced the image of women as sex objects and as tending to be subordinate to men (Wallis 2011). Some popular magazines and books also reinforce the power differences between men and women, portray women as sex objects, and perpetuate the ideal of thinness (Zimmerman, Haddock, and McGeorge 2001; Krassas, Blauwkamp, and Wesselink 2001). An analysis of 100 top income-grossing films found that middle-aged men were more likely than their female counterparts to play leadership roles and to have occupational power (Lauzen and Dozier 2005).

Such portrayals in the media have an impact. Men who watch television programs that portray women as sex objects are more likely to engage in sexual harassment (Galdi, Maass, and Cadinu 2014). Girls and women exposed to the thinness ideal on television and in magazines have an increased likelihood of lowered self-esteem, depression, eating disorders, and approval of cosmetic surgical procedures such as liposuction and breast augmentation (Botta 2003; Vaughan and Fouts 2003; Bessenoff 2006).

fallacy   Another practical consequence of media portrayal of the sexes is that people who engage in the *fallacy of circular reasoning* find support for their arguments. Consider the following exchange we once had with an older man who made the statement: "Everyone knows that men are rational and women are emotional." We asked the man how he knew that. "Everyone knows that. Look around you. Look at television." When the man was told that television is fiction, he replied: "But it is based on fact, on what is real about people. And men are really rational and women are really emotional."

A third social structural factor is the economics of gender inequality. Situations that continue in the nation are *likely profitable* for someone, and gender inequality is no exception. The kind of gender inequalities we have discussed are beneficial for men in a variety of ways. They increase men's job opportunities, incomes, and power. It has

Someone has said, "You are what you read." As noted in this chapter, one factor in perpetuating gender-role inequality is the books that you read as a child. Conduct your own research into children's literature. The librarian at a local public library can help you make a selection. Decide on what age level you want to investigate first. Then find five books written for this age level before 1975 and five of the most recent.

Compare the books in terms of the number of male and female characters and the gender roles portrayed. How do the earlier books differ from the more recent ones? To what extent do you believe that the later books overcome gender inequality? Identify two or three aspects of traditional gender roles in the earlier books that are either maintained or eliminated in the later ones.

If the entire class does this project, assign people to cover different age levels (beginning with picture books for preschool children) and see whether there are any differences by age.

been said that the hand that rocks the cradle rocks the world (which suggests that real power belongs to women). In most people's experience, however, the hand that holds the biggest purse holds the most power—and this hand typically belongs to a man.

Furthermore, the present amount of income inequality between men and women means that men benefit by having to work less to earn the same amount of money. In essence, a woman might work seven days or more to earn what a man makes in five days (because, as noted earlier, the median income of white women is 77 percent that of white men, and the median income of black and Hispanic women is even less).

Since the end of World War II, women and men have been engaged in an ongoing struggle over the extent of women's participation in the workplace. That the struggle is one for the better positions is illustrated by the relative ease with which women can secure menial and low-paying jobs. Such jobs must be done by someone if other jobs are to be highly paid and employers are to maintain high levels of profit. Who will take such jobs?

As we shall see in the next chapter, racial and ethnic minorities also are likely to cluster in these low-level jobs, which means that **sexism** *and racism are functional substitutes* with respect to such work. Where racial or ethnic minorities are available, they provide that labor. Where they are not available, women provide it. This doesn't mean that women are equal to men in the labor market where racial or ethnic minorities are available for low-paying jobs. Rather, the point is that women are the next-to-the-lowest group on the hierarchy rather than the lowest.

sexism
prejudice or discrimination against someone because of his or her sex

One other social structural factor in gender inequality is religion. Justification for gender inequality is found in both the teachings and the practices of many religious groups (Crandall 2006). In those groups, which are found in all the world's major religions, the leaders assert or imply that men are superior to women and/or that women should be subservient.

In recent decades, a number of Christian theologians, both male and female, have argued that biblical teachings have been misinterpreted by generations of people who used them to justify and maintain patriarchal systems (Meyers 1988; Clifford 2001). Nevertheless, many religious people, but particularly the most conservative ones (known as fundamentalists), justify sexism on religious grounds (Peek, Lowe, and Williams 1991; Bendroth 1994). Religious conservatism and social conservatism tend to go hand in hand. Thus, 85 percent of religious liberals, but only 59.6 percent of religious conservatives, disagree that men are better suited emotionally to politics than are women (McConkey 2001); and 81.2 percent of the liberals, but only 68.1 percent of the conservatives, disagree that it is more important for wives to help their husband's careers than to have careers themselves.

Sexism in religion is also seen in the fact that women generally do not hold the most honored positions—minister, priest, rabbi. It is true that an increasing number of women are assuming places of leadership (Fiedler 2010). And a number of Protestant denominations technically allow women to hold top positions. Nevertheless, very few women have actually held these positions (Sandstrom 2016). Lay religious leaders are also likely to be men, even though women may be more numerous and more consistently involved in the activities of the group. In some fundamentalist groups, women are not even allowed to speak before a group or lead public worship.

Social Psychological Factors.   While American attitudes toward gender roles have become more *egalitarian,* some attitudes detrimental to women's continued progress still exist. In particular, some believe that there is no longer any discrimination, that women have opportunities equal to those of men, and that those who continue to complain are troublemakers or "radical feminists."

Such attitudes fly in the face of the realities of women's lives. We have already discussed the amount of sexual harassment with which women must deal. We have also noted the fact that discrimination in the workplace, in spite of the progress made, continues to depress the income of women. And women continue to face *negative attitudes in the workplace* with regard to their competence and commitment to the job.

Many women feel compelled to perform better than men in order to prove themselves and be accepted. For example, there is evidence that women must work harder to prove that they have the ability because men expect women—including women in supervisory and managerial positions—to be less competent than men and this bias enters into the evaluation of women (Martell, Parker, and Emrich 1998; Heilman 2001).

As we noted earlier, many women also fear that they will be penalized in their careers if they become mothers. In fact, some employers do place women into two categories: achievers and mothers. Those who opt for motherhood may find themselves on the "mommy track" of their career. The mommy track means that working mothers follow a modified career line in which they continue their work but do not advance as rapidly as men or those women without children. Thus, for example, women lawyers who take time off to attend to child care are less likely to become partners in their firms and earn less even if they do become partners (Noonan and Corcoran 2004).

Ideology is also a factor in gender inequality. Many Americans still believe that a woman's place is in the home and that when she leaves the home to pursue higher education or a career, she leaves her post as one of the guardians of the social order. The ideology that *women's abdication of the home* can only result in *social disorganization* was expressed by those who insisted that women return to their homes after World War II. They identified working women as a primary cause of delinquency and argued that for women to continue in the labor force would mean instability in the social institutions of the nation. More recently, in the surveys of religious people noted earlier, 81.2 percent of religious liberals, but only 44.2 percent of conservatives, disagreed that everyone is better off if the man is the achiever outside the home and the woman cares for her home and family (McConkey 2001:162). A study of 349 American adults found two nonreligious ideologies that foster prejudice against working women (Christopher and Wojda

2008). The "social dominance orientation" includes the belief of superior-inferior groups (with men, of course, being superior). Right-wing authoritarianism includes deference to established authority, which means that women and men fulfill complementary roles but that women need to be protected and cared for by men. Adults in the research with a social dominance orientation tended to have a "hostile sexism," viewing women in negative, disparaging terms; those with a right-wing authoritarian ideology tended to have a "benevolent sexism," viewing women in the traditional terms of those whose proper place is in the home.

Many books and magazines also continue to extol the virtues of the stay-at-home mother and to warn mothers of the dangers of going to work while they have children in the home (Johnston and Swanson 2003). Some books portray employed mothers as tired, busy, and guilty, whereas other books laud the bliss of stay-at-home mothers. And although some Americans believe that women's magazines promote a feminist agenda, the image of women that comes from an examination of those magazines is a person who is focused on consumption, is beautiful, and is domestic.

Is it true, as an important part of the ideology asserts, that children are harmed when their mothers work? Many Americans agree with the idea that a mother with small children (and, in some cases, with any children) should remain at home. A review of research conducted throughout the 1990s, however, concluded that there was little relationship between maternal employment and child outcomes (Perry-Jenkins, Repetti, and Crouter 2000). In fact, maternal employment may be beneficial for the children of single mothers and lower-income families.

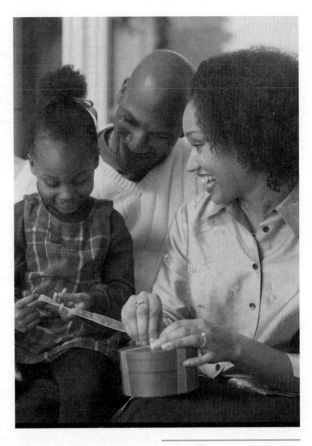

Working mothers have children as happy and healthy as do stay-at-home mothers.

©Ryan McVay / Getty Images

There are circumstances, however, that might foster negative consequences. For one thing, the effects *depend in part on how family members define the mother's working.* Agreement that it is a good thing for the mother to work minimizes any negative effects and can even have positive outcomes for the children in terms of their educational and career aspirations. Disagreement can create some serious problems.

A second important circumstance is the nature of the mother's work, including the pay, the hours worked, and the time of day spent working. In general, children of working mothers do as well academically as those of nonworking mothers (Goldberg, Prause, Lucas-Thompson, and Himsel 2008). However, research on welfare-reliant single mothers found that when the number of hours worked increased, the children were more likely to skip school and less likely to perform above average (Gennetian, Lopoo, and London 2008). And a national study of single mothers found that part-time, low-wage work and working nonstandard hours can both lead to poorer home environments (Lleras 2008).

The consequences of maternal employment also may vary by age of the child. Available research indicates no negative consequences for infants at least 2 years old. In some cases, day care may even be better than home care because it offers the children various kinds of enrichment not available in their homes. For infants under the age of 2, however, the research is contradictory and not always encouraging for those who prefer to work. Some research suggests that babies cared for by others are less securely attached to their mothers. Such children may have to cope with problems of insecurity for years or even a lifetime. In addition, there is evidence of some detrimental effects on cognitive development for children whose mothers go to work during the first year of their lives (Baum 2003). Such children score lower on measures of cognitive development than do children whose mothers stayed at home.

In sum, the evidence is that children over the age of 2 will probably not be harmed by a mother working and may even be helped by it, as long as the family defines the work as appropriate activity and the children have adequate supervision and care. For infants 2 and under, more research is needed. But it is *a myth that there are inexorable, undesirable consequences for the children when the mother works.*

Public Policy and Private Action

fallacy

Like other social problems, gender inequality is so pervasive and so entrenched that pessimists may commit the *fallacy of retrospective determinism* and argue that the nation will never be rid of it. Whether a perfectly equitable society is achievable may be debatable, but it is clear that progress can be made.

What kind of action can address the problems of women? What kind of public policy is needed, and what other forms of private initiative in addition to consciousness-raising groups can help?

Clearly, the federal government needs to be involved. Federal antidiscriminatory laws have helped American women. But the Council on Contemporary Families (2003) compared American husbands and the American government to their counterparts in Germany, France, Italy, and Japan. The council concluded that American husbands do more housework and child care than do husbands in the other nations, but the U.S. government does the least of all the governments to help employed wives. In France, women workers have a government-mandated and protected benefit of a fully paid leave 6 weeks prior to and 10 weeks after the birth of a child. Both parents can also receive some additional paid leave until the child's third birthday. The United States needs more and better *child care centers* and more extensive *family leave laws* (laws that allow people time off from their jobs without penalty when a child is born, adopted, or seriously ill). The right to parental leave in the United States covers only about half of the private sector workforce and is generally short and often unpaid. Some other nations offer universal, paid leaves of 10 months or more.

The importance of such measures is underscored by the fact that more than 10 million women in the labor force have children under the age of 6. The well-being of employed mothers is dependent on adequate child care. Employed mothers who have no problems in arranging for child care and whose husbands participate in child care have very low depression levels, whereas those who have difficulties and who have sole responsibility for child care tend to have very high levels of depression.

The children of satisfied mothers are better adjusted whether the mothers stay at home or work away from home. Women who prefer, or who feel the need, to work will not be satisfied to stay at home; but the option of working is closed to many women unless child care centers are available. Such centers are a part of the "bill of rights" of the National Organization for Women (NOW).

As more women become politically involved and are elected to public office, the government is more likely to enact measures that help women. As Swers (2002) has found, women legislators engage in more, and more intense, action in behalf of women's interests than do men. And this finding is true in both political parties.

Changes in education are crucial in order to alter notions of the "proper" roles of the sexes and to attack the ideology that restricts women's sphere of appropriate activity to the home. As presently structured, education affects women's attitudes more than men's and does more to help people recognize gender inequality than to support remedies for that inequality (Kane 1995). Education needs to be restructured to aid people's understanding about the capabilities of women. Educators need to treat males and females equally from kindergarten through graduate training; they need to teach people how to parent so that females are no longer socialized into a subordinate role; and they need to help people develop new norms about women's participation in all sectors of the economy.

In addition, educational institutions should find ways to increase the amount of mentoring women receive. A study of chemists reported that the women believed they had received less mentoring than the men at every level of their training—the undergraduate, graduate, and postdoctoral levels (Nolan, Buckner, Marzabadi, and Kuck 2008). Such differences in mentoring can easily carry over into different degrees of advancement and achievement in one's career.

Still another form of action involves changing the policies and practices of organizations. A controversial proposal to eliminate income inequalities is the notion of *comparable worth* (Barko 2000). In essence, the idea is that women should receive equal pay not just for equal work but for work that is judged to be of comparable worth. The basis for such a proposal is the fact that women are overrepresented in such areas as nursing and clerical work, whereas men are overrepresented in such jobs as pilot and truck driver. The occupations in which women are overrepresented tend to pay less than those in which men are overrepresented, even though they may require similar amounts of training. The argument is that when jobs are of comparable worth, they should pay equal salaries. Otherwise gender inequality in income will continue indefinitely.

Why, for example, should beginning engineers (mostly men) earn 30 to 70 percent more than beginning teachers (mostly women) (Barko 2000)? Is a truck driver (probably a man) 45 percent more valuable than a child care worker (a college graduate and probably a woman)? Proponents of comparable worth raise such questions. They argue that experts can examine jobs in terms of their difficulty, responsibility, and education and experience requirements; rate the jobs accordingly; and equalize the pay for equivalent work.

Although both federal laws and laws in most states reflect a basic principle of comparable worth by prohibiting gender-based differences in pay, the inequality persists. But at least there is a legal basis for unions and individuals to pursue cases against organizations whose policies and/or practices perpetuate inequality.

Action by work organizations is also needed to deal with the problem. The majority of employers responded in the 1990s to the problem by instituting grievance procedures and sensitivity training (Dobbin and Kelly 2007). Victims now have legal redress, and employers are held responsible for harassment that occurs in their places of work. Among other changes, employers have been encouraged to avoid legal problems by making policy statements to employees, setting up grievance procedures for alleged victims, and educating employees on appropriate behavior between the sexes. Such procedures are designed to correct one of the basic reasons for the continuation of harassment: people's ignorance of the problematic nature and consequences of harassment and of the recourse available to victims. Harassment also can be reduced if work organizations assume the responsibility for training all employees to be supportive of women's dignity and intolerant of harassment.

Legal change can be effective in reducing inequality. Antidiscrimination laws have brought about significant changes on the nation's college and university campuses. Among other changes, discrimination in official policies and practices and admissions quotas have been abolished. Accordingly, students are to be treated equally in terms of rules and services; married women, for instance, are no longer excluded from financial aid because they are married, and sexual harassment is explicitly forbidden. As we noted earlier, covert discrimination still occurs, and the problems of women on the campus are by no means fully resolved, but gains have been made as a result of legal change.

Finally, business and industry can take the important step of *ensuring women equal career opportunities.* In particular, the business world can reject the "Mommy Track" notion and allow women to be mothers without sacrificing a professional career. An example is the "family plan" implemented by Johnson and Johnson to help its employees cope with family responsibilities (Deutsch 1990). Included in the plan are a nationwide resource and referral system for child care and elder care; a year's family care leave, with full benefits for an employee who has to care for a child, a spouse, or a parent; training of supervisors to make them aware of the needs and problems involved in balancing work and family demands; and benefits that pay some of the costs of adopting a child. Some companies offer reduced work hours or other kinds of help for employees with family responsibilities. But such programs are available to only a small minority of women employees.

Follow-Up.   Set up a class debate on this topic: Comparable worth offers the most promising solution for ending gender inequality in the United States.

The LGBT Community

heterosexual
having sexual preference for persons of the opposite sex

homosexual
having sexual preference for persons of the same sex; someone who privately or overtly considers himself or herself a homosexual

homophobia
irrational fear of homosexuals

In American society, the fulfillment of intimacy needs is often framed in terms of a **heterosexual** relationship. In this section, we will look at people who find fulfillment in other kinds of relationships, such as the **homosexual**. We will see the problems homosexual individuals encounter because of irrational fears and disdain, as illustrated by **homophobia**, and we will look at factors that perpetuate the problems.

The LGBT Community: Definitions and Numbers

lesbian
a female homosexual

bisexual
having sexual relations with either sex or both together.

transgender
having a gender identity different from one's anatomy

Not everyone who engages in a homosexual act can be considered a homosexual. Boys commonly engage in homosexual activity during adolescence, but most of them become exclusively heterosexual. We define a homosexual as an individual both who has a sexual preference for those of the same sex and who also defines himself or herself as homosexual. *Gay* is a synonym for homosexual, though some use it to refer primarily to males. **Lesbian** is the term for female homosexuals.

Some people are **bisexual,** finding gratification with both sexes and having no strong preference for either, but bisexuals are not as common as those who are exclusively heterosexual or homosexual. **Transgender** refers to those who have a gender identity that differs from their anatomy. The body may be male, but the person feels like a woman, or the body is female but the person feels like a man.

Homosexuality is found throughout the world. It is difficult to estimate the proportion of people who are homosexual. In some societies, homosexuality is still a crime and homosexuals must keep their sexual orientation secret. Many studies have examined only small populations, such as college students, that are not representative of the nation as a whole. Moreover, as noted earlier, many people are either bisexual or have a homosexual experience at some point but prefer heterosexual relations. For example, a survey of same-sex activity among American teenagers and young adults (ages 15 to 21) who had never married or cohabited reported that 11 percent of females and 4 percent of the males had had some same-sex experience (McCabe, Brewster, and Tillman 2011). Most of those who reported same-sex experience also preferred it exclusively, but some of those who acknowledged same-sex activity indicated they preferred only heterosexual relationships.

One of the most comprehensive studies of sexual behavior in recent decades was the National Health and Social Life Survey, conducted by researchers at the University of Chicago (Laumann et al. 1994). Using a sample of 3,432 American men and women between the ages of 18 and 59, the researchers found that 2.7 percent of sexually active men and 1.3 percent of sexually active women had a homosexual experience in the past year. Further, they reported that 9.1 percent of men and 4.3 percent of women have had a homosexual experience since puberty, and 7.7 percent of men and 7.4 percent of women said they felt some degree of same-sex *attraction* or interest. More recently, a researcher used various sources of data and estimated that about 5 percent of men are gay (Stephens-Davidowitz 2013). And a national study of U.S. adults that were asked about any same-sex experience since age 18 reported a doubling of the proportion from the early 1990s (3.6 percent of women and 4.5 percent of men) to the early 2010s (8.7 percent of women and 8.7 percent of men) (Twenge, Sherman, and Wells 2016). Bisexual behavior also increased, from 3.1 to 7.7 percent. The increase could represent increasing homosexual behavior or increasing willingness to acknowledge homosexual behavior or both.

At any rate, it is safe to say that a minimum of 3 to 4 percent of American men and 2 to 3 percent of American women prefer to be exclusively homosexual. The proportions are not high, but in absolute terms we are talking about 17 or more million Americans at a minimum.

It is even more difficult to estimate the number of transgender individuals. Two incidents brought transgenderism into focus in recent years. One was when the Olympic decathlon champion Bruce Jenner announced in 2015 that he identified himself as a female. He changed his name to Caitlyn and his appearance to female. The other incident was the public restroom battles that began in 2007 centering on the issue of whether someone, for example, who is anatomically a male can use the women's room. We'll discuss the matter further below. Here, we simply want to note that a group of researchers at UCLA has estimated the number of transgender people in the United States to be 1.4 million adults, which is less than 1 percent of all adults.

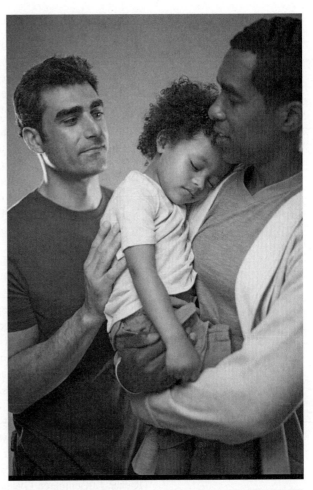

Many homosexuals lead well-adjusted lives even when faced with negative social reaction.
©Image Source/Veer

Why Are Some People Homosexual?

Enormous pressures exist in American society for people to be heterosexual. Few of you have grown up without hearing the word "homosexual" or a slang term meaning homosexual applied to someone in a disparaging way. Moreover, books, television, and observation all reinforce the expectation of heterosexual relations. Why, then, do some people prefer homosexual relations?

Biological Explanations.   A number of observers believe that *homosexuality is genetically programmed into some people.* Balthazart (2012), for example, has forcefully argued that homosexuality is not an individual's free choice but is the result of "embryonic endocrine/genetic phenomena" that fashion the individual's sexual desires and needs. Let's examine some of the evidence that leads to such a conclusion. A number of researchers have identified differences between homosexuals and heterosexuals in the structure of their brains, and genetic differences in a region on the X chromosome (Swaab and Hofman 1990; Pool 1993; Harrison, Everall, and Catalan 1994; McCormick and Witelson 1994; Mustanski, Chivers, and Bailey 2002).

The possibility that homosexuality is biological rather than sociocultural is also supported by some behavioral studies. Bell, Weinberg, and Hammersmith (1981) reported finding none of the usual sociocultural factors in their study of 979 homosexuals. Rather, the single most important factor they identified is gender nonconformity at an early age. That is, gay men and lesbians both recall having different preferences and behaviors than most of their peers, suggesting the possibility that they were different from birth. The difference is confirmed in research with parents of gay men, who also recall much atypical gender behavior in their sons, including a lack of interest in sports (Aveline 2006).

Subsequent studies lend further support (Landolt et al. 2004). Studies of lesbians report that, as children, they preferred masculine roles and "boy's games" (Palzkill and Fisher 1990; Whitam and Mathy 1991). Similarly, among a sample of adults who still had home videos from their childhood, both lesbian and gay adults were more gender nonconforming than heterosexual adults in the home videos they watched as children (Rieger, Linsenmeier, Gygax, and Bailey 2008). In short, gender nonconformity in children is a strong predictor of homosexuality.

Additional evidence emerges in studies of twins (Dawood et al. 2000). In a study of male twins in which at least one brother was gay, two researchers found that in 52 percent of 56 sets of identical twins, both brothers were gay, compared to 22 percent of 54 sets of fraternal twins (Bailey and Pillard 1991). They also looked at 57 families in which a gay son had an adoptive brother and found that only 11 percent of the adoptive brothers were also gay.

The point is that the chances that both siblings will turn out to be homosexual increases dramatically according to the amount of genes they share. At the same time, as the researchers acknowledge, the fact that not all the identical twins were homosexual suggests that sociocultural factors play a role. Let's look at some of those factors.

Sociocultural Explanations.   Some social scientists argue that homosexuality is a *learned pattern of behavior* rather than the natural outgrowth of an innate drive. Because there are strong pressures toward heterosexuality, these social scientists look for factors in family life or in patterns of interaction that differ for homosexuals and heterosexuals.

Some researchers have found that homosexuals have *disturbed relationships with their parents.* Harry (1989) reported that gays were more likely to suffer abuse by their parents, though the abuse may have been a result rather than a cause of the son's sexual

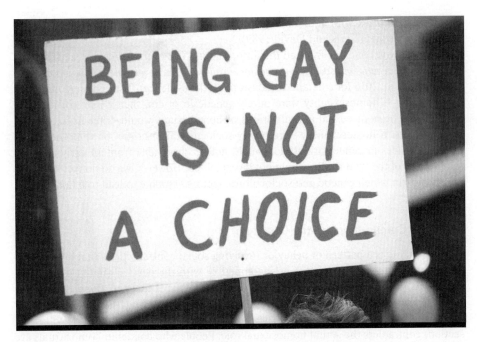

Gay activists parade to protest the negative societal reaction they must often endure.
©Jack Star/PhotoLink/Getty Images

preference. Others have found that homosexuals were more likely than heterosexuals to have been the victims of incest (Cameron and Cameron 1995). Note, however, that only a minority of the homosexuals indicated an incestuous experience. Studies of lesbians also report family problems, including physical and sexual abuse (Sang, Warshow, and Smith 1991; Bradford, Ryan, and Rothblum 1994).

The issue of problematic family experiences remains clouded. Most studies rely on the recollections of adults. Earlier ones, conducted from the 1950s through the 1970s, tended to find deficiencies in the family life of homosexuals, whereas subsequent studies tend to find no differences between homosexual and heterosexual backgrounds. Thus, we cannot say with certainty whether family experiences contribute to the development of homosexuality.

One family factor that is intriguing but has not so far been convincingly explained either biologically or socioculturally is birth order in a family with two or more sons. There is a correlation between sexual orientation and the number of older brothers (Cantor, Blanchard, Paterson, and Bogaert 2002; McConaghy et al. 2006). Each older brother that a man has raises his odds of being homosexual by about 33 percent. This fraternal birth order effect accounts for the sexual orientation of about one of every seven gay men.

A sociocultural factor that may be important, however, is the *norms of one's peers during adolescence.* Some young males engage in homosexual activities with adults to earn money. It may be a purely financial transaction for the boys that is approved by group norms. The same norms, on the other hand, define the adult homosexuals as "queers." The boys do not regard themselves as homosexuals and do not continue homosexual activity when they become adults.

By contrast, if an adolescent participates in a *homosexual clique,* homosexuality may be defined as preferable, and the individual may accept a homosexual identity as he or she internalizes the norms of the group. Some, perhaps a majority, of young male prostitutes engage in sex with adults not merely for money, but because their own orientation is homosexual (Earls and David 1989).

What can you conclude from all this information? The overall evidence suggests that *there are both genetic and sociocultural factors involved in the development of homosexuality* (see Bailey et al. 2016 for a detailed analysis of all the evidence). The genetic component is strong, but if homosexuality were purely genetic in origin, then all sets of identical twins would be homosexual and all brains of homosexuals would differ from those of heterosexuals. If homosexuality were purely sociocultural in origin, on the other hand, then differences in gender orientation would not be observable from an early age, and the findings of the twin studies could not be explained. However, we do not yet know the precise way in which genetic and sociocultural factors combine to lead to a homosexual identity.

The LGBT Community and the Quality of Life

Homosexuality is a pattern of behavior involving social contradictions that both homosexuals and heterosexuals define as incompatible with the desired quality of life. Homosexuals point to two contradictions in particular. One is that the *American ideology of equality contradicts American attitudes and behavior toward homosexuals.* The other is that the stereotyped homosexual role (see the discussion of myths in the following section) contradicts the actual homosexual role. People who condemn homosexuals are frequently condemning the stereotyped rather than the actual role.

Myths about Homosexuality.   A contradiction exists between the ideal of the *dignity of human beings and the prevalent ideology about homosexuals.* This contradiction is manifested in a *number of myths about homosexuality,* myths that involve the *fallacies of personal attack and appeal to prejudice.* Perhaps the most common myth is that homosexuals have characteristics that are normal for the opposite sex—males are "effeminate" and females are "masculine." While it is true, as noted earlier, that gender nonconformity among children is a strong predictor of homosexuality, that nonconformity does not persist for the majority of homosexuals. As Taywaditep (2001) pointed out, most gay men who are gender nonconforming as children "defeminize" during adolescence. They may do so to avoid social stigma or because it is a natural part of growing up. In any case, the majority of adult homosexuals are not gender nonconforming in their mannerisms and behavior.

A second myth about homosexuals is that they fear, and are incapable of, having heterosexual relationships. Homosexuality is commonly attributed to unsatisfactory heterosexual experiences that cause fear of relationships with the opposite sex.

Although experiences with people of the opposite sex may be a factor in the development of homosexuality, there does not seem to be any evidence that homosexuals are incapable of relating to the opposite sex. By definition, a homosexual prefers sexual relations with those of his or her own sex exclusively. However, homosexuals do make and maintain good relationships with people of the opposite sex. Research by the Institute for Sex Research, founded by Kinsey, showed that about one-fifth of homosexuals in the sample had been married at one time and about half of them had intercourse from two to four times a week during the first year of marriage (Bell and Weinberg 1978). Bell, Weinberg, and Hammersmith (1981) reported that the lesbians in their sample had early histories of heterosexual experiences that were virtually identical to those of straight women.

A third myth is that people typically become homosexual by being seduced by a homosexual. No evidence supports this myth.

fallacy

Still another myth is that a homosexual is attracted to, and will make advances to, anyone of his or her own sex, children as well as adults. The homosexual, however, is as selective as a straight person and is unlikely to be a pedophile. A study of erotic age preference reported that gay males, who prefer mature partners, respond no more to male children than do heterosexual males, who also prefer mature partners to children (Freund, Watson, and Rienzo 1989).

Finally, there is the myth that homosexuals do not form the same kinds of long-term attachments as heterosexuals. When homosexuality was even more of a stigma than it is today, it would have been difficult to maintain such a relationship without rousing suspicions. But researchers have found that homosexuals want essentially the same things as heterosexuals in intimate relationships. There are few differences between homosexual and heterosexual couples at any stage of the relationship from dating to long-term commitment (Roisman et al. 2008). And that includes a long-term relationship with the same partner; long-term homosexual couples resemble long-term heterosexual couples in virtually everything except their sexual orientation (Gottman et al. 2003). In short, *homosexual couples have the same hopes, the same needs, the same desires, and, indeed, the same problems as heterosexual couples* (Patterson 2000). The problems include instances of verbal and physical abuse (Lockhart, White, Causby, and Isaac 1994).

Homosexuals may want, like heterosexuals, to be parents and may find great satisfaction in parenting. Of 47 lesbian couples studied by Koepke, Hare, and Moran (1992), 40 percent had children and were more satisfied with their relationship and their sexual relations than were the childless couples. Gay men who are fathers are similar to heterosexual fathers in both parenting style and attitudes (Bigner and Jacobsen 1992).

Independent of desire and satisfaction is the question of the *well-being of children raised in a homosexual family*. A national study of gay and lesbian parents found more similarities than differences between them and heterosexual parents (Johnson and O'Connor 2002). Where they did find differences, moreover, the gay and lesbian parents had, in a number of areas, more positive child-rearing practices: they were, compared to the heterosexual parents, more responsive to their children, more child-oriented, and more egalitarian in sharing household tasks between the partners. In sum, the research available so far indicates that the overall well-being of children raised in a homosexual family is as high as that of children raised in heterosexual families (Patterson 2000; Wainwright and Patterson 2006, 2008). And contrary to what some people believe, children raised by a homosexual pair are no more likely to be homosexual themselves than are children raised by a heterosexual pair (Fulcher, Sutfin, and Patterson 2008).

Equality of Opportunity. The American ideology of *equality of opportunity contradicts the norms about the hiring of homosexuals and about their rights to equal treatment in such things as* housing. Until the start of this century, the homosexual was a criminal under state **sodomy** laws. Legally, the term "sodomy" was ambiguous. Depending on the state, it referred to anal intercourse, mouth-genital sex, or sex with animals. Sodomy laws were established to prevent what people considered to be "unnatural" kinds of sexual behavior. In practice, however, the laws were used mainly to prosecute homosexuals. The laws were not always enforced, and were finally overturned by the Supreme Court in 2003. But homosexuals and lesbians have had to contend with a number of barriers to equal opportunity within both the government and the business sectors.

The lack of equal opportunity is not based on any lack of ability or inferior performance by homosexuals. In fact, homosexuals may *suffer discrimination in spite of*

sodomy
intercourse defined as "unnatural"; particularly used to refer to anal intercourse

proven adequate or even superior performance. They may experience harassment, stalled careers, or other sanctions if their sexual orientation is known. Tilesik (2011) sent fictitious pairs of résumés to 1,769 postings of available jobs in seven different states. In each pair, one of the résumés included experience in a gay campus organization, and the other listed experience in an organization that had nothing to do with sexual orientation. Otherwise, the two applicants had the same experience and qualifications. The researcher found that employers in some of the states—those with stronger antigay attitudes and weaker antidiscrimination laws—were significantly more likely to reject the gay applicants. And a study of physicians' experiences in the practice of medicine found that among physicians who were lesbian, gay, bisexual, or transgender, 10 percent said they were denied referrals from heterosexual colleagues, 15 percent reported being harassed by a colleague, and 22 percent said they were socially ostracized (Eliason, Dibble, and Robertson 2011).

In addition to the workplace, homosexuals are sometimes the victims of discrimination in the housing market. A Canadian study looked at inquires about renting available apartments and found significant discrimination of same-sex couples relative to heterosexual couples (Lauster and Easterbrook 2011).

sanctions
mechanisms of social control for enforcing a society's standards

Negative Sanctions.   **Sanctions** are rewards (positive sanctions) or punishments (negative sanctions) designed to influence behavior. Homosexuals are subjected to *numerous negative sanctions,* including ridicule, suppression, physical abuse, and ostracism. Negative sanctions contradict the American ideology that every citizen has a right to life, liberty, and the pursuit of happiness. All the sanctions, of course, are aimed at changing the homosexual into a heterosexual. Transgender people experience many of the same kind of negative sanctions. Transgender youth are punished for public displays of affection and for violating gender norms (Snapp et al. 2015). And transgender adults report arrests and incarceration and abuse while in the custody of law enforcement (Stotzer 2014).

Transgender rights became the focus of national attention after an Illinois transgender girl athlete demanded the right to use the girl's locker room to change (Stolberg et al. 2016). The federal Department of Education's support of the girl raised the issue elsewhere, including the use of public rest rooms by transgender people. The federal government ordered all public schools to let transgender people use the bathroom of their choice, leading to a series of lawsuits by states that wanted to require students to use bathrooms in accord with their anatomy. As of this writing, the controversy continues.

Negative sanctions can come from parents or caretakers, other family members, friends, acquaintances or strangers (Balsam, Rothblum, and Beauchaine 2005). Rejection by parents may be one of the reasons for the high rate of homelessness among gay and lesbian youth. A representative sample of public school students in Massachusetts in grades 9 through 12 reported that 25 percent of lesbian/gay students, compared to 3 percent of heterosexual students, were homeless (Corliss, Goodenow, Nichols, and Austin 2011). Lesbian/gay youth also experience a disproportionate amount of other kinds of victimization (Button, O'Connell, and Gealt 2012). One study of 528 gay, lesbian, and bisexual youth found that because of their sexual orientation nearly 80 percent had been verbally abused, 11 percent had been physically abused, and 9 percent had been sexually victimized (D'Augelli, Grossman, and Starks 2006). A study using a national probability sample of gay, lesbian, and bisexual adults reported that 20 percent had been victimized by a personal or property crime because of their sexual orientation,

50 percent had suffered verbal harassment, and more than 10 percent reported an experience of employment or housing discrimination (Herek 2009).

The verbal abuse includes such things as being *labeled perverts or called mentally ill.* The physical abuse may be sufficiently severe to result in injuries or even death (D'Augelli and Grossman 2001). In fact, FBI (2015b) statistics show that 18.6 percent of the thousands of hate crimes in 2014 were based on bias against people because of their sexual orientation.

Fear. It is little wonder that *homosexuals live with a certain amount of fear,* including the fear of making their sexual identity known to physicians because of possible negative reactions (Lehmann, Lehmann, and Kelly 1998). One of the freedoms cherished by Americans is the freedom from fear. For the homosexual, this ideal is contradicted by the norms and laws that apply to gay people as well as by the experience of being abused. Lesbian/gay youth are 2.4 times more likely than heterosexuals to miss school out of fear (Friedman et al. 2011). And, depending on the community in which they function, the fear continues into adulthood.

In other words, the homosexual is subject to fear of exposure if he or she decides to remain secretive and to fear of negative sanctions if he or she decides to come out. Not every homosexual goes around constantly haunted by fear. Nevertheless, all homosexuals must come to terms with realistic fears. These fears are realistic because all homosexuals are familiar with stories of harassment and attacks. For example, imagine what it must be like to be a homosexual and read in a national magazine of a gay man who, because he led a campaign against an antigay resolution passed by the local government in the area where he and his partner lived, received anonymous telephone calls that threatened to "slit your throat and watch your faggot blood run in the street" (Henry 1994:57). Gays know that such incidents are neither rare nor confined to isolated areas of the nation. Nor are they confined to the United States. Homosexuals in other nations struggle with similar sanctions and fears, even in societies like Sweden that are more tolerant of diverse kinds of sexual behavior (Röndahl, Innala, and Carlsson 2007).

Psychological and Emotional Problems. You might expect that it is difficult for those in the LGBT community to avoid psychological and emotional problems as they wrestle with the contradictions that impinge upon their lives. In fact, a number of studies have identified problems that result from the *stress generated by the societal reaction to an individual's homosexuality.* Among other things, homosexuals and transgender people have higher rates than heterosexuals of isolation, depression, anxiety, substance abuse, posttraumatic stress disorder, and suicide proneness (Bostwick, Boyd, Hughes, and McCabe 2010; Langhinrichsen-Rohling, Lamis, and Malone 2011; McCallum and McLaren 2011; Baams, Grossman, and Russel 2015; Miller and Groffman 2015; Mustanski, Andrews, and Puckett 2016).

It is important to underscore the point that these psychological and emotional problems are the result of stress imposed by the social environment rather than because of any innate flaws in homosexuals themselves. For example, those who are in legally recognized relationships (marriages or civil unions) have fewer and less severe mental health problems and higher levels of general well-being than those homosexuals who are single (Riggle, Rostosky, and Horne 2010). Homosexuals in states that have laws and policies that protect homosexuals against hate crimes and employment discrimination have significantly fewer psychiatric disorders (Hatzenbuchler, Keyes, and Hasin 2009). And homosexuals who have strong social support in the form of a social network have fewer mental health issues than those with little social support (Teasdale and Bradley-Engen 2010).

In spite of the greater prevalence of psychological and emotional problems, homosexuals generally function quite well in society. Three conclusions follow from the varied evidence we have presented in this section. First, there is no basis, in other words, for claiming that a homosexual orientation per se is associated with clinical symptoms of mental illness. As the American Psychiatric Association has underscored by removing homosexuality from its list of mental disorders, the notion that gays are inherently disturbed individuals who need therapy in order to change their sexual preference is no longer tenable. Second, the stress induced by societal reaction to the individual's homosexuality creates emotional and psychological problems (I. H. Meyer 2003). Third, many homosexuals come to terms with the societal reaction, cope with the problems, and lead well-adjusted and productive lives.

Contributing Factors

Without the societal reaction to the LGBT community among Americans, we could not speak of their behavior as a social problem. In this section we look at some of the multilevel factors that account for this societal reaction and that create stress for homosexuals and transgender people.

Social Structure Factors.   In the United States, *normative sexual behavior* is heterosexual. The norms of society define homosexuality as deviant, but such norms do not reflect universal standards or innate biological imperatives. In fact, even when heterosexual relations are dominant, a society may not disapprove of or *punish homosexuality.* In her study of a variety of primitive societies, Brown (1952) found that 14 of 44 of the societies for which data were available did not punish male homosexuality, and 8 of 12 did not punish female homosexuality.

Many modern societies refrain from formally punishing homosexual acts that are conducted in private between consenting adults. These acts, for example, are not considered a crime in Japan, Korea, Mexico, Argentina, Uruguay, Egypt, and the Sudan.

The United States is the only large Western nation that allows the punishment of adults who privately engage in consensual homosexual acts. This attitude reflects the English heritage of America, particularly the views of the Puritans, who saw homosexuality as one symptom of the moral corruption of England in the 17th century (Mitchell 1969). Changes have since occurred in England. In 1967 the House of Commons reformed the laws on homosexuality and removed private, consensual homosexual acts between adults from the criminal statutes.

The changes in England were facilitated by the support of prominent Anglican and Catholic clergymen. In the United States, many religious leaders, particularly fundamentalist Christians, stress that homosexuality is a "vice" condemned by various biblical teachings. In general, although most religious people are becoming more tolerant, the more conservative people are in their faith, the more negative their views on homosexuality (Barna Research Online 2001).

Gay Christians and Jews have formed a number of organizations, including Evangelicals Concerned, and Dignity (Roman Catholic), in an effort to win acceptance for themselves. Some religious leaders have spoken out in support of homosexuals. And some theologians have constructed a religious justification for homosexuality (Lowe 2009). Nevertheless, by and large, religious groups continue to view homosexuality in negative terms.

The result is that trying to attend church or a synagogue can be a stressful experience for a homosexual. It may only intensify a sense of guilt. At the least, it underscores the fact that official religion is likely to be as much a problem as a comfort.

FIGURE 7.3
Attitudes about Homosexuality.
Source: Polling Report 2016.

Social Psychological Factors. The homosexual's stressful environment is maintained by social psychological factors that support and reinforce norms and institutional arrangements. Attitudes about homosexuality and homosexual behavior generally have been negative throughout most of our history. A majority of Americans now believe that homosexual marriages should be legal, and that homosexuals should have the same civil rights as other Americans (Figure 7.3). At the same time, many people distinguish between the formal rights and the informal privileges (such as public displays of affection) (Doan, Loehr, and Miller 2014). Some who support the formal rights are not as accepting of the informal privileges. And a study of health care providers found a preference for treating heterosexual over homosexual patients (Sabin, Riskind, and Nosek 2015). Finally, attitudes about the rights of transgender individuals are ambivalent. In a national poll, more Americans (46 percent) believed that transgender people should use the public bathrooms of the gender they were born with than those (41 percent) who agreed that they should be able to use the public bathrooms of the gender they identify with (Polling Report 2016).

In sum, the LGBT community still has to deal with many negative attitudes. But we expect the shift to positive attitudes will continue. That shift has been considerable. Surveys by the National Opinion Research Center at the University of Chicago show that by 2010 less than a majority (43.5 percent) agreed that sexual relationships between two adults of the same sex is "always wrong." This represents a dramatic shift from 1987, when 75 percent of the respondents said such relationships are always wrong. The trend of increasingly positive attitudes should continue because of the differences in age groups. For example, the percentage of those saying that homosexual behavior is always wrong varied from 62.5 percent of those aged 70 and above to only 26.0 percent of those aged 18 to 29 years. And the percentage approving of same-sex marriage varied from 12.5 percent of those aged 70 and above to 64.2 percent of those aged 18 to 29 years.

Various other studies confirm this pattern of increasing acceptance and approval. Research comparing college students living in a residence hall in 1985 with those living there in 2001 found the 2001 group more accepting of lesbians, more likely to have contact with lesbians, and more likely to say their parents had positive views about lesbians (Newman 2007). Those who continue to hold negative attitudes are more likely to be found among older age groups, political conservatives, and fundamentalist Protestants (Wood and Bartkowski 2004). Negative attitudes are also more likely among those who believe that homosexuality is a choice or the result of nurture rather than a genetically based predisposition (Smith, Zanotti, Axelton, and Saucier 2011).

For some people, the negative reaction to homosexuality is legitimated by the ideology that homosexuals are "sick." For the professional, this attitude means that people who prefer homosexual relations suffer from an emotional disorder and need to be treated in the same way as any other emotionally disturbed individual. We heard a therapist analyze homosexuals as people who can never be happy because heterosexual relations are basic to human development and well-being. This view implies that *those who prefer homosexual relations should be identified, treated, and cured.*

fallacy   Some nonprofessionals view homosexuals as not only sick but also perverse *(the fallacy of personal attack).* Just as some Americans believe that alcoholics could stop drinking "if they only wanted to," they also believe that homosexuals could change their sexual behavior "if they only wanted to." In other words, some Americans view homosexuality as a personal problem, not a social one. They believe that the norms, institutional arrangements, attitudes, values, and ideology that work together to condemn and oppress homosexuals are legitimate.

Public Policy and Private Action

An important way to deal with the oppression and discrimination experienced by homosexuals is to *change the legal status of homosexuals.* In the early 1980s, the gay rights movement began to focus on national policies, giving priority to such things as extending the Civil Rights Act to prohibit discrimination based on sexual orientation. Gay rights advocates continue to press for antidiscrimination laws and policies in all spheres of life. In other words, homosexuals are striving to acquire the status of a recognized and protected minority group in American life. That effort was greatly helped by the Supreme Court's decision to make same-sex marriage legal in all states. The challenge now is to work on people's attitudes and practices that still denigrate and discriminate against those in the LGBT community.

To help the LGBT community combat the problems that still exist, there must be additional research and educational programs. People need to understand the nature of homosexuality and the perspectives of homosexuals. They need to understand what it means to be a transgender person. Fortunately, some helpful efforts already exist. There are college seminars on homosexuality as well as gay and lesbian programs. Articles in the print media and television and movie programs are powerful tools for combating antigay attitudes. Such educational efforts help people recognize that prejudice and discrimination achieve nothing but trauma. They also help young homosexual and transgender people to receive the social support from friends and family that will enable them to deal with the challenges and stresses in their lives. Educational efforts helped bring about dramatic changes in attitudes in the past (Loftus 2001). But those efforts must continue until the LGBT community is as fully accepted as heterosexuals in American society.

Follow-Up.   Investigate whether your school has any classes or seminars on homosexuality. Ask the instructors about the content of the classes, the assigned reading materials, and how effective the courses are in developing understanding of and tolerance for homosexual lifestyles.

Summary

Because they have suffered some of the same problems as minorities, women have been called America's "largest minority." In fact, they compose a slight majority of the population. Until recently, much of professional and popular opinion viewed the disadvantages of women as rooted in biology rather than in society. But the bulk of evidence points to sociocultural rather than biological factors for most differences between men and women.

Gender inequality means that women do not have the same opportunities for work and career as do men. Women's income is also less than men's. And women are victimized by the beauty myth and by harassment and violence.

The normative role of the female in American society is an important structural factor perpetuating women's problems. That role is reinforced by socialization at home, at school, and through the mass media. Discrimination is also practiced because it is economically profitable to men. Finally, some religious groups help maintain women's subordination by both their teachings and their practices.

Among social psychological factors in gender inequality are attitudes, such as the belief that women now have equal opportunities with men, and the ideology that asserts that wives and mothers who work outside the home pose a threat to their own families and to the well-being of the entire society.

Homosexuality, the sexual orientation of 2 to 3 percent of American women and 3 to 4 percent of American men, is also associated with inequality. Both biological and social factors are involved in sexual orientation. But some Americans view homosexuality as nothing more than a perverse choice.

The quality of life for homosexuals is diminished by such things as the myths that detract from their human dignity, negative sanctions, fear, and problems resulting from societal rejection and oppression. Social structural factors that tend to perpetuate the problem include societal norms and the legal and religious policies and practices that support those norms. Social psychological factors include a number of attitudes and the ideology that homosexuals are either sick or perverse.

Key Terms

Bisexual
Gender
Gender Role
Heterosexual
Homophobia
Homosexual
Innate
Lesbian
Sanctions
Sex
Sexism
Sexual Harassment
Sodomy
Transgender

Study Questions

1. What is the evidence for both biological and social factors as the basis for sex differences?
2. To what extent do women have equal economic opportunities with men?
3. How does the "beauty myth" affect the lives of women?
4. How does socialization affect the role of women?
5. Discuss the stance of religion on women's role in society.
6. What are the attitudes and ideologies that tend to perpetuate gender inequality?
7. What steps can be taken to reduce gender inequality?
8. What is meant by homosexuality and homophobia?
9. What is the evidence for biological and sociocultural factors in someone becoming homosexual?
10. What kind of negative sanctions do homosexuals face?
11. What attitudes and ideologies help you understand the problems homosexuals face?

Internet Resources/Exercises

1. Explore some of the ideas in this chapter on the following sites:

http://www.infoplease.com/ipa/A0001523.   This site has information about most of the issues related to gender, to the LGBT community, and to the problem of abuse.

http://www.now.org   The site of the National Organization for Women has information on a wide range of issues affecting women, including economic justice, abortion and reproductive rights, ending discrimination, and stopping violence.

http://www.glaad.org/   Defends gays and lesbians against defamation; offers publications and other resources as well as ongoing reporting of news about homosexuals from media around the nation.

2. Use a search engine to explore "gender equality." Find materials on the problem of equality and inequality between men and women in other nations. How would you compare the United States with those other nations? In what kinds of nations do women seem to have the most equality? The most inequality?

3. Explore the Internet for sites that condemn homosexuality and those that assert that sexual orientation can be changed. How would you respond to these sites using the materials in your text?

For Further Reading

Cruse, Sheryle. *Thin Enough: My Spiritual Journey Through the Living Death of an Eating Disorder.* Birmingham, AL: New Hope, 2006. A woman shares her torturous struggle with anorexia and bulimia, and her use of self-discipline and faith to overcome her eating disorders.

Flexner, Eleanor. *Century of Struggle: The Woman's Rights Movement in the United States.* New York: Atheneum, 1972. An excellent and thorough history of the struggle of American women—both white and black—from colonial times to 1920.

Hesse-Biber, Sharlene Nagy, and Gregg Lee Carter. *Working Women in America: Split Dreams.* New York: Oxford University Press, 2004. An examination of every facet of the issue of women working,

including the impact of globalization, the problems of the glass ceiling and sexual harassment, and the management of multiple roles.

Gibson, Michelle A., Jonathan F. Alexander, and Deborah T. Meem. *Finding Out: An Introduction to LGBT Studies,* 2nd edition. Thousand Oaks, CA: Sage, 2013. A text, but very readable and a must read for an in-depth study of the LGBT community, including history, politics, literature and the arts, and the media as they relate to LGBT life.

Stiers, Gretchen A. *From This Day Forward: Commitment, Marriage, and Family in Lesbian and Gay Relationships.* New York: St. Martin's Press, 2000. Interviews with 90 gay men and lesbians, who offer their perspectives on making a commitment, getting married, and having a family in a homosexual relationship.

Wharton, Amy S. *The Sociology of Gender.* New York: Blackwell, 2004. An overview of gender issues, including theory and research on gender at the individual, interactional, and institutional levels.

Williams, Joan. *Unbending Gender: Why Family and Work Conflict and What to Do about It.* New York: Oxford University Press, 2000. A discussion of the contradictions between the economy and family life, and policy suggestions for resolving the problems. Williams advocates what she calls "reconstructive feminism."

chapter 7 review

CHAPTER 8

Race, Ethnic Groups, and Racism

©Plush Studios/Blend Images LLC

Will It Ever End?

Daryl is in his 50s, black, and a college administrator. He was a teenager when the civil rights movement began to have a strong impact. Daryl has lived in two different worlds, because he spent his early years in the segregated South, but, as he recounts, there are some disturbing continuities:

I can remember going into a department store and finding the drinking fountain that said "colored only" on it. We couldn't drink out of the same fountains or go into the same bathrooms as the whites. I've achieved a place in society that neither my grandfather nor my father could have ever dreamed of being.

But it hasn't been easy. I guess I could forget those segregated water fountains if white people didn't keep reminding me that I'm different. I served in the army for a time in Germany. I married a white, German woman. We came back to this country so I could pursue a graduate degree. We took a trip down South in 1969 so I could show my wife where I grew up. We drove around my old neighborhood, then went into a restaurant in the suburbs. It was the last time we tried that. I had come back here to pursue my graduate degree, not to get into conflict with a lot of hostile people. They couldn't tolerate an interracial couple. Their glares made us both extremely uncomfortable during dinner. We wound up eating hurriedly and getting out.

I've had a lot of other incidents to contend with, sometimes with my wife and sometimes just on my own. You'd think it would be over by now, wouldn't you? But recently I attended a conference of black college administrators in a resort area. There was a convention of doctors there at the same time. One morning I came down into the lobby to meet a friend and saw one of our female administrators in a heated argument with a doctor. I stepped in and broke it up. It turned out that she was just standing at the desk when he came up and started making remarks to her about how hostile and arrogant blacks are. He said blacks keep causing trouble because we cry about discrimination when we have just as many opportunities as anyone else.

Instead of going out for a pleasant morning with an old friend, I wound up calling a meeting of our officers and trying to decide what to do about the incident. I don't think white people realize what it's like to be vulnerable to those kinds of things just because of the color of your skin. And I really wonder sometimes if it will ever end.

Introduction

Are people with white skin biologically inferior? Are they inherently less capable, less deserving, or less willing to work to get ahead than others? These questions may sound absurd to some of you, but millions of Americans who are minorities confront such questions about themselves. Throughout American history, minorities have been treated as if they were somehow inferior human beings, but racial inequalities are rooted in sociocultural rather than biological factors. We are all one species—human.

Before discussing the race problem (which is a shorthand phrase for the problem of relationships between people of diverse racial and ethnic backgrounds), we explore the meaning of race. Then we look at the origin and distribution of America's minorities, what the "race problem" means for them, what factors contribute to the problem, and how the problem can be attacked.

The Meaning of Race, Ethnic Groups, and Racism

race
a group of people distinguished from other groups by their origin in a particular part of the world

biological characteristic
an inherited, rather than learned, characteristic

We define **race,** in accord with the U.S. Census Bureau, as a group of people who are distinguished from other groups by their origin in a particular part of the world (Grieco and Cassidy 2001). As such, they tend to share a particular *skin color* (blacks originated in Africa, whites in Europe, the Middle East, or North Africa, etc.). Many people use the single **biological characteristic** of skin color to identify races, but there are so many shades of skin color that classifying someone as a member of one or another race solely on skin color is arbitrary.

In addition, if race were a purely biological phenomenon, a number of other biological characteristics could be used: blood type, the presence or absence of the Rh factor in the blood, or the ability to taste the chemical phenylthiocarbamide. In each case the groups would be composed of different people. For instance, people who can taste the chemical (as opposed to those who cannot taste it) include large numbers of Europeans,

Americans, American Indians, and Chinese. The point is that any biological basis for distinguishing among people is arbitrary and results in different groupings, which is why geneticists view race as more of a sociological than a biological phenomenon (Lewis 2002).

All human beings belong to one biological species—*Homo sapiens.* The breakdown of that species into subcategories is arbitrary. As Jefferson Fish (1995:55) sums it up: "The short answer to the question 'What is race?' is: There is no such thing. Race is a myth. And our racial classification scheme is loaded with pure fantasy." Nevertheless, people continue to identify different races primarily on the basis of skin color, and the inequalities people experience follow directly from that identification. We follow the categories of the U.S. Bureau of the Census, which uses people's self-identification to place them into one of the following: white or non-Hispanic white, black, Asian/Pacific Islander, American Indian/Eskimo/Aleut, other, and two or more races. In addition, the Census Bureau collects data on one ethnic group—Hispanic origin, which includes people of any race.

The term **ethnic group** refers to people who have a shared historical or cultural background that leads them to identify with each other. Although the Census Bureau routinely gathers data only for Hispanics, numerous ethnic groups have been involved in the growth of the nation. Many, such as the Irish and the Polish, have faced problems of acceptance. At present, Hispanics are the largest ethnic group struggling with integration into American society.

ethnic group
people who have a shared historical and cultural background that leads them to identify with each other

Keep in mind that *all people have more shared than different characteristics, and no group is biologically superior to another.* Nevertheless, **racism,** the belief that some racial groups are inherently inferior to others, has been common and is used to *justify discrimination and inequality.* Essed (1991) identified three forms of "everyday" racism: *marginalization* is making people of other races feel excluded and unimportant; *problematization* is imputing racial problems to those of other races rather than to one's own race; and *containment* refers to efforts to deny the existence of racism. We'll explore various forms of racism throughout this chapter.

racism
the belief that some racial groups are inherently inferior to others

Extent and Origin of Races and Racism in America

As Table 8.1 and Figure 8.1 show, the composition of the American population is changing. Racial minorities and Hispanics make up more than a third of the total population of the nation, and their proportion continues to grow. By the middle of the 21st century, they will comprise half or more of the total population. Both the Hispanic and Asian American population are growing faster than the population as a whole. In fact, by 2010 the Asian population was the fastest growing of all. From 2000 to 2010, the Asian population grew 43 percent, more than four times faster than the overall population (Hoeffel et al. 2012).

The increase in the minority population reflects not only differing birthrates among various groups but also changing immigration patterns. In 1960, 75 percent of the foreign-born population was from Europe and 9.4 percent was from Latin America; by 2013, only 11.1 percent was from Europe and 52.5 percent was from Latin America (U.S. Census Bureau website).

In addition to the changing proportions of various racial/ethnic groups, the United States is becoming more diverse in the sense that an increasing number of Americans identify themselves as multiracial. According to the Census Bureau, more than 9 million Americans claim to be of two or more races.

TABLE 8.1

U.S. Resident Population, by Race and Hispanic Origin, 1980 and 2015

Race	Number (1,000)		Percent Distribution	
	1980	2015	1980	2015
All races	226,546	321,419	100.0	100.0
White	194,713	247,785	85.9	77.1
Black	26,683	42,633	11.8	13.3
Hispanic origin	14,609	56,600	6.4	17.6
Asian/Pacific Islander	3,729	18,792	1.7	5.8
American Indian, Eskimo, Aleut	1,420	4,011	0.6	1.2

Note: Persons of Hispanic origin may be of any race and are included in the figures for the other races.
SOURCE: Humes, Jones, and Ramirez 2011, and U.S. Census Bureau website.

FIGURE 8.1

Composition of U.S. Population, 2000–2050.

Source: "Projected population of the United States," U.S. Census Bureau website.

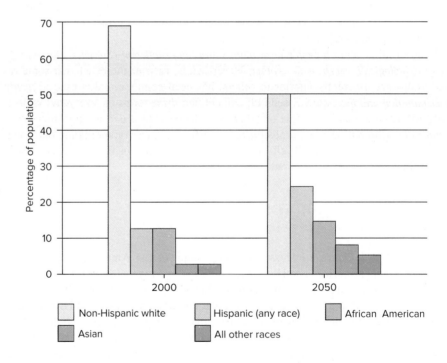

As we discuss the quality of life of the racial and ethnic groups, it is important to keep in mind the diversity within groups. Among Hispanics, for example, there are clear and often considerable differences between Mexicans, Puerto Ricans, Cubans, and other Hispanics in such matters as their citizenship status, educational attainment, marriage and divorce rates, employment status, and household income (U.S. Census Bureau 2010a). Similarly, although Asians as a group are among the more educated and higher-income groups in the nation (including whites), some of the immigrants from Southeast Asia, such as the Vietnamese, have lower education levels and higher unemployment and poverty rates.

Racism in American History

Why do problems exist among the various races and ethnic groups in the United States, the supposed "melting-pot" nation of the world? In part, the problems stem from historical circumstances. For example, the high rates of poverty and other problems among American Indians cannot be separated from events that began with the European colonization of the Americas. The colonists decimated both the population and the culture of the various Indian groups. Indians were defrauded of, or forced off, their traditional lands. Solemn treaties between tribes and the American government were repeatedly broken by the latter with little or no compensation to the Indians. And granting tribes a certain autonomy on reservations is a mixed bag at best. They are free from much federal law, but they are also isolated to a considerable extent from the mainstream of the nation's economy.

Minorities continue to use nonviolent protest to gain equal rights.

©Susan See Photography

Similarly, the problems of African Americans cannot be separated from their historical experience of slavery and segregation. The first African Americans to arrive, in 1619, were indentured servants, not slaves. However, states soon passed laws that legitimated slavery, and *those brought here as slaves were legally defined as property, not as persons.* Their enslavement was justified by various kinds of "evidence" of the inherent inferiority of the black race.

The system of slavery ultimately gave way to a castelike system. In a caste system, people are categorized into groups according to some characteristic over which they have no control, such as their race or the status of their parents. The groups have differing amounts of power, status, and access to those things that are valued. In the United States, whites formed one caste and African Americans another, with the whites having the bulk of the power, status, and financial resources. Of course, there were also differences within the two races. But even lower-class whites could be better off than higher-class blacks. That is, the two races were like two separate class systems, with the great majority of African Americans in the lower levels of their class system, and with the black upper class at roughly the same level as the white middle class in terms of material advantages. Segregation in such things as housing, schools, and public accommodations helped maintain the system.

Finally, in the 1950s, black leaders, including Martin Luther King Jr. led a civil rights movement designed to break down segregation and give African Americans all the rights and privileges enjoyed by whites. They fought the notion of inferiority, rejected discrimination and prejudice, and insisted upon nothing less than full equality of opportunity for all of America's citizens. Their efforts resulted in many significant gains. Nevertheless, severe problems of racial and ethnic inequality continue to tarnish the American dream of freedom and justice for all.

In sum, despite our *ideology of equal opportunity for all,* racism or ethnic hostility confronts many people who hope to take advantage of the American dream. The United States is not a melting pot. Someone has suggested that a more apt metaphor is a salad bowl, since the various groups tend to retain their identity even as they mix together in the society.

Even the salad bowl metaphor overstates the case, however. For *racial and ethnic segregation persist* in the nation. There may be less, and different patterns of, segregation in metropolitan areas, but segregation is not disappearing (Farley and Squires 2005; Roscigno, Karafin, and Tester 2009). The predominant pattern is still segregation. Unfortunately, segregated children who grow up in segregated areas are likely to define this as both normal and desirable and perpetuate the pattern of segregation—a pattern that works against the American dream of equal opportunity and freedom from discrimination.

Immigration

Immigration illustrates well the ongoing struggles of minorities to gain full acceptance into American society. Historically, every racial and ethnic group that has come to the United States in large numbers has faced suspicion, nonacceptance, discrimination, and harassment. Whether the Chinese laborers who worked on the railroads in the West, or the Irish who swarmed into the East coast, or the Vietnamese who fled to this country in hopes of finding freedom, or any of the many other groups, none were greeted with welcoming, open arms by those already living here.

Two major concerns regarding immigrants have always been the economic threat they seem to pose (they take away "our" jobs) and the danger of cultural corrosion (they will change our way of life because their ways are not our ways). A national poll reported that a third of Americans see immigrants as a burden to the nation because they take "our jobs" and they take advantage of the health care system (Jones 2016). In response to these concerns, advocates of immigration point out that the immigrants typically do jobs that most Americans don't want to do anyway. In addition, immigrants can have a very positive effect on the economy, thereby benefiting all Americans. Indeed, immigrants comprised a significant proportion of the industrial workforce from 1880 to 1920 and, thus, were a disproportionate part of the laborers who fueled the industrial revolution in the United States (Hirschman and Mogford 2009). As far as the concern about cultural corrosion is concerned, immigration advocates note that American culture has always included influences from a variety of sources. Moreover, American culture has had a greater impact on immigrants than immigrant culture has had on American society.

In recent decades, the *major concern has been with unauthorized immigrants,* frequently called "illegals." Hundreds of thousands of people enter the country illegally every year, primarily to find work and the income and opportunities that they cannot get in their own countries. Early in this century, the number of unauthorized immigrants exceeded that of legal immigrants (Passel and Cohn 2008). By 2010, an estimated 11.2 million unauthorized immigrants were living in the United States (Passel and Cohn 2010). This represents a decrease from 2007, when the estimate was 12.05 million. More stringent efforts to halt immigration and to deport those discovered, along with reduced opportunities in the United States as a result of a severe recession, account for the lower number.

Unauthorized immigration is a racial/ethnic problem because most entrants are Hispanics, Asians, or Africans. The largest number of unauthorized immigrants (58 percent) are from Mexico, although from 2009 to 2014 more Mexicans left than entered; there was a net loss of 140,000 Mexicans (Gonzalez-Barrera 2015). Despite the decrease in numbers and lack of evidence about serious detrimental effects of the unauthorized immigrants (see the discussion below), anti-Mexican attitudes were widespread by 2015. Millions of Americans supported the plan of one of the presidential candidates to deport all illegals and to build a wall across the entire U.S.-Mexican border. Some unauthorized immigrants travel back and forth between the United States and their native country, but many have remained here for 10 or more years. By 2014, unauthorized immigrants made up 3.5 percent of the nation's population (down from 4 percent in 2007) and 5.1 percent of the labor force (Krogstad and Passel 2015).

Is Unauthorized Immigration a Threat?   Many Americans define unauthorized immigration as a threatening situation. Some argue, particularly those who live in areas of high unemployment, that the immigrants take away jobs from natives (Esses, Brochu, and Dickson 2011). Others believe that their taxes are higher because they are paying for social benefits (such as health care and in-state tuition at state schools) received by unauthorized immigrants (Berg 2009).

Responding to the perceived threats, a majority of state legislatures have passed or introduced anti-immigration legislation. Arizona led the way in 2010, with a law that authorized deportation of all undocumented immigrants. To facilitate the process, the law included the following provisions: local police are to make immigration checks; immigrants who are authorized must carry papers with them; it is illegal for an unauthorized immigrant to live, or to look for work, in the state; and it is illegal for anyone to knowingly shelter, transport, or hire unauthorized immigrants.

Interestingly, not only states with a large number of unauthorized immigrants, like Arizona, but states with a relatively small number, like Alabama, have enacted such legislation. In Alabama, the new law became effective in 2011. It eliminated all state and local services (driver's licenses, tuition help, enrolling in college, securing employment, etc.) to anyone who was undocumented (Symmes 2012). The law was popular with the residents, and many of the unauthorized immigrants left the state. But some Alabamans soon began to question its effects. Businesspeople couldn't find enough people to do the low-wage work that the unauthorized immigrants had done; they wanted the immigrants back. In addition, a couple of police stops that questioned foreign employees (who were, it turned out, authorized) led to concern about backlash and withdrawal of foreign firms with plants in the state. The combination of disruption of businesses, potential loss of industrial plants, and the high costs of enforcing the law resulted in the legislature working on modifications in early 2012. Nevertheless, state legislatures continued to propose legislation that would restrict the freedom of the immigrants to live at peace in their states. In 2016 alone, 19 states considered legislation that the American Civil Liberties Union called "misguided, mean-spirited, and, in many instances, unconstitutional" (ACLU 2016).

The point is, as with all social problems there are conflicting positions about how to deal with unauthorized immigration. Some—including businesspeople, advocates of the free market, and ethnic advocacy groups—want a policy of amnesty and eventual citizenship for unauthorized immigrants. Others—including cultural conservatives, unions, and people concerned about employment and taxes—advocate deportation and greater border security to prevent the unauthorized from entering the country.

The Myths of Unauthorized Immigration.   There are legitimate points made by both sides of the issue of unauthorized immigration, but we need to frame the debate in light of the increasing amount of evidence about the actual impact immigrants have on our society. Weeks and Weeks (2010) studied the impact of unauthorized immigration from Latin America on states in the South. The researchers identified a number of myths people hold about the impact of such immigration. One myth is the idea that tighter border security will reduce the numbers. Actually, before the recent state and federal efforts to make the borders more secure, many of those from Mexico would travel back and forth to be with family on holidays and special family occasions. Their long-range plans might include eventually settling back in their own country. With the tightening of the borders, however, many no longer take the risk of traveling back and forth, but choose to remain in this country. They have children here (thereby making the children legal American citizens), work here, and become more Americanized over time.

A second myth is the assertion that the unauthorized are an economic drain on our resources. On the contrary, as the situation in Alabama illustrates, the immigrants are a needed labor supply; some agricultural business has relocated to Mexico because of the lack of workers in this country. Other researchers have come to the same conclusion about the economic impact. Overall in the nation, unauthorized immigrants have *not* increased the number of Americans living in poverty, and the states in which the new laws have been passed have, at this point, suffered adverse economic consequences rather than lessened their economic burden (Peri 2011; Esses, Brochu, and Dickson 2011).

A third myth is that the culture is diluted and altered by the large number of unauthorized immigrants. Many believe that the immigrants don't bother to learn English, that they expect bilingual education in the schools for their children, and that they promote foreign ideas about political and social life. In point of fact, most of the immigrants do learn English and are far more affected by American culture than American culture is affected by them.

Finally, some Americans fear that the influx of unauthorized immigrants is bringing unknown numbers of "undesirable" people into the country, such as criminals and even terrorists. The inevitable consequence, it is believed, is an increase in crime and violence. However, Sampson (2008) showed that as immigration numbers increased after the 1990s, the number of homicides decreased. He estimated the probability of violence in differing kinds of neighborhoods in Chicago and concluded that some of the safest places in our nation are areas of cities with concentrations of immigrants.

Race, Ethnicity, and the Quality of Life

What does it mean to be a minority in America? How does being a minority affect the *quality of life?* We will look at four areas in which all Americans are supposed to have equal rights:

1. Certain rights as citizens.
2. Equal economic opportunities.
3. The right to life, liberty, and the pursuit of happiness.
4. The right to dignity as a human being.

In each of the four areas, being white is a distinct advantage. Although the advantage is not as great as it was in the past, discrimination is still a part of the life experiences of minorities. In a national survey, 71 percent of African Americans and 52 percent of Hispanics said they have regularly or occasionally experienced discrimination or have been treated unfairly because of their race or ethnicity (Krogstad and Lopez 2016).

The Rights of Citizenship

The mass media often remind you of the *rights and privileges attached to your citizenship:*

1. This is a nation governed by laws rather than by individuals.
2. As a citizen, you have both the privilege and the responsibility of participating in the political process to ensure that laws reflect the will of the people.

3. The people do not exist to serve the government; the government exists to serve the people, and to serve all equally.

All these statements break down when we consider minority groups.

The Right to Vote.   If you don't like the way things are going, it is said that you can express your disapproval at the polls. Indeed, voting is the responsibility of every citizen because one way that Americans are presumably able to change things is by exercising their right to vote. However, this right and privilege, basic as it is to our notions of government, has often eluded African Americans and was long withheld from American Indians.

When the Fifteenth Amendment to the Constitution was ratified in 1870, all male Americans over age 21 had the right to vote, regardless of their race, creed, color, or prior condition of servitude (Rodgers and Bullock 1972). In the latter part of the century, however, various steps were taken to keep African Americans from voting. The southern states passed laws that effectively **disfranchised** black voters. Some of the laws required literacy and property tests. Others imposed a poll tax. Such laws excluded poor whites as well as African Americans, however, so loopholes were created. One loophole was the "understanding clause," which allowed a registrar to enroll any individual who could give a "reasonable" explanation of a part of the state constitution that was read to him. Similarly, the "grandfather clause" exempted from the literacy test those who descended from pre-1865 voters.

Intimidation also was used to keep African Americans from registering and voting. Sometimes the threat of violence or actual violence (including even murder) discouraged African Americans. The pressure of economic intimidation also was applied. They faced the possibility of losing their jobs or of being refused supplies at local stores.

Nor is all of this disfranchisement mere history now. From time to time, a report appears in the news media about efforts to keep various minorities from voting. Rather than intimidation, however, a tactic more likely to be used is drawing voting district lines in a way that neutralizes the power of minority votes (by, for example, splitting areas with heavy concentrations of minorities into separate districts so that whites are in the majority in each of the areas). Various other measures may be used at the state and local level. Laws have been enacted in recent years that make it more difficult to register and/or to vote. Registration has become a more rigorous process with particular kinds of required identification. With regard to voting, beginning in 2001, more than a thousand voter ID laws have been proposed and hundreds have been adopted in various states (Hicks et al. 2015). Proponents of such laws claim they are necessary to prevent voter fraud. As of this writing, however, there is no evidence of significant voting fraud, and what fraud we know about is likely to occur with absentee ballots rather than with people who come to the polls to vote (Fogarty et al. 2015). Proponents still argue that the laws are necessary as a preventive measure. Opponents counter that the laws essentially function to disfranchise certain segments of the population—in particular the poor, seniors, and racial and ethnic minorities, all of whom are less likely than others to have a government-issued photo ID card (Rosenfeld 2007). As of this writing, the issue of whether photo ID laws violate the constitutional right to vote is being fought in the courts.

The Rule of Law.   Another right and privilege of citizenship is to live in a land governed by laws rather than by individuals. The laws, however, have failed to fully protect minority rights in the areas of *housing and school desegregation.*

With regard to housing, the laws forbid discrimination in the sale, rental, or financing of any housing. Legally, a home that is for sale should be available to anyone who

disfranchise
to deprive of the right to vote

can afford it. However, some white property owners have "restrictive covenants" in their deeds that bar racial minorities from purchasing their homes (San Francisco Bureau 2001), and a certain amount of *racial steering* (diverting minorities away from predominantly white neighborhoods) still occurs. A study of 20 major metropolitan areas found racial steering of African Americans and discrimination against Hispanics in access to rental housing (Ross and Turner 2005). A survey of the literature on housing discrimination concluded that both institutional (such as banks, real estate agents, and insurance companies) and individual (such as landlords and homeowners) factors contribute to the problem (Roscigno et al. 2009). The result is continuing residential segregation. To be sure, the extent to which residential areas are segregated has declined over the past few decades. Nevertheless, by 2010 non-Hispanic whites lived in areas in which 75 percent of the other residents were also non-Hispanic whites (Farley 2011). Another way to look at it is that African Americans account for about 14 percent of urban residents, but are only 8 percent of the residents in areas in which the majority is white.

Even if minorities don't encounter obstacles in obtaining the kind of housing they prefer, they may find themselves at a disadvantage in the financing process. In the study of 20 major metropolitan areas, the researchers reported that Hispanics got less help in obtaining financing (Ross and Turner 2005). Lending agents may reject minority applicants at a higher rate than that for whites (the rejection rate for high-income minorities is often as high as that for low-income whites) and may exact higher interest rates from minorities than from whites (Williams and Nesiba 2005).

Ironically, during the early 2000s minorities appeared to be getting help in housing by securing subprime mortgages. These mortgages became available as government regulations eased. They were a high risk for investors. They were also a high risk for those obtaining them, because most were adjustable rate mortgages. When the housing market changed in 2006, refinancing became more difficult and many homeowners could no longer afford to pay their mortgages. Minorities were particularly affected by the situation because mortgage brokers tended to target them as customers for the risky subprime loans (Rugh and Massey 2010).

Finally, *segregated educational facilities* were declared illegal in the now-famous 1954 Supreme Court decision in the *Brown v. Board of Education of Topeka* case. Such facilities were ruled unconstitutional on the grounds that they are *inherently unequal,* but the desegregation process has been agonizingly slow. In recent years, moreover, there has been a reversal of the gains that were made in the years immediately after the Supreme Court decision, such that segregation is as much a problem now as it was in the 1950s (Fiel 2013; Heilig and Holme 2013; Kucsera, Siegel-Hawley, and Orfield 2014; Ayscue et al. 2016). The segregation would be less if all children attended nearby public schools, but a large number go to private, magnet, and charter schools and thereby increase the segregation in local, public schools (Saporito and Sohoni 2006). African Americans and Hispanics tend to be more segregated than Asians, but all minorities still experience segregated schooling to some extent.

Equality before the Law.   All Americans are supposed to stand as *equals before the law.* Most people, of course, quickly recognize that not all Americans are treated equally. The wealthy are rarely accorded the harsh treatment endured by the poor. Probably few people are aware of the extent to which minorities receive unequal treatment in virtually every aspect of civil and criminal proceedings (Butterfield 2000).

For example, police are more likely to be verbally abusive and to use excessive force against Hispanics and African Americans (Weitzer and Tuch 2004; Durose, Smith, and

Langan 2007). Hispanic and black youth are more likely to be detained by the police and the courts than are white youth (Demuth and Steffensmeier 2004). For example, although white, black, and Hispanic youth report using drugs at similar rates, black youth are detained at nearly five times the rate, and Hispanic youth at twice the rate, of white youth (Bell, Ridolfi, Finley, and Lacey 2009). A study of youths on probation found that the officers consistently described black youths differently from white youths in their written reports, attributing blacks' offenses to negative attitudes and personality traits and whites' offenses to the social environment (Bridges and Steen 1998).

Federal courts mete out harsher penalties for black and Hispanic than for white perpetrators (Demuth and Steffensmeier 2004; Alexander 2010). Minorities are more likely than whites to be stopped while driving and to be imprisoned, even for the same offense (Daniels 2004; Rojek, Rosenfeld, and Decker 2012). As a result, there is a disproportionate number of African Americans and Hispanics in jails and prisons. Two researchers estimated that for men born between 1965 and 1969, 3 percent of whites and 20 percent of African Americans served time in prison by their early thirties (Pettit and Western 2004). It is estimated that about 1 in 3 black males, 1 in 6 Hispanic males, and 1 in 17 white males will spend time in prison over their lifetime (Bonczaar 2003). Put another way, the number of years that black, Hispanic, and white males can expect to spend in prison or jail over their lifetime are 3.09, 1.06, and 0.5, respectively (Hogg et al. 2008).

Finally, a disproportionate number of minorities, particularly African Americans, are given the death penalty. Although only a minority of those who receive a death sentence are actually executed, minorities convicted of killing whites are more likely than other capital offenders to be executive (Jacobs, Qian, Carmichael, and Kent 2007). As we noted in Chapter 3, from 1977 through 2015, 1,422 prisoners were executed, and 44.5 percent of them were racial/ethnic minorities.

The Right to Equal Economic Opportunities

Among other factors, racial and ethnic discrimination means that minorities are more likely to be poor, unemployed, or—if they work—underemployed. Minorities also receive, on average, less income than whites.

Employment. A group might have *unequal access to employment* in at least five ways. First, the group might have a higher rate of unemployment than other groups. Second, a greater proportion of the group might be *underemployed*. Third, members of the group might be clustered at the lower levels of occupational categories (i.e., even if the proportion of minorities in a category is the same as that of whites, the minorities cluster at the lower levels). Fourth, members of the group might have less job security than whites. And, fifth, a disproportionate number of the group might become disillusioned and drop out of the labor market.

All five kinds of inequality apply to minorities in the United States (Herring 2002; Coleman 2004; Fullerton and Anderson 2013). And the *inequality is maintained by practices at the job candidate, job entry, and job promotion stages.* At the job candidate stage, many of the better jobs are still discovered through informal methods such as friends as much as through a formal recruitment process. Those without such an informal network of people who can exercise influence in the job market will be at a great disadvantage. Immigrants dramatize the extent of the disadvantage. For example, many Asian immigrant women have only been able to secure employment in garment sweatshops on the West Coast (Kim et al. 1992). The nature of the jobs is described by Helen Wong,

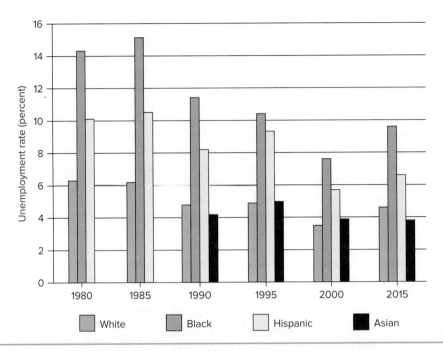

FIGURE 8.2   Unemployment Rates, 1980–2015.

Source: Various editions of the *Statistical Abstract of the United States* and the Bureau of Labor Statistics website.

who came with her husband and five children from Hong Kong in 1988 and found work in a small shop (Louie 1992). She worked on women's dresses and pantsuits for piece rates, which means that any breaks and other time off were unpaid. She worked Monday through Saturday, and came in on Sundays when there was a special rush order. The pay was the same regardless of how many hours or days she worked. On average, she made between $1 and $2 an hour.

Even with a formal recruitment process, minorities are disadvantaged when tacit hiring preference is given to whites. Three researchers had white and racial minority applicants with equal qualifications apply for waiter/waitress jobs in a number of fine dining restaurants in New York City (Bendick, Rodriguez, and Jayaraman 2010). Although the overt treatment of all the applicants was courteous, the minorities were only 54 percent as likely as the whites to receive a job offer.

Among the most accessible data on inequality in employment are unemployment rates (Figure 8.2; in this and other figures and tables in this chapter, all groups are included for which data are available). The unemployment rates for African Americans have been double or more those of whites since 1948, and unemployment rates for Hispanics (available since 1973) have been between one and a half and two times those of whites. American Indians tend to have the highest unemployment of all groups— about 46 percent in 2004 (Center for Community Change 2005). And in addition to higher rates, the unemployment spells of minorities are longer than those of non-Hispanic whites (Palumbo 2010). In short, minorities are far more likely to be out of work and looking for a job, and are likely to be out of work for a longer period of time, than are non-Hispanic whites.

Occupation	Percent of Total That Is		
	African American	Hispanic	Asian
Total	11.7	16.4	5.8
Managerial and professional	9.2	9.1	7.7
Service occupations	16.8	23.5	5.4
Sales and office occupations	12.3	15.3	5.2
Natural resources, construction, maintenance	7.3	29.0	1.9
Production, transportation, material moving	15.3	22.3	4.7

TABLE 8.2
Employed Persons, by Race and Occupation, 2015

SOURCE: Bureau of Labor Statistics website.

Underemployment (working fewer hours than desired or at a job for which the worker is overqualified) is also more common among minorities, and it is detrimental to the well-being of workers (see Chapter 10). In 2009, underemployment rates were: white, non-Hispanic, 5.2 percent; African American, 7.5 percent; and Hispanic, 12.0 percent (Sum and Khatiwada 2010).

Table 8.2 offers additional evidence on the problem of *discrimination in job opportunities*. As with most economic data, among the minority groups for which figures are given here, Asian Americans are found disproportionately in the highest group (managerial and professional). But African Americans and Hispanics are more likely to be found in the lower-prestige and lower-income categories (if there were perfect equality, the proportion for each job category in the table would be the same as the group's proportion of the labor force: 11.7 percent for African Americans and 16.4 percent for Hispanics). Moreover, a detailed inspection of each of the categories shows that minorities tend to cluster in the lower levels of those categories.

For example, in the managerial and professional category, the proportion of African Americans and Hispanics who are chief executives, physicians, and lawyers are less than half the two groups' proportion of the population. On the other hand, their proportion in some of the less prestigious and less rewarding occupations in that category—such as tax examiners, community and social service specialists, and teacher assistants—is greater than their proportion of the total population.

Furthermore, once in a job or a career line, minorities are likely to find advancement more difficult for them than for their white peers. A study of female workers found that African Americans and Hispanics experienced less job mobility than did whites (Alon and Tienda 2005b). And a researcher who investigated promotion experiences reported that, compared to white men, black men had to work longer periods of time after leaving school and Hispanics had to have more years with their current employer before getting a promotion (Smith 2005). And black and Hispanic women, compared to white men, needed more job-specific experience and more overall work experience in order to get a promotion.

Clearly, *race and ethnic background are factors in all aspects of employment.* And that includes the loss of work and change of job or career. Here, again, minorities may suffer more than their white counterparts. For one thing, minorities are more vulnerable to

TABLE 8.3

Money Income of Households, 2015: Percent Distribution by Income Level, by Race, and Hispanic Origin

Income	Percentage of Households			
	White	Black	Hispanic	Asian
Under $15,000	9.3	21.7	13.6	9.7
$15,000 to $24,999	9.6	14.2	13.6	6.7
$25.000 to $34,999	9.4	11.9	12.7	6.2
$35,000 to 49,999	12.2	13.6	15.1	10.2
$50,000 to $74,999	16.7	15.9	18.1	15.5
$75,000 to $99,999	13.0	8.9	10.8	12.2
$100,000 to $149,999	15.9	8.8	9.7	16.8
$150,000 to $199,999	7.1	2.8	3.7	10.5
$200,000 and over	6.9	2.3	3.2	12.1

SOURCE: Proctor, Semega, and Kollar 2016.

losing their jobs (Wilson 2005). For another thing, minorities are less likely than whites to benefit when finding new employment. Among workers displaced from some high-technology industries, African Americans and Hispanics suffered greater earnings losses than did whites, whether their new jobs were within or outside the high-tech sector (Ong 1991).

Income and Wealth.   Wealth includes all the assets of a family—housing equity, investments, insurance, and so on. Great disparity exists between the races in wealth. The Census Bureau does not regularly publish data on wealth, so the following median net worth of households are the latest available as of 2016 (U.S. Census Bureau 2013). The numbers change over time, but the relative position of the racial/ethnic groups stays roughly the same. In 2011, the net worth of households was as follows: non-Hispanic whites, $110,500; African Americans, $6,314; Asian Americans, $89,339; and Hispanics, $7,683. Thus, non-Hispanic white households had 17.5 times the wealth of black households and 14.4 times the wealth of Hispanic households.

An important component of wealth is income. Table 8.3 shows the extent to which minorities are concentrated more heavily than whites in the lower income brackets. Some people believe that minorities have made significant progress. However, although the income of all racial groups has been increasing, the gap between whites and minorities other than Asian Americans is greater than it was in the 1970s (Figure 8.3). In 2015, black household income was 58.6 percent and Hispanic household income was 71.6 percent that of non-Hispanic whites Proctor, Semega, and Kollar 2016).

In general, income inequality is widespread across occupations and is certainly a consequence of discrimination. Black income is lower than that of whites even for those workers with the same education, occupation, experience, authority, and number of hours worked (Coleman 2003). The gap increases in the higher-income occupational categories (Grodsky and Pager 2001). Rank (2009) summed up the consequences of the "economic racial divide" for African Americans: compared to whites, they are far more likely to experience poverty and far less likely to achieve affluence, less likely to be able to buy a home at an early age or to accumulate a large amount of equity in a home, and more likely to have low levels of wealth across all phases of their lives.

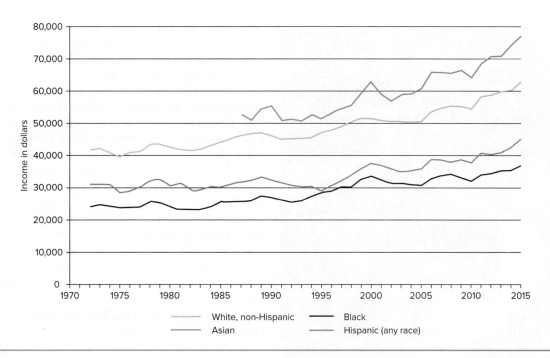

FIGURE 8.3 Median Household Income, by Race and Hispanic Origin, 1972–2015.
Source: Proctor, Semega, and Kollar 2016. (Data on Asian income only available after 1986.)

The Right to Life and Happiness

The right to "life, liberty, and the pursuit of happiness" was affirmed in the Declaration of Independence. However, those rights are not distributed equally in the United States. In particular, although the differences between whites and the racial/ethnic minorities are declining, there is still less reported happiness and life satisfaction among African Americans and Hispanics than among whites (Coverdill et al. 2011). The lower levels for minorities, in turn, are related to significant inequalities in life chances and in freedom from fear.

Life Chances. Insurance companies and government agencies compile large amounts of information on **life chances,** which include probability of divorce, disease, suicide, mental illness, and premature death. The life chances of whites are generally better than those of minorities (Williams, Neighbors, and Jackson 2003; Geronimus, Bound, and Colen 2011; Spence, Adkins, and Dupre 2011; Herne, Bartholomew, and Weahkee 2014; Buchmueller et al. 2016). For example, compared to whites, minorities tend to have (1) lower levels of physical and mental health; (2) a higher rate of infant deaths and deaths from tuberculosis, AIDS, homicide, and suicide; (3) a lower median family income; (4) lower-level jobs; (5) proportionately fewer full-time and white-collar jobs; and (6) fewer people with health insurance and fewer who receive old age and survivor insurance benefits. Many of the differences are striking. Black and Puerto Rican women have particularly high rates of infant mortality (Hummer et al. 1999). A black baby's life expectancy is nearly five years less than that of a white baby, and this gap has changed little in more than half a century (Carr 2005). The risk of a black youth being murdered is four times that of a white youth (Snyder and Sickmund 2006). And Native

life chances
the probability of gaining certain advantages defined as desirable, such as long life and health

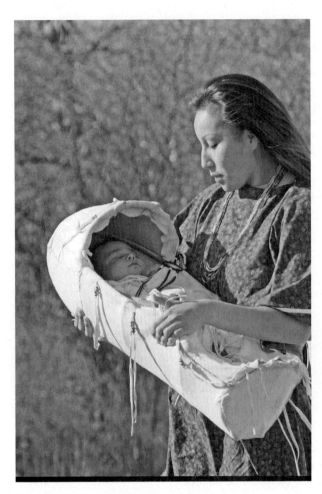

Native Americans are the poorest minority group in the United States.

©Nancy G. Western Photography/ Alamy

Americans have rates of alcohol abuse and alcohol-related rates of death that are five or more times as great as the rates for whites (Landen et al. 2014).

Disadvantages with respect to life chances are rooted in a number of factors. Racism and perceived discrimination are major contributors to problems of both physical and mental health (Flores et al. 2008; Chou, Asnaani, and Hofmann 2012; Gibbons et al. 2014; Hunter et al. 2016). Minorities are more likely to live near hazardous waste facilities and be exposed to toxic materials (Mohai and Saha 2007; Downey and Hawkins 2008). Finally, minorities are disadvantaged in life chances because of their lower economic levels (Meckler 1998; McLaughlin and Stokes 2002). People who live in poverty or who try to survive at low income levels have higher rates of physical and emotional problems. Impoverishment combined with racism takes a dreadful toll on poor African Americans in high rates of cirrhosis of the liver, homicide, accidents, and drug and alcohol abuse.

Minorities are also more likely to be victims of both property and violent crimes (Truman and Langton 2015). In 2014, for every 1,000 persons aged 12 or older in the group, 7 whites, 10 African Americans, and 8 Hispanics were victimized by a violent crime. In an interesting examination of the higher rates of violent crime in neighborhoods with a high percentage of minorities, Hipp (2011) raised the question of whether the minorities increased the rates or the rates increased the number of minorities. He found that whites are more likely than minorities to move out of neighborhoods with high rates of crime, whereas minorities are more likely than whites to move into neighborhoods that already have a high rate of crime. For some people, the only financially practical choice is to move into a house in a high-crime neighborhood or to be homeless.

Of all the racial/ethnic groups, American Indians/Alaska Natives are the most deprived in terms of life chances. They are more likely than others to be poor and unemployed (Castor et al. 2006). They have higher rates of criminal victimization than any other group (Pavkov et al. 2010). They have disproportionately high rates of sexual assault (Arnold 2014). A survey of Indian and Alaska Native women in New York City found that 65 percent had experienced some form of interpersonal violence, including childhood physical abuse (28 percent), rape (48 percent), or domestic violence (40 percent) (Evans-Campbell, Lindhorst, Huang, and Walters 2006). The women reported high levels of emotional trauma resulting from the violence. In addition to abuse, American Indians have serious problems of neglect, alcoholism, fetal alcohol syndrome, mental and physical disabilities, depression, school problems, and delinquency (Grant et al. 2004).

Freedom from Fear. One of the four basic freedoms proclaimed by President Franklin Roosevelt was freedom from fear. No one should have to live in constant fear of offending someone who claims to be superior. Yet, for decades black mothers and fathers taught their children to fear offending white people. Richard Wright related an incident from his own childhood that illustrates the point (Bernard 1966). A group of white boys threw broken bottles at him and some of his friends, and the two groups fought. Wright was badly cut. He went home and sat on his steps to wait for his mother to come home from work. Rather than sympathy, he received a severe beating. Had a white mother treated her son in this way, you might have questioned her love; but Wright's mother was teaching him what she regarded as a most important lesson—to avoid such encounters at all costs. She was teaching him what it meant to be black in America: that he would always be the loser in battles with whites.

Violence and threats of violence against people because of some characteristic of a group to which the people belong are now called *hate crimes* (Harlow 2005). The characteristic may be religion or sexual orientation or being a member of a gang, but the majority of hate crimes are motivated by the victim's race or ethnicity. Such crimes remind minorities that some people despise them and are willing to use violent means to intimidate them. You need only read the daily papers to realize that the victims of hate crimes include African Americans, Hispanics, Jews, Asians, and Indians. The crimes range from verbal abuse to physical violence and even murder. People who survive hate crimes are likely to suffer severe emotional problems (McDevitt, Balboni, Garcia, and Gu 2001). In recent years, the incidents have included chaining a black man to the rear of a truck and dragging him to his death, shooting Jewish children at a day care center, and brutally beating a Hispanic boy with a metal pipe.

Many hate crimes are committed by members of the hundreds of racist and neo-Nazi groups in the nation who proclaim the superiority of the white race and the threats posed by the varied minorities. Some hate crimes are committed by local groups of vigilantes. In 2014, the FBI recorded 6,727 hate crimes that were reported to the police. That figure is far below the number that comes from victimization studies. A 2012 victimization report put the number of hate crimes at 293,800 (Wilson 2014). Over half the victimizations were motivated by the race or ethnicity of the victim.

The cherished rights of Americans to move about as they please, to live according to their means, and to enjoy the use of all public facilities has not yet been fully extended to minorities. Minorities who try to break down old barriers are still subject to threats of violence and efforts at intimidation. Freedom from fear is an unmet promise rather than a reality.

The Right to Dignity as a Human Being

Most of the material already discussed in this chapter illustrates how minorities are directly *deprived of their dignity as human beings.* A majority of Hispanics and African Americans believe they have experienced some kind of discrimination during their lives. What kind of discriminatory behavior do they encounter? Much of it is what Eddings (1995) called **stealth racism,** which involves hidden or subtle acts of prejudice and discrimination, acts that may be apparent only to the victim. Examples of stealth racism include taxis that never stop for minorities; suspicious stares from clerks in stores; the assumption that the minority individual is in a subordinate role (like the couple who came out of an expensive restaurant and asked an African American man to get their car, not realizing he was a senior editor at a national magazine); the sense of being unwelcome (such as when looking for a new home in a well-to-do neighborhood); and the surprise expressed when the minority person is articulate and sophisticated.

stealth racism
hidden or subtle acts of prejudice and discrimination that may be apparent only to the victim

Some of the incidents are irritating and demeaning. For instance, a black woman returning a rented video is ignored by the clerks until she speaks up and asks for help (St. Jean and Feagin 1998). Or consider the problem of "dwb"—driving while black. There is evidence that black drivers are far more likely to be stopped by police than are white drivers, and are more likely to have their cars searched (Kowalski and Lundman 2007). Stealth racism can also be hazardous for the victims, such as when black and Hispanic women are less likely than white women to get the proper care in the early stages of breast cancer (Bickell et al. 2008). At that point, the right to dignity may mean the right to life-saving measures.

The right to dignity also includes the right to truthful representation of one's group. Two often-heard myths violate this right.

The Myth of Success around the Corner.   A common American myth is that *success is "just around the corner" for anyone who is willing to work for it.* The implication is that the minorities can end their impoverishment merely by being willing to work as hard as other people. "If they want to get ahead," it is said, "let them work for it and earn it." The point, of course, is that if they do not get ahead, it is their own fault. The *fallacy of personal attack* is used to defend an unjust social order. The reasoning is that if the minorities have as many opportunities as everyone else and yet remain in the lower levels of society, something is wrong with the minorities.

Unfortunately, many people do believe that minorities have the same opportunities as whites. A national poll asked whether blacks have as good a chance as whites to get any job for which they are qualified. White respondents overwhelming agreed (81 percent) that they do, but fewer than half (45 percent) of black respondents agreed (Polling Report 2016).

Many whites believe not just that minorities have an equal opportunity, but that minorities now possess an advantage. These whites see themselves as hampered in their access to the best education and the most desirable jobs and careers because of their race (Cohen 2003; Flynn 2003). They believe they have lost out, or potentially could lose out, to people less qualified than they are simply because the other people are part of a minority. In other words, they see themselves as victims of *reverse discrimination,* with their own opportunities becoming restricted as minority opportunities have opened. They cite cases in which minorities (including women) have been given preference over white males even when the white males have seniority or somewhat better qualifications. According to such beliefs, if minorities do not achieve success, it is clearly their own fault.

Associated with the myth that success is readily available to those willing to work for it is the notion that African Americans prefer welfare to hard work. This notion is also a distortion of the truth. African Americans did not appear on welfare rolls in large numbers until the late 1940s. Furthermore, few able-bodied men of any race are receiving welfare. Poor African Americans are, like anyone else, eager to escape their poverty. There is no evidence that minorities prefer welfare to work or that they are failing to take advantage of work opportunities available to them. Quite simply, the notion that success is just around the corner for anyone willing to work for it is a myth.

The Myth of Inferiority.   The insidious myth that minorities are *inherently inferior* is still around. The argument about inferiority takes a number of different forms. One argument is that minorities are, and always have been, biologically inferior. This argument

fallacy

can take the form of the *fallacy of circular reasoning.* An individual argues that African Americans are inferior because their IQs are lower than those of whites. "But," one could reply, "they are only lower for those who live in deprived conditions." "No," is the response, "they are lower because they are inferior people."

The theory of biological inferiority has also been claimed in a few scientific circles. The most recent attempt to argue for innate inferiority is *The Bell Curve,* by Herrnstein and Murray (1994). Herrnstein, a psychologist, and Murray, a political scientist, claimed that about 60 percent of IQ is genetic. Differences in achievement, therefore, are both inevitable and unchangeable. The work of Herrnstein and Murray has been criticized and refuted on various grounds. One is the lack of any evidence of a gene that is conclusively linked to intelligence, so that it is not possible to prove any genetic link of intelligence with race (Sternberg, Grigorenko, and Kidd 2005). Another is the fact that African Americans made gains of from four to seven IQ points on non-Hispanic whites between 1972 and 2002, indicating that the gap reflected social rather than genetic differences (Dickens and Flynn 2006).

The argument of a second form of the inferiority myth is that minorities are *culturally inferior.* Whatever may or may not be true biologically, it is argued, the culture of a particular people is obviously inferior and the people therefore are unfit to rise above their low status.

African Americans, Hispanics, and American Indians are all perceived to have cultural characteristics that make them different and less committed to such traditional American values as education and hard work; but most people in America tend to have the same aspirations for themselves and their families. Thus, a study of the life goals of graduating high school seniors found similar educational and occupational aspirations among the white, black, Hispanic, and Asian youths (Chang et al. 2006). The aspirations were high for all groups. And a Pew Research survey reported that 86 percent of Hispanic parents, 79 percent of black parents, and 67 percent of white parents said that it is extremely or very important that their children get a college degree (Stepler 2016). The fact that minorities have not achieved such aims cannot be attributed to cultural inferiority nor to cultural values that differ from those of white America.

Contributing Factors

The problems of minorities in America are well described by the title of Gunnar Myrdal's classic work *An American Dilemma* (Myrdal 1944). The author, a Swedish social economist, came to the United States in 1938 to direct an analysis of the problem. The book that resulted defined the problem as a moral issue and stated that the *dilemma involved a contradiction between the American creed and our racial behavior.* The creed proclaims the primacy of individual dignity, equality, and the right of all citizens to the same justice and the same opportunities, but the racial behavior systematically denies minorities the same rights and benefits accorded to whites.

The problem also involves *contradictory value systems.* Some people define the segregated and deprived state of African Americans as a problem, but others define efforts to "mix" the races as the real problem. The latter vigorously resist efforts of the former to alter the existing structure of segregated relationships. They fear an integrated society for various reasons. They argue that such a society will lack the strength and vigor of the present society.

BECOMING COLOR BLIND

We were once involved in arranging an exchange of ministers and choirs between a black and a white church. After the black pastor had spoken at the white church, one of the members said to us, "You know, the longer that man preached, the less I thought of him as black." It was her way of saying that the contact had broken down some of the prejudice she had harbored all her life.

Social scientists have long known that interracial contact is one way to deal with prejudice. Arrange for a visit with a group of a race other than your own. It might be a local church, a student organization on campus, or some kind of community organization. Talk with some of the members and explore how they feel about the current racial situation. Ask them about their aspirations for themselves and their children. Discuss their outlook on the future. Do they feel that the situation for their race has improved or worsened in the 2000s? Why?

What insights into the life of the other race did you gain from the visit? Do they have any needs and aspirations that are fundamentally different from your own? How does America's race problem look from their point of view? Can you see the basis for their point of view?

If possible, you might arrange some kind of exchange visit with the group. As the people from the different races mingle with each other, note any changes in prejudicial attitudes and any increases in mutual understanding.

Finally, the problem involves *contradictions in the social structure.* Minorities today are hampered by the changed economy, for our economy has developed to the point where the demand for unskilled and semiskilled labor is relatively small. Unlike the immigrants earlier in our history, therefore, people cannot better their lot today by going to work in vast numbers in the factories, where few or no skills are required.

Social Structural Factors

The tables in this chapter show that minorities occupy a *low position in the stratification system.* This finding raises the question of whether the main problems facing minorities are due to social class, racial or ethnic identity, or both. The answer seems to be both. Minorities share some characteristics with lower-class whites, but, as you have seen, even those who achieve higher socioeconomic levels still face various disadvantages and assaults on their dignity.

institutional racism
policies and practices of social institutions that tend to perpetuate racial discrimination

The disadvantages are not always due to biased individuals. The term **institutional racism** was coined to refer to the fact that established policies and practices of social institutions tend to perpetuate racial discrimination. In other words, whether or not the people involved are prejudiced or deliberate in their discriminatory behavior, the normal practices and policies themselves guarantee that minorities will be short-changed. Policies and practices are set by those in power, and minorities typically have lacked the power necessary to control institutional processes. We examine institutional racism in four important areas: the media, education, the economy, and government.

Mass Media. *The portrayal of minorities in the media has tended to perpetuate various negative stereotypes.* The problem was particularly severe in the past when movies and radio and television programs—such as the *Amos 'n Andy* radio show—portrayed African Americans as lazy, inferior, stupid, and dishonest. After the mid-1960s, the portrayals changed, and various racial minorities appeared more frequently and in more positive roles.

Racial and ethnic minorities still do not receive equitable treatment in the media, however. A study of prime-time television programs found (Children Now 2004):

- Most white youth interacted with their parents, but only a fourth of Hispanic youth did.
- A homogenous and segregated world was portrayed in the eight p.m. programs.
- The number of Hispanics increased over past seasons, but nearly half were in low-status positions and jobs.
- Virtually all service workers and unskilled laborers were people of color.

Another study of prime-time television programs concluded that there were no longer significant differences in appearance and conversational style between the races (Monk-Turner et al. 2010). But only 5 percent of the actors were Hispanic, and 16 percent African American. Most of the Hispanics were in main roles, but only 61 percent of the African Americans had main roles. In addition, the Hispanics were the objects of ridicule more than were either whites or African Americans, and more Hispanics (18 percent) and African Americans (9 percent) than whites (2 percent) were portrayed as immoral or despicable rather than admirable characters.

Other media also contribute to the problem of negative stereotypes. A content analysis of best-selling video game magazines and video game covers found that minority males were underrepresented and were more likely than whites to be shown as athletic or aggressive or thugs, and less likely than whites to be shown in military combat or using technology (Burgess et al. 2011). Even college textbooks can be misleading. In her examination of economics textbooks, Clawson (2002) found black faces "overwhelmingly portrayed" among the poor (recall that, in terms of numbers, there are far more poor whites than poor blacks).

One thing that could help would be for more minorities to be in positions of influence in the media. The minority cause is not helped by the proportion of minorities who work in newsrooms of newspapers. According to the Pew Research Center (2016), the proportion of black workers in newsrooms actually declined from 5.4 percent in 2003 to 4.7 percent in 2014, and the proportion of Hispanic workers declined from 4.4 percent in 2005 to 4.2 percent in 2015. In sum, some progress has been made, but the mass media as a whole continue to either neglect minorities or reinforce negative stereotypes.

Education.   Four primary and secondary educational practices that perpetuate discrimination are *segregated schools, so-called IQ testing, so-called ability-grouping of children, and differential treatment of children based on racial or ethnic identity.* All these practices discriminate against people in the lower socioeconomic strata, and because most minorities are disproportionately in the lower strata, they suffer disproportionately from such practices. The discrimination begins early in the school career. A study of fifth-grade students reported that 15 percent of the children perceived racial or ethnic discrimination, and 80 percent of the discrimination occurred at school (Coker et al. 2009). And those who perceived discrimination were more likely than others to have symptoms of depression and other mental disorders.

Schools continue to be more segregated than integrated. Nearly three out of ten Hispanic and black students attend schools with fewer than 5 percent of white students (an increase from the early 1990s, when the proportion was one out of four) (Fry 2007). The resegregation of schools is due, in part, from the assumption that school districts no longer need court oversight; once released from that oversight, school districts become increasingly segregated again (Reardon 2012). Attending a segregated school depresses the achievement of minorities (Quillian 2014; Quinn 2015). Among other things, segregated minority schools tend to offer a poorer education because of inadequate resources and, in some cases, lower expectations of the students' interests and abilities. For example, a study of three Los Angeles high schools with a high proportion of minority students found that while the school had an ample number of computers, the computer science program itself was poor (Margolis et al. 2008). In part, the quality of the program reflected the fact that teachers, counselors, and even some of the students had low expectations about both minority student interest and minority student ability in the field of computer science.

IQ testing also works to the disadvantage of minorities. A child may do poorly on an IQ test, for example, because little in his or her home environment has served as preparation for tests constructed by middle-class educators. Then, when placed in a group of lower ability, a child may accept the label of mediocrity or even inferiority.

At the college level, efforts are made to recruit more minority students than have attended in the past. Some of the efforts have been successful, but minorities (other than Asian Americans) still lag considerably behind non-Hispanic whites. By 2015, the proportion of adults 25 years and older who had a college degree was 53.9 percent of Asian Americans, 32.5 percent of whites, 22.5 percent of African Americans, and 15.5 percent of Hispanics (Ryan and Bauman 2016).

Finally, as noted previously, teachers may treat minority students differently from white students. In her qualitative study of white student teachers, Marx (2006) found the future teachers' knowledge of the history and culture of the varied origins of the minority students to be sparse at best. For example, they thought that speaking Spanish in the home was a sign of low intelligence and that the cultural context in which minority students were raised was at best an obstacle to be overcome and at worst a sign of innate inferiority.

Differential treatment also occurs in discipline. Schools with a larger proportion of black students tend to have more punitive disciplinary practices and to implement zero tolerance policies (Welch and Payne 2010). Nationally, 51 percent of students in elementary and high schools are white, but white students account for only 33 percent of expulsions and 29 percent of those with multiple suspensions (Brenchley 2012). Black students are 18 percent of the total, but they make up 35 percent of students suspended once and 39 percent of students expelled. Such differences do not simply reflect differing behavior patterns but teacher and administrator attitudes. Morris (2005) studied an urban school intensively and drew a number of informative conclusions about discipline. First, teachers and administrators tended to view black girls' behavior as "unladylike," and attempted to discipline them into dress and manners more acceptable to the adults. Second, school officials tended to define the behavior of Hispanic boys as threatening, so that the boys were often disciplined in strict, punitive ways. And third, school officials tended to see the behavior of white and Asian American students as both nonthreatening and gender appropriate; discipline for these students was likely to be less strict and punitive.

It is difficult to learn if your school makes you feel more vulnerable to disciplinary action simply because of your race. It is also difficult to learn if your school's cultural values and teaching methods are contrary to the cultural values of your family and community. Such an incongruity helps explain why 25 to 60 percent of all American Indian students drop out of high school each year (Klug and Whitfield 2002).

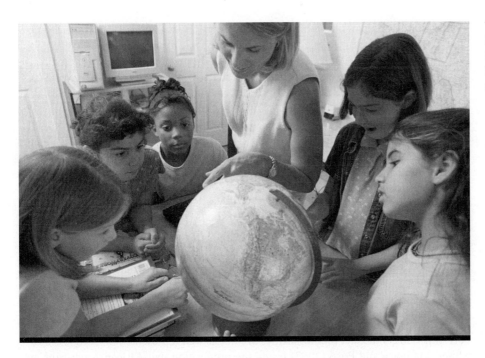

Minority students tend to have higher academic achievement in integrated classrooms.
©Creatas/PunchStock

The Economy.   Institutional racism has pervaded the economy in at least three ways: **exploitation** *of minority labor, exclusion of minorities from full participation in the economy, and exploitation of minority consumers.* Some gains have been made, of course. For example, racial/ethnic segregation in employment has declined since the 1960s (Tomaskovic-Devey et al. 2006). Nevertheless, as we noted earlier, minorities tend to secure the lower-paying jobs, a tendency that was reinforced by the shift from an industry- to a service-based economy (Jaret 1991). And even in the same occupational categories, a gap exists between minority and white income (McCall 2001).

exploitation
use or manipulation of people for one's own advantage or profit

As for participation in the economy, minorities come out best during economic booms and worst when the economy falters. Even in the best of times, they lag considerably behind non-Hispanic whites in terms of employment and income. In the worst of times—during recessions—their unemployment rate goes up more than that of non-Hispanic whites. For example, the nation lapsed into a severe recession in the first quarter of 2008. Bureau of Labor statistics show that from then until 2010, the rise in unemployment rates were as follows: white, 6.3 percent to 8.7 percent; Hispanic, 8.9 percent to 12.5 percent; and black, 11.5 percent to 16.0 percent. Moreover, African Americans tend to be the first fired when the economy sinks into recession (Couch and Fairlie 2010). Once unemployed, they are much less likely to be reemployed than are white workers with equivalent characteristics and experience (Moore 2010).

Minorities also fail to participate fully in the economy as entrepreneurs, a fact that is closely related to credit practices and policies. Lending institutions traditionally demand credit history, some kind of collateral, and some evidence of potential success before they lend money to prospective businesspersons, whether or not they are white. These are standard practices, defined as necessary and practical when giving credit, but applying them to minorities, who may have poor credit records because of exploitation and who may have nothing to use as collateral because of poverty, means that the standard practices only ensure continued white domination of the economy.

Insisting on comparable "sound" business practices when the prospective customers are minorities results in exploitation of the minority consumer. It is true that the poor are greater credit risks and that businesses in ghetto areas must pay higher insurance premiums because of the greater probability of theft and property damage; yet it is also true that these higher costs of doing business exploit the minority consumer, who must then pay more than others for the same quality of goods.

The most serious exploitation may be in housing, however. African Americans are often forced to pay more than whites for the same quality of housing. In fact, ghetto housing is sometimes costlier in terms of square footage and is frequently costlier in terms of quality square footage than is housing in suburban areas. When minorities attempt to find better housing, they may find themselves, as noted earlier, steered into some areas and kept away from other areas by real estate agents.

Economic deprivation of minorities has meant economic gains for whites. When minorities are kept in a subordinate position, whites are able to secure a higher occupational status, lower rates of unemployment, and higher family income (Tomaskovic-Devey and Roscigno 1996). At least some of those who resist equal opportunities are not unaware of such implications.

Government.   The government is supposed to protect and help all citizens equally. But minorities do not always benefit from the government as much as whites do. In part, this reflects the fact that minorities are not as well represented in Congress as are whites. Malhotra and Raso (2007) tested the proposition that African Americans and Hispanics are not as well served as are whites by the equal representation of each state in the Senate. They concluded that both groups are underrepresented because they tend to be concentrated in a few high-population states.

To be sure, civil rights legislation has greatly helped minorities in, among other things, government employment, particularly at the federal level. According to data gathered by the Equal Employment Opportunity Commission (2013), African Americans had a greater proportion (18.8 percent) of the jobs in state and local governments than their proportion (13.3 percent) of the population. However, Hispanics (17.6 percent of the population) had a lower proportion (11.3 percent).

If minorities are to make headway in their efforts to achieve equality of opportunity, they must be able to secure *political power* and find help in the courts. However, minorities have barely begun to infiltrate positions of political power in spite of the election of the nation's first black president in 2008. As of 2016, minorities continued to make gains—17 percent of Congress was nonwhite (Krogstad 2015). However, only six Senators were minorities. And minorities were 38 percent of the total population. No minority group had representation in Congress in accord with their proportion of the population.

There has been some progress, of course. The numbers of minorities in elected offices have risen dramatically since 1970. And with the election of Barack Obama, they have reached the highest office in the land. But the bulk of minorities are in local and state positions. Overall, then, the record of minority participation in the political process shows only modest gains over the past half century.

Social Psychological Factors

We said previously that ideology affects social interaction. Why does the ideology of equal opportunity not alter the superior/inferior kind of interaction between whites and minorities that results from the social structure? It might, except for the many ideologies in any society. Some of the ideologies of America have helped shape and sustain the traditional interaction patterns between the races. In fact, some values, attitudes, and ideologies among both whites and minorities tend to perpetuate the race problem. We examine those of the whites first.

Majority Perspectives. The initial low position of minorities in America stems from the circumstances of their arrival—as indentured servants, slaves, or unskilled laborers. The *ideology necessary to legitimate the enslavement or subordination of minorities was already present.* The first white settlers in America believed in their own racial superiority and certainly considered themselves superior to the "savages" who were native to America. Similarly, the English, on first making contact with Africans, considered them very "puzzling" creatures and tried to determine why the people were black. In one explanation, blacks were said to be the descendants of Ham, whom the Bible says God had cursed. Actually, as stated in the ninth chapter of Genesis, the curse was pronounced by Noah, not God, and it was against Ham's son, Canaan. The fact that many people have accepted the argument underscores the power of the *fallacy of the appeal to prejudice,* for those who accepted the argument undoubtedly acted out of prejudice rather than knowledge of the Bible. In any case, Africans were a different kind of people, and the difference was seen to be undesirable.

A number of white groups entered the country in low-status, low-power positions (and were to some extent the objects of prejudice), but none of them were so looked down upon as the minorities. A number of additional factors worked against minorities but not against whites: (1) the economy needed less and less unskilled labor, (2) their skin color was a "visible" disability, (3) the political system no longer offered jobs for votes so freely, and (4) their smaller households probably did not have several wage earners.

Prejudice, a "rigid, emotional attitude toward a human group" (Simpson and Yinger 1965:15), is an attitude that is widespread in the white majority (Bonilla-Silva, Goar, and Embrick 2006). Prejudice against any group legitimates different treatment of group members, generates resistance to programs designed to help the group (such as affirmative action programs that increase the number of minorities in higher education and the workplace), creates the desire to live in areas with few or none of the group members, and resists such things as interracial dating and marriage that would break down the racial barriers (Loury 2005; Iceland and Wilkes 2006; Kreager 2008; Lewis, Emerson, and Klineberg 2011). White prejudice, then, helps perpetuate white dominance.

Prejudice is an individual characteristic, but its causes lie outside the individual—no one is born with prejudice. Simpson and Yinger (1965:49–51) identified a number of sources of prejudice. The sources included personality needs; the usefulness of prejudice for certain groups (low-status whites, for instance, who have been better off than African Americans); group tradition (children learn to hate without knowing precisely why); and certain attributes possessed by the minority group. "Group attributes" are questionable as a source, however. They may serve as a useful rationalization for prejudice, but they do not generally cause that prejudice.

Prejudice does not necessarily have so rational a basis as a consistent set of beliefs about or a well-defined image of the target group. Social psychologists have known for a long time that certain groups can be defined as undesirable even when the attributes of those groups are vague. This insight is expressed in an old poem:

> I do not love thee, Dr. Fell,
> the reason why I cannot tell.

fallacy

prejudice
a rigid, emotional attitude that legitimates discriminatory behavior toward people in a group

But this I know and know quite well,

I do not love thee, Dr. Fell.

fallacy

One consequence of prejudice is that it facilitates fallacious thinking. To the prejudiced person, certain *fallacies of non sequiturs* come easily: They are on welfare, therefore they don't want to work; they have more children than they can properly care for, therefore they show themselves to be immoral; they don't speak proper English, therefore they are intellectually inferior; and so forth. The "they," of course, is whichever minority group the speaker wants to castigate. The same arguments have been used about many different groups.

Such prejudicial thinking continues in spite of decades of efforts to combat it. There is, consequently, *a racial divide in attitudes about America's racial situation.* When polls are taken related to the issue of racial equality (e.g., are people treated equally in the justice system and do people have equal opportunities for success), typically a majority of whites but a minority of African Americans believe that racial equality exists in this country (Maniam 2016).

Prejudicial thinking is reflected in interracial behavior, including such things as interaction in classrooms and stores, encounters on the streets, and the process of securing housing (Emerson, Yancey, and Chai 2001; Krysan 2008; Lynn et al. 2011). Discriminatory behavior in these varied settings is the result of, and is justified by, the stereotypes created by prejudice (Frederico 2006). Even positive stereotypes can be used to maintain white dominance. For example, Asian Americans are frequently viewed as the "model minority." In this view, they succeed because of their strong family life, their hard work, and their high value on education. Although the stereotype has some validity, it has been used to dismiss the need for programs that help minorities by providing more educational and work opportunities (Yu 2006). The idea is: if Asian Americans can do it, why can't the other minorities? The argument that if one does it, all can, is another example of a *non sequitur.*

The insidious nature of prejudice is illustrated by the way it legitimates and helps perpetuate the interaction patterns occurring in institutions. In the schools, for instance, a black child may perform poorly because, in part, he or she senses a teacher's hostility, born of prejudice. The teacher labels the child as having mediocre ability and places him or her in an appropriate group. The child may accept the teacher's definition of his or her ability, and that definition may be further reinforced through IQ tests and subsequent teachers' reactions. Thus, prejudice further reduces the chances of academic success for a poorly prepared child, and the normal policies and practices of the school, such as IQ testing and grouping by ability, reinforce an official definition of the child's ability. If a child rebels against this hostile and repressive environment and becomes a "behavior problem," the teacher will conclude that his or her initial hostility is fully justified.

Minority Perspectives.   In the face of disparaging attitudes and ideologies, minorities can get trapped in a vicious circle. By experiencing disparagement, deprivation, and powerlessness, members of a minority group may develop attitudes of alienation and cynicism about society. We have already noted that far more minorities than whites agree that minorities suffer from discrimination. They are also less satisfied than whites with the treatment they receive in American society. In a 2016 poll, 65 percent of African Americans, compared to 27 percent of whites, agreed that it is a lot more difficult to be black than white (Maniam 2016).

Such attitudes can lead minorities to despair of being able to make significant advances in their lives. They may accept their low position rather than struggle against it. In turn, remaining deprived and powerless confirms their perspective. How does this situation compare with our earlier observation that African Americans place an even higher value on education than whites do? Matthew's (2011) research answers the question. In essence, whites tend to equate success with personal factors such as effort, whereas African Americans tend to see structural barriers that can negate their efforts. In other words, African Americans are more likely to believe that education will not pay off for them as it does for whites, that they will be treated unfairly in the workplace regardless of their education. In other words, many minorities who might otherwise aspire to higher education will not go through the struggle to get it because they are convinced that they still live in a racist society in which they face unfair treatment.

For Hispanics, the attitudes and values underlying their high dropout rates come from their peer groups. As a study of Mexican American students found, Mexican American students are much less involved in informal and extracurricular activities at school than are white students (Ream and Rumberger 2008). They tend, instead, to form street-oriented friendships that place little or no value on formal schooling. As a consequence, Hispanics have considerably lower levels of educational attainment than whites, African Americans, or Asian Americans (U.S. Census Bureau 2009).

Asian-Americans are often viewed as the "model minority."

©McGraw-Hill Education./Lars A. Niki, photographer

Finally, for minorities in ghetto areas, there is the additional problem of a *lack of role models* (Parker and Reckdenwald 2008). This lack contributes to the amount of violence in ghetto areas as well as depriving the youth of people they could emulate in order to have a more meaningful life. An ironic reason for the lack is the civil rights legislation of the 1960s that gave middle- and upper-class African Americans the opportunity to move out of segregated and impoverished areas. As a result, ghetto youth no longer see people who get a good education, work at good jobs on a regular basis, and thereby become examples of what can be accomplished. Instead, those who remain in the ghettoes see a pervasive hopelessness, cynicism, and rejection of educational and occupational aspirations. They live in a climate of low expectations, and many social psychologists argue that the expectations are crucial, virtually guaranteeing continued deprivation unless the expectations are somehow changed.

Public Policy and Private Action

Minority groups themselves have launched attacks on the forces that discriminate against them to the detriment of their desired quality of life. The result has been *intergroup conflict* as minorities strive to alter values, attitudes, ideologies, and social structural arrangements.

Resolution of the problem requires more than the actions of the minorities, however. What kind of actions may be taken, keeping in mind that any action will probably involve some conflict (verbal debate at the very least)?

PREJUDICE IN EUROPE

Prejudice is found everywhere. It varies from one country to another as well as within countries. In the United States, the fear of economic competition (for jobs and income) has often fanned the flames of prejudice and led to racial tensions and riots. The threat—real or not—of economic competition is also a factor in prejudice in other nations.

Quillian (1995) studied prejudice in a number of European countries. He found that the average prejudice scores varied from one country to another (Figure 8.4). He also looked at the extent to which the people in each nation defined the threat from people of other races and nationalities as being due to such things as adding to problems of delinquency and violence,

leading to lower educational quality, and creating a drain on social security benefits.

Quillian's analysis showed that perceived threat explained most of the variations in average prejudice scores in the 12 European nations. He found that such individual characteristics as education, age, and social class had little impact on prejudice and explained none of the variations between countries. Rather, the economic conditions in each country and the size of the racial or immigrant group were the significant factors, and the more problematic the economy, the more the minorities are perceived to be an economic threat and the higher the level of prejudice.

SOURCE: Quillian 1995.

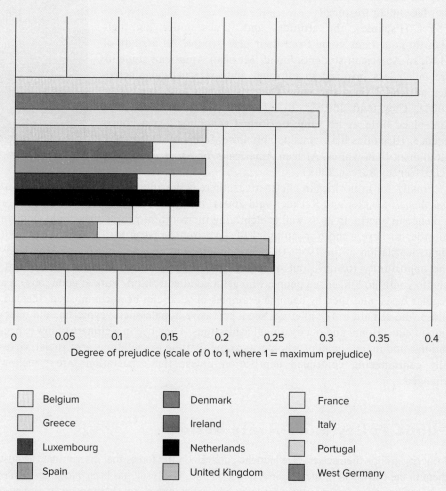

Degree of prejudice (scale of 0 to 1, where 1 = maximum prejudice)

- Belgium
- Denmark
- France
- Greece
- Ireland
- Italy
- Luxembourg
- Netherlands
- Portugal
- Spain
- United Kingdom
- West Germany

FIGURE 8.4 Racial Prejudice in Europe.
Source: Adapted from Quillian 1995.

First, attitudes and ideologies can be changed through a policy of persistent education in schools and the mass media. Many efforts have already been initiated, of course, but throughout the country there still are extensive prejudice and adherence to ideologies that disparage minorities. Educational efforts, incidentally, should attack not only the negative attitudes and ideologies about minorities but also the unrealistic ideas that many whites have about the consequences of an integrated society. Many are unaware that school desegregation brings benefits to whites as well as to minorities (Mickelson 2001). Private initiatives that bring whites and minorities together in social and religious settings also can reduce prejudice (Vora and Vora 2002).

Second, minorities need to continue to mobilize for political action that will shape public policy. It is imperative to exercise expanded influence in the government at all levels. Political action is particularly important in the area of employment (Herring 2002). Even though job discrimination is against the law, it continues to occur. New policies and programs are needed to increase workplace equality. Local and state governments could help with the auditing of companies to ferret out instances of discrimination. Funding can be restricted and contracts withheld from firms that repeatedly discriminate against racial and ethnic minorities.

Third, equal educational opportunities must be guaranteed to all minorities. In the late 1980s, Asian Americans protested about discrimination when their numbers were restricted in the California University system. Asian Americans were qualifying in disproportionate numbers for university admission; officials restricted their entry to maintain room for other racial groups. But why should people who are performing well be penalized?

The problem of other groups—notably African Americans and Hispanics—is different. Too few are seeking and gaining entrance to higher education. Programs are needed to keep minorities in school (Hispanics have particularly high dropout rates) and encourage them to seek the highest possible level of attainment. Among other factors, having a higher proportion of faculty and administrators who are minorities and increasing the contact of student affairs officers with minority students help raise the retention rate (Opp 2002). Educators can also recruit those minority students who are in higher education to help analyze the situation and develop strategies for redressing the problem (Hobson-Horton and Owens 2004).

Fourth, legislation must be continually introduced and backed up by the commitment of the federal government to enforce the law. Many beneficial changes have occurred in the wake of such legislation and commitment. Some observers despair of the law having any force, but they often expect too much from law. Laws can change attitudes and alter behavior, but only by increments. A law is passed, people find ways to circumvent it, and a new law is passed to address the contradiction between the intended and the actual results of the first law. Over time the intent of the law is increasingly realized.

Programs must attack institutional racism directly. For example, *affirmative action programs* attempted to increase minority participation in business, industry, education, and service agencies. In essence, affirmative action was a preemptive policy, preventing discrimination before it ever occurred. In spite of considerable evidence that such programs can be effective (Davidson and Lewis 1997; Button and Rienzo 2003; Alon and Tienda 2005a; Fischer and Massey 2007), they have been dismantled and their legality denied in the courts. Some new programs that achieve the same aims are needed.

One aspect of the race problem that has broad implications is *residential segregation*. The majority of American Indians live on reservations. Most Hispanics live in their own segregated neighborhoods, or "barrios." African Americans are concentrated in the inner cities of metropolitan areas. Residential segregation virtually guarantees segregated social life and education (unless there is busing), and it inhibits the kind of intergroup contact that can break down myths, prejudice, and racist ideologies (Ellison and Powers 1994). It follows that a program designed to achieve residential integration could have a significant influence on the problem. One such effort, the Gautreaux Program, was designed to help low-income black families move into better housing in white suburbs and black inner-city neighborhoods (Rosenbaum, Popkin, Kaufman, and Rusin 1991). Both the families who moved into the white areas and those who moved into the black areas reported making friends and finding support from their neighbors. Those who moved into the suburbs did report more experiences of harassment, but they were relatively minor and decreased over time. Thus, it is possible to move low-income minorities into middle-class white communities with minimal problems.

Follow-Up.   Think about the relationships you have had with people of other racial groups. What factors made some of these relationships more positive than others?

Summary

America's black, American Indian, Asian, Pacific Islander, and Hispanic minorities compose a substantial and growing proportion of the population. Inequalities between the majority white race and minority races are primarily the result of sociocultural factors. Skin color is a minor biological characteristic, but it is a major sociocultural factor.

The meaning of the problem and the diminished quality of life it imposes on minorities may be summed up in terms of citizenship rights; economic opportunities; the rights of life, liberty, and the pursuit of happiness; and the right to dignity as a human being. In each of these four areas, it is a distinct advantage to be white. Minorities have been deprived of basic citizenship rights, such as the right to vote and the right to be governed by and be equal before the law. Economically, minorities have suffered discrimination in employment opportunities and income. With respect to the value Americans place on life and happiness, minorities have been disadvantaged in terms of life chances. They often have lived in fear and been treated as though their lives were of less value than the lives of whites. Their right to dignity has been violated by the myth of "success around the corner" and the myth of inferiority.

An important social structural factor that contributes to the problem is institutional racism. Minorities are kept clustered in the lower levels of the stratification system and are exploited by the normal policies and practices of institutions, including the mass media, education, the economy, and government. Social psychological factors of attitudes, values, and ideologies of both the white majority and the minorities compound the structural discrimination. Whereas the social structural factors lead to devaluation of minorities, the social psychological factors can lead, in addition, to self-defeating behavior on the part of minorities.

Key Terms

Biological Characteristic
Disfranchise
Ethnic Group
Exploitation
Institutional Racism

Life Chances
Prejudice
Race
Racism
Stealth Racism

Study Questions

1. What do social scientists mean by "race"?
2. Discuss the extent and origin of races, ethnic groups, and racism in America.
3. How do prejudice and discrimination affect minorities' rights of citizenship?
4. Do minorities have equal economic opportunities?
5. In what sense do prejudice and discrimination violate minorities' rights to life and happiness and to dignity as human beings?
6. How is their position in the stratification system a factor in the problems of minorities?
7. Discuss the ways in which social institutions diminish minorities' quality of life.
8. What are the social psychological aspects of the white majority that are involved in the problems of minorities?
9. What kinds of attitudes on the part of minorities exacerbate the race problem in America?
10. Discuss some of the institutional changes that are needed to address the problems of America's minorities.

Internet Resources/Exercises

1. Explore some of the ideas in this chapter on the following sites:

http://www.naacp.org Site of the National Association for the Advancement of Colored People, with the latest news on racial issues and a variety of other resources.

http://www.census.gov The U.S. Census Bureau site, with special reports and comprehensive statistics on racial and ethnic groups.

http://www.hrw.org Information on race problems throughout the world by the Human Rights Watch.

2. Find a Hispanic site—a Hispanic magazine or journal, a Hispanic advocacy group, or a Hispanic news site—and make a list of the concerns expressed over the last year or so on the site. To what extent do those concerns reflect and/or address the inequalities identified in the text?

3. Compare the situation of African Americans with that of Asian Americans. Gathering materials from

sites for each of the groups, compare both their griev-ances and their achievements. On the basis of your findings, what kinds of recommendations would you make to each group?

For Further Reading

Bowser, Benjamin P., and Raymond G. Hunt, eds. *Impacts of Racism on White Americans.* 2nd ed. Thousand Oaks, CA: Sage, 2002. Various chapters show that, far from disappearing, racism is still strong in America, and there are both advantages and disadvantages for white Americans in racist practices.

Cafferty, Pastora San Juan, and David W. Engstrom, eds. *Hispanics in the United States: An Agenda for the Twenty-First Century.* New Brunswick, NJ: Transaction, 2002. A comprehensive overview of the quality of life of Hispanics in the United States and their role in various social institutions.

Camacho, Julian Segura. *Higher Education as Ignorance: The Contempt of Mexicans in the American Educational System.* Lanham, MD: Hamilton Books, 2008. An account by a Mexican American professor of his own experiences and those of other Mexican Americans in the educational system from kinder-garten through graduate school. Criticizes the "forced Americanization" and anti-Hispanic bias in schools.

Carens, Joseph H. *Immigrants and the Right to Stay.* Cambridge, MA: MIT Press, 2010. A proposal by the author to grant amnesty to unauthorized immigrants who have been in this country a long time, including a chapter on the responses of other scholars.

Ehrlich, Howard J. *Hate Crimes and Ethnoviolence: The History, Current Affairs, and Future of Discrimina-tion in America.* Boulder, CO: Westview Press, 2009. An expert in ethnoviolence discusses such matters as the social conditions that give rise to and justify hate crimes, and the need to include verbal and emotional as well as physical assaults as crimes.

Feagin, Joe R. *Racist America: Roots, Current Realities and Future Reparations.* New York: Routledge, 2001. A so-ciological analysis of racism that shows how it is em-bedded in the system, including a discussion of the historical roots of racism in our European heritage.

PART 4

Problems
of Social
Institutions

©Dynamic Graphics/JupiterImages

Social institutions exist in every society to solve the problems and meet the needs of people. The government should protect people, secure social order, and maintain an equitable society. The economy should provide the basic necessities of life. Education should fulfill people and train them to function well in society. The family should nurture its members and provide them with emotional stability and security. The health care system should maintain emotional and physical well-being.

Unfortunately, social institutions create as well as solve problems. In this section, you'll learn how the government and the political system fail in some of their functions; how the economy, including work, is detrimental to the quality of life for some people; how education fails to fulfill its functions for some individuals; how family life can detract from, rather than enhance, well-being; and how the health care system does not adequately meet the physical and emotional needs of some Americans.

Society cannot exist without social institutions, but not everyone benefits equally from those institutions. Some even become victims. Institutions need reshaping in order to maximize the well-being of all Americans.

Government and Politics

1 Know the functions of government.

2 Identify reasons why government and politics are problems.

3 Discuss how the problems of government and politics affect the quality of life.

4 Explain how size, organization, economics, the media, and interest groups contribute to the problems of government and politics.

5 Show the way in which attitudes and ideologies contribute to the problems of government and politics.

6 Suggest ways to deal with the problems of government and politics.

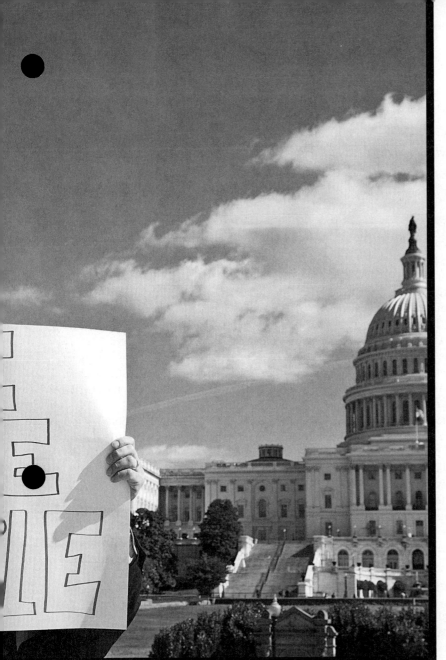
©fStop / Alamy

"Why Isn't There Help for People Like Me?"

Jacquelyn is the single mother of two preschool children. Shortly before her second child was born, her husband, Ed, lost his job. He was unable to find another one. About the time they had exhausted their savings, he announced that he couldn't take it anymore and disappeared. Jacquelyn, who only has a high school education, is struggling to survive:

We lost our home. The kids and I are living in a cheap apartment. We're barely getting by. I don't have enough money to even buy my kids any new toys. And when I go to the grocery store, I see other mothers putting all kinds of good food into their baskets that I can't afford. My parents give us a little, but my dad is on disability and they have a hard time meeting their own bills. I married Ed right out of high school. So I've never worked, and I don't have any skills. I can't even use a computer.

I remember that we were promised the government would give us a safety net. Well, where is it? I'm in a job training program now, but who's going to take care of my kids while I work? And how am I going to pay for someone to take care of my kids? How much do they think I'm going to make from the kinds of jobs they're training me for?

What I'd like to know is, why isn't there some real help for people like me? The government tells me I have to get a job in a couple of years or I won't get any more welfare. Why doesn't the government find Ed and make him help support his kids? For all I know, he's found work somewhere else and has plenty of money. Or why doesn't the government make sure that I get a job that will pay me enough so I can give my kids a decent life? Our country goes all over the world helping people in need, and forgets about people like me. I'd like to see some of those politicians take my place for a while. Maybe then they would realize how some of us die a little bit every day from worrying about what's going to happen to us and our kids and how we're going to survive.

Introduction

What adjectives would you use to describe American government? How about American politics? If you are like many students we have taught, you probably came up with such adjectives as "huge," "inefficient," "corrupt," and "self-serving." However, we have also had students who described government and politics as "effective" and "helpful."

Let's follow up with another question: What role does government play in social problems? Some students see government as a major contributor to social problems. Others see it as the only hope for resolving them. Most students agree that the government should take a leading role in attacking various problems.

Each of these responses has some validity. Throughout this book, we note various ways in which the government and politics enter into both the causes and the resolution of social problems. In this chapter, we concentrate on the ways in which government and politics are themselves problems. We begin by examining the functions of government—what people believe they can legitimately expect from government. We then look at four specific ways in which government and politics are problems, how those problems affect people's quality of life, and various structural and social psychological factors that contribute to the problems. Finally, we explore possible ways to attack the problems of government and politics.

Why Government?

anarchism
the philosophy that advocates the abolition of government in order to secure true freedom for people

Can you imagine a society without any government? Some people can. **Anarchism** is a philosophy that advocates the abolition of government in order to secure true freedom for people. According to anarchists, people are free only when they can cooperate with each other to achieve their ends without the restraints of government and law. To be sure, history provides abundant examples of governments that have deprived people of freedom. Nevertheless, we agree with the student who said: "When I look at the way that governments have exploited and oppressed people throughout history, I am sympathetic to the idea of anarchism. But I still think we need government."

The question is, why do we need government? What do people expect from their government? What functions does it fulfill? We shall discuss four important functions. Keep in mind that government at all levels—federal, state, and local—is involved in fulfilling these functions.

Protect the Citizenry

The first function of government is to protect the citizenry. Americans expect government to protect them from foreign aggressors. This function will be explored in greater detail in Chapter 14. They also expect the government to protect them from various threats to their well-being, *threats that come from sources more powerful than any individual* (Sypnowich 2000). For example, people look to government for protection from environmental hazards, unsafe or unfair business practices, and corporate exploitation of consumers. In recent years, many Americans have looked to government to stop the flow of illegal immigrants into the nation. As noted in the last chapter, hundreds of thousands enter illegally each year, and some Americans believe that they take away jobs from citizens and use services that increase taxes and costs to citizens. In addition, some fear that terrorists will be among those who sneak into the country. Some state and local governments have enacted, or are considering enacting, laws that punish employers who hire illegals and landlords who rent to them.

Protection at the federal level comes in the form not only of laws but of regulatory agencies. A **regulatory agency** is an organization established by the government to enforce statutes that apply to a particular activity. For instance, the Securities and Exchange Commission (SEC) monitors the trading of stocks and bonds, whereas the National Labor Relations Board (NLRB) monitors employer-employee issues. Although many people complain about the irrational and autocratic procedures of the regulatory agencies, they were established mainly in response to demands from citizens who felt the need for protection.

An example of the way the protective function works is seen in the Food and Drug Administration's (FDA) monitoring of prescription drugs. In the early 1960s, the world was shocked at the news of babies being born without arms or legs. The tragedy took place, for the most part, in Europe and Australia and was linked to mothers' ingestion of the drug thalidomide. Thalidomide had been used as a tranquilizer and to treat nausea in pregnant women (Colborn, Dumanoski, and Myers 1997), but it was eventually shown that the drug also caused terrible deformities in children who were exposed to it while in the womb. Although Americans didn't avoid the tragedy altogether, they did escape the large number of cases that occurred in other nations because a physician at the FDA delayed approval of

regulatory agency
an organization established by the government to enforce statutes that apply to a particular activity

The police are one way the government performs its function of regulating behavior and maintaining civil order.
©McGraw-Hill Education./John Flournoy, photographer

the drug, insisting on more safety data before the agency would agree to its use. The action of the agency protected a great many children from serious handicaps.

Secure Order

A second function of government is to *secure order.* In contrast to anarchists, many observers argue that government is necessary to control individuals so that society does not degenerate into chaos and violence. By regulating people's behavior in the economy and other areas of social life, government helps prevent the destructive disorder that would result from a situation in which individuals acted to benefit themselves (Durkheim 1933).

Although there may be disagreement about whether government is necessary for social order, there is no disagreement about the importance of that order. Imagine what it would be like to live in a society in which there were no consensual rules about such matters as traffic, education of the young, or the right to private property. *Order is essential to both emotional and physical well-being.*

Distribute Power Equitably

A third function of government is to distribute power equitably so that every citizen has *an equal opportunity for life, liberty, and the pursuit of happiness.* In other words, a person's freedom and aspirations should not be constricted because of his or her sex, race, age, religion, or socioeconomic background. A person should not have more power than others simply because he is male rather than female, white rather than nonwhite, and so on.

We have shown in previous chapters that such factors have and do affect people's life chances. In fact, a survey of a number of nations in the world has shown a direct relationship between the way the government functions and the reported happiness of the citizenry (Ott 2011). One way for a government to function well is to redress inequities. In our nation, a good example involves the right to vote (Burns, Peterson, and Cronin 1984). In the early years of the nation, the right to vote was limited to white, male adults who were property owners and taxpayers. Thus, in the first election for which a popular vote was recorded (1824), less than 4 percent of the population voted. In response to public demands, federal and state governments took action to broaden voting rights. For example, a number of constitutional amendments assisted in gradually enlarging the franchise. The Fifteenth Amendment, ratified in 1870, gave black males the right to vote, although state and local governments found numerous ways to subvert this right. In 1920 women gained the right as a result of the Nineteenth Amendment. Finally, the Twenty-sixth Amendment, ratified in 1971, extended the right to vote to 18-year-olds.

Provide a Safety Net

Finally, government functions *to provide a safety net, a minimum standard of living below which it will not allow citizens to fall.* Even if opportunities abound, some people—because of such things as the economy and life circumstances—are not able to achieve what most Americans define as a minimal standard of living. In addition, as Americans discovered in the Great Depression that followed the stock-market crash in 1929, there are times when opportunities are severely limited. It was in response to the hardships of the Depression that, in the 1930s, President Franklin Roosevelt initiated the New Deal, which featured programs like the Social Security system. Since that time, Americans have come to expect government actions to provide a safety net that secures a minimum standard of living (Kryzanek 1999).

Differences exist over what should be included in the safety net. Currently, safety-net benefits include, for example, Social Security and Medicare for the retired, short-term financial aid for the unemployed, subsidized lunches for poor schoolchildren, and health insurance for children who otherwise would be uninsured (Long and Marquis 1999; Felland et al. 2003).

Problems of Government and Politics

The problems discussed in this section reflect the fact that *political parties and government bureaucracy play a central role in the way representative democracy functions in the United States.* **Political parties** are organized groups that attempt to control the government through the electoral process. A **bureaucracy** is an organization in which there are specific areas of authority and responsibility, a hierarchy of authority, management based on written documents, worker expertise, management based on rules, and full-time workers. The government bureaucracy includes those government employees whose jobs do not depend on elections or political appointment.

Inequalities in Power

The actual distribution of power in American society contradicts the expectation that the government should ensure equity. But exactly how is power distributed? This question is not easy to answer.

Pluralism or Power Elites?   Who holds the most power in the United States? Many social scientists believe that America is a *pluralistic society* in terms of the distribution of power. **Pluralism** means that power is distributed more or less equally among **interest groups,** which are groups that attempt to influence public opinion and political decisions in accord with the particular interests of their members. Thus, an interest group such as the National Rifle Association (NRA) exercises power in the political sphere to protect its members' insistence on the right to own firearms. The National Organization for Women (NOW) exercises power to protect and advance the rights of women.

In contrast to the pluralist view, the **power elite model** asserts that power is concentrated in a small group of political, economic, and military leaders (Mills 1956). In essence, the top leaders in government, in business, and in the military determine the major policies and programs of the nation—and they do this in a way that furthers their own interests and solidifies their power. A variation, held by Marxists and some others, is that capitalists wield the power, including power over the government (Barry 2002). Most of the people who hold to the power elite view argue that interest groups have some power, but mainly in their capacity to lobby members of Congress, whereas the great bulk of individuals is an unorganized, powerless mass controlled by the power elite.

Evidence can be gathered in support of both the pluralist and the power elite positions. Domhoff's (1990) analysis of decision making, for example, concludes that the upper class generally rules the nation. Many observers found support for the power elite model in the ties between political leaders and the oil industry during the George W. Bush administration. President Bush himself owned an oil company. Vice President Cheney was head of Halliburton, an energy and construction firm. And Condoleezza Rice, the national security adviser, had been on the Chevron board of directors for a decade. Critics charged that the U.S. Middle East policy, including the war on Iraq, was shaped by the

political party
an organized group that attempts to control the government through the electoral process

bureaucracy
an organization in which there are specific areas of authority and responsibility, a hierarchy of authority, management based on written documents, worker expertise, management based on rules, and full-time workers

pluralism
the more or less equal distribution of power among interest groups

interest group
a group that attempts to influence public opinion and political decisions in accord with the particular interests of its members

power elite model
a model of politics in which power is concentrated in political, economic, and military leaders

administration's close ties to the oil industry. Further evidence of the ties was the awarding of billions of dollars of government contracts to Halliburton for various projects in rebuilding Iraq and servicing U.S. troops still in Iraq (Burger and Zagorin 2004).

Power and Inequality.   Although there is some validity to both the pluralist and the power elite positions, neither seems to capture fully the realities of power distribution. *People are not powerless, particularly when they organize.* Mothers Against Drunk Driving (MADD) has influenced the passage of new legislation on drinking while driving, helping to reduce the number of deaths caused by drunk drivers.

At the same time, *there clearly are power inequities;* otherwise the poor, women, and minorities, among others, would not have had to struggle for so long against their various disadvantages. It is true that women and minorities have made some inroads into the power elite (Zweigenhaft and Domhoff 2006). There are more women and more minorities (particularly more African Americans) among corporate CEOs and directors, in the higher ranks of the military, and in national political and governmental positions. Nevertheless, the struggle for equality has been torturously slow. In spite of its efforts, for example, the National Organization for Women could not get the Equal Rights Amendment (ERA) ratified; and in spite of the work of numerous civil rights organizations, African Americans and other minorities have made only modest headway in their efforts to achieve equity in the economy.

In other words, regardless of which model of power distribution most accurately reflects the realities of social life, the government clearly has not maintained an equitable distribution of power. The longstanding deprivations of certain groups show that Americans have not yet achieved the ideal of liberty and justice for all.

The Failure of Trust

An important part of the task of securing order is building trust (Levi 1998). Trust in this context means having confidence that others will fulfill their responsibilities. Citizens need to trust each other, and they need to trust the government. Trust is essential if people are to cooperate and work together in maintaining the norms and the laws of society. If citizens distrust their government, they are more apt to resist and even ignore government policies and laws.

How much do Americans trust their government? Over the last half century, public confidence in all the major institutions has declined markedly. By 2014, as Figure 9.1 shows, only the military and the police had half or more of Americans express "a great deal" or "quite a lot" of confidence in the nation's institutions. Slightly less than a third expressed such expressed such confidence in the Supreme Court and the presidency, and the results for Congress were a dismal seven percent.

Why do Americans view government with more skepticism than they do other social institutions? Unfortunately, researchers who survey people on their level of confidence do not probe into the reasons for their responses. It is probably true, as Levi (1998) asserts, that such factors as the breaking of campaign promises, incompetence, and the lack of responsiveness to people's interests and needs lead to distrust. Scandals and corruption also contribute to distrust. Scandals and corruption have never been absent from American political life, but the Watergate scandal of the Nixon administration seems to have had a particularly strong impact on people. Public confidence in government began to decline dramatically after the media exposed the break-in at the office of the Democratic National Committee and the attempts to cover up the involvement of President Nixon and officials in his administration (Kryzanek 1999).

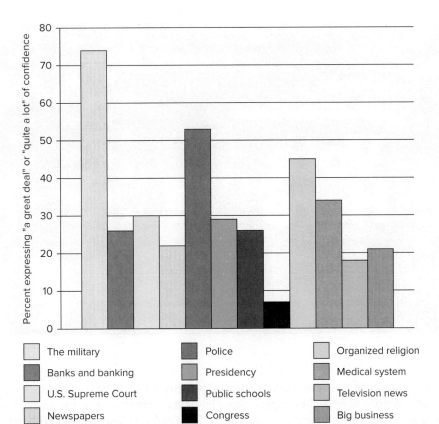

FIGURE 9.1
Public Confidence Levels in Selected Institutions, 2014.

Source: Rifkin 2014.

Other events in the 1960s and 1970s—including the growing disillusionment with the Vietnam War and with the truth of official reports about the war—also contributed to the decline in confidence. Moreover, Americans have continued to learn about instances in which the government has not been truthful. What are people to think, for example, when they hear that the Central Intelligence Agency (CIA) admitted lying about the nature of unidentified flying objects (UFOs) in order to keep secret its growing fleet of spy planes, or that the Bush administration created an Office of Strategic Influence that would create news items, some of which would be false, in order to gain support for government decisions (Broad 1997; Wilson 2002)? It is not surprising that in response to the question of how much of the time you can trust the federal government to do what is right, 2 percent of Americans in 2012, compared to 16 percent in 1958, said "just about always," whereas 76 percent in 2012, compared to 23 percent in 1958, said only "some of the time" (American National Election Studies 2016).

Whatever the reasons for the distrust, it has produced at least four consequences we need to examine: the emergence of the Tea Party, the lack of citizen participation in the political process, altered voting patterns, and political alienation.

Emergence of the Tea Party.   In 2009, Tea Party protests erupted around the nation. The dominant type of person in the movement was older, male, lower middle-class, and far-right Republican (Hood, Kidd, and Morris 2015). As part of their protests, some Tea Party members dressed like 18th-century American revolutionaries. They claimed that the government, including many politicians in their own party, no longer worked in a

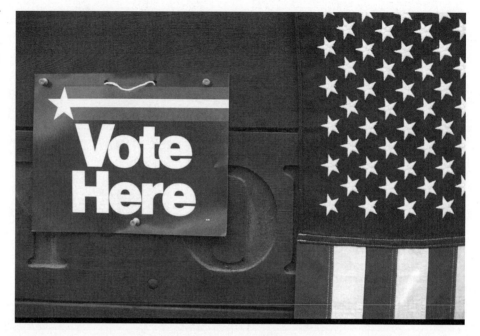

way that was acceptable to them. They called for reduced government interference in people's lives and a no-compromise approach to governing. Buttressed by funds from wealthy conservatives and by support from far-right commentators in the media, they were able to influence a number of races in the 2010 elections (Skocpol and Williamson 2012). Members of Congress aligned with the Tea Party were able to force out the Republican Speaker of the House from office in 2015, and their no-compromise approach has contributed to governmental gridlock (see below). The future power of the Tea Party, however, is in doubt. Gallup polls show that support for it declined from 32 percent in 2010 to 17 percent in 2015 (Norman 2015).

Lack of Citizen Participation.   If the approach of the Tea Party was to protest and work for candidates who support its viewpoint, the approach of others who distrust the government is to simply drop out. After all, why participate in the political process if you lack confidence in the government? Why vote if you believe that no matter who is elected the government will not function as it ought?

Although it is not the only reason for not voting, the *failure of trust is certainly one reason* for the relatively low proportion of Americans who vote (Jamieson, Shin, and Day 2002). It is not true, as some people believe, that low voter turnout is a new phenomenon in American politics. Rather, the proportion of people voting has fluctuated over time. Between 1840 and 1908, the proportion who voted in presidential elections varied from about 65 to 82 percent of eligible voters (U.S. Census Bureau 1975:1071–72). The proportion then began to fall. As Table 9.1 shows, the proportion continued to vary between 1932 and 2008 but was never more than 62.8 percent for president or 58.5 percent for representatives. Voting proportions for representatives in nonpresidential year elections (these years are not shown in the table) are even lower, ranging from about 33 to 38 percent since 1974 (U.S. Census Bureau 2012). In general, then, *about half or less of the voting-age population participates in national elections, and the proportion is much lower for state and local elections.*

Year	Percentage of Voting-Age Population Casting Votes For:		Year	Percentage of Voting-Age Population Casting Votes For:	
	President	U.S. Representatives		President	U.S. Representatives
1932	52.5	49.7	1976	53.5	48.9
1936	56.9	53.5	1980	52.8	47.6
1940	58.9	55.4	1984	53.3	47.8
1944	56.0	52.7	1988	50.3	44.9
1948	51.1	48.1	1992	55.1	50.8
1952	61.6	57.6	1996	49.0	45.8
1956	59.3	55.9	2000	51.2	47.2
1960	62.8	58.5	2004	55.5	51.4
1964	61.9	57.8	2008	57.1	53.3
1968	60.9	55.1	2012	61.8	n.a.
1972	55.2	50.7			

TABLE 9.1
Participation in Presidential Elections, 1932–2012

SOURCE: U.S. Census Bureau website.

The proportion of people who vote varies considerably by a number of demographic factors. In the 2012 election, for example, the proportion who voted varied by age from 41.2 percent of those 18–24 years to 73.5 percent of those 65–74 years; by gender from 59.7 percent of males to 63.7 percent of females; by race/ethnicity from 64.1 percent of non-Hispanic whites, to 66.2 percent of African Americans, 48.0 percent of Hispanics, and 47.3 percent of Asian Americans; by marital status from 69.3 percent of those married to 50.0 percent of those never married; and by education from 81.3 percent of those with an advanced degree to 37.1 percent of those with less than a high school diploma.

At one time, many politicians believed that an important reason for low participation was the *difficulty of registering to vote.* In 1993, therefore, Congress passed the National Voter Registration Act, which required states to register voters at driver's license and motor vehicle bureaus, welfare offices, and military recruiting stations. The new law made it easier to register but has not had a significant impact on voting participation. In fact, when asked why they did not vote, the most common reason given by a national sample was that the individual was "too busy" or had a schedule conflict (U.S. Census Bureau website). Clearly, more than ease of registration is needed to bring more people to the polls.

Altered Voting Patterns.   A third consequence of the failure of trust is altered voting patterns. That is, whereas some people neglect to vote, others *change the way they would have voted under conditions of high levels of trust.* In particular, third parties are likely to benefit when people do not trust the government. A study of the third-party nominees such as George Wallace, John Anderson, and Ross Perot concluded that lower citizen trust levels strongly predicted a vote for them (Hanenberg and Rojanapithayakorn 1998). The number of votes received by third-party candidates has varied from as few as 9,000 (for the People's Party in 1972) to as many as 19.7 million (for H. Ross Perot of the Independent Party in 1992) (U.S. Census Bureau 2012). When the number of people voting for third-party candidates is large, it can change the outcome. An analysis of the 2000 election concluded that the 2.5 million votes cast for Ralph Nader were crucial to the election of George Bush over Al Gore for the presidency (Magee 2003).

WHY DON'T PEOPLE TRUST THE GOVERNMENT?

As noted in the text, researchers who have surveyed people about their confidence in American institutions have not asked about the reasons for their responses. Why do most people have little confidence in the government, whereas others still have a good deal of confidence?

Conduct your own survey. Ask 10 people how much confidence they have in the federal, state, and local governments. Have them respond to one of four choices: a great deal, quite a lot, some, or very little. Then ask them why they responded as they did. Use follow-up questions until you feel you fully understand their reasoning.

We hope that you found people whose responses fell into each of these four categories. Why did they respond as they did? Can you categorize their responses (e.g., "Politicians are self-serving." "The whole system is flawed.")? How do your respondents' answers differ by level of government? What conclusions would you draw about Americans' views of their government if your respondents are typical?

If the entire class participates in this project, assign different social categories for the interviews. Assign the following kinds of respondents to various class members: males, females, whites, African Americans, Hispanics. Tabulate all the results and note any gender, racial, and ethnic differences.

In elections with no third-party candidates, distrustful voters are more likely to vote against the incumbent—whatever the incumbent's party affiliation (Hetherington 1999).

Some political scientists see third parties as a threat because they believe that the two-party system is best for the United States (Bibby and Maisel 1998). Other political scientists disagree, arguing that a responsible three-party system would work well (Lowi and Romance 1998). All agree that government and politics would be different under a three-party system. The three-party system might work better than the present two-party system, or it might create the kind of instability and inaction that have plagued some European nations.

If the failure of trust continues to intensify, Americans may well find out how they will be affected by a three-party system. Whether such a system will restore people's confidence in the government or simply plunge them into even deeper disillusionment is something that no one can say with certainty.

political alienation
a feeling of political disillusionment, powerlessness, and estrangement

Political Alienation. The fourth consequence of the failure of trust is **political alienation,** *a feeling of political disillusionment, powerlessness, and estrangement.* Alienated people lose interest in political life (Southwell 2008). They do not necessarily blame individual politicians for the sorry state of affairs in political life. And they are not merely turned off by the mudslinging and broken promises and endless conflict in the political arena. Rather, they are *disillusioned with the entire system,* including the voting process. For example, just before the 2006 elections, only 49 percent said they were "very confident" that their vote would be accurately counted (Polling Report 2012). The rest were unsure or lacked total confidence that they could vote and have it counted!

In short, alienated people believe that the system itself is fundamentally flawed (Scher 1997). For such people, it will take more than appeals to civic duty to involve them once again in the nation's political life.

Waste, Corruption, and Scandals

Americans believe they have a right to expect effectiveness, efficiency, and honesty from the politicians who are running their government. Unfortunately, Americans believe they observe contrary qualities—waste, corruption, and scandals—in those politicians. In a Gallup poll, 75 percent of Americans believed government corruption in the United States is widespread (Clifton 2016)! Moreover, professional assessments of government effectiveness and efficiency do little to change those beliefs. In 2000, for example, various news media reported the results of a study by the Government Performance Review Project of Syracuse University's Maxwell School of Citizenship and Public Affairs (Allen 2000). The researchers looked at the 20 federal agencies that have the most contact with the public and gave them an overall grade of B−. Work done by the agencies includes such activities as cleaning up New York Harbor, administering the national park system, overseeing air traffic, and ensuring that immigrants are in the nation legally. Some agencies did much better than others, but all suffered from such problems as reduced funding in the face of expanded workloads and political interference with their tasks.

Some government tasks, in other words, are not being carried out effectively or efficiently because of political decisions. "Government waste," on the other hand, refers to such things as excessive *paperwork, excessive costs, and unnecessary expenditures.* A number of groups and individuals, including politicians, work on identifying and publicizing examples of wasteful spending by the government. For example, a U.S. senator put together a "Waste Book" that lists $6.5 billion worth of projects he considers pointless (Kristof 2011). It includes such things as $30 million to help mango farmers in Pakistan hire workers and boost sales; nearly $766,000 to build a House of Pancake franchise in a toney area of Washington, D.C.; $652,740 to build a fourth visitor's center on a scenic highway in Oklahoma; $484,000 to a private developer to build a pizza business in Texas; and $702,558 to bring television into 14 remote Vietnamese villages so researchers could investigate how television affects family formation and reproductive health.

You want to beware of the *fallacy of non sequitur* at this point. It does not follow that, when a particular project sounds pointless or unreasonable, it clearly represents government waste. What one group calls "waste," such as some environmental projects, might

fallacy

be considered important and needed by another group. Nevertheless, no one disputes the fact that waste is a serious problem of government at all levels.

Nor does anyone dispute the *existence of fraud, corruption, and scandals.* A government official estimated that 5 percent of all federal spending in 2005 was lost to fraud, much of it to defense contractors and companies with contracts to rebuild Iraq (Kopecki 2006). In the early 2000s, a number of members of congress were indicted and jailed or forced out of office by various kinds of corrupt practices and ethics violations, including a sex scandal (homosexual overtures to a Congressional page), bribery, exchanging favorable legislation for campaign contributions, using legislative power to enhance their personal wealth, and using their positions to obtain financial benefits for family members (Sloan 2006). For example, one congressman went to prison for amassing personal wealth by agreeing to get government contracts for various businesses in return for monetary payoffs. Another congressman named his wife as his campaign fund-raiser. She had no other clients and no experience in fund-raising. But she received 15 percent of all funds raised for his campaign.

Such things are not new, of course. There is a long history of corruption and scandals in government at every level. In general, the instances of corruption or scandal involve *a politician acting in terms of self-interest or particular interests to the detriment of the politician's constituency or the general public.* The outcome is not only economic waste but also negative attitudes toward the government and lower levels of trust in government officials (Anderson and Tverdova 2003). In fact, public corruption is so threatening to the well-being of government that it is a top-priority item in FBI criminal investigations. According to the agency website, the FBI is investigating more than 2,000 cases of corruption involving public officials in the nation, and in 2010 it recorded more than 900 convictions.

A corrupt practice that is less common today than earlier in the nation's history is **patronage,** giving government jobs to people who are members of the winning party. Recall that one of the fundamental characteristics of a bureaucracy is the expertise of workers. Yet politicians have often hired, or used their influence to obtain employment for, relatives, friends, and party workers no matter their level of expertise. This practice is less common than it once was because the bulk of government jobs now come under civil service. But the fundamental principle of rewarding those who support the winners is still carried out in other ways. Thus, states that support the winning presidential candidate, or that have a governor of the same party as the winning candidate, are likely to receive more federal funds than are other states (Larcinese, Rizzo, and Testa 2006). A study of contracts awarded to companies to engage in postwar reconstruction in Afghanistan and Iraq found that campaign contributions and political connections were important factors in securing a contract (Hogan, Long, Stretesky, and Lynch 2006). And a study of states reported that politicians used state-level patronage to increase their chances of maintaining control over various state elective offices (Folke, Hirano, and Snyder 2011).

Corruption may also take the form of "stuffing the ballot box" or other methods of rigging elections. The outcome of the 2000 presidential election was delayed for weeks by disputed votes in Florida (Cannon, Lavelle, and Ragavan 2000; Slevin and Kovaleski 2000). Initially, the news media projected a Democratic victory. Later, they said it was too close to call. After some recounts, the final tally gave George W. Bush an extremely narrow edge over Al Gore. Charges of impropriety quickly surfaced, including flawed ballots, improper instructions, questionable counting methods, and discrimination against nonwhite voters. Democrats took their case to the Florida Supreme Court and, eventually, to the U.S. Supreme Court, whose ruling ensured a

patronage
giving government jobs to people who are members of the winning party

narrow victory for George W. Bush. Florida subsequently changed its voting system and abolished the use of punch-card ballots. Americans may never know for certain which candidate was actually preferred by a majority of the Florida voters.

What we do know is that many people were illegally purged from voters rolls (a list sent to election officials included the names of 8,000 Florida residents who had committed misdemeanors rather than the felonies for which they could legitimately be purged) (American Civil Liberties Union 2004). There were also efforts to intimidate black and Hispanic voters (Miller 2005).

Gridlock

Frequently, the government seems *mired in inaction,* unable to legislate new policies because of ideological conflict, party differences, or a standoff between the executive and legislative branches of the government. Such a situation is known as **gridlock** (Brady and Volden 1998). Gridlock may reflect the fact that politicians are taking stands in accord with contradictory values and are unable to reach a compromise. However, gridlock also occurs when politicians are engaged in power struggles in which who is in control is more important than what gets done (Chiou and Rothenberg 2003).

gridlock
the inability of the government to legislate significant new policies

Gridlock can occur at any level of government. In the late 1990s, a number of states experienced gridlock because they had an increased number of decisions to make after the federal government deferred certain issues to the state level (Levy 1999). For example, in New York the 1999 gridlock prevented passage of the state budget, which was three months late. This delay hampered planning by schools and other nonprofit groups, and important health care proposals languished in political limbo. At the federal level, partisan gridlock in Congress prevented legislation that would fix defects in the No Child Left Behind law, which deals with how schools prepare and evaluate students. Both political parties agreed that changes were needed, but they could not agree on how to fix the problems. By 2012, President Obama began giving states waivers on meeting the existing law's requirements until the gridlock could be broken (Associated Press 2012).

Gridlock is likely to maintain or even intensify the failure of trust. A government mired in inaction appears weak to the public it supposedly serves.

Government, Politics, and the Quality of Life

As with all the problems we are examining, government and politics affect the quality of life of great numbers of people. We consider here the way government action or inaction leads to three problem areas that affect quality of life: unequal opportunities for a high quality of life, inadequate protection of freedoms and rights, and the lack of responsiveness to needs.

Unequal Opportunities for a High Quality of Life

Today, Americans generally expect government to maintain an equitable distribution of power so that they have an equal opportunity to secure a high quality of life. Politicians themselves acknowledge their role in this quest for a high quality of life. As we wrote this chapter, we searched the Internet for "quality of life and government." The following are among the tens of thousands of items we found:

- The New York City site encouraged citizens to record complaints related to, and point out problems that detract from, their quality of life.
- A Los Angeles news item discussed local government's role in the city's quality-of-life goals.
- A Kansas City report discussed local elections and their consequences for the area's quality of life.
- A Jacksonville, Florida, annual report considered the quality of life in the community.
- An item from Chicago talked about the county government's role in the area's quality of life.
- A report from Philadelphia noted receipt of a grant to combat crimes that depress the city's quality of life.

Clearly, *politicians and citizens alike expect government at all levels to have a role in those matters that affect the quality of life.* Yet government has not measured up to these expectations and maintained a system in which all Americans have an equal opportunity to reap the benefits deemed necessary for a high quality of life. We noted in the previous three chapters various ways in which some groups benefit to the detriment of others: how, for instance, the wealthy benefit more than the poor from tax laws and other government policies and practices and how white males have more opportunities than do women or people of either sex from racial and ethnic minorities.

These disadvantages mean a lower quality of life for whole groups of people. For example, African Americans, Hispanics, and people in the lower socioeconomic strata have higher rates of negative mood, such as feelings of sadness, than do whites and people in the higher strata (Blackwell, Collins, and Coles 2002).

The relationship between advantages and quality of life holds true in other nations as well. Surveys of people's sense of their well-being in 55 nations, representing three-fourths of the earth's population, found that the higher the income and the greater the amount of equality in the nation, the higher the people's sense of well-being (Diener, Diener, and Diener 1995).

In essence, then, *the government has failed to maintain a social system in which all individuals, regardless of their social origins, have equal opportunities.* People do not expect equal outcomes. The nation's ideology is that anyone can succeed, but no one expects the government to ensure that every individual achieves the highest quality of life. However, Americans do expect the government to ensure a system in which no one's quality of life is diminished automatically because of his or her sex or social origins.

Inadequate Protection of Individual Rights

There is also *a contradiction between the value of individual rights and the way government functions to protect them.* As we noted in the last two chapters, government has not always protected the rights of women and of racial and ethnic minorities. In addition, government has threatened or violated certain basic rights that every citizen ideally possesses. For example, for many years the FBI secretly gathered information and kept files on thousands of Americans who openly opposed certain government programs and policies. Some of this information was secured by illegal means, such as breaking and entering or unauthorized taps of telephone lines. Among those under surveillance by the bureau were Martin Luther King Jr. and others in the civil rights movement.

It is important to acknowledge that at least a part of the problem of inadequate protection of individual rights lies in the *dilemma faced by government—how can individual rights and social order both be preserved?* A classic instance of the dilemma is the clash between individual rights and national security. During World War II, the clash was decided in favor of national security, resulting in the internment of around 100,000 Japanese Americans. Even though they were American citizens, they were viewed as a threat because of the war with Japan. Some observers still believe that the internment was the appropriate course of action (Rehnquist 1998). Others, however, have concluded that Japanese American citizens were deprived of their rights; in fact, lawsuits were instituted in the 1990s to obtain reparations for the injustice.

Individual rights versus national security remains a prominent issue. In the 1990s, various right-wing militias, fringe groups, and Islamic militants engaged in acts of violence against the government. These acts increased the pressure for measures that are likely to violate individual rights such as more covert domestic spying and information gathering by the government. We explore this issue in more detail in Chapter 14.

Additional areas in which individual rights may be threatened or suppressed by government include the criminal justice system, free speech on—and use of—the Internet, drug policies, the rights of immigrants, the rights of homosexuals, police practices, the right to privacy, and religious freedom (American Civil Liberties Union 1999). Consider, for example, the situation of some immigrants. The Immigration and Naturalization Service (INS) uses secret evidence in a small number of cases to deport people considered potential threats (American Civil Liberties Union 1999). Most of the cases involve Arabs or Muslims who cannot fight the deportation order because they do not have access to the "evidence."

Immigrants' rights have also been suppressed by the 1996 Personal Responsibility and Work Opportunity Reconciliation Act, which resulted from perceptions in Congress that immigrants and refugees abuse the welfare system (Hing 1998). The act effectively curbs benefits available to immigrants and refugees. It ignores the fact that immigrant labor serves an important economic function and that second-generation immigrants have significantly lower rates of welfare use than did the first generation.

The Freedom of Information Act of 1966 addressed at least some of the problems of individual rights (Unsworth 1999). The act gave the public access to government records and documents. Access is limited to records of the executive branch and only to those materials that have been "declassified" (i.e., that are not a threat to national security). The number of documents declassified has varied depending on the president. Presidents Nixon and Carter expanded declassification, whereas President Reagan restricted it. President Clinton tried to expand it once again. Unfortunately, even if material is declassified, there is no penalty imposed on an agency that refuses to comply with a citizen's request. The issue of the protection of individual rights continues to be a nettlesome one.

Lack of Responsiveness to Needs

Any satisfying relationship, including the relationship individuals have with organizations, *requires give and take.* If you find school a satisfying experience, for example, it is because you have given your time, money, and energy to complying with the school's requirements and have gained from your classes the knowledge and credentials needed to pursue your goals. People expect the same sort of give and take from government. Yet some Americans perceive the government to be all "take"—in the form of taxes and the demand for compliance with laws and regulations—and no "give"—in the sense of being unresponsive to the needs of the citizenry (see "Why Isn't There Help for People Like Me?" at the beginning of the chapter). Of course, a substantial number of Americans believe that both the "take" and the "give" should be minimal. That is, they accept the ideology that the smaller and less intrusive the government is, the better off people will be. However, three researchers examined data from a number of developed countries around the world over the period from 1981 to 2007 (Flavin, Pacek, and Radcliff 2014). They concluded that the citizenry finds life more satisfying as governmental intervention in the economy increases.

In the United States, there is often considerable opposition to any additional action by the government. The opposition can come from within the government itself, and it may take the form of a refusal to act or a public promise to action without the action ever taking place. For example, in 2005 when Hurricane Katrina devastated the city of New Orleans, officials at all levels, from the president to the governor to the mayor, promised full and rapid aid to victims. Yet the aid was minimal and slow in coming. When President Bush visited New Orleans shortly after the hurricane struck, he promised "one of the largest reconstruction efforts the world has ever seen" (Krugman 2006). The governor of Louisiana and the mayor of New Orleans also issued statements promising aid. However, two researchers who investigated the efforts to rebuild the city and help the citizenry recover described the outcome in terms of "malfeasance, official deviance and the failure to serve and protect a community" (Herron and Smith 2012). One of the researchers visited one of the city's wards six years after the disaster and found it "overgrown like a jungle, containing only about 20 percent of the houses that were there before the hurricane struck."

Although government at all levels shared some blame for the inadequate response to the disaster, attention focused in particular on the federal government and the Federal Emergency Management Agency (FEMA). FEMA was set up to deal with such crises, but the agency's response was so inept that its leader (a political appointee) and a number of others had to resign. Perhaps some of the best help received by the people of New Orleans and other hard-hit areas in the region came not from government but from the hundreds of thousands of volunteers from across the nation who contributed (and continue to contribute) money and their time to assist in the rebuilding efforts (Schwartz 2006).

An evaluation of state governments on such things as the management of employees, budgets, and finances, and the provision of information and infrastructure gives further evidence of inadequate responsiveness (Pew Center on the States 2008). The team of journalists and academics who did the research graded the states and found the national average to be a B−. Three states—Utah, Virginia, and Washington—received an A−. The grades of the rest ranged from B+ to D+.

When government responds so slowly and inadequately, or fails to respond at all, people understandably become cynical. They begin to view *government not as their protector and safety net, but as their competitor for the good things of life, or even as their enemy.* The citizens lose an important source of security and confidence, and the government loses a substantial amount of commitment to civic duty as people ignore or subvert laws and regulations whenever they feel they can do so with impunity.

Contributing Factors

Although many Americans blame inept or self-serving politicians, the problems of government cannot be reduced to defects in elected officials. You don't want to engage in the *fallacy of personal attack* and claim that the problems of government will be solved when present officials are replaced with better ones. Rather, you must recognize and deal with the varied social structural and social psychological factors that create and help perpetuate the problems of government.

Social Structural Factors

Size. "There is no country in the world today where the entire government establishment of 1910 could not comfortably be housed in the smallest of the new government buildings now going up, with room to spare for a grand-opera house and a skating rink" (Drucker 1968:172). This assessment, now five decades old, dramatizes the growth of government. Figure 9.2 illustrates that growth. Note that, contrary to the beliefs of many Americans, the federal government has not been growing (at least, in terms of the number of people employed). There are fewer people working for the federal government now than there were in the 1980s. Employment by state and local governments, on the other hand, has increased considerably over the past few decades. In 1982, federal civilian employment stood at 2.85 million; by 2014, the number had dropped to 2.7 million. In contrast, there were 12.99 million state and local government employees in 1982, and 17.66 million by 2014.

Of course, the number of people employed is not the only way to measure size. In addition to those directly employed, there are those who provide goods and services under contracts, grants, and mandates (Light 1999). If these are added, the size grows by tens of millions of people.

The growth of government reflects both a growing population and a growing number of functions and services assumed by government. Government was smaller and simpler in the early

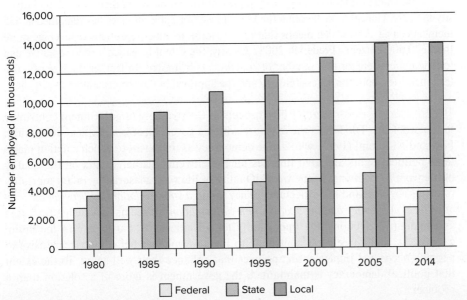

FIGURE 9.2
Government Employees, 1980–2014.
Source: U.S. Census Bureau website.

years of the nation. There were far fewer people and a more homogeneous population. There were also no income taxes to collect, no services to the poor to regulate, no monitoring and regulating of the conduct of businesses, no governmental health care obligations, no elaborate defense system to support, and so on. Whether the size of government today is necessary may be debatable, but a substantial amount of the growth was either inevitable because of the growing population or a response to public demand for protection or assistance.

Still, *size—both the size of government and size of the population—has consequences for functioning.* Consider the size of government. It is more difficult for large organizations to be efficient and responsive to the needs of people. Questions must be addressed and procedures must be followed that are not necessary when individuals help each other or small community organizations help people locally. When an individual seeks assistance from the federal government, for example, such questions as the following arise: What agency is responsible for helping? Who in the agency should handle the situation? What procedures (including filling out necessary paperwork) must be followed to meet the requirement of accountability? Who in the agency and/or other government organizations must approve the assistance? And so on. In the case of entire groups who need help (the poor, those suffering discrimination, those without health insurance, etc.), the questions and answers become even more complicated and demanding.

The size of the governed population also affects function. It is more difficult to gain compliance and enforce rules when regulating a large number of people. For instance, Ehrenhalt (1997) reported that there were nearly 3.1 million outstanding violations of the New York City housing code in 1996. However, the city's 200 inspectors could make only about 160,000 inspections per year. Most of the violations, therefore, can never be addressed. As Ehrenhalt noted, the city government's failure to respond to these violations is rooted in neither indifference nor ineptness. Rather, there are simply more citizens violating the law "than even the most efficient government can possibly keep track of." It may be that the difficulties of effectively governing large cities is one reason two researchers found in a study of 55 American cities that the larger the size of the city, the less trust the citizens had in their local government (Rahn and Rudolph 2005).

It is also more difficult to adequately represent the people when their number and diversity increase. Consider the fact that the U.S. House of Representatives has remained at 435 members since 1911, which means that now a House member represents on average more than 640,000 citizens (Frederick 2008). Clearly, the extent to which a representative can function effectively for that number of constituents is limited. In fact, as the size of a district increases, both the accessibility to and the approval of the representative diminishes.

The Structure of Government.   Two aspects of the structure of government contribute to the problems. The first is the extent to which a government is a political democracy. Frey and Al-Roumi (1999), who define democracy as the extent to which a nation maintains political rights and civil liberties for the citizenry, gathered data on the quality of life from 87 countries of the world. Quality of life was measured by infant mortality rate, literacy rate, and life expectancy. They found *a strong relationship between the level of political democracy and the quality of life in the nations.* It seems that such advantages as competitive elections, the opportunity for all citizens to participate in the political process, and a free press contribute to the government's being more responsive to people's needs and implementing policies that enhance their well-being. To the extent that political democracy is maintained, the government is more of a solution than a problem.

The other aspect of structure is *the way the government is organized to fulfill its functions.* In the United States, the federal system provides a constitutional separation of powers between the national and state governments. In addition, there are county, municipal, and township governments. All have direct authority over individuals. This arrangement creates unity without enforcing uniformity, encourages experimentation, and keeps government close to the people (Burns et al. 2005).

However, there are disadvantages as well. What level of government is best equipped to provide efficient and effective service? What level of government is responsible for dealing with various social problems? Consider, for example, the following questions: Is a safety net for the poor the primary responsibility of the federal government or of state and local governments? Who is going to handle problems of discrimination based on race/ethnicity, gender, age, or sexual orientation? Should there be national standards for education, or should education be completely under the control of local school boards?

An ongoing struggle among various levels of government over responsibility, or the efforts of government at one level to shift responsibility for a problem to government at another level, can result in an inadequate response to people's needs. As we discussed in Chapter 6, the current transfer of major responsibility for poverty from the federal to the state and local level in the form of workfare is having a negative impact on the quality of life of many of America's poor.

Finally, *the government is organized along bureaucratic lines in order to fulfill its various functions.* Look back at the characteristics of a bureaucracy that we discussed earlier, and you will see that it should be a highly efficient and effective form of large-scale administration. If people in a bureaucracy function according to the criteria we listed, the organization should help people expertly and impartially.

In practice, however, bureaucracies never measure up to the ideal. As a result, and in spite of many positive achievements, the very term "bureaucrat" has become a term of disparagement, and a wide variety of government problems are blamed on the bureaucrats. To blame bureaucrats, however, is to substitute the *fallacy of personal attack* for a realistic appraisal.

There are various reasons for the disparity between the ideal and the reality. Middle-class bureaucrats may not treat lower-class citizens with the same respect and concern that they do citizens in higher classes. Bureaucrats who try to be impartial in their dealings with people face severe pressure and potential reprisals from individuals who want special consideration. Some government bureaucrats may be in positions for which they have not been properly trained and for which they lack needed expertise.

Other bureaucrats may rigidly follow the rules of the organization even if the rules don't apply well to particular cases. Two business writers call such bureaucrats the "white-collar gestapo," arguing that they mindlessly enforce a growing number of arbitrary rules and regulations (McMenamin and Novack 1999). Indeed, even though the bureaucratic rules and regulations are supposed to cover all circumstances, you can raise the question of whether this is possible when dealing with a large, heterogeneous population. Perhaps bureaucrats need the flexibility to exercise more discretion.

Furthermore, in spite of the highly bureaucratic nature of government, *the government is not organized in a way to deal effectively with waste and corruption.* One way to stop waste and corruption would be to encourage employees to act as internal watchdogs and report such practices (to be "whistleblowers" in contemporary terminology). From time to time this happens. But in spite of the Whistleblower Protection Act, most government employees fear reprisals if they blow the whistle on

fallacy

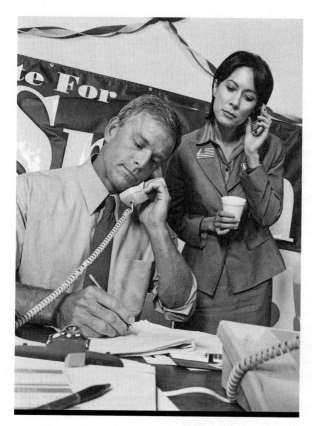

Campaigning for elective office is expensive, and critics argue that the wealthy are at an advantage when they have millions of dollars of their own money to spend in their efforts to be elected.

©Digital Vision/Getty Images

corrupt or wasteful practices. Such fears are justified because whistleblowers are as likely to suffer retaliation (including demotion, loss of career, and even threats to their well-being) as to bring about a rectification of the problem they identify (Dehaven-Smith 2011).

The Economics of Campaigning. How much would it cost you to become a U.S. senator? It would depend on the state in which you ran, of course, and the amount of opposition you faced. But political advisers can put a price tag—and the price is steep—on every race from the presidency to local offices.

The cost of political office is not only high but has, as shown in Figure 9.3, been on an upward path. By the time of the 2012 election, one analysis found that the average amount raised for the campaign was $1,689,580 for a House seat and $10,476,451 for a Senate seat (Costa 2013). The total amount spent in the races for Congress and president in 2012 was $6.3 billion (*New York Times,* October 19, 2014).

The cost of political office will continue to soar because of the 2010 Supreme Court decision to allow corporations and individuals to spend as much as they want on political advertising as long as the ads are not coordinated with the candidates' campaigns. The controversial ruling led to the creation of so-called Super PACs, organizations that create ads in support of particular candidates (and sometimes are run by former advisers or staff members of those candidates). The Super PACs are often able to pour enough money into particular campaigns to literally buy offices for their preferred candidates.

In light of the costs of running a campaign, *it is evident that people without access to considerable sums of money or money-raising skills are unlikely to win an election.* In recent decades, some very wealthy individuals have invested millions from their own fortunes as they sought political office. Such a use of personal wealth raises the concern that the nation may be entering a time when only the rich can successfully run for office.

In order to gain and remain in office, whether they are personally rich or not, politicians need massive amounts of money. This need makes politicians beholden to the wealthy and to various interest groups. A politician may be able to vote against the interests and preferences of those who support him or her only at the cost of continuing in office. The fact that poor people in a politician's district have pressing needs for various kinds of aid is not likely to take priority over the interests of the wealthy individuals and interest groups that provide the money that keeps the politician in office.

Some measures have been taken to *reform campaign financing,* which became a hotly debated issue in the late 1990s. In the 1970s, Congress set up the Federal Election Commission and limited the amount that individuals can contribute to a campaign. However, wealthy individuals and interest groups circumvent the intent of the law by giving so-called soft money, contributions directly to the party instead of to an individual candidate. Legislation in 2002 banned national parties from raising soft money. But politicians circumvented the law through "527 political organizations," which are political interest groups that are tax-exempt under Section 527 of the Internal Revenue Code and have not been

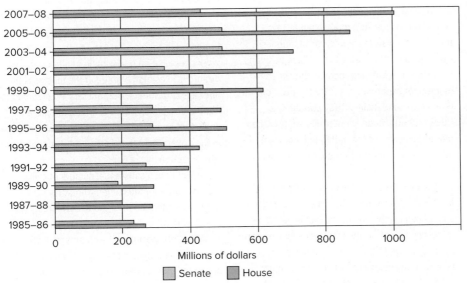

FIGURE 9.3
Cost of Congressional
Campaigns.
Source: U.S. Census Bureau
website.

regulated by the Federal Election Commission. Clearly, campaign financing remains problematic.

The Media. In the first of the televised presidential debates in 1960, Richard Nixon looked unkempt and nervous in contrast to John F. Kennedy, who appeared crisp and confident. Although Nixon won the debate among radio listeners, Kennedy came out ahead among television watchers. This event began a new era in the relationship between media coverage and election results.

The media have always played a role in American politics, of course—but *both the nature of the coverage and the influence of the media have changed as radio, network television, cable television, and now the Internet have been added to the print media as factors in the political process.* Let's explore the impact of the media on three aspects of political life: elections; political agendas and action; and public trust.

First, the media are important in political campaigns. For one thing, advertising by candidates accounts for a substantial proportion of the enormous costs of campaigns. Television advertising is particularly expensive, but it is necessary *because a substantial proportion of Americans rely on television for their political news* and television ads affect the outcome of elections (Drew and Weaver 2006). Relying on television means that voters get less information than is provided by the print media or radio because they depend heavily on "sound bites"—those brief excerpts from the campaign trail that, in the opinion of television editors, capture something informative about the candidate's position or something newsworthy or sensational about the candidate's activities. Sound bites generally consume less than 10 seconds, raising the question of how much accurate information they convey about a candidate's position.

In addition to television, the social media of candidates are an important source of information. In the 2016 election, about a fourth of U.S. adults turned to social media posts by the two presidential candidates (Shearer 2016). That was far more than the 10 percent who relied on the candidates' websites or the nine percent who relied on e-mails from the candidates. Overall, a third of Americans got most of their election news from at least one of the three sources.

BUREAUCRACY IN INDONESIA

As noted in the text, bureaucrats are supposed to have expertise and act impartially in accord with written rules—but they do not always function that way. In some areas of Indonesia, for example, people are able to purchase positions in the government bureaucracy; they need money, not expertise, to secure the position (Kristiansen and Ramli 2006). Dwight King (1998a, 1998b) made an intensive study of the Indonesian civil service and found a number of additional reasons the bureaucracy falls short of the ideal.

The Indonesian civil service is organized in 17 ranks. Each employee has a grade and a step ranking within the grade that is based on education and seniority. Employees who perform their duties well advance one step every four years and eventually can qualify for a higher grade. At a certain level, however, the employees must acquire additional education or pass a test in order to continue their advancement.

In spite of this apparently well-organized arrangement, there is often a disparity between an individual's qualifications and the requirements of the position that he or she holds. For instance, an individual who has a graduate degree in liberal arts might be promoted to the head of the agency on public works because no one with an engineering degree is in as high a grade at the time as is the liberal arts graduate. Bureaucrats' educational attainment and civil service grade are more important in determining where they work in the government than is their educational specialization.

In addition, a substantial number of civil servants are promoted even when they have not reached the required grade. Two practices are at work here. One is to promote someone to an "acting" position. The other is to utilize an exception clause in the regulations that allows individuals who have performed in an "extraordinary" way for two years to be promoted even when they are not in the necessary grade.

The point is, voters' knowledge of candidates and their positions comes either from the candidates' brief postings or from the other electronic media. What appears in the media, therefore, affects how people vote. The way the media interpret an incumbent president's performance, for example, strongly influences his or her chances for re-election (Dover 1998). Similarly, a study of House elections and the media concluded that incumbents have an advantage, particularly among less educated voters, because they have had more television coverage and much of that coverage is positive (Prior 2006). In fact, the more television stations in a district, the greater the advantage of the incumbent.

While television continues to be a major source of political information, the Internet has become an increasingly powerful political tool. By the time of the 2010 elections, 24 percent of Americans (compared to 7 percent in 2002) said that the Internet was their main source of campaign news (Smith 2011). The proportion was highest among the young (35 percent of those aged 18–29), the college educated (34 percent), and those in the higher ($75,000 and above) income brackets (32 percent). In the 2008 election, Barack Obama supporters were far more active on the Internet than were supporters of John McCain, which was one of the factors in Obama's election to the presidency.

It was not the first time the Internet played a key role in a campaign. In 2004, bloggers and sites such as the Drudge Report helped George W. Bush defeat John Kerry by raising doubts about such matters as Kerry's status as a war hero (Feld and Wilcox 2008). In fact, the large, active number of political activists on the Internet, and the clear nature of the impact they can have, has given rise to the term *"netroots."* Netroots (from Inter*net*

For some functions, the Indonesian government bureaucracy is also hampered by the lack of clearly defined areas of responsibility. For example, three different agencies have responsibility for education: the Ministry of Education and Culture (MOEC), the Ministry of Home Affairs (MOHA), and the Ministry of Religious Affairs (MORA). MOEC is responsible for secondary and higher education, but shares responsibility for primary education with MOHA. MORA is responsible for the Islamic schools, which are mainly at the post-primary level.

This dispersion of responsibility has negative consequences for Indonesian education. First, little effort is made to improve primary education because neither MOEC nor MOHA seeks the resources needed. MOHA secures funding for primary education, but has not sought additional funds because it is responsible for funding, not for quality. MOEC is aware of the need for improvement, but funding is not part of its responsibility.

Second, some schools do not receive the resources they need. For example, MOEC publishes textbooks and sends them to regional warehouses. From there, the regional government is supposed to distribute them to the schools. But the regional governments complain that they do not have the necessary funds to distribute books. Thus, some schools, particularly those in relatively isolated areas, may not receive needed texts and materials.

Third, career advancement for primary school teachers occurs in the context of the contrary decisions of MOEC and regional governments. MOEC evaluates the teachers' performance. Regional governments, however, make promotion and transfer decisions—often independently of MOEC evaluations.

In sum, government bureaucracy in Indonesia is similar to that in other nations: It falls short of the bureaucratic ideal. Yet it does no good to simply complain of "bureaucrats." A different set of people in the same system would make little or no difference in the outcome. It is the way the bureaucracy is organized, not the kind of people in it, that is primarily responsible for the problems.

and grass*roots*) refers to the networks of those who use the Internet as their primary medium to engage in political discussion and action. It is imperative for a candidate for political office to have (and most do) a netroots coordinator who can both monitor and try to influence information being passed around the Internet.

The second impact of the media is on political agendas and government actions. The influence of the media is not limited to elections. As Cook (1998) has argued, *the media are an integral part of the governing of the nation.* Government officials use the media to shape public opinion and gain support for decisions and programs. In turn, officials are influenced in their decision-making process by the information they glean from the media (Edwards and Wood 1999). To a considerable extent, the media help decide what are the issues, problems, and crises to which political leaders must respond (Dye 1995).

If the media were impartial and always accurate, their influence would not be a cause for concern. *However, nine corporations control most of the nation's media* (Foerstel 2001). Does that matter? Clearly it does, as illustrated by an investigation into Fox News (Coyle 2004). The television network is owned by Rupert Murdoch, a wealthy conservative. But Common Cause, a nonpartisan watchdog group, and a liberal political advocacy group filed a petition with the Federal Trade Commission arguing that Fox should stop using its slogan of being "fair and balanced" in the news. In fact, the groups maintained, the news on Fox is consistently biased in favor of the Republican Party and right-wing perspectives. That such a biased perspective affects voters is shown in an analysis by two economists, who found that when Fox News becomes available in a town, Republicans gain votes (DellaVigna and Kaplan 2006).

fallacy

This point does not mean that media information is always biased or distorted. It does mean, however, that people must be careful not to engage in the *fallacy of authority* and assume that what comes to them through the media is *ipso facto* accurate and impartial. It also means that serious problems, affecting considerable numbers of citizens, may be largely invisible because they are ignored by the media.

Finally, the media have contributed to the failure of trust. Is government more corrupt, unreliable, and unresponsive now than it was in the past? On the one hand, such factors as the civil service, term limits, and extension of the right to vote are evidence that government and political life are more democratic and more effective now than in the past. On the other hand, all too frequent scandals and deceptions at the various levels of government raise questions about the integrity of government and undoubtedly contribute to the failure of trust. Still, such scandals are not new.

What is new is *the way in which the media give so much coverage to scandals, including matters that would have been glossed over as private affairs in past decades.* The mainline media play up stories of scandals and potential scandals in ways similar to those of the tabloids. During the Clinton administration, for example, the media gave enormous attention to the president's sexual improprieties. The media also provided extensive coverage when a number of members of Congress resigned because of sexual or other scandals.

Many Americans indicated a weariness with this extensive coverage, noting its negative impact on their trust in government. At the same time, many Americans admitted to an almost *insatiable curiosity about the scandals* (Ricchiardi 1998). As long as this public demand exists, the media will continue to provide in-depth reports that may expose problems in politics but may also contribute to the growing distrust in government.

Interest Groups. The most effective way to influence a massive organization like government is through other organizations. The lone individual has little chance of bringing about change, but an organization can put considerable pressure on politicians. For that reason, *interest groups have become an increasingly important factor in American political life.*

There are at least 30,000 interest groups in the United States. Many have political action committees (PACs) that are registered with the government and legally entitled to raise funds and make contributions to election campaigns and political parties (Table 9.2). The number of political action committees grew considerably after 1980. PACs contribute hundreds of millions of dollars to candidates each presidential election year. A substantial amount of that money comes from a relatively few wealthy donors.

TABLE 9.2
Number and Type of Political Action Committees

Type	Number			
	1980	1990	2000	2016
Corporate	1,206	1,795	1,523	1,621
Labor	297	346	316	278
Trade, membership, and health	576	774	812	926
Nonconnected	374	1,062	902	1,786
Cooperative	42	59	39	41
Corporation without stock	56	136	114	92
Total	2,551	4,172	3,706	5,819

SOURCE: Federal Election Commission 2016.

Interest groups also hire **lobbyists,** individuals who try to influence legislation in accord with the preferences of the interest groups. *Lobbyists use various means to influence politicians.* They may provide a politician with information that supports the interest group's position on a given issue. They may try to cultivate personal friendships with particular politicians. They may treat a politician to expensive dinners and trips. In addition, there is always the promise of support through votes and contributions by members of the interest group.

lobbyist
an individual who tries to influence legislation in accord with the preferences of an interest group

The number of lobbyists in Washington, D.C. declined for the first time in decades in 2011, perhaps a reflection of legislative gridlock and a fragile economy (Eggen 2012). Still, the number of registered lobbyists was 12,600 (not all lobbyists register because the rules are unclear and the penalty for not registering is light), and the various interest groups who hired the lobbyists spent about $3.27 billion on lobbying efforts during the year. The money is not merely to pay the salaries of the lobbyists. One of the lures the lobbyist uses is a substantial contribution to a politician's campaign. The money is also used to wine and dine politicians, provide them with tickets to sporting events and concerts, offer them free trips, and provide them with gifts of various kinds.

The abuses of the practice were dramatized in 2006 when a powerful lobbyist, Jack Abramoff, pleaded guilty to fraud, tax evasion, and conspiring to bribe public officials (Stone 2006). Abramoff gained enormous personal wealth while funneling money and other perks to lawmakers in return for favorable legislation. Linkages with Abramoff cost a number of politicians their positions either through resignation or through defeat at the polls.

Another aspect of lobbying that most Americans find troublesome is the fact that many lobbyists are relatives of lawmakers or members of their staff (Eisler and Kelley 2006). In a poll, 80 percent of Americans agreed that it's wrong for relatives to lobby lawmakers. Nevertheless, an investigation reported 53 cases in one year in which members of the House or Senate appropriations committee or their top aides had relatives who were lobbyists. And of those relatives who attempted to get money in appropriations bills for their clients, 22 were successful.

Social Psychological Factors

Public Attitudes. The American ideal is that government is of the people, by the people, and for the people. This statement means that government originates in the people, involves the people, and effectively represents them. Government is meant to be the people's ally, not their opponent. But consider some of the results of national polls in recent years:

- only 30 percent of Americans have a great deal, or quite a lot, of confidence in the Supreme Court;
- only 7 percent of Americans have a great deal, or quite a lot, of confidence in Congress;
- 69 percent believe Super PACs should be illegal;
- only 23 percent are satisfied with "the way things are going in the United States at this time."

While the numbers fluctuate and can even change rapidly, such attitudes reflect the failure of trust. They also help perpetuate the failure of trust. Instead of stimulating people to get involved in government and make necessary reforms, *negative attitudes lead to alienation and withdrawal from political life* (Plane and Gershtenson 2004).

The irony here is that people who believe that the government does not help them become alienated and do not bother to vote. But research shows that members of Congress not only strive to direct resources into their districts but also try to put those resources where they appear to pay off in terms of votes (Martin 2003). In other words, *alienation becomes a self-fulfilling prophecy* because negative attitudes lead to nonparticipation and nonparticipation results in fewer benefits.

In addition to negative attitudes about government and politics, a set of *contrary attitudes* contribute to the problem. Cronin and Genovese (1998) have identified a number of these contrary attitudes in their discussion of the "nine paradoxes" of the American presidency:

Americans want strong leaders, but they also fear the abuse of power that a strong leader might bring to the office.

Americans have favorable attitudes toward ordinary people holding political office (thus, the traditional appeal of the candidate who was born in a log cabin), but they also value charisma in their leaders.

Americans want leaders who will unify the people, but they do not want to compromise their own positions in order to forge the unity.

Americans admire leaders with vision, but they also believe that leaders should be responsive to public opinion.

Moreover, Americans tend to approve of such items as lower taxes, reduced government spending, and less government interference in daily life. Yet Americans also resist proposals to reduce government or government spending in those areas from which they benefit or which they support for ideological reasons (Young 1998). In essence, the nation is quite ambivalent about the role of government. As shown in a Gallup poll (Newport 2011), roughly the same proportion (35 percent) support an activist government that strives to improve life in all ways as the proportion (37 percent) that believes government should provide only the most basic of services.

Such contrary attitudes pose *a dilemma for politicians.* In essence, no matter what a politician does, some segment of the population will be disappointed and frustrated. The easiest course of action is to follow his or her conscience when possible and, at other times, follow the desires of those who contribute the funds necessary to stay in office.

Ideologies.   Americans, for the most part, are suspicious of extreme ideologues and value compromise in resolving political conflicts. Indeed, when politicians of opposing ideologies work together, the result is usually compromise; but under some circumstances, the result may be gridlock. Brady and Volden (1998) studied legislative gridlock in the U.S. Congress. They concluded that members of Congress fall at various points on a liberal-conservative continuum. The median ideology of Congress is also somewhere on this continuum. Recall that the median is the point at which half the cases are above and half are below. For example, if you use −10 as the extreme conservative position, and +10 as the extreme liberal position, then calculate the average of all the members of Congress, you might find that the median position of a particular Congress is −2 (slightly conservative).

Let's say that a new policy is proposed, and that it can be placed at +1 (slightly liberal). It has a good chance of passing because it is not that far from the median. It has an even better chance of passing if the existing policy is more liberal than the proposed one. It has less chance if the existing policy is −2, that is, right at the median.

The situation is compounded by Senate filibusters and presidential vetoes. Taken together, these factors indicate a "gridlock region," an area on the continuum that results in gridlock if a proposed new policy falls in this region. The gridlock reflects the fact that there is a sufficient number of politicians on both sides of opposing ideologies so that the issue cannot be resolved.

Public Policy and Private Action

Many of the factors that contribute to the problems of government pose an ongoing dilemma. For example, you cannot reduce the size of the population served. It is doubtful that the overall size of government can be reduced (the number of federal employees declined in the 1990s, but government employees at other levels increased, so that there was a net increase in the total).

Although selected restructuring might be helpful, it is always a trial-and-error process. For example, some people believe that term limits will enable politicians to function more effectively because they will not be hampered by catering to special interests or their own ambitions to pursue long-term careers. However, in states that have instituted term limits for legislators, the tendency is for more power to go to the governor (Mahtesian 1999). With little time to gain political savvy, legislators are likely to have far less influence than the executive branch of state government. At this point, therefore, it is not clear whether term limits for state legislators make state governments more or less responsive to people's needs.

Campaign finance reform is one of the most needed areas for addressing the problems of government. Individuals and groups with money have the most power in government because politicians are dependent on them to gain, and remain in, office. In recent elections, the candidate who raised the most money was also most likely to win. In spite of reforms in recent years, such as certain limits on contributions to specific candidates, huge amounts of money flow from individuals and interest groups into the political coffers as corporations and rich donors find ways to *circumvent the laws on contribution limits* (Rosen 2000).

A number of states have implemented campaign financing reforms that could serve as a model for the federal government. Maine and Arizona became the first states to have a completely subsidized public finance system for legislative candidates (Francia and Hernson 2003). A number of other states offer partial funding. Candidates who accepted the full funding spent less of their time raising money than did other candidates, including those who had partial public funding. Many European nations also have publicly financed elections (Kryzanek 1999). If the United States adopted such a system, it would mean that campaigns would be shorter, less expensive (fewer television ads, etc.), and more likely to focus on issues rather than on personal attacks and extravagant events. To enact such a change, Congress will have to overcome the resistance of interest groups, wealthy individuals, television executives, and others. Without a change, however, politicians will continue to be captive to their sources of money.

Greater citizen participation is another step needed to address the problems of government. The Internet is a powerful tool for building greater citizen participation in political decision making (Leighninger 2011). It facilitates debate and discussion, can be used to gather support for particular points of view, and could increase the number of people who vote. When large numbers of people get involved and vote, they can overcome some of the shortcomings of politicians. For example, publicity about the absentee rates of senators and representatives in votes on legislation led voters in many areas to reject at the polls those politicians with high rates of absenteeism (Mintz 1998). As a result, participation in voting on congressional legislation rose steadily over the last 30 years of the 20th century.

At the state and local levels, a number of cases of citizen participation in the governing process illustrate the value of the practice (Kramer 1999). For example, officials in a county in Florida wanted to attack several social problems, including juvenile crime in a poor community composed mostly of racial and ethnic minorities. At first, they made no progress. But when they worked with citizens of the community and included representatives of the racial and ethnic groups in the discussions, the project was not only successful but became a model for other communities. Only when the people became involved were the government officials able to fully understand the situation and become responsive to the people's needs.

The problem is, given the political alienation of so many citizens, how do you secure more participation? One way you can change attitudes is to encourage citizens to become part of a group that engages in political discussions. The National Issues Forum (NIF) sponsors deliberative forums and study groups on national issues. A study of people who participated in NIF discussions found that, at the end of their participation, they had a much more coherent understanding of issues and much less attitudinal uncertainty about political issues (Gastil and Dillard 1999).

Certainly, politically alienated people have little motivation to join such a group. Thus, to increase citizen participation in the governing process, it is necessary to educate people about the effectiveness of such groups and to publicize efforts at various levels of government that have brought about change.

Other measures that increase citizen participation include easing the registration process and allowing citizen-initiated ballot measures at the state level. Increased numbers of people vote in those states that now permit registration on election day (Brians and Grofman 2001). A comparison of states that allow citizen-initiated ballot measures with those that do not showed considerably higher turnout in the former (as much as 35 to 45 percent higher in presidential elections) (Tolbert, Grummel, and Smith 2001).

Still another measure that can increase voting is *the use of social pressure*. Three researchers carried out an interesting experiment in which they sent a series of mailings to hundreds of thousands of registered voters (Gerber, Green, and Larimer 2008). They found a substantially higher proportion of actual voting among those who received mailings that promised to publicize that they voted to members of their household or to neighbors.

Finally, *face-to-face canvassing increases the number who vote* (Michelson 2003). Voters who are contacted are significantly more likely to vote than those who are not. And this contact may have a long-term payoff. In a field experiment with 25,200 registered voters, researchers found that those people who were urged to vote either through direct mail or face-to-face canvassing not only voted in significantly higher proportions but also were more likely to vote in subsequent elections (Gerber, Green, and Shachar 2003).

Follow-Up.   What recommendations would you make to government and school officials to increase voter participation?

Summary

Government is necessary because it fulfills a number of important social functions, functions that reflect people's expectations of their government. First, government is expected to protect the citizenry from foreign aggressors and from threats to individual well-being. Regulatory agencies were established to protect citizens from threats to their well-being. Second, government is expected to secure social order. Third, government is expected to distribute power equitably so that citizens have an equal opportunity for life, liberty, and the pursuit of happiness. Fourth, government is expected to provide a safety net, a minimum standard of living below which it will not allow citizens to fall.

A number of problems of government and politics exist in the United States. There are inequalities in the distribution of power. Social scientists disagree about whether power is distributed in accord with a pluralistic or a power elite model. The failure of trust is a second problem. Americans trust most other institutions far more than they trust the government. This distrust has a number of consequences: it leads to a lack of citizen participation in the political process; it alters people's voting patterns; and it leads to political alienation, a feeling of political disillusionment, powerlessness, and estrangement.

A third problem involves waste, corruption, and scandals in government. Waste refers to such problems as excessive paperwork, excessive costs, and unnecessary expenditures. Corruption and scandals usually involve a politician acting in terms of self-interest or particular interest to the detriment of the politician's constituency or the general public.

Gridlock is a fourth problem. Gridlock means that the government is mired in inaction, unable to legislate significant new policies because of ideological conflict, party differences, or a standoff between the executive and legislative branches. Gridlock is likely to intensify the failure of trust.

Problems in government and politics affect the quality of life in a number of ways. Such problems mean that people have unequal opportunities for a high quality of life. They mean that the freedoms and rights of citizens are not always adequately protected and that the government is not adequately responsive to people's needs.

Various factors contribute to the problems of government and politics. The size of the population served and the size of the government itself both affect how well the government can function. The way the government is organized to fulfill its functions—the separation of powers between the national and state governments and the bureaucratic nature of government agencies—also creates some difficulties in effective functioning. On the other hand, the government is *not* organized so as to deal effectively with waste and corruption.

The costs and financing methods of campaigning have particularly adverse effects. Many social scientists believe that campaign finance issues threaten the democratic process itself and virtually ensure politicians' unresponsiveness to people's needs.

The media also contribute to the problems. They are a substantial part of the cost of campaigns, and they determine the information and perspectives that voters receive about the candidates. The media affect political agendas and actions of those in office, which gives them an integral part of the governing of the nation. They also contribute to the failure of trust.

Interest groups have become an increasingly important part of American political life through contributions, lobbyists, and influence on voting blocs. Interest groups can affect legislation in a way that protects particular interests to the detriment of the general well-being.

Social psychological factors that contribute to the problems include the attitudes of the public and the ideologies of politicians. Negative attitudes of the public lead to alienation and withdrawal from political life; contrary attitudes pose a dilemma for politicians. Ideological positions of politicians can lead to gridlock.

Key Terms

Anarchism	Pluralism
Bureaucracy	Political Alienation
Gridlock	Political Party
Interest Group	Power Elite Model
Lobbyist	Regulatory Agency
Patronage	

Study Questions

1. What is meant by anarchism, and why does it appeal to some people?
2. What are the functions of government?

3. Explain the different views on the distribution of power in the United States.

4. What is meant by the "failure of trust," and what are the consequences of this failure?

5. Give some examples of waste, corruption, and scandals in government.

6. How can legislative gridlock occur?

7. In what ways do problems of government and politics affect Americans' quality of life?

8. What social structural factors contribute to the problems of government and politics?

9. How do public attitudes affect the political life of the nation?

10. Explain how political ideologies can lead to gridlock in the government.

11. What are some of the important steps to be taken in order to deal with the problems of government and politics?

Internet Resources/Exercises

1. Explore some of the ideas in this chapter on the following sites:

http://www.gao.gov   Access reports of the General Accounting Office, the congressional watchdog of federal spending.

http://www.uspirg.org   Reports plus access to information and programs of state organizations associated with the Public Interest Research Group.

https://fedstats.sites.usa.gov   The gateway site to all the statistical data published by the federal government, including data on government at all levels.

2. Go to the PIRG site listed above. Select one of the state PIRGs. Then read their materials on an area of interest to you (higher education, health care reform, government reform, etc.). If you live in the state, write a letter to your representative advocating one or more of the changes or programs in the PIRG materials. If you live in a different state, try to locate materials on the same topic and compare them with the state PIRG materials.

3. Find information on corruption, scandals, or waste in one or more other countries. How does the information you get compare with materials in the text on such problems in America? Do other nations have the same or different kinds of problems? Which nation seems to have the most serious problems?

For Further Reading

Haidt, Jonathan. *The Righteous Mind: Why Good People Are Divided by Politics and Religion.* New York: Vintage, 2013. A social psychologist draws on a number of disciplines to provide understanding into the polarization that exists today in politics and other areas as well.

Iyengar, Shanto. *Media Politics: A Citizen's Guide.* 2nd ed. New York: W. W. Norton & Company, 2011. A critical examination of the role of the media in American politics, including how politicians use the media to get elected and to stay in office, the role of the FCC, and the impact of the media on framing news and politics.

Lakoff, George. *Moral Politics: How Liberals and Conservatives Think.* 2nd ed. Chicago: University of Chicago Press, 2002. An examination of the worldviews and ways of thinking of liberals and conservatives, including their differing views of morality and their diverse approaches to such issues as taxes, crime, the death penalty, and the environment.

Light, Paul C. *A Government Ill Executed: The Decline of the Federal Service and How to Reverse It.* Cambridge, MA: Harvard University Press, 2008. Using Alexander Hamilton's seven "tests" of a good government, Light discusses why the federal government increasingly has difficulty passing these tests and suggests what can be done to rectify the situation.

Maisel, Sandy L., and Mark D. Brewer. *Parties and Elections in America: The Electoral Process.* 5th ed. New York: Rowman & Littlefield, 2009. Discusses political parties and the electoral process at all levels (local, state, and national); includes an examination of the role of the media and the issue of campaign financing.

Terry, Janice J. *U.S. Foreign Policy in the Middle East: The Role of Lobbies and Special Interest Groups.*

London: Pluto Press, 2005. A case study of the pro-Israel lobby and the way it affects foreign policy, illustrating the power of special interests and lobbyists on the U.S. government.

Wilensky, Harold L. *Rich Democracies: Political Economy, Public Policy, and Performance.* Berkeley: University of California Press, 2002. Uses a variety of data, including hundreds of interviews, to analyze differing styles of conflict resolution and the common social, economic, and labor problems of modern governments.

CHAPTER

10

Work and
the Economy

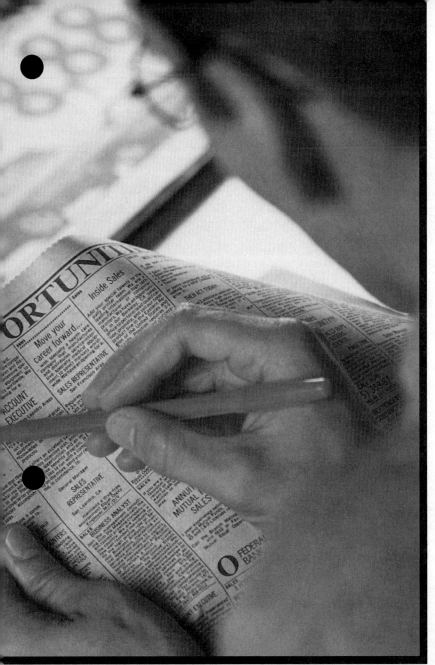
©Photodisc/Punchstock

"I'm Not a Worrier. But . . ."

Some people are optimistic by nature. They tend not to worry even when they are struggling with problems. But, as Ted points out, unemployment can strain even the most optimistic of outlooks. Ted is in his late 40s. He has been out of work for more than a year, a situation that was inconceivable to him only a few months before he lost his job:

I'm an engineer. I've never been out of work before. In fact, only a few months before I was laid off, I was planning to stay in my job until I retired. A group of us were laid off at the same time. We were all completely taken by surprise. We knew things were slack, but there was no talk of any layoffs. They just called us each in one day and told us they didn't have a job for us anymore.

At first, I was kind of cocky about it. I was hurt, because I really liked working there. But I was also sure that I would have another job in a few weeks. Probably even with better pay. I fantasized about writing them a letter and thanking them for giving me the opportunity to advance myself. You know, rub it in, and make them sorry.

That was over a year ago. It was about a hundred résumés and applications ago. I'm not a worrier. But I'm really worried now. And every month when the mortgage comes due, I worry a little more. My wife's job keeps us afloat, but we've about exhausted our savings, and we're now thinking about selling our house and moving into an apartment.

But you know what the worst part of it is? Just waiting and waiting and not hearing, and feeling more and more useless and more and more helpless. I've lost the chance at jobs for which I'm a perfect fit because they could hire someone younger and cheaper. It's really depressing. I'll keep trying, but it gets harder all the time to make yourself go through the application process, and it gets harder all the time to feel hopeful, to really believe that this could be the place that will finally hire me.

Introduction

Many Americans fantasize about becoming independently wealthy so that they can do whatever they please. Moreover, they believe that the American economy offers that possibility. Think about this fantasy for a moment. Do you believe that the American economy offers you the possibility of becoming independently wealthy? If so, what are your chances? If it happens, what will you do? Will you continue to work?

When we pose such questions to social problems classes, virtually everyone agrees that he or she could become independently wealthy. Many do not think the chances of this are very good, however, and nearly all the students say they would continue to work.

In general, the students believe that the American economy is the best economy, and they are committed to it and to the work ethic. The **work ethic** involves the notion that *your sense of worth and the satisfaction of your needs are intricately related to the kind of work you do.*

In this chapter we explore evidence related to these beliefs about work and the economy. We look at the changing nature of the economy, work, and the workforce as well as the diverse meanings people attach to their work. We consider the kinds of problems associated with work, discuss how they affect the quality of life, and note the factors that contribute to and help to perpetuate those problems. Finally, we outline a few approaches to resolving the problems.

work ethic
the notion that your sense of worth and the satisfaction of your needs are intricately related to the kind of work you do

The Economy, Work, and the Workforce in America

All things change. The American economy, the nature of work, and the nature of the workforce are vastly different today from what they were at various times in the past.

The Changing Economy

Initially, the United States was *an agrarian society,* that is, a society in which agriculture is the dominant form of work and people and animals are the major sources of energy. It has been estimated that as late as 1850, 65 percent of the energy used in American work was supplied by people and animals (Lenski 1966). After the middle of the 19th century, the nation industrialized rapidly. In simple terms, *industrialization is economic development through a transformation of the sources and quantities of energy employed.*

American industrialization, like that of most nations, occurred in the context of **capitalism,** an economic system in which there is private, rather than state, ownership

capitalism
an economic system in which there is private, rather than state, ownership of wealth and control of the production and distribution of goods; people are motivated by profit and compete with each other for maximum shares of profit

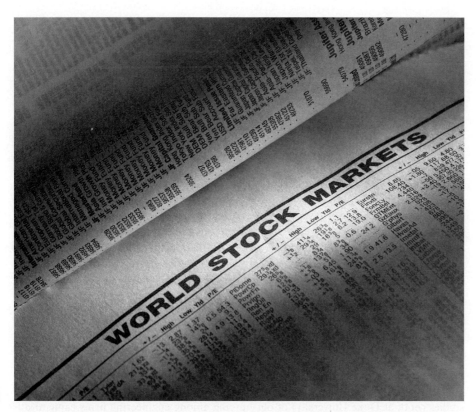

The global economy now drives the U.S. economy.

©Brand X Pictures

of wealth and control of the production and distribution of goods. In a capitalist system, people are motivated by profit and they compete with each other to maximize their share of the profits. The premise is that the combination of private ownership and the pursuit of profit benefits everyone, because it motivates capitalists to be efficient and to provide the best goods and services at the lowest possible prices.

In a pure capitalist system, government involvement in the economy is minimal. In the United States, the government role in the economy has grown over the past century. In addition, our economy is affected by various other factors such as the global economy, weather, and wars. *The global economy has become particularly important.* In simplest terms, globalization of the economy means a significant increase in the amount of international trade and investment (Weisbrot 2000). In the United States, for example, trade provides an increasingly large percentage of the gross domestic product, so much so that some observers claim global markets are now necessary to keep the U.S. economy healthy (Griswold 2010). Supermarkets have become more important than superpowers for key economic decisions. When governments try to impose restrictions to protect or enhance the national economy, enterprises simply shift the work to another setting. For instance, when Japan raised postage rates, direct mailers sent their mailings to Hong Kong, which mailed them back to Japan at considerably less cost to the mailers; and when the United States put limits on the number of work permits given to foreign computer programmers, some companies changed the work location to other nations.

Technology has driven down the cost of international communication and travel. Thus, there has been a growth in trade, the flow of capital across national borders, foreign investment, shared research and development, and movement of personnel (including students attending universities in foreign countries). Business enterprises maximize their profits by locating the best markets and the least expensive places for operations. As a result, a particular product may have components made in various parts of the world.

In other words, the economy is now truly global. The amount of international trade in goods and services is enormous. In one month in 2016, for example, the United States exports totaled $183.5 billion, while the imports totaled $225.6 billion (U.S. Bureau of Economic Analysis 2016). Many large U.S. firms, including Exxon, Colgate-Palmolive, and Coca-Cola, obtain the majority of their income from overseas markets. Economists differ on the effects of trade and on whether we should strive for "free" trade agreements or a system of restrictions on what and how much can be imported and exported. The public, on the other hand, looks at trade as good for the economy as a whole, but only one in five believe that trade creates jobs for Americans (Stokes 2015).

The consequences of globalization, then, are controversial. On the one hand, researchers have identified positive consequences such as a reduction in occupational sex segregation and gender inequality (L. B. Meyer 2003). On the other hand, many observers argue that globalization has led to a growing gap between the world's rich and poor (Amin 2004). Whatever the consequences for the world as a whole, globalization and new technologies combine to present the U.S. economy and the American worker with new challenges. *Globalization means that businesses shift their operations to other nations where the employees work for lower pay than Americans and other business expenses are less, thus lowering the costs of products and services.* The results of this process, called *outsourcing,* are debatable. It is argued that, on the one hand, outsourcing helps American companies stay competitive in the global market, while, on the other hand, it also increases unemployment in the United States (Amadeo 2016b). Research has not resolved the issue. For example, two studies (both at Duke University) of outsourcing among engineering firms came to different conclusions (Engardio 2006). One study reported that the companies resort to outsourcing because they need more talent and they shift some of their more complex work to countries such as India and China because they can decrease the time it takes to get their products to market. The other study, however, argued that the outsourcing reflects no shortage of talent in the United States; rather, the only motivation is to reduce costs.

In any case, it is undeniable that one outcome of outsourcing is that well-paid, lower-skilled jobs in the United States are increasingly difficult to find. Indeed, the prospects for lower-skilled workers are more bleak than they were in the early 1990s (Bartik and Houseman 2008). Other kinds of work have also been affected, such as that in science, engineering, and technology. Many of the jobs in these areas have moved to other countries (Hira 2009). One CEO of a large high-tech company even stated that his company could succeed without ever hiring another American.

Globalization has also contributed to what Kalleberg (2009:2) calls "precarious work," work that is "uncertain, unpredictable, and risky from the point of view of the worker." The precarious nature of work is dramatized by the fact that literally tens of millions of Americans lost their jobs involuntarily in the two decades between the early 1980s and the early 2000s.

In the competitive context of the global economy, then, *a number of changes have occurred that are detrimental to the well-being of many American workers* (Caskey 1994; Harrison 1994; U.S. Department of Labor 2000):

downsizing
reduction of the labor force in a company or corporation

- Businesses and corporations have used both outsourcing and **downsizing** (reduction of the labor force) to reduce costs and maximize profits.
- An increasing number of jobs are temporary or part-time, with no fringe benefits such as health insurance.

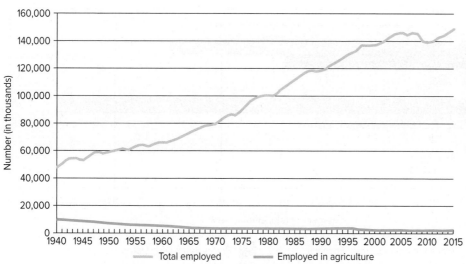

FIGURE 10.1
Civilian Employment,
1940–2015.

Source: "Employment status
of the civilian noninstitutional
population," Bureau of Labor
Statistics website.

- Unions continue to decline in membership and power.
- Corporate tax obligations have been reduced, cutting back on revenues necessary to support social programs.
- When corrected for inflation, the income of many American families has declined.

As a result of such changes, many Americans are not only unable to better their lot in comparison to their parents, but are finding themselves worse off than their parents.

In sum, the nature of the changes in the economy means that many American families are worse off financially in the early 2000s than they were in the 1970s. For many, the American dream seems more remote than ever.

The Changing Workforce

The **labor force** (defined as all civilians who are employed or unemployed but able and wanting to work) has increased enormously since the founding of the nation. The number of those actually employed has also risen fairly steadily (Figure 10.1). It was the rapid increase since the beginning of the 19th century that made the nation's swift industrial growth possible. The workforce was low in 1800 because all but a small proportion of Americans lived on farms, and the family farmer along with his wife and children is not counted—only those who work for pay outside the home are included in the workforce. Since 1940 the labor force has been growing faster than the population. This growth has been fueled by population growth, by the rapid entry of women into the labor force, and by the fact that more older workers are staying in the labor force beyond the age of 65 (Desilver 2016).

The *occupational structure* also has changed with an increasing **division of labor,** or *specialization*. There are now more than 30,000 different occupations. This change is not due to growth in all job categories, however. If you look at the categories of occupations used by the Census Bureau, you will find that since the beginning of the 20th century the proportion of workers in professional, technical, managerial, clerical, and service jobs has increased greatly. The proportion of workers classified as farm workers, on the other hand, has declined dramatically. In 1900, 17.7 percent of all employees worked on farms (U.S. Census Bureau 1975:144). As Figure 10.1 shows, the number of agricultural employees continues to decline, comprising less than 2 percent of all employees in 2015.

labor force
all civilians who are employed or unemployed but able and desiring to work

division of labor
the separation of work into specialized tasks

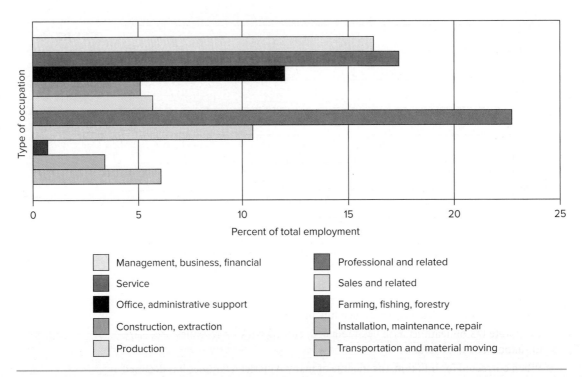

FIGURE 10.2   Distribution of Occupations.

Source: Bureau of Labor Statistics website.

Jobs requiring more skill and training have tended to increase at a faster rate than others. In other words, there has been a general upgrading of the occupational structure. With increased industrialization and technological development, the need for farmers and unskilled workers has diminished and the need for skilled workers and clerical and other white-collar workers has increased. The United States has moved into a service and, some would argue, an informational society, in which growing numbers of workers are needed outside the manufacturing areas (Figure 10.2). It is increasingly likely that workers will engage in tasks involving *substantive complexity* such as verbal and math skills and abstract thinking rather than motor skills such as lifting, stooping, coordination, or finger dexterity. Unfortunately, many new jobs, particularly those in the service area, do not pay well. According to the Bureau of Labor Statistics, in 2016 7.23 million workers supplemented their income by working two or more jobs. Thus, many American workers either work longer hours or face a lower standard of living.

The Changing Composition of the Labor Force

Data from the Bureau of Labor Statistics website show how the demographics of the labor force have changed over time. First, as the general skill level increases, *the educational level of the workforce also increases.* In 1970, 38.7 percent of the labor force had less than four years of high school, whereas 12.0 percent had four or more years of college. By 2014, only 8 percent of whites and African Americans, 6 percent of Asian Americans, and 28 percent of Hispanics had less than four years of high school. And the proportions of those with four of more years of college increased to 60 percent of

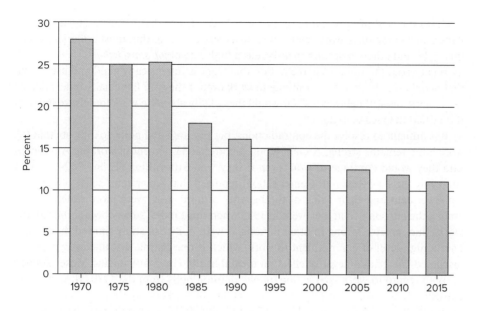

FIGURE 10.3
Membership in Labor Unions as a Proportion of the Labor Force, 1970–2015.
Source: Bureau of Labor Statistics website.

Asian Americans, 38 percent of whites, 27 percent of African Americans, and 19 percent of Hispanics.

Another substantial change in the labor force involves the *proportion of workers who are female.* From 1950 to 2014, the participation rate of men fell from 82.4 percent to 69.2 percent, whereas that of women rose from 32.0 percent to 57.0 percent.

A third change is the increasing number of undocumented immigrants in the workforce. The exact number is not known. But the Bureau of Labor Statistics reports that in 2015 there were 26.3 million "foreign-born" workers in the labor force, composing 16.7 percent of all workers. The foreign-born population includes legally admitted immigrants, refugees, temporary residents such as students and temporary workers, and undocumented immigrants. The majority of the undocumented come in from Mexico and other Latin American nations. They are generally concentrated in the lower-paying occupations, such as farming, cleaning, construction, and food preparation.

Finally, the labor force also became more *unionized* until the 1960s. Since then, however, the proportion of workers who are union members has declined (Figure 10.3). By 2015, only 11.1 percent of wage and salary workers were union members. The type of workers who are unionized has changed as well (Bureau of Labor Statistics 2012). Unions no longer involve mainly blue-collar workers. Federal, state, and local government workers comprise a substantial proportion of all union workers: 4 out of 10 government workers are in unions, compared to about 1 out of 12 private-sector employees. Among occupational groups, unionization is highest among government workers in protective services such as the police and firefighters. In private industry, the highest union membership rates are found in public utilities, transportation, and construction.

The Changing Meaning of Work

When we try to determine the *meaning of work* for Americans, we find ourselves in a morass of contradictions. Some people argue that work is one of the most important activities in an individual's life. They maintain that those who do not have a satisfying job do not have a fully satisfying life. Others insist that work is purely instrumental, a way to attain the goal of *maximum consumption.* There is also disagreement about whether Americans enjoy their work, with some observers claiming that most Americans hate their jobs and others asserting that there is a high rate of *job satisfaction.*

What about the *work ethic,* the notion that work is intrinsically good and useful and that people should therefore continue to work even if they are financially independent? Do Americans still believe this? Or would they gladly abandon work for leisure pursuits if they had the means to do so?

It is difficult to resolve the contradictions, but research and polls do indicate that the work ethic remains strong. A Gallup poll found that 55 percent of working Americans said they would continue to work even if they won $10 million (Lyons 2004). And a survey by the Pew Research Center (2003) reported that Americans' sense of personal empowerment and their value of the benefits of hard work were more widely spread among the citizenry than they were in 1987 when this kind of survey began. Indeed, the work ethic remains strong in other nations as well. A British study showed that people have a high level of commitment to work, which is one reason that unemployment (as discussed later) has a negative effect on mental health (Ingmar-Paul and Moser 2006).

With regard to work satisfaction, public opinion polls from the 1970s through 2011 consistently reported that more than 80 percent of workers say they are "satisfied" or "very satisfied" with their jobs. Thus, a 2011 Gallup poll (which only gave the choices as satisfied or dissatisfied) put the proportion of satisfied workers at 87.5 percent (Mendes 2011). Unfortunately, as of this writing Gallup has not conducted a more recent poll of job satisfaction among American workers. A marketing research group, however, published a survey in 2015 that found a 75 percent satisfaction rate with "current employment" among workers (Koenig 2015). At this point, we can't be sure if worker satisfaction is declining or the results indicate differences in the research design. In any case, it appears that a majority of American workers are satisfied with their jobs.

At the same time, an increasing number of Americans no longer accept the notion that their self-worth is tied in with their work or that they have a moral duty to work. On the contrary, Americans increasingly expect their work to have *meaning,* to be emotionally and intellectually *stimulating,* and to offer an opportunity to feel *good about themselves and the products of their labor.* Income is no longer the most important facet of an individual's work.

In evaluating job quality, an individual is likely to consider not just income, but such nonincome factors as job duties and working conditions, job satisfaction, period of work, job status, and job security (Moen and Yu 2000). *Job duties and working conditions* refers to such matters as whether the job is hazardous, repetitive, stressful, closely supervised, and isolated (versus working with a team). *Job satisfaction* increases when the worker engages in problem solving, has the opportunity to be creative, gains recognition, can fully utilize skills and learn new skills, and has the chance for advancement.

Period of work is the extent to which the job involves weekend or shift work, overtime, or flexible work hours. *Job status* includes both social status (being recognized by outsiders as having a more prestigious or less prestigious job) and status within the organization. *Job security* means that workers can be confident of retaining their jobs as long as their performance is satisfactory. Where, for whatever reason, such security is lacking, there will be an increase in distress and burnout among workers (Jiang and Probst 2016).

Americans, then, are not rejecting work. They are rejecting meaningless work and low-quality jobs. To say, as we have heard from some students and employers, that Americans today "just don't want to work anymore" is the *fallacy of personal attack.* In a national survey, only 5.1 percent of those not working said it was because they were "not interested in working" (Weismantle 2001). The great majority wants work, but work that is important and that fosters a sense of achievement.

fallacy

Work as a Social Problem

Because most Americans want to work and expect their work to provide some degree of personal fulfillment, there are three basic problems associated with work in America today. First, there is the problem of *unemployment and* **underemployment.** People are underemployed if they work full time for poverty wages, work part time when they desire full-time work, or work at jobs that are temporary or below their skill levels. Second, there is the problem of *dissatisfaction and alienation.* Finally, there is the problem of various kinds of *work hazards.*

underemployment
working full time for poverty wages, working part time when full-time work is desired, or working at a job below the worker's skill level

Unemployment and Underemployment

Underemployment is perhaps as serious as unemployment for people who look to work for meaningful activity. Underemployment results in frustration, financial worry, and lowered job satisfaction (Vaisey 2006). Moreover, there is a stigma attached to being underemployed. For example, recent research found that underemployed college graduates who tried to get better jobs had a 30 percent lower callback rate than those who were adequately employed (Nunley et al. 2016). It is difficult to measure how many Americans are underemployed, but two researchers estimated the proportion to be 13.1 percent (Jensen and Slack 2003). The proportion varies by various demographic factors, with the highest rates occurring among the 18- to 24-year-old workers (29.1 percent) and workers with less than a high school education (29.0 percent). Rates are also higher for women than for men and for racial and ethnic minorities than for non-Hispanic whites.

A substantial number of the underemployed are working part time, which means that they have no benefits (including health insurance). Lacking the kind of social benefits available in countries such as Sweden, such workers *cannot achieve their desired quality of life without working full time* (Reynolds 2004). Another large group of the underemployed are those in temporary jobs. And professionals—lawyers, accountants, engineers, and so on—make up an increasing proportion of the temporary market (Thottam 2004). Businesspeople claim that temporary work serves the interests of those people who want something other than a permanent work situation. However, *temporary workers are underemployed because most of them are looking for full-time permanent employment* and most dislike the lack of stability and the degradation of being a temporary worker. However, it isn't the workers but the owners who are most likely to benefit from temporary employees. The temps are cheaper, easier to deal with, and easier to get rid of than are full-time employees (Hatton 2011).

With regard to those out of work, reliable data exist on the **unemployment rate.** The rate fluctuates considerably (Table 10.1). By 2015, the overall rate was 4.8 percent, or 7.9 million workers. The statistic does not mean, however, that only 7.9 million Americans were affected by unemployment in that year. Many people are unemployed for only a portion of the year. The length of unemployment may rise during times of economic recession. Thus, between 2007 and 2010, the length of time the unemployed spent looking for work before finding a job increased from 5.2 weeks to 10.4 weeks (Ilg and Theodossiou 2012).

unemployment rate
the proportion of the labor force that is not working but is available for work and has made specific efforts to find work

In addition, a good many Americans who want to work are not counted as part of the labor force or the unemployment rate because they are not actively looking for work. In 2011, 6.1 million Americans wanted to work but were not considered unemployed or part of the labor force for various reasons (Theodossiou 2012). They were discouraged by such things as lack of education or training or the inability to find a job, or because other factors such as family responsibilities or health problems prevented them. When

TABLE 10.1
Unemployment Rates,
1950–2015

Year	Total	White	Black	Hispanic	Asian
1950	5.3	4.9	9.0		
1955	4.4	3.9	8.7		
1960	5.5	4.9	10.2		
1965	4.5	4.1	8.1		
1970	4.9	4.5	8.2		
1975	8.5	7.8	14.8		
1980	7.1	6.3	14.3	10.1	
1985	7.2	6.2	15.1	10.5	
1990	5.5	4.7	11.3	8.0	4.2
1995	5.6	4.9	10.4	9.3	5.0
2000	4.0	2.6	5.4	4.4	2.7
2005	5.1	4.4	10.0	6.0	4.0
2010	9.5	8.7	16.0	12.5	7.5
2015	4.8	4.2	8.3	5.6	3.8

SOURCE: Bureau of Labor Statistics website.

you take into account those who want to work but are not counted in the unemployment rate as well as those who are unemployed for only a part of the year, the number of people affected by unemployment becomes far higher than the official figures.

As Table 10.1 shows, *unemployment does not strike all groups the same.* Typically, the rates are higher for minorities than for whites and are higher for younger than for older workers. In some years, the unemployment rate for workers 16 to 19 years of age is double, triple, or more the rate for the workforce as a whole. In 2015, the overall unemployment rate was 4.8 percent, but the rate for workers 16 to 19 years of age was 16.1 percent.

Unemployment also varies by occupational category, with rates tending to be higher among blue-collar and service workers. The lowest rates are likely to be found in the higher-status, high-income occupations of the managerial and professional category.

Dissatisfaction and Alienation

In Chapter 3, we defined *alienation* as a sense of estrangement that is usually measured by an individual's feelings of powerlessness, normlessness, isolation, and meaninglessness. This definition is a subjective approach to alienation. Alienation is an objective phenomenon, according to Karl Marx. In a capitalist society the worker is *estranged from his or her own labor* (because work is something that is coerced and external to the worker rather than a fulfillment of the worker's needs), from other people, and from his or her own humanity. The worker sinks to the level of a commodity and becomes the most wretched of commodities. Because capitalism wrenches the means of production from the control of those intimately involved in production, workers are necessarily alienated whether or not they feel any sense of alienation.

The amount of alienation in the workplace, therefore, depends on whether you take a Marxist or a social psychological approach to the question. For Marxists, all workers in a capitalist society are alienated by definition. For social psychologists, workers are alienated to the extent that they perceive themselves as powerless and isolated. Social psychological studies indicate that some American workers, but by no means the majority, are alienated. In fact, some researchers have found that many workers say they would rather continue their jobs than get the same wages for not working.

Nevertheless, indications are that dissatisfaction is still a problem. First, no matter which polls are used to measure job dissatisfaction, the results translate into tens of millions of dissatisfied American workers. Second, there is evidence of various troublesome issues. For example, workers who have low control over their work situation may experience dissatisfaction and anger (Fitzgerald, Haythornthwaite, Suchday, and Ewart 2003). And, as noted earlier, workers in a situation of insecurity (e.g., where some of the workforce is being laid off or workers are being asked to take unpaid leave) may experience dissatisfaction and anxiety (Berkshire et al. 2011).

Work Hazards and Stress

According to the Office of Safety and Health Administration (OSHA), there were 2.9 million cases of nonfatal work-related injuries and illnesses in 2015. The following industries had the highest number of incidents per 100 full-time workers: aquaculture (13.8), nursing and residential care facilities (12.0), police protection (11.3), household furniture manufacturing (10.8), manufactured home manufacturing (10.2), and fire protection (10.2). The number of injuries and illnesses has declined in recent years. But many of the injuries still involve temporary or permanent disability or even death—in 2015, there were 4,836 fatal work injuries.

Unemployment is higher for minorities and younger workers.

©Jack Star/PhotoLink/Getty Images

Not included in the government report are the risks posed to adolescents who work. A national survey of working adolescents revealed that over a third reported a violation of guidelines for hazardous occupations (such as working at a job or using equipment that is prohibited for them), 11 percent reported working past the latest hour allowed on a school night, and 15 percent reported working off the clock (Rauscher, Runyan, Schulman, and Bowling 2008).

We use the term "work hazards" broadly to include *work-induced stress* as well as *work-related injuries and illnesses.* For example, a spot welder on an auto assembly line told about some of the daily hazards to which he is exposed.

> I pulled a muscle in my neck, straining. This gun, when you grab this thing from the ceiling, cable, weight, I mean you're pulling everything. . . . This whole edge here is sharp. I go through a shirt every two weeks, it just goes right through. My overalls catch on fire. I've had gloves catch on fire. (Indicates arms.) See them little holes? That's what sparks do. I've got burns across here from last night. (Terkel 1972:224)

Psychological as well as physical hazards occur in the workplace. Some occupations are particularly likely to expose workers to stress. For instance, many taxi drivers work

UNEMPLOYMENT RATES IN INDUSTRIAL NATIONS

Unemployment is a huge and ongoing problem in many underdeveloped nations. For one thing, economic growth lags behind population growth, so that even a robust economy cannot absorb all the new workers coming into the labor force each year. In the developed nations, unemployment tends to be smaller but is still an enduring problem. The unemployment rate varies considerably, however, depending on how the economy is structured. Note in Table 10.2 that some nations have lower rates than the United States, and others have higher rates.

Although the rates are strikingly low in some cases, every nation confronts the problem in which a segment of its population wants but is unable to obtain employment—and in every nation, unemployed people face some of the same problems of stress and self-worth as do Americans. One major difference is that in countries such as Sweden and Japan, more benefits are available for the unemployed, so that unemployment is not as likely to be associated with abject poverty.

Country	2000	2005	2010	2015
United States	4.0	5.1	9.6	5.3
Canada	6.8	6.8	8.0	6.9
Australia	6.3	5.0	5.2	6.3
Japan	4.7	4.4	5.1	3.3
France	n.a.	8.9	9.3	10.6
Germany	7.8	11.1	7.1	4.6
Italy	10.2	7.7	8.4	12.1
Netherlands	3.0	4.7	4.5	6.1
Sweden	4.7	7.1	8.4	7.4
United Kingdom	5.4	4.9	7.9	5.5

TABLE 10.2

Unemployment Rates, by Country, 2000–2015

SOURCE: International Labor Organization website.

under the continual threat of robbery. Salespeople often endure harassment from customers. Many high-tech workers feel ongoing pressure to produce and to make their work the consuming focus of their lives. Psychiatrists and psychotherapists often find their work to be emotionally draining. In other jobs, stress is associated with such conditions as lack of communication and delegation of authority by management, fast-paced work in poor environmental conditions, frequent overtime, conflict between workers, recent reduction of employee benefits, and downsizing (Koretz 1997; Grunberg, Anderson-Connolly, and Greenberg 2000).

Work and the Quality of Life

Many people thoroughly enjoy their work. They find it meaningful and satisfying, thus providing them with a higher quality of life. They are more likely to enjoy their work when they perceive themselves to be included in the information network and the decision-making processes of their workplace (Barak and Levin 2002).

There are also many people for whom the effect of working is a kind of *emotional and spiritual malaise.* They do not despise their work, but neither are they excited by it. They may simply be apathetic or resigned. Finally, there are some who find their work to be disturbing or frustrating or even destructive to their well-being. The point is, then, that work can have very positive or very negative consequences for the worker (Campione 2008). And one of the areas that work effects is the mental and physical health of the worker.

Work, Unemployment, and Health

Ironically, both working and not working can adversely affect your health. What are the risks?

Work and Health. Work can have a *negative impact on both the emotional and the physical well-being of workers* (Dalgard et al. 2009; Hauke, Flintrop, Brun, and Rugulies 2011; Nixon et al. 2011). Feelings of alienation or high levels of job dissatisfaction or job stress may lead to heavy drinking in an effort to cope (Greenberg and Grunberg 1995; Martin and Roman 1996) or to burnout (Fragoso et al. 2016). People whose work provides relatively low rewards (including low job security or advancement possibilities) for high levels of effort may increase their risk of cardiovascular disease three- to fourfold (Siegrist 1995). Regardless of the level of effort, job insecurity puts workers under continual stress and can produce various kinds of health problems (Heaney, Israel, and House 1994; Bernhard-Oettel, Sverke, and De Witte 2006). In some high-stress occupations, such as physicians and law enforcement, suicide rates are high (Kulbarsh 2016; American Website for Suicide Prevention website). A study of death rates across various occupations found that high-risk occupations (those associated with higher death rates at earlier ages) include taxi drivers, cooks, longshoremen, and transportation operatives (Johnson, Sorlie, and Backlund 1999). Finally, exposure to various kinds of hazardous conditions can impair both physical and mental health. A variety of cognitive and physical disabilities have been linked with such work conditions as repetitive loading, and exposure to heat, pesticides, and other toxic chemicals or metals (Ross et al. 2016).

Underemployment also poses health risks. People who are underemployed, in the sense of being overeducated and overqualified for their jobs, are likely to lack job satisfaction and to leave their jobs sooner than other workers (Tsang, Rumberger, and Levin 1991). Further, they are more likely than adequately employed workers are to report lower levels of health and well-being and exhibit symptoms of depression (Dooley, Ham-Rowbottom, and Prause 2001; Friedland and Price 2003).

The risks to health are related both to job satisfaction and to working conditions. Those who are less satisfied are more likely to exhibit various kinds of physical and mental health problems (see, e.g., Bovier, Arigoni, Schneider, and Gallacchi 2009). And a study by the National Safe Workplace Institute concluded that more than 71,000 Americans died in one year from diseases such as cancer and from cardiovascular and neurological problems induced by work conditions (Scott 1990a). The study called job-related illnesses "America's invisible killer." A national study of workers reported that, although Americans generally like their jobs, the majority of them admit to one or more problems that reflect stress (Bond, Galinsky, and Swanberg 1998). Finally, another national study found that a third of all workers feel chronically overworked (Galinsky et al. 2005). The study also reported that the overworked have higher levels of stress, a higher proportion of depression, and more reports of poor health than do other workers.

There is, in sum, a strong relationship between stressful working conditions and physical and emotional illness. And the stress occurs in all kinds of work. A Protestant minister described his own health problems caused by stress at work. The stresses he experienced could occur in virtually any kind of job, and his story shows that no one is immune.

> I arrived at my new church with an intense anticipation of a rewarding and fruitful ministry. I brought the enthusiasm and recklessness of youth to a job that demanded the caution and wisdom of age. For about a year, the enthusiasm was sufficient. It carried me through some discouragements and minimized any overt criticism. Then I made the mistake of criticizing an older member of the church. The criticism was neither harsh nor malicious, but the member was quite sensitive and quite influential. I also plunged ahead and pushed programs and began projects without first consulting the officers. At the beginning of my second year, criticism erupted and quickly mushroomed.
>
> For about the next five years, I had problems with various people in the church. And I had a series of things go wrong with myself, both emotionally and physically. At one point, it seemed that everything was coming to a head and there would be a final all-out struggle to see whose way would prevail—mine or those that felt I was taking the church down the wrong road. Just before this culminating battle, I lost about 20 pounds from my slender physique. One week I broke out in a rash. I had severe sinus problems. Worst of all, I nearly developed a phobia about being in an enclosed area with a lot of people. I found it torturous to go to a crowded restaurant. One day I had to leave a church conference because my heart was pounding and I felt intense panic. Sometimes I even felt serious anxiety when I led the worship service.
>
> As it turned out, the "final" battle was not really the final one after all. It had only served to trigger the various physical and mental ailments that I endured for the next few years. Ultimately, we were able to work out the differences we had. I think I gained some in wisdom and lost some of my recklessness. The church began to stabilize and then grow, and some of those with whom I had fought became my best friends. After about eight years or so, I finally lost my fear of crowded places. In a way, I suppose you could say it all had a happy ending. But I wouldn't go through that again for anything. It was the only time of my life when the thought of suicide entered my mind as an appealing option.

Unemployment and Health.   The stress of being forcibly unemployed can be as serious as the stress of working in undesirable conditions or in an unfulfilling job. For most people, *unemployment* is a traumatic experience. Millions of Americans are affected by unemployment every year. Two researchers looked at work in the early 2000s and called it the era of the "disposable worker" (Dixon and Van Horn 2003). They pointed out that nearly a fifth of American workers lost their jobs and that the great majority of these workers had no advance notice, no severance pay, and no career counseling from their employers. Some workers who lose their jobs are unemployed for only a portion of the year. Some find employment, but the work is not meaningful to them. Some have dropped out of the labor force, discouraged by their inability to find employment in their line of work. Some are the victims of downsizing that eliminated their jobs (Uchitelle and Kleinfield 1996).

Whatever the reason for being out of work, *unemployment is detrimental to both physical and emotional well-being* (Reine, Novo, and Hammarstrom 2004; Burgard, Brand, and House 2007). Unemployment can result in high levels of stress and lowered life satisfaction. It can lead to such problems as depression, lowered self-esteem, anger and resentment, shame and embarrassment, social isolation, serious mental illness, physical health problems, alcohol abuse, criminal behavior, and suicide (Mossakowski 2009; Morin and Kochhar 2010; Pellegrini and Rodriguez-Monguio 2013). A study of women in Texas who gave birth reported that, compared to those who were working, the unemployed gave birth to children with lower birth weights and they experienced higher

Stress Indicator	Percent Increase
Suicide	4.1
State mental hospital admissions	3.4
State prison admissions	4.0
Cirrhosis of the liver mortality	1.9
Cardiovascular-renal disease mortality	1.9

TABLE 10.3
Impact of a Sustained 1 Percent Rise in Unemployment

SOURCE: Brenner 1976.

rates of infant mortality (Scharber 2014). The negative consequences are likely to be more severe for workers who experience a second job loss (or who lose three or more jobs) than for those who experience their first loss (Chen, Marks, and Bersani 1994). And, finally, the trauma of being unemployed is likely to result in long-term negative consequences for well-being (Young 2012).

Brenner (1978) calculated the impact for a sustained 1 percent rise in unemployment in the United States from about 1940 to the early 1970s. The corresponding increases in various physical and emotional ills are shown in Table 10.3. Similarly, other researchers (Luo et al. 2011) examined suicide rates from 1928 to 2007 and found that the rates generally rose during economic recessions and fell during times of economic expansion.

The detrimental physical and emotional consequences of unemployment also are seen in other nations. In Canada and England, researchers found an association between unemployment and rates of illness (including cardiovascular disease), mortality, and suicide (Jin, Shah, and Svoboda 1995; Bartley, Sacker, and Clarke 2004). A Swedish study reported higher tobacco and drug use, increased crime rates, and higher mortality rates (especially by suicide and accidents) among unemployed youth (Hammarstrom 1994). In Australia, researchers found youth unemployment to be associated with such psychological symptoms as depression and loss of confidence, and with suicide (Morrell, Taylor, and Kerr 1998). A comparison of unemployed with employed people in Spain reported that the unemployed had higher rates of respiratory illness (Kogevinas et al. 1998).

Interpersonal Relationships

A number of studies support the notion that both work-related stress and unemployment *can adversely affect interpersonal relationships.* Work in stressful conditions can lead to marital tension and conflict at home (Story and Repetti 2006; Ferguson 2011). The stress can be rooted in various factors, including the general conditions under which the work is performed and the kind of relationships the worker has with coworkers. A particularly stressful condition is shift work, which may *create both personal stress and interpersonal problems* (Grosswald 2003; Presser 2004). Researchers have found that shift work tends to increase conflict in the family, depress marital happiness and interaction, and increase various problems such as conflict over sexual and child-rearing matters and a lower quantity and quality of parent–child interaction (Demerouti, Geurts, Bakker, and Euwema 2004; Han, Miller, and Waldfogel 2010).

Underemployment is also stressful and is associated with varying degrees of both physical and emotional health (Cassidy and Wright 2008). Moreover, the strains and frustrations of stressful work conditions or of underemployment often carry over into family life, increasing tension and conflict and decreasing satisfaction.

Unemployment tends to place even more strain on an individual's relationships, including relationships within the family. During the Great Depression, when the unemployment rate went as high as one-fourth of the labor force, many workers blamed themselves for their unemployment, became disillusioned with themselves, and began to have trouble within their homes (Komarovsky 1940). Even in less serious economic recessions, workers are embarrassed by being unemployed, may begin to withdraw from social contacts, and may direct some of their hostility toward members of their families. It is, of course, not merely the embarrassment and stress of being unemployed but also the strain of trying to meet the expenses of food, clothing, housing, and health care that contributes to the conflict between spouses and between parents and children.

Not all the problems are due to unemployment or job dissatisfaction. Some situations are simply a *conflict between work and family responsibilities* (Voydanoff 2004; Forma 2009). For men, the conflict generally focuses on excessive work time—they are spending too much of their time and energy on their work. For women, the conflict is more likely to be one of scheduling problems or fatigue and irritability. In any case, the outcome is a certain amount of conflict between family members.

Contributing Factors

The factors that contribute to unemployment are generally different from the factors involved in work dissatisfaction, alienation, and work hazards. Although we focus on the latter factors, we also examine the political economy of unemployment.

Social Structural Factors

The Capitalist Economy.   We noted earlier that people in a capitalist economy are motivated by profit. *In business and corporations, profit tends to be the "bottom line."* That is, the goal is profit, and managers do whatever is necessary to maximize profits. This bottom-line approach has led owners, executives, and managers to act in ways that have adverse consequences for large numbers of people. One type of action is longstanding: the subservience of workers' needs to organizational needs. Three other actions changed in nature or increased greatly after 1980: union busting, downsizing, and the use of temporary workers.

The *subservience of workers' needs to organizational needs* is illustrated by the other three actions. Workers need well-paying and meaningful jobs, but union busting, downsizing, and the use of temporary workers are ways to meet the organization's need for profits at the expense of the workers' needs. In addition, workers may be abused and exploited by tyrannical managers and supervisors who focus on efficiency and productivity rather than the workers' needs for self-esteem, encouragement, and fulfillment (Ashforth 1994).

Union busting has been going on since the unions were first formed, but a change occurred in the 1980s (Rosenblum 1995). In 1981, the Reagan administration fired and permanently replaced more than 1,200 striking air-traffic controllers. Thereafter, an increasing number of companies dealt with strikes by hiring permanent replacements rather than by negotiating with the union.

Downsizing and outsourcing also reflect the drive to maximize profits. Downsizing, however, has taken on a different character—because it increases profits, it now occurs independently of whether a company is doing well or poorly and of whether the economy is booming or in recession (Simone and Kleiner 2004). Ironically, executives are rewarded for downsizing, because to the extent that profits increase as a result of the lower costs of a smaller workforce, executive bonuses go up. Similarly, outsourcing has economic benefits not only to the company but to the economy as a whole (Smith 2006). There is, therefore, little incentive on the part of either business or government to regulate the practice.

Finally, *there is increasing use of temporary and part-time workers.* Temporary employment grew rapidly during the 1980s and 1990s. By the turn of the century temporary help accounted for about 2.5 percent of all nonfarm payroll employment (Bureau of Labor Statistics website). Interviews with managers of temporary employment firms show that the higher demand for temporaries does not reflect workers' preference but rather employers' desire for flexibility and lower costs (Parker 1994). Some temporary workers are former employees who return as "rentals" to the company for which they formerly worked (Uchitelle 1996). Not surprisingly, they often struggle with resentment over now doing the same work at lower pay and with few or no fringe benefits.

A June 2016 report from the Bureau of Labor Statistics (2016c) put the number of part-time workers at 26.3 million, 16.6 percent of the labor force. The majority preferred part-time work (because of such things as child care or other family responsibilities, being in school or training, and health). But a substantial minority were involuntary part-time workers, unable to find full-time work because of the economy.

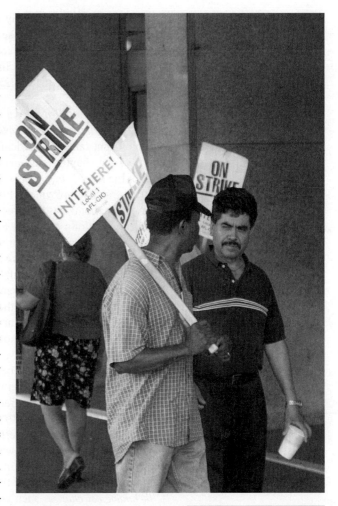

The power of labor unions has been weakened by antilabor government policies.
©McGraw-Hill Education./Andrew Resek, photographer

The Political Economy of Work. The traditional notion of man as the breadwinner assumed that a man's work would allow him to support his family. One of the problems of work today is that *a large number of jobs provide inadequate support and benefits to enable a family to live well.* A substantial number of Americans have to work longer hours or hold more than one job in order to provide sufficient income for their families. The Bureau of Labor Statistics noted that in August 2016, 7.2 million Americans held two or more jobs. A majority had a full-time and a part-time job, but 279,000 held two full-time jobs."

Many workers also struggle with wages that have not kept pace with inflation, or they have to contend with reduced employee benefits. Median household income in the United States. reached a peak in1999, then declined through 2014 until it rose again in 2015 (Proctor, Semega, and Kollar 2016). The 2015 median of $56,516, however, was still below the 1999 median of $57,909. One reason for the lagging household incomes is the increasing number of workers in low-wage work (Surowiecki 2013). As noted in Chapter 6, it is not possible to adequately support a family if the breadwinner works for the minimum wage. Unfortunately, it is extremely difficult to get legislation passed that raises the minimum. Ironically, when adjusted for inflation, the minimum wage was lower by 2012 than it was in the late 1960s (Shierholz 2013). And to add to the irony, worker productivity increased continuously over that period, such that if the minimum wage kept pace with increases in productivity, the minimum in 2012 would have been $18.67 per hour rather than $7.25.

The Political Economy of Unemployment.   It is important to distinguish between *structural and discriminatory unemployment.* Discriminatory unemployment involves high unemployment rates for particular groups, such as women and minorities, and is discussed in the chapters that deal with those groups. Structural unemployment is the result of the *functioning of the political-economic system itself.*

Structural unemployment takes various forms. Since the Great Depression, the American economy has been regulated basically in accord with the theories of the English economist John Maynard Keynes. In Keynes's view, governments can *control the swings of the economy,* greatly moderating the inflationary and deflationary trends, programs, and taxation. There is *an inverse relationship between unemployment and inflation.* When the rate of inflation is high, the government may take steps that will result in an increase in unemployment. Some unemployment is necessary, and some fluctuations are inevitable. Yet because of the moderating impact of government intervention, fluctuations need not be as severe as they were earlier in U.S. history.

The unemployment rates shown in Table 10.1 reflect in large part the government's efforts to regulate the economy. There will always be some unemployment in a capitalist economy. The amount can be controlled and perhaps lessened by government intervention, but unemployment cannot be eliminated.

In addition to the overall rate of unemployment, the functioning of the political-economic system contributes to the high rates of unemployment in particular areas or in particular occupations at certain times. *Government spending* can create many jobs and then eliminate those jobs when the priorities change. For example, massive federal funding of the space program in the 1960s created many jobs, some of which vanished when the priorities changed in the 1970s.

Technological changes such as automation or the introduction of computers into a business can displace workers and lessen the need for them in the future. Old industries in the United States are in serious trouble. Numerous workers in the auto and steel industries have lost their jobs or have been indefinitely laid off. The problem may worsen as humans are replaced by robots in basic industries. Pioneered by the Japanese, robots are effective mechanisms of production in such industries as automobile manufacturing.

The Organizational Context of Work: Unions.   The union movement has been instrumental in bringing about higher wages, fringe benefits, and safer conditions for workers (Doyle 2002). For example, in 2015, union members had median weekly earnings of $980, compared to $776 for those not members of a union (Bureau of Labor Statistics 2016d). A study of the 50 states found an inverse correlation between the proportion of the working poor and the level of unionization (i.e., that fewer the unions the more working poor). There is also an inverse relationship between unionization and income inequality, and it exists both in the United States and in countries round the world (Jacobs and Myers 2014; Kerrissey 2015). Finally, research by Flavin and Shufeldt (2016) found evidence that union members have higher levels of life satisfaction than those who are not members.

Given this research, then, it is not surprising that with the dramatic decline in union membership since the 1970s, inequality between wage earners has increased considerably

(Western and Rosenfeld 2011) and the subjective well-being of people has declined some-what (Flavin, Pacek, and Radcliff 2010). Various factors have brought about the decline of unions. Some losses occurred as a result of layoffs in manufacturing. In addition, unions have faced adverse rulings by conservative federal judges and the National Labor Relations Board (NLRB) regarding the right of unions to organize and strike. Meanwhile, management often has been supported by the legal system in efforts to keep unions out or to break existing unions. The globalization of the economy also has weakened the bargaining power of unions by allowing employers to opt for foreign locations for a part or all of the work. Finally, some unions have failed to engage in vigorous recruiting efforts.

The obstacles faced by unions are illustrated by a study of an Arizona miners' strike (Rosenblum 1995). The miners, who were largely Mexican Americans, went on strike against one of the world's largest copper producers. The strike was a reaction to the company's demand that cost-of-living adjustments and some other benefits be eliminated. The company replaced all the workers, and the replacements voted to decertify the union. The National Labor Relations Board ruled in favor of the company when the union protested.

Union membership has declined, then, not because workers have become disillusioned with their unions but because of various social factors and processes. If the unions continue to decline, there may be an increase in the kinds of work problems we have discussed.

Contemporary Work Roles and Environments. Job dissatisfaction and alienation reflect the *nature of work roles and work environments* in contemporary society. Workers suffer when they lack such benefits as positive relationships at the workplace, clear definitions of their work, physical comfort in the work environment, and just treatment (Turnipseed 1992; Gershon et al. 2009). They particularly suffer when they feel they have no control over their work lives and no security in their jobs, a situation that is exacerbated by a growing tendency to use part-time and temporary workers.

Work roles in American society result from a combination of factors, including *technological developments, efforts to maximize profits, and the bureaucratization of work.* The disposable worker is one consequence of the effort to maximize profits. At least three consequences of the technological developments bear upon the meaningfulness of work. First, technology brought with it *highly specialized tasks,* with the result that many workers focus on a narrow range of tasks and may have little or no sense of the overall project.

Second, and associated with the intense specialization, many jobs are stressful. A survey of American workers found that 5 percent reported being "extremely" stressed at work, 14 percent said they were stressed "quite a bit," and 33 percent regarded themselves as "somewhat" stressed (Yung 2004). The other 47 percent reported their stress level at work as "a little or not at all." Reasons for the stress include too much responsibility, too many demands, too much pressure, and jobs that involve *extremely repetitious, routine tasks.* Quite a few workers must *come to terms with the boredom of their work.* The tactics they use include such activities as daydreaming, playing, singing, and talking.

Barbara Garson (1975) described the *coping mechanisms* utilized by people who work in routine jobs ranging from typists, to keypunchers, to workers who stack Ping-Pong paddles all day, to tuna cleaners in a seafood plant. The deadly routine of many jobs is portrayed in the account of Cindy, a girl who worked for a time in the Ping-Pong factory.

> My job was stacking the Ping-Pong paddles into piles of fifty. Actually I didn't have to count all the way up to fifty. To make it a little easier they told me to stack them in circles of four with the first handle facing me. When there got to be thirteen handles on the second one from the front, then I'd know I had fifty. . . . As soon as I'd stack 'em, they'd unstack 'em. Maybe it wouldn't have been so bad if I could have seen all the piles I stacked at the end of

the day. But they were taking them down as fast as I was piling them up. That was the worst part of the job. (Garson 1975:1–2)

Such jobs are stressful. They may also be physically and emotionally harmful. Interviews with 52 women with *repetition strain injury,* the result of work in either a telecommunications organization or a chicken processing factory, found the women to report reduced capacity for housework, troubled family relationships, mental distress, and lowered self-esteem (Ewan, Lowy, and Reid 1991).

Third, technological developments are associated with *depersonalization* within the workplace. Workers tend to be *isolated* in certain kinds of jobs. For instance, isolation may occur when the work is computerized or automated. In such cases, the workers may have to pay closer attention to their work, have less interaction with people, and engage in fewer tasks that require teamwork.

Work roles also are affected by *bureaucratization of work.* Perhaps the majority of Americans work in bureaucratic organizations, which tend to be *authoritarian.* A defining characteristic of a bureaucracy is the hierarchy of authority. Workers in an authoritarian organization are likely to experience negative emotions and attitudes ranging from job dissatisfaction to alienation. People prefer to be *involved in decisions that affect them and their work.* Their satisfaction with their work, their motivation, and their effectiveness all can be enhanced by participation in the decision-making process (Schnake, Bushardt, and Spottswood 1984; Barak and Levin 2002).

Participation gives the worker some control over his or her work. The more control that workers have, the more likely they are to be satisfied and the more likely the work is to enhance their health, while less control means less satisfaction and more physical and emotional problems are likely (Spector 2002; Gelsema et al. 2006; Brand, Warren, Carayon, and Hoonakker 2007).

Unfortunately, workers are unlikely to have the opportunity for participation and a sense of control in many bureaucratic organizations. Lacking that opportunity, they are likely to have lower levels of job satisfaction, lower morale, and lower levels of motivation.

In addition to the frustrations of working in an authoritarian organization, workers must deal with a certain amount of *built-in conflict* that bureaucracies tend to generate. In theory, such conflict is unnecessary because the chain of command is clear: All workers are experts in their own jobs, and there are rules to cover all tasks and any problems. In reality, a certain amount of conflict is invariably found in work roles. There may be *role ambiguity* (a lack of clear information about a particular work role) that results in lower job satisfaction and higher stress levels (McCleese and Eby 2006). There may be *role conflict* because different groups in the workplace have different expectations for a particular work role or because the role expectations are excessive. Role conflict, like role ambiguity, leads to lower satisfaction and higher stress levels. The important point is that these problems are not the result of the individual worker's cantankerous nature but of contradictions that are part of the work role itself. The individual falls victim to the role and suffers the consequences of lowered satisfaction and higher stress levels.

The Political Economy of Work Hazards.   Some jobs necessarily entail more risk than others, and others entail more risk than necessary. Many work-related illnesses and injuries could be prevented or at least minimized if the health and well-being of workers took priority over profit. Historically, untold numbers of American workers have died in the name of profit and with the approval or apathy of the government.

The government has not yet engaged in the vigorous efforts needed to maintain a safe work environment. Both the federal and state governments have been lax in the

criminal prosecution of companies in which workers die because of inadequate safety measures. Further, the federal government tends to prosecute employers on civil rather than criminal grounds.

One government program that has been effective is the Occupational Safety and Health Administration (OSHA). OSHA (1996) was established in 1970 to protect the health and lives of workers. OSHA inspectors work with other professionals such as investigators, engineers, and physicians to establish and enforce safety standards. Overall, the workplace death rate has been cut by more than half since 1970; more than 100,000 workers could have died on the job but did not because of the improved safety and health conditions required by OSHA.

Although the results of OSHA are impressive, accidents and deaths in the workplace continue to be a problem. As long as the issue remains a civil rather than a criminal matter, work hazards probably will continue to put many workers at risk.

Social Psychological Factors

Attitudes.   Attitudes toward unions hurt many workers. We noted that union power may be diminishing along with declining membership. In addition, public opinion about unions and union leaders is not strongly positive. Polls by the Pew Research

FUN AND GAMES AT WORK

As various studies in this chapter indicate, many Americans find little pleasure in their jobs, though most expect their work to be enjoyable and fulfilling. By young adulthood, most people have worked at some job. Consider how much enjoyment and fulfillment you have received from your own work experiences. With respect to any job (or jobs) you have had, think about your feelings toward the work, the impact that the work had on your life, and the problems and satisfactions connected to the work. Imagine that someone is interviewing you about your experiences. Write out your answers to the following questions about a job you have had or now have.

What did you most like about the job?

What did you most dislike about the job?

How would you feel about working at the job for all or the major portion of your life? Why?

How were you treated by others in your work role?

Did the job make any difference in the way you feel about yourself? Why or why not?

How could the job be made more meaningful to workers?

Gather with other class members working on this project and summarize the results. What do the results say about the amount of worker dissatisfaction and alienation in America? If the only jobs available were the kinds discussed by the class, would most Americans prefer not to work? Could all the jobs be made into meaningful and fulfilling experiences?

Center show that since 1985 the proportion of Americans who have a favorable view of unions has fluctuated a little above and below the 50 percent level (Desilver 2014). In other words, at any given point in time roughly half of Americans look favorably and half look unfavorably on the union movement.

The negative attitudes that many Americans have about unions sometimes lead them into the *fallacy of circular reasoning,* as exemplified by the following exchange between two students in a social problems class:

"Unions hurt the economy and they hurt the workers."

"But the workers are much better off than they were in the past, before they had unions."

"They're not better off than they would be without the unions."

"How do you know? How can you say that?"

"Because unions hurt people. They keep workers from getting the best deal for themselves in the free market."

Negative thinking about unions is interesting in view of the union movement's achievements. The power of labor unions, along with government intervention, has helped eliminate many lethal work situations and has greatly improved the conditions of labor. Without the support of the public, labor unions will find themselves increasingly unable to gain further benefits for their members and for labor as a whole. Public opinion vacillates, of course, and may shift again in a more favorable direction. However, the decline in public approval of labor unions is an unwelcome sign to people who strive to improve the lot of workers.

Another attitude that enters into work problems is the sense of superiority that people might have toward certain workers. The attitudes of many Americans toward service workers, manual laborers, and clerical workers range from patronizing to contemptuous. If some workers are dissatisfied or alienated, it is in part because others *treat them with little or no respect because of their jobs.* For example, we have seen many instances of secretaries and clerks being treated with contempt by their superiors or by customers who feel they should quickly respond to demands from those who "pay your salary."

Socialization. One of the more important reasons Americans desire interesting work that makes full use of their skills and abilities is that they have been socialized to expect it. *The socialization process in the United States involves an emphasis on achievement,* and that achievement involves a job that will enable you to do better than your parents and to fulfill yourself (Chang et al. 2006). Work—the right kind of work—is an integral part of the American dream. That is why parents will forgo some of their own pleasure in order to send their children through college, and why professionals frequently prefer for their children to follow them in some kind of professional career.

In other words, you learn at an early age that if you are going to engage seriously in the pursuit of happiness that is your right, you must secure the kind of work that is conducive to the pursuit. As long as work is an integral part of individual fulfillment, and as long as the economy does not yield sufficient numbers of jobs that facilitate fulfillment, Americans will continue to have the quality of their lives diminished by the contradiction between socialized expectations and the realities of society.

The Ideology and Reality of Work. A final factor in work problems is the incongruity between the ideology about work and the reality of work. One line of thought, which dates back to the first Protestants, insists on the *value of all work.* The classic devotional writer William Law (1906:32) said, "Worldly business is to be made holy unto the Lord, by being done as a service to Him, and in conformity to His Divine will." This ideology regards work as a sacred obligation and implies that all work is equally good.

Although American ideology emphasizes the value of work and the equal value of all work, in practice not all work is given equal value. As we noted in the previous section, some kinds of work are disparaged by people who have jobs with higher prestige. Many Americans accept the ideology that work of any kind is intrinsically superior to nonwork, only to find themselves disparaged by other Americans who have "better" jobs. This ideology compounds the problems of the unemployed, who tend to define a social problem as personal and blame themselves for their plight. In addition, the work ideology may make the unemployed feel guilty about not working, even though they are the victims of a political-economic system rather than blameworthy violators of the American way.

Public Policy and Private Action

The problems of work can be attacked in a number of different ways. First, with regard to unemployment, it is unlikely that the rate can go much lower than it was from the late 1990s through 2001 or the below 5 percent of 2016. The challenge is not to bring the unemployment rate down to zero; this won't happen (even economists do not mean zero unemployment when they use the term "full employment"). The challenge is to keep the rate low by maintaining a strong economy while supporting those who are unemployed.

Government programs to train, or retool, and find jobs for the unemployed are one form of support. Although such programs often benefit people, they also are usually controversial in terms of cost and effectiveness. Finding an effective job-training program is as much a political as a technical matter and, thus, requires a strong commitment from politicians.

Unemployment benefits are another form of support. Such benefits depend on action by both federal and state governments. Contrary to what some people believe, unemployment benefits are not automatically available to anyone who loses a job. Although the proportion varies by state, nationally fewer than half of the unemployed receive benefits (DeParle 2009).

The government could also require other kinds of benefits for workers. As we noted earlier in this chapter, nearly one out of five American workers has no health insurance. The lack of insurance is a serious problem for those who are currently employed and is a particular concern of the unemployed. A national health plan could provide such coverage both for them and for the workers who do not now receive such a benefit. Time off from work is another benefit that is important to the well-being of workers (Etzion 2003). But American workers have fewer days of paid vacation than workers in many other nations. After a year on the job, blue-collar workers tend to receive an annual paid vacation of 5 days, and white-collar workers receive 10 days. Longer paid vacations come only after years on the job. By contrast, all the European Union nations have a statutory minimum vacation of at least 20 days a year after one year on the job (Worklife Report 2003). Public holidays add another 10.8 days per year to the average time off.

Various measures can alleviate the problem of work–family conflict. These measures can be voluntarily undertaken by firms or mandated by the government. Work–family conflict can be minimized, for example, among those people who are able to work from their homes (e.g., via computer), those parents who are able to work part-time for a few years without jeopardizing their careers, and those workers who have more control over their hours and work conditions (Work and Family Newsbrief 2003; Hill, Martinson, and Ferris 2004).

Regarding the problem of work hazards, governmental and union actions have significantly reduced the incidence of occupational injuries and illnesses. The Occupational Safety and Health Administration of the Department of Labor acts as a watchdog group to enforce safety regulations. As a result of OSHA's activity, the rate of injuries and the number of workers killed on the job have both declined dramatically. Some employers resent the OSHA regulations and complain about government intervention in their business. Yet the data on diminishing injuries and deaths support the continuing efforts of OSHA to provide workers with a safe working environment.

Various measures can help address the problems of job dissatisfaction and alienation. From this chapter's discussion about the causes of the problems, you can see that more challenging work, greater worker participation and control, and more worker autonomy are needed. In addition, the quality of the relationship between bosses and coworkers is closely related to job satisfaction. Workers who are on good terms with and feel supported by others at the workplace have higher levels of satisfaction than do other workers (Ting 1997; El-Bassel, Guterman, Bargal, and Su 1998). Thus, programs that engage in team-building and conflict resolution skills can enhance the quality of workplace relationships.

Job enrichment efforts also can reduce dissatisfaction and alienation. Job enrichment involves such changes as more worker responsibility and less direct control over the worker. It also includes the upgrading of skills required for a job and enlargement of the job so that the worker is not confined to a single, highly specialized task. Some job enrichment programs have resulted in higher job satisfaction, higher levels of worker morale, fewer grievances, and less absenteeism and turnover.

Still another measure for dealing with dissatisfaction and alienation is *flextime,* which made its debut in America in 1970 after being used successfully in Europe. There are at least three different types of flextime systems, varying by the amount of choice given to the worker. In one type, the employer lets the workers choose from a range of times to start their eight-hour workdays. A second type allows employees to choose their own schedules. Once chosen and approved, the schedules must be followed for a specified length of time. In a third type, employees can vary their own schedules on a daily basis without prior approval of supervisors. All types have limits within which employees must function. Millions of Americans now work under flextime, and the results include greater satisfaction, higher morale, increased productivity, and less stress driving to work (Kelloway and Gottlieb 1998; Lucas and Heady 2002). At the same time, one researcher found that employees who request flextime, particularly when the reason is something other than childcare, were evaluated more negatively than those not making such a request (Munsch 2016). Employers must make it very clear that any request for flextime will be treated with respect and can be made with impunity.

Dissatisfaction and alienation also can be addressed through *participatory management or organizational democracy, which involves worker participation in the decision-making process.* Of course, there are many executive decisions that must be made without such participation. But employees may participate in the decision-making process in four areas: setting organizational goals, solving problems, selecting from alternative courses of action, and making changes in the organization. In more extreme forms of involvement, employees participate in decisions about hiring and firing and about their own wages and benefits.

Employees may participate in the decisions as individuals, as part of manager-employee pairs, or as members of a group of managers and employees. Such participation fulfills the needs of employees for some degree of control over their lives, for more meaningful work, and for the kind of involvement that attacks the problem of alienation. Participation programs can be costly to implement and conflict with the traditional management–worker relationship. However, they can improve productivity, quality control, and a company's market share of the product (Levin 2006).

A final measure is *employee ownership,* including the more radical form of *employee takeover of a company.* Thousands of companies now offer workers an employee stock ownership plan (ESOP). There are three types of employee ownership plans in the United States. In *direct ownership,* employees simply own shares in the company. This is the most common form of employee ownership in the United States (Blasi and Kruse 2006). In *trust ownership,* employees acquire some portion of shares over time as stock is transferred to them as a part of their benefits. In *cooperative ownership,* employees get votes in accord with the number of shares they hold; this type of ESOP gives the employees some control of the enterprise. These plans generally lead to increased job satisfaction and worker performance (Yates 2006).

In a few cases, employees have assumed ownership and full responsibility for a company or have been allowed to work without supervisory personnel. The results tend to be uniformly positive: higher productivity, lower costs, and greater worker satisfaction and morale.

Follow-Up.   Some critics say that Americans expect too much from their work. They not only want good pay, they also want their jobs to be fulfilling. What do you think? Should people just be grateful that they have paying jobs, and find their fulfillment in after-work activities?

chapter 10 review

Summary

The American economy, the nature of work, and the nature of the workforce all have changed over time in America. Some recent changes in the economy that are detrimental to many Americans are corporate downsizing, increased use of temporary workers, declining union strength, reduced corporate tax obligations, and decline in income for some families. The labor force and the division of labor have increased substantially. The educational level and the proportion of females in the labor force are also increasing. The work ethic remains strong, but workers now insist that their jobs be a source of fulfillment and not solely a source of income.

Work is a social problem because of unemployment and underemployment, work hazards, and dissatisfaction and alienation. Each year millions of Americans are unemployed, though the rate varies for different groups and different occupations. Many Americans are not deeply dissatisfied with or alienated from work, but many also desire a job different from the one they have. Among the hazards of work are work-induced stress and work-related injuries and illnesses.

Work is intimately related to the quality of life because it involves the worker's health. Work-induced stress, injuries and illnesses, and job dissatisfaction can all adversely affect the worker's health. Unemployment tends to be a traumatic, stressful experience that adversely affects the worker's interpersonal relationships and health.

Capitalism with its emphasis on profit is one of the factors that contributes to problems in the American economy. Subservience of workers' needs to organizational needs, union-busting, downsizing, and increased numbers of temporary jobs all reflect the drive for profit. Structural unemployment is also a product of the capitalistic system, which includes the natural swings of the economy, technological change, government spending priorities, and the growth of multinational corporations. The nature of work roles in the American technological, bureaucratic society produces much dissatisfaction, stress, and conflict. Work hazards are frequently more common than necessary because companies give priority to profit, not to worker health and safety.

Among social psychological factors that add to the problems of work are the attitudes of Americans toward unions and toward other Americans whose jobs they regard as inferior to their own. The contradiction between the ideology and reality of work is another contributing factor. The ideology glorifies work and working and places an equal value on all work. The reality is disparagement of some work and a political-economic system that guarantees a certain amount of unemployment.

Key Terms

Capitalism	Underemployment
Division of Labor	Unemployment Rate
Downsizing	Work Ethic
Labor Force	

Study Questions

1. How have the economy, work, and the workforce been changing in America?
2. What are some consequences for workers of the globalization of the economy?
3. Discuss whether the meaning of work is changing.
4. How much and what kinds of unemployment are there in the United States?
5. How serious are the problems of work dissatisfaction and of hazards at work?
6. How do work problems affect people's health and interpersonal relationships?
7. How does the political-economic system affect the problems related to the American economy and work?
8. In what ways do contemporary work roles increase job dissatisfaction and alienation?
9. What kinds of attitudes toward work, workers, and unions contribute to the problems of work?
10. Discuss the contradiction between the ideology and the reality of work in America.
11. What can Americans do to reduce unemployment, job hazards, and job dissatisfaction?

Internet Resources/Exercises

1. Explore some of the ideas in this chapter on the following sites:

http://www.dol.gov   The U.S. Department of Labor site has the latest numbers from the Bureau of Labor Statistics plus reports on every aspect of work in the United States.

http://www.bls.gov The Monthly Labor Review site provides abstracts of all articles from 1988 to the present.

http://aflcio.org/ News and information about various aspects of work, including safety, from the AFL-CIO.

2. The text points out that studies are inconclusive about the degree of worker satisfaction. Use a search engine to research the topic "worker satisfaction." What would you conclude about the topic on the basis of the text materials and the materials you found?

3. Use the government sites listed above to explore work and working conditions in other nations. What kinds of problems exist in other nations that are largely or totally absent in the United States? What kinds of benefits do workers have in other nations that are lacking in the United States? On the whole, which nations do you believe have the best working conditions?

For Further Reading

Blank, Rebecca M., Sheldon H. Danziger, and Robert F. Schoeni, eds. *Working and Poor: How Economic and Policy Changes Are Affecting Low-Wage Workers.* New York: Russell Sage Foundation, 2008. Various authors discuss all aspects of the economic well-being of low-skilled workers, including their opportunities, their patterns of consumption, and how they are affected by government policies.

Heckscher, Charles, and Paul Adler. *The Corporation as a Collaborative Community.* New York, Oxford University Press, 2006. An examination of the way the vital quality of "community" (in the form of loyalty)—both within and between businesses—has been eroded through such things as downsizing and restructuring, and a description of the new form of community that is emerging.

Janoski, Thomas, David Luke, and Christopher Oliver. *The Causes of Structural Unemployment.* Cambridge, UK: Polity Press, 2014. A discussion of the causes of unemployment in modern industrial nations, including the impact of the global economy and what can be done to address the problem.

Maynard, Douglas C., and Daniel C. Feldman, eds. *Underemployment: Psychological, Economic, and Social Challenges.* New York: Springer, 2011. An examination of the problem of underemployment from various points of view, including the issue of why underemployment is found even in healthy economies and the effects of underemployment on economic growth and human well-being.

Rogers, Jackie Krasas. *Temps: The Many Faces of the Changing Workplace.* Ithaca, NY: Cornell University Press, 2000. A critique of the temporary worker trend, dispelling some of the myths about why people work part time and showing the stress experienced by those unwillingly caught up in temp work.

Rubery, Jill, and Damian Grimshaw. *The Organisation of Employment: An International Perspective.* New York: Palgrave Macmillan, 2003. A readable introduction to the way employment and labor markets are organized in advanced capitalist countries. Compares such things as trends in labor market participation, vocational training systems, the regulation of the labor market, and the ways firms deal with work and employment.

Zlolniski, Christian. *Janitors, Street Vendors, and Activists: The Lives of Mexican Immigrants in Silicon Valley.* Berkeley, CA: University of California Press, 2006. An exploration of the use of Mexican immigrants for low-wage jobs in the high-tech industry, showing both how the workers are exploited and how they are affecting such things as the political process and union activity.

chapter 10 review

CHAPTER

Education

©Design Pics / Don Hammond

"I Kept My Mouth Shut"

In theory, all Americans have an equal chance to prove themselves in school. In practice, you are disadvantaged if you come from a poor or minority-group family. Marcia is an undergraduate student who comes from a middle-class family. She remembers with some regret about the time she learned how others are disadvantaged:

I was in the first grade when I learned that we weren't all really equal at school. It was recess and I was playing on the monkey bars. One of my classmates was playing beside me. Her name was Ramona. She came from a poor family. I didn't think about it at the time, but she was very ill-kept. Neither she nor her clothes were very clean. But I liked her. I enjoyed playing with her at recess.

As we were playing, and Ramona was turning around on the bars, some of the other girls began to make fun of her and talk about her dirty underwear. I felt sorry for her and mad at the other girls for saying such mean things to her. I hollered to them: "She can't help it if her underwear is dirty." No sooner had I said it than the strong voice of our teacher came booming at us: "Yes, she can."

I could see the embarrassment on Ramona's face. She got off the monkey bars and went over and sat by herself on a bench for the rest of the recess. I'm ashamed to say that the teacher really intimidated me. I felt really bad about Ramona, but I was very careful to keep my mouth shut about it after that. I didn't want to incur the teacher's wrath, and I didn't want all the other girls to reject me.

I think it was about the fourth grade when I no longer saw Ramona. I don't know if she dropped out or her family moved or what. I do know that she never did well in school. But I don't think it was because she wasn't smart. Ramona just never had much of a chance.

Introduction

Historically, Americans have viewed education as an answer to many social ills; but a series of Gallup polls since 1974 shows a trend of declining public confidence in public schools (Morales 2011). In 1974, 58 percent said they had a great deal or quite a lot of confidence in the nation's schools; by 2016 only 30 percent affirmed such confidence (Norman 2016).

Americans apparently have a sense that education is a problem as well as a solution to other problems. When education is in trouble, it is a very serious matter because education is the foundation of American life.

In what sense has education become a problem? In this chapter we first look at the functions of education and the high value typically placed on education. We also show how the high value is reflected in the continually "higher" amount of education attained by Americans.

In light of the functions and value of education, we look at how certain problems such as unequal opportunities bear upon the quality of life of Americans. We then examine some structural and social psychological factors that contribute to the problems and conclude with some examples of efforts to resolve the problems.

Why Education?

What do Americans expect their educational system to achieve for them personally and for their society? In 1787 the Northwest Ordinance included a provision for the encouragement of education on the grounds that "religion, morality, and knowledge" are "necessary to good government and the happiness of mankind." The significance of this, as Parker (1975:29) pointed out, is that "a people, not yet formed into a nation, declare education to be an essential support of free government and set aside western lands for schools and education."

Thus, one function of education is to create *good and effective citizens* (Tyack 2003). There is some dispute about what it means to be a good citizen, however. Some people believe that education should produce citizens who will accept traditional values and protect the "American way of life" (which obviously means different things to different people). Education achieves this function when it transmits the **culture** from one generation to the next, that is, when it *socializes the young into the basic values, beliefs, and customs of the society.* Others believe that education should equip the citizenry to reshape their society so that the flaws and inequities are eliminated. In any case, education has been held to be essential in the process of creating effective citizens in the republic.

A second function of education is to provide the individual with the *possibility for upward mobility.* For a long time Americans have associated education with good jobs. Most students in colleges and universities are there to prepare for the better-paying and

culture
the way of life of a people, including both material products (such as technology) and nonmaterial characteristics (such as values, norms, language, and beliefs)

more prestigious jobs, not for the love of learning. Education achieves this function when it *instructs the young in knowledge and skills.*

The third function of education is personal development, including a sense of personal control (Schieman and Plickert 2008). Education *liberates people from the bonds of ignorance and prepares them to maximize their intellectual, emotional, and social development.* This function is important to educators, but few people set educational goals with personal development in mind.

Whatever their views of the primary aim of education, most Americans would probably agree that all three functions are legitimate. The schools should produce good citizens. They should help the individual to better himself or herself, and they should prepare the individual to maximize his or her own development. Because all three functions are related to the *quality of life* of the individual, if any person or group is not given the opportunity to secure an education that fulfills the functions, education becomes a social problem. Quality of life is diminished when the individual lacks the tools necessary to participate effectively in political processes, to achieve some measure of success in work or a career, or to develop his or her potential to its fullest.

Educational Attainment and Payoff

Because of its importance to quality of life, you would expect Americans to secure an increasing amount of education over time. Most do aspire to a high level, but what about the **attainment?** Once attained, does education yield the expected payoff? Is the high value on education reflected in concrete results?

attainment
as distinguished from educational "achievement," the number of years of education completed by a student

Levels of Attainment

In 1870, 57 percent of youths 5 to 17 years old were enrolled in school, and 1.2 percent were in high schools. In 2014, 93.4 percent of 5- and 6-year-olds, 97.6 percent of 7- to 13-year-olds, 97.8 percent of 14- and 15-year-olds, and 92.9 percent of 16- and 17-year-olds were enrolled in school (Digest of Educational Statistics website).

A few generations ago, completion of elementary school was considered a good *level of attainment.* Today, completion of high school is the minimal level considered appropriate. As Figure 11.1 shows, an increasing proportion of the population has been reaching that level. In fact, an increasing proportion of the population is attaining a college degree. And many students find they need or desire an advanced degree—between 1985 and 2014, enrollment in graduate programs increased more than 73 percent to 2.9 million students (Kena et al. 2016). The increasing amount of education is reflected in the data on different age groups in Table 11.1. Compare, for example, the rates for people aged 65 and older with those in the 35 to 49 age group.

Another way to look at the increasing education attainment is to note the diminishing *dropout rate.* Students begin to drop out of school after the fifth grade. Since the 1920s, the proportion dropping out, especially before completing elementary school, has decreased greatly. The likelihood of dropping out varies among different groups. Males are more likely to drop out than are females. Students in the lower socioeconomic strata are more likely than those in higher strata to drop out. And minorities have higher rates than do whites.

One factor that has aided educational attainment is the proliferation of two-year colleges. Their enrollment increased fivefold from 1960 to 1970 and more than doubled

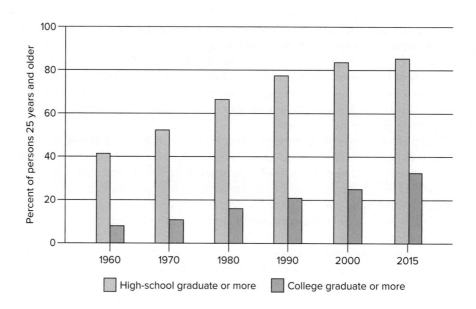

FIGURE 11.1

Educational Attainment of Adults (25 years and older).

Source: Digest of Educational Statistics website.

TABLE 11.1

Years of School Completed, by Age, Sex, Race, and Hispanic Origin, 2015 (persons 18 years old and older)

	Percent of Population				
	High School Graduate	Some College, but No Degree	Associate's Degree	Bachelor's Degree	Advanced Degree
Total	29.6	19.1	9.3	19.2	10.6
Age					
25–34 years	25.5	18.5	10.4	25.2	10.9
35–49 years	26.9	15.9	7.5	22.3	13.5
50–59 years	31.1	16.3	10.8	19.6	11.4
60–64 years	30.7	17.4	10.3	18.6	12.9
65 years and over	34.6	15.7	7.4	15.4	11.3
Sex					
Male	30.8	18.9	8.3	18.8	10.5
Female	28.5	19.2	10.2	19.6	10.7
Race/Ethnicity					
White	29.4	19.0	10.2	21.7	12.2
Black	34.3	22.9	9.3	13.2	7.1
Asian	18.3	7.8	6.2	30.9	19.4
Hispanic	30.7	17.2	6.8	9.6	4.0

SOURCE: Digest of Educational Statistics website.

from 1970 to 1980 (Figure 11.2). After 1980, enrollment continued to rise, but much more slowly. By 2014, there were 7.1 million students enrolled in two year colleges in the nation. Community colleges offer both preparation for four-year colleges and universities and numerous terminal programs. Many students use the community college experience to decide on their educational and career goals.

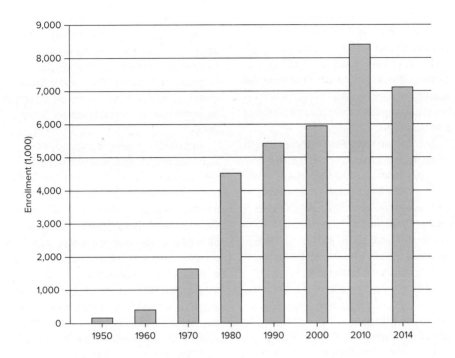

FIGURE 11.2
Enrollment in Community (two-year) Colleges, 1950–2014.

Source: Digest of Educational Statistics website.

Attainment and Payoff

In some ways you cannot talk about the *payoff of education.* You cannot, for instance, measure the personal development of individuals and correlate that with education. However, there is a positive relationship between happiness and educational level; that is, the higher the level of education, the higher the reported happiness and satisfaction with life (Pew Research Center 2006). Of course, happiness and life satisfaction are not measures of personal development—the fulfillment of an individual's potential. At best, you can say that the greater happiness and satisfaction reported by the better educated may reflect a tendency toward greater fulfillment of potential.

Similarly, there is only minimal evidence that education creates an effective citizenry. We know, for instance, that there is a *direct correlation between level of education and voter participation.* In fact, there are dramatic differences in voting rates between people in differing educational categories. As we pointed out in Chapter 9, for example, in the 2012 election the percentage of those who voted was 81.3 percent of Americans with an advanced degree and only 37.1 percent of Americans who had less than a high school diploma.

More educated people are also more likely to hold democratic values and to support democratic practices. Although such relationships indicate positive contributions of education to citizenship, they do not tell us whether education helps people to detect and reject demagoguery and to participate meaningfully in the defense of freedom and the shaping of a just social order. Education does increase political participation and understanding. However, the more educated people usually are the political and corporate heads who accept and maintain the institutional policies and practices that can contribute to the various social problems of the nation.

There is more evidence with respect to the third function of education—providing a means of upward mobility. A strong relationship exists between levels of education and

EDUCATIONAL ATTAINMENT, BY COUNTRY

A nation cannot successfully modernize or implement a political democracy without an educated populace. People must be educated in order to function effectively in the kinds of jobs associated with an industrial economy, and they must be educated in order to participate meaningfully in a democratic political process.

An economist argued that economic growth cannot begin in a country until at least 6 percent of the population is enrolled in primary school (Peaslee 1969). As the country continues to modernize, increasing educational levels are required. Thus, nations like the United States that are the most economically and technologically developed typically have the highest average levels of educational attainment.

Political leaders are aware of the crucial importance of education and in most nations are attempting to provide expanded educational opportunities. There are still some dramatic disparities, however. While the great majority of nations enroll most of their children at the elementary level—grades one through six—some nations fall far short. In 2002, for example, the proportion of children enrolled in elementary education was 90 percent or more in the majority of countries for which information was available, but it was 68 percent in Pakistan, 67 percent in Saudi Arabia, 60 percent in Sudan, and 44 percent in Niger (National Center for Education Statistics 2006).

Enrollment in higher education has also expanded greatly throughout the world. In fact, enrollment rates in developing countries are now higher than the rates were in Europe a few decades ago (Schofer and Meyer 2005). Table 11.2 shows the percent of adults aged 25 to 64 who have earned a vocational or bachelor's degree in a number of countries. As with many things, the United States is neither the most nor the least educated nation in the world. Unfortunately, data are not available for most of the developing nations. But their educational opportunities are more limited than those in the developed countries. As long

income (Table 11.3). Those differences persist throughout people's careers, so that the lifetime earnings of those with high levels of education are considerably greater than those at lower educational levels (Tamborini, Kim, and Sakamoto 2015).

Does this mean that an individual can maximize his or her income by maximizing education? In general, yes. But to assume that *anyone* can reach the highest levels of income by maximizing education is the *fallacy of non sequitur.* Your background, including your racial or ethnic identity, and the economy are among the factors that affect your chances. We discuss this situation in some detail later in this chapter, but our point here is that the high correlation between education and income does not mean that education is the open road to success. People who attain high levels of education are likely to be those whose parents had a relatively high level of education. There is mobility in the United States, but education is more useful to the privileged as a means of passing on their privileges to their children than as a means for the underdog to be upwardly mobile.

Some people have argued that education is of no use in reducing inequality in America, that schools do virtually nothing to help the poor be upwardly mobile, and that education has little effect on the future incomes of people. Rather, they feel that economic opportunities depend upon the state of the economy; one's family background; and various other noneducational factors, such as the contacts one is able to make.

It is true that education alone is not sufficient to deal with economic inequality in America, and it is true that the best way to "get ahead" in America is to start from a high socioeconomic position (obviously something over which the individual has no control). This argument overstates the case, however. The advantaged child will not maintain his or her advantage without an education, and at least some people gain new as such disparities exist, it is unlikely that the inequalities between nations in such factors as income, employment, and standard of living will diminish.

Country	Percent of Adults, 25–64 Years, Who Have	
Earned	Vocational Degree	Bachelor's or Higher Degree
Australia	11.5	29.8
Austria	7.3	12.7
Canada	24.9	27.7
France	11.9	18.9
Germany	11.1	17.0
Greece	8.8	17.9
Japan	20.2	26.4
Mexico	1.2	16.9
Norway	2.4	36.2
Spain	9.7	22.7
Switzerland	10.8	25.8
United Kingdom	10.0	31.0
United States	10.4	32.6

TABLE 11.2
Educational Attainment, by Country

SOURCE: Digest of Educational Statistics website.

TABLE 11.3
Median Income of Persons 25 Years and Older, by Educational Attainment, 2014

Educational Attainment	Males	Females
Less than 9th grade	$26,580	$20,990
9th to 12th grade (no diploma)	$30,890	$21,990
High school graduate	$40,930	$30,650
Some college, no degree	$46,900	$34,380
Associate's degree	$51,110	$37,480
Bachelor's degree	$68,160	$55,940
Master's degree	$84,760	$60,830
Professional degree	$121,750	$91,810
Doctorate degree	$80,660	$80,540

SOURCE: Digest of Educational Statistics website.

advantages through education (Hao and Pong 2008). Most Americans recognize this, particularly those who have themselves benefitted from education. Thus, parents with a college education are likely to pass on to their children a sense of need for a similar level of attainment. As a result, students whose parents went to college are more likely to enroll in college themselves and are also likely to expect that their education will yield some kind of prestigious work (Goyette 2008).

You may conclude, then, that although many people are upwardly mobile through educational attainment, those most likely to benefit from education are already in the middle and upper strata. In terms of mobility, the payoff from education is not equally likely for all groups.

Education and the Quality of Life

Ideally, as we have shown, education performs a number of valued functions that enhance the quality of life for Americans. Nevertheless, education is a problem because there are inequalities and the expected payoff does not always occur.

Inequality of Opportunity and Attainment

Besides the inequality of attainment we have touched on, there is *inequality of opportunity*—a debatable and ambiguous notion, as you will see. Such inequalities contradict *the American value of education and the ideology of equal opportunities* for all. Ideally, every American ought to have equal opportunity to maximize his or her education. However, minorities and the poor do not attain the same educational levels as white males. Is this inequality of attainment a reflection of unequal opportunities or of some characteristics of the groups themselves? You have seen in previous chapters that the answer is both but that the characteristics of the groups do not include an inferior level of intelligence. Part of the reason a son of a poor white farmer does not go to college may be his own lack of motivation, but even that lack must be seen as a social phenomenon that is rooted in a complex situation in which multiple factors work together. In other words, unequal educational attainment does not mean that those groups with lower levels of attainment are incapable of extending their education. It is important to keep this aspect in mind as we explore the ways in which educational opportunities and attainment are distributed in society.

The Meaning of Unequal Opportunities.   There is debate over the meaning of inequality of opportunity. Most Americans, including most social scientists, would affirm the *ideal of equal educational opportunity* for all. But what does that ideal mean? Does it mean that a child should have the opportunity to attend a nonsegregated school? Does it mean that all children should be schooled with equal amounts of money? Does it mean that the proportion of people of various kinds (minorities and those from different socioeconomic strata) in the differing educational levels should be the same as their proportion in the total population? Does it mean that each child should have access to the same quality and the same amount of education? Does it mean that the same amount of education should yield the same payoff in terms of income or personal development?

Or are all these matters important? If, for instance, you define equality as all children attending nonsegregated schools, there may still be considerable inequality of funding among various schools. If you define equality as equal funds per student, children could still attend segregated schools or be less likely to attend college if they are black or poor.

Because the meaning of unequal opportunities is debated, it is unlikely that we can settle on a definition that will be acceptable to everyone. Nevertheless, it is important to select a meaning so that we can explore the extent of inequality in America. For our purposes, equality of educational opportunity means that every child has access to quality education and is not deterred from maximizing that education by social background or economic factors. Social background factors include race, ethnic origin, sex, and socioeconomic status. Economic factors include the funding of education and the cost to the student. In brief, equality means that all Americans, whatever their background, have the opportunity to attain fairly equal amounts of education. It also means that students attend schools that are equally funded and that the cost of education (college or graduate school) does not force some students to drop out before they have reached their goal. In these terms, how much inequality is there?

Inequality of Attainment.   We have given figures in previous chapters on *differences in educational attainment.* A measure of inequality may be the proportion of various groups that has attained different levels of education. Table 11.1 shows some of the differences. Note, for example, the proportions of those having an advanced degree. The proportion for whites is three times, and the proportion for Asians is almost five times, that of Hispanics. Overall, the table makes it clear that whites and Asians get far more education than do African Americans and Hispanics.

A word of caution is in order here. Variations exist among Hispanics in the extent to which educational attainment is low. A Pew Research Center (2013) report on the educational attainment of Hispanics found that those from a Venezuelan background were the most educated (50 percent have a bachelor's degree or more) and those from a Salvadoran background the least educated (8 percent have a bachelor's degree and 74 percent have less than a high school diploma). The reasons for these variations are unclear, but they do caution us against the assumption that ethnicity per se is the only important variable in understanding attainment levels of America's minorities.

Funding and Costs.   The second aspect of unequal opportunities is the *funding and cost of education.* Children do not have equal educational opportunities if they attend schools with unequal resources or if they are forced to drop out at some point because they cannot pay for the cost of their education.

There are considerable inequalities of resources, both among the states and among school districts within a state. In 2013, the average expenditure per pupil ranged from $6580 in Utah to $19,979 in New York (Digest of Educational Statistics website). The school expenditures in a state, of course, tend to reflect such things as the overall wealth of the state, the cost of living in the state, and the personal income of the residents of the state. The expenditures also reflect the ideology of the people and the state government. Although Arizona spends less than any other state per pupil on education, there are many other states with a lower median household income. In any case, the amount spent on a child's education varies enormously between the states.

We are cautious about our conclusions. A particular school in a state with lower-than-average funding may offer an immeasurably better education than a ghetto school in New York, but to conclude from this example that the lower-than-average state offers a better education is the *fallacy of dramatic instance.* The point is not that every school in the better-funded state is better than every school in the more poorly funded state. Rather, overall, the schools in the better-funded state have an advantage in resources for educating students, so that the typical student is likely to experience an education backed by greater resources.

Funding also varies considerably within states. Schools have been funded by the property tax (discussed in more detail later in this chapter). Property tax funding means that a school district populated largely by people from lower-income groups who live in cheaper homes will have a low tax base. School districts that encompass affluent areas, on the other hand, may actually have a lower rate of taxation (number of dollars of

fallacy

school tax per assessed value of the property) but a much higher per-pupil income. An affluent school district may have double, triple, or quadruple the funds per pupil than an adjacent poor school district has. Should the funds available for a child's schooling be considerably less because of the neighborhood in which he or she happens to be born?

Similarly, you may ask whether an individual should drop out of college because of inadequate financial resources even though he or she is quite capable of doing the work. There is not sufficient money to provide scholarships and loans for all students who would like to go to college, and the cost of attending college has risen rapidly. For a number of decades, now, the cost of a college education has been rising much faster than the overall cost of living. This increase means that millions of American families have annual incomes less than the cost of room, board, and tuition at an average private university. Obviously, many Americans are priced out of the better colleges and universities in the nation. Moreover, the disparity between those who can and those who cannot afford college is expected to grow. There are no signs yet that the spiraling costs of higher education will stop.

There are, of course, sources of aid for those from lower-income families. This does not mean that all can afford college. There is not enough aid available to offset the cost for every low-income family that wants the help. At the same time, the group hardest hit by the rising costs are those from middle-income families (Houle 2014). Their family income is too high for them to receive tuition waivers but not high enough to avoid the huge debt acquired by borrowing money to attend college.

In sum, the quality of life for many Americans is depressed because of unequal opportunities at all levels of education. Many children cannot afford to go to a better college or even to any college. Their level of attainment will be less than their abilities warrant and often less than they desire. Those same children probably attended elementary and secondary schools that spent less on them than other schools could spend. Inequality in education exists from kindergarten to the university.

The Atmosphere: Learning or Surviving?

atmosphere
the general mood and social influences in a situation or place

Another kind of inequality that contradicts the American ideology of equal opportunity involves the **atmosphere** of the school. Some atmospheres are conducive to learning, some inhibit learning, and some require the student to focus on surviving, on merely getting through the institution with body and sanity intact.

Education as Boring.   One frequently heard criticism is that education is boring (Wurdinger 2005; Kass, Vodanovich, and Khosravi 2011). For example, boredom often results when students are required to memorize large amounts of data that are not integrated with each other and not linked to important principles or ideas. Thus, history students may be required to memorize names, dates, and events without discussing their significance for understanding the processes of social life.

Boredom can afflict students at any level. The slowest students may be bored because they cannot grasp the materials. Others may be bored because they see no point to what they are doing. Gifted children may also suffer from boredom (Long 2013). Gifted elementary students typically master from a third to a half of the curriculum in five basic subjects before they even begin the school year. Boredom leads to a variety of negative consequences. Students may behave as if they lack interest or the ability to focus their attention (Webb 2000). Or they may cut classes or even drop out of school (Fallis and Opotow 2003).

The Atmosphere of Fear.   Perhaps worse even than boredom is the *atmosphere of fear* in which some students must function. Without a safe environment, teachers find it difficult to teach and students find it difficult to learn. Unfortunately, a considerable amount of crime and violence exists in the schools.

In the previous edition of this text, we wrote that students are safer at school than away from school. That is no longer the case. In 2014, according to a national survey, students aged 12 through 18 experienced 33 nonfatal victimizations per 1,000 students at school and 24 per 1,000 students away from school (Zhang, Musu-Gillette, and Oudekerk 2016). The survey reported the following about school victimizations for the year 2012–2013:

- Students aged 12 through 18 experienced 850,100 nonfatal victimizations at school.
- About 43 percent of the victimizations were thefts; the remainder were violent incidents of assault.
- 7 percent of students in grades 9 through 12 reported being threatened or injured with a weapon, such as a gun, knife, or club, on school property.
- About 5 percent of students said they avoided at least one school activity or class or one or more places in school because they feared being attacked or harmed.
- 22 percent of students in grades 9 through 12 said that drugs were offered, sold, or given to them.
- 22 percent of 12- to 18-year-old students reported having been bullied at school; this is a lower figure than those reported in prior years, but it still means that one of every five students experiences bullying.
- 31 homicides and 6 suicides of school-age youth (ages 5–18) occurred at school during the year.

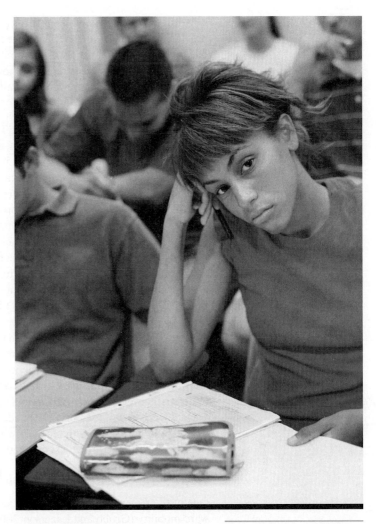

Education doesn't yield a high payoff when students are bored.

©BananaStock/JupiterImages

The kind of atmosphere created by such problems contributes to the difficulty of learning, to dropping out of school, and to entertaining thoughts of suicide (Hay and Meldrum 2010; Peguero 2011). Moreover, they are likely to have long-term negative consequences. For example, a survey of adults who had been bullied between the ages of 9 and 16 years found elevated rates of psychiatric disorders (such as phobias, anxiety, depression) among the victims (Copeland et al. 2013).

It is also important to keep in mind that all these problems are more severe in poor, inner-city schools where they create what Shanker (1994) called the "crab bucket syndrome." This syndrome refers to the fact that inner-city students who try to free themselves from the culture of gangs, drugs, and violence and do good work face enormous pressure, harassment, and even violence as others try to pull them back into the bucket. In one inner-city school, names of outstanding students were kept secret prior to an awards ceremony lest the honorees refuse to show up out of fear. One recipient had to be ordered to the stage to receive his reward; he walked up amid the sneering catcalls of others.

Ritualized Deprivation.   Another condition that exists in many American classrooms is described as **ritualized deprivation.** The teacher performs in a substandard fashion and may be with the children for only a short period of time. The building and facilities are substandard and contain little if anything to stimulate curiosity or motivate the intellect. The school offers a daily ritual—some of the motions of teaching and learning are present. However, the ritual occurs in such a deprived context that the student is more concerned about surviving the process than learning.

The kind of school that has an atmosphere of ritualized deprivation is most likely to be found in the urban ghetto or other dominantly low-income area. Kozol (1992) describes such a school in Chicago. It is a high school with no campus and no schoolyard, though it does have a track and playing field. Forty percent of its 1,600 students are chronic truants. Only a fourth who enter ever graduate. It has some good teachers, but others who the principal admits "don't belong in education." He is not allowed to fire them, so they continue teaching.

Kozol sat in on a 12th-grade English class. The students were learning to pronounce a randomly selected list of words that are difficult, for example, "fastidious," "auspicious," and "egregious." He asked a boy who was having difficulty pronouncing "egregious" if he knew what the word meant. The boy had no idea. The teacher never asked the students to define the words or to use them in a sentence, only to try to pronounce them.

Thus, the ritual goes on. The students in the school struggle not only with fear, threats, and drugs, but with teachers who take them through pointless exercises. There seems to be little learning, just survival.

The Payoff: A Great Training Robbery?

One of the American expectations about education is that it will pay off in terms of upward mobility (Grubb and Lazerson 2004). Historically, the correlation between education and income has been strong, but in the early 1970s a *contradiction developed between education and the economy.* Educational attainment outstripped the capacity of the economy to absorb the graduates into jobs commensurate with their training. Even when the unemployment rate is very low, many workers cannot find employment that utilizes the skills and training they have (Livingston 1998). *The disparity between educational attainment and the skill demands of the workplace means that some workers are underemployed.*

Another part of the problem is the assumption that greater educational attainment guarantees career advancement. In fact, employers do not routinely reward educational attainment; rather, they reward it only when they believe it will contribute to the employee's productivity (Spilerman and Lunde 1991).

However, keep in mind the strong correlation between education, occupation, and income (Table 11.3). Also keep in mind that those in occupations that require higher levels of education will gain more, and more rapid, increases in income than those in lower-level occupations. This means that over a lifetime, those with a bachelor's degree will have about double, and those with a doctorate will have about triple, the total income of those with only a high school diploma. In short, it is still true that education is associated with upward social mobility (Pfeffer and Hertel 2015).

ritualized deprivation
a school atmosphere in which the motions of teaching and learning continue, while the students are more concerned about surviving than learning

You also should keep in mind that the diminished payoff refers strictly to employment and income. Unfortunately, Americans have focused so strongly on the economic payoff that many consider their college education useless if it does not yield a desirable, well-paying job. Only in this sense can we speak of an "oversupply" of college graduates. We could argue that all or at least the majority of Americans would profit by some college because higher education can enable the individual to think more deeply, explore more widely, and enjoy a greater range of experiences; but as long as education is valued only for its economic payoff, any failure to yield that payoff will depress the quality of life of those involved.

American Education: A Tide of Mediocrity?

Periodically, there are severe criticisms of American education. Over the past few decades, a series of reports criticized education at every level, and all the reports suggested that the educational system is marred by mediocrity. This mediocrity means a *contradiction between the American value of and expectations about education,* on the one hand, and *the functioning of the educational system,* on the other hand.

The criticisms cover every aspect of education. For example, a 1997 report by *Education Week*—a journal that regularly evaluates and grades various aspects of American education—graded the 50 states on achievement (fourth-grade reading scores and eighth-grade math scores), standards and assessments (what students are expected to know and how they are evaluated), quality of teaching, school climate, and resources (*Education Week* 1997). Among the grades were: B for standards and assessments; C for quality of teaching; C+ for school climate; and C− for spending sufficient funds. No grade was given for achievement, but the report called the evidence "discouraging." The report noted, for example, that Iowa led the nation on a national math test, but 69 percent of its eighth-grade students fell below the proficient level.

A report on the condition of education in 1999 looked at the quality of teaching (*Education Week* 2000). The report concluded that millions of American students have teachers who lack the minimum requirements set by the states to teach in public schools. Various loopholes and waivers are used (probably under the pressure of obtaining sufficient numbers of teachers) to put teachers into classes for which they are inadequately prepared. A follow-up study (*Education Week* 2003) described efforts to recruit and retain competent teachers, but also pointed out that the efforts were not directed toward the problem in high-poverty, high-minority, or low-achieving schools. Students in those schools were still far more likely than others to have incompetent, inexperienced, or inadequately trained teachers.

By 2016, the situation had not improved significantly. *Education Week*'s annual evaluation of education gave grades from B+ to D to the various states, and gave the overall system a C (Education Week Research Center 2016).

One area of concern to critics is achievement in math and science. Data from the Digest of Educational Statistics showed that among 50 educational systems around the world, the United States ranked 10th in average math scores and 7th in average science scores of fourth grade students (Digest of Educational Statistics website). At the eighth grade level, among 42 international systems, U.S. students ranked 9th in average math scores and 10th in average science scores. In part, the American scores reflect the fact that a larger proportion of American students who take the tests come from a disadvantaged social class background (Robelen 2013). But even correcting for that difference, American students are behind those of a number of nations in math and science.

A substantial number of Americans see yet another deficiency in the schools—the lack of a religious perspective. A Gallup poll reported that 61 percent of Americans support allowing daily prayer at school (Rifkin 2014b). In response to the perception that the schools are spiritually deficient, there is a growing number of Christian schools. The Digest of Education Statistics website reports over 5 million students enrolled in elementary and secondary religious schools. A little over 2 million of these were in Catholic schools. What is the quality of education in these schools?

The nation, of course, has always had religiously based schools. *The parochial school tradition has been strong among Roman Catholics and Lutherans.* Some people believe that such private schools offer a better education. However, a study that compared achievement in grades four and eight between public and private schools found little difference in reading and math scores (Braun, Jenkins, and Grigg 2006). Eighth-grade students in private schools did score higher on reading. Otherwise, when taking into account characteristics of the students (such as gender and race/ethnicity), the differences in reading and math scores were insignificant.

Such scores are not, of course, the only measure of effectiveness. We need to raise the question of how religious schools, and conservative Christian schools in particular, teach the various disciplines, including the sciences. Since the schools teach pupils to think and behave in accord with particular religious doctrines (Wagner 1990), religious ideology enters into every facet of the curriculum. Such schools may teach creationism instead of (not along with) evolution and Darwinism.

In short, religious ideology is pervasive throughout the educational process, and for that reason critics charge that the Christian schools not only fail to address the issue of mediocrity, but also increase the amount of miseducation in the nation. They say the schools promote racial segregation (some began in the 1960s in the face of court-required integration), use outmoded methods of teaching (discipline is often strict), and give students distorted views of human knowledge (everything is filtered through religious doctrine).

To some extent, one's evaluation of the conservative Christian schools depends on one's values. It seems clear, however, that the schools do violate some of the basic principles of education, including free inquiry. The emphasis is not on raising questions and learning to think creatively, but on accepting answers and learning to think narrowly in accord with a particular religious doctrine.

Contributing Factors

Why are there inequalities in educational opportunities and attainment? Why hasn't education yielded the expected payoff for some people? As you will see, part of the answer does lie in the structure and processes of the educational system. A greater part of the answer lies in nonschool factors. The problems of education are only partially a problem of the schools.

Social Structural Factors

Social Class, Family Background, and Educational Inequality. In our discussion of poverty, we pointed out that *families in the lower strata* of society are different in a number of respects from those in the middle and upper strata. Certain characteristics of the lower-strata family tend to depress **cognitive development.** Consider, for example, such a simple fact as the number of books in the family home. There are likely to be far fewer in lower-strata homes, and a study of families in 42 nations discovered a strong relationship between the number of books in a home and the children's academic performance (Evans, Kelley, and Sikora 2014).

> **cognitive development** growth in the ability to perform increasingly complex intellectual activities, particularly abstract relationships

Children who come from lower-strata families, then are more likely to enter school with an intellectual disadvantage that tends to depress their performance and academic achievement (Petrill, Pike, Price, and Plomin 2004; Noble, Farah, and McCandliss 2006). Their school work is further hurt by the fact that they come to school with a background that includes poor health care, parents who are minimally involved with them, few preschool opportunities, unsafe neighborhoods, and some degree of malnourishment (Alvarado 2016; Burdick-Will 2016). As a result, they may be *unprepared to learn* when they come to kindergarten. They lack the vocabulary and sentence structure skills necessary for success in school. Even if they attend equally good schools and receive equal treatment from teachers, children from such a disadvantaged background cannot have educational opportunity equal to that of others.

Thus, *the position of the family in the stratification system has a close relationship to the educational attainment of the children.* Parental educational attainment and parental influence and expectations for children strongly affect children's educational aspirations and achievement (Räty 2006; Keller and Tillman 2008; Augustine 2014). In turn, the parental behavior is related to social class; the higher the social class, the more likely parents are to have high attainment, hold high expectations, and positively influence the child to attain a high degree of education. The greater the parental income and the fewer children in the family (both of which tend to characterize the higher strata), the more willing the parents are to pay for higher education (Steelman and Powell 1991).

Socioeconomic background affects a child at every point in his or her academic career. Students from low-income backgrounds are less likely to graduate from high school, less likely to go to college even if they do graduate (in part because they are more likely to marry at an early age), less likely to complete college if they enroll, and less likely to go to a prestigious school regardless of their ability or aspirations (Davies and Guppy 1997; Roscigno, Tomaskovic-Devey, and Crowley 2006). Children from high-income families, in contrast, can gain admission to elite colleges and universities even though academically they do not do as well as some from low-income families who are rejected (Golden 2006). Among other things, the well-to-do gain admission through donations to the school, and because they are the children of alumni or celebrities or politicians.

Socioeconomic status is also one of the prime factors in unequal educational **achievement** at all levels of education, from elementary school through college (Betts and Morell 1999; Hossler, Schmit, and Vesper 1999; Lee and Burkham 2002). We are not saying that students from a lower socioeconomic background can never succeed. Some poor youths who have had strong parenting and sufficient opportunities have risen above their circumstances and carved out a better life for themselves (Furstenberg et al. 1999).

Yet the poor will always have a greater struggle. The struggle begins at the "starting gate" of kindergarten. The children enter a lower-quality school with less well-prepared and less-experienced teachers, less positive attitudes on the part of those teachers, and little in the home or neighborhood to nurture whatever motivation and aspirations they have (Lee and Burkham 2002). For such children, the school may be an alien setting. They and their teachers from the middle strata of society may be totally unprepared to deal with each other. The teachers may react to the children's range of experiences with astonishment and perplexity. The children may not even be able to distinguish the various colors when they enter school, and they may appear to have little grasp of abstract qualities such as shape and length. They may be unfamiliar with such cultural phenomena as Frosty the Snowman and *Green Eggs and Ham,* which teachers may take for granted are known to all students. Most teachers' training does not prepare them for these kinds of students.

As these children progress through school, their academic problems become more rather than less serious. Learning depends increasingly on the ability to deal with abstractions. What is a society? What is a nation? What happened in the past? Children from a deprived background may even have difficulty with such fundamental distinctions as bigger and smaller, higher and lower, round and square.

Such children could be looked upon as a challenge, but teachers may be more likely to react to them with despair or contempt. Indeed, one of the reasons that children from poor families do not achieve in school is that their *teachers may not like them.* Poor children have, if anything, a greater need for acceptance and warmth but are less likely to receive it than are middle-class children.

In addition to socioeconomic level, a number of other family background factors are important in achievement. One is the extent to which parents are involved in the process of education. The more that parents are involved in their children's education, the higher the children's level of achievement tends to be (Jimerson, Egeland, Stroufe, and Carlson 2000). "Involvement" includes such things as attending school functions, meeting with teachers, seeing that their children have adequate meals and rest so they are prepared to learn, and expecting their children to be diligent students with aspirations for high educational attainment.

For example, a study of more than 2,000 sixth-grade students in 11 middle schools in North Carolina found that the students' perceptions of their parents' expectations about school behavior was reflected in the students' math and reading scores three years later (Bowen, Hopson, Rose, and Glennie 2012). Specifically, the students were asked how upset their parents would be about such matters as a D or F on a report card; cutting classes; being late with homework; getting suspended; engaging in a fight or classroom misbehavior; and arguing with their teachers. Students who believed their parents would be very upset with such behavior tended to get higher reading and math scores than those who perceived a lesser amount of upset from parents.

achievement
as distinguished from educational "attainment," the level the student has reached as measured by scores on various verbal and nonverbal tests

Finally, *living with both biological parents* is associated with higher levels of achievement than living with a stepparent or a single parent (Cavanagh, Schiller, and Riegle-Crumb 2006; Jeynes 2006). Children who live with a single parent or a stepparent during adolescence receive less encouragement and less help with schoolwork and achieve less than children living with both birth parents (Hanson 1999; Xu 2008). Among those in single-parent households, grades are lower than for those living with both parents, and grades are lowered even more by father absence than by mother absence (Mulkey, Crain, and Harrington 1992; DeBell 2008).

The Organization of Education. The gap between children from the lower socioeconomic strata and those from the middle and upper strata tends to increase with the level of school. This finding suggests that the schools *may somehow contribute to educational inequality—children who are disadvantaged by their social background when they enter school become even more disadvantaged as they progress through school.*

At least two factors contribute to the disadvantage. One is the quality of teaching. Many instructors are teaching subjects for which they are not trained (*Education Week* 2000). Where there is a shortage of teachers or a need for quick action, teachers may be hired with emergency or substandard certification. Such teachers are more likely to be in schools serving the lower strata. Even if the teachers are competent, other problems may thwart the learning process. A national study of K–12 teachers reported that two out of five were disheartened and disappointed with their jobs (Yarrow 2009). More than half of them were teaching in low-income schools, and they were frustrated with the administration, classroom disorder, and an overemphasis on testing. Another national survey reported that teacher job satisfaction dropped 23 percent between 2008 and 2012 (Resmovits 2013). In 2012, only 39 percent of teachers reported being very satisfied with their jobs. Still another problem is the middle-class background of so many teachers, making it difficult for them to understand, relate to, and help children from disadvantaged backgrounds (Halvorsen, Lee, and Andrade 2009). They may believe that children from low-income families are uninterested in learning when, in fact, there is evidence that even in the face of negative teacher attitudes and low expectations for them, many if not most disadvantaged children in elementary school want teachers who care about them and help them learn (Lewis and Kim 2008).

A second factor is the *evaluation and labeling of ability.* This grouping by ability, or *tracking,* of students has been common in public schools, beginning in the first grade. It is a controversial practice. Proponents point out that tracking is necessary for dealing with the boredom and lack of adequate progress among bright students when course work proceeds too slowly in order to accommodate slower students. Tracking allows students to proceed at their own pace. "Detracking," they argue, not only hurts the brighter students but also can harm the self-confidence of low achievers when they are forced to compete with the bright students (Loveless 1999).

Opponents of tracking argue that high achievers do not benefit that much, and low achievers are stigmatized and deprived of opportunities for success (Romo 1999; Oakes 2005). Tracking also hurts minorities, a disproportionate number of whom are placed in the low-achieving tracks. Once in a low-achievement track, it is difficult for students to escape it. Among other things, they take the kind of classes that ensure that they will remain in the same track, and their teachers tend to label them as low achievers and to expect them to perform accordingly.

Both the advocates and the critics of tracking make valid claims. Putting a student in a high track, or in an advanced or honors class, has a positive impact on that student's performance (Karlson 2015). Unfortunately, the opposite is also true—putting a student in a low track can depress educational aspirations. Consequently, the question should not be one of tracking or not tracking. Rather, the real question is how to organize schools and classrooms in light of the fact that children learn differently and at different rates. The important point to keep in mind is that inequality of achievement during the first years of school does not mean that the low achievers lack the capacity to attain high educational levels. Low achievement, as we have shown, tends to follow from a particular kind of social and family background. We also have shown, in previous chapters, the effects of labeling. If the low achiever is labeled as one with a low capacity, both the reaction of the teacher and the self-expectations of the child are negatively affected. In effect, labeling becomes a form of the *fallacy of personal attack,* blaming the students rather than the system for their lack of achievement.

The effects of labeling on children's achievement are dramatized in an elementary school experiment that showed that teachers' expectations about the intellectual abilities of their students were reflected in the students' IQ scores (Rosenthal and Jacobson 1968). A student whom the teacher expected to do poorly tended to get lower scores, and a student whom the teacher expected to do well got higher scores. The performance of people, whether children or adults, can be significantly influenced by the expectations of others and can reflect those expectations more than any innate abilities.

Thus, labels can become *self-fulfilling prophecies,* retarding or stifling the achievement of able students. Is there any evidence that the labels are inaccurate? Can't teachers detect and encourage children who are bright but who perform poorly on achievement tests? No doubt some teachers can and do. However, children from lower socioeconomic backgrounds may have a capacity that is masked by their initial disadvantage and by their subsequent experiences and performance in the school. The evidence is scattered and, in some cases, indirect. We will furnish some evidence when we discuss the effects of desegregation in the last section of this chapter.

The Politics of School Financing.   We have noted the large differences in the money allocated per child among various school districts. Although money per se is not the answer to all the problems of education, the funding per child makes a difference in the quality of teachers hired and the physical conditions of the school. These factors, in turn, raise attendance rates and student achievement (Condron and Roscigno 2003; Pinkerton 2003).

Both the amount of funding and the equitable distribution of the funding among districts are important. As far as the amount is concerned, some resist any increase on various grounds (such as the notion that teachers are already overpaid). It is instructive to note that between 1979 and 2013, funding for prisons and jails increased 324 percent, while funding for pre-K-12 education increased by 107 percent (Wheaton 2016). Every state in the union increased correction funding far more than education funding.

As far as distribution is concerned, one way to deal with the inequality is to *equalize the money available* to various districts. Such equalization cannot occur because public education is financed largely by the property tax. As a result, pupils in wealthier districts with more expensive homes have more money available for their education. Moreover, when states make cuts in funding for education, the poor districts may suffer a disproportionate loss. In 2011–2012, Pennsylvania cut more than a billion dollars from the state's budget for schools (Litvinov 2015). And the cuts were four times larger ($532 per student) in the 50 poorest districts than in the wealthiest districts ($113 per student).

The result of such practices is that throughout the nation children in more advantaged areas are likely to have clean, well-staffed schools with good facilities and up-to-date books and technological aids, whereas children in more disadvantaged areas are likely to attend class in dilapidated school buildings staffed by less than fully qualified teachers and supplied with outdated textbooks and few, if any, technological aids. The differences in resources are illustrated by the availability of computers. A child today whose early education is devoid of computer use lacks an important resource and has a serious deficiency in his or her education. Yet schools in poorer areas are likely to have far fewer computers available to the students than are schools in more advantaged districts. The point is that *even if the student in a lower socioeconomic area overcomes the handicaps of a disadvantaged family, he or she faces obstacles to educational attainment in the school itself.*

In principle, many Americans support the idea of equalizing the funds available to school districts—but how would that be done? Some have argued that it can be accomplished only by eliminating the property tax as the basis for funding. They point out that no child should be denied a quality education simply because his or her parents happen to live in a poorer area.

Such arguments finally have begun to effect change in a number of states. In the late 1980s and early 1990s, a number of state courts ruled that existing methods of financing schools were unconstitutional. Montana, Kentucky, Michigan, and Texas were the first states to construct alternative financing systems. In Kentucky, the court decision led to a comprehensive school-reform effort that included channeling more money into poorer schools and restructuring the state education department so that its primary task is to assist local school districts rather than issue directives to them. An assessment of the situation a few years later concluded that more financial resources were available to districts but that patterns of resource allocation had not changed (Adams 1997). Clearly, the process of gaining equity in funding

will be a slow and difficult one. And simply getting more equitable funding may or may not be sufficient to improve the quality of education. In 2004, Maryland began providing more resources for school districts that had larger shares of disadvantaged students (Chung 2015). The funding was more equitable, but so far it has not made a difference in student performance.

Poorer school districts cannot provide the resources enjoyed by wealthier districts.

Source: National Archives and Records Administration

There is another aspect to the politics of financing—the extent to which political leaders give high priority to education. School districts get revenues from local, state, and federal sources. Of all revenues received by the public schools, states provide the most, and the federal government the least. When support at one of the levels declines for whatever reason, education is likely to suffer.

The Economics of Education.   The politics of school financing interact closely with the economics of education. As with so many important areas of American life, *education is affected by the ups and downs of the economy,* and political and economic factors are intertwined as they affect the educational process. Educational decisions may be made on the basis of economic considerations. For example, a Texas survey found that 68 percent of the elementary teachers had students who were promoted to the next grade even though they had failed the class, and 61 percent of middle school and junior high teachers had students who moved on without repeating a course they had failed (Shanker 1996). In part, the practice was justified by the social stigma attached to being held back, but another part of the justification was economic: It costs a good deal to fail students and add a year or more to their schooling.

Economic factors can become even more powerful in times of recessions, when political leaders look with jaundiced eyes at the costs of education and resist any changes that involve more money. Inflation also can be troublesome. Inflation may rapidly outstrip the fiscal resources of schools and result in problems regarding salaries and the purchase of supplies.

As we pointed out in the previous section, *economic problems are also political problems.* Not everyone and not everything suffers equally in times of economic difficulty—political leaders make decisions that bear upon the resources available. The governor of a state must decide whether education, mental health, highway maintenance, or a number of other areas will receive priority consideration when budgets must be cut.

Obviously, the problems of education cannot be separated from other problems in a time of national economic difficulty. When resources are scarce, the decision to more fully fund one area—such as education—is a decision not to adequately fund another area—such as health programs. A faltering economy, therefore, inevitably means an intensification of at least some social problems.

Social Psychological Factors

Attitudes.   We have already noted some *attitudes that contribute to educational problems.* Parental attitudes are particularly important, because parental expectations are one of the factors in a child's educational achievement (Jacobs and Harvey 2005). Minority parents generally are very positive in their attitudes. A Pew Research Center survey reported that 86 percent of Hispanic parents and 79 percent of black parents, compared to only 67 percent of white parents, consider a college degree to be very important (Stepler 2016). Such attitudes may help account for the increasing educational attainment of those groups.

Social class differences, on the other hand, remain problematic. Even if children from lower-class families aspire to high levels of attainment, they may not be able to realize their aspirations (Hanson 1994). And, unfortunately, they have living examples in their network of friends and acquaintances that prove the futility of high aspirations. Only 5 percent of Americans aged 25 to 34 whose parents had less than a high-school education have a college degree (Porter 2015).

The attitudes of students toward schoolwork also affect their achievement. Three researchers who did an extensive study of 20,000 high school students and hundreds of parents in California and Wisconsin reported *widespread student apathy toward learning* (Steinberg, Brown, and Dornbusch 1997). About 40 percent of the students indicated that they were simply "going through the motions" in school and had little interest in what happens in the classroom. These attitudes are reinforced by a teen culture that disparages academic success. Large numbers of students strive to be a part of some social clique, such as the "populars" or "jocks" or "partyers," each of which tends to scorn high academic achievement. Nearly 20 percent of students admitted that they don't try as hard as they could because they are concerned about what their friends would think if they got good grades.

The attitudes of teachers also contribute to educational problems. The attitudes of teachers are rooted in the conditions under which they must work. Low salaries, inadequate resources, and other poor working conditions may lead teachers to change professions. Others remain in teaching, but they develop jaded attitudes about their work and education generally; and sinking teacher morale usually is accompanied by lower student achievement (Black 2001).

Values. Many educational problems, such as segregation and school financing, are difficult to resolve because they involve a conflict of values. In essence, Americans have tried to address educational issues in the context of a *clash between the value on individualism and the value on egalitarianism* (Hochschild and Scovronick 2003). "Individualism" means that Americans expect their schools to be the means to individual advancement, and this belief translates into such attitudes as "I should be able to choose the kind of school—public or private—that my children attend without being penalized by the tax system" and "I should be able to veto any policies or practices that I deem harmful to my child's education." "Egalitarianism," on the other hand, means that Americans expect their schools to help equalize opportunities for all students, and this belief translates into such attitudes as "Poor schools should get as much money as rich schools" and "No child should be denied entrance into any school because of the child's color or social standing."

Resolving the issues that are caught up in the matrix of clashing values will never be easy. Rather, such clashing values illustrate why efforts to deal with social problems are typically accompanied by intergroup conflict.

A Concluding Note on Inequality in Education

We have suggested that if the various factors we identified are all taken into account, then children of different racial, ethnic, and socioeconomic backgrounds should be able to show about the same levels of achievement. Earlier research by the Office of Education supports this conclusion. Figure 11.3 shows the achievement scores for sixth graders when various factors in their backgrounds are taken into account. If we look only at the scores of unequalized whites, Asian Americans, American Indians, African Americans, Mexicans, and Puerto Ricans in the United States, we see considerable differences in their achievement. The Puerto Rican students had the lowest average score and the white students the highest, about 50 percent higher.

Suppose we control for socioeconomic background. What will the differences be for children of different racial and ethnic groups but the same socioeconomic level? The answer is in the second set of points in Figure 11.3, labeled "Equalized for socioeconomic status." The spread narrows considerably, showing that a good part of the

FIGURE 11.3

Racial and Ethnic Group Achievement Means of Sixth-Grade Pupils, Adjusted for Social Background Conditions.

Source: Adapted from Mayeske, G. W. et al., A Study of Achievement of Our Nation's Schools (Washington, DC: Government Printing Office, 1973), p. 137.

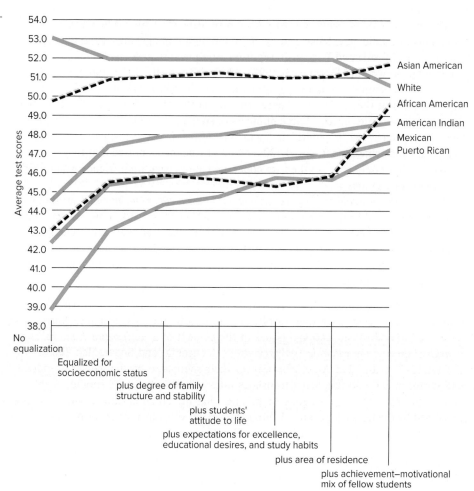

differences that were observed among the groups was really rooted in different socio-economic backgrounds. As we continue to move to the right in the figure, each set of points takes progressively more background factors into account, and the differences in scores diminish correspondingly. The third set of points adjusts the scores to equalize for socioeconomic status *plus* degree of family structure and stability. The next set of points adds the students' attitude to life (as described in this chapter). The fifth set of points takes in the students' expectations for excellence, educational desires, and study habits. The sixth adds to those factors the area of residence. The last set includes the achievement-motivational mix of fellow students, which means if the students were to come from the same socioeconomic background, have the same family experiences, and exhibit the same social psychological processes, the differences between the scores of the various racial and ethnic groups would be about 1 percent.

Thus, unequal educational achievement in the United States is a sociocultural matter, not a racial-genetic one (Farkas 2004; Sampson, Sharkey, and Raudenbush 2008; Cheadle 2008). As efforts have been made to help disadvantaged minorities, the gap between their scores and those of white, non-Hispanic children has narrowed. For example, comparing math scale scores on standardized tests for 9-year-olds, in 1972 whites scored on average 35 points higher than African Americans and 23 points higher than

Hispanics; by 2015, the gaps were 24 and 18, respectively (Digest of Educational Statistics website). For 13-year-olds, the gaps between white–minority scores were 46 points for African Americans and 35 points for Hispanics in 1972, but down to 32 points for African Americans and 22 points for Hispanics in 2015. Such results underscore both the social nature of the problem and the importance of social action for addressing it.

Public Policy and Private Action

Our analysis suggests a variety of ways to attack the various problems of education. Clearly, it must be a multifaceted attack. Undoubtedly, parental involvement is one of the crucial factors in children's educational attainment. Among other parental factors, having high expectations for the children's education, creating an educationally rich environment in the home, and helping with homework will make a difference in how much children achieve academically (Okagaki and Frensch 1998).

Another obvious need is *reform of school financing.* The inequities between school districts must be addressed. Action taken by the state of Vermont suggests one possible way. In 1997, the Vermont legislature passed the Equal Education Opportunity Act, which drastically increased the proportion of state money designated for public education and altered the taxation system (Proulx and Jimerson 1998). A statewide property tax now provides a general state support grant to school districts.

In addition, a variety of other efforts and proposals exist that hold promise: vouchers, quality enhancement measures, efforts to reduce racial and ethnic inequality, and compensatory and other innovative programs. Some are quite controversial.

Use of Vouchers and Tax Credits

A good deal of controversy exists over the *use of school vouchers and tax credit programs* (Medler 2002). A **voucher system** enables parents to use tax funds to send their children to private as well as public schools. Tax credit programs offer state tax credits for contributions to organizations that award scholarships to children from families with limited resources. In some states, tax credit scholarship programs send more low-income students to private schools than do voucher programs (Figlio and Hart 2011). Any program that enables children to go to private rather than public schools raises issues, including the capacity of private schools to absorb all those who want to attend them (Zehr 2011). But the most controversial issue is whether being able to choose the school that one's child attends will result in higher-quality education not only for that child but for all children.

voucher system
a system that allows parents to use tax money to send their children to a school, private or public, of their choice

Thus, in terms of voucher systems, proponents argue that the system will bring about higher academic achievement, increased parental involvement in children's education, better use of tax monies, and pressure on the public schools to improve the quality of education. Opponents argue that vouchers will mainly subsidize parents who can already afford to send their children to private schools, violate the separation of church and state (because most private schools are religious), and ultimately destroy the public school system. But states that have tried to implement a voucher system have encountered problems of administration and of courts that have declared it unconstitutional. Furthermore, studies of the educational outcomes in states that have set up voucher systems have not found clear, positive effects on students' academic achievement, nor improved performance by the public schools, and have reported mixed results for students overall (Anrig 2008; Usher and Kober 2011). The potential for voucher or tax credit programs to improve education substantially is not supported by the evidence we have thus far.

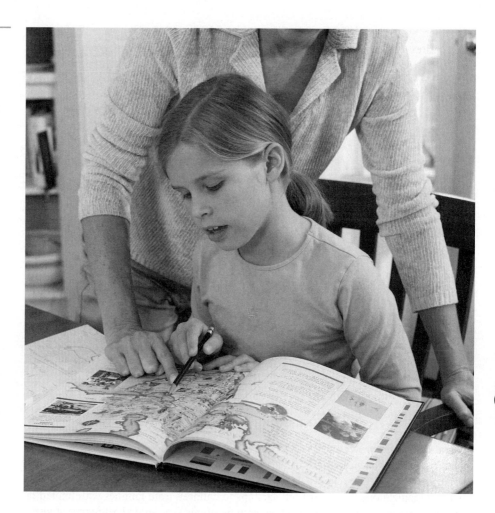

Some parents have sought to maximize their children's education by homeschooling them.

©Big Cheese Photo/PunchStock

Quality Enhancement Measures

A variety of suggestions exist for enhancing the quality of education. Lengthening the number of days in the school year could help poor children, who lose ground in the summer when they lack the intellectual demands of the classroom (Entwisle and Alexander 1992). Establishing standards-based education, which includes testing and accountability for meeting minimum standards in subject areas, has yielded gains in student achievement in a number of states (Editorial Projects in Education Research Center 2006). Improving the school atmosphere by ensuring student safety and making schools drug- and gun-free could facilitate learning (Ingersoll and LeBoeuf 1997). Providing all children with the opportunity to attend preschool can enhance both their emotional and intellectual well-being, and can be particularly helpful to those from disadvantaged backgrounds (Scott and Delgado 2005; Arnold et al. 2006). Finally, placing all children in small classes can improve performance, because from kindergarten on those in small classes do better academically than those in large classes (Finn, Gerber, Achilles, and Boyd-Zaharias 2001; Konstantopoulos 2009).

Some analysts believe that all such efforts are only "tinkering" with the system, and that *what is needed is a complete restructuring of the schools and even the community itself*

(Emery 2006). There are varied ideas on what restructuring would involve, but most advocates agree that it requires decentralization (whether in the form of school-site management, a choice plan, or some variation on privatization).

Restructuring through decentralization gives parents and local schools greater control over the educational process. The idea is that schools will function better when they reflect the realities of the community in which they are embedded rather than conforming to some uniform set of policies and procedures. This worked well in an experiment with elementary schools in Chicago (Bryk et al. 2010). The schools were given local control with greater discretionary funding, resulting in improved student learning as reflected in reading and math scores. Decentralization also worked well for "community schools" in Oregon (Samuels 2012). As an example, one school that served low-income students utilized various nonprofit and county agencies to provide such things as homework assistance, academic enrichment, free breakfast and dinner for students, a food pantry, health screenings, dental care, and information on how to make use of various social services.

A different way to enhance quality is to start from scratch with a school—namely, establish a **charter school.** *Charter schools are nonreligious public schools that are approved by the local school district but are free of many regulations and policies that apply to other public schools.* Charter schools can be converted public schools or entirely new facilities. They are operated by educators, parents, and/or community members. In essence, the district and the school negotiate a contract or "charter" that covers a specified number of years and that spells out the school's mission, program, goals, type of student body, and method of accountability.

The first state charter-school law was passed in Minnesota in 1991 (National Study of Charter Schools 2000). By 2014 there were 6,500 charter schools, representing 5.1 percent of all schools (National Center for Education Statistics 2016). Most of the schools are relatively small, enrolling between one and two hundred students.

Some charter schools are successful, as measured by improved scores on standardized tests, whereas others do no better or even worse than the traditional public schools (Bowman 2000; American Federation of Teachers 2002; Shah 2011). An analysis of 2003 test scores found that students at charter schools had lower scores in both reading and mathematics than did students in regular public schools (Robelen 2006). And a California study concluded that the state's charter schools neither closed the achievement gap for minorities nor had any positive effect on the performance of other public schools (Schutz 2007). Finally, a survey of the research on the effect of charter schools concluded that charter schools overall are producing higher gains in math achievement than are traditional schools, but reading achievement is about the same as in traditional schools (Betts and Tang 2016).

One quality-enhancement measure that seemed promising was the "No Child Left Behind Act" of 2002, which required all schools receiving federal money to meet certain standards and to educate low-income students to improve student test scores every year (Moran 2002). Students in a school in which scores did not improve for two consecutive years could receive free transportation to a school that did meet the standards. Unfortunately, the federal government failed to adequately fund the program.

In addition to inadequate funding, the program was severely criticized on various other grounds and was finally revised into the Every Student Succeeds Act (ESSA), which was passed in 2015 (Welch 2016). ESSA is too new as of this writing to know how it will affect the quality of education. It tries to address the needs of all students—the gifted and the challenged, the poor and the well-to-do, and those from the various

charter school
a nonreligious public school approved by the local school district but free of many regulations and policies that apply to other public schools

racial/ethnic groups. It requires state educational systems to: be clear about what they expect students to learn; help all students meet or exceed the standards; regularly assess whether schools are teaching the standards; and make information about the schools (including assessment results) publicly available (Chenoweth 2016).

Reducing Racial and Ethnic Inequality

Racial and ethnic inequalities in education must be reduced in order to create a society of equal opportunity. One crucial step is desegregation of schools. In the 1954 case *Brown v. Board of Education of Topeka, Kansas,* the U.S. Supreme Court ruled that segregated education imposed by governments was not legal. This ruling reversed a 19th-century decision that argued that "separate but equal" facilities may be provided by the states. The 1954 decision, which declared that separate facilities were inherently unequal and thus unconstitutional, furnished momentum for the movement to desegregate the nation's public schools.

Does desegregation help disadvantaged students? There is evidence that achievement levels of black children are raised by attending desegregated schools (Mickelson 2001; Mickelson 2015). Moreover, those who attend desegregated schools are more likely to secure jobs in desegregated workplaces (Braddock, Dawkins, and Trent 1994).

Unfortunately, after some small and slow gains in the 1960s and 1970s, the desegregation process went into reverse. *Segregated housing patterns, white flight to the suburbs, resistance to busing children from their neighborhoods in order to integrate schools, and the establishment of private schools all helped subvert the desegregation efforts* (Saporito and Sohoni 2006). From 2000 through 2014, the proportion of K-12 schools with high percentages of minority students grew from 9 to 16 percent (U.S. Government Accountability Office 2016). These schools, compared to others, offered fewer math, science, and college prep courses. With the increase in segregation, the gap between white and minority test scores increased again (Berends and Penaloza 2010).

Some efforts have been made to bring white children to black schools rather than the reverse, but those efforts were stopped by the courts. Court decisions also dismantled affirmative action programs, decreasing the enrollment of minorities in higher education. The result is a pattern of resegregation over the past two decades (Cohen 2004). On average, white students attend schools that are 78 percent white, black students attend schools that are only 30 percent white, and Hispanic students attend schools that are only 28 percent white (Orfield and Lee 2005).

State and local governments need to devise plans to reverse the resegregation process. In the area of higher education, for example, the state of Texas initiated a plan that brought more minorities to colleges and universities (Yardley 2002). In essence, the plan guarantees slots in state universities to the top 10 percent of graduates in each high school without regard to SAT scores or grade-point averages. A student in the top 10 percent of a disadvantaged school may have a lower SAT score and/or grade-point average than a student who ranks at the 75th percentile of another high school. However, the student from the disadvantaged school will still be guaranteed a place in a public college or university.

Compensatory and Other Innovative Programs

compensatory programs programs designed to give intensive help to disadvantaged pupils and increase their academic skills

Compensatory programs are aimed at *disadvantaged pupils.* They focus on skills such as reading and speech and attempt to offer an intensive program of help so that the disadvantaged pupil can approach the level of others in the school. Some compensatory programs are remedial. They attempt, among other benefits, to reduce the number of students per teacher, to provide the student with extra help (including after-school hours), and to use special teaching materials. The Head Start program stimulates learning of verbal and social skills among preschool disadvantaged children (Zhai, Brooks-Gunn, and Waldfogel 2011).

Another program aimed at disadvantaged children is called CIS, or Communities in Schools (Cantelon and LeBoeuf 1997). The program uses resources from the local, state, and national levels to provide at-risk youths with four items basic to the child's well-being and academic performance:

A personal one-on-one relationship with a caring adult.

A safe place to learn and grow.

A marketable skill.

An opportunity to give something back to peers and the community.

Evaluations of the CIS program find that a majority of students with high absenteeism and low grades prior to their participation have lower dropout rates and improved attendance, grades, and graduation rates (ICF International 2010).

The Deschooling Movement

The *deschooling movement* aims at providing students with a situation in which they will maximize their learning. The movement emphasizes the necessity of a break with the existing educational structure and the creation of new schools where the children can be free to learn.

The most common manifestation of deschooling today is *homeschooling*. People decide for various reasons to teach their children at home rather than send them to the schools (Stevens 2001). Initially, most homeschooling was done by conservative Christians who felt that their children were not given sufficient moral guidance in the schools (Hawkins 1996). As a 5-year-old girl explained to the author, she would not go to public school because "they don't teach about God there." The second wave of homeschoolers, however, includes more people who are either dissatisfied with the quality of teaching in the schools or with the potential for emotional or physical harm to their children in the schools (Cloud and Morse 2001).

According to the Digest of Educational Statistics website, there were 1.8 million children, aged 5 through 17, being homeschooled in 2012. The number is 3.4 percent of all children in that age bracket. How well are these children educated? There is not a great deal of evidence, but what we have suggests that homeschooled children do well on the whole. They score well on standardized tests of achievement, and they appear to be as socially and emotionally adjusted as children in public or private schools (Collom 2005; Ray 2013).

Undoubtedly, some children receive an inadequate education through homeschooling; but, on average, those who are homeschooled appear to be benefiting. Parents who opt for it, however, need to recognize the extent to which they are committing themselves to their children's lives. Parenting is a consuming task as it is; when homeschooling is added, parenting becomes more than a full-time job.

Follow-Up. In what ways were your parents involved in your elementary and high school education? Which of these ways were helpful? Were any harmful? What will you do differently to enhance your own children's education?

chapter 11 review

Summary

Education is a problem when it fails to fulfill its expected functions: creating good and effective citizens, providing the possibility for upward mobility, and facilitating individual development. For these purposes education is highly valued by Americans. Lack of education is frequently associated with failure to achieve one's ambitions in life.

America has become an increasingly educated society. Whether this education has yielded the expected payoffs is not always clear. The greater degree of happiness reported by the highly educated may reflect a tendency toward greater fulfillment of individual potential. Education increases political participation and understanding. There is a strong relationship between education and income, but those most likely to benefit from education are already in the middle and upper strata.

Education is a problem because there are inequalities, and the expected payoff does not always occur. Educational attainment is unequally distributed among various groups. Educational funding is unequally distributed among states and school districts within states. The cost of education prices many Americans out of the better colleges and universities. The learning atmosphere of some schools (critics would say nearly all schools) is rigid and joyless and precludes individual schedules of learning; sometimes students suffer an atmosphere of fear and threat or ritualized deprivation.

A series of reports have charged that American education is in danger of being overwhelmed by mediocrity. The mediocrity affects education at every level and applies to student performance, faculty performance, administrative functioning, and academic programs. Many Americans believe that a particular kind of deficiency afflicts the schools—a non- or anti-Christian bias—and they have opted to send their children to Christian schools.

Among the social structural factors that contribute to the problems of education, social class and family background are particularly important. The organization of education also makes a difference in students' achievement and attainment. Particularly important are the distribution of funds, the assignment of teachers, the socioeconomic composition of the student body, and the evaluation and labeling of ability. The inequitable distribution of funds is a political issue that must be resolved by political action. Finally, the quality of education varies with the economy. Both recessions and inflation drain the resources available to schools.

Attitudes of parents, students, and teachers are important social psychological factors that contribute to the problems of education. The attitudes of parents and students toward school and intellectual activities, and toward the educational potential of the students are strongly related to achievement. Teacher attitudes can inhibit or facilitate student achievement.

Our analysis implies that when the various contributing factors are taken into account, children of different social backgrounds have the same capacity for achievement. The Office of Education survey supports this position. Given the same socioeconomic background, family background, attitudes, and the like, there is only about a 1 percent difference in the achievement scores of the various racial and ethnic groups.

Key Terms

Achievement	Compensatory Programs
Atmosphere	Culture
Attainment	Ritualized Deprivation
Charter School	Voucher System
Cognitive Development	

Study Questions

1. What are three functions of education?
2. Discuss the levels of educational attainment in America and the varied payoffs from that attainment.
3. How much inequality of opportunity is there in America, and how does it affect attainment?
4. What kinds of school atmosphere contribute to the problems of education?
5. Is education a "great training robbery"? Why or why not?
6. Explain the meaning of "a tide of mediocrity."
7. In what ways is family background important for education?
8. What aspects of the organization of education contribute to the education problem?
9. What are the political and economic factors involved in educational problems?
10. Discuss attitudes and values involved in education problems.
11. What are ways to resolve education problems?

Internet Resources/Exercises

1. Explore some of the ideas in this chapter on the following sites:

http://nces.ed.gov Site of the National Center for Education Statistics, a government effort to collect and analyze data about education in the United States and other nations.

http://www.eric.ed.gov Access to ERIC, the comprehensive collection of research and ideas about all facets of education.

http://www.edweek.org Site of *Education Week* on the Web, a weekly journal with news, evaluation, and analyses of various aspects of education.

2. Select an educational level that interests you, from preschool through graduate school, and research it on the Internet. Find five things that are fitting or useful at that level and five things that are troublesome or problematic. Comparing your two lists, how would you evaluate the educational level you have researched?

3. The text points out that American elementary and high school students do not score as high on tests of math and science as do students in many other nations. Find information on math and/or science education in Japan or one of the European nations. What are they doing that can help explain the higher scores? What recommendations would you make for American schools in order to close the gap in the scores?

For Further Reading

Banks, James A., ed. *Diversity and Citizenship Education: Global Perspectives*. New York: Jossey-Bass, 2007. Case studies and examples of successful programs and practices from 12 nations in which there are schools that have addressed the problems of education of a diverse population for living and working together as citizens of one nation.

Graham, Patricia Albjerg. *Schooling America: How the Public Schools Meet the Nation's Changing Needs*. New York: Oxford University Press, 2006. An examination of the way in which public education, from kindergarten through college, changed in the United States over the 20th century in order to meet changing expectations; includes accounts of both failure and success in the process.

Kozol, Jonathan. *Savage Inequalities: Children in America's Schools*. New York: Crown Publishers, 1992. A comparison of schools in some poor areas in the nation with others in well-to-do districts, dramatizing the way in which students who come from a disadvantaged background continue to struggle in a deprived educational setting.

Kupchik, Aaron. *Homeroom Security: School Discipline in an Age of Fear*. New York: New York University Press, 2010. Shows how the challenge of maintaining security in the schools has led to the use of various surveillance methods and punitive measures to control behavior, which, in turn, has negative consequences for the atmosphere of the school, for student behavior, and for the way students will function in society when they become adults.

Lois, Jennifer. *Home Is Where the School Is: The Logic of Home-schooling and the Emotional Labor of Mothering*. New York: New York University Press, 2013. Analysis of the mother's role in home-schooling, and the emotional and temporal demands with which the mothers must cope.

Oakes, Jeannie and Marisa Saunders, eds. *Beyond Tracking: Multiple Pathways to College, Career, and Civic Participation*. Cambridge, MA: Harvard Education Press, 2008. An argument for the radical reform of secondary education in the United States by providing multiple pathways that recognize the diversity of the population and our responsibility to adequately address the needs of the poor and minorities.

Sexton, Robert. *Mobilizing Citizens for Better Schools*. New York: Teachers College Press, 2004. An in-depth analysis of the changes in Kentucky schools after the state's Supreme Court declared the school system unconstitutional. Includes lessons learned that can be used in other states.

Smith, Mary Lee. *Political Spectacle and the Fate of American Schools*. New York: Routledge/Falmer, 2003. Case studies that illustrate the ways in which educational policies and practices have been shaped by political considerations as much as by reasoning, research, and discussion.

chapter 11 review

CHAPTER

Family Problems

©Pixland / PunchStock

"I Survived the Abuse"

Patricia is a self-confident, middle-aged, professional woman. Yet she could have turned out quite differently because she grew up in a home in which she suffered ongoing verbal abuse from her mother. To most people, Patricia's mother was a genteel southern lady. Patricia knew a different side of her mother:

My mother was beautiful. She looked like a movie star. I grew up with her and my grandparents after she divorced my father when I was an infant. And I remember the verbal abuse vividly. She never shouted. She never sneered. In her pleasant, soft voice, she simply said things that were gut-wrenching to me. Like the time she took me to buy some shoes, and told the clerk in a giggly voice that he should just bring a shoe box because he probably didn't have shoes that were big enough to fit my feet. Do you know what that does to an adolescent girl?

When I was a teenager, my mother and I were about the same size. She would buy dresses for herself, then try them on me. I didn't say, "Let me try them on," because I never volunteered nor wanted to do it. I knew what her reaction would be. It was always the same—she would look at me in her dress, sigh, and shake her head as though it were hopeless. It was her way of letting me know how ugly I was compared to her. She also let me know this once when we were looking at a picture of us together when I was younger. She said it was too bad I was smiling and showing my big, ugly teeth.

One thing that saved me was my schoolwork. I was always good in school. I loved to read. I studied hard. My mother acknowledged my intelligence, but said it was a good thing I was smart because I would never be pretty. So I grew up thinking I was the world's best example of the ugly duckling. Except I expected to stay ugly. And in my mother's book, it was looks, not brains, that were a woman's most important asset. But at least I knew I was not a total loss.

The other thing that saved me was my husband. It took me a long time to accept his compliments as sincere. I still remember the first time he told me I was beautiful. I thought he was just trying to con me into something. Eventually, I began to see myself in a different light. And now when I look at pictures of myself as a child, my first thought is: "That's no ugly duckling. You were a lovely child. How could your mother have done that to you?"

A lot of my childhood pictures show a girl who is unsmiling and unhappy. That's the way I was. In some ways, I feel that I lost a good deal of my childhood. But I feel good about myself now. Most of the time, anyway. I still have occasional doubts. But I have a man in my life who keeps telling me I am beautiful. And I have a career that is going well. I only wish I had a mother whom I felt really loved me. But I guess you can't have everything.

Introduction

Is the family a dying institution? Some observers say yes, arguing that the family is doomed. Others go further, maintaining that the family *should* be doomed because it no longer functions in a useful way. The family, according to this argument, contributes more misery than benefit because it is ill adapted to modern social life.

Still others argue that the family is essential and ineradicable. What is needed, they argue, is help for troubled families, not radical changes or the abolition of family life. In this chapter we consider the argument that the family is doomed. Then, taking the position that it is not doomed, we look at the family as a problem. In previous chapters we asked how the family contributed to other problems. Now we examine the nature and extent of family problems. We also describe how those problems affect the quality of life. Finally, we identify the structural and social psychological factors that contribute to family problems and inquire into ways to resolve the problems.

family
a group united by marriage, blood, and/or adoption in order to satisfy intimacy needs and/ or to bear and socialize children

nuclear family
husband, wife, and children, if any

Is the Family Doomed?

A **family** is a group united by marriage, blood, and/or adoption in order to satisfy intimacy needs and/or bear and socialize children. The family, thus, is a crucial factor in both individual well-being and social life. Nevertheless, if prophecies could kill, the family would have died long ago. The popular and the professional literature continues to forecast the *death of the family,* at least the death of the **nuclear family** consisting of a married couple, and their children, if any. The evidence used to support the notion that the nuclear family is dying typically includes factors such as **divorce rates,** birthrates, runaway children, people who abandon their spouses and/or children, and **cohabitation** (in 2015, the U.S. Census Bureau reported 8.4 million cohabiting couples). The high rate of family disruption, combined with various other changes going on, makes family life appear to be in peril to some observers. At the same time, the fact that alternative forms of family life, including cohabitation, have proliferated suggests that *intimate relationships* must and will continue. Some people are merely finding alternate ways to express their intimacy needs.

divorce rate
typically, the number of divorces per 1,000 marriages

cohabitation
living together without getting married

Alternative Forms of the Family

Many alternatives to the traditional nuclear family have been explored by Americans (Lauer and Lauer 1983). One alternative is group marriage, which has been tried in some communes. In this arrangement, all males and females have access to each other for sex and companionship. Other proposed alternatives include trial marriages with renewable contracts for specified periods of time, and "open marriages" in which each partner has the right to sexual and companionate relationships with someone other than the spouse.

Another arrangement, which has increased enormously since the 1970s, is cohabitation. As we just noted, 8.4 million unmarried couples are living together. The *reasons for cohabiting* are varied: as an alternative to marriage, as a preparation for marriage and family living, or as a way to deal with loneliness (Popenoe and Whitehead 1999). Those who view cohabitation as a preparation for marriage may be cautious because of the high divorce rate or because they have been previously married and divorced. What happens if a cohabiting woman gets pregnant? If the pregnancy was unintended, or the couple disagreed on the desirability of a child, they may end their relationship (Guzzo and Hayford 2014). In other cases, the couple may opt to marry. And still others may decide to continue to cohabit and raise the child. As a result, a substantial number of cohabiting couples have children in the home. Census Bureau data show that in 2015 3.1 million of the cohabiting couples had children under 18 in the home.

Although some couples cohabit as a test for whether to marry or not, a number of studies have found that, contrary to expectations, cohabitation does not enhance the chances for a more stable or more satisfying marriage (Heaton 2002). In fact, compared to those who married, cohabitors have higher rates of violence and abuse, lower rates of relationship happiness, higher rates of depression, less commitment to the relationship, a greater chance of breaking up even if the relationship is relatively satisfying, and lower levels of emotional and behavioral well-being of children living with them (Skinner, Bahr, Crane, and Call 2002; Stanley, Whitton, and Markham 2004; Shackelford and Mouzos 2005; Brown 2004). In addition, those who cohabit before marriage report less satisfying relationships after marriage and are more likely to have an extramarital affair (Thomson and Colella 1992; Treas and Giesen 2000).

However, a more recent study of those married since 1996 found no difference in divorce rates between those who had and those who had not cohabited before marriage (Manning and Cohen 2012). It is possible, as the researchers speculate, that as cohabitation has become widespread (about two-thirds of newlyweds cohabit prior to their first marriage), there is no longer a relationship between cohabiting and marital stability. And another study (Kuperberg 2014) concluded that a substantial part of the reason for higher rates of breakup was the young age at which a couple begins to cohabit (as we shall note below, the younger the age at marriage, the more likely there will be a divorce). We must wait on any firm conclusions until we have additional research. Moreover, even if stability is no longer an issue, there are still the questions of the quality of the relationship and of the well-being of children.

To return to the initial question: Is the family doomed? Clearly, the American family is changing in important ways. Yet, as we discuss later in this chapter, most Americans retain some traditional values about the family. Both in the United States and in Western European countries, cohabitation rates have increased dramatically, but the vast majority of people still marry at some point (Billari and Liefbroer 2016). Indeed, even those who divorce are likely to remarry. It's been estimated that about 20 percent of Americans marry two or more times during their lives (Siordia 2014a). We take the position that, despite the critics and the changes, the family remains strong and crucial to the well-being of people. At the same time, it is clear that fewer people opt for the traditional form of the family in which there is a breadwinner husband, a housewife, and children. Precisely how, then, is the American family changing?

The Changing American Family

Among the important changes in American families in recent times are *increases* in (1) age at first marriage, (2) proportion of young adults remaining single, (3) divorced adults, (4) adults living alone, (5) unmarried couples, (6) families maintained by adults with no spouse present, (7) children living with only one parent, (8) wives and mothers working, and (9) dual-career families (in which both husband and wife pursue careers, with minimal, if any, interruption of the wife's career for childbearing). At the same time, there has been a *decrease* in the number of children couples have. One effect of the various changes has been to dramatically alter the typical composition of American households over the past decades. As Figure 12.1 shows, the proportion of households with married couples has declined significantly, while the proportions of other kinds of families and of nonfamily households (such as people living alone, friends living together, and same-sex couples) have increased significantly. Consider some specific data (U.S. Census Bureau website):

- From 1970 to 2015, the proportion of people who were never married increased from 18.9 percent to 34.8 percent of adult males and from 13.7 percent to 28.4 percent of adult females.

FIGURE 12.1

Composition of American Households, 1970 and 2015.

Source: "Households, Families, Subfamilies, and Married Couples" (U.S. Census Bureau 2007 and U.S. Census Bureau website).

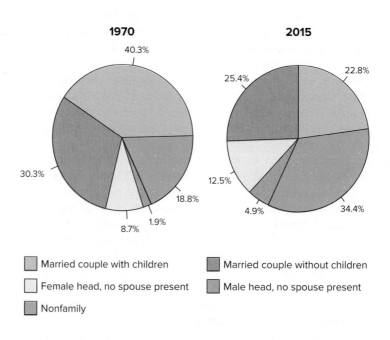

- From 1970 to 2015, the proportion of Americans who were married dropped from 71.1 percent to 50.3 percent.
- From 1970 to 2014, the birthrate per 1,000 women decreased from 87.9 to 62.9; the average size of families is smaller than it has ever been.
- Since 1970, the proportion of all births that occur out of wedlock has more than tripled: 4 of 10 births are to unmarried women.
- The divorce rate rose dramatically after 1965; it declined from a high of 5.2 per 1,000 people in 1980 to 3.2 per 1,000 people in 2014, but is still far higher than the rate of 2.5 per 1,000 people in 1965.
- Among women, 64.8 percent of those with children under age 6 and 70.4 percent of those with children between ages 6 and 17 are in the labor force.

Although such changes may be interpreted as threatening to the traditional nuclear family, you also must consider other evidence. First, many of the statistics that we just cited reflect a reversal rather than a continuation of a trend. For example, the divorce rate has tended to decrease since 1980. Second, most Americans marry at some time in their lives. Only a minority of those who are single are so by choice. Third, the bulk of Americans rate a good marriage and family life as extremely important to them (White-head and Popenoe 2001). Fourth, most Americans are satisfied with their own family life. A 2004 Harris poll of adults reported that 98 percent felt good about their relations with their family and 66 percent felt good about their marriage (Polling Report 2012).

Indeed, married people generally are happier and healthier than the nonmarried. More than 130 studies have reported that both married men and married women are happier and less stressed (as measured by such factors as alcoholism rates, suicide rates, and physical and emotional health) than are the unmarried (Lauer and Lauer 2018).

Clearly, then, Americans still value the traditional nuclear family. Just as clearly, there is an increasing tendency to prefer nontraditional roles, particularly an egalitarian arrangement (in which husband and wife both work and share responsibility for home and children).

Functions of the Family

Whether Americans opt for a traditional or a nontraditional family arrangement, they face certain problems. The problems reflect not only the expectations and values about family life but also the *functions of the family.* Those functions, like other aspects of the family, have changed over time. At one time the family was primarily responsible for matters such as education, religious training, recreation, and providing the necessities of life. Those functions have been largely assumed by other institutions. However, the family continues to be an important factor in *regulating sexual behavior, reproduction, and rearing children.*

Another important function of the family is to provide a *primary group* for individuals. The **primary group,** consisting of the people with whom you have intimate, face-to-face interaction on a recurring basis, is of enormous importance. In a classic study, a children's home created "artificial" families after it was noted that the children were having developmental problems (Stanton and Schwartz 1961). Previously, all the children had been cared for by all the attendants, who carefully avoided too much involvement with any one child so as not to appear to have favorites. However, when this arrangement was abandoned and the home was divided into family groups of about four children and a "mother," the results were "astonishing."

primary group
the people with whom one has intimate, face-to-face interaction on a recurring basis, such as parents, spouse, children, and close friends

The need for individual attachment for the feelings which had been lying dormant came out in a rush. In the course of the one week all six families were completely and firmly established . . . the children began to develop in leaps and bounds. The most gratifying effect was that several children who had seemed hopeless as far as the training for cleanliness was concerned suddenly started to use the pot regularly and effectively. (Stanton and Schwartz 1961:236)

Primary groups are important for adults as well as children. You have a personal status in primary groups. You gain an understanding of the kind of person you are and learn the kind of norms by which you are to live. Primary groups, in other words, are crucial to your well-being as a functioning human. For most Americans, the family is a primary group *par excellence.*

When problems arise in the family, they arise in the group that is important to your well-being, that provides you with important emotional support, and that is of central importance to your life satisfaction and happiness (Lauer and Lauer 2009). The family is not always a solution; it is also a problem, as we will explain later in this chapter. The point is that the family is a central aspect of your well-being; thus, when family life becomes problematic, you are threatened at the very foundation of the quality of your life.

The Extent of Family Problems

The family becomes a problem when it does not fulfill its purposes, particularly its purpose as a primary group. The American ideal is that the family should be *structurally complete.* Children should have both a father and a mother in the home. The family should be a *supportive group,* providing emotional support for each member. "Ideal" in this context does not mean "perfect" (and therefore unrealistic). Rather, the ideal is defined as realistic and expected. When the actual situation falls short of the ideal, the *quality of life* is diminished. Expectations are thwarted, the most important primary group is disrupted, and family members experience stress.

For many people today, the expectations are thwarted more than once. In your lifetime, you might live in five, six, or more different families, each of which could fail in some way to fulfill your needs for structure and support. If your parents were divorced when you were young, and you lived with one parent for a while, then a stepparent for some years, you would have three different family experiences before adulthood. As an adult, if you cohabited, married, divorced, and remarried one or more times your family experiences would rise to six or more.

Consider next the extent of structural and supportive problems. *Structural problems* relate to the breaking up of husband and wife and/or parent and child. *Supportive problems* involve the lack of emotional support.

Disrupted and Reconstituted Families

Divorce rates, one measure of structural problems, have fluctuated in the United States, but the *general trend of number of divorces per 1,000 population from 1860 to 1980 was upward.* A surge occurred after World War II and again after 1965, so that by the mid-1970s the United States had the highest divorce rate in the Western world.

However, as Table 12.1 shows, the rates began to decline after 1980. The 2014 figure of 3.2 was lower than any since the late 1960s. Even so, millions of Americans continue to be affected by divorce. Children as well as adults are affected. According to the U.S. Census Bureau, in 1970, 85 percent of children lived with both parents; by 2015, as seen in Table 12.2, only 69.2 percent lived with both parents.

Divorces	1960	1965	1970	1975	1980	1985	1990	1995	2000	2011
Total (1,000)	393	479	708	1,026	1,189	1,190	1,182	1,169	944	877
Rate per 1,000 population	2.2	2.5	3.5	4.8	5.2	5.0	4.7	4.4	4.1	3.6
Rate per 1,000 married women, 15 years and over	9.2	10.6	14.9	20.3	22.6	21.7	20.9	19.8	18.8	20.9
Percent divorced, 18 years and over:										
Male	2.0	2.5	2.5	3.7	5.2	7.6	7.2	8.0	8.8	9.0
Female	2.9	3.3	3.9	5.3	7.1	10.1	9.3	10.3	10.8	11.0

TABLE 12.1
Divorces, 1960 to 2011

SOURCE: U.S. Census Bureau 2009 and National Marriage Project 2012.

During the 1960s and 1970s, divorce was the major cause of single-parent families. Since then, however, delayed marriage and out-of-wedlock births are responsible for more mother-child families than is divorce (Bianchi 1995). As we noted earlier, 4 out of 10 children are born to unmarried mothers. A parent also may be lost through death, separation, and abandonment. The combination of all these factors has meant a dramatic increase in the number of single-parent families since 1970. Table 12.2 shows the proportion of children living in various arrangements. The proportion living with both parents has decreased for all groups but is particularly low for African Americans and, to a lesser degree, Hispanics. We show later in this chapter some of the consequences of living in a single-parent family.

About three-fourths of people who divorce eventually remarry. If the remarriage includes children from a previous marriage of one or both partners, a **stepfamily** is formed. We do not know exactly how many stepfamilies there are in the nation, because the government does not gather that information. However, by the late 1990s estimates were that more than one of five families with two parents in the home were stepfamilies, involving between 7 and 8 million children under the age of 18 (Lauer and Lauer 1999). At some point in the future, according to demographers, the stepfamily could become the main type of American family.

stepfamily
a family formed by marriage that includes one or more children from a previous marriage

Strain and conflict with or about stepchildren is common in such families (Stoll, Arriaut, Fromme, and Felker-Thayer 2005). As a result, the marital relationship is stressed, and the divorce rate among second marriages is even higher than that among first

	Both Parents	Mother Only	Father Only	Neither Parent
All races	69.2	23.1	3.7	3.9
Non-Hispanic White	77.5	15.5	4.1	2.9
African American	38.7	49.4	4.2	7.7
Asian	85.7	10.6	2.0	1.7
Hispanic	67.0	25.9	3.0	4.1

Percent living with—

TABLE 12.2
Living Arrangements of Children Under 18 Years, by Race and Hispanic Origin

SOURCE: U.S. Census Bureau website.

Severe violence occurs in some families.

©Ingram Publishing

marriages. White and Booth (1985) found that the percentage who divorced over a four-year period was slightly higher for re-married (8 percent) than for first-married (6 percent) couples if one of the partners in the remarriage was previously unmarried. The chances of divorce went up (to 10 percent) if both partners were previously married (with no children) and went up considerably (to 17 percent) if both were previously married and one or both brought stepchildren into the marriage.

Family Violence

Information on the amount of *violence in families* shows that it is not a rare phenomenon. Violence, of course, represents an alarming example of the failure of support-iveness. It is found in every kind of family and can reach extreme levels. For example, family fights are one of the most frequent reasons for police calls. Almost a fourth of murders are against a family member, and aggravated assaults by family members comprise about 10 percent of all aggravated assaults (Durose et al. 2005). *The likelihood of being a victim of family violence varies by a number of demographic characteristics.* Nearly three-fourths of the victims are fe-males. Whites and African Americans have higher rates of victimization than do Hispanics and those of other races. And those in the 35- to 54-year-old age group have higher rates than do other age groups.

Studies of *spouse abuse* and *child abuse* were rare until the 1960s. Since then, numer-ous studies, including some national surveys, have been undertaken. The first national survey of family violence occurred in 1975, and the second took place in 1985 (Gelles and Straus 1988). The researchers found that the overall rates declined during this 10-year period, perhaps because of such factors as an increase in the average age at marriage (violence is more common among younger couples), a more pros-perous economy (financial stress increases violence), and less willingness to tolerate violence in the family (shelters for battered women rose from 4 to more than 1,000).

Still, there is a *high level of violence in intimate relationships generally and in families in particular.* A national survey found that 620,850 women and 191,540 men were victims of intimate partner violence in 2011 (Catalano 2013). Between 2003 and 2012, domestic vio-lence accounted for 21 percent of all violent crime (Morgan and Truman 2014). Children who witness violence between parents are also victims, for it is a traumatizing experience

MARITAL QUALITY AND WELL-BEING OF CHILDREN

The family is a central element for individual well-being. In nations throughout the world, the more stable and harmonious family life, the higher the life satisfaction of family members. Four researchers surveyed 2,625 male and 4,118 female college students from 39 nations on six continents (Gohm, Oishi, Darlington, and Diener 1998). They categorized the nations by whether they have a collectivist or individualist culture. In individualist cultures (such as the United States, Germany, Australia, Japan, and Spain), people perceive their lives as depending largely on their own actions. They see society as a collection of individuals rather than as a highly integrated group. They believe that the course of their individual lives has no necessary relationship to the course of social life. Thus, they see possibilities for individual success and happiness even if the society as a whole is deteriorating.

In collectivist cultures (such as China, Brazil, India, and Tanzania), people perceive their lives as inextricably bound up with what happens in groups and in the nation as a whole. They cannot conceive of individual success that is independent of the groups to which they belong. Individual happiness, for them, is not as important as group well-being.

The researchers thought that the well-being of the college students in their survey might vary not only by the kind of family in which they grew up but also by the kind of culture in which they lived. Some of their results are shown in Figure 12.2.

Clearly, there were both cultural and state-of-marriage differences in student well-being. Generally, students in individualist cultures scored higher on a life satisfaction test than did students in collectivist cultures. But regardless of the type of culture, students from intact homes (with two natural parents or a remarriage) in which there was low interparental conflict tended to score higher than those from homes with a single parent or with high interparental conflict. The highest scores of all were those in homes headed by a married couple with low conflict.

In sum, for people everywhere, the family is important for individual well-being. If the family is functioning well, the well-being of each member is maximized. If the family is functioning poorly, all members are adversely affected.

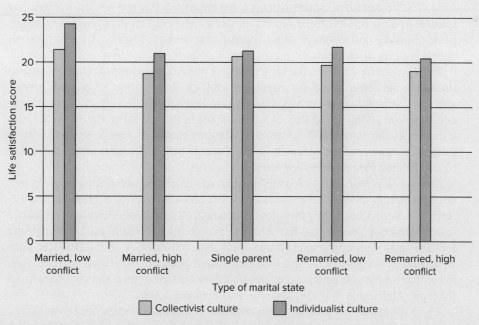

FIGURE 12.2 Marital Status and Child Well-Being in 39 Nations.
SOURCE: Gohm et al. 1998.

to see one's parents in a violent confrontation. A national survey found that more than 1 in 9 (11 percent) children saw some kind of family violence in the year prior to the survey, including 1 in 15 (6.6 percent) who were exposed to violence between their parents (Hamby, Finkelhor, Turner, and Ormrod 2011). The researchers concluded that about a fourth of children are exposed to at least one form of family violence during their lifetime.

Of course, family violence is not an exclusively American problem. In Canada, for example, a survey of women in Quebec found that 6.1 percent had suffered physical violence and 6.8 percent had experienced sexual violence perpetrated by their male partners (Rinfret-Raynor et al. 2004). A Korean national study found that 29.5 percent of women had experienced violence from their husbands, resulting in serious mental health problems among the victims (Kim, Park, and Emery 2009). In the Middle East, wife abuse is not only pervasive but widely accepted (Boy and Kulczycki 2008); nearly 90 percent of ever-married women accept at least one reason that justifies wife beating.

Family violence is, then, a worldwide problem. A United Nations report on violence against children around the world found that "physical violence against children in the home is widespread in all regions" (Pinheiro 2006:52). For instance, 38.5 percent of students aged 11 to 18 in the Kurdistan Province of Iran reported being victimized by violence at home that caused physical injuries, and in Korea "kicking, biting, choking and beating by parents are alarmingly common, with a high risk of physical injury—and for a small proportion, disability—as a result" (Pinheiro 2006:52).

Sexual victimization in the family also occurs throughout the world. According to a United Nations (2015) report, one in three women in the world experience physical/sexual violence at some point in their lives, and two out of every three victims of intimate partner/family related homicides are women. Depending on the nation, from 7 to 36 percent of females and 3 to 29 percent of males report being victimized during their childhood. The perpetrators include parents, grandparents, aunts and uncles, siblings, and cousins. And the results for the victims include alcohol or other drug abuse, depression, panic disorders, posttraumatic stress disorder, and attempted suicide. Clearly, for some people in all societies "intimate" means threat and harm as much as it means fulfillment.

Family violence may take the form of spouse abuse, child abuse, or abuse of parents (including the abuse of elderly parents by adult children). Abuse of parents is probably less common than the others. Still, in a survey of 469 university students, Browne and Hamilton (1998) found that 14.5 percent acknowledged using violent tactics with a mother and/or father, and 3.8 percent admitted that they were severely violent. A substantial number of the violent students, it should be noted, also reported being maltreated by their parents in earlier years.

Spouse abuse involves wives beating husbands as well as husbands beating wives. In fact, more incidences of husband abuse than of wife abuse are reported. However, the violence of women against their husbands is frequently a case of self-defense or, at least, a response to prior abuse by the husband. The probability of being injured is also greater for the woman than for the man (Bookwala, Sobin, and Zdaniuk 2005). However, interviews with 90 women and 10 men who filed assault charges against an intimate partner found that the adverse emotional effects on the victimized women and men were about the same (McFarlane, Willson, Malecha, and Lemmey 2000).

Child abuse, another form of family violence, is more likely when one of the natural parents is missing. Children in a single-parent home, or those with a stepparent, are much more likely to be victims of abuse (Snyder and Sickmund 1999). Estimates of the amount of child abuse in the nation vary widely. One problem in getting reliable figures is that mandatory reporting laws were not passed in the states until the 1960s. Government data call the abuse "maltreatment" and show that there are hundreds of thousands of substantiated cases each year. The rate of maltreatment is slightly higher for girls than for boys (Federal Interagency Forum on Child and Family Statistics 2015). By age, the highest rate occurs for children 1 year or younger. By race/ethnicity, the highest rate occurs for black children, followed by American Indians, whites, Hispanics, and Asian Americans (whose rate was quite low). A small number of children die from maltreatment, most of them 4 years old or younger.

These numbers are undoubtedly conservative. How many cases go unreported? One way to obtain more accurate information is to ask the victims themselves. For child abuse, this means asking them when they are older whether they have ever been abused. Some still will not remember or will have repressed the memory, so even the results from victimization research will underestimate the amount. A national study of adolescent health asked American youth, among other things, about their experiences of maltreatment (Hussey, Chang, and Kotch 2006). Being left home alone as a child (a possible case of neglect) was named by 41.5 percent. It was the most common kind of maltreatment. In addition, 28.4 percent reported experiencing physical assault, 11.8 percent said they had been physically neglected, and 4.5 percent reported sexual abuse. Clearly, maltreatment is more prevalent than the number of cases officially substantiated by state agencies.

Incest, which we discussed briefly in chapter 4, is likely to be an extremely traumatizing experience for a child (Sheinberg and Fraenkel 2001). The effects tend to be long lasting. A study of 17 incest survivors who became mothers found that the women had poorer relations with their own mothers and lower psychological adjustment than a comparable set of mothers who had not been sexually victimized (Fitzgerald et al. 2005). In addition, although the incest survivors appeared to be mothering as well as the others, they did not see themselves as being very effective mothers.

Girls are more likely than boys to be victims (Russell 1986), but we do not know how many victims there are in the United States. A survey of 1,672 male and female adolescents in Korea, however, reported that 3.7 percent had been victimized (Kim and Kim 2005). The families of the victims had high levels of other kinds of problems, such as mental illness, criminal behavior, and alcoholism. The victims, compared to adolescents not so victimized, had higher rates of emotional and social problems.

Besides the observable and measurable supportive problems in family violence, a considerable amount of supportive failure cannot be measured—intense conflict or alienation within families. In addition is the problem of neglect, which affects over a half million children each year. Neglectful parents abuse their children psychologically through lack of feeling and caring. They are emotionally distant from their children. They may be struggling to retain their own sanity or totally absorbed in their own pleasures. For whatever reason, they provide none of the support that parents typically give. Neglected children may never learn to trust adults. They may suffer various physical ailments because of inadequate nutrition, clothing, and sleep. They are likely to have retarded intellectual development and be insecure, withdrawn, and unable to express emotions.

Family Problems and the Quality of Life

The effect of family problems on the *quality of life* is sometimes obvious and sometimes not. As with all social problems, the effects impact more than just those immediately involved in the problem. For example, consider the economic costs associated with divorce. Research by David Schramm and his associates (Schramm et al. 2013) assessed the economic costs of divorce in terms of various kinds of state help available to those who find themselves financially strapped after a divorce. They found that Texas spent some $3.2 billion on the consequences of divorce each year, representing about 12 percent of the total budget in 2008. In other words, even Texas families that remain intact are helping, through their taxes, to sustain those involved in family disruption. Thus, there is an economic cost of divorce for all citizens.

Moreover, other and often even more severe problems occur. Physical violence against a person by someone in his or her primary group produces emotional trauma as well as physical pain. *Alienation from those in one's primary group is emotionally traumatic.*

Less obvious is the effect of a broken home on children and their parents. Parenting is demanding and stressful even when there are two parents in the home. Not surprisingly, both single parents and their children face a broad range of stresses, including feelings of responsibility, task, and emotional overload on the part of the parent; and emotional, interpersonal, and school problems on the part of the children (Dunifon and Kowaleski-Jones 2002; Bramlett and Blumberg 2007).

Supportive problems mean, by definition, that family members endure some degree of stress. But the consequences of structural problems are less clear. Consequently, much of this section examines structural problems. You will discover that supportive problems also have some not-so-obvious consequences for the quality of life.

Most of the effects that we discuss later in this section involve a *contradiction between interaction patterns and American values.* Supportive problems mean that interaction patterns within the family contradict the value of emotional and physical health. Structural problems result in interaction patterns that contradict the value of social adjustment. Because children who grow up in broken homes lack experience with either a mother or a father, they often have various problems of adjustment and have to cope with such problems as illness, poverty, and deviant behavior more than others do.

The structural characteristics peculiar to the stepfamily, on the other hand, can lead to different types of problems (Lauer and Lauer 1999). Each member of a stepfamily may have lost an important primary relationship. Children may be angry about the loss and focus that anger on the stepparent. The noncustodial parent may interfere with the stepfamily's adjustment. The children and the stepparent also might compete for the custodial parent's attention and affection; the stepparent, after all, is entering an ongoing relationship as an "extra" member. The stepparent and children may even have difficulty because the role of stepparent is still somewhat ambiguous. Is the stepparent to be like a parent, a friend, or a teacher? Finally, the children may try to work their natural parents one against the other to gain various ends. Thus, both in single-parent and stepfamilies, interaction patterns may diminish the quality of life.

Physical and Emotional Difficulties

Physical and mental illnesses are rooted, in part, in family arrangements. Children growing up with both biological parents receive more social, emotional, and material support than children in any other kind of family. In contrast, broken homes (structural failure) and homes in which parents frequently quarrel (supportive failure) have been linked to stress in children, often resulting in physical or emotional illness (Vandervalk et al. 2004).

Divorce. For adults, adjustment to divorce has *striking similarities to the bereavement process.* Contrary to a popular notion that divorce may be an avenue to freedom and therefore an exhilarating experience (at least once the legal procedure has been

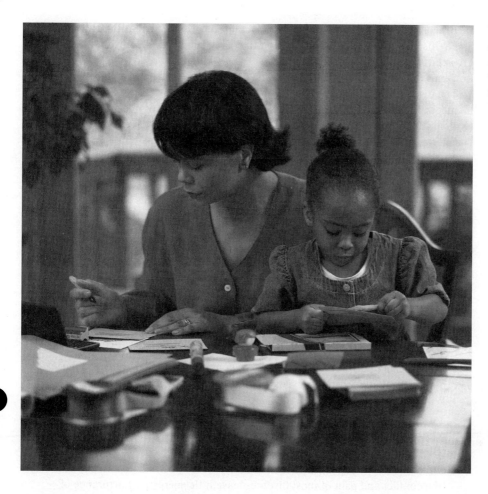

completed), divorced people typically face a painful process of adjustment not unlike that which occurs after a death in the family. In both death and divorce, a *primary relationship has been disrupted,* and the disruption of a primary relationship is always traumatic. The consequences include a sense of loss and bewilderment, various kinds of deprivation (including financial and emotional support), and susceptibility to emotional problems such as depression (Hilton and Kopera-Frye 2006). The disruption, incidentally, is not only with an intimate partner but also with one's children. Thus, nonresident fathers have much higher emotional distress than either single mothers or married parents (Yuan 2016).

Particularly in the first months, divorce is more likely to bring emotional and physical disturbances than a sense of freedom. In fact, various studies report that divorced people have higher rates of suicide, accidents, death from various causes, physical and mental ailments, and alcoholism (Yip and Thorburn 2004; Lorenz, Wickrama, Conger, and Elder 2006; Stack and Scourfield 2015). Of course, these problems are not always the result of a divorce. In some cases, they existed prior to, and helped bring about, the divorce, but they also can result from the divorce (Wade and Prevalin 2004). Those who divorce are highly likely to experience at least some of these negative outcomes in the short run and, for some people, the outcomes may persist for years or decades.

Because of such outcomes, divorce is a major health problem in the nation (Chatav and Whisman 2007). It is not surprising that divorced people, compared to those not divorced, report themselves as less happy and as having more insecurity in their relationships (Schneller and Arditti 2004).

The distress of divorce involves not just the couple but also their friends and family members. The parents of those who divorce may experience problems with depression (Kalmijn and De Graaf 2012). Adult children whose parents divorce later in life report a change to a negative relationship with one or both of their parents during the initial stages of the divorce (Greenwood 2012). But young children and adolescents suffer the most. The negative consequences for young children and adolescents whose families are disrupted by divorce include the following problems:

- Children in divorced families are more likely to be anxious, depressed, and withdrawn than those in intact families, and their mental health problems tend to persist when they become adults (Amato 2001; Kim 2011).
- Children in divorced families are more likely to have behavior problems, sleep disorders, fear of abandonment, and aggressive tendencies (Amato and Cheadle 2008; Guinart and Grau 2014).
- Adolescents from divorced homes are more likely to engage in delinquent behavior, use alcohol and illegal drugs, and pursue a life style that tends to result in various health problems (Holmes, Jones-Sanpei, and Day 2009; Thuen et al. 2015).
- Adolescents in divorced families worry about having enough money to meet both present and future needs and aspirations (Koerner, Korn, Dennison, and Witthoft 2011).
- Young women from divorced families rate themselves as less attractive and report more dissatisfaction with their bodies than do women from intact families (Billingham and Abrahams 1998).
- Children in divorced families tend to receive less maternal warmth and empathy (the conflict and pain of most divorces leave little energy for nurturance of children), which contributes to various emotional and behavior problems (Kline, Johnston, and Tschann 1991).
- Children in divorced families rate themselves lower in social competence, and, in fact, are likely to have poorer interpersonal skills (Peretti and di Vitorrio 1993; Kim 2011).
- Children and adolescents in divorced families tend to have lower levels of educational attainment and achievement and more problems in school than children from intact families (Center for Marriage and Families 2005; Sun and Li 2011; Soria and Linder 2014).
- Children in divorced families have lower levels of emotional well-being when they become adults (Amato and Sobolewski 2001; Wauterickx, Gouwy, and Bracke 2006).
- Children in divorced families have more negative attitudes about marriage, less optimism about the possibility of a long-lasting, healthy marriage, and, in fact, have a higher probability of divorce when they become adults and marry (Wolfinger 2005; Whitton, Rhoades, Stanley, and Markman 2008).

Children also face *problems of adjustment.* They confront questions from peers, particularly when they are in elementary school, about why they have only one parent at home. They have to adjust to a change in primary relationships and possibly to restricted interaction with one of the parents (generally the father). They may have to cope with parental conflict, which often continues after the divorce, and with attempts by each parent to gain the child's loyalty and affection at the expense of the other. It is not surprising, then, that children whose parents are divorced are prone to both emotional and physical problems.

The severity of the negative consequences for children depend on a number of factors, including how well the parents handle the divorce. Some older research showed that the consequences are more severe for younger children. This may be because divorce is harder on the parents of young children (Williams and Dunne-Bryant 2006). The emotional strain of becoming a single parent (even with shared custody) and of being separated from one's child for a good deal of the time make the adjustment to divorce more difficult than it is for those without children or without children in the home.

Nevertheless, the discord that leads to divorce is probably more stressful for the child than is divorce itself. Parents who stay together "for the children's sake" may actually harm the children more than if they were to separate. A home with continual conflict or emotional coldness can be more damaging to the children than a home that is broken. Children from divorce-disrupted families have higher rates of depression and withdrawal than others, but the rates are even higher for those who live in a home with persistent conflict than for those who live in a single-parent home. A study of college students concluded that being in a conflicted home as a child significantly increased the chances of subsequent distress and emotional disorders such as depression and alcohol abuse (Turner and Kopiec 2006). Consequently, if the family is a severely dysfunctional one, the children may actually benefit by a divorce (Strohschein 2005b).

Thus, the intact home may have supportive problems that are far more damaging to the child or to the spouses than a structural problem would be. In other words, structural problems of broken homes are associated with various kinds of physical and emotional problems, but the intact home is not free of such problems.

What about the stepfamily? Does remarriage mitigate the negative health effects of divorce? As noted earlier, the stepfamily has its own peculiar set of problems. In the long run, stepchildren seem to do as well as those who grow up with both biological and adoptive parents. However, in the short run, children in stepfamilies do exhibit more behavior problems of various kinds (Hetherington 1993; Thomson, Hanson, and McLanahan 1994); but they are not lower than those in intact families in self-esteem, psychological functioning, or academic achievement—although the outcome may vary by type of stepfamily (whether the mother or the father is the stepparent).

Abuse. The effects of abuse tend to lead to both *short-term and long-term trauma.* Abused children may become withdrawn and isolated; feel shame, guilt, or unworthiness; and become anxious and depressed (Cole 1995; Stroebel et al. 2012). They are also likely to exhibit, to a greater degree than nonabused children, a variety of problem behaviors, such as quick anger, frequent fighting, resisting of parental authority, school problems, and violence (Markward 1997; Kotch et al. 2008). And they may suffer impaired brain functioning (Teicher 2002). Many of the negative consequences occur because of emotional abuse as well as physical abuse (Panuzio et al. 2007; Melançon and Gagné 2011).

The problems of abused children tend to persist into adulthood. Physical or sexual abuse during childhood is associated with a wide assortment of problems among adults: physical ailments, emotional problems, problems of establishing meaningful intimate relationships, substance abuse, posttraumatic stress disorder, becoming an abuser, and attempted suicide (Afifi et al. 2008; Fang and Corso 2008; Green and King 2009; Larsen,

Sandberg, Harper, and Bean 2011). Emotional and physical problems also occur in children who witness violence between their parents and/or who try to intervene in the adult violence (Jarvis, Gordon, and Novaco 2005). When they grow up and marry, abused children tend to have lower marital satisfaction and a higher probability of marital disruption (Whisman 2006).

Adults as well as children suffer physical and emotional harm from both psychological and physical abuse (Taft et al. 2006). Abused adults have higher rates of impaired mental health, impaired physical functioning and health, and problems in social functioning (Laffaye, Kennedy, and Stein 2003; Loxton, Schofield, and Hussain 2006). A study of Hispanic women in the southeastern part of the United States asserted that so many of the women are victims of domestic violence that the abuse is a "major health problem" for them (Murdaugh, Hunt, Sowell, and Santana 2004).

Thus, the damage from abuse can be severe. The physical harm ranges from bruises and broken bones to permanent brain damage and even death. The emotional harm is more difficult to measure. Yet some indication may be seen in the high rates of both mental disorders and attempted suicide.

Poverty

We previously noted that *female-headed families* are more likely to experience *poverty* than male-headed families. Because most single-parent families have a female head, they have a higher probability of being in poverty than do other households. Moreover, the never-married single mother is even more likely than the divorced single mother to be in poverty. Because of low welfare payments and low wages in available jobs, the single mother may be caught in a bind: Whether she works or stays home and receives welfare, she may find herself and her family living in poverty (Tucker and Lowell 2015). In recent years, the rate of poverty among families headed by a female with no husband present has been more than twice that of the general population. About half of the millions of children living in poverty are in female-headed families.

Children who grow up in poverty have challenges in many areas of their lives. Here, we look briefly at one area that is important because it will tend to perpetuate their poverty as they grow older—education. Poverty is associated with lower educational achievement, which, in turn, results in lower earnings in the labor market when the child eventually goes to work (Borjas 2011). In part, the lower educational achievement reflects the fact that children living in poverty are unprepared for school; fewer than half of poor children are ready for school at age 5 compared to 75 percent of children not living in poverty (Isaacs 2012). And once in school, 22 percent of children who lived some of the time in poverty and 32 percent of those spending more than half their childhood in poverty drop out before finishing high school, compared to 6 percent of those who have never been poor (Hernandez 2011).

Deviant Behavior

Sexual variance, drug and alcohol abuse, and juvenile delinquency have been associated with disturbed family life (Bjarnason et al. 2003; Fagan 2003). We pointed out in earlier chapters that prostitutes and drug and alcohol abusers often have a background of disturbed relationships with their parents. There are, in fact, higher rates of a wide range of deviant behavior among children in single-parent homes (Ellis et al. 2003;

Barton 2006; Wen 2008; Magnuson and Berger 2009). Compared to those in two-parent families, children in single-parent families:

- have higher rates of antisocial behavior, aggression, anxiety, depression, and school problems.
- are less likely to complete high school.
- are more likely to get involved in early sexual activity and adolescent pregnancy.
- are more likely to use illicit drugs.
- are likely to have poorer mental and physical health.

The deviant behavior is likely to continue into adulthood. Researchers examined the records of a group of 1,575 children over a period of years. The children had all been physically or sexually abused or neglected in their early years. By the time they were in their mid- to late-20s, 49 percent had been arrested, compared to 38 percent of those in a control group of the same age, gender, race, and social class, and 18 percent had been arrested for a violent crime (National Institute of Justice 1996b).

Maladjustment

People who come from disturbed families tend to have various difficulties that we subsume under the category of **maladjustment:** antisocial behavior (such as aggression and bullying), insecurity, overconformity to one's peers, a tendency to withdraw from relationships, difficulties in relating to others, problems with one's personal identity, and various problems as adults. The maladjustment affects all areas of a child's life. Divorce, severe parental conflict, and abuse all are associated with higher rates of conduct disorder and problems with both adults and peers (Flisher et al. 1997; Bing, Nelson, and Wesolowski 2009). Such children have problems trusting others, and therefore it is difficult for them to establish effective relationships.

maladjustment
poor adjustment to one's social environment

The problems of maladjustment continue to afflict the children as they grow into adulthood. Adults who were physically punished during childhood tend to have more physical and verbal aggression with their spouses, to be more controlling of their spouses, and to be less able to see things from the spouse's perspective (Cast, Schweingruber, and Berns 2006). And a significant number of abused children will become abusers, including the abuse of their own children.

From the point of view of the child, *abuse is a form of rejection.* It is, however, not the only way in which parents can reject and distress a child. Parental hostility is a form of supportive failure that can result in maladjustment as the child attempts to relate to others. Inconsistency—including inconsistency in discipline—in how the parent treats the child is another form of supportive failure. Inconsistency means the child lives in a capricious environment, and no one functions well with chronic uncertainty. Consequently, parents who are inconsistent in the way in which they relate to and discipline their children foster various kinds of maladjustment, including hostility and difficulties in relating to peers and to adults (Gross, Sambrook, and Fogg 1999).

The *child's sense of self-esteem,* so important in his or her social functioning, is crucially related to family experiences. Self-esteem tends to be high when a child has nurturing parents and a harmonious family environment (Scott, Scott, and McCabe 1991). Parents build self-esteem through such actions as affirming and supporting their children, showing their children how to constructively express their feelings, taking an interest in their children's activities, showing respect for their children's point of view, and teaching their children how to exercise self-control and handle responsibility. In contrast, supportive failure, including abuse, is related to low self-esteem, and low self-esteem tends to lead to emotional and interpersonal problems.

Contributing Factors

The factors we examine in this section contribute to both structural and supportive problems. Some families suffer from both types of problems. The two types can be independent, but more often are interdependent. Structural problems, for instance, may either make supportive failure more likely or reflect supportive failure in the past.

Social Structural Factors

Social Norms.   An important factor in the divorce rate is that divorce is more "respectable" now than it was in the past. In other words, the *norms about divorce have changed.* In the past, religion and the law both said, in effect, "You should not get a divorce. You should make every effort to work it out and stay together." Today the norms about divorce reflect a loosening of the laws ("no-fault" divorce) and greater tolerance among religious groups. In contrast to the *stigma* formerly attached to divorce and to divorced people, most Americans now agree that divorce is an acceptable option if the marriage isn't working out. This new attitude is based on the norm of happiness, the notion that each individual has the right, if not the obligation, to be happy. The *fallacy of non sequitur* may be involved in the process: "I have a right to be happy; therefore, I must get a divorce." Even if you agree to the individual's right to happiness, it doesn't follow that divorce is necessary. All marriages have troubled times. Couples who have achieved long-term, satisfying marriages point out that happiness comes by working through problems, not by avoiding or leaving them (Lauer and Lauer 1986). Of course, some marriages may be hopeless, but many break up too quickly because people believe the marriage is infringing on their right to happiness.

Divorce is more likely if people marry at a young age and have a short or no engagement period. In particular, people who marry as adolescents have higher rates of divorce than those who marry as adults (Amato and Rogers 1997). Age at marriage is one of the more important factors in marital instability. One study reported that 59 percent of women who married when they were younger than 18 years, compared to 36 percent of those who married when they were 20 years or more, either separated or divorced within 15 years (Bramlett and Mosher 2001).

Both structural and supportive problems are more common among the very young. In fact, adolescent marriage and parenthood has been called a case of "children raising children." Not only is the marriage more likely to break up, but problems of childrearing are likely to be serious, including a greater probability of child abuse. A study of infanticide reported that whereas young women under the age of 17 have 2 percent of all births, their babies are 7 percent of all infant homicide victims (Overpeck et al. 1998). The study also reported that having more than one child before the age of 19 involves a ninefold increase in the risk of an infant homicide compared to having children after the age of 25.

Why do adolescents marry at a young age? Social norms define the appropriate time for marriage. For most Americans, that time has been soon after high school graduation or, at the latest, soon after college. In the 1950s, people lowered the ideal age for getting married. Females who were not married by the time they were 20 could develop a sense of panic that they would become old maids. Males who waited until their late

fallacy

20s or after to get married might be suspected of having homosexual tendencies or an inadequate sex drive (which was an affront to their manhood). Subsequently, however, the norm about marital age has reverted to earlier notions. It is now acceptable for an individual to be and to remain single. Yet the average age for marriage is still relatively young, and the single individual may not be wholly acceptable to many businesses and corporations who still prefer their young executives to be married. As long as these attitudes persist, structural and supportive problems due to marriage at a young age will continue.

Norms also contribute to the amount of family violence in the nation. A common norm in families is that it is proper to hit someone who is misbehaving and who does not respond to reason. Many Americans consider the use of physical punishment in the rearing of children as virtually an obligation (Gelles and Straus 1988). Recall the old saying "Spare the rod and spoil the child." In some cases it is applied with a vengeance. But as a French-Canadian study showed, rather than being an effective method of discipline, harsh punishment—both physical and verbal—only increases the likelihood of aggression by the child against the parent (Pagani et al. 2009).

Role Problems. A number of *role problems* contribute to both structural and supportive problems. Indeed, whatever else may be true of modern marital roles, they place an *emotional burden on people that is probably unprecedented in human history.* Modern couples often do not have the proximate interpersonal resources available to those in extended families or to those in small, preindustrial communities. Instead, they rely heavily on each other for advice, intimacy, and emotional support in times of difficulty or crisis.

Divorce rates are higher among those who marry at a young age.
©McGraw-Hill Education./ Christopher Kerrigan, photographer

Moreover, the marital role is ambiguous as well as demanding. *Role obligations* in a changing society are not as clear-cut as those in more traditional settings. Couples who disagree on role obligations of husband and wife are more prone to divorce than are those who agree. The nature of these obligations is not as important as whether the couple agrees on them and whether each feels that the other is fulfilling them. A gap between expectations and perceived behavior increases dissatisfaction.

The majority of American couples are willing to participate in activities once regarded as the domain of the opposite sex, but some may not want to give up their own traditional gender roles. A husband's expectations may still carry more weight than a wife's in determining the division of labor. Wives may be more accepting of noncompliance with expectations than husbands are. Again, however, the crucial factor is not whether the couple is traditional or nontraditional, but whether they agree on their arrangement of role obligations.

For women, *role flexibility* is important for well-being. That is, women need to be free to choose whether to work outside the home. The number who make that choice will probably continue to increase inasmuch as women who work full time outside the home have greater work satisfaction than women engaged in full-time housekeeping (Treas, van der Lippe, and Tai 2011).

The divorce rate is higher among women who work outside the home (South 2001). Financial independence allows women to escape from unhappy unions, such as those in which they perceive severe inequity in the relationship. When wives work outside the home, then, negotiation over role obligations may be required to effect a more equal sharing of both responsibilities and privileges. In particular, working wives expect an equitable sharing from their husbands of responsibility for household tasks, and they are much more likely to be happy with their marriage when they perceive such sharing exists (Frisco and Williams 2003; Khawaja and Habib 2007).

Finally, role problems can be critical in the reconstituted family. Exactly what is the relationship between stepparent and stepchild? People often bring unrealistic expectations to stepfamilies. Women who become stepmothers, for example, tend to expect themselves to:

- Somehow compensate the children for the distress caused by the death or divorce.
- Create a happy and close-knit family unit.
- Maintain happiness and contentedness in all family members.
- Demonstrate through appropriate behavior that the notion of the wicked stepmother is just a myth.
- Love, and be loved by, the stepchildren almost immediately as if the stepchildren were her own natural children. (Lauer and Lauer 1999)

People who impose such role obligations on themselves, or who have them imposed by others, are certain to encounter problems. Thus, stepmothers vexed by role problems have higher rates of depression and anxiety than biological mothers (Dodson and Davies 2014).

Family Continuity.   People who are reared in problem families tend to perpetuate the problems in their own families. Those who come from families in which one or more parents died tend to have rates of disruption similar to those who come from intact families. But people who come from families in which the parents were divorced or separated have higher marital disruption rates than do those coming from intact families (Amato and DeBoer 2001). And those who grow up in families that have parental conflict or parental infidelity are more likely to engage in infidelity themselves when they are adults (Weiser et al. 2015).

Similarly, family violence tends to be continued from one generation to the next (Stith et al. 2000; Coohey 2004). Parents who abuse their children were often abused by their own parents. The battered child of today is likely to become the battering parent of tomorrow, perpetuating the problem of family violence. Marital abuse also is transmitted from one generation to another. The husband who abuses his wife is likely to be a man predisposed to violence because he learned such behavior from his parents. He may have been abused, or he simply may have witnessed violence between his parents (Carlson 1990). Unfortunately, some children learn from watching their parents that those who love you also hit you, and that this action is an appropriate means to get your own way and deal with stress. Such children are *modeling their behavior* after that of their parents, although that behavior may be considered undesirable or immoral by most others.

Even if the child does not grow up to be an abuser, *the mere fact of witnessing violence between one's parents tends to lead to problems of adjustment.* This effect occurs in infants as young as 1 to 3 years of age (McDonald et al. 2006). And the effects can persist into adulthood (Henning et al. 1996). Witnessing violence in the home is associated with such maladies as depression and other emotional ills, delinquency and behavior problems, and posttraumatic stress disorder (O'Keefe 1994; Crusto et al. 2010). And boys that witness violence between their parents have higher rates of dating violence (Gage 2016).

A family can perpetuate its problems into the next generation simply because it is such an important factor in the *socialization* of the child. The family is an important place for learning what it means to be a male or a female, how to function as a parent, and generally how to relate to others. Thus, there is some continuity in parent–child relationships and husband–wife relationships from generation to generation.

Stratification and Family Problems.   Families in different social classes exhibit different problems. For one, *divorce is more common in the lower strata than in the middle and upper strata.* A government survey found that the proportion of women whose marriage broke up within 10 years was 44 percent in the low-income group, 33 percent in the middle-income group, and 23 percent in the high-income group (Bramlett and Mosher 2002). Because of the relationship between racial and ethnic background and income, variations exist in the probability of divorce among racial and ethnic groups. The same government study reported that the proportion of marriages that broke up within 10 years was 32 percent for white women, 47 percent for black women, 20 percent for Asian women, and 34 percent for Hispanic women.

The relationship between income and divorce may seem contrary to common sense, as the well-to-do can afford the costs of divorce more easily than the poor, but financial problems put enormous strains on marital and family relationships. In fact, income is one of the best predictors of family stability. The increasing rates of structural failure as you go down the socioeconomic ladder reflect the greater potential for financial difficulties. Economic difficulties, in turn, tend to generate more discord in the home, increasing the amount of hostile, contemptuous, and angry behavior (Williams, Cheadle, and Goosby 2015; Masarik et al. 2016).

Another factor that bears on the divorce rate is jointly owned property and financial investments, both of which are more likely to be held by people in the middle- and upper-income levels. Divorce is more difficult and expensive when it involves a division of assets. Middle- and upper-income people are also more likely to have a network of friends and relations who will resist their divorce and who may support them as they try to work through their problems.

Finally, the combination of the higher rates of unmarried mothers and higher divorce rates means that fewer children in the lower socioeconomic strata live with both parents (Table 12.3). Thus, the undesirable consequences of living in a disrupted or single-parent home are more prevalent in the lower socioeconomic strata.

Family Income	Percent with Both Parents
Under $10,000	29.0
$10,000 to $19,999	36.0
$20,000 to $29,999	49.9
$30,000 to $49,999	62.6
$50,000 to $74,999	73.7
$75,000 to $99,999	83.6
$100,000 and over	91.2

TABLE 12.3
Proportion of Children Living with Both Parents, by Income

SOURCE: U.S. Census Bureau website.

Supportive failure is suggested by data on abuse and neglect. A certain amount of abuse occurs in middle- and upper-class families, but both neglect and abuse seem to be more prevalent in the lower than in the middle or upper strata (Kruttschnitt, McLeod, and Dornfeld 1994; Berger 2005).

The Family in a Changing Structure.   Rapid change of the social structure creates its own problems, including problems for families. Certain kinds of change can affect the divorce rate. If roles are in a state of flux, the potential for conflict within the family is increased and the probability of divorce becomes greater. Rapid change may involve confusion and ambiguity about what it means to be a husband, a wife, or a parent, which leads to more stress, more conflict, and more structural and supportive problems.

Most observers agree that the current society is in a time of rapid change. Any family can put down an anchor somewhere and suddenly find that there is nothing solid to hold it in place. A family moves into a neighborhood in the hope of having a better life, only to find the neighborhood deteriorating. A family moves to a new city because the father or mother is offered a better job, only to face unemployment when an economic reversal occurs. To compound the problem, the family has no roots in the area and the family members are wholly dependent on each other for emotional support. Moreover, even if the new job opportunity works out well, the family still may be strained by the lack of a social support system. Thus, the divorce rate in the United States is positively related to urbanity, population change, and lack of church membership (Amato and Rogers 1997; Vaaler, Ellison, and Powers 2009), all of which are indicators of a lack of integration into a local community.

Social Psychological Factors

Attitudes.   In general, Americans' attitudes about the single-parent family have become somewhat less negative over time (Usdansky 2009). Nevertheless, the single-parent family is considered, at best, less than what is desirable and, at worst (particularly in the case of an unmarried-mother single-parent family), something that exists but should not exist or be approved. Such attitudes contribute to the problems of the single-parent family if the parent and/or children sense the disapproval or rejection of others. In essence, the disapproval or rejection means a loss of social support, and social support is essential for well-being even in the best of circumstances.

Attitudes are also a factor in problems of abuse. Men who sexually abuse their children come up with a variety of rationales that minimize or even justify the incest (Hartley 1998). In situations in which there is no intercourse, they may dismiss the seriousness of the relationship on the grounds that it "wasn't really sex." In situations in which intercourse occurs, they may define it as an adult-to-adult rather than an adult-to-child relationship or maintain that the child was a willing participant who gave permission for the incest.

Some Americans agree that violence in intimate relationships is acceptable or even necessary at times (Simon et al. 2001). Although few Americans believe that women are the *cause* of their own abuse, a fourth still believe that at least some women *want* to be abused, and most are convinced that women can end abusive relationships (Worden and Carlson 2005). Abusive husbands maintain their spouses deserve the beatings for some reason (Eisikovitz, Edleson, Guttmann, and Sela-Amit 1991). *Blaming the victim is one of the more common characteristics of husbands who abuse their wives.* A small proportion of abused women agree that they deserved to be beaten.

How could a woman justify wife beating? Unfortunately, many victims have attitudes that lead them to remain in a violent relationship (Marano 1996; Barnett 2001). Some of these attitudes are understandable: The women may fear that they will lose their children (courts have been known to award custody to the father when a battered woman leaves the home), or be unable to protect their children, or risk their own lives. The risk to their own lives is a real one: Abusers threaten to kill their wives if they try to leave, and in fact, more abuse victims are killed when trying to leave their abusers than at any other time.

Battered women may have rationales that are difficult to counteract. Ferraro and Johnson (1983) interviewed more than 100 battered women. The women who opted to remain in their relationships justified the decision in six ways, many of which involve fallacious modes of thinking. Some of the women had a "salvation ethic"; they viewed their husbands as troubled or "sick" individuals who needed them in order to survive. Some said that the problem was beyond the control of either the women or their husbands; the violence was caused by some external factor or factors such as work pressure or loss of a job. Of course, this is the *fallacy of non sequitur.* It does not follow that a man will necessarily abuse his wife when he has problems with his work. A third explanation involved a denial of injury; some women insisted that the beatings were tolerable and even normal. Fourth, some of the women used the *fallacy of personal attack against themselves,* blaming themselves for the abuse. They said that the violence could have been averted if they had been more passive and conciliatory. A fifth reason was the women's insistence that they had no other options; some of the women believed that they were too dependent on their husbands either financially or emotionally. Finally, some of the women used the *fallacy of an appeal to authority,* claiming that a "higher loyalty"—such as a religious faith or a commitment to a stable family—motivated them. Such attitudes may be rationalizations that disguise a deeper reason for maintaining an abusive relationship, or they may be potent factors in their own right. In any case, they are used by the victims to justify and perpetuate the violence.

Finally, *attitudes toward the self* are important factors in abuse. Mothers who abuse their children tend to have lower levels of self-esteem than other mothers do (Wolfner and Gelles 1993). Husbands who abuse their wives tend to be dissatisfied with their lives, believe that the man should be the head of the family but lack the resources to be the head, and assault their wives in order to establish their control over them (Felson and Messner 2000; Atkinson, Greenstein, and Lang 2005).

If negative attitudes can contribute to family conflict and disruption, positive attitudes can contribute to family health and stability. Stafford (2016) found that people who consider their marriages as sacred tend to put more effort into protecting their marriages. This enhances the spouse's marital satisfaction and the probability of maintaining a healthy and lasting union.

Values and Homogamy.   When you marry, you undoubtedly hope that the relationship will last and be rewarding to both you and your spouse. Is marital happiness more likely to happen if you and your spouse have similar or dissimilar backgrounds? The answer to this question has been debated by social scientists. Some have argued that couples with *dissimilar backgrounds* (**heterogamy**) will be attracted to each other and will *complement* each other so that the marriage is more rewarding and successful. Others have argued that *similar backgrounds and shared rather than different values* (**homogamy**) are more likely to produce a rewarding and lasting marriage.

Research generally supports the view that homogamy is more conducive to a lasting marriage. Although homogamy does not mean that the couple must have similar backgrounds in every respect, it appears that the greater the similarity, the greater the likelihood of a satisfactory marriage (Mullins, Brackett, Bogle, and Pruett 2004). This

heterogamy
marriage between partners with diverse values and backgrounds

homogamy
marriage between partners with similar values and backgrounds

ONE BIG HAPPY FAMILY

Some utopian communities that have arisen in the United States have considered traditional family arrangements detrimental to human well-being. The 19th-century Oneida community, for instance, was founded on the notion of "Bible communism." Private property was abolished, including the private property of a spouse or child. The entire community was a family. Every adult was expected to have sex relations with a great variety of others. Women who bore children cared for them for the first 15 months and then placed them in the children's house where they were raised communally and taught to regard all adults in the community as their parents.

Obtain literature about utopian communities of the present or past (see Lauer and Lauer 1983). For example, you might investigate Bethel, Brook Farm, Oneida, Ephrata, the Icarians, the Rappites, the Shakers, or any one of numerous contemporary communes. Consider what kinds of family arrangements they have created. Do any of these arrangements solve the kinds of problems discussed in this chapter? Why or why not? Do the utopian arrangements appear to create other kinds of problems? Would the utopian arrangement be practical for an entire society? What is your own ideal after reading about the utopians and the alternatives mentioned earlier in this chapter?

kind of relationship is more likely to result when there is similarity in family background, socioeconomic background, cultural background, personality traits, and religion. Homogamy tends to correlate with marital happiness. Perhaps the more similarity between spouses, the fewer areas of conflict. In any case, shared rather than dissimilar values are important in securing a satisfactory marriage. Structural and supportive problems are more likely to occur when the couple come from dissimilar backgrounds and hold diverse values.

The Value of Success. The American *value of success* can lead to supportive failure in the family. Merton (1957:136) showed how the "goal of monetary success" pervades society so that Americans "are bombarded on every side by precepts which affirm the right or, often, the duty of retaining the goal even in the face of repeated frustration." In families, schools, and the mass media, Americans are urged to pursue the goal with unrelenting diligence. Most Americans share this value of success. Even in the lower socioeconomic strata, where people often do not *expect* success, they still *wish* for it.

Monetary success often requires long hours at work and minimal contact with family. What are the consequences? A survey of employees in a Fortune 500 company found that the more time an individual spent at work, the greater was the interference with family life and the higher was the level of distress (Major, Klein, and Ehrhart 2002). In addition, family members may feel neglected by the person who is working the long hours. Clearly, then, a strong emphasis on success that leads to spending long hours at work can result in supportive failure in the family. Individuals who are attaining such success may be neglecting their families. Individuals who are severely frustrated in their attempts to attain success may react with violence in the family setting. In either case, the family members are the victims of a value that is deeply ingrained in American society.

Ideology of the Family. Unfulfilled or conflicting expectations about role obligations can lead to marital dissatisfaction and dissolution (Pasley, Kerpelman, and Guilbert 2001). *The American ideology of the "good" family generates a set of expectations* that may create problems if the expectations are not met. Two versions of this ideology exist, each of which can give rise to unrealistic or conflicting expectations.

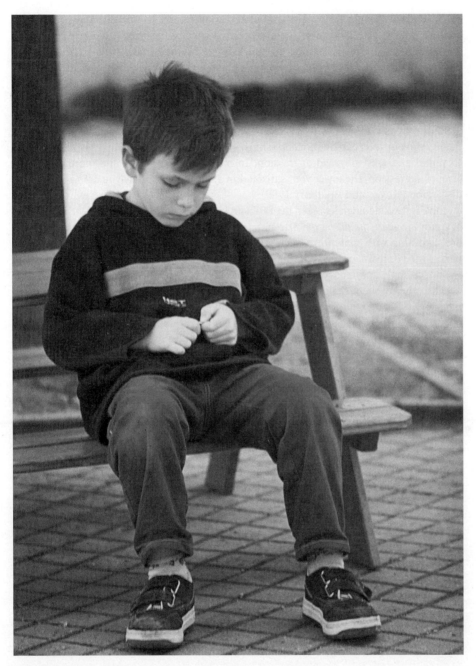

One version asserts that *a good family is a happy family* and that *happy families are harmonious* and free of conflict. Further, the family is a kind of miniature society in which all important human relationships and feelings can be experienced. Each person can find within the family a complete range of experiences in the context of harmony and happiness. This view of family life is unrealistic, and the result is a higher rate of emotional stress when conflict is suppressed because of the ideology.

A different version of the ideology of the good family stresses the need to express feelings and engage in creative conflict. This ideology has grown out of small-group work and says, in effect, that the good family maintains *healthy relationships* and that healthy relations can be obtained only when people give *free expression to their feelings.* People should "level" with each other and accept each other.

If the first ideology errs by condemning conflict in the family, the second one errs by encouraging too much *anger and aggression* in the home. Giving free expression to feelings may provide you with a sense of release and relief, but it does not enhance the quality of your interpersonal relationships. The free expression of anger is likely to lead to verbal and even physical aggression. In marriage, the higher and more severe the level of aggression, the lower your satisfaction and the more likely you are to experience disruption (Rogge and Bradbury 1999).

Finally, two ideologies worsen the problem of abuse within the family. One is the *ideology that the man should be the breadwinner.* Men who accept this ideology and equate breadwinning with masculinity may resort to violence if their wives earn a significant part of the family income (Atkinson et al. 2005). In such cases, the violence is an attempt to reassert male dominance in the relationship and in the family.

The other is the *ideology of nonintervention,* which asserts that outsiders should not interfere in family affairs. People who might aid a woman being beaten by a man would not interfere if that same man were beating his wife. People who might stop a woman from abusing a child would not intervene if that child were her own.

The ideology of nonintervention affects the police as well. As Ferraro (1989) found, the police may use their ideologies about battered women and family fights to evaluate specific incidents. The police officers with whom Ferraro worked believed that if battered women opted to stay in their situations, it was not the responsibility of the police to control the violent behavior. One male officer even insisted that because a man's home is his castle, he should be able to do whatever he wants there. Furthermore, the officer asserted, most wife abuse is provoked by the woman herself. Thus, in spite of a presumptive arrest policy (arrests are required when there is probable cause and the offender is present), the police frequently did not arrest the offender. Rather, they would reassure the woman and tell her to call them if anything further happened.

We should note that educational efforts are changing the ideology, so that most victims have positive and helpful experiences with the police now (Apsler, Cummins, and Carl 2003). But negative experiences still exist (Johnson 2007; Kim and Gray 2008). And such experiences can make some women hesitant about trying to get help from the police. Research with victims who came to a battered women's shelter found that two-thirds of the women had contact with the police some time during the previous six months, but most did not have as much contact as they had needed (Fleury, Sullivan, Bybee, and Davidson 1998). The women gave various reasons for not calling the police, including *fear of even greater violence* and *previous negative experiences with the police themselves.*

Public Policy and Private Action

As with all problems, *both therapeutic and preventive measures* can be applied to family problems. Therapeutic measures include the more traditional counseling services as well as newer efforts involving discussion and interaction in small-group settings. Public policy could require intervention, counseling, and needed protection in cases of abuse and divorce. Such measures, of course, attempt to resolve problems after they have already begun.

What kind of preventive measures could be taken? That is, what measures might minimize the number of family problems in the nation? Consider, first, what government and business can do. Much has been said about "family values" in the political arena in recent years. The question is, what are political and business leaders doing to strengthen American families?

We pointed out in the chapters on poverty and work some of the ways in which government and business can help families that are poor (some of the problems of family life are intertwined with the problem of poverty) and can address the problems created by work conditions (e.g., too much time at work and too stressful work both have negative impacts on family life). Some other nations do far better than the United States on these and other matters; some countries offer day care for workers' children and paid time off for new parents (Remery, van Doorne-Huiskes, and Schippers 2003). If businesses do not adopt such family-friendly policies on their own, they may need to do so by government mandate (Gray and Tudball 2003). Single-mother families are particularly in need of help because most have already suffered the pain of disruption and because they have the highest poverty rate of any group in the nation. The United States desperately needs policies and programs that support and help single working mothers through such benefits as child care and flexible work hours (Albelda, Himmelweit, and Humphries 2004).

The arguments against government-mandated policies include the resistance to any expansion of government into the private sector and the claim that the additional costs will harm business. The answer to the first argument is simply that if the government does not require these changes, they will not happen. With a few exceptions, business leaders are not known for voluntarily taking steps to enhance the well-being of workers when those steps involve additional costs. With regard to the second argument, a survey of 120 employers in New York found that the employers who offered flexible sick leave and child care assistance had significant reductions in turnover, offsetting some of the costs involved in the benefits (Baughman, DiNardi, and Holtz-Eakin 2003).

Numerous other courses of action also fall into the category of preventive measures. For example, states could experiment with a legalized system of trial marriage. Couples would contract to marry for a specific period of time and then have the option of renewing the contract. However, you need to be aware of the nature of experiments. They are searches—often blind gropings—for answers, and not firm guidelines. Some experiments may work, but others may not (and perhaps may even make a problem worse).

A contrary approach would be to make it harder to divorce. Some states presently allow *covenant marriages,* in which spouses sign a legal contract that they will not seek divorce except for abuse or adultery. If they want to divorce for any other reason, they agree to first undergo counseling and wait two years before finalizing the decision. A researcher tracking 600 newly wed couples, half of whom were in covenant marriages, reported that after the first two years the rate of divorce was much lower among those in the covenant marriages (Perina 2002).

Beneficial *family life education* at all stages of the life cycle, through the schools and the mass media, could change negative attitudes about single-parent families and the legitimacy of violent behavior as well as break down harmful ideologies about the "good" family. Family life education could also change some norms, and new norms can affect family life in crucial ways. For example, consider our norms about roles and the division of labor in the home. It is true that husbands today are more willing than in the past to agree with greater role freedom for their wives. Yet even women who have careers still tend to take major responsibility for home and children. Americans are egalitarian in theory but not yet in practice.

A great many false or counterproductive ideas can be attacked through educational programs. *Marriage enrichment programs* can help couples confront and work through the common issues in marriage and family life. Such programs teach couples, for example, how to create and maintain good communication patterns, handle conflict constructively, work out an equitable division of labor in the home, and manage their finances.

The problem of family violence needs to be addressed through the law, education, and practical aids like shelters for battered women. These efforts need to be buttressed by bringing about ideological changes in the culture. Religious groups can help in these efforts; a lower amount of domestic violence occurs among families who report regular attendance at religious services than among those who are not regular or who are nonattenders (Ellison, Bartkowski, and Anderson 1999; Cunradi, Caetano, and Schafer 2002).

Ideologies of the family in which authorities and others (such as neighbors or relatives) regard domestic violence as a private matter need to be changed. If domestic violence is a private matter, then people will be hesitant to intervene and offer help to the victim, particularly when the ideology is combined with the *fallacy of personal attack.* The fallacy of personal attack is the argument that the woman has done something to deserve the violence. A former victim of abuse told us that she stayed in her marriage for many years because everyone she knew, including her priest and her own family, kept telling her that she must be doing something wrong to make her husband act so violently! Education through schools and the mass media can change people's understanding of family violence, get rid of the old ideologies, and lead to an open confrontation of the problem. Spouse and child abuse must be seen for what they are: crimes of violence and not justifiable acts within the confines of a group—the family—that is off limits to outsiders.

Finally, shelters for battered women also address the problem of violence. They provide many services, including emergency shelter, crisis counseling, support groups, child care, and assistance with housing, employment, and education. These shelters help reduce the amount of domestic violence. The very existence of shelters warns batterers that their wives have an alternative to remaining in an abusive relationship. Although the number of shelters has increased over the past few decades, there are still too few and the funding is too little to meet the demand (Wasley 2009). Even when the shelters have room, they may require women to find alternative housing within weeks; and the waiting lists for public or subsidized housing can be anywhere from seven months to years. The lack of alternatives ultimately forces many of the women to return to the men who battered them. Additional shelters would allow more women to escape abusive relationships, and the shelters also would stand as a visible reminder to men that violence against women is no longer tolerable.

Follow-Up.   Set up a debate in your class on the topic "Divorce is too easily attained and too readily accepted in the United States today."

fallacy

Summary

Family problems are so common that some observers have argued that the family is doomed. Those who predict the end of the present type of family suggest a number of alternatives, such as group marriages, trial marriages, open marriages, or cohabitation. But most Americans continue to marry and establish homes, and to prefer that option over alternatives.

The problems of the family stem from the fact that it is one of the most important primary groups. Americans believe the family to be the cornerstone of society and that an ideal family provides stability, support, and continuity for American values. We identify two basic types of problems: structural (disruption and reconstitution of families) and supportive (lack of emotional support).

Several kinds of data suggest the extent and seriousness of family problems. Structural problems may be measured by the divorce rate, by the number of single-parent families, and by the number of reconstituted families that contain a stepparent–stepchild relationship. Supportive problems are evident in the amount of family violence, including child abuse.

All family problems diminish the quality of life. Physical and emotional difficulties may result from family conflict. Additional problems of adjusting to a broken home result from separation or divorce. And problems of adjustment to new and ambiguous roles must be confronted in the stepfamily. Poverty is more frequently associated with a female-headed than with a two-parent family, and the poverty tends to be perpetuated because the child from a single-headed family does not perform as well academically as other children do. Several kinds of deviant behavior have been associated with disturbed family life: sexual deviance, drug and alcohol abuse, and juvenile delinquency. People who come from families with problems tend to develop various kinds of maladjustment: antisocial behavior, interpersonal problems, and low self-esteem.

Norms that are permissive about divorce and that encourage young marriages are two social structural factors that contribute to family problems. Role problems contribute to marital dissatisfaction and thereby lead to both structural and supportive failure. Family problems are especially likely to occur when there is disagreement on role obligations and when expectations are in conflict and unfulfilled for one or both spouses. The stepfamily has its own peculiar set of problems, stemming from the difficulties of the stepparent-stepchild relationship. The family itself also contributes to future family problems. Because parents act as role models for their children, the children may learn patterns of behavior that will create future problems.

Family problems are generally more prevalent in the lower social strata, partly because of financial strains and partly because of different norms and roles. Rapid social change is yet another structural cause of family problems.

Among the social psychological factors, attitudes are important. A number of attitudes contribute to family problems, including negative attitudes about single-parent families and attitudes that justify abuse. Values are also a significant factor in family problems. A couple with similar values based on similar backgrounds is more likely to have a satisfactory marriage. The value of success in American culture, on the other hand, puts a strain on marriages and family life because certain occupations can consume family members who are striving for that success.

Two "good family" ideologies generate expectations and behavior that strain marriage and family relationships. One says the good family is happy and free of conflict, which can lead to a suppression of conflict and guilt. The other claims that in the good family, people can freely express their feelings, including aggression; this ideology can perpetuate debilitating conflict. Both ideologies tend to result in supportive problems. Families need a balance between excessive openness and free expression of feelings, on the one hand, and suppression and guilt, on the other hand. Finally, the ideologies that the man should be the breadwinner and that outsiders should not intervene in family affairs both worsen the problem of abuse within the family.

Key Terms

Cohabitation	Maladjustment
Divorce Rate	Nuclear Family
Family	Primary Group
Heterogamy	Stepfamily
Homogamy	

Study Questions

1. What are some alternative forms of the family?
2. In what ways is the American family changing?
3. What are the important functions of the modern family?
4. What are the various kinds of problems that afflict families, and how extensive are those problems?

chapter 12 review

5. How does family disruption affect the physical and emotional well-being of people?

6. How do family problems relate to deviant behavior and maladjustment in families?

7. What norms contribute to family problems?

8. Explain the role problems that can result in both structural and supportive difficulties in families.

9. What are the relationships between the stratification system and family problems?

10. Name and explain the kinds of attitudes, values, and ideologies that contribute to family problems.

11. What are the therapeutic and preventive measures that can address family problems in the United States?

Internet Resources/Exercises

1. Explore some of the ideas in this chapter on the following sites:

http://www.nationalmarriageproject.org/wordpress Publications and links from the National Marriage Project at Rutgers University.

http://www.childtrends.org   Site offering publications and links to information that helps strengthen families and increases the well-being of children.

http://www.divorcemag.com   News, information, and links about all aspects of divorce.

2. Most of the information in this chapter involves what can go wrong in a family. Search the Internet for information about healthy family life. What are the characteristics and qualities of such families? Design a one-day "healthy family" seminar based on your findings.

3. Choose one or more nations other than the United States and find information about divorce laws and/or divorce statistics. How do your findings compare with information in this chapter on divorce in the United States? How would you explain any differences and similarities between nations?

For Further Reading

Booth, Alan, and Ann C. Crouter, eds. *Just Living Together: Implications of Cohabitation on Families, Children, and Social Policy.* Mahwah, NJ: Lawrence Erlbaum Associates, 2002. An exploration, by a variety of experts, of individual, familial, and social causes and consequences of cohabitation.

Casper, Lynne M., and Suzanne M. Bianchi. *Continuity and Change in the American Family.* Thousand Oaks, CA: Sage, 2002. An examination of various facets of change and continuity in family life in America in the last half of the 20th century, including cohabitation, work, parenting, and single-mother families.

Daniels, Cynthia R., ed. *Lost Fathers: The Politics of Fatherlessness in America.* New York: St. Martin's Press, 2000. A collection of diverse perspectives on how the lack of a father in the home intersects with such issues as welfare, poverty, sexuality, family values, children's well-being, and the race problem.

DePaulo, Bella. *Single Parents and Their Children.* CreateSpace Independent Publishing Platform. 2015. Although this is a self-published book, the author is an academic psychologist who brings together a number of her own and others' writings, based on research and experience, of life in the single-parent family.

Hertz, Rosanna. *Single by Choice: How Women Are Choosing Parenthood Without Marriage and Creating the New American Family.* New York: Oxford University Press, 2006. Based on in-depth interviews with 65 middle-class, single women who chose to be single mothers, Hertz explores different ways to become a mother and how the women balance parenthood with work.

Lauer, Robert H., and Jeanette C. Lauer. *'Til Death Do Us Part: How Couples Stay Together.* New York: Haworth Press, 1986. A study of 362 couples who have been married 15 years or more, showing how they keep their marriage intact. Compares happy, long-term marriages to those in which one or both partners are unhappy.

Wolfinger, Nicholas H. *Understanding the Divorce Cycle: The Children of Divorce in Their Own Marriages.* New York: Cambridge University Press, 2005. Explores the ways in which the divorce of one's parents affects every facet of one's intimate relationships; includes a discussion about the effects of no-fault divorce laws.

CHAPTER

13

Health Care and Illness

Physical and Mental

OBJECTIVES

1 Understand the meaning and extent of physical and mental illness.

2 Know the kinds of undesirable consequences of illness, including suffering, disrupted interpersonal relationships, constraints on personal freedom, and economic costs.

3 Discuss the ways in which Americans receive inadequate

health care, including deinstitutionalization.

4 Show how roles and social institutions affect the health care problem.

5 Describe the attitudes, values, and ideologies that contribute to the health care problem.

6 Identify some ways to address America's health care problem.

©Photodisc Collection/Getty Images

Tami, in her 40s, has what she calls a "bizarre, cruel disease." She also says the disease may be helping her live a long life: "If you want to live a long life, get a chronic disease and take care of it." Tami's story illustrates both the trauma of chronic illness and the ability of some people to triumph over the trauma and live a reasonably normal life:

I have lupus. It is intermittent and recurrent, and I know it can destroy my life, my will to live, and my ability to cope. In lupus, your body and soul are enmeshed in a web of pain and desperation. When the symptoms first appeared, people thought I was a hypochondriac. Doctors said nothing was wrong with me. They labeled me a neurotic, and I began to think of myself that way. Friends and family saw me looking well one moment and distressed the next. My internist finally turned me over to a psychiatrist. Nothing helped.

Then I got a new physician, and I had the shock of learning that I had a complicated, chronic illness that would alter all my plans and dreams for my life. I was both relieved and in panic. It was a relief to finally identify the problem. It was panic to know what the problem was. I suddenly had to confront the possibility of my own death. A feeling of emptiness spread throughout my body.

Before I got sick, I was full of life. Now I was physically, emotionally, and spiritually exhausted. At times, I could barely raise my arms to attend to personal needs. My husband remained optimistic. My daughter was angry. But as time passed, I was forced to make a decision: I had to try to take charge of my life, or waste away into nothing. I began a program of educating myself. Slowly, I got stronger. I went into

383

remission. No one knows if it was the treatment or my changed attitudes or just a natural process.

I harbor no false hopes. I know I'm not cured. Sometimes, when the sun is shining I feel sad. I want to go out and bask in it. I want to forget that the sun is my enemy, that it can kill someone with lupus. But I get over the sadness. I can't make the lupus disappear by an act of my will, but I can refuse to let it destroy my spirit. I don't know what the future holds. For now, I just focus my energy on what I can control, and live moment to moment.

Introduction

If you were living before 1910, were sick, and randomly chose a doctor, your chances of benefiting from that doctor's ministrations were less than 50 percent. Your chances today are much better, but they vary according to such factors as whether you are physically or mentally ill, live in the city or a rural area, and are poor or well-to-do. The unequal probabilities of all Americans having good health and good health care contradict the *value of equality*. Inequality of care, then, is one reason health care is a social problem.

Another reason health care and illness are social problems is that both physical and mental illness may be induced by social factors. For instance, poverty may force an individual to live in an unhealthy physical environment. Rapid social change may generate anxiety, depression, or other mental disorders.

Adverse effects on health are serious because Americans place a *high value on good health*. Indeed, good health is one of the most important factors in happiness and life satisfaction (Michalos, Zumbo, and Hubley 2000; Pew Research Center 2006). Yet many Americans are less than fully satisfied with the health care system: in a national poll, 42 percent of Americans cited cost or access as an urgent health problem (Riffkin 2015).

In this chapter, we examine health care and illness by first drawing the distinction between physical and mental illnesses and then discussing their **prevalence** in American society. (Prevalence is the number of cases of a disease that exist at any particular time; **incidence** is the number of new cases that occur during a particular period of time.) Next, we show how the problem affects the quality of life. Then we consider the **epidemiology** of physical and mental illness—the factors that affect the incidence, prevalence, and distribution of illnesses. Finally, we discuss ways to deal with the problem.

prevalence
the number of cases of an illness that exist at any particular time

incidence
the number of new cases of an illness that occur during a particular period of time

epidemiology
the study of factors that affect the incidence, prevalence, and distribution of illnesses

Nature of the Problem: Health Care and Illness

Are Americans unnecessarily concerned about their health and health care system? After all, we spend more on health care (measured either on a per capita basis or as a proportion of the gross domestic product) than any other industrial nation (Park 2008).

Nevertheless, although there have been considerable improvements in health in the nation, Americans have a higher infant-mortality rate and lower life expectancy than those in many other developed nations (Brill 2013). A survey that compared the United States with 16 other wealthy, developed nations reported that the American system was at, or near, the bottom in life expectancy and in the prevalence and mortality rates for various diseases (Woolf, Laudan, and Aron 2013).

As we examine the nature and extent of physical and mental illness, keep in mind that the two are not really separable (Jacobsen et al. 2002; Whooley 2006; Keyes and Simoes 2012). Physical illness can cause emotional problems. Mental illness can be manifested in physical distress (Ruo et al. 2003). Both physical and mental illness have social causes. However, the methods used to assess the extent of physical and mental illnesses are different and must be discussed separately.

Physical Illness

Important indicators show that Americans have made significant advances in health matters. For instance, **life expectancy,** the average number of years a person can expect to live, has increased dramatically (Table 13.1). In 1900, life expectancy was less than two-thirds of the present figure. In large part, this increase in life expectancy *reflects reduced infant mortality and lower rates of infectious diseases.* It isn't that the majority of people only lived until their late 40s in the early 1900s. Rather, the large number of infant deaths combined with the high rate of infectious diseases among the middle-aged severely depressed the average length of life. Sanitation, better diet, reduced fertility, and advancing medical knowledge and technology greatly reduced both the prevalence and the seriousness of infectious diseases. Despite the progress, however, physical illness is a major problem. It is even a problem for the young. According to the National Center for Health Statistics (2016), 4.9 percent of children under 18 years of age suffered an asthma attack in the year prior to the survey, 11.8 percent had a skin allergy,

life expectancy
the average number of years a newborn can expect to live

TABLE 13.1
Expectation of Life at Birth, 1900–2014

Year	Total	Male	Female
1900	47.3	46.3	48.3
1910	50.0	48.4	51.8
1920	54.1	53.6	54.6
1930	59.7	58.1	61.6
1940	62.9	60.8	65.2
1950	68.2	65.6	71.1
1960	69.7	66.6	73.1
1970	70.9	67.1	74.8
1980	73.7	70.0	77.5
1990	75.4	72.0	78.8
2000	76.8	74.1	79.3
2010	78.3	75.7	80.8
2014	78.8	76.4	81.2

SOURCES: *Historical Statistics of the United States, Part I* (Washington, D.C.: Government Printing Office, 1975), p. 55, and National Center for Health Statistics 2016.

Cause	Percent of Deaths among—				
	Whites	Hispanics	Blacks	Asians	American Indians
Diseases of the heart	23.4	20.1	23.7	21.6	18.3
Malignant neoplasms	22.5	21.5	22.4	26.8	17.5
Cerebrovascular diseases	5.0	5.1	5.5	7.0	3.6
Chronic lower respiratory diseases	6.0	2.8	3.2	3.0	4.4
Accidents	5.2	7.3	4.6	4.3	11.1
Alzheimer's disease	3.8	2.9	2.1	2.7	1.7
Diabetes mellitus	2.7	4.6	4.3	3.8	5.2
Influenza and pneumonia	2.1	2.3	1.8	3.1	2.3

SOURCE: National Center for Health Statistics 2016.

TABLE 13.2
Leading Causes of Death, by Race/Ethnicity

5.6 percent had a food allergy, 16 percent had a respiratory allergy, and 5.2 percent had three or more ear infections.

Table 13.2 shows the diseases primarily responsible for death. Cardiovascular diseases, including high blood pressure, coronary heart disease, rheumatic heart disease, and strokes, afflict millions of Americans and have been at the top of the list since the beginning of the 20th century.

Chronic diseases are the major cause of death in the United States. A national survey found that 45 percent of American adults are living with one or more chronic conditions (e.g., high blood pressure and diabetes) (Fox and Duggan 2013). Chronic diseases are of long duration and may be classified along a number of dimensions (Rolland 1987). They may be *progressive* (worsening over time) or *constant.* Lung cancer is progressive, whereas stroke is constant. Their onset may be *acute* (short-term) or *gradual* (occurring over an extended period of time). Stroke is acute, whereas lung cancer is gradual. They may be *fatal* (lung cancer), *possibly fatal or life-shortening* (stroke), or *nonfatal* (kidney stones). Although heart disease and cancer are the leading causes of death, the most common chronic conditions are arthritis and sinusitis. Dementia, including Alzheimer's disease, afflicts a third or more of those people who live to age 85 (St. George-Hyslop 2000). Increasing concern has developed over health problems created by obesity (more than a third of adults and 17.5 percent of children aged 6 through 11 are obese) and diabetes (11.9 percent of adults have diabetes) (National Center for Health Statistics 2016).

There is also concern about a *resurgence of infectious diseases.* Infectious disease mortality declined during the first eight decades of the 20th century from 797 deaths per 100,000 to 36 deaths per 100,000 (Armstrong, Conn, and Pinner 1999). However, the rates began to increase in the 1980s and 1990s. Today, infectious diseases are a serious problem throughout the world (see the Global Comparison box in this chapter). Infectious diseases cause more deaths worldwide than heart disease and cancer combined. In addition to increasing rates of such diseases as tuberculosis, at least 30 previously unknown diseases have emerged in recent decades, including Lyme disease (caused by a tick bite), AIDS (discussed next), Legionnaires' disease (caused by air-conditioning systems), toxic shock syndrome (caused by ultra-absorbent tampons), SARS (severe acute respiratory syndrome, caused by a virus), and Zika (also caused by a virus, passed on by the bite of certain mosquitoes or by sexual relations with an infected person). Among the pernicious effects of Zika is brain damage of the fetus in a pregnant woman. What these varied outbreaks mean is that new infections whose source may be obscure and for which there is no known treatment continue to appear. Infections are caused by bacteria, including bacteria that mutate, and by new strains of diseases like tuberculosis that are resistant to antibiotics and other drugs now available (Simon 2006; Barry and Cheung 2009). If we are entering a new era of infectious diseases for which we have no effective antibiotics, it is possible that by 2050 there will be as many as 10 million deaths each year from microbes that are drug resistant (Khatchadourian 2016).

The health problems you are likely to face vary according to your gender. In general, women have higher rates of acute diseases (such as respiratory ailments and viral infections), short-term disabilities, and nonfatal chronic diseases. Men have more injuries, more visual and hearing problems, and higher rates of life-threatening chronic diseases such as cancer and the major cardiovascular diseases.

Health problems also vary according to racial or ethnic origin. This may be due as much to socioeconomic differences as to racial factors per se (Haywood, Crimmins, Miles, and Yang 2000). Table 13.2 shows some interesting variations between racial and ethnic groups in the causes of death. Note, for instance, that Hispanics and Asian Americans are the only groups for which cancer causes more deaths than does heart disease. Whites are more likely than others to die from chronic lower respiratory diseases, but less likely than the others to die from diabetes. Still, for all groups except American Indians, heart disease and cancer account for close to half of all deaths.

Finally, *health problems vary by age and tend to intensify with age.* Older people are more likely than those in other age groups to define their health as only "fair" or "poor"; 21.7 percent Americans aged 65 and older do so (National Center for Health Statistics 2016). The fact that people are living longer does not mean that they all have a better quality of life.

AIDS
acquired immune deficiency syndrome, a disease in which a viral infection causes the immune system to stop functioning, inevitably resulting in death

AIDS. **AIDS** is caused by a virus (HIV) that attacks certain white blood cells, eventually *causing the individual's immune system to stop functioning.* The individual then falls prey to one infection after another. Even normally mild diseases can prove fatal. Many AIDS patients develop rare cancers or suffer serious brain damage.

There is no cure for AIDS. Drugs can prolong the lives of some AIDS victims, but each infection takes its toll, and the immune system continues to collapse. In the advanced stages of HIV infection, 15 to 20 percent of patients develop a type of dementia that involves slow mental functioning (Portegies and Rosenberg 1998). Eventually, the individual succumbs and dies.

How does AIDS spread? The two primary ways are through sex (oral, anal, or vaginal) with someone infected with the AIDS virus and by sharing drug needles and syringes with an infected person. Some people were infected through blood transfusions before blood was tested for the virus. Infected mothers can transmit the disease to their babies before or during birth or while breast feeding. Primarily, then, the *virus is spread through blood or semen.* Females who get the disease are either intravenous drug users or sex partners of an infected male. In fact, a woman is 12 times as likely as a man to be infected with the AIDS virus during heterosexual intercourse and, once infected, is likely to die more quickly (Ickovics and Rodin 1992).

In spite of the "cocktail" of drugs available to treat AIDS patients, the disease continues to have a devasting impact on society.
©McGraw-Hill Education./ Christopher Kerrigan, photographer

THE WORLDWIDE CHALLENGE OF INFECTIOUS DISEASES

Most research money in the United States is devoted to the study of chronic diseases, the primary cause of death for Americans. In many of the developing nations, particularly in Africa, infectious diseases are more prevalent and far more likely to be the cause of death. Worldwide, about 11 million people a year die from infectious disease (Figure 13.1). Some of these diseases are relatively rare in the United States and other Western nations. Many, not shown in the figure because they afflict fewer numbers (such as tropical diseases), are unknown in the United States. Nevertheless, the developed nations are vulnerable to these diseases because of such things as international travel and bioterrorism (Becker, Hu, and Biller-Andorno 2006).

Both new and reemerging infectious diseases afflict both the developed and the developing nations (Peleman 2004). Their spread is rapid because of such factors as pathogens that are resistant to antibiotics and disease-carrying insects that are resistant to insecticides.

The problems of dealing with these diseases are illustrated by efforts to stop malaria in Africa. For a number of years, mosquito-killing insecticide reduced the number of deaths from malaria. But the insects could not be effectively controlled in the long run, and the incidence of malaria increased again in the 1990s. As Figure 13.1 shows, malaria once again is a serious health problem, causing about a million deaths a year. Children account for a majority of the deaths.

An increasingly more deadly infection worldwide is tuberculosis (Weber 2016). Scientists estimate that a third of the world's population is infected with tubercle bacilli, and that there are 8 to 10 million new cases of tuberculosis each year. The great majority of the new cases and the deaths occur in the developing nations. Tuberculosis is difficult to treat because bacterial mutations make it resistant to any single drug, and drugs that are effective at one point in time eventually become ineffective as the bacilli become resistant.

Although the U.S. death rate from tuberculosis is now quite low, the disease presents a challenge to Americans as well as to other nations because of the new strains that are resistant to formerly effective drugs. Tuberculosis

HIV infection and AIDS are a worldwide problem. According to the World Health Organization (2016), 35 million people have died of AIDS since 1981, making it one of the most destructive illnesses in the history of humankind. The rate of new infections has declined, but as of 2015 there were still about 2 million new infections each year and about 36.7 million people living with HIV.

In the United States, the number of new AIDS cases peaked in the early 1990s, then declined. More than a million Americans have been diagnosed with HIV, and more than 40,000 new infections are reported each year (National Center for Health Statistics 2016). Homosexual activity is the most common way the disease is contracted. Thus, 81 percent of new infections in 2014 were men.

The reaction to AIDS has varied from skepticism about its importance to near-panic. Some researchers have warned of an AIDS epidemic sweeping over the nation and over the world. The extent to which Americans are concerned is seen in a number of ways. New dating services have appeared that test people regularly and issue them cards showing that they are free of sexually transmitted diseases. Many people are afraid even to be around individuals with AIDS.

Some people believe that the concern over AIDS is overdrawn. Certainly, it seems an exaggeration to say that AIDS is an *epidemic.* The incidence is low compared to other diseases. Death rates are down. Moreover, there are ways to minimize the risks. Health experts advise the use of condoms as one of the best preventive measures (condoms are not foolproof, however). Others argue that the disease can be eliminated only is also more likely to develop in people who are infected with HIV (the virus that causes AIDS). As a result, tuberculosis could once again become a leading cause of death in the world (as it was in the early years of the 20th century). In any case, it is clear that, looking at the world as a whole, infectious diseases are still a major (and increasingly serious) health problem.

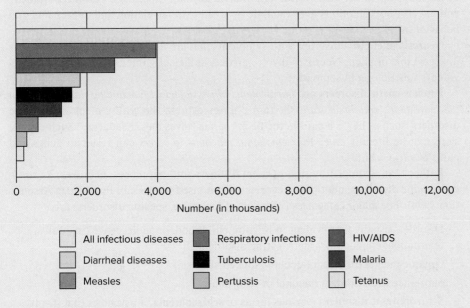

FIGURE 13.1 Worldwide Deaths, by Selected Infectious Diseases.
Source: World Health Organization website 2007.

Legend:
- All infectious diseases
- Diarrheal diseases
- Measles
- Respiratory infections
- Tuberculosis
- Pertussis
- HIV/AIDS
- Malaria
- Tetanus

X-axis: Number (in thousands) — 0, 2,000, 4,000, 6,000, 8,000, 10,000, 12,000

if people change their sexual and drug-use behavior. Unfortunately, too many people ignore the preventive measures. People continue to share drug needles and to have unprotected sex (in some cases, even those who know they are HIV positive) (Semple, Patterson, and Grant 2002; Osmond, Pollack, Paul, and Catania 2007). It is likely that AIDS will be a matter of great concern for some time to come.

Mental Illness

Types of Mental Illness.   Some sociologists prefer the term "mental disorder" to mental illness. "Illness" suggests to them a medical model, a problem deeply rooted in an individual that may also have an organic basis. "Disorder" suggests to them a problem that is more social in its origin and resolution. We believe that both perspectives are valid in part. A particular individual's problem may be a biologically based illness, or it may be behavior that results from the actions and reactions of others (see the discussion of labeling at the end of this chapter). Or it may be a combination of both. Thus, we use the terms "mental illness" and "mental disorder" interchangeably to avoid any simplistic assumptions about the problems.

Before 1980, mental disorders were separated into three broad categories: psychoses, neuroses, and psychosomatic disorders. This breakdown is still a useful way to get a general sense of the kinds of disorders that afflict people. In a **psychosis,** the individual is unable to distinguish between internal and external stimuli. The individual's

psychosis
a disorder in which the individual fails to distinguish between internal and external stimuli

thinking and perceptions are disordered. In everyday terms, he or she has "lost touch with reality." The individual may have hallucinations or fantasize in a way that has no relationship to the real world. The individual may experience chronic perplexity and uncertainty. Emotions may vacillate between extreme elation and depression, and behavior may involve either hyperactivity or extreme inactivity.

neurosis
a mental disorder involving anxiety that impairs functioning

Neurosis refers to a disorder with symptoms that are distressing, and are defined as unacceptable or alien. Neuroses involve anxiety sufficiently intense to impair the individual's functioning in some way.

psychosomatic disorder
an impairment in physiological functioning that results from the individual's emotional state

Psychosomatic disorders are *impairments in physiological functioning that result from the individual's emotional state.* Certain phrases express the reality of psychosomatic disorders, such as he "is a pain in the neck" or she "gives me a headache." Such expressions can be literally true. *Your emotional reactions to others* can result in aches and pains of various kinds.

Rather than a simple division of mental illness into psychoses, neuroses, and psychosomatic disorders, multiple categories are now used (American Psychiatric Association 1994). The major categories (with some illustrative, specific disorders) are:

Disorders usually first evident in infancy, childhood, or adolescence (mental retardation, conduct disorders, eating disorders).

Organic mental disorders (alcohol-induced amnesia).

Substance use disorders (alcohol or drug abuse).

schizophrenia
a psychosis that involves a thinking disorder, particularly hallucinations and fantasies

Schizophrenic disorders (various forms of **schizophrenia,** a psychosis that involves a thinking disorder, particularly hallucinations and fantasies).

Paranoid disorders (various forms of paranoia).

bipolar disorder
a disorder involving fluctuation between emotional extremes

Mood disorders (depression; **bipolar disorder,** in which the individual fluctuates between emotional extremes).

Anxiety disorders (panic disorder, phobias).

Somatoform disorders (the conversion of emotional into physical problems, as in hysteria).

Dissociative disorders (multiple personality).

Psychosexual disorders (paraphilias).

Disorders of impulse control (pathological gambling, kleptomania).

Personality disorders (narcissism, an absorbing preoccupation with one's own needs, desires, and image).

Extent of Mental Illness.   *Mental illness is a problem in all societies.* It is found among preindustrial people and in small, relatively isolated communities as well as in modernized societies. How many Americans suffer from mental disorders? There are two ways to estimate. We can examine the data on *hospitalization rates,* or we can research communities to get estimates of *"true" prevalence* ("true" because only a minority of people with mental disorders are hospitalized).

deinstitutionalization
a movement to change the setting of treatment of mental disorders from hospitals to the community through rapid discharge of patients

Rates of hospitalization must be interpreted cautiously because they reflect changing styles of treatment as well as changing levels of prevalence. Therapy with new drugs became common in the late 1950s. In the 1960s, **deinstitutionalization**—a movement to change the setting of treatment from the state mental hospital to the community— began. (We discuss deinstitutionalization later in this chapter.) Thereafter, the number of patients in hospitals decreased, although the number of admissions increased until the 1970s. Since the mid-1980s, the proportion of Americans admitted to mental

EXCEPT ME AND THEE?

There is an old saying that all the world is crazy except "me and thee, and sometimes I am not too sure of thee." As we point out in this chapter, it is probable that only a minority of the population is free of any psychiatric symptoms. To say that someone has symptoms, of course, does not mean that the individual requires psychiatric care or has problems functioning in his or her responsibilities. Nevertheless, the ideal for Americans would be the very best health—freedom from all symptoms.

How do you stack up? You can test yourself on a set of symptoms suggested by Walter Gove and Michael Geerken (1977). For the symptoms listed, write "often," "sometimes," or "never" beside each to indicate how often you have experienced them during the past few weeks.

1. I felt anxious about something or someone.
2. I was bothered by special fears.
3. I felt that people were saying things behind my back.
4. I felt it was safer not to trust anyone.
5. I couldn't take care of things because I couldn't get going.
6. I was so blue or depressed that it interfered with my daily activities.
7. I was bothered by nervousness.
8. I was in low spirits.
9. I was bothered by special thoughts.
10. I was so restless I couldn't sit for long in a chair.
11. I felt that nothing turned out the way I wanted it to.
12. I felt alone even when I was among friends.
13. I felt that personal worries were getting me down, making me physically ill.
14. I felt that nothing was worthwhile anymore.

Give yourself two points for each "often," one point for each "sometimes," and no points for each "never."

Your total score can range between 0 and 28. A score of 0 would mean that you are completely free of psychiatric symptoms. A score of 28 would mean that you have serious levels of those symptoms. If the entire class participates in this exercise, each score can be given anonymously to the instructor, who can give you the range and compute the average for the entire class. What do you think the results say about the prevalence of psychiatric symptoms in the population? Do you think students' scores would be higher or lower than those of the population at large? Why?

hospitals has remained at a low level. Even some chronically mentally ill people are not hospitalized, and those who are admitted are staying a shorter time. Thus, the total population in hospitals is less than it was from 1965 to 1975.

Surveys are a better way to estimate prevalence. National surveys conducted by the Substance Abuse and Mental Health Services Administration (2015; Karg et al. 2014) found:

About 22.5 percent American adults (51.2 million people in 2014) suffer from a mental disorder in any given year.

The prevalence of mental disorders varies by racial/ethnic group: 19.2 percent of whites, 15.6 percent of Hispanics, 16.3 percent of African Americans, 13.1 percent of Asian Americans, and 21.2 percent of American Indians.

In 2014, 4.1 percent of adults had a "serious" mental disorder, with a mean of 88.3 days when they couldn't carry out their normal daily activities.

The prevalence of serious mental disorders varies by gender (3.1 percent of men and 5.0 percent of women) and age (4.8 percent of those 18–25 years, 5.1 percent of those 26–44 years, 4.2 percent of those 45–64 years, and 1.5 percent of those 65 years or older).

Major depressive disorder, which affects 6.3 percent of the adult population in any given year, is the leading cause of disability; it is more prevalent in women than in men.

Anxiety disorders are the second most common type, affecting about 5.7 percent of the population.

Mental disorders tend to appear early in life; in 2014, 11.4 percent of adolescents aged 12-17 years had at least one major depressive episode.

Variations exist in both the prevalence of the different disorders and in the at-risk background factors. The prevalence doesn't remain stable over time. The rates of some disorders are going up. For example, anxiety disorders have increased among children and young adults (Twenge 2000). Rates of depression have also increased. As far as at-risk background factors are concerned, socioeconomic status and gender are both important. Rates tend to be higher among the lower social classes, and rates vary between men and women. In general, men have more problems with substance abuse and higher rates of antisocial personality disorder, whereas women have more anxiety disorders and depression. Depression affects twice as many women as men. This higher rate among women, incidentally, seems to be universal. An examination of 29 different nations found that females have more depression than males in all of them (Hopcroft and Bradley 2007).

Finally, mental disorders are so prevalent that they cost the nation more than $200 billion each year (McCarthy 2016). The cost includes such things as the care of nursing home residents, long-term patients in mental hospitals, and prisoners.

Health Care, Illness, and the Quality of Life

One effect that illness has on the quality of life is this: People must endure considerable stress and suffering because of illness, which is a contradiction to Americans' value of good health. In addition, illness affects interpersonal relationships, involves people in inadequate health care, interferes with individual freedom, and costs the individual and the nation economically.

Stress and Suffering

The obvious impact of illness on the quality of life is the *stress and suffering* that illness imposes on people. Consider Anton Boisen's (1936:3) account of his psychotic episode:

> [T]here came surging in upon me with overpowering force a terrifying idea about a coming world catastrophe. Although I had never before given serious thought to such a subject, there came flashing into my mind, as though from a source without myself, the idea that this little planet of ours, which has existed for we know not how many millions of years, was about to undergo some sort of metamorphosis. It was like a seed or an egg. In it were stored up a quantity of food materials, represented by our natural resources. But now we were like a seed in the process of germinating or an egg that had just been fertilized. We were starting to grow. Just within the short space of a hundred years we had begun to draw upon our resources to such an extent that the timber and the gas and the oil were likely soon to be exhausted. In the wake of this idea followed others. I myself was more important than I had ever dreamed of being; I was also a zero quantity. Strange and mysterious forces of evil of which before I had not had the slightest suspicion were also revealed. I was terrified beyond measure and in terror I talked. . . . I soon found myself in a psychopathic hospital. There followed three weeks of violent delirium which remain

indelibly burned into my memory. . . . It seemed as if I were living thousands of years within that time. Then I came out of it much as one awakens out of a bad dream.

Physical illness also involves *stressful disruptions* in a person's life. If the person's work is disrupted, he or she may experience economic anxiety. If the illness is chronic, the individual may struggle with his or her identity (what kind of person am I?) and with alterations in lifestyle (Charmaz 1995). Protracted or chronic illness also affects the rest of the family (Lundwall 2002). Taking care of a chronically ill individual is demanding and stressful (Adams, Aranda, Kemp, and Takagi 2002). The marital relationship may suffer (Woods and Lewis 1995). Family patterns may be altered and highly constrained by the sick member, particularly if other family members must become caregivers over an extended period of time. For example, a study of the parents of children with cancer reported a significant worsening of the parents' health following the diagnosis of the cancer (Wiener et al. 2016).

Because physical and mental health are intertwined, physical health problems can generate *long-term fears* and even *serious emotional problems.* A substantial number of people experience high levels of psychological distress before or after surgery (Glosser et al. 2000). People diagnosed with serious diseases such as AIDS may develop high levels of anxiety and depression, problems with their work and social lives, and thoughts of suicide (Griffin, Rabkin, Remien, and Williams 1998).

Heart attack victims and cancer patients may have problems readjusting to normal routines. They often experience depression and anxiety even when the prognosis for the future is good, and they may have serious reservations about returning to a normal routine (Peleg-Oren and Sherer 2001). Patients with arthritis report a *significantly lower quality of life* than those without chronic disease (Anderson, Kaplan, and Ake 2004).

Serious *emotional problems* often are involved in cases of *organ transplants* (Dew et al. 2001). Severe depression and even psychosis have been reported. Men who receive organs from women may fear that their characters will be altered or that they will be feminized. Some patients develop fantasies about the transplanted organ and think of it almost in human terms as a living being within them. Some develop an image of the organ as a malevolent or hostile being; others conceive of it as life-giving. Not every patient has such serious problems, of course, but some long-term fears are probably common.

The *disabled* also endure stress and suffering because they are often *socially disvalued.* Social devaluation is particularly acute when the disability is visible. The visibly disabled individual may be treated as inferior and may be subject to serious disadvantages in job opportunities. Such experiences result in insecurity and anxiety.

The close relationship of physical and mental illness works both ways, because emotional problems can lead to physical illness. It is well-known, for example, that chronic negative emotions such as hostility, cynicism, and anxiety are risk factors for heart disease (Grewal, Gravely-Witte, Stewart, and Grace 2011; Stauber et al. 2012). To some extent, the problem can become a vicious circle for the individual, who may become entangled in the interaction between physical and mental disorders.

Interpersonal Relationships

There is a contradiction between the *sick role* and Americans' attitudes and values about desirable behavior; this contradiction can result in disrupted interpersonal relationships. Although people realize that illness is inevitable, they are reluctant to allow illnesses of others to disturb their routines. Furthermore, some illnesses, such as cancer and various kinds of mental illness, carry a social **stigma** (Angermeyer, Beck, Dietrich, and Holzinger 2004; Sandelowski, Lambe, and Barroso 2004; Wright, Wright, Perry, and

stigma
that which symbolizes
disrepute or disgrace

Foote-Ardah 2007). A survey of parents and spouses of 156 first-admission psychiatric patients found that half of them concealed the hospitalization to some degree (Phelan, Bromet, and Link 1998). They did not want people to know that someone in their immediate family had a mental disorder.

The *strain on interpersonal relationships* when one of the interactants is ill is also seen in patterns of family relationships. Both physical and mental illness can lead to disruption in the family. In families with a chronically ill member, the ill member can become a focal point of family life. If the mother is ill, the husband and children may experience an emotional void in their lives. If the father is ill, there is a likelihood of economic problems and a lowered standard of living. Moreover, the father may tend to monopolize the attention of his wife, leaving the children feeling neglected. If the family develops a subculture of illness, they withdraw into themselves, isolated from outsiders.

Not all families respond to serious illness in this way, of course. Some families become more integrated, and the members experience a greater richness of family life. Others experience a temporary breakdown but recover and return to normal. Still others disintegrate in the face of the challenge, especially if the family was already weakly integrated. In every case, however, illness presents a serious challenge to the family.

One reason serious illness tends to disrupt family life is that it *precludes proper role functioning.* The physically or emotionally ill may be incapable of adequately fulfilling the role of spouse, parent, or breadwinner (Peleg-Oren and Sherer 2001). The normal functioning of family life may give way to a focus on the ill person. In extreme cases, most activities of family members reflect the ill person's needs and limitations.

As with the interplay between mental and physical illness, the relationship between interpersonal relations and illness can become a vicious circle. Poor interpersonal relationships can be a factor in the onset of a mental disorder, and mental disorders adversely affect interpersonal relationships. On the other hand, *good interpersonal relationships are associated with better health* (Berkman 2000). Those who have satisfying, close relationships have better mental and physical health, fewer problems of drug and alcohol abuse, and higher levels of satisfaction with their lives.

In sum, there is a relationship between patterns of interaction and health. Illness, whether physical or mental, tends to be associated with disturbed interpersonal relationships. The relation between interaction and illness may be a vicious circle: bad interpersonal relationships being a factor in the onset of illness, and illness being a factor in causing disturbed relationships.

Inadequate Care

The value of good health is contradicted by the *inadequate care* that many Americans receive for both physical and mental illnesses (a national study about the latter concluded that *most* people with mental disorders are either untreated or poorly treated) (Wang et al. 2005). Inadequate care may result from a variety of factors. One important factor is the *lack of health insurance,* including 5.2 percent of all children under the age of 18 (Barnett and Vornovitsky 2016). Medicare provides seniors with some coverage, but, despite the Affordable Care Act, in 2015 10.5 percent of Americans under the age of 65 were uninsured (Figure 13.2).

The proportion who lack health insurance varies by racial/ethnic group as well as by age. In 2015, non-Hispanic whites had the lowest uninsured rate (6.7 percent) and Hispanics had the highest (16.2 percent) (Barnett and Vornovitsky 2016). The African American rate was 11.1 percent and the Asian American was 7.5 percent.

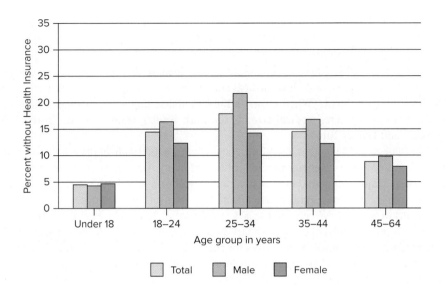

FIGURE 13.2
Percent of Persons under
65 without Health Insurance
Coverage, 2015.
SOURCE: Cohen, Martinez, and
Zammitti 2016.

Lack of insurance can lead people to delay or avoid needed health care, or to find questionable or useless kinds of care (e.g., the use of a copper bracelet to treat arthritis). In 2014, nearly a third of uninsured Americans delayed or failed to get needed medical care, and about one of six failed to get a needed prescription drug, because of the cost (National Center for Health Statistics 2016).

Errors by the medical establishment are another factor in inadequate care. Errors include **iatrogenic** problems, those caused by the physician in the course of a patient's treatment. Physicians may misdiagnose a case, prescribe the wrong medication, and even order unnecessary surgery (Pilippo et al. 1999; Shojania, Burton, McDonald, and Goldman 2003; Waldman and Smith 2012). In a five-year study of patient safety in 10 North Carolina hospitals, researchers found 588 incidents of patient harm among the 2,341 patients admitted (Landrigan et al. 2010). This amounts to 25 harmful incidents per 100 patients. The incidents included such things as severe bleeding during surgery, serious breathing problems due to an incorrectly performed procedure, injury and nerve damage resulting from a fall, and vaginal cuts caused by a device used to help deliver babies.

iatrogenic
caused by the physician in the course of his or her treatment of a patient

Women seem to be particularly prone to iatrogenic problems. One study concluded that 81.2 percent of the caesarean sections performed in four hospitals were unjustified (Gomez and Carrasquilla 1999). Another study drew the same conclusion about 70 percent of the hysterectomies performed on 497 California women (Broder, Kanouse, Mittman, and Bernstein 2000).

Hospital personnel, including medical lab technicians, also make mistakes. An analysis of critical care patients reported that medication error was the most common kind of medical error (MacFie, Baudouin, and Messer 2016). A study of medication in 36 hospitals reported that nearly one of five doses were in error—given at the wrong time, not given, given in the wrong amount, or were an unauthorized drug (Barker et al. 2002). A national study concluded that on average a hospital patient suffers at least one medication error each day, and that such errors harm 1.5 million patients and kill thousands each year in the United States (Aspden, Wolcott, Bootman, and Cronenwett 2007). And a survey of 134 Wisconsin hospitals found that 3.4 percent of the children discharged had one or more medical injuries, injuries resulting from medications, procedures, devices, implants, or grafts (Meurer et al. 2006).

Overall, medical errors probably cause more deaths than car accidents, breast cancer, suicide, homicide, or AIDS. A study by HealthGrades, an organization that rates doctors and hospitals, reported that 195,000 patients die in hospitals each year from preventable errors (Allen 2004). "Preventable errors" include such problems as overdoses, postsurgical infections, and slow medical staff responses to signs of infection or other life-threatening problems. When errors in the hospital setting are combined with errors generally in health care, medical error is the third leading cause of death in the U.S. (Makary and Daniel 2016)!

The value of good health is also contradicted by the actual state of the science of medicine. Contrary to the expectations and attitudes of many Americans, *medicine is an inexact science.* Many symptoms, such as extreme fatigue or a pain in the back, are difficult to diagnose. Moreover, diagnoses are affected by who—in terms of age, sex, and race—physicians expect to have certain diseases (Lutfey et al. 2010). For example, a physician could miss the diagnosis of coronary heart disease in a middle-aged woman because such individuals are not known as high risks for the problem. Diagnosing mental disorders is even more problematic. Psychiatry is a field of *competing ideologies* rather than a science of mental therapy. There are various schools of therapy with different ideologies of health and illness and different views about diagnostic categories. A psychiatrist's diagnosis of a case will depend partly on *which school of therapy* he or she follows, but even within a particular ideology, diagnosis of mental disorders is difficult.

A psychiatric diagnosis also may be influenced by stereotyped thinking. That is, the **fallacy** diagnosis may be a perfect illustration of the *fallacy of non sequitur:* "because this is a woman, her symptoms show her to be hysterical," and so forth. It isn't that the therapist consciously thinks in those terms, of course, but the diagnosis does reflect stereotypes, whether the stereotype involves gender, race, or social class (Dixon, Gordon, and Khomusi 1995; Wang, Demler, and Kessler 2002).

For example, 209 psychiatrists evaluated two cases of patients with a schizophrenic disorder (Loring and Powell 1988). All the symptoms were presented, but the researchers varied the race and gender of the patients. Some of the psychiatrists thought they were evaluating two white males, whereas others evaluated two white females, two black males, two black females, or two clients with unnamed sex and race. A majority correctly identified the disorder as schizophrenia when no sex or race was listed. For the other cases, less than a majority made the correct diagnosis. Only 21 percent diagnosed the white females correctly. The race and gender of both the psychiatrist and the patient tended to affect the diagnosis. In general, when the race and sex of psychiatrist and patient were the same, the diagnosis tended to be the same as if there were no information about the patient's sex and race. In other cases, however, the psychiatrists were affected by stereotypical thinking.

In addition to incompetence, errors, and the fact that medicine is an art as well as a science, many Americans do not receive the quality of care they desire because of the *maldistribution of medical care.* Both economic and geographic factors enter into the maldistribution. *Maldistribution of doctors* means that people in certain areas have less access to doctors than those in other areas. There are a disproportionate number of doctors and nurses in cities and in the more well-to-do areas of the cities, leaving many rural areas and impoverished urban neighborhoods with inadequate care. For example, in 2013 the number of physicians per 10,000 population varied among the states from a low of 19.2 in Idaho to a high of 47.0 in Massachusetts (the highest was Washington, D.C., with a rate of 74.7) (National Center for Health Statistics 2016).

Deinstitutionalization

The inadequate care of the mentally ill has been compounded by the deinstitutional-ization movement that began in the mid-1950s (Lamb 1998). Partly because of newly available drugs, state and county hospitals began discharging a great many patients, including some with serious mental disorders and some who could not be effectively treated without 24-hour care. The goal was to provide a more humane, more effec-tive, and less costly method of treating the disorders by using a community setting rather than a mental hospital. The drugs would keep the patients from harming oth-ers or themselves and enable them to function relatively well while they recovered. Their recovery would be facilitated by more normal living conditions. Further, their civil rights would be respected. In other words, the movement seemed to offer a new and enlightened approach that would transform the care of the mentally ill. Unfortunately, the reality diverged sharply from the ideal, adding to the problem of inadequate care.

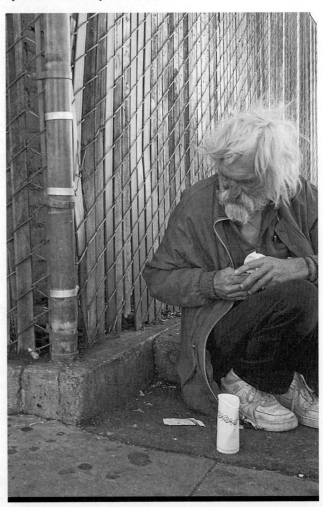

One goal was met: A great many patients were re-leased from hospitals. Patients who now go into hos-pitals are likely to stay only a short time compared to those who were institutionalized before 1960. As a result, the hospitals are treating more people than for-merly, but they also have fewer patients in residence at any one time.

Nevertheless, deinstitutionalization has not only failed to solve many problems, it has also created new ones. In fact, many observers regard the movement as a total failure because it has basically taken the men-tally ill out of the hospitals and put them on the streets or in the jails (Isaac and Armat 1990; Gilligan 2001). Recent research indicates that there are more than 2 million of the deinstitutionalized mentally ill who receive no treatment, and more than 300,000 of them are in prisons or jails (Amadeo 2016a).

Studies of the homeless illustrate the way in which deinstitutionalization has failed. A majority of the homeless have serious problems of mental ill-ness, including drug addiction (National Coalition the Homeless 2009). Homeless shelters are avail-, but they are hardly adequate to provide treat-t for the mentally ill even if the staff had the

Thus, large numbers of the deinstitutionalized
lly ill are lost and homeless or in jails. The problem is compounded by laws
th ake it difficult to involuntarily hospitalize the mentally ill. Thus, the legal
bas r the deinstitutionalization movement—the rights of patients—keeps some
men ill individuals at liberty until they act violently toward themselves or others
(Isaa d Armat 1990). Unfortunately, most individuals with severe mental disorders r ire medication, and the disorders are likely to impair their judgment and
make i likely that they will voluntarily submit to treatment.

As a result of deinstitutionalization, many severely mentally ill patients have become homeless.

©McGraw-Hill Education./ Christopher Kerrigan, photographer

Individual Freedom

Americans are an individualistic people. They cherish the *freedom of the individual* and tend to react strongly to anything that threatens that freedom. However, there is sometimes a contradiction between the value of individual freedom and the value of good health. Some religious groups, for example, resist medical procedures such as blood transfusions and vaccinations on the grounds that these procedures violate their religious beliefs. If they are forced to undergo such medical treatment, their religious convictions and freedom of choice are violated. However, a counterargument is made that they may jeopardize the health or the lives of others by their refusal; thus, their freedom cannot extend to the point at which it affects the well-being of others. The same issue of individual freedom versus public well-being arises in such issues as providing a health identification number for every individual, mandatory notification of the parents of adolescents who use health care services, and the right of noncompliance with treatment of tuberculosis and other infectious diseases (Netter 2003; Adams 2004; Senanayake and Ferson 2004).

The issue of freedom is also raised by advances in biological engineering. The 1972 National Sickle Cell Anemia Control Act required people to submit to a screening blood test to determine the likelihood of their producing children with sickle cell anemia. Many people felt that this law was a clear invasion of privacy. Many more would probably consider it an invasion of privacy if the next step were taken: preventing people with certain genetic deficiencies from having children or even from marrying. Certain genetic diseases can be controlled only by forbidding certain couples to have children. Which, then, is more important: individual freedom or public health and welfare?

The history of medicine is marked by ongoing conflict between the advocates of medical advance and those who defend the freedom of the individual. Greater advances in medicine will intensify the conflict and compound the problems.

Economic Costs

An increasing amount of the nation's *economic resources* is channeled into the effort to combat illness and promote good health. And the costs are growing rapidly. Americans spent $4,121 per capita (or a total of nearly $1.2 trillion) for health care in 2000 and $8,054 per capita (or a total of nearly $2.6 trillion) in 2014 (National Center for Health Statistics 2016). The cost of health is not limited to expenditures, of course. There are also such factors as the loss of income and productivity when people are ill. Mental disorders alone cost the nation about $200 billion each year in lost earnings.

The personal cost can be massive. About a fifth of Americans live in families in which health care costs more than 10 percent of family income (Banthin and Bernard 2006). And 7.3 percent are living in families in which the costs are 20 percent or more of family income. Such burdensome costs often result from long-term chronic diseases and diseases requiring the use of *sophisticated medical technology*. Even with health insurance, an individual or a family may *find the cost of illness oppressive*. Why the dramatic increase in costs? Three factors can account for the increase in expenditures on medical care since 1950: inflation, population growth, and technological advances and the increasing use of medical services involving these expensive advances (Callahan 1998).

Thus, an increasing portion of the economic resources of individuals, families, and the nation are consumed by medical care (Toner and Stolberg 2002). The cost of that care includes the value of goods and services not produced because of illness. For example, workers with depression cost employers an estimated $44 billion per year in lost productive time (Stewart et al. 2003). Physical illness also results in lost productive time; in a national study, 13 percent of the workforce experienced a loss in productive time during a two-week period because of a common pain condition (headaches, back pain, arthritis pain, etc.) (Stewart et al. 2003). With the costs of both physical and mental health care continuing to rise each year, an interesting question arises. Despite the high value placed on good health, is there a point at which Americans will forgo some measure of health care in order to retain more of their economic resources?

Contributing Factors

We have pointed out that there are sociocultural factors in illness. In this section we examine some of those factors in detail. We show that sociocultural factors are involved not only in the **etiology** (causes of diseases) but also in inadequate care and the maldistribution of care.

etiology
the causes of a disease

Social Structural Factors

Roles. Many studies have shown that *stress* leads to a variety of physical and mental health problems, including cardiovascular disease, digestive problems, heightened susceptibility to infection, problems of the skeletal-muscular system, and mental disorders (Mayer, Craske, and Naliboff 2001; House 2002). Stress can be a product of roles that are excessively demanding, contradictory, or overly restrictive. Not everyone who occupies a particular role will experience the same amount of stress, nor will everyone who occupies a particular role get sick. Nonetheless, *certain roles are considered stress-inducing* because they have been associated with a disproportionate amount of illness, particularly the female role and certain occupational roles in American society.

Women seem to have more health problems than men. Health statistics consistently show that women in the United States and other Western nations have higher rates of **morbidity,** health service usage, and certain mental disorders (Ladwig, Marten-Mittag, Formanek, and Dammann 2000; Kendler, Thornton, and Prescott 2001; National Center for Health Statistics 2016). In part, these health problems reflect the fact that women generally suffer more distress (sadness, anger, anxiety, aches, etc.) than men (Mirowsky and Ross 1995)—and this, in turn, may be rooted in the female role.

morbidity
the prevalence of a specified illness in a specified area

One characteristic of the female role is that *women are more emotionally involved than are men in the lives of the people around them* (Shih and Eberhart 2010). Women are more likely than men to be stressed by "network" events (events in the lives of loved ones) such as the death of a spouse, divorce, and illness of a family member. The cost of this caring is greater vulnerability to stress and illness.

The *traditional role of married women* is another reason for higher rates of illness (DeStafano and Colasanto 1990). Married women have higher rates of mental disorders than married men, but single or widowed women tend to have lower rates than their male counterparts. (Among both sexes, married people have lower rates than unmarried people [see, e.g., King and Reis 2012; Uecker 2012].)

We have noted that the majority of married women now work outside the home. Is it, then, a problem of overload? Interestingly, working tends to enhance rather than diminish the health of women (Schnittker 2007). In other words, *multiple roles are associated with better health* (Hong and Seltzer 1995; Ahrens and Ryff 2006). The point is, the restrictions of the traditional role—staying at home and taking care of the house and children—are more stressful for many women than taking on additional responsibilities. To be sure, some women find the traditional role fulfilling, but others do not. Women who are confined to, but dissatisfied with, the traditional role of housewife exhibit higher rates of illness (Shehan, Burg, and Rexroat 1986). This conclusion is supported by research showing that when men and women have equivalent gender roles, the gender differences in health tend to disappear (Bird and Fremont 1991; Gutierrez-Lobos 2000). In sum, for both men and women, role satisfaction is associated with better health (Wickrama et al. 1995).

We noted in Chapter 10 that certain occupational roles generate considerable physical and/or mental risks. In some cases, the occupational role may carry intrinsic risks— for example, mining occupations or high-pressure sales jobs. In other cases, the risks reflect the particular shape the role is given by the people in the workplace. For example, an engineer told us:

> I love my work. But I hate this job. My boss terrorizes everyone. If it was just the work I do, I would love going in. But I get a feeling of dread when I go through the gates every morning because I never know from one day to the next what new craziness we'll all have to endure from the boss. His demands are unreasonable, and you can't sit down and discuss things with him. He has managed to turn enjoyable work into a daily grind.

The Family Context of Illness.   Among the institutional arrangements that contribute to illness are family patterns of interaction and **socialization** (the process by which an individual learns to participate in a group). We noted in the previous section that married people of both sexes have lower rates of mental illness than the unmarried. The mental health of the married couple depends on the quality of the marriage, however. When the intimate relationship between a man and a woman is defined by both as basically rewarding, the pair is more likely to enjoy positive mental and physical health (Lee and Bulanda 2005; Kaplan and Kronick 2006; Tower and Krasner 2006). Infidelity or a conflicted relationship, in contrast, is associated with major depression (Cano and O'Leary 2000).

For children, both physical and mental health are crucially related to the *quality of the relationship between the child and parents* (Feeney 2000). Children who have a good relationship with their parents and who feel themselves to be an integral part of family life are less likely to engage in various kinds of health risk behavior, including the use of alcohol, tobacco, and other drugs (Thuen et al. 2015).

Family disruption is stressful for children and typically leads to higher rates of physical and emotional problems. A study of 2-year-olds, for example, reported a higher proportion of accidents and higher rates of treatment for physical illnesses among those in single-parent and stepfamilies than those in intact homes (Dunn, Golding, Davies, and O'Connor 2000).

The adverse effects of a troubled family life may continue into adulthood. Thus, researchers found that the mental health of mothers of newborn infants had an impact on their children's romantic relationships 30 years later (Slominski, Sameroff, Rosenblum, and Kasser 2011). Mothers with mental health problems were more likely to raise children who had difficulty establishing meaningful, secure, romantic attachments.

Siblings as well as parents are important to a child's well-being. Thus, in a community study, researchers found that children who had siblings with a substance abuse problem were more likely both to use drugs themselves and to suffer from depression (Reinherz et al. 2000). They also found more depression among children whose parents were depressed.

The Industrial Economy.   Certain aspects of the American economy, and indeed of the world economy, are involved in the onset of illness. In an increasingly industrial, technological world, people and materials move around the globe in great numbers. An infectious virus can now travel around the world in a few hours.

socialization
the process by which an individual learns to participate in a group

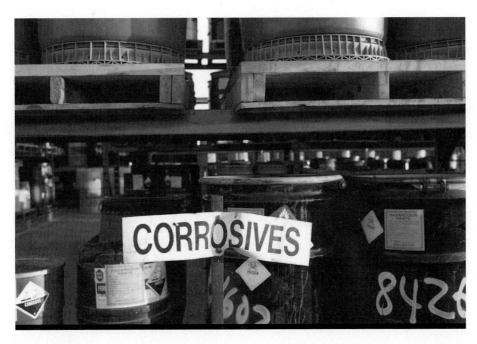

In the modern economy, both agricultural workers (because of the use of artificial fertilizers, herbicides, and pesticides) and other workers are exposed to materials that are **carcinogenic** (cancer-causing). Some common carcinogens in nonagricultural occupations are shown in Table 13.3. People who work in industries using carcinogenic materials are more likely to get cancer than are others.

carcinogenic
causing cancer

An industrial economy also exposes the citizenry to illness through *different kinds of pollution.* Lead poisoning can have disastrous effects on children: mental retardation, behavioral difficulties, perceptual problems, and emotional instability. Lead poisoning is most common among ghetto children, who ingest chips of paint from flaking walls or other substances containing lead (Richardson 2002). Use of lead in paint was discontinued for the most part by 1950, but leaded paint still exists in older buildings. Craving for such unnatural substances—a condition called **pica**—is frequently associated with impoverished living. In rural areas, pica may lead to eating dirt and clay, which is not healthful but is probably less damaging than leaded paint.

pica
a craving for unnatural food, such as dirt or clay

The most familiar pollutant to many Americans is automobile exhaust, which contains carbon monoxide. Carbon monoxide poisoning can lead to apathy, headaches, perceptual problems, retardation, and even psychosis. However, the precise effects of carbon monoxide poisoning are unclear. The amount of carbon monoxide released into the air from automobile exhaust varies considerably from one area to another. We discuss chemical pollutants further in Chapter 15.

Noise is another kind of pollution linked to the industrial economy that can have deleterious effects. The noise level endured by some workers can create mental stress, as can road traffic noise and the noise associated with living near an airport (Stansfeld and Matheson 2003). Children appear to be particularly vulnerable to noise pollution. Environmental noise can impair reading comprehension, long-term memory, and motivation and may also be associated with elevated blood pressure (Haines, Brentnall, Stansfeld, and Klineberg 2003; Stansfeld and Matheson 2003). A study of German

Agent	Organ Affected	Occupation
Wood	Nasal cavity and sinuses	Woodworkers
Leather	Nasal cavity and sinuses; urinary bladder	Leather and shoe workers
Iron oxide	Lung; larynx	Iron ore miners; metal grinders and polishers; silver finishers; iron foundry workers
Nickel	Nasal sinuses; lung	Nickel smelters, mixers, and roasters; electrolysis workers
Arsenic	Skin; lung; liver	Miners; smelters; insecticide makers and sprayers; tanners; chemical workers; oil refiners; vintners
Chromium	Nasal cavity and sinuses; lung; larynx	Chromium producers, processors, and users; acetylene and aniline workers; bleachers; glass, pottery, and linoleum workers; battery makers
Asbestos	Lung (pleural and peritoneal mesothelioma)	Miners; millers; textile and shipyard workers
Petroleum, petroleum coke, wax, creosote, shale, and mineral oils	Nasal cavity; larynx; lung; skin; scrotum	Workers in contact with lubricating oils, cooling oils, paraffin or wax fuel oils or coke; rubber fillers; retort workers; textile weavers; diesel jet testers
Mustard gas	Larynx; lung; trachea; bronchi	Mustard gas workers
Vinyl chloride	Liver; brain	Plastic workers
Bis-chloromethyl ether, chloromethyl methyl ether	Lung	Chemical workers
Isopropyl oil	Nasal cavity	Isopropyl oil producers
Coal soot, coal tar, other products of coal combustion	Lung; larynx; skin; scrotum; urinary bladder	Gashouse workers, stokers, and producers; asphalt, coal tar, and pitch workers; coke oven workers; miners; still cleaners
Benzene	Bone marrow	Explosives, benzene, or rubber cement workers; distillers; dye users; painters; shoemakers
Auramine, benzidine, alpha-naphthylamine, magenta, 4-aminodiphenyl, 4-nitrodiphenyl	Urinary bladder	Dyestuffs manufacturers and users; rubber workers (pressmen, filtermen, laborers); textile dyers; paint manufacturers

TABLE 13.3

Common Occupational Carcinogens

SOURCE: American Public Health Association; *Health and Work in America* (Washington, DC: Government Printing Office, 1975).

children concluded that high exposure to traffic noise, especially at nighttime, stimulates bodily processes that increase the problem of bronchitis (Ising et al. 2004).

As we noted in Chapter 10, *fluctuations in the state of the economy* also have been identified as having adverse effects on people's health. Unemployment is associated with health problems and increased mortality rates in all societies (Rodriguez 2001; Brenner 2005). In fact, a study of 42 nations showed that unemployment lowers well-being even in those countries with high levels of social security (Ouweneel 2002).

The Politics of Illness. Usually people do not think of illness as a political issue, but *government policy* is a crucial factor in health care. For example, after President Obama signed the Affordable Care Act in 2010, there was an immediate political response from opponents that was designed to sabotage the legislation (Lanford and Quadagno 2016). Lawsuits were filed in 26 states that challenged some of the key provisions. Among those provisions was the expansion of Medicaid in order to insure those in the lower-income brackets. But the Supreme Court ruled that provision unconstitutional, and many states opted not to expand. In addition, a succession of bills to repeal the act were introduced in Congress. Criticism has been so strong and so vocal that a substantial number of Americans disapprove of the law. While the law significantly reduced the proportion of those without any health insurance, the future of health insurance is uncertain because of the political wrangling.

Political factors also enter into the struggle against various health problems and diseases. American infant mortality rates, for example, are higher than the rates of many other nations, and the rate for African Americans is more than double that for whites (National Center for Health Statistics 2016). Yet the African Americans most at risk—those in impoverished areas—are least likely to have the political influence necessary to secure federal funds for infant health programs.

Another example is provided by a physician, Jane Hightower (2008). She was concerned about the health problems of some of her patients, and eventually traced the source to the mercury-laden fish they had eaten. Although the toxic nature of mercury is well-known, industry and government had colluded to obscure the danger of eating the fish, working to protect the profits of those who caught and sold the fish rather than the health of those who were consuming it. Thus, scientific findings may be ignored or downplayed or rejected by politicians and businesspeople (and by scientists whose work is funded by corporations—recall the notorious few scientists whose work was funded by tobacco companies and who persisted in downplaying the hazards of smoking in the face of overwhelming evidence to the contrary).

Funding for research into causes and cures of diseases reflects political as well as scientific and humanitarian considerations. Of course, political decisions may reflect ideological considerations as well as economic ones, as well illustrated by the controversy over stem cell research during the Bush administration (Rosenberg 2002). Stem cells are obtained from human embryos, which are destroyed in the process. The medical value of embryonic stem cells lies in the fact that they can become any type of cell in a child or adult, which means that they have the potential to cure a variety of diseases that result from particular cells in the body being disabled or destroyed (diabetes, Parkinson's disease, cirrhosis of the liver, etc.).

But the embryos are destroyed in the process, and many of those who believe that human life begins at conception consider the destruction of an embryo an act of murder. Based on this reasoning, the government limited federal funding of research to existing stem cell lines, which most researchers considered inadequate and of poor quality. This decision was reversed in the Obama administration, which once again allowed the creation of new stem cell lines.

From a strictly scientific point of view, the years when no new stem cell lines could be created were a setback to important medical research. From an ideologically informed view, depending on your beliefs, they were either years of high moral ground or of the subservience of medical considerations to political ones. In any case, it is clear that political decisions are at least as important as scientific ones in research that bears upon the health of Americans.

Finally, there is the issue of governmental regulations that can reduce exposure to a number of known health threats. Fagin and Lavelle (1999) ask why no regulations exist on such actions as the use of certain toxic weed killers that have been linked with cancer and birth defects in farming communities, the use by dry cleaners of a chemical that pollutes homes, and "dry clean only" labels in clothing that can now be cleaned by cheaper and safer water-based alternatives. Of course, the answer to these and the other examples they cite is that political considerations outweigh public health needs.

The Stratification of Illness.   When we speak of the stratification of illness, we are referring to the *different patterns of illness* and *variations in health care among the socioeconomic strata.* People in the lower strata tend to have more, and more serious, health problems than those in the middle and upper strata. With regard to physical health problems, for example, those in the lower strata have higher rates of chronic illnesses such as asthma, hypertension, diabetes, and heart disease; suffer more days of restricted activity due to illness; are less likely to use health care services (including fewer visits to physicians and dentists); are less likely to use preventive health measures such as vaccinations; are more likely to report daily pain as a result of financial worries; and have higher risks of death from all causes in each age category (Stringhini et al. 2010; Johnson and Schoeni 2011; Ferraroa, Schafer, and Wilkinson 2016; National Center for Health Statistics 2016).

Ironically, then, poor and uneducated Americans have the fewest resources to meet medical expenses and the greatest likelihood of discovering that they have a serious, chronic, disabling, or even fatal illness. The pattern of physical illness in American society—more problems and less help as people descend the socioeconomic ladder—is likely to continue because of both the lack of information and resources among the poor and the concentration of medical services outside the areas where they live.

The pattern for mental illness is similar. In general, the rates of psychiatric disorders are higher in the lower strata (Wheaton and Clarke 2003; Strohschein 2005a; Wickdrama, Conger, Lorenz, and Jung 2008; McLaughlin et al. 2012).

The higher rates of illness in the lower strata reflect in part their lower likelihood of having health insurance and regular health care. They also reflect, however, the greater number and intensity of stressors in their lives: more role problems, more family disorganization, more financial stress, a greater number of stressful life events, and a more unhealthy lifestyle (such as smoking, abuse of drugs and alcohol, and poor eating habits (Grzywacz, Almeida, Neupert, and Ettner 2004; Clouston et al. 2015; Mirowsky and Ross 2015; Lippert 2016).

Social Change and Health   As a society changes, the nature of health problems also changes. For example, new technologies (such as vaccines, new drugs, better tests, new kinds of surgery) clearly affect our health status. Many of them contribute to better health. But some can have adverse effects as well. The Internet, for instance, can enhance people's ability to understand health issues. It can also cloud understanding by offering conflicting or erroneous information. Also the compulsive use of the Internet by teenagers leads to problems of mental health (Ciarrochi et al. 2016). Adults who are compulsive users can also develop mental health issues such as depression (Dokoupil 2012).

It is not only change per se that can be problematic. The *rate of change* also affects our well-being. One effort to measure the effects of rate is the Social Readjustment Rating Scale. A respondent indicates which of the 43 events composing the scale have occurred to him or her within the last year. The events include role changes (such as death of spouse, divorce or marriage, beginning or stopping work) and changes in institutional participation (school, church activities, financial status). Each event is rated in terms of how much adjustment it requires. Scores range from 100 for the most stressful event (death of a spouse) to 11 for the least stressful (a minor violation of the law). The total score reflects the number and kinds of events that have occurred in an individual's life during the previous year. In one study, 79 percent of people scoring 300 or above, 51 percent of those scoring between 200 and 299, and 37 percent of those scoring between 150 and 199 had changes in their health in the following year (Holmes and Masuda 1974).

Considerable research since the early 1970s supports the thesis. For example, a high rate of change in life events can result in more injuries (Lee, Niemcryk, Jenkins, and Rose 1989), panic attacks (Pollard, Pollard, and Corn 1989), a lessening of the body's ability to ward off disease (Zautra, Okun, Robinson, and Lee 1989), and various other physical and emotional disorders (Turner and Lloyd 1999; McQuaid et al. 2000; Tiet et al. 2001; Malik and Malik 2016).

Note, however, that although a rapid rate of change does increase stress, the stress may be moderated if the people perceive the changes as desirable (Lauer 1974; Vinokur and Selzer 1975). It is *undesirable life events,* rather than change per se, that are likely to cause illness. People may function in a context of rapid change with minimal effects on their physical and mental health as long as they desire the changes that are occurring (and, perhaps, as long as they have areas of stability in the midst of the change).

Social Psychological Factors

Attitudes and Values.   Certain attitudes and values of individuals who are ill, of the public, and of medical personnel affect rates of illness and the nature of health care. Negative attitudes toward one's work can increase the risk of illness. An individual's work is a focal point of his or her existence as well as one of the most time-consuming areas of life. If it is defined in negative terms, the risk of illness is increased (Spector 2002).

A particular personality type, identified by a cluster of attitudes and values, has an increased probability of coronary heart disease (Eaker et al. 2004). Men who are ambitious, highly competitive, and self-driving and who impose frequent deadlines on themselves have a higher incidence of coronary heart disease than do men with opposite characteristics (Rosenman 1990). All these characteristics are admired in American society; they are long-standing American values. Unfortunately, when accepted and followed diligently, they are also the precursors of illness.

The sick person's attitudes about his or her illness and prospects for recovery are another important factor. Some people are skeptical about the ability of medical care to affect their health (Fiscella, Franks, and Clancy 1998). Such skepticism is stronger among young, white males in the lower socioeconomic strata. In contrast, other people believe that their prospects for recovery from illness are very good. They rely confidently on medical help and, in some cases, also believe that God is at work to bring about healing. Positive attitudes, especially ones that are grounded in spirituality, are associated with shorter and fewer illnesses, improved immune functioning, better mental health, and longer life (Phillips, Ruth, and Wagner 1993; Oxman, Freeman, and Manheimer 1995; Braam et al. 2004; Kliewer 2004).

The attitudes of other people may be as important as the ill person's own attitudes. We have noted the stigma associated with certain kinds of physical and mental illness, a stigma that creates adverse reactions in individuals who are ill. For example, people with Parkinson's disease tend to feel ashamed and want to withdraw from public situations because, among other difficulties, they are unable to control their saliva and have difficulty speaking (Nijhof 1995). They are aware of the embarrassment and unease created in people with whom they interact.

Mental illness tends to be even more of a stigma, so much so that many Americans who would benefit from therapy either refuse to seek help or drop out before the therapy is complete (Corrigan 2004). The stigma of mental illness is fueled by a number of myths (Socall and Holtgraves 1992; Wahl 2003). The myths are a form of the *fallacy of personal attack,* because they stigmatize current and past mental patients. The following are some of the common myths:

A person who has been mentally ill can never be normal.

Persons with mental illness are unpredictable.

Mentally ill persons are dangerous.

Anyone who has had shock treatment must be in a really bad way.

When you learn that a person has been mentally ill, you have learned the most important thing about his or her personality.

A former mental patient will make a second-rate employee.

These statements are myths. Note, however, that although the vast majority of people with serious mental illness are no more dangerous than those in the general population, there is a subgroup of the mentally ill that does pose a risk of acting violently (Torrey 1994; Swanson et al. 2002). People with a history of violent behavior, those who do not take their medication, and those with a problem of substance abuse are more likely than other people to engage in violent behavior. Yet for the great majority of the mentally ill, all the statements just listed, including the statement that they are dangerous, are myths.

The myths illustrate the way in which people who are troubled or different tend to be labeled. Thomas Scheff (1966) made the most thorough use of labeling theory to analyze mental illness. According to Scheff, the mentally ill are *rule breakers,* though the rules they break are different from the rules criminals break. The mentally ill break rules that govern normal social interaction, rules that define "common decency" and indicate an acceptance of social reality as defined by the group. Everyone occasionally breaks such rules with impunity. You may, for example, overreact to an insult, refuse to talk to someone who has angered you, or talk too loudly or too softly. The person who consistently breaks the rules of conventional interaction runs the risk of being labeled mentally ill.

Yet not everyone who breaks the rules is labeled mentally ill. In fact, most rule breaking is "denied and is of transitory significance" (Scheff 1966:51). A certain amount of rule breaking always goes unnoticed or unpunished. The response of other people varies in accord with the kinds of rules that are broken. Loud speech, for example, is less likely to be negatively sanctioned than the refusal to speak at all.

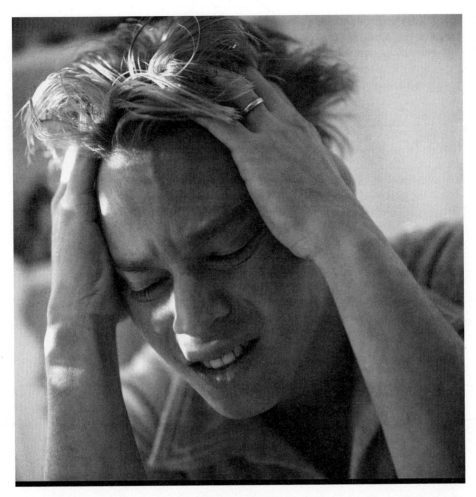

How do people know when to label someone as mentally ill when there are various kinds of behavior that break rules? Scheff points out that *stereotyped imagery of mental illness* is learned early in life and that these stereotypes are reinforced in normal interaction. People avoid behavior that is a stereotype of mental illness and thereby reinforce the image of that behavior as a symptom of mental illness. Furthermore, they evaluate others according to the stereotype.

If an individual behaves in accord with the stereotype, he or she may be labeled mentally ill and rewarded for playing out the stereotyped role. Moreover, the individual may be punished for any attempt to abandon the role and adopt more conventional behavior. This objection occurs because people desire a *predictable social order;* that is, they expect to know how a mentally ill person behaves even if they do not define that behavior as desirable. Just as criminals who avow they are beginning new, law-abiding lives are likely to be treated with some suspicion (their behavior is no longer predictable), the mentally ill who seem to be recovering may be told that they are not as well as they think. In other words, once an individual is labeled as ill, the responses of other people tend to perpetuate the behavior involved.

Scheff denied that his is a complete explanation of mental illness. His aim was not to supplant psychiatric approaches but to supplement them and to stimulate new thinking about mental illness.

Evidence shows that labels do have a significant impact (Markham 2003). Even when the label may enhance sympathetic understanding and help among those with whom the individual has relatively close ties, it is likely to lead to rejection and discrimination by those with whom the individual has more casual ties (Perry 2011). In addition to having to cope with the social stigma, those who are labeled may accept the labels as legitimate and label themselves accordingly. This has further negative consequences. Moses (2009) studied 54 adolescents who were receiving integrated mental health services. Only a minority of the adolescents engaged in self-labeling using psychiatric terms; the majority talked about their problems in nonpathological terms or indicated that they were uncertain or confused about their problems. Those who self-labeled, compared to the others, scored higher on self-stigma and depression. Thus, labeling is a powerful social factor, and even if it does not directly lead to mental illness, it clearly seems to have negative outcomes (Rosenfield 1997).

Attitudes and values also affect medical care of physical illness. The *distribution of physicians* in the United States does not reflect medical need. Physicians, of course, are attracted to places that have desirable resources, abundant professional opportunities, and an active medical community. They also cluster in areas where they are likely to maximize their income. This pattern has been characteristic for some time, and it implicitly means that many Americans are receiving inadequate medical care. Apparently, physicians' attitudes toward working with the less affluent and the value physicians place on income outweigh their commitment to good medical care for all.

The attitudes and values of physicians have inhibited development of governmental programs that would reduce the maldistribution of medical care. Although most physicians now accept and even support Medicare, the American Medical Association (AMA) vigorously opposed the program when it was first proposed. Earlier, organized medicine had opposed Blue Cross plans for many of the same reasons. In both cases the financial benefits to physicians have been enormous. The programs also have provided more Americans with better medical care. Yet this result has often been in spite of, rather than because of, the attitudes and values of physicians.

Public Policy and Private Action

As in the case of drug and alcohol abuse, more money and effort have been expended on the treatment of ill health than on its prevention. In order to change this focus, there needs to be an expansion or improvement of existing programs and the development of new, innovative programs. An example of an existing program that can be expanded is the neighborhood health center, which addresses the maldistribution of care by bringing medical services to previously neglected groups. Poor people, minority groups, and residents of rural areas have benefited from these federally funded centers (Wright et al. 2000). However, the centers have faced difficulties in maintaining a stable professional staff and receiving adequate funding from the federal government.

Health Care Reform

As we noted earlier in this chapter, in 2010 Congress enacted legislation (popularly called "Obamacare") to address some of the serious deficiencies in the American health care system. One of those deficiencies involved the tens of millions of Americans without any health insurance. The lack of health insurance has detrimental effects on both the uninsured individual and on society. As far as the individual is concerned, the need for insurance is dramatized by the fact that when uninsured people reach the age of 65, their health improves significantly because of Medicare (McWilliams, Meara, Zaslavsky, and Ayanian 2007). But the need is also dramatized by the fact that the uninsured are more likely than those with insurance to die before they reach the age of 65 (Wilper et al. 2009b).

With regard to social effects, the uninsured are treated by hospitals in their emergency rooms. The costs of such care are borne by the hospitals; this means that those costs are passed on to insurance companies, who then pass them on to those they insure in the form of higher premiums. In other words, to have a segment of the population uninsured raises the costs of health care for the insured.

The Affordable Care Act reduced the number of those without insurance by, among other things, allowing more of the poor to secure coverage (Sommers 2016). But the lack of insurance is still a deficiency in the system. And there are other deficiencies. One is the lack of adequate care throughout the nation (recall, for example, the wide variation in number of physicians and dentists among the states). Another is the rapidly rising costs to the nation (the United States spends a larger proportion of its gross domestic product on health care than any of the major industrialized nations) and to individuals (in the form of increasingly higher insurance premiums and higher out-of-pocket expenses for care not covered by insurance). The societal cost of health care can be, and has been, exacerbated by overuse of the system. For example, an investigation of a Texas city found that in one recent year Medicare spent $15,000 per enrollee, nearly twice the national average and $3,000 more per year than the average person in the city earned (Gawande 2009). The problem was overuse—far more doctor visits, tests, and medical procedures than in a nearby city in the same state. Clearly, any system can be misused or abused. Regulation and oversight are necessary.

While the challenges are vexing, the need is pressing. In fact, since the administration of Franklin D. Roosevelt, most presidents have argued for some kind of national health insurance program (Pear 2009). Until very recently, however, all efforts at reform failed because of the power of various interest groups. Now those interest groups, including employers, business groups, and insurers, appear ready for change. Still to be hammered out is what kind of change is acceptable. Some want the federal government to offer a plan that would compete with private insurers, but others find this idea abhorrent. Some would prefer the coverage to be dealt with at the state level, but others argue that the states cannot or will not accept such responsibility. Some want whatever system is implemented to be regulated by the free market, but others argue that the system will require close federal regulation. Virtually everyone agrees on one point—health care reform is desperately needed and the federal government will have a crucial role in the reform.

Innovations in the Delivery of Health Care

There is a need for ongoing innovations that effectively deliver health care. For example, an innovation that has emerged in the face of escalating costs is the *managed-care plan, which includes health maintenance organizations (HMOs), point-of-service (POS) plans, and preferred provider organizations (PPOs).* The original idea of the HMO was to offer people a comprehensive, prepaid health care plan. The individual pays an annual fee and receives total medical care, including necessary hospitalization and/or surgery. There are different kinds of HMOs, but one of the important distinctions for the quality of care is that of the not-for-profit versus the investor-owned HMO. A national survey found that patients in the not-for-profit HMOs were more likely to be very satisfied with their care than were patients in the investor-owned groups (Tu and Reschovsky 2002).

There are problems with care by an HMO. One is that administrators who are not physicians or therapists are making decisions about the kind and the length of treatment that will be allowed. Their decisions may be based on keeping costs at a minimum rather than on doing what the physician or therapist considers best for the patient.

Another problem is *capitation,* which means that the doctor receives a fixed monthly amount for each patient (Kuttner 1998). Any additional costs incurred in the treatment of patients must be absorbed by the physician or group of physicians involved. Therapists face the same dilemma in treating mental disorders.

Dissatisfaction with HMOs has led to a growth in the use of the point-of-service (POS) and preferred provider organization (PPO) plans. The *point-of-service* plan allows a patient to go to a health care provider outside the HMO, but the patient must bear the additional cost. The *preferred provider organization* is composed of a network of physicians and hospitals that offer care at discounted rates. A particular PPO may contract with HMOs to treat their patients. The difference is that the physicians remain in their own offices and have patients other than those who come from the HMO.

Innovations in Treatment

Innovations in treatment are also needed. There are, of course, continuing technological innovations that facilitate diagnosis and treatment of various physical illnesses, but there is a need for innovations that consider the close relationships between physical and mental health and between mind and body. The mind plays a key role in health, a fact that needs further exploration and exploitation (Jacobs 2001).

Innovations in the treatment of mental disorders also have been developed in an effort to achieve quicker, more effective results. One approach is the *community support system* (Roskes, Feldman, Arrington, and Leisher 1999). In essence, a variety of services, supports, and opportunities are set up within communities to enable mental patients to function. Among other benefits, the support system can include therapy, health and dental care, a crisis-response service, housing, income maintenance, family and community support, and protection and advocacy services. Community support systems can be more effective than hospitalization in dealing with mental illness (Chinman, Weingarten, Stayner, and Davidson 2001).

Another program offers support to the patient's family when the family is the primary caretaker of the chronically ill person (Bull and McShane 2002). Family care, which is an alternative to hospitalization, generates various kinds of stress. Groups of families entrusted with the care of a chronically ill member meet for support, skill training, and information. With the aid of a mental health professional, the families are able to form a support group that enables each of them to cope with the difficult task.

Prevention

It is usually much less costly and always more beneficial to people to *prevent illnesses* than to treat them once they have emerged. Preventive medical care includes such things as the neighborhood or community health centers that provide checkups for early detection or prevention of physical illness. Similarly, "preventive psychiatry" has emerged as an effort at early detection of mental disorders. Any realistic effort at prevention has to address the sources of stress in society. Stress-inducing roles must be changed. Help must be provided for troubled families. Economic deprivation must be eliminated. Government policy and its agencies must be responsive to health needs rather than to business interests. And people need to be educated about, and encouraged to pursue, those kinds of activities that foster better health, including such things as recreation, finding a social support system, and being a part of groups and organizations like churches that provide a network of friends (Koenig and Vaillant 2009).

One program of prevention that gained momentum in the 1980s is aimed at minimizing or eliminating smoking. Spurred by reports from the surgeon general and antismoking groups, the federal government has banned or restricted smoking in all federal facilities. Many states have done the same, or have gone even further. California, for example, forbids smoking in all public buildings, including restaurants. Such measures, along with increased education and higher taxes on cigarettes, have resulted in a substantial decline in the number of Americans who smoke.

Finally, *a crucial aspect of prevention is lifestyle.* In fact, the three leading causes of death in America are all related to lifestyle. In 2000, the leading causes of death were tobacco (18.1 percent of all deaths), poor diet and physical inactivity (16.6 percent of all deaths), and alcohol consumption (3.5 percent of all deaths) (Mokdad, Marks, Stroup, and Gerberding 2004). Or to put the matter in positive terms, national data show that people with four kinds of low-risk behavior (never smoked, a healthy diet, adequate physical activity, and moderate alcohol consumption) lived an average 11.1 years longer than those with none of the low-risk behaviors (Ford, Zhao, Tsai, and Li 2011). Nevertheless, in spite of considerable information about the value of a healthy lifestyle, *the lifestyle of Americans has tended to become less rather than more healthy.* Only 21.5 percent of adults engage in both aerobic activity and muscle strengthening exercises (National Center for Health Statistics 2016). Nearly half of adults do neither. In addition, in 2014, 34.7 percent of adult men and 36.4 percent of women were obese (a Body Mass Index of 30 or greater). And 20.6 percent of adolescents (12 to 19 years of age) were obese (Ogden et al. 2016). The high rate of obesity is a significant factor in the nation's relatively poor world ranking in longevity (Preston and Stokes 2011). Obesity makes people more vulnerable to disability and various diseases, including arthritis, diabetes, and cancer (Ferraro and Kelley-Moore 2003; Calle, Rodriguez, Walker-Thurmond, and Thun 2003; Leveille, Wee, and Iezzoni 2005). Researchers estimate that obesity causes more than 100,000 excess deaths in the United States each year, and is the seventh leading cause of death (Flegal, Graubard, Williamson, and Gail 2005; Johnson 2005).

The point is, you have a good deal of control over your own health, and you choose to ignore that control at your own peril. A healthy lifestyle is essential for both physical and mental health.

Follow-Up. In what ways do you try to manage your lifestyle in an attempt to prevent illness? What more could you do?

Summary

Good health is a primary value of Americans. Some advances have been made, as indicated by the increasing life expectancy. The main problem of physical health today is chronic diseases rather than the infectious diseases that plagued society in earlier times. Millions of Americans are limited in their activities because of chronic conditions. There is general agreement about the classification of mental disorders, which are found in all societies.

Illness affects the quality of life in many ways. The illness itself and the inadequate care that many Americans receive cause stress and suffering. Interpersonal relationships are adversely affected. Individual freedom is threatened by certain medical advances. Often, heavy economic costs are involved for the nation and for individuals. Both physical and mental illnesses cause fears and anxiety. There is, in fact, a close relationship between physical and mental illness; each can be a factor in bringing about the other, so the individual can be caught in a vicious circle.

Structural factors contribute to the problem. Certain stress-inducing roles have been associated with illness, especially the female role and certain occupational roles. Patterns of interaction and socialization in the family can promote or inhibit good physical and mental health. The industrial economy exposes people to carcinogenic materials and to various pollutants. Fluctuations in the economy generate stress. Political decisions reflect economic interests rather than health needs.

Health care problems are more serious for individuals in the lower than the higher socioeconomic strata. People in the lower strata suffer higher rates of mental and physical illness and receive less adequate care for both. Also, different kinds of illness characterize the various socioeconomic strata.

One other important structural factor is change, and the rate of change, of the structure itself. There is evidence that rapid change may result in illness. A crucial factor in the effects of a changing structure is whether the people define the changes as desirable.

Among social psychological factors, attitudes and values are related to illness. The ill person's attitudes about the illness and his or her prospects for recovery are important. Negative attitudes toward work and certain attitudes rooted in traditional American values increase the probability of illness. Once a person is ill, negative attitudes of other people can inhibit recovery—a problem stressed by labeling theory. The attitudes and values of physicians have contributed to the maldistribution of care and have delayed federal programs designed to correct that maldistribution. These attitudes and values are supported by the ideology of free enterprise, which stresses governmental noninterference in medical care.

Key Terms

AIDS	Morbidity
Bipolar Disorder	Neurosis
Carcinogenic	Pica
Deinstitution-alization	Prevalence
Epidemiology	Psychosis
Etiology	Psychosomatic Disorder
Iatrogenic	Schizophrenia
Incidence	Socialization
Life Expectancy	Stigma

Study Questions

1. What are the various kinds of physical and mental illness, and how prevalent are they?
2. What kinds of suffering are associated with illness?
3. How does problematic health affect interpersonal relationships?
4. In what sense can it be said that Americans have inadequate health care? How has deinstitutionalization contributed to this problem?
5. How does illness affect individual freedom?
6. What are the economic costs of health and illness?
7. How do gender and occupational roles contribute to health and illness?
8. In what ways is the health problem affected by the family, the economy, and the polity?
9. What kinds of attitudes and values on the part of those who are ill, the public, and health personnel affect rates of illness and the nature of health care?
10. What innovations could help ameliorate the health problem?

Internet Resources/Exercises

1. Explore some of the ideas in this chapter on the following sites:

http://www.cdc.gov/nchs The National Center for Health Statistics site has the most comprehensive collection of health data available.

http://www.mentalhealth.org The site of the U.S. Substance Abuse and Mental Health Services Administration, with full coverage of news and data about mental health.

http://medlineplus.gov The National Library of Medicine site, which has information about all health topics.

2. Many nations have national health coverage. Search the Internet for programs in at least two industrialized nations. Compare information about coverage and health conditions in those nations with the United States. What facts could you use to support or to reject a national health program in this country?

3. There is an ongoing struggle in the United States between consumer advocate groups, big business, and politicians over government regulations or potential regulations that bear upon health. Research a recent controversial issue. What were the arguments pro and con for federal regulation? What measures were taken by various groups to get acceptance for their position? Did the outcome, in your judgment, benefit or harm public well-being? Report your findings to the class.

For Further Reading

Bendelow, Gillian. *Health, Emotion and the Body.* Cambridge, UK: Polity, 2009. An examination of the relationship between physical and mental illness, focusing on stress as the key factor in understanding the interaction between body and mind, and emphasizing the fact that illness is a social and emotional phenomenon.

Blanc, Paul D. *How Everyday Products Make People Sick.* Berkeley, CA: University of California Press, 2007. A discussion of the kinds of everyday products, such as glue, bleach, a rayon scarf, or the wood in a patio deck, that can be hazardous to your health, including the difficulty of getting controls or alerting the public to the dangers.

Budrys, Grace. *Unequal Health: How Inequality Contributes to Health and Illness.* Lanham, MD: Rowman and Littlefield, 2003. Illustrates the various ways in which differing kinds of inequality, separately and in combination with each other, significantly affect health and illness throughout an individual's lifetime.

Goodman, John C., Gerald L. Musgrave, and Devon M. Herrick. *Lives at Risk: Single-Payer National Health Insurance in Countries around the World.* Lanham, MD: Rowman and Littlefield, 2004. Examines the national health insurance systems of various countries and the problems that typically arise with such systems, particularly the way in which the problems intersect with politics.

Himmelstein, David, Steffie Woolhandler, and Ida Hellender. *Bleeding the Patient: The Consequences of Corporate Health Care.* Monroe, ME: Common Courage Press, 2001. A critique of profit-driven health care, showing the varied ways in which patients are victimized by the system.

Kreider, Katherine. *The Big Fix: How the Pharmaceutical Industry Rips Off American Consumers.* New York: Public Affairs, 2003. A detailed study of the prescription drug industry, including the methods used to market the drugs and the reasons that prices are so high.

Whitaker, Robert. *Mad in America: Bad Science, Bad Medicine, and the Enduring Mistreatment of the Mentally Ill.* Cambridge, MA: Perseus Publishing, 2002. A history of how psychiatrists have treated schizophrenics, underscoring the fact that treatment is a trial-and-error process that changes from generation to generation.

PART

5

Global Social Problems

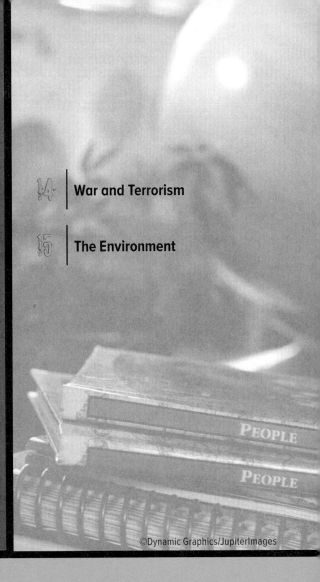

©Dynamic Graphics/JupiterImages

Is there hope for civilization? Ever since the invention of gunpowder, pessimists have been predicting that humans will destroy themselves with their own technology. Their pessimism doesn't seem all that far-fetched, particularly because war, terrorism, and environmental problems all pose serious threats to the quality of human life, if not to the very existence of the human race.

In this final part, we examine these problems. We cannot discuss them meaningfully without seeing them in their global context. The threat they pose goes beyond any particular nation and inevitably includes all nations. We examine war and terrorism first. Then we explore the vexing environmental problems that are not only threatening but also involve painful dilemmas.

War and Terrorism

1 Distinguish between war, civil war, and terrorism, and know the extent of each.

2 Discuss the varied ways in which war and terrorism detract from the quality of life.

3 Identify the political and economic factors that contribute

to the problems of war and terrorism.

4 Explain the kinds of attitudes and ideologies that legitimate war and terrorism.

5 Suggest steps that can be taken to address the problems of war and terrorism.

Source: Department of Defense photo by Sgt. David Foley, U.S. Army

"I Didn't Want to See It"

Steve is 22. He is a veteran of the 1991 war against Iraq. In many ways, Steve is fortunate. He was not wounded, and he has not suffered from posttraumatic stress syndrome. He returned home to a wife and baby girl with minimal problems of adjustment. But in another way, Steve also suffers from the war. His suffering is the memory of things he wished he had never seen:

When we chased the elite Iraqi forces back into their own country and literally overwhelmed them, we all felt a sense of pride and exultation. It was the sweet taste of victory. A victory that cost us very little in terms of lives. I wish I had come home immediately after that. But we were stationed for a time within the borders of Iraq, guarding against any return of their forces. That's when I saw the real costs of the war. I didn't want to see it. But I couldn't avoid it.

Every day we would face Iraqi children begging for food. We saw hundreds of refugees camped out in the desert, living in burned-out cars and trucks. When I came through one of the refugee camps, I nearly got ill.

But it was the children that really got to me. I have my own little girl. I couldn't help but think about her when I saw those Iraqi kids. Some of them would look at our guns and start crying. And then there were the mothers holding crying babies who needed food or medicine. And there was nothing at all we could do.

One day an Iraqi professor came up to us. She spoke English, and she went on and on about how miserable their lives were. They had no food, she said, and nothing but dirty water to drink. They had no drugs, no hospitals, and no way to treat people who were wounded or sick.

I tell you, the combat was frightening at times. But it was far easier than dealing with those hurting people. I don't think I'll ever be able to forget the children begging for food. I'm home. I'm safe. I guess the war is still going on for some of them.

Introduction

On September 11, 2001, four American passenger jets were hijacked by terrorists. Two of the planes crashed into the Twin Towers of the World Trade Center and a third slammed into the Pentagon. A fourth plane, headed for the White House, went down in Pennsylvania after passengers tried to stop the hijackers. With more than 3,000 deaths from this terrorist attack, "war" took on a new meaning for Americans.

The next month, the United States launched an attack on Afghanistan, where the perpetrators of the September 11 attack were believed to be in hiding. And in March 2003, the United States and Great Britain invaded Iraq, calling it Operation Iraqi Freedom and justifying the action on the grounds that the Iraqi government had ties with the terrorists and also had weapons of mass destruction that were threatening our two nations. Over the next few years, opposition to the war grew dramatically. By 2007, when asked about the nation's most pressing problems, more Americans named the war in Iraq than any other issue. By 2016, the United States was still involved in conflicts with the radical Islamic group, ISIS, but was not officially at war with another nation. The most important problem for the nation, according to a Gallup poll in October 2016, was the economy (Auter 2016). But "national security" came sixth on the list and terrorism was eighth (ahead of such matters as the federal debt, health care, crime, and the environment). So war and terrorism have been, and continue to be, considered a more important problem than many other issues facing the nation.

In this chapter, we begin by looking at the nature and extent of the problem. We show the ways that war and terrorism detract from the quality of life. We identify the sociocultural factors that contribute to the problem. Finally, we discuss some proposals for minimizing or eliminating war and terrorism.

War, Civil War, and Terrorism

When you hear the word "war," your first thought may be of armies from two opposing nations clashing with each other. However, this definition doesn't best describe present-day wars, which are more likely to be civil wars or wars of terrorism.

The New Face of War

Modern warfare is no longer confined to opposing armies facing each other on the battlefield. Nor is it merely a matter of nuclear powers confronting each other with the threat of mass destruction. Rather, the small armaments that have flooded the world can be used by dissidents to destroy a nation's infrastructure. And:

> Civilians are targets as much as combatants, often more so. . . . Children fight alongside adults. The front line may be someone's bedroom. Hospitals and libraries are fair game. Even humanitarian aid workers become pawns. (Musser and Nemecek 2000:47)

Not only have the struggles spread from the battlefield to the bedroom, but increasingly they have involved civil wars and terrorism. *Civil war* is rebellion by dissident groups within a nation. If the groups are small, they may simply engage in acts of domestic terrorism (discussed in Chapter 4). **International terrorism** is politically motivated violence against citizens of political entities different from those of the perpetrators in order to coerce and intimidate others into accepting the perpetrators' goals. Terrorism is not new, but the September 11, 2001, attacks made Americans painfully aware both of its destructive potential and of their vulnerability to it.

The "new face" of war also includes some controversial methods of waging war. One is the use of drones to target and kill individuals deemed a threat (Kaag and Kreps 2014; Horowitz 2016). Those who oppose the drones argue, among other things, that killing someone outside a war zone is an assassination and therefore it is illegal. They also note that drones are known to have killed the wrong targets, including innocent bystanders. Those who support drones argue that they provide us with a safer way to confront and destroy our enemies.

Another controversial method is the use of such techniques as waterboarding to torture captured enemy combatants in order to gain information (Del Rosso 2014). Proponents insist that any such method is legitimate in the defense of freedom. Opponents stress the point that such a method is inconsistent with a humane, democratic society, and only gets the victim to say anything that will stop the torture, whether or not the information is accurate.

international terrorism politically motivated violence against citizens of political entities different from those of the perpetrators in order to coerce and intimidate others into accepting the perpetrators' goals

The Extent of the Problem

Wars and Civil Wars. When the United States is not involved in war, Americans tend to think that the era is one of relative peace. Yet at any point in time the world experiences a large number of armed conflicts, including both wars and minor armed conflicts. A **war** is defined as a major armed conflict between nations or between organized groups within a nation in which 1,000 or more people are killed (Renner 1997). Minor armed conflicts may involve the same kind of weaponry and fighting, but they result in fewer deaths. The total number of armed conflicts has fluctuated over time, but between 2006 and 2015 there has always been at least 30 each year; in 2015, there were 50 active conflicts (Stockholm International Peace Research Institute 2016).

war a major armed conflict between nations or between organized groups within a nation in which a thousand or more people are killed

Most wars in recent decades involve the developing nations of the world, but the United States and other developed nations can be drawn into the conflicts under certain circumstances. One such circumstance occurred in late 1990, when Iraq invaded and took over Kuwait. When Iraq refused to respond to U.N. demands to withdraw, a multinational force began a massive air bombardment in January 1991, thus starting the Gulf War.

Although the war was brief, the damage was massive and it should serve as a reminder that war is always possible. In fact, current events threaten future wars. Pakistan and India continue to struggle over Kashmir. Palestinians and Israelis continue to kill each other. Islamic terrorists in various parts of the world are calling on all Muslims to engage in a holy war against Israel and the United States. And the list goes on. The point is that *you live in a world that is never free of war or the threat of war.*

The bloodiest wars in recent years have been civil wars and wars involving just two nations (Renner 1999). More than 1.5 million died in the civil war in the Sudan (97 percent of them civilians), more than 1 million died in the Mozambican civil war from 1981 to 1994, nearly 4 million died in the war that broke out in the Democratic Republic of the Congo in 1998, and about 1.5 million died in the Soviet intervention in

Afghanistan between 1978 and 1992. The incidence of civil wars has increased since the end of World War II (Fearon and Laitin 2002). Rebellion against dictators occurred in the "Arab spring" of 2011. It began in December 2010 when a Tunisian street vendor committed suicide after local officials confiscated his vegetable cart. Thousands of Tunisians went into the streets to demand the end of the 23-year dictatorship of the nation. Their action prompted similar protests in Egypt, Libya, and other Arab nations, leading to the downfall of a number of dictatorial governments. Tens of thousands died as the protests turned into civil wars. Overall, millions have died in civil wars over the last 60 years.

We should note that "civil war" does not mean that only one nation is involved. In the civil war that ravaged Syria beginning in 2012, Russia and Iran gave support to the existing regime, while the United States and others supported the rebels. In the modern era, few, if any, civil wars are ignored by the rest of the world.

Terrorism.   For most Americans prior to September 11, 2001, terrorism was something that was a problem elsewhere. Little was made in our news media about terrorism other than the acts of various leftist movements, the Irish Republican Army, and the attacks on U.S. embassies in Kenya and Tanzania in 1998 that killed 301 people. Since the end of the Cold War, attacks by leftist groups have declined, while those by Islamist groups have increased dramatically (Robison, Crenshaw, and Jenkins 2006). The September 11 attack was the worst terrorist attack ever in terms of the number killed.

Nevertheless, Americans have suffered far fewer attacks and far fewer casualties than the rest of the world. According to the U.S. Department of State (2016), there were 11,774 terrorist attacks in the world in 2015, resulting in more than 28,300 deaths, 35,300 injuries, and 12,100 kidnappings. The attacks took place in 92 different countries, but nearly three-fourths occurred in just five: Iraq, Afghanistan, Nigeria, Syria, and Pakistan.

Of course, the main purpose of terrorism is not merely to kill people. It is to use the killings and the destruction to dramatize a condition that the terrorists find unacceptable (Northern Ireland remaining under British control; Israel's domination of Palestinians; American troops in Muslim countries; etc.), and to warn people that none of them is safe as long as the condition persists. Thus, terrorist attacks in recent years have included a school in Russia in which 323 people, half of them children, were killed; suicide bombings in Egyptian resorts; the bombing of four commuter trains during morning rush hour in Madrid, Spain; the bombing of the Australian embassy in Jakarta, Indonesia; subway bombings in London, England; and more than 400 small bombs exploding in cities and towns in Bangladesh.

It is unlikely that terrorist attacks will decline significantly in the near future. An important reason is that there is no single group or cause involved. Even though the radical Islamist group responsible for the 9/11 attack, al-Qaida, has been greatly weakened by the killing of Osama bin Laden and other key leaders and the disruption of base operations in Afghanistan, the group is still regarded as a significant terrorist threat because of other radical groups with whom it cooperates and shares resources. In addition, a number of smaller, loosely organized terrorist groups have emerged in various parts of the world. Thus, at this point terrorism appears to be something with which we will have to deal for an unforeseeable number of years.

Although bombings have been the most common form of terrorism, there is concern that other, possibly even more destructive, forms will emerge, including biological terrorism (Kuhr and Hauer 2001). A vast number of biological, chemical, and radioactive materials are capable of causing mass illness and death, and terrorists are capable of securing many if not most of these materials.

War, Terrorism, and the Quality of Life

Like the impact of violence at the interpersonal and intergroup levels, it is not possible to fully capture in writing the impact of war and terrorism. To give you a sense of what people are doing to each other through such violence, consider a few reported experiences. You will see that war and terrorism destroy and dehumanize.

Human Destruction and Injury

Human destruction reaches a peak in war. The 20th century was the bloodiest in human history. More than 100 million deaths occurred, compared to 19.4 million in the 19th century and 3.7 million from the 1st to the 15th centuries (Renner 1999:10). The figures for American casualties in various wars are shown in Table 14.1. From the Civil War (including Union troops only) to the present, nearly 1 million American military personnel have died as a result of wars. And nearly 1.5 million more have been wounded.

Increasingly, civilians are the main victims of war through a combination of direct injuries, starvation, and disease. Civilians accounted for half of all war-related deaths in the 1950s, three-fourths of deaths in the 1980s, and nearly 90 percent of deaths in 1990 (Renner 1993a:9). Estimates of the number of civilians who died in the war against Iraq range from 100,000 to 600,000 or more. In addition, more than a million Iraqi citizens fled their homes and their country to escape the violence.

Similarly, an analysis of death in the Congo's civil war reported that for every combat death there were 62 nonviolent deaths, 34 of them children (Lacey 2005). These deaths are caused by such things as malnutrition and various diseases resulting from the chaos and deprivation.

Civilians are also the main victims in terrorist attacks. The great majority of Americans killed by terrorists have been civilians. The thousands of Palestinians and Israeli casualties in the ongoing terrorist attack–retaliation cycle in Israel and the occupied territories also have been mainly civilians.

In addition, *children are increasingly the likely victims of war and terrorism.* Children are victims in a number of ways. First, they are often among those killed. Second, they suffer severe and sometimes permanent injuries, are left without parents and/or homes, or fall prey to hunger and disease. Third, children are recruited for, or forced into, being

TABLE 14.1
War Casualties of American Military Personnel (in thousands)

War	Battle Deaths	Nonbattle Deaths	Wounded
Civil War*	140	224	282
World War I	53	63	204
World War II	292	114	671
Korean War	34	3	103
Vietnam War	47	11	153
Persian Gulf War	**	**	1
War on Iraq	4.4	0.9	32.0
War on Afghanistan	2.2	0.4	20.0

*Union troops only
**Fewer than 500
SOURCES: U.S. Census Bureau 2009; U.S. Department of Defense website.

combatants in wars and terrorist activities. Hundreds of thousands of children, some as young as 7 years old, have fought in armed conflicts or participated in terrorist attacks around the world. Palestinian children, for example, are taught the virtue of self-sacrifice, are encouraged to throw stones at Israeli soldiers and to become suicide bombers, and are assured that if they die they will receive the reward of martyrs (Burdman 2003). Finally, children may be victimized when women who participate in war have babies with birth defects. Women who served in Vietnam, for example, were far more likely to have children with birth defects than were other women (Brooks 1999).

A United Nations report summarized the situation with regard to children and war and terrorist activities as follows (United Nations General Assembly 2006:4):

> Today, in over 30 situations of concern around the globe, children are being brutalized and callously used to advance the agendas of adults. It has been estimated that over 2 million children have been killed in situations of armed conflict; another 6 million have been rendered permanently disabled; and, more than 250,000 children continue to be exploited as child soldiers. Increasingly, children and women are the casualties of war, with the fatalities of civilians disproportionately higher than ever before in the history of warfare.

The report also notes that thousands of girls are raped and sexually exploited, and both boys and girls are being seized and taken away from their homes and communities in large numbers. Such suffering and death of children are among the most agonizing effects of war (see "I Didn't Want to See It" at the beginning of this chapter).

Various factors account for the human destruction in war. The obvious factor, of course, is the use of weaponry, including bombs. Even when bombs are aimed at military targets, a certain number will hit civilians. For instance, the 1991 war against Iraq, with its "smart" bombs and missiles that hit military targets with pinpoint accuracy, was heralded as an example of the wonders of modern military technology. However, many hospitals also were hit, including the only hospital in the nation that performed kidney transplants and advanced heart surgery (Burleigh 1991). In addition, the

Each year, land mines kill or maim more than 25,000 people, many of them children like this young Afghan girl.
©Peter Turnley/Corbis/Getty Images

destruction of power plants prevented some hospitals from operating even basic equipment like incubators and refrigerators.

Land mines are also responsible for many civilian deaths and injuries. There are more than 100 million land mines in more than 70 countries; an estimated 10 million mines are in Afghanistan alone (Rieder and Choonara 2012). The mines remain lethal for decades (Henig 2012), and more are being planted every year. Land mines kill or maim at least one person every hour (Williams 2004). One in every 236 people in Cambodia is an amputee because of land mines. A study of victims of land mines admitted to an emergency surgical center in Cambodia from 2003 to 2006 found that a little over a fourth were children (Bendinelli 2009). Compared to the adults, the children were more likely to require a blood transfusion; suffer blindness; be maimed in their upper limbs; and die from their injuries. As with war generally, women and children are at greater risk from land mines than are soldiers.

Land mines cause suffering and destruction indirectly as well. An investigation of the Nuba people in the Sudan found serious problems resulting from the mere existence of the mines (Sultan 2009). Knowing that the mines had been planted, the Nubas avoided the area. That meant they no longer had the same access to water or to farmland. Greater numbers concentrated in more inaccessible areas, resulting in economic hardship, loss of local markets, insufficient food, and outbreaks of disease among both animals and humans.

Despite the dire consequences, and despite the fact that 134 countries have signed a mine ban treaty and 18 countries have destroyed their stockpiles, 47 other countries (including the United States, China, and Russia) have not signed the treaty and have stockpiled as many as 200 million mines.

The more recent version of land mines is the *improvised explosive device,* or IED (Bryce 2006). IEDs are homemade bombs designed to kill or incapacitate the opposition. They can be hidden and camouflaged so effectively that they are extremely difficult to detect. They are usually triggered by the victims, but can also be triggered remotely. They have emerged as major weapons in the war in Iraq. About 3 percent of American combat deaths in World War II were due to mines or booby traps. The figure for the Vietnam War was 9 percent. But in Iraq, IEDs accounted for fully 65 percent of U.S. combat deaths and about half of all nonfatal injuries.

Another reason for the destructiveness of war is that, throughout human history, conquering armies have considered the vanquished to be undeserving of humane treatment. Girls and women experience a higher probability of being raped. Rape occurs in all wars, including civil wars. A survey of households in Sierra Leone reported that 94 percent contained at least one person who had suffered abuse in the previous 10 years of the nation's civil war, and one of eight of the households contained someone who had been victimized by some kind of war-related sexual violence (Physicians for Human Rights 2002). Such rape in wartime, like rape generally, is most often a hostile act. Farr (2009) calls it "extreme war rape." The point is that the rapists intend to inflict emotional and physical injury on their victims. Farr examined war rape in 27 countries engaged in armed conflicts and concluded that extreme war rape was found in all of them.

Finally, war is destructive because, in their quest for military power or military victory, governments may act in ways that harm their own people. In 1993 the Department of Energy acknowledged that the United States had conducted about 800 radiation tests on humans between 1945 and 1970—and some of these people were unaware of the risks (Wheeler 1994). Part of the justification for the research, which was often supported financially by the Department of Defense or the Atomic Energy Commission, was the presumed threat of nuclear war and, thereby, the need to know the effects of radiation on the human body as well as ways to counter those effects.

Wars always have been destructive, but they are more destructive now than they were in the past. Clearly, one reason for the increasing number of people killed, as well as the increasing proportion of civilians among those killed, is the *changed nature of war,* which now involves the total population of nations rather than military personnel only.

Another reason for the increased destructiveness of war is the *increasingly sophisticated nature of military technology* compared to past weaponry. It is now possible to kill people in numbers that are staggering. In World War I, fewer than 3 people per 100,000 were killed by bombs in England and Germany. In World War II, nearly 300 people per 100,000 were killed by bombs (Hart 1957:44). World War II also saw the introduction of atomic weapons. Two Japanese cities, Hiroshima and Nagasaki, were each decimated by a single bomb. About 140,000 people in Hiroshima and 70,000 in Nagasaki died immediately or within a few weeks, and another 130,000 died within five years after the attack (Committee for the Compilation of Materials on Damage Caused by the Atomic Bombs in Hiroshima and Nagasaki 1981). It is sobering to realize that whereas the Hiroshima bomber delivered 25,800 tons of TNT-equivalent explosives, a bomber today can deliver *literally hundreds of times more destructive power,* and that the missiles carried by just one Russian Delta 4 submarine could kill 6.7 million people in the first 30 minutes after detonation, and an additional 6 to 12 million would die of radiation sickness in the following weeks (Helfand 1999).

In addition to the destruction of bombs and bullets, there is the horror of biological and chemical warfare. During the Iran-Iraq war from 1980 to 1988, the Iraqis used mustard gas, breaking a 63-year-old international agreement that forbids the use of any chemical weapons (Willems 2002). The gas initially causes sneezing and coughing and sometimes nausea and vomiting. Within hours, the victim suffers tightness in the chest and shortness of breath as a result of respiratory inflammation. Painful blisters appear on the body, causing patches of skin to fall off. Some victims recover, but some die and others suffer bone marrow or gastrointestinal problems for years.

The destructiveness of war goes beyond that inflicted by weaponry. As studies of Palestinian and Lebanese children have shown, children who witness military violence may become more aggressive and antisocial in their behavior (Qouta, Punamäki, Miller, and El-Sarraj 2007; Tarabah et al. 2015). An investigation of American soldiers who were parents found that when the soldiers were combat deployed the rate of maltreatment of their children by their spouses rose significantly (Gibbs, Martin, Kupper, and Johnson 2007). And the rates of violence within a society tend to go up in the aftermath of war. Some of the violence involves homicides by veterans (Purdy 2008). But, for reasons unknown, the violence extends to nonveterans as well. An analysis of U.S. violence during the 1980s, when the nation conducted four major foreign military operations, showed that yearly rates of murder, rape, and aggravated assault rose dramatically (Bebber 1994). However, *the increase in the rate of criminal violence occurred only in the years immediately after the four military operations.* The legitimation of violence that occurs during war apparently carries over into the postwar years.

A different kind of carryover involves the increased rates of physical problems among veterans. About 1 out of every 10 living veterans was seriously injured while serving in the military (Morin 2011). Most of the injuries happened during combat. Compared to veterans who were not seriously injured, the seriously injured are more than twice as likely to report difficulty readjusting to civilian life and nearly twice as likely to say their current health is only poor to fair. Veterans of the Gulf War developed a number of persistent physical symptoms: chronic fatigue, skin rashes, muscle and joint pain, shortness of breath, headaches, and diarrhea (Clark 1994; Gray et al. 2002). And Gulf

War veterans who may have been exposed to nerve agents in Iraq have elevated rates of death from brain cancer (Bullman, Mahan, Kang, and Page 2005).

Finally, the destruction of human life and well-being is affected by the threat of war as well as by war itself. *The production and storage of weapons of war are hazardous even if the weapons are never used.* Radioactive wastes from the production of nuclear weapons contaminate water and soil, posing hazards to human health (Baverstock 2005; Shrader-Frechette 2005). Arms plants in the United States have been known to routinely release large amounts of radioactive particles into the air. Some government nuclear-production facilities disposed of radioactive waste as though it were harmless; the result was the contamination of some water supplies. Even apart from carelessness, however, no nation has yet solved the problem of safely disposing of the wastes. The result is an increased risk of cancer, leukemia, and genetic damage.

Psychological and Interpersonal Disruption and Dehumanization

Psychological and interpersonal disruption and dehumanization occur during and after war and terrorist attacks—both of which are disruptive for military and civilian personnel. No one escapes the trauma.

The Trauma for Civilians. Civilian trauma of the severest kind followed the atomic bombings of the Japanese cities of Hiroshima and Nagasaki during World War II. Hiroshima was a city accustomed to crises, having experienced periodic disastrous floods. Nevertheless, the social order of the city collapsed after the atomic bomb was dropped. The city was rebuilt mainly through the work of migrants from the hinterland rather than through the efforts of the surviving residents. The survivors

> suffered from extreme shock and fatigue that lingered for a year. . . . Demoralization was so extreme that industrial alcohol was sold as a substitute for saki; many citizens died or went blind from drinking it. (Dentler and Cutright 1965:420)

Civilians are the emotional and physical victims of war in massive numbers.
Source: U.S. Navy/Photograph cleared for public release by LT John Gay, Combined Press Information Center

Drugs were used to escape reality. Children who survived developed a fear of becoming attached to others and of having their own children when they became adults. Crimes of violence and thefts of precious water and other scarce goods were common. Four months after the bomb had been dropped, the number of reported crimes for one month was as high as all reported crime throughout the entire war. Years later, the survivors were still not capable of leading normal, happy lives. Most of them carried a *deep sense of guilt,* including the guilt of surviving when so many had died.

Hiroshima became a city of chaos, pain, crime, anxiety, and deep-rooted fear. So many people continued to feel sick a month after the bomb fell that a rumor spread that the bomb had left a poison that would give off deadly fumes for seven years (Hersey 1946:94). Such rumors, of course, intensified the already pervasive anxiety and fear of the people and contributed to an atmosphere that drained people of the necessary psychological strength to function normally and proceed with the work of rebuilding.

The suffering need not be on the scale of Hiroshima for people to experience the emotional trauma of war. Civilians in war zones suffer emotional problems in large numbers (Cardozo, Vergara, Agani, and Golway 2000), and the problems may continue even after they are out of the war zone. Increased depression and posttraumatic stress disorder were found in a study of 124 Cambodian refugees living in Utah (Blair 2000). A team of researchers interviewed nearly a thousand Cambodians living in a refugee camp on the Thailand-Cambodia border. Many of them had witnessed the murder of a family member, had been raped, or had been physically assaulted during the civil war in their country. More than 80 percent felt depressed (with 55 percent meeting the criteria for clinical depression) and 15 percent had symptoms of posttraumatic stress syndrome (Mollica et al. 1994). Similarly, a survey of Guatemalan refugees living in Mexico 20 years after a long civil conflict in Guatemala found that the refugees had high rates of mental problems, including anxiety, depression, and posttraumatic stress disorder (Sabin et al. 2003). Widespread mental health problems not only exist among civilians who endured the war in Bosnia, but worsened among some of them as they aged (Carballo et al. 2004). Among Iranian Kurds, being exposed to chemical weapons during the Iran-Iraq war of the 1980s resulted in long-term high rates of major anxiety, severe depression, and posttraumatic stress syndrome (Hashemian et al. 2006). Finally, a national survey in Iraq found that 17 percent of the adult population suffered some kind of mental disorder, particularly depression, phobias, posttraumatic stress syndrome, and anxiety (Rubin 2009). And nearly 70 percent of those with one of the disorders said they had thoughts about suicide.

Civilians can suffer even if they are not directly exposed to conflict, because great numbers of civilians flee an oncoming battle and become refugees in another area or another country. In 2016, when the Syrian civil war raged, about 6 in 10 Syrians were displaced from their homes (Connor 2016a). Worldwide, an estimate 60 million or more people were displaced from their homes as of the end of 2015 (Connor 2016b). Whatever trauma a war inflicts on the civilian population, the effects are even stronger for those displaced (Shemyakina and Plagnol 2013).

Children as well as adults are traumatized by war. Consider, for example, what it must have been like to have been a Jewish child in a Nazi concentration camp during World War II. In Czechoslovakia, the camp at Terezin had 15,000 children. Only 100 of the 15,000 survived, but some of their drawings and writings also survived. Following is part of a poem written by a 15-year-old boy:

> I was once a little child
> Three years ago.
> That child who longed for other worlds.

But now I am no more a child
For I have learned to hate.
I am a grown-up person now,
I have known fear.

Somewhere, far away out there, childhood sweetly sleeps,
Along that path among the trees,
There o'er that house
Which was once my pride and joy.
There my mother gave me birth into this world
So I could weep. . . .[1]

Or consider what life is like for Lebanese children who have grown up in a land wracked by war and civil war. Those children who experienced the death of a family member or the forced displacement of their family, or who saw their home destroyed or someone killed, were about 1.7 times more likely than other children to be nervous or depressed and to exhibit aggressive behavior (Chimienti, Nasr, and Khalifeh 1989). Continued shelling and killing were also responsible for depression among Lebanese mothers, and their depression, in turn, was associated with the illness of their children (Bryce, Walker, Ghorayeb, and Kanj 1989). Among young people injured by shelling in 1996, half suffered some kind of impairment and 29 percent who had been enrolled in school did not continue their education (Mehio Sibai, Shaar Sameer, and el Yassir 2000).

Many children and young people in the Middle East have never experienced an extended time of peace. It is little wonder, then, that children in the Gaza Strip who have been exposed to war conflict have a high rate of emotional and behavioral problems (Thabet and Vostanis 2000). Studies of children in other war situations yield similar results (Brajs-Zganec 2005; Hoge et al. 2007).

The Trauma for Combatants. During the latter days of World War II, the American Air Force launched a massive air attack on German positions near Saint Lo, France. The famous war correspondent Ernie Pyle was there to record his reaction as the planes began to come:

> [T]hey came in a constant procession and I thought it would never end. . . . I've never known a storm, or a machine, or any resolve of man that had about it the aura of such a ghastly relentlessness. . . . It seems incredible to me that any German could have come out of the bombardment with his sanity. When it was over I was grateful, in a chastened way that I had never before experienced, for just being alive. (Commager 1945:441, 444)

In part, because of the horror of battle, there is *a high rate of posttraumatic stress disorder, major depression, and drug abuse among veterans* (Dohrenwend et al. 2006; Eisen et al. 2012; Shen, Arkes, and Williams 2012). They may reexperience the war trauma in dreams, have recurring images and thoughts related to the trauma, feel a lack of involvement in life, experience guilt about having survived in situations in which others died, and struggle with sleep disturbances. The rates are higher, and the symptoms are more severe, among veterans who experienced combat and those who were prisoners of war (Neria et al. 2000; Wallis 2004; Solomon, Dekel, and Zerach 2008).

It is possible that the rate of traumatization among combatants is increasing. Hayman and Scaturo (1993) reported higher rates of posttraumatic stress disorder among Vietnam veterans than those reported by studies of veterans of other wars. A study of Gulf War veterans also noted rates of disability compensation two to three times higher than those of World War II, the Korean conflict, or the Vietnam War (Haley, Maddrey, and Gershenfeld 2002). There is as yet no explanation for these increasing rates.

The psychological problems vary in their severity but affect a substantial number of veterans. Among the returning troops who fought in Afghanistan or Iraq, 21.8 percent had posttraumatic stress disorder, and 17.4 percent struggled with depression (Seal et al. 2009). The rate of those with a mental health problem varied considerably depending on the number of times deployed: 12 percent after the first deployment, 19 percent after the second, and 27 percent after the third or fourth (Thompson 2008). Those who experienced combat also were at increased risk for heavy weekly drinking, binge drinking, and alcohol-related health problems (Jacobson et al. 2008).

In addition to the personal distress, veterans experience a variety of interpersonal problems, including decreased satisfaction with romantic, marital, and family relationships; increased sexual dissatisfaction; higher rates of extramarital affairs; higher rates of intimate partner violence; higher rates of divorce; a diminished capacity to work once they return to civilian life; and higher rates of homelessness and suicide (MacLean 2010; Solomon, Shimrit, Zerach, and Horesh 2011; London, Allen, and Wilmoth 2013; Hoyt, Wray and Rielage 2014; Peterson et al. 2015; Department of Defense 2016; Karney and Trail 2016). Younger soldiers may be more likely than older ones to develop serious problems. A study of 57 veterans of the Vietnam War found that those who were adolescents (17 to 19 years old) at the time of their tour of duty were more likely than older soldiers to have problems of adjustment (Harmless 1990). The younger soldiers experienced later on a greater number of conflicted relationships and work problems.

As we noted in Chapter 13, there is an integral relationship between physical and emotional health. Continued emotional problems will adversely affect physical health. Thus, an examination of 605 male combat veterans of World War II and the Korean War found that posttraumatic stress symptoms were associated with increased onset of various physical problems, including arterial, gastrointestinal, skin, and musculoskeletal disorders (Schnurr, Spiro, and Paris 2000).

Combatant trauma stems from more than battle conditions, however. Military personnel may be traumatized and dehumanized by their own acts. Consider, for example, some of the acts that took place during World War II, such as mass extermination of and "medical" experiments on Jews. Some of the worst acts of the war were committed in the infamous *concentration camps,* especially Dachau (Gellhorn 1959:235–42). For example, Nazi Germans wanted to know how long their pilots could survive without oxygen. At Dachau they put prisoners into a car and pumped out the oxygen. Some prisoners survived for as long as 15 minutes. Nazi Germans also wanted to see how long pilots could survive in cold water if they were shot down over the English Channel or some other body of water. Thus, prisoners were placed in vats of ice water that reached to their necks. Some subjects survived for two and a half hours. Both experiments resulted in painful deaths for all the subjects.

Inhuman punishments were meted out to prisoners at Dachau who violated such rules as standing at attention with their hats off when an SS trooper passed within six feet. Prisoners were lashed with a bullwhip, hung by bound hands from a hook, or placed in a box that prevented them from sitting, kneeling, or lying down.

Perhaps the most disquieting aspect of all was the crematorium. A reporter who was in Dachau after it had been captured by the Allies wrote her reaction on seeing piles of dead bodies:

> They were everywhere. There were piles of them inside the oven room, but the SS had not had time to burn them . . . the bodies were dumped like garbage, rotting in the sun, yellow

and nothing but bones, bones grown huge because there was no flesh to cover them, hideous, terrible, agonizing bones, and the unendurable smell of death. . . . Nothing about war was ever as insanely wicked as these starved and outraged, naked, nameless dead. (Gellhorn 1959:240)

Dehumanizing acts are not confined to any one people. Americans learned during the Vietnam War that they too are capable of atrocities. That war was particularly vicious for soldiers because there were no "lines" in the usual sense of the word. The enemy was everywhere and could not be distinguished from allies. Americans and some Vietnamese were fighting other Vietnamese. As we heard a Vietnam veteran put it: "After a while you get so sick of the trouble that you start killing everyone. It gets so you don't feel so bad about shooting at a six-year-old kid because the kids are throwing grenades at you." The South Koreans who fought with the Americans and South Vietnamese reportedly wiped out entire villages, including men, women, and children, when they suspected that enemy forces were present. In Iraq, American guards at Abu Ghraib prison subjected Iraqi prisoners to abuse and humiliation of a kind that enraged people throughout the Arab world and led President Bush to express a "deep disgust" and a promise to bring to justice the guards who were responsible (Roston and McAllister 2004).

Soldiers who perform such acts may have *serious psychological problems* once they reflect on what they have done. They have treated other human beings as objects, dehumanizing them, and they are appalled at their own actions. Even soldiers who do not participate in such actions may be traumatized. Just being in combat seems to bring some individuals to the point of irrationality, if not insanity. Since the time of the ancient Greeks, soldiers have succumbed to madness as a result of the horrors of combat (Gabriel 1987). Anything from fatigue to hysterical paralysis to psychosis may afflict them.

Terrorism and Trauma. *Terrorist acts* also generate emotional trauma (Pfefferbaum et al. 2001, 2002; Verger et al. 2004). A number of studies of Americans after the September 11, 2001, attacks reported an increase in emotional distress, including depression (Stein et al. 2004; Knudsen, Roman, Johnson, and Ducharme 2005). Telephone interviews with 1,008 Manhattan residents between one and two months after the attacks found that 7.5 percent reported symptoms consistent with posttraumatic stress syndrome and 9.7 percent reported symptoms of depression (Galea et al. 2002). Some of these symptoms existed prior to the attacks, but the researchers were able to determine that the rate of posttraumatic stress syndrome tripled in the weeks following the attacks. Researchers have found persistent posttraumatic stress disorder and other emotional problems a decade later among those with high exposure to the terrorist attacks (Neria, DioGrande, and Adams 2011).

Other research showed an increase in smoking and in alcohol and marijuana use after the attacks (Vlahov et al. 2004), and a survey of adolescents reported a sharply increased sense of vulnerability to dying than was found among adolescents prior to the attacks (Halpern-Felsher and Millstein 2002). These negative consequences can persist for years afterward (Richman, Cloninger, and Rospenda 2008).

Studies of other nations also find various kinds of trauma resulting from exposure to terrorist acts. A survey of Jewish and Palestinian citizens in Israel found that those exposed to terrorist acts had higher rates of depression and of posttraumatic stress disorder (Hobfoll, Canetti-Nisim, and Johnson 2006). And a study of Israeli adolescents found that being exposed to terrorism significantly increased the level of violent behavior by the youth (Even-Chen and Itzhaky 2007).

Environmental Destruction

environmental destruction
alterations in the environment
that make it less habitable or
useful for people or other living
things

As you will see in the next chapter, a precarious balance exists between natural resources and the growing demand for energy. *Conservation of natural resources throughout the world is essential, but there is a contradiction between this need and the willingness of people to engage in war,* because war always involves a certain amount of **environmental destruction.** The environment has been called "an invisible casualty of war" (Hynes 2011), and the increasing destructive power of weaponry has made war an ever-greater disaster for the land.

Before the war, Vietnam was the "rice bowl of Asia," but the land was so decimated by bombing that the nation had to import rice after the war. The military also sprayed millions of gallons of herbicides on fields and forests in an effort to flush out guerrillas. We do not yet know the long-term effects on the environment, but the short-term effects included serious disruption of agriculture.

The Gulf War also turned into an environmental disaster when the Iraqis dumped hundreds of millions of gallons of crude oil into the Persian Gulf and set fire to hundreds of wellheads in Kuwait. At one point, Kuwaiti officials estimated that the fires were burning 6 million gallons of oil a day, about 9 percent of the total world consumption of petroleum (Renner 1991:28). The smoke caused daytime April temperatures to drop as much as 27 degrees below normal and created severe smog as far as 1,000 miles away. Black rain (soot washed out of the air) coated people, animals, buildings, and crops with a black, oily film (Renner 1991:28).

The longer the warfare lasts, the more severe the environmental consequences. In 2001, the United States and other nations launched an attack on Afghanistan to unseat the ruling Taliban because they had harbored terrorists. The Taliban were defeated and a new government was installed within a matter of months, but the nation had already endured 23 years of wars and the warfare of opposing factions. The resulting environmental destruction has been severe (Garcia 2002). Irrigation canals were destroyed, dense forests were decimated, and a number of species of birds and mammals are close to extinction. Without the trees, the ground has eroded. Dust often hangs in the air, blocking sunlight and causing respiratory problems and other diseases.

Although much of the environmental destruction is the result of intensive bombing, the evidence suggests that such bombing contributes little to winning a war. A study of the strategic bombing of Germany during World War II concluded that at least 300,000 Germans were killed (including adults and children) and 780,000 injured; 155,546 British and American airmen also died in the assaults. Nevertheless, "the slaughter made little contribution to victory" (Wilensky 1967:25), and although the United States dropped more bombs in Vietnam than all the Allied forces dropped in World War II, the United States did not win in Vietnam.

As with other effects, it is not only wartime itself that results in environmental destruction; the years of preparation and the years following a war also have deadly consequences for the environment. Thus, it may take decades to repair the damage in nations such as Vietnam and Afghanistan. A 2002 report noted that more than half a century after the naval battles of World War II, the oil, chemicals, and unexploded ammunition on sunken ships in the Pacific still pose a serious peril to people and fisheries.[2] Land also continues to be contaminated by materials from World War II, including land on which armaments were made. Each new war adds to the peril.

You will see in Chapter 15 that one of the serious environmental problems is that of toxic waste dumps. One of the worst polluters is the U.S. government's various weapons laboratories and assembly plants (Morain 1990). Experts estimate that it will require decades and hundreds of billions of dollars to clean up toxic wastes at federal facilities throughout the nation. At other sites, including military bases, a range of toxic wastes such as pesticides, asbestos, old fuel, chemicals, and even radioactive materials threaten the environment and pose hazards to human health and life. In fact, the hazards may be far greater than those created by bombings.

The Economic Costs

War is *one of the greatest devourers of economic resources.* The total cost to the United States, in 2002 dollars, of World War I, World War II, the Korean War, the Vietnam War, and the Persian Gulf War was $6.33 trillion (Ericson and Hossain 2003). The cost of all the wars between September 11, 2001, and the end of 2010 amounted to $1.15 trillion (Bumiller 2010). The waging of wars is increasingly expensive.

Consider also the cost of stockpiling weaponry and preparing for possible wars. The lengthy arms race between the United States and the Soviet Union that lasted until 1996 cost Americans a staggering $5.5 trillion (Newman 1998). A look at military spending throughout the world (see "Global Comparison") makes it clear that an enormous amount of the world's resources is being channeled into paying for past wars and preparing for future wars.

National defense spending continues to be high (Office of Management and Budget 2016). For the 2016 federal budget, national defense was set at $604 billion, by far the largest single item in the discretionary part of the budget. Veterans' benefits added another $72 billion to the cost.

One reason for the *high cost of preparedness* as represented by the defense budget is the technological advances made in weaponry, which cost considerably more than weapons of the past (Wood 2004). Still, it is sobering to realize that the world's per capita military spending is larger than the per capita gross domestic national product of some of the poorest nations of the world. Some nations allocate more to their military than they do to health and/or education. It's all part of a frantic effort by most of the nations of the world to gain **military parity** if not military superiority.

The economic costs are more than the money spent, of course. Indirect economic costs include the money spent to combat the emotional and physical problems resulting

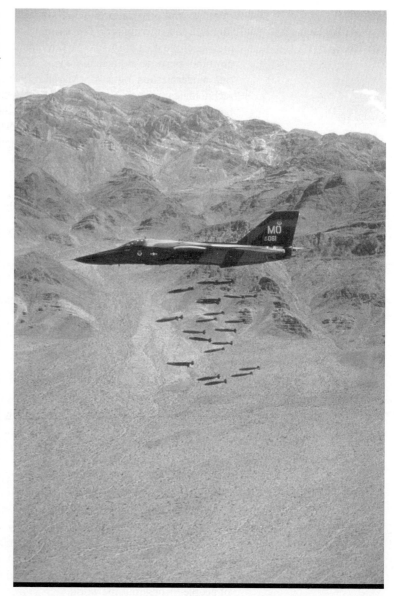

Some people argue that military spending increases the number of jobs. Others point out that the same expenditure of funds in other sectors would create far more jobs.

©Purestock/SuperStock

military parity
equality or equivalence in military strength

from war and preparations for war. Indirect costs also result from so much money being funneled into the military. For example, although military contracts produce jobs, they are one of the least cost-effective ways to create jobs: "Government programs for virtually any other purpose produce more jobs, and more less-specialized jobs, than nuclear weapons modernization outlays" (Marullo 1987:138). Military research has yielded many technological advances, but some of the technology does not get to the civilian sector because of secrecy requirements. Finally, the growth of some industries has been retarded because of the heavy investment in defense-related industries.

What if the United States invested the billions spent on military preparedness in electronics, education, health, and other sectors that benefit human beings? What if those nations in which substantial numbers of adults are illiterate and chronically hungry invested their resources in health, education, and industrial development? What could be accomplished?

Consider first what needs to be accomplished. Each year:

- Hundreds of thousands of children become partially or totally blind because of vitamin A deficiency.
- Millions of children die of diseases that could have been prevented by relatively inexpensive immunization.
- Millions of children die before they reach the age of 5.
- Millions of children are deprived of a primary education.
- Hundreds of millions of women are illiterate.
- Hundreds of millions of people are chronically malnourished.
- More than a billion people lack access to safe drinking water.

If only a relatively small part of the billions of dollars expended every year on the military were diverted to social programs, many of these needs could be addressed. Weighing the cost of modern military equipment and personnel against nonmilitary needs can dramatize this trade-off (Military Education 2016). For example, the cost of one submarine is the same as the sum of: the total annual income of 46,516 average households; plus the cost of four years of college education for 109,597 students; plus the cost of health insurance for 152,591 families; plus the cost of 10,370 new homes!

Ironically, you live in a world in which there are more soldiers than physicians per capita, a world in which military technology makes the distance between western Europe and Russia a matter of minutes while poor women in Africa must walk for hours each day just to get the family's water supply. A military mentality results in an enormous waste of resources that could be channeled into the enhancement of the quality of life of people throughout the world.

Terrorism also has economic costs, and it has become particularly costly since September 11, 2001. The most dramatic economic loss was the World Trade Center—about $40 billion (Friedman 2002). But the costs of terrorism involve far more than the facilities damaged or destroyed. Since September 11, 2001, governments and businesses have invested huge sums of money to increase security (Moritsugu 2001). Businesses also must bear the costs of such things as reduced revenues (because of decreased activity of consumers who may fear leaving their homes), higher insurance rates, and impeded international trade because of tighter security at borders. A survey that looked at the cost of terrorism estimated that for Standard and Poor's 500 companies alone, the direct and indirect costs are $107 billion a year for the United States (Byrnes 2006).

There is also the additional cost to the government. The Department of Homeland Security spends tens of billions of dollars each year. The money is used for a wide variety of purposes, including better screening of baggage and people at airports, more vaccines and bioterrorism antidotes, tighter border security, new bomb-detection machines, and more FBI agents. Clearly, the threat of terrorist activity has made the world as a whole, including the United States, a much different economic environment.

War, Terrorism, and Civil Liberties

The right of free speech is a longstanding American value. However, there *is a contradiction between this value and the perceived need for consensus and security during a war and in the face of terrorism.* In fact, governments tend to frame the issue in such terms: We must choose between freedom and security because we cannot have a full measure of both (Donohue 2008). Davenport (1995) examined events in 57 nations over a 34-year period and found that "increasing the resources given to the army enhanced the likelihood that censorship and political restrictions would be applied by governments." These restrictions occurred in nations with democratic as well as autocratic governments.

In the United States, both citizens and government officials have participated in the suppression of civil liberties during wartime. During World War I there was mob violence against dissenters and numerous prosecutions of people who spoke out against American involvement. In the later years of the Vietnam War, there were cases of mass protests against the war, mob violence against war protestors, massive arrests of demonstrators, and resultant court cases in which the issue of civil liberties was fought.

Violations of civil liberties were less severe for most Americans during World War II, but some German Americans were imprisoned in the early days of the war, and Japanese Americans were almost totally deprived of their civil rights. In 1942, more than 100,000 Japanese Americans were relocated from their homes into detention camps in isolated areas. They had committed no crimes. There was no evidence that they supported Japan rather than America in the war, but they were defined as potential sources of subversion. Longstanding prejudice against the Japanese Americans and jealousy of their landholdings, especially on the West Coast, played into this decision. The relocations caused serious economic and psychological problems for many of the victims. The wholesale deprivation of civil liberties was upheld as legal by the U.S. Supreme Court, which ruled that the government did not have to respect traditional rights during a national emergency.

Unfortunately, if a war is considered legitimate or if terrorism is considered an imminent danger by the majority of people, they may passively or even gladly accept restrictions on their civil liberties (Davis 2007). Furthermore, their institutions, including religion and the mass media, may actively help build consensus. During the Gulf War, the mass media facilitated consensus by not informing the public of Middle Eastern history, by "the jingoistic behavior of American reporters and anchorpersons," and by biased reporting (Stires 1991). For example, just before the bombing began in January 1991, polls showed that the American public was evenly divided between using military and economic sanctions against Iraq to try to force it out of Kuwait, but a content analysis of network news programs between August 8, 1990, and January 3, 1991, reported that of 2,855 minutes of coverage of the Gulf crisis, only a little over 1 percent noted grassroots dissents from presidential policies, only 1 of 878 news sources was a peace organization, and more professional football players than peace activists were asked about their attitudes toward the war (Stires 1991:141–42).

Terrorism poses as severe a threat to civil liberties as does war (Lacayo 2003). Government actions following the September 11, 2001, attacks alarmed civil libertarians (Liptak, Lewis, and Weiser 2002). More than 1,200 people suspected of violating

MILITARISM: "A WORLD GONE INSANE"

We were discussing the problem of war in a social problems class, focusing on the militarism of American society. A student objected: "Let's not make this an American problem. It's a *world* problem. Even the poorest nations are spending their resources on the military. We live in a world gone insane with arms."

He was right. Militarism is not a problem of any single nation but of the entire world. From the poorest to the richest of nations, military expenditures are consuming resources that could be used to enhance the quality of life of the citizenry.

In 2013 military expenditures of the nations of the world totaled an estimated $1.75 trillion (Perlo-Freeman and Solmirano 2014). The United States was by far the biggest spender—36.6 percent of the world total. By contrast, China, which ranked second in terms of total military spending, accounted for 10.8 percent of the total. After China, the top military spenders were Russia, Saudi Arabia, France, and the United Kingdom.

Those who defend the amount the United States spends on the military point out that the expenditures are necessary and that as the richest country in the world we can afford them. Whether they are necessary is a matter

of considerable debate. Whether we, or other nations, can afford them must be examined in light of both the total amount (imagine what those enormous sums could do for such things as health care, education, and the infrastructure) and of the proportion of the nation's gross domestic product consumed by military spending.

When we look at the proportion of the gross domestic product represented by military spending (see Figure 14.1), the United States is not at the top of the list. There are eight nations that spend a larger proportion (Central Intelligence Agency 2016). And the nation that spent the highest proportion in recent years is also one of the poorer nations—South Sudan's military spending was 10.3 percent of its gross domestic product.

Of course, whether a nation can "afford" its military expenditures is a matter of values. But one measure of well-being in a nation is the infant mortality rate (number of deaths of children under one year of age per 1,000 live births in a given year). Higher rates typically reflect poverty and inadequate health care. For 2016, the infant mortality rate in the United States was 5.8 per 1,000 live births. Compare that with the rates in those nations that are considerably poorer than the United States but that spend a higher proportion of their GDP on the military: South Sudan, 64.6; Iraq, 37.5; Azerbaijan, 24.7; Jordan, 14.7; Algeria, 20.3

immigration laws or of being material witnesses to terrorism were detained for weeks or months without being charged. The attorney general altered federal rules to allow the monitoring of communications between inmates and their lawyers if the government believed there was a reasonable suspicion of terrorist information. The government considered trying suspected terrorists by military tribunals rather than in the courts.

Within weeks of the attack, Congress passed what the attorney general called the "Patriot Act," which gave officials nearly unprecedented peacetime authority to "nullify the constitutional rights of individual citizens" (Van Deerlin 2003). And the administration created the Department of Homeland Security, which is responsible for preventing terrorist attacks and reducing the nation's vulnerability to terrorism. The department must gather information on citizens to fulfill its mandate. Invasive surveillance measures by government agents increased immediately after September 11 (Gould 2002). They continued under the Patriot Act and the department. And the fears of civil libertarians seemed to be justified because the Patriot Act was used by prosecutors to deal with people charged with common crimes (Caruso 2003). The Patriot Act expired in 2015, and was replaced by the USA Freedom Act, which modified some of the Patriot Act's provisions and allowed many of the questionable practices to continue.

(Central Intelligence Agency 2016). Improvements in infant mortality rates and other health matters, in educational opportunities, and in other economic benefits cannot be implemented when military spending consumes so much of a nation's resources, a situation that one of our students called "a world gone insane with arms."

Not to be overlooked in this is the fact that the United States is also one of the world's leading suppliers of arms. As Table 14.2 shows, the total amount of arms sales to other nations has fluctuated since 1995, but more often than not has remained in excess of $1 trillion.

Year	Total Amount (millions of dollars)
1995	$12,100
1996	11,710
1997	15,663
1998	13,179
1999	16,888
2000	10,436
2001	12,001
2002	10,240
2003	9,315
2004	10,681
2005	10,985
2010	8,098
2016	10,484

TABLE 14.2
U.S. Military Sales Deliveries to Other Countries

SOURCES: U.S. Census Bureau 2012, and Stockholm International Peace Research Institute website.

In 2005, news broke that President Bush had authorized domestic spying by the National Security Agency without court approval (Condon 2005). The president defended the need for such spying (including such things as eavesdropping on telephone calls and e-mail between the United States and other nations) and called the leaking of the program a "shameful act." Had the news not leaked out, the spying would have probably continued. But after resisting the critics for some time the president relented and declared in early 2007 that the government would disband the warrantless surveillance program and that future spying would be overseen by the secret court that governs clandestine spying in the nation.

Not everyone is concerned about the violations of civil liberties that have occurred since 2001. In fact, some observers argue that Americans face a trade-off. As one jurist put it, "it stands to reason that our civil liberties will be curtailed. They *should* be curtailed to the extent that the benefits in greater security outweigh the costs in reduced liberty" (Posner 2001:46). And, in fact, many Americans agree. The greater the perceived threat of terrorism, the more people are willing to give up civil liberties in order to gain more security (Davis and Silver 2004).

For civil libertarians, this argument is the *fallacy of non sequitur*. To say that Americans need increased security does not mean that the government must necessarily curb

fallacy

traditional civil liberties. As the American Civil Liberties Union (2002) argued, without civil rights and privacy protections, "What's to stop the Department [of Homeland Security] from abusing the very citizens it is responsible for protecting?"

Undoubtedly the debate will continue. The extent to which civil liberties are curtailed by the effort to deal with terrorism remains to be seen.

Contributing Factors

War and terrorism are complex phenomena. Some thinkers have tried to make them, like violence, a simple outgrowth of a *human need for aggression.* Yet, like aggression and violence, they are linked with *cultural values and patterns.* Some societies, for example, have no notions of organized warfare. The Hopi Indians traditionally had no place for offensive warfare and did not idealize the warrior as did other tribes. Furthermore, the Hopi conceived of the universe as a harmonious whole, with gods, nature, people, animals, and plants all working together for their common well-being.

Why do people support wars? In particular, why do they support wars in view of the consequences we have described? Why do people support terrorism? What makes a terrorist willing to commit suicide in order to hurt or kill civilians? In the following sections, we examine various factors that help answer these vexing questions.

Social Structural Factors

The Economics of War and Terrorism.   The idea that wars have an *economic cause* is an ancient one. The Greek philosophers Plato and Aristotle both argued that economic factors are fundamental in the outbreak of war. Plato believed that the quest for unlimited wealth brings on not only war but a number of other human problems. Aristotle saw economic competition as the root of wars. In particular, poverty is the "parent" of both revolution and crime. The same economic inequality that leads to revolution within a nation results in wars between nations.

Marxist
pertaining to the system of thought developed by Karl Marx and Friedrich Engels, particularly emphasizing materialism, class struggle, and the progress of humanity toward communism

Marxists also argue that war has an economic basis. The **Marxist** view is that war is a *mechanism for maintaining inequalities* in a struggle for control of raw materials and markets. The inequalities are necessary because capitalism requires an ever-expanding market to endure. Warfare is one way to ensure that a nation will have control over adequate resources and an expanding market. Consequently, war is an inevitable outcome of capitalism.

Although the Marxist explanation of war is debatable, economic factors are probably always at work in war and in preparations for war (Renner 1999). High military budgets mean considerable profits to a number of industries, offering them literally hundreds of billions of dollars in military prime contracts. With such funds at stake, it is not surprising that there are intense lobbying efforts in Congress to maintain and even increase military expenditures. One way that members of Congress can pump money into their districts or states is to maintain a military presence (in the form of a base) or secure military contracts for local industries. The military presence may no longer be needed and the military contracts may be wasteful, but the economic benefits to the district or state outweigh such considerations.

Economic factors are also at work in civil wars and terrorism. Some nations experience sharp economic inequality between racial, ethnic, or religious groups. *These racial, ethnic, or religious divisions may form the basis for civil war or terrorist activities* (Bonneuil and Auriat 2000; Reynal-Querol 2002).

A prime example is the Palestinian suicide bombers in Israel (Ratnesar 2002). Between 2000 and 2002, more than 70 bomb attacks or suicide bombings killed or injured hundreds of civilians. Although even some top leaders of the Palestinians have condemned the bombings, the majority of Palestinians defend the killing of Israeli citizens on the grounds that Palestinians are killed by Israeli troops.

Why do the majority of Palestinians defend what many people in the world community denounce as terrorism? They do so because these terrorist activities have developed in a context of what a United Nations human rights official has called daily experiences of discrimination, inequality, and powerlessness. Palestinians have lost land, work opportunities, freedom of movement, and access to water. The ongoing cycle of violence and retaliation between Palestinians and Israelis has greatly increased Palestinian poverty. After 2006, a political and economic boycott of the elected Palestinian administration increased unemployment, poverty, and conflict and also made access to health care more restrictive (Rahim et al. 2009). By 2014, according to a World Bank (2014) report, unemployment in the Palestinian territories was 26.3 percent, and about a fourth of the population was living in poverty. The cycle of violence and the cycle of increasing inequality have fed on each other.

The Politics of War: Militarism. From a political point of view, there are advantages to both militarism and war (Marullo 1987). The presence of a foreign threat, whether real or fabricated by politicians, can create cohesion within a society, including support for both domestic and foreign policies that might otherwise be resisted. One important source of unity in American foreign policy has been the support of both Republicans and Democrats for anticommunist policies.

In the international arena, a strong military gives a nation higher status and more power. The nuclear arsenal of the United States, for example, is a "big stick" that can be used to facilitate the nation's diplomatic efforts and economic trade relations with its allies as well as its enemies. Some observers see this as necessary and proper in order to spread democracy in the world. Others see American foreign policy over the last century or so (including the 2003 war on Iraq) as an expression of imperialism. Chalmers Johnson (2004) argued that the nation has been on a steady path to imperialism, building an empire not through colonies but by establishing military bases throughout the world—there are at least 725 U.S. bases outside the nation's borders. Imperialism is manifest in such things as the justification of interference in the affairs of other nations (including the overthrow of governments that are said to be hostile to our interests) and of preemptive war (Walt 2005).

Militarism is seen not only in foreign policy, but also in the resources allocated to defense. Some defend the defense budget on the basis that it has consumed an increasingly smaller proportion of the total federal budget. Yet the U.S. military budget is vastly higher than that of any other nation. In fact, it is close to half of all military spending in the world. As a proportion of the gross domestic product, however, the U.S. budget is not the highest but is still about 60 percent higher than that of the world average (Figure 14.1). Moreover, through arms sales the United States, along with Britain, France, Russia, and China, is contributing to the high level of weaponry throughout the world. Two-thirds of arms sales are to developing nations, which desperately need their resources for social, educational, and health programs (Grimmett 2006).

Why is an arms buildup, or the maintenance of high levels of arms, in other nations of concern? When the communist governments in Eastern Europe fell during the 1990s and the United States and Russia engaged in an arms limitation agreement in 1990, a

FIGURE 14.1
Military Budgets, by Country.

Source: Perlo-Freeman and
Solmirano 2014.

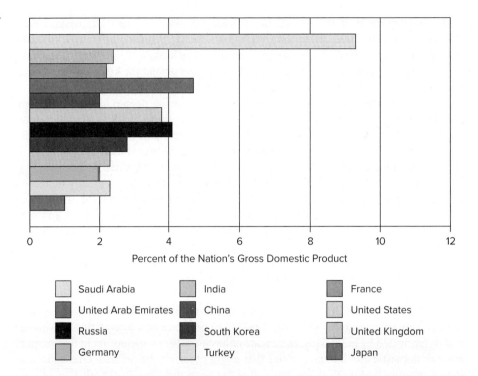

Percent of the Nation's Gross Domestic Product

Saudi Arabia	India	France
United Arab Emirates	China	United States
Russia	South Korea	United Kingdom
Germany	Turkey	Japan

new era of peace appeared to be at hand. Wars and civil conflicts continued in various parts of the world, but there seemed little likelihood of a world war breaking out. Since 2001, however, peace once again appears to be precarious. The U.S. wars against Afghanistan and Iraq have angered many Muslims throughout the world. Anti-American sentiment worldwide is at a high level (Fuller 2011). And it is particularly high in predominantly Muslim nations (Stokes 2014).

In addition, a number of nations continue to build up their weaponry. Iran and North Korea, neither of which is friendly to the United States or the West in general, are working hard to build new biological, chemical, and nuclear weapons along with long-range missiles. In short, militarism is flourishing throughout the world.

The Politics of Terrorism: Autonomy.   Throughout the world are groups who both desire and lack political autonomy—the right of people to govern their own affairs. Generally, when people press for autonomy, they believe that their interests are not adequately represented (or are even ignored) by the current government. Indeed, the United States became a nation under such circumstances.

The lack of political autonomy is a major factor in terrorism. For example, much bloodshed occurred in the struggle by East Timor to gain independence from Indonesia and the attempt by Yugoslavia to suppress the political autonomy of Kosovo. East Timor was finally granted the right to govern itself, and the Yugoslav Republic broke apart when U.N. forces took military action to stop the political oppression of minorities.

The early years of the 21st century are rife with examples of the struggle for political autonomy, including:

• Terrorist acts arising from the dispute between India and Pakistan over Kashmir, and the desire of Kashmir to be independent.

• The Chechnyan revolt against Russia.

- Terrorist acts by Palestinians who want to be free of Israeli control.
- Terrorist acts by the Irish who want Northern Ireland to be free of English control.
- Basque separatists' terrorist acts against Spain.
- Terrorist acts by Islamic extremists who want the Muslim world to be free of all influence and control by the West.

A careful analysis of every suicide terrorist attack in the world from 1980 through the early 2000s concludes that suicide bombers are not primarily the result of Islamic fundamentalism (Pape 2005). The great bulk of suicide bombings take place in the context of campaigns that strive to get rid of foreign military forces from territory that the terrorists regard as their own. Moreover, contrary to assumptions, suicide bombers are not impoverished, uneducated religious fanatics, but more often are educated, middle-class political activists.

In support of these conclusions, Pape notes such things as the fact that prior to Israel's invasion of Lebanon in 1982 there was no Hezbollah suicide campaign against Israel. Nor were there any suicide attacks in Iraq until after the American invasion in 2003. Other observers agree that suicide bombers are driven primarily by the conviction that only through such desperate tactics as killing themselves in order to kill and instill fear into the enemy can their people achieve the political ends that are needed for their well-being (Brym 2007).

Sometimes governments get involved in helping terrorists—providing such things as sanctuary, personnel, weapons, and economic aid—with whose cause they sympathize. According to the U.S. Department of State (2016), Iran, Sudan, and Syria are *state sponsors of terrorism*. This means that these countries have repeatedly provided support for acts of international terrorism through such means as training, arms, and giving shelter for individual terrorists and terrorist groups. But there is also a cluster of independent, cell-based units that do not rely on particular states for their support (Benjamin and Simon 2005). Instead, terrorist groups use various methods to gain financial support for their activities, including "charities" and illegal enterprises such as drugs, extortion, and kidnapping (Perl 2006).

Social Psychological Factors

Attitudes. Militarism and war are legitimated by a number of attitudes. The concept of a "just war" has a long history in the West. A just war is one that meets a number of tests, such as whether it has a just cause and whether all peaceful alternatives have been exhausted. If the war is just, the people are expected to support it fully. Shortly before the 1991 war against Iraq, some religious leaders questioned whether the notion of a just war is still valid in the face of the awful destructiveness of modern weapons (Day 1991). Indeed, Stires (1991) called the subsequent war against Iraq a "sanctioned massacre" because of the way in which the U.S. military technology overwhelmed the Iraqi forces. In spite of disparities in the military technology of nations and the incredible destructiveness of modern weapons, most people accept the notion that at least some wars are just.

The attitude that the United States has a mission to be "number one" in the world helps the country justify militarism. "We feel a collective strength and confidence that comes from being 'number one' in military power" (Marullo 1987:143). National pride is involved in attaining a place of military superiority. Gibson (1994) has argued that this need for being a "winner" facilitated U.S. involvement in Grenada, Panama, and the Persian Gulf. These military actions reflected the American dream of "redeeming

"WHAT A GREAT WAR THAT WAS"

A friend of ours served as a navigator in the Air Force during World War II. "Those," he says "were some of the best days of my life." He recalls his days in the military as a time of adventure. He does not desire war, but neither does he think of it in terms of the detrimental consequences discussed in this chapter.

Interview a number of armed forces veterans. If possible, find veterans who served in different wars, and include some who did have combat experience as well as some who did not. How do they describe the experience of war? Do they mention any of the consequences discussed in this chapter? Would they be willing to serve in another war or to have their children serve? Note any differences based on service in different wars or on combat versus noncombat experience. If everyone felt as your respondents did, would the probability of future wars be greater or less?

Vietnam and recovering from all the other disappointments and traumas of the late 1960s and 1970s" (Gibson 1994:269). After the Gulf War in particular, Americans purchased a spate of military-type items: commemorative handguns, rifles, knives, and T-shirts and uniforms. Many of those who made the purchases were celebrating the restoration of the nation as the supreme military power of the world.

International misperception is a set of attitudes that legitimate both militarism and war. In a classic analysis, White (1966) identified six forms of misperceptions that recur in cases of international wars:

1. The *diabolical-enemy image* imputes flagrant evil to the enemy, who is conceived to be thoroughly criminal in behavior. Prior to the 1991 war against Iraq, the nation's political leaders "indulged in personal name-calling, false analogies to past wars and demonic leaders of earlier times" (Mack and Rubin 1991). In 2002, when President Bush urged new action against Iraq, he said that the Iraqi regime not only raped women to intimidate them but also tortured dissenters and their children and that President Saddam Hussein was a "dangerous and brutal man" who sought to acquire the destructive technologies that matched his hatred (Kozaryn 2002). Ironically, portraying the enemy as diabolically cruel can justify using the same behavior against the enemy (Dutton, Boyanowsky, and Bond 2005). Thus, Americans tortured captured terrorists with little, if any, question being raised about the moral or legal legitimacy of the practice (Shane and Mazzetti 2009).

2. The *virile self-image* implies preoccupation with one's strength and courage and the need to avoid humiliation by determined fighting.

fallacy

3. The *moral self-image* affirms the nation's goodness; Americans are the people of God and the enemy is of the devil. This attitude is the *fallacy of personal attack* and ignores the fact that among the enemy are many innocent, decent people who also are victims of the struggle between the nations.

4. *Selective inattention* means that only the worst aspects of the enemy are noticed; at the same time Americans attend to the best aspects of themselves, reinforcing the idea of the war as a conflict between black and white, good and evil.

5. *Absence of empathy* means the inability to understand how the situation looks from the other's viewpoint. An American might wonder, for example, how any German could fight on behalf of Hitler, or how any South Vietnamese could not welcome

the American effort to save Vietnam from communism. People on both sides of a war fail to understand how the war could be justified by those on the other side. In the 1991 war against Iraq, Americans denied their contribution to the problem (later reports indicated that the United States had assured the Iraqis it would not interfere if they invaded Kuwait, and it had built up the Iraqi forces during the 1980s) and placed the blame totally on Iraq's shoulders (Mack and Rubin 1991).

6. *Military overconfidence* refers to the conviction that our side can win. In the case of the 1991 war against Iraq, the Iraqi leaders boasted (and no doubt believed to some extent) that the enemy would be soundly and humiliatingly defeated. Similarly, top American political leaders predicted that the 2003 war against Iraq would be swift, would result in a decisive victory for the United States, and would establish democracy in that nation.

These attitudes can be found on both sides of a conflict and are encouraged by the opposing leaders. For decades, American leaders portrayed the Soviet Union as an evil empire that threatened the nation's fundamental (and righteous) values. On the other hand, *Pravda,* the Soviet Communist Party's daily newspaper, discussed attempts at arms control with the United States in terms of dealing with "militaristic ambitions," "hotheads in the Pentagon," and "insane anti-logic" (Lichter, Lichter, Amundson, and Fowler 1987:12).

Misperceptions were also at work in the 2003 war against Iraq (Kull, Ramsay, and Lewis 2003). Many Americans accepted the notion that Iraq was involved in the September 11, 2001, terrorist attacks, that Iraq had developed and was prepared to use weapons of mass destruction, and that a good part, if not most, of world opinion favored the American position. The news media, particularly Fox News, helped shape these misperceptions. People who watched Fox network were three times more likely to hold those misperceptions than were people who watched other networks. Misperceptions were also fostered among the Iraqi people. They were told that the United States was the "Satan" of the world and that American forces would be soundly defeated if they invaded Iraqi soil.

In any confrontation between nations, the perceptions on both sides are remarkably similar, and people will support war to the extent that they accept such attitudes. Because both sides have the same attitudes, the attitudes obviously cannot be realistic. Nevertheless, they have typically been defined as valid and have served to legitimate international violence.

We noted earlier in this chapter that the majority of Palestinians support the suicide bombers and other acts of terror against Israel. Even though most Muslim leaders (both religious and political) condemn terrorism, the people take the attitude that the terrorists are only acting in defense of the Palestinian people and are doing nothing worse than what is being done to them.

Other terrorists also justify their actions on the grounds that they are really defending rights and seeking the well-being of the oppressed. They may also believe that change is nonexistent or too slow and that attention needs to be called to their cause (Jacobs 2001).

War, Terrorism, and Ideology. *Ideologies* support militarism and war. In particular, Bacevich (2010) has identified an ideology about national security to which every president since 1945 has subscribed. The ideology consists of four assertions. First, the world needs to avoid chaos through order. Second, only the United States has the necessary power and resources to create and maintain global order. Third, only the United States is capable of identifying the principles (which, of course, are American principles) that are valid for a proper global order. Fourth, most of the world understands and accepts this role for the United States. Such an ideology, Bacevich argues, is why the United States repeatedly has gotten, and will continue to get, involved in wars.

This ideology was a part of the rationale for initiating the war against Iraq in 1991. It was necessary, Americans were told, for the United States to take steps to protect the world against dictators like Saddam Hussein. Of course, the ideology is used selectively. In other situations in which dictators and totalitarian governments have initiated action against another country or against a segment of their own country, the United States has responded only with moral support or arms. In Iraq, however, the ideology was used to justify a massive assault.

The Islamic extremists who resort to terrorism use a fundamentalist interpretation of the Koran to help motivate their followers (Del Castillo 2001; Hassan 2001). They represent what one researcher called "political Islam" rather than "personal religiosity" (Haddad 2003). For them, religion and politics are intertwined and inseparable. Their ideology includes a rejection of Western culture, a belief in Islamic law as a basis for the state, and the assertion that believers who are martyred in the cause of pursuing those aims are ensured entrance to eternal paradise. Many of the extremists received their education in fundamentalist religious schools, where they learned only a particular interpretation of the Koran and little that was modern except for the use of armaments.

Public Policy and Private Action

Inequalities of wealth and power among nations and between groups within nations, political and ideological conflicts, and economic factors all contribute to the likelihood of war and terrorism. An important step toward solving the problem would be to negotiate treaties that reduced the weaponry and armaments in the world. Current stockpiles, which are more than sufficient to eradicate life on the earth, need to be cut back. Military spending must be reduced. The sale of weapons of mass destruction is not an acceptable way to boost the supplier nation's economy. The massive number of weapons in the world also aids the cause of terrorists, who are able to secure sufficient arms to carry out their attacks.

Nations that thwart the effort to reduce arms or that abet terrorism can be subjected to economic sanctions through the United Nations. Such sanctions should be used judiciously. They eventually worked against Libya, which seems to have withdrawn from the ranks of those countries that sponsor terrorism (Collins 2004). Sanctions did not work to overthrow the Iraqi regime of Saddam Hussein, however. The main outcome of the sanctions was "enormous human suffering, including massive increases of child mortality and widespread epidemics" (Gordon 2002:44).

One problem with fighting terrorism is the sophisticated and strong financial infrastructure of some groups (Basile 2004). Terrorists have the economic resources they need to train their people, purchase arms, and pay the expenses needed to carry out their missions. International cooperation will be necessary to break up the financial base of terrorism because it is rooted in both legitimate and illegitimate businesses and charities and it transfers money around the world through poorly regulated banking networks.

Although the United States has tried to take the lead in committing the world's nations to a concerted fight against terrorism, cooperation will be difficult because of unilateral actions the country has taken in the name of its own interests (Cameron 2002). The 1989 Convention on the Rights of the Child was ratified by every nation except Somalia and the United States. The Comprehensive Test Ban Treaty of 1996 to halt nuclear testing and the development of new nuclear weapons was ratified by all the NATO nations and Russia but rejected by the United States. The United States rejected the Ottawa Treaty to Ban Landmines, while 142 other countries approved it. In 2002, the Bush administration gave notice that the United States was pulling out of the 1972 Anti-Ballistic Missile Treaty, which limited the testing and deployment of antimissile weapons. A day later, Russia announced that it was no longer bound by the 1993 START II agreement, which outlawed multiple-warhead missiles and other weapons in the strategic arsenals of the two nations.

In essence, U.S. foreign policy in recent decades reflects more a determination to protect what political leaders define as the nation's self-interest (defined, in part at least, in terms of the international misperceptions described earlier) than a desire to be a leader in the construction of world peace. It is questionable how long the nation can continue to press for cooperation in fighting terrorism while asserting its right to take unilateral action on other issues whenever it pleases.

The United States also needs to stop the ongoing sale of arms to nations throughout the world. As Renner (1993a) has argued, armaments may simply be a symptom of deep conflicts between people, but curbing the availability of arms is still crucial for three reasons. First, arms proliferation tends to gain a momentum of its own; no nation is satisfied with just being equal to others but wants an advantage over its enemies or potential enemies.

Second, if arms are readily available, nations will more likely rely on them than on diplomacy and negotiations to settle their disputes (recall that in Chapter 4 we noted that the availability of a weapon makes it more likely that it will be used). Third, when arms are readily available, the ensuing hostilities are likely to be far more devastating

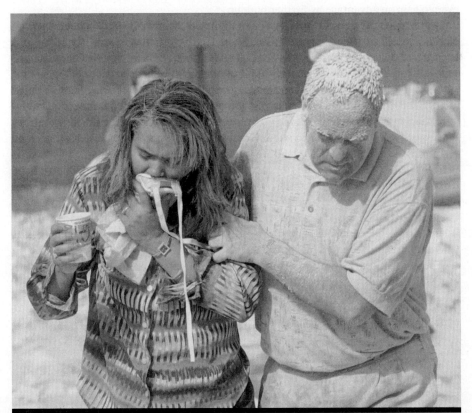

Innocent bystanders are the main victims of terrorist attacks.
Source: Library of Congress Prints and Photographs Division [LC-DIG-ppmsca-01813]

than they would be otherwise. For instance, the United States and the Soviet Union both shipped large amounts of arms to Somalia during the Cold War, each trying to lure the country into its sphere of influence. After the Cold War ended, a civil war broke out in Somalia in 1991, decimating the country and turning it into a nightmare of heavily armed, competing factions.

Of course, it is risky for any nation to demilitarize unless its potential adversary does the same, but there is some evidence to suggest that the risk is minimal. In the process called *Graduated Reciprocation in Tension-Reduction* (GRIT), one nation initiates an action that visibly reduces the way it threatens the other nation without at the same time endangering its own security. The action is an invitation to the other side to reciprocate (Elms 1972). Will such reciprocation occur? Following the 1962 Cuban missile crisis, President John F. Kennedy announced that the United States would stop atmospheric nuclear tests and would resume them only if another country's action compelled it to do so. The next day the Soviet Union agreed to a Western-backed proposal in the United Nations to send observers to Yemen (a proposal the Soviets had been blocking). America reciprocated by agreeing to restore the Hungarian delegation to full status in the United Nations. A few days later Khrushchev announced that Russia would stop producing strategic bombers. Shortly thereafter the "hot line" between the White House and the Kremlin was installed. This series of concessions was the result of each side taking a step that led the other to reciprocate.

Subsequently, Soviet President Gorbachev initiated a number of efforts to reduce tensions and to engage in arms reductions. The United States responded to each effort positively. Neither nation used concessions by the other as an opportunity to attack or even to gain an advantage by further buildup.

In contrast, the reverse process occurred in the Israeli-Palestinian conflict. Each side believed it had the right to—indeed, that it *must*—retaliate against the other after each attack. Clearly, such a process has no end (Brym and Araj 2006). There can be a graduated reciprocation in tension building as well as in tension reduction.

In addition to a halt to unilateral action and the breaking of international agreements, and to actively working to reduce arms and demilitarize the world, there is a need in the United States for changed attitudes and ideologies. More contact between peoples—cultural, educational, and political contact—could alter some of the misperceptions that abound in the world. Education should include an international perspective, so that Americans become increasingly aware of the smallness of the world and of the similarities among human beings everywhere. Instead of viewing other countries as adversaries or as problems, Americans should view them as partners working together on common problems. If the United States strives to be a world leader, let it be a leader in peace and in promoting the well-being of people rather than a leader who uses strength for pursuing self-interest.

The effort to avoid war and terrorism and to reduce the costs of preparing for war entails a great deal of work and frustration, but the alternatives to making the effort are grim. A noted man of peace, Martin Luther King Jr., put it this way:

> In a day when sputniks dash through outer space and guided ballistic missiles are carving highways of death through the stratosphere, nobody can win a war. The choice today is no longer between violence and nonviolence. It is either nonviolence or nonexistence. (quoted in Weinberg and Weinberg 1963:74)

Follow-Up.   What kind of measures would you like to see become a matter of public policy to maximize your own protection from terrorist attacks?

Summary

Americans are greatly concerned about war and terrorism. Warfare is no longer just a matter of opposing armies on the battlefield, but increasingly involves civil wars and terrorist activities.

War diminishes the quality of life of people and destroys the lives of many. From the Civil War to the present, nearly a million American military personnel have died as a result of wars. And nearly 1.5 million more have been wounded. During the 20th century, the bloodiest of all centuries, wars killed more than a hundred million people. War and terrorism cause psychological disruption and dehumanization of everyone involved. As illustrated by posttraumatic stress disorder, the effects last after the war or terrorist act is over. Much environmental destruction is involved. The economic costs of war, of preparation for possible wars, and of terrorism are staggering. The costs of fighting war and stopping terrorism inevitably mean that certain social needs will be neglected. War and terrorism always pose a threat to civil liberties, as illustrated by sanctions against dissenters and the detention of Japanese Americans in isolated camps during World War II and measures taken by the U.S. government after the September 11, 2001, attacks.

Social structural and social psychological factors help bring about war and terrorist activities and motivate people to support them. Economic factors are involved in wars and terrorism. Military spending is highly profitable to some industries, and people who profit from such spending tend to exercise considerable power in the government. Severe economic inequality between racial, ethnic, or religious groups within nations can give rise to civil war or terrorism.

Militarism is a political factor that can lead to war. The military influence in America is strong. The military, the government, and the corporations have some shared interests. This military-industrial-governmental linkage tends to maintain high levels of defense spending. Arms races tend to be self-perpetuating because each side views developments of the other with alarm and responds with its own efforts, which then become the stimuli to the other side to make further advances.

The desire for autonomy is a political factor in terrorism. People everywhere want the right to govern themselves and may assert that right through civil war or terrorist activities when they believe their interests are not represented in the government.

A number of attitudes justify war and terrorism, including the notion of a just war, the idea that Americans have a mission to be number one in the world, the set of attitudes called "international misperception" held by people on both sides of a potential conflict, and the belief that terrorist acts are a necessary form of self-defense. Finally, the ideology that Americans must protect national security by taking responsibility for creating and maintaining a global order that is consistent with American ideals supports militarism and war, and Islamic extremists use a religion-based ideology to justify terrorist acts.

Key Terms

Environmental Destruction	Marxist
International Terrorism	Military Parity
	War

Study Questions

1. How extensive is the problem of war and terrorism?
2. How has the amount of human destruction and injury during war changed over time?
3. What is meant by "psychological and interpersonal disruption and dehumanization" as a consequence of war and terrorism?
4. What effects does the problem have on the environment?
5. What are the economic costs?
6. How do war and terrorism affect civil liberties?
7. How do economic factors enter into war and terrorism?
8. What kinds of political factors contribute to the problem?
9. What attitudes and ideologies legitimate wars and terrorism?
10. What steps could be taken to diminish the possibility of war and terrorist acts?

Internet Resources/Exercises

1. Explore some of the ideas in this chapter on the following sites:

http://www.terrorism-research.com   The International Terrorism and Security Research site has news, essays, and links to other sites that deal with terrorism throughout the world.

http://www.fbi.gov   The FBI site features the latest news and information about terrorist activities.

http://www.iwpr.net   The Institute for War and Peace Reporting site has news about conflicts throughout the world.

2. Go to the site of the Institute for War and Peace Reporting. Summarize the various wars and armed conflicts currently reported there. Where are the trouble spots in the world? What are the more common kinds of conflicts—wars between nations or civil wars? What materials in the text could you use to help understand the reasons for the conflicts?

3. Search the Internet for a particular aspect of terrorism, such as the history of terrorism, terrorism in the United States, the war on terrorism, or terrorist groups. Make a report to the class showing how your findings fit in with, or modify, the text materials.

For Further Reading

Cole, David, and James X. Dempsey. *Terrorism and the Constitution: Sacrificing Civil Liberties in the Name of National Security.* 2nd ed. Washington, DC: First Amendment Foundation, 2002. Two constitutional scholars show how civil liberties are threatened by the government's response to real or perceived threats, from the communists of the 1950s to the Islamic terrorists of the 21st century.

Grynberg, Michal, ed. *Words to Outlive Us: Eyewitness Accounts from the Warsaw Ghetto.* New York: Henry Holt, 2002. Detailed accounts from individual diaries, journals, and other writings show life in the Jewish community from the first bombardments of the capital to the razing of the Jewish ghetto. The struggles, deprivations, and suffering are graphically portrayed in these previously unpublished accounts.

Harwayne, Shelley. *Messages to Ground Zero: Children Respond to September 11, 2001.* Portsmouth, NH: Heinemann, 2002. A compilation of poems, drawings, and essays that illustrate children's reactions to the terrorist attacks, ranging from admiration for the heroic rescuers to personal feelings of anxiety and grief.

Honigsberg, Peter Jan. *Our Nation Unhinged: The Human Consequences of the War on Terror.* Berkeley, CA: University of California Press, 2009. A professor of law analyzes the ways in which executive power was abused, the Constitution was subverted, and civil liberties were eroded as the government responded to the September 11, 2001, attacks by terrorists.

Howard, Russell, and Reid Sawyer, eds. *Terrorism and Counterterrorism: Understanding the New Security Environment.* Guilford, CT: McGraw-Hill/Dushkin, 2002. A collection of articles by terrorism experts analyzing terrorism from many perspectives, including suggestions on how to deal with the current terrorist groups.

Margulies, Joseph. *Guantanamo and the Abuse of Presidential Power.* New York: Simon & Schuster, 2006. A close examination of a major point of contention over civil liberties—the American prison at Guantanamo Bay, Cuba, including abuses at the prison and the efforts of the president to defend the situation by extending the bounds of presidential authority.

Tirman, John. *The Deaths of Others: The Fate of Civilians in America's Wars.* New York: Oxford University Press, 2011. Beginning with the seldom-recognized fact that the millions of foreign civilians who have died in America's wars receive little notice, Tirman explores the extent of those deaths in various wars, the ways in which our tactics brought about such destruction, and the reason for minimal concern on the part of the American people for such a massive amount of killing.

Endnotes

1. *I Never Saw Another Butterfly: Children's Drawings and Poems from Terezin Concentration Camp, 1942-1944.* New York: McGraw-Hill, n.d.

2. *Oil Spill Intelligence Report,* April 11, 2002, pp. 1-3.

CHAPTER

The Environment

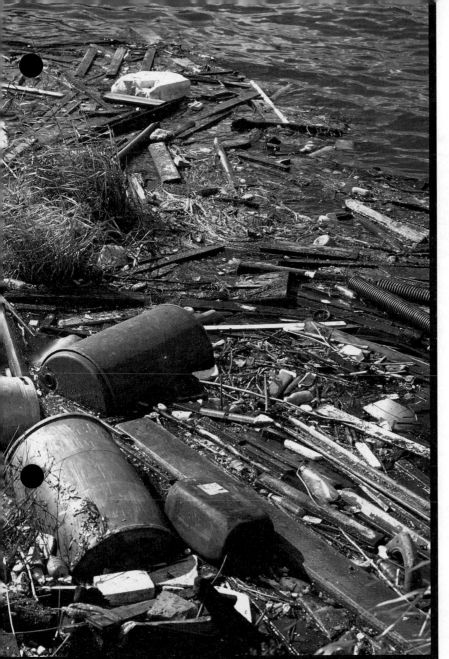

©Steve Allen/Brand X Pictures

"We're Not Safe Here Anymore"

Karl is a civilian employee on an air force base in a western state. Karl lives in a home that was occupied by his great-grandparents—built long before the air force base. Yet Karl isn't sure whether his children or his grandchildren will live in this place.

I can't imagine living anywhere else. But I can't imagine my children or grandchildren living here. I don't even want them to. We're not safe here anymore. The hazardous wastes from the base have contaminated our water supply. We can't grow our gardens anymore. We can't drink the water. We don't even feel safe taking a bath in it.

And it's not just the water. When you know that stuff is all around you, you feel like you're living in poison. Of course, I try not to think about it most of the time. But you can't keep it out of your mind altogether. And whenever I do think about it, I can feel myself getting nervous. Or sometimes I just get depressed.

I love this place. It's my home. But sometimes I hate it. At least, I hate what's happened to it. I don't know yet what we're going to do. But I do know that even if my wife and I don't leave, our kids will. And that will be the end of generations of my family on this land.

Introduction

In 2004, the Nobel Peace Prize was awarded to an environmentalist activist, Wangari Maathai of Kenya. She founded and led a movement to plant millions of trees to replenish the dwindling forests that provide Africans with cooking fuel. To many observers, declaring an environmentalist the winner of the Peace Prize seemed strange. But Christopher Flavin, president of Worldwatch Institute, declared it a most fitting award, because "the insecurity the world struggles with today is inextricably linked to the ecological and social problems" that Maathai strives to address (Flavin 2005:xix). In other words, although Americans tend not to consider them as serious as other matters we have addressed in this book, the problems we deal with in this chapter are crucial to the security and general well-being of people everywhere.

We look first at the ecosystem to set the stage for an understanding of environmental problems. Then we examine various kinds of environmental problems and how extensive they are. We show how these problems affect the quality of life and what structural and social psychological factors contribute to them. Finally, we consider several proposed as well as actual efforts to resolve these problems.

The Ecosystem

ecosystem
a set of living things, their environment, and the interrelationships among and between them

The **ecosystem** refers to the interrelationships between all living things and the environment. The emphasis is on the interdependence of all things: people, land, animals, vegetation, atmosphere, and social processes. Commoner (1971:16–17) called the ecosystem of the earth a "machine" and described some of the crucial interrelationships:

> Without the photosynthetic activity of green plants, there would be no oxygen for our engines, smelters, and furnaces, let alone support for human and animal life. Without the action of the plants, animals, and microorganisms that live in them, we could have no pure water in our lakes and rivers. Without the biological processes that have gone on in the soil for thousands of years, we would have neither food crops, oil, nor coal. This machine is our biological capital, the basic apparatus on which our total productivity depends. If we destroy it, our most advanced technology will become useless and any economic and political system that depends on it will founder. The environmental crisis is a signal of this approaching catastrophe.

Nature is not "out there" to be conquered for human benefit. Rather, people, nature, and the earth form a delicately balanced system. What is done at one place can have serious consequences for the system at that place or in other places. For example, companies that drill for natural gas in Texas and Oklahoma use fracking—pumping massive amounts of water and other materials into the ground to crack rock and release the gas (Kuchment 2016). An increase in the amount of drilling has resulted in a dramatic jump in the number of earthquakes in the region. Between 2008 and 2015, Texas had a sixfold and Oklahoma had a 160-fold increase in the number of earthquakes, some of which have resulted in injuries and damage to buildings and highways.

The interrelationships between human activity and the environment are also illustrated by the problems of acid rain and the threat to the ozone layer. The problem of acid rain was originally caused by sulfur dioxide emissions from coal-burning plants and factories and by nitrogen oxides from automobile exhaust and some industries. These chemicals, as they rise, mix with water vapor to form sulfuric and nitric acids that then fall to the earth as rain or snow. Acid rain threatens lakes and forests, kills fish and birds, reduces crop yields, contributes to health problems, and damages buildings and monuments (see the U.S. Environmental Protection Agency website; see also Bright 2000; Leslie 2003; Youth 2003). Moreover, the damage may occur hundreds or thousands of miles away from where the sulfur dioxide emissions occurred.

In recent decades, tougher air pollution regulations have significantly reduced sulfur dioxide emissions. Some damaged lakes and forests are beginning to recover. However, acid rain continues to be a problem, but more in the form of nitric acid rather than sulfuric acid (Tennesen 2010). The nitric acid is produced not only by coal-burning plants and automobiles but also by farming (bacteria work on fertilizer to create nitric acid).

The threat to the ozone layer is another example of current environmental problems. Ozone is a rare form of oxygen that is poisonous to human beings at ground level but is necessary in the upper atmosphere to absorb the deadly ultraviolet radiation of the sun. There is a natural balance of ozone distribution from ground level to the stratosphere. However, human activity disturbs that natural balance. High-voltage electrical equipment, including electrostatic air cleaners used to reduce other kinds of air pollution, create ground level ozone, and higher than normal concentrations at ground level pose health problems to the eyes, throat, and lungs.

The ozone in the upper atmosphere is reduced as a result of a number of human activities, including the use of nitrogen fertilizers, supersonic airplanes, fluorocarbons from aerosol spray cans (now banned in most nations), and nuclear explosions in the atmosphere. The effects of a depleted ozone layer are far reaching, involving changes in the earth's climate, destruction of some plant and animal life, reduced crop yields, increased incidence of skin cancer, possible genetic damage to plants and humans, and an impact on the food chain of the oceans (McGinn 1999).

Environmental problems dramatize the interdependence in the ecosystem. A poet once wrote that one cannot stir a flower without troubling a star. It is imperative that individuals make every effort to evaluate all the implications of human action for their delicately balanced ecosystem.

Types of Environmental Problems

Environmental problems can be divided into two types: **environmental pollution** and **environmental depletion.** "Pollution" refers to degradation of air, land, water, climate (global warming), aesthetic environment (eye pollution), and sound environment (noise pollution). "Depletion" refers to the diminishing supply of natural resources, illustrated well by the challenge of meeting the ever-increasing demand for energy.

Environmental Pollution

Pollution is any alteration of the environment that is harmful to the ecosystem and/or to human well-being. **Pollutants,** those things that cause the pollution, are by-products of human activity (e.g., industrial production, war, farming, and the use of hazardous materials). In this chapter, we discuss numerous kinds of pollution and pollutants. It is important to keep in mind that in an ecosystem the overall impact of pollutants is greater than the impact of particular pollutants in particular places.

Pollution can occur in two ways: through catastrophes and through the slower, more insidious poisoning that occurs as a result of various processes and activities. The catastrophes dramatize the problem. In 1984, vapors from a deadly chemical used to manufacture pesticides escaped through a faulty valve into the air in Bhopal, India.

environmental pollution
harmful alterations in the environment, including air, land, and water

environmental depletion
increasing scarcity of natural resources, including those used for generating energy

pollutant
anything that causes environmental pollution

Within a few hours, more than 2,500 people were dead, and thousands were critically ill. It was one of the worst industrial disasters in history. The accident underscored the horrendous consequences of exposure to toxic substances. Yet even more important than the catastrophes are the countless ways in which industries are exposing millions of people to high levels of toxic materials. Many of the victims in Bhopal died quickly. Others died more slowly or suffered long-term health problems as the result of regular exposure to toxic materials in the air, water, and land. Twenty years later, in 2004, survivors and their supporters demonstrated because people were still suffering, and 24 years later, in 2008, hundreds of tons of toxic waste still lay within a warehouse on the grounds of the old factory (Sengupta 2008). And three decades later, residents continued to exhibit both physical and mental health problems arising from the disaster (Howard, 2014; Murthy 2014).

Air Pollution.   Millions of tons of pollutants are released into the air every year in the United States and are visible in the smog that darkens urban areas. Much other pollution is not visible to the naked eye because it results from the discharge of gases and tiny particulate matter into the air. In some areas, atmospheric conditions tend to concentrate pollutants in the air. Even when winds blow the pollutants away from the populated area in which they are generated, damage still occurs.

Major air pollutants include suspended particulates (dust, pollen, ash, soot, chemicals, etc.), sulfur dioxide (from industrial processes), carbon monoxide (from motor vehicle exhaust, forest fires, decomposition of organic matter, etc.), and nitrogen dioxide (from motor vehicle exhaust, atmospheric reactions, etc.). The burning of fossil fuels—oil, natural gas, and coal—is the primary source of air pollution (Flavin and Dunn 1999).

While many people think of air pollution in terms of outside air, *a major problem throughout the world is indoor air pollution* (World Health Organization 2005). In developing countries, the indoor smoke resulting from burning solid fuels pollutes indoor air and is responsible for much illness and early death. In the United States and other developed nations, there are numerous sources of indoor pollution, including the polluted outdoor air but also including numerous everyday products found in all buildings, from offices to homes (Figure 15.1). For example, formaldehyde, which emits toxic vapors that can lead to respiratory ailments and cancer, is used in a great many products, including bed sheets, permanent press shirts, fingernail hardeners and polishes, latex paints, plywood and particle-board cabinets, and plastic-laminated kitchen counters (Horowitz 1999; Raloff 1999). We don't know how many homes are polluted by excessive levels of formaldehyde, but a survey of homes in Japan reported that a fourth of them had concentration levels above the value set by the Ministry of Health, Labor, and Welfare as acceptable (Osawa and Hayashi 2009).

Water Pollution.   There are eight different kinds of water pollution (Sampat 2000). First is organic sewage, which requires dissolved oxygen in order to be transformed into carbon dioxide, water, phosphates, nitrates, and certain plant nutrients. Less oxygen is needed if the sewage is treated, but the amount of treatment varies and in some places there is no treatment at all.

eutrophication
overfertilization of water due to excess nutrients, leading to algae growth and oxygen depletion

Eutrophication, a second kind of water pollution, is overfertilization of water from excess nutrients, leading to algae growth and oxygen depletion. Eutrophication threatens aquatic life. It has already killed great numbers of fish in the United States and in other nations.

A third type of water pollution results from infectious agents. Many water-borne bacteria that cause disease have been eliminated in the United States, but there is still danger from infectious viruses such as hepatitis. Organic chemicals such as insecticides,

OUTDOOR SOURCES	BUILDING EQUIPMENT	COMPONENTS/ FURNISHINGS	OTHER POTENTIAL INDOOR SOURCES
Polluted Outdoor Air • Pollen, dust, mold spores • Industrial emissions • Vehicle and nonroad engine emissions (cars, buses, trucks, lawn and garden equipment) **Nearby Sources** • Loading docks • Odors from dumpsters • Unsanitary debris or building exhausts near outdoor air intakes **Underground Sources** • Radon • Pesticides • Leakage from underground storage tanks	**HVAC Equipment** • Mold growth in drip pans, ductwork, coils, and humidifiers • Improper venting of combustion products • Dust or debris in ductwork **Other Equipment** • Emissions from office equipment (volatile organic compounds [VOCs], ozone) • Emissions from shop, lab, and cleaning equipment	**Components** • Mold growth on or in soiled or water-damaged materials • Dry drain traps that allow the passage of sewer gas • Materials containing VOCs, inorganic compounds, or damaged asbestos • Materials that produce particles (dust) **Furnishings** • Emissions from new furnishings and floorings • Mold growth on or in soiled or water-damaged furnishings	• Science laboratory supplies • Vocational art supplies • Copy/print areas • Food prep areas • Smoking lounges • Cleaning materials • Emissions from trash • Pesticides • Odors and VOCs from paint, caulk, adhesives • Occupants with communicable diseases • Dry-erase markers and similar pens • Insects and other pests • Personal care products • Stored gasoline and lawn and garden equipment

FIGURE 15.1 Typical Sources of Indoor Air Pollutants.

Source: U.S. Environmental Protection Agency Web site.

pesticides, and detergents cause a fourth kind of water pollution. These chemicals may also be highly toxic to aquatic life.

Inorganic and miscellaneous chemicals constitute a fifth category of water pollutants. These chemicals can alter the life of a body of water, kill fish, and create unpleasant tastes when the water is used as a drinking supply. Sixth, sediments from land erosion may cause pollution. These sediments can diminish the water's capacity to assimilate oxygen-demanding wastes and block the sunlight needed by aquatic plants.

Radioactive substances, a seventh kind of pollutant, are likely to become more serious if nuclear power plants to generate electricity become more common. The eighth kind of water pollution is waste heat from power plants and industry. Overheated water holds less oxygen, and fish and other aquatic life are generally very sensitive to temperature changes.

Not only are lakes and rivers being polluted, but the oceans are as well. Oil spills and the dumping of waste into the oceans have made many beaches unsafe for swimming.

Millions of barrels of oil are poured into the ocean each year from the cleaning of the bilges of tankers. In addition, thousands of oil-polluting incidents occur every year from such problems as tanker accidents. Incidents in and around U.S. waters result in various amounts of spillage. In 2009, the spillage was 195,189 gallons; the worst year was 1990 when 7.9 million gallons were spilled (U.S. Census Bureau 2012).

pesticide
a chemical used to kill insects defined as pests

herbicide
a chemical used to kill plant life, particularly weeds

Land Pollution.   **Pesticides, herbicides,** chemical wastes, radioactive fallout, acid rain, and garbage all infect the soil. Some chemicals used in pesticides, herbicides, and a number of manufactured products are hazardous to human health and are highly stable, remaining in the soil for decades (McGinn 2000).

The pesticide DDT, for example, was banned in the United States after it was found to interfere with the formation of normal eggshells in certain birds, adding to the potential extinction of some species. It is incredibly stable, having been detected in Antarctic penguins, in the blood and fat of most Americans, and in carrots and spinach sold in supermarkets more than a decade after being banned.

Nor is the threat posed only by the "active" ingredients in pesticides. The so-called inert ingredients can constitute up to 99 percent of the contents, and many of those ingredients are biochemically active. For example, an unlisted ingredient in Dibrom, a mosquito pesticide, is naphthalene, which may cause cancer and developmental problems in children (Epstein 2003).

The problem of pesticides is compounded by the fact that the pests tend to develop a resistance to them; thus, increasing quantities are required over time. And if the natural enemies of a particular pest disappear, a pest control program may require monstrous increases in dosage of the pesticide.

Global Warming.   Air pollution from carbon dioxide, methane, nitrous oxide, and a number of other gases is a primary factor in the so-called greenhouse effect (McKeown and Gardner 2009). The gases trap solar energy in the atmosphere, which, in turn, leads to global warming. Few if any scientists deny that global warming is occurring (although there is still a small amount of disagreement about the extent to which human activity is a factor in the warming). The first 15 years of the 21st century had 14 of the 15 hottest years ever recorded, and July 2016 was the hottest month ever recorded (Cullen 2016). The levels of carbon dioxide in the atmosphere "are higher than they have been at any time in the past 650,000 years" (Stix 2006). Glaciers around the world are retreating. The polar ice is melting even more rapidly than scientists anticipated (Brown 2008). Sea levels are rising and extremes of climate are increasing (World Health Organization 2007).

As the warming continues, the impact on human life will be severe (McKeown and Gardner 2009). Scientists warn that there will be:

- Increased flooding and intensity of storms on coastal areas;
- An increase in extremes, with more of both droughts and flooding;
- Reduced fresh water supplies and food production;
- Damage to ecosystems, including extinctions; and
- Increases in malnutrition, disease, and mortality.

Although, as we noted, there is some disagreement about the extent to which human activity contributes to the warming, the great majority of scientists argue convincingly that humankind has seriously affected the climate (Collins et al. 2007). For example, some of the greenhouse gases have no natural source; they are the products of processes initiated by humans. And even those that have a natural source are increased greatly by human activity. Thus, most of the increase in carbon dioxide (which had remained at roughly the same level for 100,000 years prior to the industrial revolution) is due to the burning of coal, oil, and natural gas. In short, although some politicians and skeptical observers demur, the scientific community is virtually one voice in proclaiming both the severity of, and the central role of human activity in, the problem.

Noise Pollution.　Prolonged exposure to noise of sufficient intensity can not only damage hearing but can also disturb sleep, create irritability, diminish the ability to concentrate on work, disrupt activity and communication, and cause accidents (Committee on Technology for a Quieter America 2010). Many things—from traffic to industrial processes to vacuum cleaners—contribute to noise pollution. You may find the noise level in a particular situation as anything from annoying to painful. For most people, the noise environment is worsening. Indeed, hundreds of millions of people throughout the world are exposed to unacceptable noise levels at work and at home (Skanberg and Ohrstrom 2002).

Aesthetic Damage.　An aesthetically pleasing environment is one component of a high quality of life (Sirgy, Efraty, Siegel, and Lee 2001). An attractive environment can affect mood and influence health-promoting behavior like exercise (Craig, Brownson, Cragg, and Dunn 2002). It is no minor point, then, that pollution involves *deterioration of the beauty of the environment* as well as actual physical damage.

Air pollution, for instance, leads to the deterioration of buildings, statues, and paintings. It can inhibit visibility, obscure scenic views, and produce noxious odors. This kind of aesthetic damage—whether from air and water pollution or from litter—is the effect on the environment that most people first recognize. Whatever the source, aesthetic damage signals that the environment is less pleasing, that the beauty of the natural world has been scarred by human activity.

Energy consumption per capita is higher in the United States than it is in any other country in the world.

©Shutterstock

TABLE 15.1
Energy Production and
Consumption, 1950–2015

Year	Total Production (quad. Btu)	Total Consumption (quad. Btu)	Consumption/ Production Ratio
1950	35.5	34.6	0.97
1960	42.8	45.1	1.05
1970	63.5	67.9	1.07
1975	61.4	72.0	1.17
1980	67.2	78.4	1.17
1985	67.7	76.7	1.13
1990	70.7	84.6	1.20
1995	71.2	91.5	1.29
2000	71.3	100.0	1.40
2005	69.9	100.3	1.44
2010	75.0	98.0	1.31
2015	88.1	97.4	1.11

SOURCE: U.S. Energy Information Administration 2016b.

Environmental Depletion

The Dwindling Natural Resources. Air, water, and land can be restored, but the problem of dwindling resources is another matter. If the air is cleaned, it may become just as useful as before it was polluted. But once a mine has been exhausted, an oil well pumped dry, or a patch of soil ruined for farming, you have lost a resource that cannot be reclaimed easily or quickly, if at all.

For a long time Americans tended to think that the nation had virtually unlimited natural resources. In 1973, a group of oil-producing nations temporarily suspended the sale of oil to other nations, and Americans confronted the fact that no nation in the modern world can be self-sufficient by virtue of its own natural resources. The United States does not have sufficient oil in its own reserves to meet its needs. Nor does it have sufficient supplies of various other natural resources. In 2015, the United States imported 100 percent of 19 minerals used in various manufacturing processes and products (U.S. Geological Survey 2016). And the nation imported varying amounts of dozens of other minerals, ranging from 11 percent of iron and steel slag to 95 percent of bismuth.

Energy Production and Consumption. An integral part of the pollution problem and the dwindling of resources is the production and consumption of energy. As Table 15.1 shows, energy consumption has risen rapidly in the United States. Although the United States does not have the highest per capita usage of energy, our usage accounts for 17 percent of the world's energy consumption.

There are some hopeful signs in the area of energy. Consumption declined a bit by 2015. Per capita consumption has also declined somewhat: it was lower in 2015 than it was in 1990. It remains to be seen whether this trend will continue.

How Big Are These Environmental Problems?

How serious are the environmental problems of this country? Using the same two categories of environmental pollution and environmental depletion, consider what the data reveal.

Environmental Pollution

The federal Environmental Protection Agency (EPA) has established standards for six "criteria" air pollutants: sulfur dioxide, particulate matter, carbon monoxide, ozone, lead, and nitrogen dioxide. Many states and cities have adopted the Pollutant Standards Index (PSI), which indicates when any of the six criteria pollutants are at a level considered to be adverse to human health. These six criteria pollutants are not the only sources of the problem but are the ones used by the federal government to evaluate air quality.

In general, enforcement of *air pollution standards* has been reducing the amount of the pollutants released into the air (EPA website). From 1980 to 2015, the emission of six principal air pollutants dropped by 69 percent. however carbon dioxide (a major factor in global warming) increased by 18 percent. Although progress has occurred, the problem remains severe. In 2015, 120.5 million Americans lived in a county where one or more pollutants exceeded the national air quality standards (EPA website).

Air quality has improved, but serious problems remain. In many places—particularly the developing nations—it is a more serious problem than in the United States. It is estimated that more than a billion people are exposed to outdoor air pollution each year, mainly in urban areas where about half the world's population now lives (United Nations Environment Programme 2016). This urban air pollution is responsible for a million premature deaths each year.

As noted earlier, *indoor air pollution* is also a serious problem. According to the World Health Organization (2016a), between 3 and 4 million deaths each year are caused by indoor air pollution. And about one out of every eight deaths worldwide is linked with either indoor or outdoor air pollution.

In the United States and other developed nations, indoor air pollution can cause the "*sick building syndrome.*" In a sick building, the workers suffer from acute physical and/or psychological discomfort that is eased when they leave the building (Thorne et al. 2001). The sick building syndrome includes a variety of symptoms: mucous membrane irritation, eye irritation, headaches, nausea, feelings of lethargy, fatigue, the inability to concentrate, breathing difficulties, and fainting (Abdul-Wahab 2011). The syndrome is due to such factors as inadequately maintained air conditioning and heating systems; pests (e.g., cockroaches and dust mites); moisture and mold in ceiling tiles, carpet, insulation, and furnishings; improper ventilation; and toxic vapors from copy-machine liquids, paint, flooring, and cleaning agents (Mendell et al. 2006).

In severe cases, the air quality inside the building may be far worse than the urban air outside the building. It is not known how many buildings are sick, but a number of surveys indicate that from 40 percent to 55 percent of office occupants will experience one or more sick building symptoms each week (Hood 2005).

Nor are people's homes necessarily safe. We have noted that formaldehyde is toxic and that a wide range of materials and products used in homes contain formaldehyde. In the 1970s, about half a million homes were insulated with urea formaldehyde. In addition, there are other toxic chemicals in virtually all homes, making them one of the more hazardous places to be. Some of the chemicals in the home may not be toxic in themselves but can combine with common kinds of air pollution to cause health problems (Hughes 2004).

Another problem in homes and other buildings is the *presence of radon gas, which can cause lung cancer after long periods of exposure* (Barros-Dios, Barreiro, Ruano-Ravina, and Figueiras 2002; Pawel and Puskin 2004). The Environmental Protection Agency claims that millions of homes and buildings contain high levels of the gas (EPA website). The gas is odorless and colorless and can be detected only by appropriate testing. Radon is produced by the decay of uranium in rocks and soil.

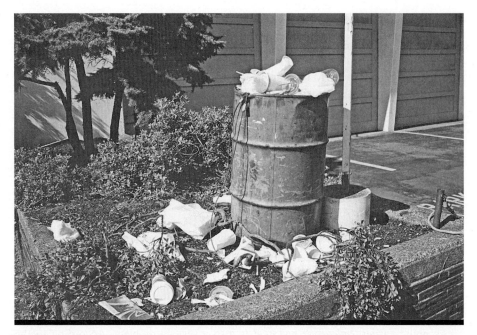

Per capita, Americans discard almost twice as much garbage as do people in Western Europe or Japan.

©S. Meltzer/PhotoLink/Getty Images

Electromagnetic radiation is another possible form of air pollution. We say "possible" because the issue is controversial. Various studies have come out with contradictory results. For example, diverse researchers have found that the use of cell phones slows cognitive function, or speeds up cognitive functioning, or has no effect on cognitive functioning (Rich 2010). Research funded by the telecommunications industry is much more likely than independent research to find no harm in cell phone use.

The problem is compounded by the fact that we don't know what levels, if any, are unsafe for humans. Researchers have reported such problems as increased rates of cancer and increased risk for Alzheimer's disease among people exposed to sustained, high levels of radiation (Gorman 1992; Sobel et al. 1995; Miller et al. 1996). On the other hand, a 16-member committee of the National Research Council examined more than 500 studies and concluded that there is no convincing evidence that such exposure is related to health problems (Leary 1996). At most, there may be a very weak connection between exposure and illness, but the issue is still unresolved (Brodsky et al. 2003; Moulder, Foster, Erdreich, and McNamee 2005; Kheifets, Afifi, and Shimkhada 2006; Genuis 2008).

Some advances have been made in *water pollution control.* The volume of pollutants discharged into the nation's waterways has decreased, and thousands of acres of lakes and thousands of miles of rivers and streams have been restored and made safe for swimming and fishing. The problem remains serious, however. An assessment of the nation's rivers and streams found that 55 percent of them do not support healthy populations of aquatic life (Environmental Protection Agency 2013). They are polluted by high levels of phosphorus and nitrogen. Water pollution also includes the oil spills noted earlier. And serious pollution occurs from various toxic materials dumped into the oceans and waterways and from nitrogen and phosphorus from agricultural runoff. The greenhouse gases that fuel the warming are also a threat to the ecosystem of the oceans (Lieberman 2004). Oceans contain increasing concentrations of carbon dioxide, which can hamper the efforts of many marine animals to form shells.

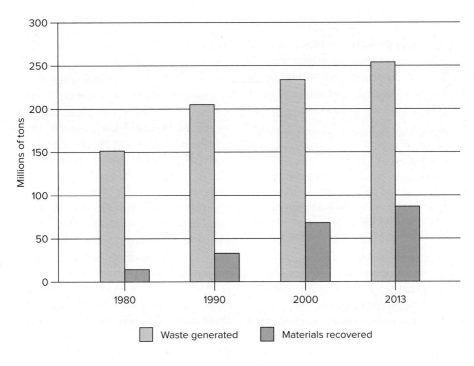

FIGURE 15.2
Municipal Solid Waste
Generation and Recovery.
Source: EPA website.

Pollution by hazardous wastes has also declined, but the problem is still severe. Literally billions of pounds of toxic chemicals are released into the environment each year. This form of pollution intersects with the problems of racial or ethnic origin and poverty because chemical plants and toxic wastes tend to be in areas where the poor and minorities live (Pine, Marx, and Lakshmanan 2002; Pais, Crowder, and Downey 2014).

Finally, there is the staggering amount of trash and garbage discarded each year. Americans discard hundreds of millions of tons of trash and garbage every year, and the amount is increasing. As Figure 15.2 shows, the amount of waste that is recovered (recycled) is also growing. But recovery has not kept pace with generation, so the net amount of waste dumped into the environment continues to increase. On average, people in the industrialized nations throw out around 1,235 pounds of trash and garbage per person per year, and Americans produce 51 percent more waste than the average resident of any other nation (Gardner, Assadourian, and Sarin 2004). Put in other terms, the *ecological footprint refers to the amount of productive land needed to produce the resources and absorb the waste for a particular economy.* The world as a whole contains 1.9 hectares of productive land per person, but the average American requires 9.7 hectares!

Trash illustrates the dilemmas of environmental problems. To help clean the air, incinerators, which once burned a good part of the trash, were phased out and "sanitary" landfills became the main method of disposal. Because a good part of the trash is paper, much that is thrown away is supposedly biodegradable. That is, it will eventually break down, decompose, and become a part of the earth.

Unfortunately, biodegradation doesn't happen in landfills. Archaeologists have discovered that so-called biodegradable trash and garbage are preserved rather than destroyed in landfills, probably because the materials are tightly packed and covered, with little exposure to light or moisture (Grossman and Shulman 1990). Most of the trash remains essentially unchanged in weight, volume, and form for at least four decades.

WORLD ENERGY PRODUCTION AND CONSUMPTION

Energy production and consumption are an integral part of the problems of pollution and dwindling resources. They also play an integral part in the quality of people's lives. For example, try to imagine a world without electricity and the internal combustion engine. It would still be a livable world, but as Flavin and Dunn (1999:23) put it:

> Homo sapiens has relied for most of its existence on a virtually limitless flow of renewable energy resources—muscles, plants, sun, wind, and water—to meet its basic needs for shelter, heat, cooking, lighting, and movement. The relatively recent transition to coal that began in Europe in the seventeenth century marked a major shift to dependence on a finite stock of fossilized fuels.

This shift affected every aspect of life—health care, education, leisure activities, and so on. People throughout the world desire the standard of living produced by the shift. As developing nations strive to achieve the standard of living now enjoyed by the developed nations, questions of practicality arise. Does the earth have enough resources for all nations to achieve such a standard? Energy use per capita varies enormously around the world (Table 15.2). Note the difference between a developing nation such as India and the developed nations such as the United States. The United States consumes over four times the amount of energy that is consumed on the entire continent of Africa!

Even among the developed nations there is a considerable difference in the amount of energy consumed per capita. Some of these differences reflect varying climates (e.g., heating and air conditioning are needed far more in some nations than in others). Yet the figures raise the question of how much energy per capita is needed for a decent standard of living. Is life in the United States, where energy consumed per capita is significantly higher than that of the United Kingdom, Austria, Germany, and Japan, far superior to that of other developed nations? Or is there a good deal of unnecessary energy use in the United States? Could Americans cut down on their energy use without seriously or even moderately diminishing the quality of their lives?

It is difficult to estimate the seriousness of all kinds of pollution, partly because measurement techniques have not been developed and partly because the potential hazards involved have been recognized only recently. Some forms of pollution, such as noise pollution and aesthetic damage, are undesirable or annoying rather than hazardous. How can their seriousness be assessed? In spite of such problems, it is clear that pollution in general is one of the serious problems confronting the nation, and it is a problem for which there are no easy answers.

Environmental Depletion

Many experts believe that the astounding pace at which people are consuming natural resources threatens the resource capacity of the earth (Assadourian 2010). We mentioned earlier that Americans now import a major proportion of many important minerals and will import even more in the future as they continue to devour their own resources at a high rate.

The problem of depletion, of course, is international (Moyer 2010). For example, a major concern for the well-being of the earth is deforestation. Between 2000 and 2005, Africa lost 3.2 percent of its forested area, and South America lost 2.5 percent (Gardner 2006). Over the course of human history, nearly half of the earth's forests have been depleted, most of which has occurred since 1970. Tropical forests may contain as many as half of the world's plant and animal species, including many plants used for medicine. In addition, they are a major impediment to the buildup of carbon dioxide and, thereby, to global warming. About 1.3 million hectares of tropical forest are cut down each year to provide fuel and land for development and agriculture

Country	Total (Quadrillion Btu)	Per Capita (Million Btu)
World total	575.4	79.3
United States	97.8	304.3
Brazil	15.1	73.9
Canada	14.6	416.0
China	129.2	94.5
India	28.0	22.4
Japan	20.6	162.3
Mexico/Chile	9.1	65.4
Australia/New Zealand	7.0	257.5
Russia	31.7	222.6

TABLE 15.2

Energy Consumption of Selected Nations

SOURCE: U.S. Energy Information Administration 2016a.

(Flavin and Engelman 2009). And that adds 6.5 billion tons of carbon dioxide to the earth's atmosphere each year.

Increasing energy use is another major concern. Energy use per capita is increasing in most of the nations of the world (U.S. Census Bureau 2012). And as Table 15.2 shows, with the exception of China, the United States uses more energy than any nation in the world and more energy per capita than the great majority of nations. With about 4.4 percent of the world's population, the U.S. proportion of the world's consumption of energy is 17 percent!

The amount of energy Americans consume driving their vehicles is staggering, and the number of miles traveled continues to increase in spite of rising gas prices and efforts to encourage car pools. In 1970, Americans drove their cars, vans, pickups, SUVs, and motor homes 1.11 trillion miles. By 2014, the number rose to 303 trillion miles. In doing so, the United States consumed 134 million gallons of gasoline and nearly 40 million gallons of diesel (U.S. Department of Transportation 2015).

How can Americans keep up with their voracious appetite for energy? Some experts believe that nuclear sources are the only hope, but reliance on nuclear power plants poses serious problems. Total reliance on nuclear power is not even feasible because of the number of plants that would have to be built and the problem of storing radioactive wastes. In addition, there is the ever-present possibility of accidents and disasters. This possibility became a reality in April 1986 when two large explosions occurred at the Chernobyl plant in the Soviet Union, "a blast heard round the world" (Flavin 1987). Within days, much of Europe reported the highest levels of radioactive fallout ever. Within two weeks, elevated levels of radioactivity were detected throughout the Northern Hemisphere. For weeks afterward, fresh vegetables in many areas of Europe were contaminated. Cows that grazed on contaminated grass soon produced milk with unhealthy levels of radioactivity. For a number of months, as many as 100 million people had to alter their diets.

The Soviet Union, of course, suffered the worst consequences. Thirty-one people were killed and 1,000 were injured immediately. Another 135,000 were evacuated from their homes. Of the 25,000 workers under the age of 35 who participated in the cleanup, 5,000 to 7,000 died (Chernousenko 1991). As many as 4 million people in the region are at high risk for cancer and other illnesses. The incidence of these illnesses began to increase within a few years after the accident (Parks 1991). Ten years after the disaster, researchers found a variety of psychosomatic symptoms and high levels of fear and stress (Specter 1996). More than two decades later, researchers linked the disaster to high rates of mental health problems, thyroid cancer (including in the Czech Republic, which had received only a moderate amount of radioactive fallout), and leukemia among the emergency workers who responded to the disaster (Murbeth, Rousarova, Scherb, and Lengfelder 2004; Bromet 2012; Ivanov et al. 2012; Tronko et al. 2012).

The Chernobyl disaster, along with subsequent accidents and near-disasters, has intensified concerns about the utility of nuclear power for generating energy. As a result, several nations—including the United States, Great Britain, and Germany—have cut back on the number of reactors in operation.

Environmental Problems and the Quality of Life

Environmental problems confront Americans with *a number of inherent contradictions:* the value of growth and progress versus the value of freedom to choose the size of one's family; the desire for abundant energy versus the value of a clean environment; the preference for reasonably low energy prices versus the value of independence in the world arena. It is impossible to have all these options, so Americans must engage in *trade-offs* between such choices as cost and abundance, national independence and abundance, and abundance and quality of the environment.

The Environmental Threat to Life and Health

The *environmental threat to both physical and emotional well-being* occurs from all the environmental problems named thus far.

The Physical Threat.   The physical threat is summarized by the U.S. Public Health Service (1995:80):

> Among the numerous diseases and dysfunctions that have a known or suspected environmental component are cancer, reproductive disorders such as infertility and low birthweight, neurological and immune system impairments, and respiratory conditions such as asthma. Exposure to environmental hazards can be through air, food, or water and covers a broad range of factors such as pesticides, toxic chemicals, and radiation.

You are surrounded by hazards of all kinds, and those hazards may be even more threatening than we have realized. A "moderate" level of pollution by ambient fine particulate matter is considered generally safe by the Environmental Protection Agency. But a study of 10 years of data on Boston, Massachusetts, found that residents had a 34 percent higher chance of having a stroke within hours of experiencing a "moderate" level of the pollution (Wellenius et al. 2012).

Among the illnesses that severe air pollution can cause or contribute to:

Permanent lung damage in children (Gauderman et al. 2007)

Genetic abnormalities in children (Fagin 2008)

Fetal deaths (Siddika et al. 2016)

Infant mortality, including sudden infant death syndrome (Dales et al. 2004; World Health Organization 2016)

Respiratory illness and death from respiratory infections (Spix et al. 1998; Samet et al. 2000)

Cardiovascular disease (Samet et al. 2000; Miller et al. 2007)

Premature deaths (Revkin 2001; World Health Organization 2016)

Asthma attacks (Sarafino, Paterson, and Murphy 1998; Schwartz 2004)

Lung cancer (Moore 1999; Parent et al. 2007)

There is also a possible link between air pollution and autism (Roberts et al. 2013) and between air pollution and tuberculosis (Lai et al. 2016). These adverse consequences may be caused by either outdoor or indoor air pollution. We pointed out earlier in this chapter that many products and materials in the home give off toxic vapors. A similar situation exists in workplaces. Workers in particular kinds of jobs may be exposed to, or may work with, one of the chemicals known to be a factor in respiratory problems, cancer, and other illnesses.

For example, a study of 125 pregnant women who were exposed to organic solvents in their jobs found an increased risk of major fetal malformations; they were thus more likely than nonexposed women to give birth to babies with major defects (Khattak et al. 1999). The researchers also found an increased risk of miscarriage among the exposed women. Other research found that the use of cleaning products can exacerbate the problem of asthma (Vizcaya et al. 2015).

Some of the chemicals to which workers are exposed are known to be neurotoxic, causing damage to the nervous system, with resulting behavioral and emotional disorders. The problem of neurotoxins came to public attention in the 1970s when workers at a fabrics plant suffered various degrees of nerve damage. The workers had been exposed to a solvent used as an ink thinner and machine cleaner. As a result, they experienced weakness in their hands and feet (so much so that some could barely turn a key or use a screwdriver), loss of weight, and problems with walking (Anderson 1982).

Exposure to toxic materials can also lead to sterility. Male sperm counts have been declining for many decades (Lemonick 1996; Swan 2006). The decline may reflect the fact that industries use a number of chemicals that can result in infertility. In Costa Rica, 1,500 banana plantation workers developed permanent sterilization from exposure to a toxic pesticide (Thrupp 1991). In the United States, children born to women who live within a quarter mile of a toxic waste dump have higher rates of birth and heart defects (Roosevelt 2004).

The depleted ozone layer raises the risk of skin cancer, whereas high ozone levels at ground level are harmful to both humans and plant life. In fact, high ozone levels are associated with breathing difficulties, asthma attacks, lung damage, and increases in the number of cardiovascular and respiratory deaths (Gryparis et al. 2004; Environmental Protection Agency 2015). In rural areas, high ozone levels reduce crop yields (Monastersky 1999).

Acid rain is a threat to forests and lakes. Eutrophication in waterways can kill massive numbers of fish, which means less food available for a world in which millions of people are starving. Ironically, some of the eutrophication problems arise from efforts to produce an adequate food supply. More than half the phosphorus that overfertilizes water comes from municipal wastes, but a substantial minority is due to urban and rural runoff. As farmers continue to apply fertilizer in increasing quantities to improve the yield of needed agricultural products, they also increase the likelihood of eutrophication of waterways and the consequent destruction of needed fish.

Routinely used pesticides and herbicides produce yet another hazard (Alarcon et al. 2005). The consequences of exposure to pesticides and herbicides include increased risk for stillbirth, birth defects, children's asthma, injury to the nervous system and reproductive organs, lung damage, problems with the immune and endocrine systems, renal disease, and cancer (Mansour 2004; Salam, Li, Langholz, and Gilliland 2004; Lebov et al. 2016).

A number of adverse consequences of global warming have already surfaced (Epstein 2000). Disease-causing bacteria, viruses, and fungi are spreading more widely; malaria and other mosquito-associated diseases have begun to appear in areas of the world where they were once absent. The problem will only intensify as the warming continues.

Finally, noise pollution is at best a nuisance and at worst a hazard to personal well-being. Excessive noise levels can result in hearing damage, high blood pressure, increased risk of cardiovascular disorders, sleep disturbance, lower work productivity, and problems in relating to others (Haines et al. 2003; Gan et al. 2016).

The Emotional Threat.   The emotional threat is illustrated by the fact that people who work around hazardous materials may suffer from increased anxiety and depression (Roberts 1993). They experience stress over potential health problems—from uncertainty about the seriousness of the exposure and from a sense of powerlessness over the situation (what can an individual do to change the situation?) (Hallman and Wandersman 1992; Matthies, Hoger, and Guski 2000).

Edelstein (1988) interviewed a number of New Jersey residents whose water supply had been contaminated by a municipal landfill. He found that knowledge of the contamination brought with it a radical change in the way the people viewed the world. They began to fear for their own and their families' health. They felt a loss of control over their lives. They viewed their homes as places of danger rather than havens of security. They lost trust in the government.

Another study of psychological consequences involved a survey of Alabama residents who lived near the Gulf of Mexico where the massive BP oil spill occurred in 2010 (Gill, Picou, and Ritchie 2012). Five months after the disaster, researchers found high levels of stress generated by such things as concern over family health, economic loss, exposure to the oil, and future financial security.

Noise also detracts from emotional well-being. People in New York City identified noise pollution as the worst infringement on their quality of life (Tierney 1998). A study of 2,844 children who lived near major airports in three different countries found a correlation between exposure to aircraft noise and hyperactivity and between traffic noise and conduct problems (Stansfeld et al. 2009).

Threat to the Ecological Balance

Many of the examples given in this chapter show that human actions can result in a whole chain of consequences for the environment. One consequence can be an upsetting of the ecological balance. Alterations occur in the ecosystem that can have adverse effects on the quality of life.

One way that the ecological system has been altered is through the *disappearance of a number of species of animals and plants* as a result of human activity. Hundreds of animals and plants have become extinct. Hundreds more are endangered (in danger of becoming extinct) or threatened (likely to become endangered). The list of endangered or threatened species includes 96 mammals, 100 birds, 504 other kinds of animal life, and 903 plants (U.S. Fish and Wildlife Service 2016). And those numbers are all rising. A declining number of species means less diversity, represents a vast biological loss, and poses a direct threat to the quality of human life. As Tuxill (1999:7–8) wrote:

> In addition to providing the genetic underpinnings of our food supply, plant diversity keeps us healthy—one in every four drugs prescribed in the United States is based on a chemical compound originally discovered in plants. Plants also furnish oils, latexes, gums, fibers, timbers, dyes, essences, and other products that we use to clean, clothe, shelter, and refresh ourselves and that have many industrial uses as well. Health assemblages of native plants renew and enrich soils, regulate our freshwater supplies, prevent soil erosion, and provide the habitat needed by animals and other creatures.

Finally, a diminishing diversity increases the likelihood of pest infestations and outbreaks of disease.

Clearly, *people depend on biological diversity for the quality of their lives* (MacDonald and Nierenberg 2003). Still, caution needs to be exercised about the loss of species. Ecosystems are dynamic, not static. Some species would disappear regardless of human activity. On the other hand, humans need to be careful not to fall into the *fallacy of circular reasoning* by arguing that only those species disappear for which there is no use or importance. Therefore, the argument would run, those species that have become extinct are not needed anyway; humans are doing just fine without them. This line of reasoning ignores the fact that some species became extinct because of human activity rather than the natural workings of nature. People need to be concerned that the ecological balance is not upset, that they do not start a chain of consequences that will be detrimental to human life.

Perhaps more important than the balance among the species is the possibility that humans will somehow intrude into the major processes of the ecosystem and cause irreversible damage that could threaten life—for the continuation of life demands certain processes, including reproduction, **photosynthesis,** and the recycling of minerals. The reproduction of some species has been affected by certain pollutants. For instance, the use of DDT caused the eggshells of some birds to become thinner and to crack before the young hatched, thus threatening the birds' reproductive capacity. DDT also has affected the reproductive capacity of some fish. Other pesticides and herbicides also may impair reproduction.

Photosynthesis may be adversely affected by air pollution, by pesticides and herbicides, and above all, by the spread of the human population, which destroys the habitat of other species. Air pollution inhibits the plant life in which photosynthesis occurs, whereas human activity such as **urbanization** destroys plants by destroying their habitat. It is also possible that the pesticides and herbicides accumulating in the oceans will disrupt the process there as well. Photosynthesis is essential in the production of oxygen; it helps maintain the carbon dioxide balance in the atmosphere and is of fundamental importance in producing the organic material needed for supporting life. It is difficult to imagine that photosynthesis would halt completely. If it did, it would be a catastrophe. But whether or not the process could totally stop, it is clearly adversely affected by certain human activities.

The Economic Costs

It is difficult to place a price tag on environmental problems. To fully assess the cost, we would have to include an enormous number of items: damage to livestock, trees, and crops; the death of wildlife; the expense of pollution-control measures; the cost of

fallacy

photosynthesis
a natural process essential to life, resulting in the production of oxygen and organic materials

urbanization
the increasing concentration of people living in cities

medical care for those whose health is adversely affected; the lost work time due to ill health; the expense of maintaining and refurbishing buildings and other structures that deteriorate because of pollution; and the cost of restoring the quality of the air and of waterways. The public is barely aware of the *innumerable ways in which economic resources are consumed by ecological problems.*

Consider the factors involved in analyzing and estimating these economic costs. First, the pollutants are emitted at a particular time and place. Second, they affect the environmental quality. (For example, the amount of sulfur dioxide in the air at a particular time and place may increase and may cause an increase in the number of people with respiratory problems.) Finally, a dollar cost must be assigned to the damages.

Every factor in this process is marked by uncertainty. We are not yet aware of all the amounts and kinds of pollutants being emitted. Nor do we yet know how all the pollutants act and interact in the environment. Thus, identifying actual damages is problematic. It is relatively easy to assign a dollar value to some damages, but extremely difficult for others. We can estimate the cost of painting a building marred by air pollution or the cost of replacing damaged crops, but what is the dollar value of a human life; a clear sky; a place for recreation; or a species that contributes to the diversity, complexity, and stability of the ecosystem?

Keeping these difficulties in mind, we can still estimate some of the economic costs of pollution. The costs, in terms of damage to property, materials, health, and vegetation, run into many billions of dollars each year for air pollution alone. For example, an analysis of the air pollution just from U.S. ships engaged in international trade between 1993 and 2001 put the costs at between $697 million and $3.9 billion from sulfur dioxide and $3.7 billion from nitrous oxide (Gallagher 2005). And a Canadian study concluded that air pollution in 2008 would result in 21,000 deaths and cost $8 billion (Canadian Medical Association 2008). The study was based on an analysis of the effects of two pollutants—ozone and particulate matter. Of course, eliminating the hazards of pollution will be extremely costly. Environmentalists argue, however, that on balance the economic benefits will be greater than the costs. They point out that although the economic costs of addressing environmental problems are considerable, they are not as great as the cost of allowing the environment to deteriorate.

Threat to World Peace

The contradictions between the demand for energy, the desire for a clean environment, the desire for reasonably low prices for energy, the struggle for natural resources, and the value on political independence are manifested on the international level in the form of a *threat to world peace.* A number of armed conflicts in the world can be traced to the struggle for control of various natural resources (Renner 2002).

Pollution results in damage to health, property, and vegetation.

©Doug Menuez/Getty Images

In addition, the developing nations of the world are demanding to share in the affluence enjoyed by the West and Japan. Inequality among nations has become a matter of international concern. On May 1, 1974, the General Assembly of the United Nations adopted the "Declaration on the Establishment of a New International Order," which asserted a determination to work for a new and more equitable international economic order. If the widening gap between the developed and the developing nations is not eliminated, many observers fear that the result will be a world war between the relatively few rich nations and the far more numerous poor nations.

Questions arise about whether the earth's resources are sufficient and whether the environmental damage can be adequately contained if the developing nations are to achieve the same standard of living as the developed nations. On the one hand, if the gap between the rich and the poor nations is not narrowed, peace is threatened by those nations or groups of nations that would resort to violence to achieve a higher economic status (Renner 1999). On the other hand, if rich nations help poor nations achieve a higher standard of living, depleted resources and a damaged environment may drastically lower the quality of life for the entire world. It appears that the contradictions inherent in these ecological problems will continue to plague us in the future.

Contributing Factors

Before looking at the sociocultural factors that contribute to environmental problems, you should note that some of the problems are caused by *ignorance and accidents.* Ignorance is involved because people often do not know and generally cannot anticipate the environmental consequences of their behavior. DDT, for instance, seemed beneficial because it controlled many pests, including the carriers of malaria. What was not known at the time was that DDT would impair the reproductive capacity of some fish and birds and would remain in the food chain with such persistence.

Accidents also contribute to environmental problems. It is not possible, for example, to avoid all oil spills. Weather conditions cannot be controlled. Human error cannot be totally eliminated. Thus, it was human error that led to a nuclear reaction in a uranium-reprocessing facility in Tokaimura, Japan, in 1999. The reaction lasted nearly 20 hours and had the potential for creating a Chernobyl-type disaster. And it was weather conditions—a tsunami created by an earthquake—that killed around 20,000 people in Japan in 2011 and damaged a nuclear plant that released huge amounts of radiation. It will be years before we know the full impact of this disaster.

In addition to ignorance and accidents, however, a number of sociocultural factors contribute to environmental problems. As with other social problems, both social structural and social psychological factors are involved.

Social Structural Factors

Population Growth. *A growing population poses a threat to the environment* (Gardner, Assadourian, and Sarin 2004). Population growth accelerates the consumption of the earth's natural resources to the point that oil, natural gas, and certain minerals may eventually be exhausted. The population could even reach a number at which it would be impossible to produce enough food. The point is, any given area on the earth has a *limited carrying capacity,* that is, a limit to the number of people who can live there without causing a collapse of the biological system. If the biological system collapses, the inhabitants must either be supported by outside resources, move from the area, or face massive deaths.

Fortunately, the rate of population growth has slowed. It has slowed so much that the population of some European nations has declined and other nations may experience a decline in the future (Carr 2009). Nevertheless, the total population of the world and of most countries (even those with declining birthrates) continues to increase. The increase reflects the fact that the number of women of childbearing age has been growing and life expectancy has been rising (Engelman 2009).

As a result, the world's population is more than double what it was in 1950. The populations of the poorer nations are among those with the highest growth rates. Given their growing populations, what are the prospects for raising the standard of living in the poorer nations and for maintaining a high standard for those in the developed nations? Most scientists doubt that the earth can sustain the number of people now living at the same standard enjoyed by the average American. In fact, Assadourian (2010) has estimated the earth can sustain only about 1.4 billion people at the U.S. standard.

The problems of population growth are compounded by the fact that the effects of increased population are more than additive. We noted earlier in this chapter that people generally, and Americans in particular, are consuming increased amounts of energy and other resources *per capita*. In other words, the impact per person on the environment is far greater today than it was in past years.

A second reason that a growing population has more than an additive impact on the environment is the *threshold effect*. Vegetation in an area may be able to survive a certain size of population and the air pollution created by that population. But further increase in the population might create just enough additional pollution to kill the vegetation. It becomes "the straw that breaks the camel's back."

The threshold effect can occur in all kinds of pollution. A number of cases illustrate this problem (Brown and Postel 1987). For example, in 1982, about 8 percent of the trees in West Germany were damaged from pollution. The figure jumped to 34 percent one year later, and then to 50 percent by 1984. Something had tipped the balance and caused a sudden surge in deterioration. Several Canadian scientists showed the effects of acid rain by deliberately acidifying a small lake. Over an eight-year period, they gradually increased the concentration of acids in the lake and found a particular point at which a dramatic change occurred in the ability of the various species of fish to reproduce and survive. The effects of population may be additive to a point, and beyond that point *the increasing quantitative changes become a qualitative change.*

The Industrial Economy.   Both pollution and depletion of the environment are rooted in the industrial economy. This finding is dramatically illustrated by the fact that the United States, with about 4.4 percent of the world's population, accounts for 16 percent of the world's carbon dioxide emissions (EPA website). Various industrial processes, from the generation of electricity to the production of goods, are responsible for a considerable part of the air pollution problem.

Water pollution is also a by-product of industrial processes. This problem includes thermal pollution, which occurs when water is taken from a waterway in large quantities and used for cooling. In the cooling process, the water absorbs heat. When this heated water is dumped back into the river or lake, it can raise the temperature to a point that is dangerous for aquatic life.

A major cause of air pollution in the United States is the *extensive use of the automobile.* The automobile also bears heavy responsibility for the rapid depletion of the world's oil reserves. America is involved in a love affair with the automobile. More than a fourth of all cars in the world are on U.S. roads; automobiles and light trucks are responsible for

40 percent of U.S. oil consumption and have an effect on climate change equal to that of all economic activity in Japan (Sawin 2004).

The burgeoning number and use of automobiles creates increasing pollution. Despite the fact that emissions per automobile have been greatly reduced over the past few decades, overall air quality has worsened in many cities because of the increased number of cars. Yet to drastically reduce the use of the automobile not only would be contrary to the American value of freedom and mobility, it also would cause serious economic problems. The automobile, a prime factor in environmental pollution and depletion, is an integral part of our affluent economy. Significant numbers of workers depend on the manufacture, distribution, service, and use of motor vehicles. An attack on the automobile is clearly an attack on the economy. Thus, a way must be found to deal with the environmental problem without ignoring the economic consequences.

As the automobile illustrates, the industrial economy operates at a pace that outstrips the ability to counteract the environmental problems it creates. Consider the chemical industry. Cancer is largely an environmental problem often *caused by carcinogenic chemicals* (Napoli 1998; McGinn 2002). There are approximately 2 million known chemical compounds, and thousands more are discovered each year. Some of these new compounds will be carcinogenic, but there are insufficient facilities to properly test them all.

These chemical compounds are one example of useful new products. Unfortunately, useful products can have undesirable environmental side effects. Because industrial technology can produce enormous quantities of any single product and an enormous range of products, and because the economy is set up to maximize growth, the whole situation is self-sustaining. Continual expansion is the goal. That goal is facilitated by (1) massive advertising; (2) the proliferation of products, many competing for the same market; (3) the planned obsolescence of products; and (4) lobbying at various levels of government to ensure that governmental decisions will be favorable to business and industry. "Planned obsolescence" refers to the fact that many products are specifically

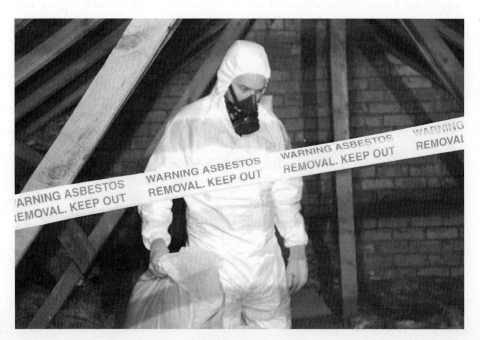

Many industrial workers are directly exposed to a variety of hazards to their health.

©Alistair Forrester Shankie/Getty Images

designed to last only a limited time. In fact, some are designed and advertised as throw-away products: clothing, pots and pans, and safety razors are to be used once or twice and then discarded. The consequences of planned obsolescence are the production of more trash that must be disposed of, the use of more resources, and the creation of more pollutants from industries that make such products.

Business and industry not only lobby for industrial growth, they also vigorously oppose pollution-control proposals and, in some cases, have managed to defeat those proposals either by lobbying or by influencing public opinion. Thus, the industrial economy intersects with the polity in environmental problems.

The Politics of the Environment.   Environmental problems have generally not been high-priority items with politicians. This lack of attention is unfortunate, because one way to get something done about environmental problems is to create positions that have specific responsibility for those problems. For environmental problems, this solution means governmental positions. Although Americans dislike the creation of new governmental positions, without them little may be done. There is little incentive for private industry to take the lead in addressing ecological problems.

Pollution is a national problem that requires federal action. In the past, the federal government either ignored the problem or delegated responsibility to the states. This attitude changed with the creation of the Environmental Protection Agency. Today, most politicians express interest and concern for environmental issues. Unfortunately, the rhetoric is not always matched by effective action.

The political nature of environmental problems is well illustrated by what has happened in the sale of timber in the national forests. As we have already noted, deforestation is a serious problem. Among other things, trees help reduce air pollution. According to one estimate, the reduction resulted in 850 fewer deaths and 670,000 fewer cases of acute respiratory symptoms over a year's time (U.S. Forest Service 2016). The federal government, however, has a history of selling forested land at a price below the value of the timber (Abramovitz 1998). At least until the end of the 20th century, timber sales by the government not only led to a reduction in the amount of forested land but also cost the government far more than it received from the sales. A recent report by the U.S. Forest Service (2016) indicates that the problem persists. The report noted that sales of forested land are made to those who are not concerned about conservation, so that "the survival of these forests and their associated ecosystem services is in question" (U.S. Forest Service 2016, p. 37).

Another example of politics affecting environmental problems involves the destruction wrought by Hurricane Katrina (Mayer 2005). The state of Mississippi wanted casinos built on the wetlands of the Gulf coast. They wanted the revenue from the casinos, but didn't want them built on dry land because of objections from local conservative moralists. The Environmental Protection Agency argued against the casinos because the wetlands are the home of aquatic life, are an important mechanism for drainage, and act as a buffer against storm damage. A U.S. senator from Mississippi was influential in having an EPA employee who was holding up the casino permits transferred. The permits were granted, the casinos were built, and the damage both to the casinos and the coast was far more severe than it would otherwise have been. In this case, politics triumphed over environmental needs. But the victory turned bitter with Katrina.

A third example of adverse environmental effects from political decisions is the Flint, Michigan, drinking water crisis that came to national attention in 2014. A political decision was made to switch the city's water supply from Lake Huron to the Flint

"Of all the problems I've studied," said one student, "the environmental problem is the most frustrating and frightening to me. It seems that no matter what you do, you're trapped. I see what it means to say that nature bats last." In spite of the seriousness of the problems and the dilemmas (such as a new technology that addresses one problem only to create another), this chapter shows that people have made some progress in dealing with environmental problems. Where does your community stand? Make a survey of the environmental problems.

Check your newspaper, your library, and local officials to get information about pollution levels. Tour your area and observe the number and, if possible, kinds of pollutants that are daily being released into the atmosphere, the waterways, and the land. Use the materials in this chapter and the data you get from your survey to write an article or a letter to the editor of your local newspaper and/or your school newspaper. Even though nature always bats last, is it possible that both human beings and nature can be winners in the long run?

River. The aim was to save money during a time of fiscal struggle. However, officials failed to apply corrosion inhibitors to the water. Soon a resident had the water tested, and it was found to have high levels of lead. The proportion of children with elevated lead levels in their blood doubled in two years from 2013 to 2015 (Hanna-Attisha et al. 2015). The city switched back to water from Lake Huron in late 2015.

Thus, the stance of the government on environmental issues is crucial. Consider, finally, the problem of toxic chemicals. Whatever your background, your body is undoubtedly contaminated with toxic chemicals (Curtis and Wilding 2007). You can't avoid them because they're found in many common household products such as shower curtains, shampoo, furniture, cosmetics, and computers. This is not to say that you are in imminent danger; your body can absorb certain levels of toxic substances without harming you. The problem is we don't know precisely what those levels are, and we don't know how many of the chemicals to which we are routinely exposed are toxic.

Some scientists believe that the increasing rates of infertility among women are due, at least in part, to toxic chemicals (Schapiro 2007). We don't know all of the long-range health consequences of exposure, but future generations may provide us with information—tests of the umbilical cords of 10 newborns in 2006 found traces of carcinogenic and gene-mutating chemicals. It may be that our ever-more-sophisticated technology is exposing us to ever-more kinds and levels of toxic chemicals.

Concern about the matter led Congress to pass the Toxic Substances Control Act in 1976, which gave the government the authority to regulate chemicals that might harm people and/or the environment. However, the chemical industry influenced the legislation so that all chemicals on the market before 1979 were not subject to federal testing. In addition, the procedures set up by the law are favorable to industry. As a result, the government has assessed the risks on less than 200 of the tens of thousands of chemicals on the market today (Schapiro 2007). For many people, this means that the government is failing in its responsibility to adequately protect the citizenry.

Social Psychological Factors

Attitudes and the Environment. Many people see the Earth as a resource to be mined rather than as a trust to be cared for. The measure of success is the amount of goods that can be consumed. People are admonished that they could be just as happy with less and warned that they are engaged in a process of self-destruction as they abuse the Earth for their own excessive gratification, but these warnings largely seem to fall on deaf ears. Environmentalism is honored more in theory than in practice. The prevailing attitude is "I must get all that I can out of this life," rather than "I must cherish and sustain the Earth that gives us life."

Existing attitudes about the importance of environmental problems are detrimental to helpful action. Gallup polls taken from 1991 through 2016 show that the percentage of Americans who identify themselves as environmentalists has continuously declined, from 78 percent in 1991 to 42 percent in 2016 (Jones 2016). There has also been a decline in the number of those who are concerned about air pollution, from 61 percent in 1989–1990 to 43 percent in 2016.

With regard to global warming, there has been a small increase in the proportion of American who express concern, from 33 percent in 1989–1990 to 37 percent in 2016 (Jones 2016). A larger proportion acknowledge that global warming and climate change is a reality, but many of them doubt that human activity is the cause. Of course, if human activity is not the cause, there is little point in trying to take any corrective action.

Given such attitudes, it is not surprising that there is little public pressure for the federal government to be more aggressive in compelling business and industry to be environmentally responsible. Such attitudes will not spur politicians to take actions necessary to deal effectively with environmental problems.

In addition, many people believe that stricter environmental regulations will force business closings and bring about a loss of jobs, a belief unsupported by evidence. There may be an occasional closing or the loss of certain jobs, but to generalize from a few cases is to commit the *fallacy of dramatic instance.* In the nation as a whole, there is no conflict between jobs and the environment (Obach 2002). On the contrary, efforts to protect the environment create new jobs. Moreover, some of the most serious environmental problems are due to industries that add relatively little to the nation's economy (Freudenburg 2009). A significant amount of toxic emissions are emitted by the chemical and primary metal industries; these account for less than 5 percent of the nation's gross domestic product and less than 1.5 percent of American jobs.

Racist attitudes contribute to a problem noted earlier: the greater exposure of minorities to hazardous materials both at work and in their homes. *Environmental racism means that African Americans, Hispanics, and other minorities are more likely to be exposed to toxic waste sites and to higher levels of air pollution* (Grineski, Bolin, and Boone 2007; Sicotte and Swanson 2007). It also means that minorities are more likely to work near toxic waste sites. In addition to racial and ethnic minorities, the poor of all races are also more likely to suffer detrimental consequences from environmental problems. The well-to-do, who have more political power than others, have the NIMBY (not-in-my-backyard) attitude that leads them to take action to minimize environmental hazards in their own places of work and housing. Thus, attitudes contribute to the greater exposure of both racial and ethnic minorities and the poor to environmental problems.

Values and the Environment.   The value of growth, "the more the better," has been a theme of American life. Sorokin (1942:255) called this aspect of American culture "quantitative colossalism." It leads to continual expansion of the perception of the "good life," which means ever-increasing goods and services and a concomitant ever-intensifying of environmental problems.

The American value of individualism also contributes to political inaction and thus to the environmental problems. As Hardin (1971) put it, our individualism involves

fallacy

us in the *"tragedy of the commons."* In the Middle Ages the "commons" was the pasture-land of a village. It was owned by no one person because it was available for use by all the people of the village. The "commons" today are the world's resources, and the "tragedy" is that it is advantageous for individuals to exploit those resources but disadvantageous to all when too many individuals pursue their own advantage. Yet, with our value on individualism (rather than on group well-being), we are, said Hardin (1971:247), "locked into a system of 'fouling our own nest,'" by behaving "only as independent, rational, free-enterprisers." The value of individualism also makes Americans reluctant to yield power to government. For many Americans, political inaction is the soul of good government, but in the realm of ecology, political inaction is the harbinger of disaster.

Public Policy and Private Action

At the outset, we need to acknowledge that environmental problems pose numerous dilemmas. There are no easy answers. Some of the "solutions" create new problems. For instance, with the surge in population growth in the 19th century, farmers began looking for ways to increase food production. One way was through the development of nitrogen-based fertilizers, which led to enormously increased food production. But those same fertilizers were, and continue to be, responsible for "poisoning ecosystems, destroying fisheries, and sickening and killing children throughout the world" (Fisher and Fisher 2001). Thus, the needed additional food is had at the expense of air and water quality.

Still, there are many ways to alleviate the problems, including many actions that individuals can take and are taking (DeSilver 2015). For example, the amount of energy expended on home heating has declined since 1993. The proportion of light bulbs in the home that are incandescent (and therefore use more energy) has declined dramatically, from about 65 percent in 2013 to 25 percent in 2015. The amount of water used by the average household has declined since 1980. And the percentage of paper, cardboard, yard trimmings, metals, and plastics that is recycled has risen substantially.

Such actions, along with changes in business and industry, have contributed substantially to progress in addressing environmental issues in recent decades. The emission of greenhouse gases into the atmosphere and the release of toxic chemicals into the environment have both declined. Blood lead levels in children have declined. Many lakes and waterways that were unsafe for fishing or swimming are once again usable. And the amount of materials recycled has increased greatly. In 2000, the nation generated 242.6 million tons of waste and recovered 69.4 million tons. In 2009, the United States generated 243 million tons, and recovered 82 million tons.

Action can also be taken to address the problem of dwindling natural resources. One way is to reduce consumption. Thus, a number of European nations reduced their oil consumption between 1980 and 2008 (Mouawad 2008). The reductions ranged from 13 percent in Italy to 33 percent in Denmark. During the same period, however, oil consumption in the United States rose 21 percent.

The reduction in various kinds of pollution, increased recycling, and reduced oil consumption by the European nations all demonstrate that environmental problems can be attacked by human action. Such action must be taken by individuals, by business and industry, and by the various levels of government.

What Can Individuals Do?

In addition to the actions of individuals mentioned above, knowledgeable people need to educate others about the seriousness of environmental pollution and depletion in order to change attitudes, values, and behavior. When people understand what they can do and the benefits of their efforts, they are more likely to engage in the appropriate behavior (Scott 1999; O'Connor, Bord, Yarnal, and Wiefek 2002).

Such education helps individuals recognize how much each one can do to alleviate the environmental problems. For example, you could stop using throwaway items such as cameras and razors. You could refuse to buy cheese that is sliced and individually wrapped in plastic. Or parents could use cloth instead of disposable diapers. MacEachern (1990) offers 750 suggestions for individuals to alleviate environmental problems. In addition, each individual can become a role model and an open advocate of environmental protection. Role modeling (such as picking up your trash at a campsite) and verbal appeals do influence others to behave responsibly (Wagstaff and Wilson 1988).

There are many ways in which you can conserve energy. Only minor changes in lifestyle can add up to substantial savings. When millions of people use automobiles that get more miles to the gallon than older models, when millions participate in recycling efforts, when millions use energy-saving appliances and methods that cut back on electricity, the savings are enormous. People could easily save a million or more barrels of crude oil every day without detracting from their standard of living.

Individuals can also work with others to find innovative ways to help the environment. An activist in San Francisco invented the "Carrotmob" (Caplan 2009). In essence, the idea is to reward businesses for green activity rather than punishing (by boycotting, for example) those that harm the environment. The first Carrotmob event took place after the activist got bids from 23 convenience stores and chose the one that promised to spend the highest proportion of profits on more energy-efficient lighting. Hundreds of shoppers were then secured to visit the store on a particular day, and the agreed-upon percentage of their purchases was used to make the store's lighting more energy efficient. Subsequently, people in other cities, including some in other nations, adopted the Carrotmob principle of reverse boycott.

What Can Business and Industry Do?

Business and industry must cooperate with governmental efforts to clean up the environment, but they must also strive to balance growth with ecological considerations and search for *alternative, clean sources of energy* upon which to base the economy. A number of alternatives are already being studied. Some people advocate nuclear power, but a total conversion to nuclear power is not feasible. Furthermore, nuclear power confronts people with the very difficult questions of how to dispose of radioactive waste and how to ensure against leaks and accidents that can release radioactivity into the atmosphere. Other possible alternatives include solar energy (the light and heat from the sun), geothermal energy (the water and hot rock beneath the earth's surface), the use of wind-driven generators, bioheat (heat derived from burning such things as wood or pellets), designing new buildings to be more energy efficient, and using seawater or lake water for cooling (Sawin and Moomaw 2009). These alternatives are not necessarily practical in every area. Rather, the advantages and disadvantages of each of these alternatives must be explored carefully but quickly, for the supply of fossil fuels is being rapidly depleted while the demand for energy is increasing throughout the world.

What Can the Government Do?

Government action at every level is crucial in dealing with environmental problems. The federal government could mandate higher gas mileage for all new cars. The government could effect savings in resources and simultaneously help the pollution problem by supporting the development of mass transit. Mass transit can carry 70 times the number of people as a highway, generate only 1 percent of the hydrocarbons, and cost one-tenth as much to build per mile as does a highway (Hagerman 1990). The government could follow through with a congressional mandate in the early 1990s to set standards for the distribution transformers that convert the high-voltage current transmitted over grids into lower-voltage current for home and business use (Kolbert 2006). More efficient transformers are available, and installing them in place of the less efficient ones now in use could save the nation about 12 billion kilowatt hours of electricity usage a year—enough to power all the households in Iowa for one year.

The federal government could also diminish or eliminate pollution caused by its own operations and by those supported by federal funds. It could provide direct funding and tax incentives for research into pollution control and alternative energy sources. It could impose tax penalties on businesses and corporations that damage the environment, a measure that has proven to reduce problems in the United States and other nations (Roodman 1999). It could support international treaties that set goals for cutting the emission of greenhouse gases. It could reduce the production of greenhouse gases like methane, which is the second largest contributor to global warming, by requiring the use of technology that captures the gas at landfills and waste management facilities and during the mining of fossil fuels (Hansen 2004; Jorgenson 2006).

Any action the federal government takes in behalf of the environment is likely to have effects beyond what any policy or program is designed to do. A study of the effects of a national environmental policy on nations in the European Union found that the citizens who live in nations that adopt strong pro-environment policies are more likely than others to drive less in order to help the environment (Borek and Bohon 2008). Moreover, the reduced driving occurs even when the policies are not directly related to the use of the automobile.

State and local governments also can play a significant role in addressing environmental problems by establishing recycling laws and policies. Recycling is now available in many if not most communities, but there are still those communities that do not provide a recycling service. Such a service is advantageous to the community itself as well as to the national and global effort to deal with environmental problems, for recycling means a lessening of the waste disposal problem. In addition, recycling reduces the demand for newly produced energy and materials, thereby saving our natural resources. And for some goods, such as paper, using recycled material saves energy in the manufacturing process.

Trimming waste disposal needs gets into an area that has almost reached crisis proportions in some cities. The volume of discarded material is surpassing the capacity to manage it. In addition, electronic waste has become the main contributor to high levels of lead in landfills (Saphores, Nixon, Ogunseitan, and Shapiro 2006). Recycling, which can address such problems to a considerable extent, may need to be mandatory. Will people cooperate? Unfortunately, some people will not. But most will, particularly when measures such as curbside pickup of materials are instituted (Domina and Koch 2002).

Follow-Up. Make a list of the actions you have personally taken to alleviate environmental problems. Which of these, or other actions, would you make a matter of law and which would you make purely voluntary?

Summary

Environmental problems arise out of the need to maintain a balanced ecosystem—a balance between people and their natural environment. Human activity can disrupt this ecosystem to the point of destruction.

Environmental problems may be broadly classified as environmental pollution and environmental depletion. Pollution includes air pollution, water pollution, land pollution, global warming, noise pollution, and aesthetic damage. Depletion refers to dwindling natural resources, including energy.

It is difficult to measure the extent of these environmental problems. Some progress has been made but the problems remain serious.

Environmental problems involve inherent contradictions among a number of American values. We do not fully understand how these contradictions are being manifested in social life, but we know that they diminish the quality of life in a number of ways. Pollutants threaten the health and life of humans, animals, and plants. The ecological balance is threatened by the potential destruction of certain processes that are necessary to sustain life on earth. The economic costs of both pollution damage and pollution control are enormous, and the contradictions between the demand for energy, the need for a clean environment, and the aspirations of the developing world pose a threat to world peace.

Rapid population growth is one of the important threats to the environment. The effects of population growth are more than additive, as evidenced by diminishing returns and the threshold effect. In addition to population growth, the industrial economy is at the root of environmental problems. The products, by-products, and continuing growth in the industrial economy create serious environmental problems. The problems are intensified by the tendency of the government to ignore them or to set up ineffective programs and policies. Federal action is imperative if Americans are to seriously attack the problems of the environment.

Among social psychological factors, attitudes that view the earth simply as a resource to be exploited and that give minimal importance to environmental problems inhibit action. Racist attitudes intensify the problem for minorities by exposing them to more hazards at work and home. The American values of growth and individualism have supported the economic and political arrangements that contribute to the problems.

Key Terms

Ecosystem
Environmental Depletion
Environmental Pollution
Eutrophication
Herbicide
Pesticide
Photosynthesis
Pollutant
Urbanization

Study Questions

1. What is the ecosystem? Why is it important to us?
2. Name and explain the three types of environmental problems people face.
3. How extensive are the environmental problems?
4. In what ways do environmental problems pose a threat to life, health, and the ecological balance?
5. Discuss the economic costs of environmental problems.
6. How do environmental problems threaten world peace?
7. What are some of the undesirable effects of population growth?
8. How does the economy and polity affect environmental problems?
9. What kinds of social psychological factors contribute to environmental problems?
10. What might be done to deal with the problems of environmental pollution and environmental depletion?

Internet Resources/Exercises

1. Explore some of the ideas in this chapter on the following sites:

http://www.epa.gov The U.S. Environmental Protection Agency has materials on all the environmental problems we have discussed.

http://www.envirolink.org The Envirolink Network offers links to thousands of resources on every environmental issue.

http://ewg.org Site of the Environmental Working Group, whose research is designed to improve health and protect the environment.

2. Most scientists agree that global warming is a severe and urgent problem. Some people still disagree. Search the Internet for arguments both for and against global warming as a serious problem. Summarize the points and the supporting data made by both sides. Identify any fallacies of thinking you find in the arguments.

3. Political action is imperative if environmental problems are to be effectively attacked. Use a search engine to explore the relationship between government or politics and environmental problems. Find information on government at all levels. Make a list of the 10 most helpful and 10 most harmful actions (or lack of action) taken by governments in recent years. Use the information to write a letter to your local paper urging governmental action on some environmental problem about which you are concerned.

For Further Reading

Dasgupta, Partha. *Human Well-Being and the Natural Environment.* New York: Oxford University Press, 2001. An economist argues that human well-being depends on the natural environment, including places of beauty, as well as on material goods and knowledge.

Kolbert, Elizabeth. *The Sixth Extinction: An Unnatural History.* New York: Henry Holt & Company. 2014. A review of past mass extinctions in the earth's history, and a description of processes at work today that make a new extinction possible.

Lerner, Steve. *Sacrifice Zones: The Front Lines of Toxic Chemical Exposure in the United States.* Cambridge, MA: MIT Press, 2010. An account of a number of American communities that have, in effect, been "sacrificed" for the economic benefit of businesses that establish plants that release toxic chemicals into the environment. The plants provide needed jobs, but the health consequences for the nearby residents are devastating.

Mauch, Christof. *Shades of Green: Environmental Activism Around the Globe.* New York: Rowman & Littlefield, 2006. Shows how political, economic, religious, and scientific factors come to bear on environmental activism, including ways that such factors can suppress, dilute, or enhance environmental action in diverse social and cultural settings.

Rischard, Jean-Francois. *High Noon: 20 Global Problems, 20 Years to Solve Them.* New York: Basic Books, 2003. Examines the environmental problems that threaten the planet—global warming, biodiversity losses, depletion of fisheries, deforestation, water deficits, and maritime pollution—as well as the issues related to those problems and ways in which nations must work together to resolve the problems.

Rogers, Elizabeth, and Thomas M. Kostigen. *The Green Book: The Everyday Guide to Saving the Planet One Simple Step at a Time.* New York: Three Rivers Press, 2007. Details the numerous small ways in which each individual can contribute to a greener earth (e.g., use one less napkin a day or reduce your shower time by just one minute), and shows the dramatic impact on the environment if massive numbers of individuals practice them.

Withgott, Jay H., and Scott R. Brennan. *Environment: The Science Behind the Stories.* 5th ed. New York: Addison-Wesley, 2014. Case studies are used to illustrate and discuss every kind of environmental problem in a way that is scientifically sound yet accessible to those not scientifically trained.

abuse improper use of drugs or alcohol to the degree that the consequences are defined as detrimental to the user or society

achievement as distinguished from educational "attainment," the level the student has reached as measured by scores on various verbal and nonverbal tests

addiction repeated use of a drug or alcohol to the point of periodic or chronic intoxication that is detrimental to the user or society

adjudication making a judgment; settling a judicial matter

aggression forceful, offensive, or hostile behavior toward another person or society

AIDS acquired immune deficiency syndrome, a disease in which a viral infection causes the immune system to stop functioning, inevitably resulting in death

alienation a sense of estrangement from one's social environment, typically measured by one's feelings of powerlessness, normlessness, isolation, meaninglessness, and self-estrangement

anarchism the philosophy that advocates the abolition of government in order to secure true freedom for people

atmosphere the general mood and social influences in a situation or place

attainment as distinguished from educational "achievement," the number of years of education completed by a student

attitude a predisposition about something in one's environment

autonomy the ability or opportunity to govern oneself

binge drinking having five or more drinks on the same occasion

biological characteristic an inherited, rather than learned, characteristic

bipolar disorder fluctuation between emotional extremes

bisexual having sexual relations with either sex or both together

bureaucracy an organization in which there are specific areas of authority and responsibility, a hierarchy of authority, management based on written documents, worker expertise, management based on rules, and full-time workers

capitalism an economic system in which there is private, rather than state, ownership of wealth and control of the production and distribution of goods; people are motivated by profit and compete with each other for maximum shares of profit

carcinogenic causing cancer

catharsis discharge of socially unacceptable emotions in a socially acceptable way

charter school a nonreligious public school approved by the local school district but free of many regulations and policies that apply to other public schools

cognitive development growth in the ability to perform increasingly complex intellectual activities, particularly abstract relationships

cohabitation living together without getting married

compensatory programs programs designed to give intensive help to disadvantaged pupils and increase their academic skills

conflict theory a theory that focuses on contradictory interests, inequalities between social groups, and the resulting conflict and change

consumer price index a measure of the average change in prices of all types of consumer goods and services purchased by urban wage earners and clerical workers

contradiction opposing phenomena within the same social system

corporate welfare governmental benefits given to corporations that are unavailable to other groups or to individuals

critical thinking the analysis and evaluation of information

culture the way of life of a people, including both material products (such as technology) and nonmaterial characteristics (such as values, norms, language, and beliefs)

cunnilingus oral stimulation of the female genitalia

cybersex sexual activity conducted via the Internet

dehumanization the process by which an individual is deprived of the qualities or traits of a human being

deinstitutionalization a movement to change the setting of treatment of mental disorders from hospitals to the community through rapid discharge of patients

dependent variable the variable in an experiment that is influenced by an independent variable

detoxification supervised withdrawal from dependence on a drug

differential association theory the theory that illegal behavior is due to a preponderance of definitions favorable to such behavior

discrimination arbitrary, unfavorable treatment of the members of some social group

disfranchise to deprive of the right to vote

division of labor the separation of work into specialized tasks

divorce rate typically, the number of divorces per 1,000 marriages

domestic terrorism the use, or threatened use, of violence by people operating entirely within the United States to intimidate or coerce the government and/or citizens in order to reach certain social or political aims

downsizing reduction of the labor force in a company or corporation

ecosystem a set of living things, their environment, and the interrelationships among and between them

environmental depletion increasing scarcity of natural resources, including those used for generating energy

environmental destruction alterations in the environment that make it less habitable or useful for people or other living things

environmental pollution harmful alterations in the environment, including air, land, and water

epidemiology the study of factors that affect the incidence, prevalence, and distribution of illnesses

erotica sexually arousing materials that are not degrading or demeaning to adults or children

ethnic group people who have a shared historical and cultural background that leads them to identify with each other

etiology the causes of a disease

eutrophication overfertilization of water due to excess nutrients, leading to algae growth and oxygen depletion

exploitation use or manipulation of people for one's own advantage or profit

fallacy of appeal to prejudice argument by appealing to popular prejudices or passions

fallacy of authority argument by an illegitimate appeal to authority

fallacy of circular reasoning use of conclusions to support the assumptions that were necessary to make the conclusions

fallacy of composition the assertion that what is true of the part is necessarily true of the whole

fallacy of dramatic instance overgeneralizing

fallacy of misplaced concreteness making something abstract into something concrete

fallacy of non sequitur something that does not follow logically from what has preceded it

fallacy of personal attack argument by attacking the opponent personally rather than dealing with the issue

fallacy of retrospective determinism the argument that things could not have worked out any other way than they did

family a group united by marriage, blood, and/or adoption in order to satisfy intimacy needs and/or to bear and socialize children

fellatio oral stimulation of the male genitalia

forcible rape the carnal knowledge of a female forcibly and against her will

frequency distribution the organization of data to show the number of times each item occurs

gender the meaning of being male or female in a particular society

gender role the attitudes and behavior that are expected of men and women in a society

ghetto an area in which a certain group is segregated from the rest of society; often used today to refer to the impoverished area of the inner city

gridlock the inability of the government to legislate significant new policies

herbicide a chemical used to kill plant life, particularly weeds

heterogamy marriage between partners with diverse values and backgrounds

heterosexual having sexual preference for persons of the opposite sex

homogamy   marriage between partners with similar values and backgrounds

homophobia   irrational fear of homosexuals

homosexual   having sexual preference for persons of the same sex; someone who privately or overtly considers himself or herself a homosexual

iatrogenic   caused by the physician in the course of his or her treatment of a patient

ideology   a set of ideas that explain or justify some aspect of social reality

incest   exploitative sexual contact between relatives in which the victim is under the age of 18

incidence   the number of new cases of an illness that occur during a particular period of time

independent variable   the variable in an experiment that is manipulated to see how it affects changes in the dependent variable

innate   existing in a person from birth

institution   a collective pattern of dealing with a basic social function; typical institutions identified by sociologists are the government, economy, education, family and marriage, religion, and the media

institutional racism   policies and practices of social institutions that tend to perpetuate racial discrimination

interaction   reciprocally influenced behavior on the part of two or more people

interest group   a group that attempts to influence public opinion and political decisions in accord with the particular interests of its members

international terrorism   politically motivated violence against citizens of political entities different from those of the perpetrators in order to coerce and intimidate others into accepting the perpetrators' goals

labor force   all civilians who are employed or unemployed but able and desiring to work

lesbian   a female homosexual

life chances   the probability of gaining certain advantages defined as desirable, such as long life and health

life expectancy   the average number of years a newborn can expect to live

lobbyist   an individual who tries to influence legislation in accord with the preferences of an interest group

maladjustment   poor adjustment to one's social environment

malnutrition   inadequate food, in amount or type

Marxist   pertaining to the system of thought developed by Karl Marx and Friedrich Engels, particularly emphasizing materialism, class struggle, and the progress of humanity toward communism

mean   the average

median   the score below which are half of the scores and above which are the other half

military parity   equality or equivalence in military strength

morbidity   the prevalence of a specified illness in a specified area

morphological   pertaining to form and structure

neurosis   a mental disorder involving anxiety that impairs functioning

norm   shared expectations about behavior

nuclear family   Parents, and children, if any

obscenity   materials that are offensive by generally accepted standards of decency

organized crime   an ongoing organization of people who provide illegal services and goods and who maintain their activities by the aid of political corruption

paraphilia   the need for a socially unacceptable stimulus in order to be sexually aroused and satisfied

participant observation   a method of research in which one directly participates and observes the social reality being studied

patronage   giving government jobs to people who are members of the winning party

pedophile   an adult who depends on children for sexual stimulation

personal problem   a problem that can be explained in terms of the qualities of the individual

pesticide   a chemical used to kill insects defined as pests

photosynthesis   a natural process essential to life, resulting in the production of oxygen and organic materials

pica   a craving for unnatural substances, such as dirt or clay

pimp   one who earns all or part of his or her living by acting as a manager or procurer for a prostitute

placebo   any substance having no physiological effect that is given to a subject who believes it to be a drug that does have an effect

pluralism   the more or less equal distribution of power among interest groups

political alienation   a feeling of political disillusionment, powerlessness, and estrangement

political party   an organized group that attempts to control the government through the electoral process

pollutant   anything that causes environmental pollution

pornography   literature, art, or films that are sexually arousing

posttraumatic stress disorder   an anxiety disorder associated with serious traumatic events, involving such symptoms as nightmares, recurring thoughts about the trauma, a lack of involvement with life, and guilt

poverty   a state in which income is insufficient to provide the basic necessities of food, shelter, clothing, and medical care

poverty level   the minimum income level that Americans should have to live on, based on the Department of Agriculture's calculations of the cost of a basic diet called "the economy food plan"

power elite model   a model of politics in which power is concentrated in political, economic, and military leaders

predatory crimes   acts that have victims who suffer loss of property or some kind of physical harm

prejudice   a rigid, emotional attitude that legitimates discriminatory behavior toward people in a group

prevalence   the number of cases of an illness that exist at any particular time

primary group   the people with whom one has intimate, face-to-face interaction on a recurring basis, such as parents, spouse, children, and close friends

promiscuity   undiscriminating, casual sexual relationships with many people

prostitution   having sexual relations for remuneration, usually to provide part or all of one's livelihood

psychosis   a disorder in which the individual fails to distinguish between internal and external stimuli

psychosomatic disorder   an impairment in physiological functioning that results from the individual's emotional state

psychotherapeutic drugs   prescription drugs, including pain relievers, tranquilizers, stimulants, and sedatives, that are used for intoxication effects rather than medical purposes

race   a group of people distinguished from other groups by their origin in a particular part of the world

racism   the belief that some racial groups are inherently inferior to others

recidivism   repeated criminal activity and incarceration

regulatory agency   an organization established by the government to enforce statutes that apply to a particular activity

rehabilitation   resocializing a criminal and returning him or her to full participation in society

reification   defining what is abstract as something concrete

relative deprivation   a sense of deprivation based on some standard used by the individual who feels deprived

retributiveness   paying people back for their socially unacceptable behavior

ritualized deprivation   a school atmosphere in which the motions of teaching and learning continue, while the students are more concerned about surviving than learning

role   the behavior associated with a particular position in the social structure

role conflict   a person's perception that two or more of his or her roles are contradictory, or that the same role has contradictory expectations, or that the expectations of the role are unacceptable or excessive

sadomasochism   the practice of deriving sexual pleasure from the infliction of pain

sanctions   mechanisms of social control for enforcing a society's standards

schizophrenia   a psychosis that involves a thinking disorder, particularly hallucinations and fantasies

self-fulfilling prophecy   a belief that has consequences (and may become true) simply because it is believed

sex   an individual's identity as male or female

sexism   prejudice or discrimination against someone because of his or her sex

sexting   sending erotic or nude photos or videos of oneself to a particular person or to a number of others via a cell phone or the Internet

sexual harassment   unwelcome sexual advances, requests for sexual favors, and other sexual behavior that either results in punishment when the victim resists or creates a hostile environment or both

socialization   the process by which an individual learns to participate in a group

social problem   a condition or pattern of behavior that contradicts some other condition or pattern of behavior; is defined as incompatible with the desired quality of life; is caused, facilitated, or prolonged by social factors; involves intergroup conflict; and requires social action for resolution

socioeconomic status   position in the social system based on economic resources, power, education, prestige, and lifestyle

sodomy   intercourse defined as "unnatural"; particularly used to refer to anal intercourse

statutory rape   sexual intercourse with a female who is below the legal age for consenting

stealth racism   hidden or subtle acts of prejudice and discrimination that may be apparent only to the victim

stepfamily   a family formed by marriage that includes one or more children from a previous marriage

stereotype   an image of members of a group that standardizes them and exaggerates certain qualities

stigma   that which symbolizes disrepute or disgrace

stratification system   arrangement of society into groups that are unequal with regard to such valued resources as wealth, power, and prestige

structural functionalism   a sociological theory that focuses on social systems and how their interdependent parts maintain order

subsidy   a government grant to a private person or company to assist an enterprise deemed advantageous to the public

survey   a method of research in which a sample of people are interviewed or given questionnaires in order to get data on some phenomenon

symbolic interactionism   a sociological theory that focuses on the interaction between individuals, the individual's perception of situations, and the ways in which social life is constructed through interaction

test of significance   a statistical method for determining the probability that research findings occurred by chance

total institution   a place in which the totality of the individual's existence is controlled by external forces

transgender   having a gender identity different from one's anatomy

trauma   physical or emotional injury

underemployment   working full time for poverty wages, working part time when full-time work is desired, or working at a job below the worker's skill level

unemployment rate   the proportion of the labor force that is not working but is available for work and has made specific efforts to find work

urbanization   the increasing concentration of people living in cities

values   things preferred because they are defined as having worth

variable   any trait or characteristic that varies in value or magnitude

violence   the use of force to kill, injure, or abuse others

voucher system   a system that allows parents to use tax money to send their children to a school, private or public, of their choice

war   a major armed conflict between nations or between organized groups within a nation in which a thousand or more people are killed

white-collar crime   crimes committed by respectable citizens in the course of their work

work ethic   the notion that your sense of worth and the satisfaction of your needs are intricately related to the kind of work you do

references

Abdul-Wahab, S.A., ed. 2011. *Sick Building Syndrome.* New York: Springer.

Abramovitz, J.N. 1998. *Taking a Stand.* Washington, D.C.: Worldwatch Institute.

Acierno, R., et al. 2010. "Prevalence and correlates of emotional, physical, sexual, and financial abuse and potential neglect in the United States." *American Journal of Public Health* 100:292-97.

Adams, B., M. P. Aranda, B. Kemp, and K. Takagi. 2002. "Ethnic and gender differences in distress among Anglo American, African American, Japanese American, and Mexican American spousal caregivers of persons with dementia." *Journal of Clinical Geropsychology* 8:279-301.

Adams, J. B., et al. 2003. "Relationships between personality and preferred substance and motivations for use among adolescent substance abusers." *American Journal of Drug and Alcohol Abuse* 29:691-712.

Adams, J. E., Jr. 1997. "Organizational context and district resource allocation." *Journal of Education Finance* 23 (Fall):234-58.

Adams, K. E. 2004. "Mandatory parental notification: The importance of confidential health care for adolescents." *Journal of the American Medical Women's Association* 59:87-90.

Afifi, T. O., et al. 2008. "Population attributable fractions of psychiatric disorders and suicide ideation and attempts associated with adverse childhood experiences." *American Journal of Public Health* 98:946-52.

AFL-CIO. 2016. "Executive paywatch." AFL-CIO website.

Agnew, R., S. K. Matthews, J. Bucher, A. N. Welcher, and C. Keyes. 2008. "Socioeconomic status, economic problems, and delinquency." *Youth & Society* 40:159-81.

Aguilera, E. 2011. "New scale shows greater poverty." *San Diego Union-Tribune*, November 8.

Ahrens, C. E., G. Cabral, and S. Abeling. 2009. "Healing or hurtful: Sexual assault survivors' interpretation of social reactions from support providers." *Psychology of Women Quarterly* 33:81-94.

Ahrens, C. J., and C. D. Ryff. 2006. "Multiple roles and well-being." *Sex Roles* 55:801-15.

Ajdukovic, M. 1998. "Displaced adolescents in Croatia." *Adolescence* 33 (Spring):209-17.

Alaimo, K., C. M. Olson, and E. A. Frongillo Jr. 2001. "Food insufficiency and American school-aged children's cognitive, academic, and psychosocial development." *Pediatrics* 108:44-53.

———. 2002. "Family food insufficiency, but not low family income, is positively associated with dysthymia and suicide symptoms in adolescents." *Journal of Nutrition* 132:719-25.

Alaimo, K., C. M. Olson, E. A. Frongillo Jr., and R. R. Briefel. 2001. "Food insufficiency, family income, and health in U.S. preschool and school-aged children." *American Journal of Public Health* 91:781-86.

Alamar, B., and S. A. Glantz. 2007. "Effect of smoke-free laws on bar value and profits." *American Journal of Public Health* 97:1400-2.

Alarcon, W. A., et al. 2005. "Acute illnesses associated with pesticide exposure at schools." *Journal of the American Medical Association* 294:455-65.

Albanese, J. 2007. "Commercial sexual exploitation of children." *NIJ Special Report,* December.

Albelda, R., S. Himmelweit, and J. Humphries. 2004. "The dilemmas of lone motherhood." *Feminist Economics* 10:1-7.

Albright, J. M. 2008. "Sex in America online." *Journal of Sex Research* 45:175-86.

Alderson, A. S., and T. Katz-Gerro. 2016. "Compared to whom? Inequality, social comparison, and happiness in the United States." *Social Forces* 95:25-54.

Alexander, K. L., D. R. Entwisle, and L. S. Olson. 2007. "Lasting consequences of the summer learning gap." *American Sociological Review* 72:167-80.

Alexander, M. 2010. *The New Jim Crow: Mass Incarceration in the Age of Colorblindness.* New York: New Press.

Al-Krenawi, A., and J. R. Graham. 2012. "The impact of political violence on psychosocial functioning of individuals and families." *Child & Adolescent Mental Health* 17:14-22.

Allard, S. W. 2008. "Rethinking the safety net: Gaps and instability in help for the working poor." *Focus,* Summer/Fall.

Allegretto, S. A. 2011. "The state of working American's wealth, 2011." *EPI Briefing Paper*, March 23. Economic Policy Institute website.

Allen, J. T. 2000. "Making the grade, or not." *U.S. News and World Report,* March 13, p. 24.

Allen, S. 2004. "Report puts hospital deaths from preventable errors at 195,000." *San Diego Union-Tribune,* July 27.

Allender, D. M., and F. Marcell. 2003. "Career criminals, security threat groups, and prison gangs." *FBI Law Enforcement Bulletin* 72:8-12.

Alleyne, E., and J. I. Wood. 2010. "Gang involvement: Psychological and behavioral characteristics of gang members, peripheral youth, and nongang youth." *Aggressive Behavior* 36:423-36.

Alon, S., and M. Tienda. 2005a. "Assessing the 'mismatch' hypothesis: Differences in college graduation rates by institutional selectivity." *Sociology of Education* 78:294-325.

——. 2005b. "Job mobility and early career wage growth of white, African-American, and Hispanic women." *Social Science Quarterly* 86:1196-1217.

Alonso, J., et al. 2004. "Health-related quality of life associated with chronic conditions in eight countries." *Quality of Life Research* 13:283-98.

Alvarado, S. E. 2016. "Delayed disadvantage: Neighborhood context and child development." *Social Forces* 94:1847-77.

Amadeo, K. 2016a. "Deinstitutionalization: How does it affect you today?" The Balance website.

Amadeo, K. 2016b. "How outsourcing jobs affects the U.S. economy." The Balance website.

Amato, P. R. 2001. "Children of divorce in the 1990s." *Journal of Family Psychology* 15:355-70.

Amato, P. R., and J. E. Cheadle. 2008. "Parental divorce, marital conflict and children's behavior problems." *Social Forces* 86:1139-61.

Amato, P. R., and D. D. DeBoer. 2001. "The transmission of marital instability across generations." *Journal of Marriage and Family* 63:1038-51.

Amato, P. R., and S. J. Rogers. 1997. "A longitudinal study of marital problems and subsequent divorce." *Journal of Marriage and the Family* 59 (August):612-24.

Amato, P. R., and J. M. Sobolewski. 2001. "The effects of divorce and marital discord on adult children's psychological well-being." *American Sociological Review* 66:900-21.

American Academy of Pediatrics. 2001. "Media violence." *Pediatrics* 108:1222-26.

American Association of University Women. 2006. "Drawing the line survey." AAUW website.

American Association of University Women. 2012. "Crossing the line: Sexual harassment at school." AAUW website.

American Civil Liberties Union. 1999. *Freedom Network.* American Civil Liberties Union website.

——. 2002. "ACLU says Homeland Security Bill step backward." Press release. American Civil Liberties Union website.

——. 2004. *Purged! How a Patchwork of Flawed and Inconsistent Voting Systems Could Deprive Millions of Americans the Right to Vote.* American Civil Liberties Union website.

——. 2016. *Nationwide, anti-Immigration legislation by state."* American Civil Liberties Union website.

American Federation of Teachers. 2002. *Do Charter Schools Measure Up?* Washington, DC: American Federation of Teachers.

American National Election Studies. 2016. "Trust the Federal Government." ANES website.

American Psychiatric Association. 1994. *Diagnostic and Statistical Manual of Mental Disorders,* 4th ed. Washington, DC: American Psychiatric Association.

American website for Suicide Prevention. 2016. "Physician and medical student depression and suicide prevention." AWSP website.

Amin, A. 2004. "Regulating economic globalization." *Transactions of the Institute of British Geographers* 29:217-33.

Andersen, S.H., L.H. Andersen, and P.E. Skov. 2015. "Effect of marriage and spousal criminality on recidivism." *Journal of Marriage and Family* 77:496-509.

Anderson, A. 1982. "Neurotoxic follies." *Psychology Today* (July):30-42.

Anderson, C. A., et al. 2008. "Longitudinal effects of violent video games on aggression in Japan and the United States." *Pediatrics* 122:1067-72.

Anderson, C. J., and Y. V. Tverdova. 2003. "Corruption, political allegiances, and attitudes toward government in contemporary democracies." *American Journal of Political Science* 47:91-109.

Anderson, J. P., R. M. Kaplan, and C. F. Ake. 2004. "Arthritis impact on U.S. life quality." *Social Indicators Research* 69:67-91.

Anderson, R. 2009. "The emerging class of the lucky-rich." *Contexts* 8:72-73.

Anestis, M. D., and J. C. Anestis. 2015. "Suicide rates and state laws regulating access and exposure to handguns." *American Journal of Public Health* 105:2049-58.

Angermeyer, M. C., M. Beck, S. Dietrich, and A. Holzinger. 2004. "The stigma of mental illness." *International Journal of Social Psychiatry* 50:153-62.

Annest, J. L., J. A. Mercy, D. R. Gibson, and G. W. Ryan. 1995. "National estimates of nonfatal firearm-related injuries." *Journal of the American Medical Association* 273 (June 14):1749-54.

Anrig, G. 2008. "An idea whose time has gone." *Washington Monthly,* April.

Apsler, R., M. R. Cummins, and S. Carl. 2003. "Perceptions of the police by female victims of domestic partner violence." *Violence against Women* 9:1318-35.

Arkowitz, H., and S. O. Lilienfeld. 2010. "Sex in bits and bytes." *Scientific American Mind*, July/August, pp. 64-65.

Armstrong, G. L., L. A. Conn, and R. W. Pinner. 1999. "Trends in infectious disease mortality in the United States during the 20th century." *Journal of the American Medical Association* 281 (January 6):61-66.

Arnold, D. H., et al. 2006. "Preschool-based programs for externalizing problems." *Education and Treatment of Children* 29:311-39.

Arnold, S. B. 2014. "Reproductive rights denied." *American Journal of Public Health* 104:1892-93.

Aronson, M., and B. Hagberg. 1998. "Neuropsychological disorders in children exposed to alcohol during pregnancy." *Alcoholism: Clinical and Experimental Research* 22 (April):321-24.

Arora, M., K. S. Reddy, M. H. Stigler, and C. L. Perry. 2008. "Associations between tobacco marketing and use among urban youth in India." *American Journal of Health Behavior* 32:283-94.

Arrington, C. 1990. "A generation of men grows up." *Men's Life* (Fall):64-70.

Ashforth, B. 1994. "Petty tyranny in organizations." *Human Relations* 47 (July):755-78.

Aspden, P., J. Wolcott, J. L. Bootman, and L. R. Cronenwett, eds. 2007. *Preventing Medication Errors.* Washington, DC: National Academies Press.

Assadourian, E. 2010. "The rise and fall of consumer cultures." In *State of the World 2010,* ed. L. Starke and L. Mastny, pp. 3-20. New York: W.W. Norton.

Associated Press. 2012. "10 states get No Child Left Behind waivers." Governing magazine website.

Association of American Medical Colleges. 2011. *Women in Academic Medicine.* AAMC website.

Atkinson, M. P., T. N. Greenstein, and M. M. Lang. 2005. "For women, breadwinning can be dangerous." *Journal of Marriage and Family* 67:1137-48.

Atwood, J. D. 2007. "When love hurts: Preadolescent girls' reports of incest." *American Journal of Family Therapy* 35:287-313.

Augustine, J. M. 2014. "Maternal education and the unequal significance of family structure for children's early achievement." *Social Forces* 93:687-718.

Auter, Z. 2016. "Americans continue to cite the economy as top problem." The Gallup Poll website.

Ayanian, J. Z., and P. D. Cleary. 1999. "Perceived risks of heart disease and cancer among cigarette smokers." *Journal of the American Medical Association* 281 (April 28):1019-21.

Aydin, Y. E., A. Altindag, and M. Ozkan. 2009. "Childhood traumatic events and dissociation in university students." *International Journal of Psychiatry in Clinical Practice* 13:25-30.

Ayscue, J. B., et al. 2016. "School segregation and resegregation in Charlotte and Raleigh, 1989-2010." *Educational Policy.* Published online.

Baams, L., A. H. Grossman, and S. T. Russel. 2015. "Minority stress and mechanisms of risk for depression and suicidal Ideation among lesbian, gay, and bisexual youth." *Developmental Psychology* 51:688-96.

Bacevich, Andrew J. 2010. *Washington Rules: America's Path to Permanent War.* New York: Henry Holt.

Bacon, O., et al. 2006. "Commercial sex work and risk of HIV infection among young drug-injecting men who have sex with men in San Francisco." *Sexually Transmitted Diseases* 33:228-34.

Baggett, T. P., J. J. O'Connell, D. E. Singer, and N. A. Rigotti. 2010. "The unmet health needs of homeless adults." *American Journal of Public Health* 100:1326-33.

Bahr, S. J., S. L. Maughan, A. C. Marcos, and B. Li. 1998. "Family, religiosity, and the risk of adolescent drug use." *Journal of Marriage and the Family* 60 (November):979-92.

Bailey, J. M., and R. C. Pillard. 1991. "A genetic study of male sexual orientation." *Archives of General Psychiatry* 48 (December):1089-98.

Bailey, J. M., et al. 2016. "Sexual orientation, controversy, and science." *Psychological Science in the Public Interest,* vol.17. Thousand Oaks, CA: Sage.

Bailey, W. C. 1990. "Murder, capital punishment, and television: Execution publicity and homicide rates." *American Sociological Review* 55 (October):628-33.

Ball, R., and K. Chernova. 2008. "Absolute income, relative income, and happiness." *Social Indicators Research* 88:497-529.

Balsam, K. F., E. D. Rothblum, and T. P. Beauchaine. 2005. "Victimization over the life span." *Journal of Consulting and Clinical Psychology* 73:477-87.

Balthazart, J. 2012. *The Biology of Homosexuality.* New York: Oxford University Press.

Banks, D., and T. Kyckelhahn. 2011. *Characteristics of Suspected Human Trafficking Incidents, 2008-2010.* Washington, DC: Government Printing Office.

Banthin, J. S., and D. M. Bernard. 2006. "Changes in financial burdens for health care." *Journal of the American Medical Association* 296:2712-19.

Barak, M. E. M., and A. Levin. 2002. "Outside of the corporate mainstream and excluded from the work community: A study of diversity, job satisfaction, and well-being." *Community, Work and Family* 5:133-57.

Barbeau, E. M., N. Krieger, and M. Soobader. 2004. "Working-class matters: Socioeconomic disadvantage, race/ethnicity, gender, and smoking in NHIS 2000." *American Journal of Public Health* 94:269-78.

Barker, K. N., E. A. Flynn, G. A. Pepper, D. W. Bates, and R. L. Mikeal. 2002. "Medication errors observed in 36 health care facilities." *Archives of Internal Medicine* 162:1897-903.

Barko, N. 2000. "The other gender gap." *American Prospect,* June 19, pp. 61-67.

Barna Research Online. 2001. "Born again adults remain firm in opposition to abortion and gay marriage." Barna Research Online website.

Barnes, S. L. 2005. *The Cost of Being Poor.* New York: State University of New York Press.

Barnett, J. C., and M. S. Vornovitsky. 2016. "Health insurance coverage in the United States: 2015." U.S. Census Bureau website.

Barnett, O. W. 2001. "Why battered women do not leave." *Trauma, Violence, and Abuse* 2:3-35.

Barron, M., and M. Kimmel. 2000. "Sexual violence in three pornographic media." *Journal of Sex Research* 37:161-68.

Barros-Dios, J. M., M. A. Barreiro, A. Ruano-Ravina, and A. Figueiras. 2002. "Exposure to residential radon and lung cancer in Spain." *American Journal of Epidemiology* 15:548-55.

Barry, B. 2002. "Capitalists rule OK? Some puzzles about power." *Politics, Philosophy and Economics* 1:155-84.

Barry, C. E., and M. S. Cheung. 2009. "New tactics against tuberculosis." *Scientific American,* March, pp. 62-69.

Bartik, T. J., and S. N. Houseman. 2008. *A Future of Good Jobs? America's Challenge in the Global Economy.* Kalamazoo, MI: Upjohn Institute for Employment Research.

Bartley, M., A. Sacker, and P. Clarke. 2004. "Employment status, employment conditions, and limiting illness." *Journal of Epidemiology and Community Health* 58:501-6.

Barton, P. E. 2006. "The dropout problem." *Educational Leadership* 63:14-18.

Basile, M. 2004. "Going to the source: Why Al Qaeda's financial network is likely to withstand the current war on terrorist financing." *Studies in Conflict and Terrorism* 27:169-85.

Bauer, J. E., et al. 2005. "Longitudinal assessment of the impact of smoke-free worksite policies on tobacco use." *American Journal of Public Health* 95:1024-29.

Baughman, R., D. DiNardi, and D. Holtz-Eakin. 2003. "Productivity and wage effects of 'family-friendly' fringe benefits." *International Journal of Manpower* 24:247-59.

Baum, C. L., II. 2003. "Does early maternal employment harm child development?" *Journal of Labor Economics* 21:409-48.

Baverstock, K. 2005. "Science, politics and ethics in the low dose debate." *Medicine, Conflict and Survival* 21:88-100.

Bayrakdar-Garside, R., and B. Klimes-Dougan. 2002. "Socialization of discrete negative emotions." *Sex Roles* 47:115-28.

Bebber, C. C. 1994. "Increases in U.S. violent crime during the 1980s following four American military actions." *Journal of Interpersonal Violence* 9 (March):109-16.

Beck, A. 2013. "Sexual victimization in prisons and jails reported by Inmates, 2011-12." Bureau of Justice Statistics website.

Beck, A. J., and P. M. Harrison. 2006. "Sexual violence reported by correctional authorities." *Bureau of Justice Statistics Special Bulletin,* July.

Beck, A. J., P. M. Harrison, and P. Guerino. 2010. "Sexual victimization in juvenile facilities reported by youth, 2008-09." *Bureau of Justice Statistics Special Report.* BJS website.

Beck, E. M., and S. E. Tolnay. 1990. "The killing fields of the deep south: The market for cotton and the lynching of blacks, 1882-1930." *American Sociological Review* 55 (August):526-39.

Beck, V. S., et al. 2012. "Violence against women in video games." *Journal of Interpersonal Violence* 27:3016-31.

Becker, H. S. 1953. "Becoming a marijuana user." *American Journal of Sociology* 59 (November):235-42.

Becker, K., Y. Hu, and N. Biller-Andorno. 2006. "Infectious diseases—a global challenge." *International Journal of Medical Microbiology* 296:179-85.

Bell, A., M. Weinberg, and S. Hammersmith. 1981. *Sexual Preference.* Bloomington: Indiana University Press.

Bell, A. P., and M. S. Weinberg. 1978. *Homosexualities: A Study of Diversity among Men and Women.* New York: Simon and Schuster.

Bell, D. 1960. *The End of Ideology.* New York: Free Press.

Bell, J., L. J. Ridolfi, M. Finley, and C. Lacey. 2009. *The Keeper and the Kept.* San Francisco, CA: The W. Haywood Burns Institute.

Bellah, R. N. 1993. "Outrageous thoughts on war and peace." *New Oxford Review* (March):15-20.

Belle, D. 2003. "Poverty, inequality, and discrimination as sources of depression among U.S. women." *Psychology of Women Quarterly* 27:101-13.

Belluck, P. 2003. "Methadone, once the way out, suddenly grows as a killer drug." *New York Times,* February 9.

Bendick, M., R. E. Rodriguez, and S. Jayaraman. 2010. "Employment discrimination in upscale restaurants." *Social Science Journal* 47:802-18.

Bendinelli, C. 2009. "Effects of landmines and unexploded ordnance on the pediatric population and comparison with adults in rural Cambodia." *World Journal of Surgery* (May) 33:1070-74.

Bendroth, M. L. 1994. *Fundamentalism and Gender: 1875 to the Present.* New Haven, CT: Yale University Press.

Benedek, E. P., and C. F. Brown. 1999. "No excuses: Televised pornography harms children." *Harvard Review of Psychiatry* 7 (November-December):236-40.

Benjamin, D., and S. Simon. 2005. *The Next Attack: The Failure of the War on Terror and a Strategy for Getting It Right.* New York: Times Books.

Bennett, T., K. Holloway, and D. P. Farrington. 2006. "Does neighborhood watch reduce crime?" *Journal of Experimental Criminology* 2:437-58.

Bennett, R. 1991. "Routine activities: A cross-national assessment of a criminological perspective." *Social Forces* 70:147-63.

——. 2008. "The statistical association between drug misuse and crime." *Aggression and Violent Behavior* 13:107-18.

Benson, M. L., G. L. Fox, A. DeMaris, and J. Van Wyk. 2003. "Neighborhood disadvantage, individual economic distress, and violence against women in intimate relationships." *Journal of Quantitative Criminology* 19:207-35.

Berends, M., and R. B. Penaloza. 2010. "Increasing racial isolation and test score gaps in mathematics." *Teachers' College Record.* TCR website.

Berg, J. A. 2009. "White public opinion toward undocumented immigrants." *Sociological Perspectives* 52:39–58.

Bergen, R. K., and K. A. Bogle. 2000. "Exploring the connection between pornography and sexual violence." *Violence and Victims* 15:227–34.

Berger, J. 1999. "Panel is proposed to fight corruption in trash industry." *New York Times,* March 16.

Berger, L. M. 2005. "Income, family characteristics, and physical violence toward children." *Child Abuse and Neglect* 29:107–33.

Bergner, R. M., and A. J. Bridges. 2002. "The significance of heavy pornography involvement for romantic partners." *Journal of Sex and Marital Therapy* 28:193–206.

Berkman, L. F. 2000. "From social integration to health." *Social Science and Medicine* 51:843–58.

Berkowitz, L. 1981. "How guns control us." *Psychology Today* (June):12–13.

Berkshire, J. C., et al. 2011. "Bad economy has strained many nonprofit workers." *Chronicle of Philanthropy* 24 (5).

Bernard, J. 1966. *Marriage and Family among Negroes.* Englewood Cliffs, NJ: Prentice-Hall.

Berner, M., T. Ozer, and S. Paynter. 2008. "A portrait of hunger, the social safety net, and the working poor." *Policy Studies Journal* 36:403–20.

Bernhard-Oettel, C., M. Sverke, and H. De Witte. 2006. "Comparing three alternative types of employment with permanent full-time work." *Work and Stress* 19:301–18.

Bernstein, E. 2007. *Temporarily Yours: Intimacy, Authenticity and the Commerce of Sex.* Chicago, IL: University of Chicago Press.

Bessenoff, G. R. 2006. "Can the media affect us? Social comparison, self-discrepancy, and the thin ideal." *Psychology of Women Quarterly* 30:239–51.

Bethke, T. M., and D. M. DeJoy. 1993. "An experimental study of factors influencing the acceptability of dating violence." *Journal of Interpersonal Violence* 8 (March):36–51.

Betts, J. R., and D. Morell. 1999. "The determinants of undergraduate grade point average." *Journal of Human Resources* 34 (Spring):268–93.

Betts, J. R., and Y. E. Tang. 2016. "A meta-analysis of the literature on the effect of charter schools on student achievement." Society for Research on Educational Effectiveness website.

Bhattacharya, J., T. DeLeire, S. Haider, and J. Currie. 2003. "Heat or eat? Cold-weather shocks and nutrition in poor American families." *American Journal of Public Health* 93:1149–54.

Bianchi, S. M. 1995. "The changing demographic and socioeconomic characteristics of single parent families." *Marriage and Family Review* 20 (1–2):71–97.

Bibby, J. F., and L. S. Maisel. 1998. *Two Parties—Or More? The American Party System.* Boulder, CO: Westview Press.

Bickell, N. A., et al. 2008. "A tracking and feedback registry to reduce racial disparities in breast cancer care." *Journal of the National Cancer Institute* 100:1717–23.

Biden, J. R., Jr. 1990. "They're out there crying for help." *Los Angeles Times,* March 14.

Biever, C. 2006. "The irresistible rise of cybersex." *New Scientist* 190:67.

Bigner, J. J., and R. B. Jacobsen. 1992. "Adult responses to child behavior and attitudes toward fathering: Gay and nongay fathers." *Journal of Homosexuality* 23 (3):99–112.

Billari, F. C., and A. C. Liefbroer. 2016. "Why still marry?" *The British Journal of Sociology.* Published online.

Billingham, R., and T. Abrahams. 1998. "Parental divorce, body dissatisfaction, and physical attractiveness ratings of self and others among college women." *College Student Journal* 32 (March):148–52.

Bimbi, D. S. 2007. "Male prostitution: Pathology, paradigms and progress in research." *Journal of Homosexuality* 53:7–35.

Bing, N. M., W. M. Nelson, and K. L. Wesolowski. 2009. "Comparing the effects of amount of conflict on children's adjustment following parental divorce." *Journal of Divorce & Remarriage* 50:159–71.

Binswanger, I. A., and A. J. Gordon. 2016. "From risk reduction to implementation." *Substance Abuse* 37:1–3.

Bird, C. E., and A. M. Fremont. 1991. "Gender, time use, and health." *Journal of Health and Social Behavior* 32 (June): 114–29.

Bitler, M. P., J. B. Gelbach, and H. W. Hoynes. 2004. "Has welfare reform affected children's living arrangements?" *Focus* 23:14–20.

Bjarnason, T., et al. 2003. "Alcohol culture, family structure, and adolescent alcohol use." *Journal of Studies on Alcohol* 64:200–208.

——. 2005. "Familial and religious influences on adolescent alcohol use." *Social Forces* 84:375–90.

Black, M. C., et al. 2011. *The National Intimate Partner and Sexual Violence Survey.* Atlanta, GA: Centers for Disease Control and Prevention.

Black, S. 2001. "Morale matters." *American School Board Journal* 188:40–43.

Blackwell, D. L., J. G. Collins, and R. Coles. 2002. *Summary Health Statistics for U.S. Adults.* Washington, DC: Government Printing Office.

Blair, R. G. 2000. "Risk factors associated with PTSD and major depression among Cambodian refugees in Utah." *Health and Social Work* 25 (February):23–30.

Blais, M., and F. Dupuis-Deri. 2012. "Masculinism and the antifeminist countermovement." *Social Movement Studies* 11:21–39.

Blalock, L., V. R. Tiller, and P. A. Monroe. 2004. "'They get you out of courage': Persistent deep poverty among former welfare-reliant women." *Family Relations* 53:127–37.

Blasi, J., and D. Kruse. 2006. "The political economy of employee ownership in the United States." *International Review of Sociology* 16:127–47.

Blau, G., and D. Tatum. 2000. "Correlates of perceived gender discrimination for female versus male medical technologists." *Sex Roles* 43:105–18.

Bletzer, K. V. 2005. "Sex workers in agricultural areas." *Culture, Health and Sexuality* 6:543–55.

Blizzard, L., A. Ponsonby, T. Dwyer, A. Venn, and J. A. Cochrane. 2003. "Parental smoking and infant respiratory infection." *American Journal of Public Health* 93:482–88.

Blumenberg, E., and A. W. Agrawal. 2014. "Getting around when you're just getting by." *Journal of Poverty* 18:355–78.

Blumstein, A., and R. Rosenfeld. 1998. "Assessing the recent ups and downs in U.S. homicide rates." *National Institute of Justice Journal* (October):9–11.

Boeringer, S. B. 1994. "Pornography and sexual aggression: Associations of violent and nonviolent depictions with rape and rape proclivity." *Deviant Behavior* 15 (3):289–304.

Boisen, A. T. 1936. *The Exploration of the Inner World.* New York: Harper and Bros.

Bolin, A., and P. Whelehan. 2003. *Perspectives on Human Sexuality.* New York: McGraw-Hill.

Bonczar, T. P. 2003. *Prevalence of Imprisonment in the U.S. Population, 1974–2001.* Washington, DC: Government Printing Office.

Bond, J. T., E. Galinsky, and J. E. Swanberg. 1998. *The 1997 National Study of the Changing Workforce.* New York: Families and Work Institute.

Bonilla-Silva, E., C. Goar, and D. G. Embrick. 2006. "When whites flock together." *Critical Sociology* 32:229–53.

Bonneuil, N., and N. Auriat. 2000. "Fifty years of ethnic conflict and cohesion: 1945–94." *Journal of Peace Research* 37:563–81.

Bookwala, J., J. Sobin, and B. Zdaniuk. 2005. "Gender and aggression in marital relationships." *Sex Roles* 52:797–806.

Booth, B. M., et al. 2010. "Longitudinal relationship between psychological distress and multiple substance use." *Journal of Studies on Alcohol and Drugs* 71:258–67.

Borek, E., and S. A. Bohon. 2008. "Policy climates and reductions in automobile use." *Social Science Quarterly* 89:1293–1311.

Borjas, G. J. 2011. "Poverty and program participation among immigrant children." *Future of Children* 21:247–66.

Boroughs, M. S., R. Krawczyk, and J. K. Thompson. 2010. "Body dysmorphic disorder among diverse racial/ethnic and sexual orientation groups." *Sex Roles* 63:725–37.

Bossarte, R. M., and M. H. Swahn. 2008. "Interactions between race/ethnicity and psychosocial correlates of preteen alcohol use initiation among seventh grade students in an urban setting." *Journal of Studies on Alcohol and Drugs* 69:660–65.

Bostean, G., D. R. Trinidad, and W. J. McCarthy. 2015. "E-Cigarette use among never-smoking California students." *American Journal of Public Health* 105:2423–225.

Bostwick, W. B., C. J. Boyd, T. L. Hughes, and S. E. McCabe. 2010. "Dimensions of sexual orientation and the prevalence of mood and anxiety disorders in the United States." *American Journal of Public Health* 100:468–75.

Botta, R. A. 2003. "For your health? The relationship between magazine reading and adolescents' body image and eating disturbances." *Sex Roles* 48:389–99.

Botteri, E., et al. 2008. "Smoking and colorectal cancer." *Journal of the American Medical Association* 300:2765–78.

Bovier, P. A., F. Arigoni, M. Schneider, and M. B. Gallacchi. 2009. "Relationships between work satisfaction, emotional exhaustion and mental health among Swiss primary care physicians." *European Journal of Public Health* 19:611–17.

Bowen, G. L., L. M. Hopson, R. A. Rose, and E. J. Glennie. 2012. "Students' perceived parental school behavior expectations and their academic performance." *Family Relations* 61:175–91.

Bower, B. 2005. "Childhood's end." *Science News* 168:200–01.

Bowker, A., and M. Gray. 2005. "The cybersex offender and children." *FBI Law Enforcement Bulletin* 74:12–17.

Bowles, S., S. N. Durlauf, and K. Hoff, eds. 2006. *Poverty Traps.* Princeton, NJ: Princeton University Press.

Bowman, D. H. 2000. "Charters, vouchers earning mixed report card." *Education Week on the Web,* May 3.

Bowman, K. H. 2004. *Attitudes about Homosexuality.* American Enterprise Institute website.

Boy, A., and A. Kulczycki. 2008. "What we know about intimate partner violence in the Middle East and North Africa." *Violence Against Women* 14:53–70.

Boynton-Jarrett, R., L. M. Ryan, L. F. Berkman, and R. J. Wright. 2008. "Cumulative violence exposure and self-rated health." *Pediatrics* 122:961–70.

Braam, A. W., et al. 2004. "Religious involvement and 6-year course of depressive symptoms in older Dutch citizens." *Journal of Aging and Health* 16:467–89.

Braddock, J. H., II, M. P. Dawkins, and W. Trent. 1994. "Why desegregate? The effect of school desegregation on adult occupational desegregation of African Americans, whites, and Hispanics." *International Journal of Contemporary Sociology* 31 (October):273–83.

Bradford, J., C. Ryan, and E. D. Rothblum. 1994. "National lesbian health care survey: Implications for mental health care." *Journal of Consulting and Clinical Psychology* 62 (April):228–42.

Brady, D., R. S. Baker, and R. Finnigan. 2013. "When unionization disappears." *American Sociological Review* 78:872–96.

Brady, D. W., and C. Volden. 1998. *Resolving Gridlock: Politics and Policy from Carter to Clinton.* Boulder, CO: Westview Press.

Braga, A. A. 2003. "Serious youth gun offenders and the epidemic of youth violence in Boston." *Journal of Quantitative Criminology* 19:33-54.

Brajs-Zganec, A. 2005. "The long-term effects of war experiences on children's depression in the Republic of Croatia." *Child Abuse & Neglect* 29:31-43.

Bramlett, M. D., and S. J. Blumberg. 2007. "Family structure and children's physical and mental health." *Health Affairs* 26:549-58.

Bramlett, M. D., and W. D. Mosher. 2001. "First marriage dissolution, divorce, and remarriage: United States." *Advance Data, May 31.* Washington, DC: Department of Health and Human Services.

——. 2002. *Cohabitation, Marriage, Divorce, and Remarriage in the United States.* Washington, DC: Government Printing Office.

Branas, C. C., et al. 2009. "Investigating the link between gun possession and gun assault." *American Journal of Public Health* 99:2034-40.

Brand, J. E., J. R. Warren, P. Carayon, and P. Hoonakker. 2007. "Do job characteristics mediate the relationship between SES and health?" *Social Science Research* 36:222-53.

Braun, H., F. Jenkins, and W. Grigg. 2006. *Comparing Private Schools and Public Schools Using Hierarchical Linear Modeling.* Washington, DC: Government Printing Office.

Brecklin, L. R., and S. E. Ullman. 2005. "Self-defense or assertiveness training and women's responses to sexual attacks." *Journal of Interpersonal Violence* 20:738-62.

Brenner, M. H. 1978. "The social costs of economic distress." In *Consultation on the Social Impact of Economic Distress,* pp. 3-6. New York: American Jewish Committee, Institute of Human Relations.

——. 2005. "Commentary: Economic growth is the basis of mortality rate decline in the 20th century—experience of the United States 1901-2000." *International Journal of Epidemiology* 34:1214-21.

Brenchley, C. 2012. "Answering questions of fundamental fairness." U.S. Department of Education blog site.

Brents, B. G., and K. Hausbeck. 2005. "Violence and legalized brothel prostitution in Nevada." *Journal of Interpersonal Violence* 20:270-95.

Brents, B. G., C. A. Jackson, and K. Hausbeck. 2010. *The State of Sex: Tourism, Sex, and Sin in the New American Heartland.* New York: Routledge.

Brians, C. L., and B. Grofman. 2001. "Election day registration's effect on U.S. voter turnout." *Social Science Quarterly* 82:170-83.

Bridges, G. S., and S. Steen. 1998. "Racial disparities in official assessments of juvenile offenders." *American Sociological Review* 63 (August):554-70.

Bright, C. 2000. "Anticipating environmental surprise." In *State of the world 2000,* L. R. Brown et al., eds., pp. 22-38. New York: W.W. Norton.

Brill, S. 2013. "Bitter pill." *Time*, March 4.

Brizendine, L. 2006. *The Female Brain.* New York: Morgan Road Books.

Broad, W. J. 1997. "C.I.A. admits government lied about U.F.O. sightings." *New York Times,* August 3.

Broder, M. S., D. E. Kanouse, B. S. Mittman, and S. J. Bernstein. 2000. "The appropriateness of recommendations for hysterectomy." *Obstetrics and Gynecology* 95 (February):199-205.

Brodsky, L. M., R. W. Habash, W. Leiss, D. Krewski, and M. Rapacholi. 2003. "Health risks of electromagnetic fields." *Critical Review of Biomedical Engineering* 31:333-54.

Brody, G. H., et al. 2001. "The influence of neighborhood disadvantage, collective socialization, and parenting on African American children's affiliation with deviant peers." *Child Development* 72:1231-46.

Bromet, E.J., 2012. "Mental health consequences of the Chernobyl disaster." *Journal of Radiological Protection* 32:71-5.

Bronner, G., C. Peretz, and M. Ehrenfeld. 2003. "Sexual harassment of nurses and nursing students." *Journal of Advanced Nursing* 42:637-44.

Bronte-Tinkew, J., K. A. Moore, and J. Carrano. 2006. "The father-child relationship, parenting styles, and adolescent risk behaviors in intact families." *Journal of Family Issues* 27:850-81.

Brook, J. S., K. Pahl, and P. Cohen. 2008. "Associations between marijuana use during emerging adulthood and aspects of the significant other relationship in young adulthood." *Journal of Child and Family Studies* 17:1-12.

Brookings Institution Metropolitan Policy Program. 2005. *The Price Is Wrong.* Brookings Institution website.

Brooks, C. 1999. "Study prompts VA to help ill kids of female Vietnam vets." *San Diego Union-Tribune,* September 4.

Brown, J. S. 1952. "A comparative study of deviations from sexual mores." *American Sociological Review* 17 (April):135-46.

Brown, L. R. 2000. "Challenges of the new century." In *State of the World 2000,* ed. L. R. Brown et al., pp. 3-21. New York: W. W. Norton.

Brown, L. R., and S. Postel. 1987. "Thresholds of change." In *State of the World 1987,* ed. L. R. Brown, pp. 3-19. New York: W. W. Norton.

Brown, P. 2008. "Climate change: Polar express." *Scientific American,* July, pp. 18-20.

Brown, S. I. 2004. "Family structure and child well-being." *Journal of Marriage and Family* 66:351-67.

Brown, T. L., G. S. Parks, R. S. Zimmerman, and C. M. Phillips. 2001. "The role of religion in predicting adolescent alcohol use and problem drinking." *Journal of Studies on Alcohol* 62:696-705.

Browne, K. D., and C. E. Hamilton. 1998. "Physical violence between young adults and their parents." *Journal of Family Violence* 13 (March):59-79.

Browning, K., and R. Loeber. 1999. "Highlights of findings from the Pittsburgh youth study." *OJJDP Fact Sheet #95.* Washington, DC: Government Printing Office.

Bryant-Davis, T. 2004. "Rape is: A media review for sexual assault psychoeducation." *Trauma Violence and Abuse* 5:194-95.

Bryce, J. W., N. Walker, F. Ghorayeb, and M. Kanj. 1989. "Life experiences, response styles, and mental health among mothers and children in Beirut, Lebanon." *Social Science and Medicine* 28 (7):685-95.

Bryce, R. 2006. "Man versus mine." *Atlantic Monthly* (January/February):44-46.

Bryk, A. S., et al. 2010. *Organizing Schools for Improvement: Lessons from Chicago.* Chicago, IL: University of Chicago Press.

Brym, R. J. 2007. "Six lessons of suicide bombers." *Contexts* 6:40-45.

Brym, R. J., and B. Araj. 2006. "Suicide bombing as strategy and interaction." *Social Forces* 84:1969-86.

Buchmueller, T. C., et al. 2016. "Effect of the affordable care act on racial and ethnic disparities in health insurance coverage." *American Journal of Public Health.* Published online.

Budig, M. J., and M. J. Hodges. 2010. "Differences in disadvantage: Variations in the motherhood penalty across white women's earnings distribution." *American Sociological Review* 75:705-28.

Bueler, C., and M. O'Brien. 2011. "Mothers' part-time employment." *Journal of Family Psychology* 25:895-906.

Bull, M. J., and R. E. McShane. 2002. "Needs and supports for family caregivers of chronically ill elders." *Home Health Care Management and Practice* 14:92-98.

Bullman, T. A., C. M. Mahan, H. K. Kang, and W. F. Page. 2005. "Mortality in U.S. Army Gulf War veterans exposed to 1991 Khamisiyah chemical munitions destruction." *American Journal of Public Health* 95:1382-88.

Bumiller, E. 2010. "The war: A trillion can be cheap." *New York Times*, July 25.

Burd, L., T. M. Cotsonas-Hassler, J. T. Martsolf, and J. Kerbeshian. 2003. "Recognition and management of fetal alcohol syndrome." *Neurotoxicology and Teratology* 25:681-88.

Burdick-Will, J. 2016. "Neighborhood violent crime and academic growth in Chicago." *Social Forces.* Published on-line.

Burdman, D. 2003. "Education, indoctrination, and incitement: Palestinian children on their way to martyrdom." *Terrorism and Political Violence* 15:96-123.

Bureau of Labor Statistics. 2009. "Persons not in the labor force by desire and availability for work, age, and sex." BLS website.

Bureau of Labor Statistics. 2015. "Women in the labor force: a databook." Bureau of Labor Statistics website.

Bureau of Labor Statistics. 2016a. "A profile of the working poor." Bureau of Labor Statistics website.

Bureau of Labor Statistics. 2016b. "Characteristics of minimum wage workers, 2015." Bureau of Labor Statistics website.

Bureau of Labor Statistics. 2016c. "The employment situation—June 2016." Bureau of Labor Statistics website.

Bureau of Labor Statistics. 2016d. "Union members summary." Bureau of Labor Statistics website.

Burgard, S. A., J. E. Brand, and J. S. House. 2007. "Toward a better estimation of the effect of job loss on health." *Journal of Health and Social Behavior* 48:369-84.

Burger, T. J., and A. Zagorin. 2004. "Did Cheney okay a deal?" *Time,* June 7, p. 42.

Burgess, A. W., and L. L. Holmstrom. 1974. "Rape trauma syndrome." *American Journal of Psychiatry* 131 (September):981-86.

———. 1979. "Rape: Sexual disruption and recovery." *American Journal of Orthopsychiatry* 49 (4):648-57.

Burgess, M.C.R., et al. 2011. "Playing with prejudice." *Media Psychology* 14:289-311.

Burke, R. J. 1995. "Work and career experiences and emotional well-being of managerial and professional women." *Stress Medicine* 11 (January):51-60.

Burleigh, N. 1991. "Watching children starve to death." *Time,* June 10, pp. 56-58.

Burnette, M. L., R. Schneider, C. Timko, and M. A. Ilgen. 2009. "Impact of substance-use disorder treatment on women involved in prostitution." *Journal of Studies on Alcohol and Drugs* 70:32-40.

Burns, J. M., et al. 2005. *Government by the People.* 20th ed. Upper Saddle River, NJ: Pearson/Prentice Hall.

Burns, J.M., J.W. Peterson, and T.E. Cronin. 1984. *Government by the People.* 12th edition. Englewood Cliffs, NJ: Prentice-Hall.

Bush, P. J., K. P. Weinfurt, and R. J. Iannotti. 1994. "Families versus peers: Developmental influences on drug use from grade 4-5 to grade 7-8." *Journal of Applied Developmental Psychology* 15 (July-September): 437-56.

Butterfield, F. 2000. "Report indicates 'juvenile injustice.'" *San Diego Union-Tribune,* April 26.

Butterfield, H. 1949. *Christianity and History.* London: Fontana Books.

Button, D. M., D. J. O'Connell, and R. Gealt. 2012. "Sexual minority youth victimization and social support." *Journal of Homosexuality* 59:18-43.

Button, J. W., and B. A. Rienzo. 2003. "The impact of affirmative action: Black employment in six Southern cities." *Social Science Quarterly* 84:1-14.

Byrnes, N. 2006. "The high cost of fear." *Business Week,* November 6, p. 16.

Caetano, R., S. Ramisetty-Mikler, and L. A. Rodriguez. 2008. "The Hispanic Americans baseline alcohol survey." *Journal of Studies on Alcohol and Drugs* 69:441–48.

Cairney, S., A. Clough, M. Jaragba, and P. Maruff. 2007. "Cognitive impairment in Aboriginal people with heavy episodic patterns of alcohol use." *Addiction* 102:909–15.

Calder, J., A. McVean, and W. Yang. 2010. "History of abuse and current suicidal ideation." *Journal of Family Violence* 25:205–14.

Callahan, D. 1998. *False Hopes: Why America's Quest for Perfect Health Is a Recipe for Failure.* Berkeley: University of California Press.

Calle, E. E., C. Rodriquez, K. Walker-Thurmond, and M. J. Thun. 2003. "Overweight, obesity, and mortality from cancer in a prospectively studied cohort of U.S. adults." *New England Journal of Medicine* 348:1625–38.

Cameron, F. 2002. "Utilitarian multilateralism." *Politics* 22:68–75.

Cameron, P., and K. Cameron. 1995. "Does incest cause homosexuality?" *Psychological Reports* 76 (April):611–21.

Campbell, J. C., et al. 2003. "Risk factors for femicide in abusive relationships." *American Journal of Public Health* 93:1089–97.

Campbell, R. 2006. "Rape survivors' experiences with the legal and medical systems." *Violence against Women* 12:30–45.

Campbell, R., S. M. Wasco, C. E. Ahrens, T. Sefl, and H. E. Barnes. 2001. "Preventing the 'second rape.'" *Journal of Interpersonal Violence* 16:1236–59.

Campenni, C. E. 1999. "Gender stereotyping of children's toys." *Sex Roles* 40:212–38.

Campione, W. 2008. "Employed women's well-being: The global and daily impact of work." *Journal of Family and Economic Issues* 29:346–61.

Canadian Medical Association. 2008. "No breathing room: National illness costs of air pollution." CMA website.

Cancian, M., et al. 2003. "Income and program participation among early TANF recipients." *Focus* 22:2–10.

Cannon, A., M. Lavelle, and C. Ragavan. 2000. "In the court of last resort." *U.S. News and World Report,* November 27, p. 33.

Cano, A., and K. D. O'Leary. 2000. "Infidelity and separations precipitate major depressive episodes and symptoms of nonspecific depression and anxiety." *Journal of Consulting and Clinical Psychology* 68:774–81.

Cantelon, S., and D. LeBoeuf. 1997. "Keeping young people in school: Community programs that work." *Juvenile Justice Bulletin, June.*

Cantor, J. M., R. Blanchard, A. D. Paterson, and A. F. Bogaert. 2002. "How many gay men owe their sexual orientation to fraternal birth order?" *Archives of Sexual Behavior* 31:63–71.

Caplan, J. 2009. "Boycotts are so 20th century." *Time,* June 8, p. 54.

Carael, M., E. Slaymaker, R. Lyerla, and S. Sarkar. 2006. "Clients of sex workers in different regions of the world." *Sexually Transmitted Infections* 82:26–33.

Carballo, M., et al. 2004. "Mental health and coping in a war situation." *Journal of Biosocial Science* 36:463–77.

Cardozo, B. L., A. Vergara, F. Agani, and C. A. Golway. 2000. "Mental health, social functioning, and attitudes of Kosovar Albanians following the war in Kosovo." *Journal of the American Medical Association* 284:569–77.

Carlson, B. E. 1990. "Adolescent observers of marital violence." *Journal of Family Violence* 5:285–99.

Carmody, D. C., and L. M. Washington. 2001. "Rape myth acceptance among college women." *Journal of Interpersonal Violence* 16:424–36.

Carr, D. 2005. "Black death, white death." *Contexts* 4:43.

———. 2009. "Worries over a population implosion." *Contexts* 8:58–59.

Carroll, J. S., et al. 2008. "Generation xxx." *Journal of Adolescent Research* 23:6–30.

Carson, E. A. 2015. "Prisoners in 2014." Bureau of Justice Statistics website.

Carter, B. D., et al. 2015. "Smoking and mortality." *New England Journal of Medicine* 372:631–40.

Caruso, D. B. 2003. "Patriot Act reach now extends beyond terrorism." *San Diego Union-Tribune,* September 15.

Caskey, J. P. 1994. *Fringe Banking: Check-Cashing Outlets, Pawnshops, and the Poor.* New York: Sage.

Cassidy, T., and L. Wright. 2008. "Graduate employment status and health: A longitudinal analysis of the transition from student." *Social Psychology of Education* 11:181–91.

Cast, A. D., D. Schweingruber, and N. Berns. 2006. "Childhood physical punishment and problem solving in marriage." *Journal of Interpersonal Violence* 21:244–61.

Castilla, E. J. 2008. "Gender, race, and meritocracy in organizational careers." *American Journal of Sociology* 113:1479–526.

Castor, M. L., et al. 2006. "A nationwide population-based study identifying health disparities between American Indians/Alaska Natives and the general populations living in select urban counties." *American Journal of Public Health* 96:1478–84.

Catalano, S. 2013. "intimate partner violence." Bureau of Justice Statistics website.

Caton, C. L. M., et al. 2005. "Risk factors for long-term homelessness." *American Journal of Public Health* 95:1753–59.

Cavanagh, S. E., K. S. Schiller, and C. Riegle-Crumb. 2006. "Marital transitions, parenting, and schooling." *Sociology of Education* 79:329–54.

Ceballo, R., T. A. Dahl, M. T. Aretakis, and C. Ramirez. 2001. "Inner-city children's exposure to community violence." *Journal of Marriage and the Family* 63:927–40.

Center for Community Change. 2005. *"Issues: The Native American project."* CCC website.

Center for Marriage and Families. 2005. "Family structure and children's educational outcomes." Institute for American Values website.

Center On Budget and Policy Priorities. 2016. "Chart book: TANF at 20." COBP website.

Centers for Disease Control. 1995b. "Health-care provider advice on tobacco use to persons aged 10-22 years—United States, 1993." *Morbidity and Mortality Weekly Report,* 44 (November 10).

——. 2006b. "Youth exposure to alcohol advertising on radio." *Morbidity and Mortality Weekly Report,* 55 (September 1).

Central Intelligence Agency. 2016. *The World Factbook.* CIA website.

Cha, Y. 2010. "Reinforcing separate spheres: The effect of spousal overwork on men's and women's employment in dual-earner households." *American Sociological Review* 75:303-29.

Cha, Y. 2013. "Overwork and the persistence of gender segregation in occupations." *Gender & Society* 27: 158-84.

Chan, D. K., C. B. Lam, S. Y. Chow, and S. F. Cheung. 2008. "Examining the job-related, psychological, and physical outcomes of workplace sexual harassment." *Psychology of Women Quarterly* 32:362-76.

Chang, E., C. Chen, E. Greenberger, D. Dooley, and J. Heckhausen. 2006. "What do they want in life? The life goals of a multi-ethnic, multi-generational sample of high school seniors." *Journal of Youth & Adolescence* 35:302-13.

Chang, M. L. 2004. "Growing pains: Cross-national variation in sex segregation in sixteen developing countries." *American Sociological Review* 69:114-37.

Chapman, S., P. Alpers, and M. Jones. 2016. "Association between gun law reforms and intentional firearm deaths in Australia, 1979-2013." *Journal of the American Medical Association* 316:291-99.

Chapple, C. L. 1997. "Dow Corning and the silicone breast implant debacle: A case of corporate crime against women." In *Masculinities and Violence,* ed. Lee H. Bowker, pp. 179-96. Newbury Park, CA: Sage.

Charmaz, K. 1995. "The body, identity, and self: Adapting to impairment." *Sociological Quarterly* 36 (4):657-80.

Chatav, Y., and M. A. Whisman. 2007. "Marital dissolution and psychiatric disorders." *Journal of Divorce & Remarriage* 47:1-13.

Cheadle, J. E. 2008. "Educational investment, family context, and children's math and reading growth from kindergarten through the third grade." *Sociology of Education* 81:1-31.

Cheadle, J. E., and L. B. Whitbeck. 2011. "Alcohol use trajectories and problem drinking over the course of adolescence." *Journal of Health and Social Behavior* 52:228-45.

Chen, E., K. A. Matthews, and W. T. Boyce. 2002. "Socioeconomic differences in children's health." *Psychological Bulletin* 128:295-329.

Chen, H., M. R. Marks, and C. A. Bersani. 1994. "Unemployment classifications and subjective well-being." *Sociological Review* 42 (February):62-78.

Chen, M. J., B. A. Miller, J. W. Grube, and E. D. Waiters. 2006. "Music, substance use, and aggression." *Journal of Studies on Alcohol* 67:373-81.

Chen, R. 1996. "Risk factors of sexual abuse among college students in Taiwan." *Journal of Interpersonal Violence* 11 (March):79-93.

Chenoweth, E., and M. J. Stephan. 2011. *Why Civil Resistance Works.* New York: Columbia University Press.

Chenoweth, K. 2016. "ESSA offers changes that can continue learning gains." *Phi Delta Kappan* 97:38-42.

Chernousenko, V. M. 1991. *Chernobyl: Insight from the Inside.* New York: Springer-Verlag.

Children Now. 2004. "Study finds more Latinos, fewer Asians on prime-time TV." Children Now website.

Chimienti, G., J. A. Nasr, and I. Khalifeh. 1989. "Children's reactions to war-related stress." *Social Psychiatry and Psychiatric Epidemiology* 24 (6):282-87.

Chinman, M. J., R. Weingarten, D. Stayner, and L. Davidson. 2001. "Chronicity reconsidered: Improving person-environment fit through a consumer-run service." *Community Mental Health Journal* 37:215-29.

Chiou, F. Y., and L. S. Rothenberg. 2003. "When pivotal policies meets partisan politics." *American Journal of Political Science* 47:503-22.

Chiroro, P., G. Bohner, G. T. Viki, and C. I. Jarvis. 2004. "Rape myth acceptance and rape proclivity." *Journal of Interpersonal Violence* 19:427-42.

Chou, T., A. Asnaani, and S. G. Hofmann. 2012. "Perception of racial discrimination and psychopathology across three U.S. ethnic minority groups." *Cultural Diversity and Ethnic Minority Psychology* 18:74-81.

Choudhary, E., J. Cohen, and R. M. Bossarte. 2010. "Adverse health outcomes, perpetrator characteristics, and sexual violence victimization among U.S. adults males." *Journal of Interpersonal Violence* 25:1523-41.

Christopher, A. N., and M. R. Wojda. 2008. "Social dominance orientation, right-wing authoritarianism, sexism, and prejudice toward women in the workforce." *Psychology of Women Quarterly* 32:65-73.

Chung, H. 2015. "Education finance reform, education spending, and student performance." *Education and Urban Society* 47:412-32.

Ciarrochi, J., et al. 2016. "The development of compulsive internet use and mental health." *Developmental Psychology* 52:272-83.

Clark, C. 1994. "VA secretary vows to find cause of Gulf War syndrome." *San Diego Union-Tribune,* March 30.

Clarke, R. V. 2008. "Improving street lighting to reduce crime in residential areas." *Problem-Oriented Guides for Police*

Response Guide No. 8. Washington, DC: Center for Problem-Oriented Policing.

Clawson, R. A. 2002. "Poor people, black faces." *Journal of Black Studies* 32:352-61.

Clement, M., M. Schwarzfeld, and M. Thompson. 2011. *The National Summit on Justice Reinvestment and Public Safety.* Bureau of Justice Statistics website.

Clifford, A. M. 2001. *Introducing Feminist Theology.* Maryknoll, NY: Orbis Books.

Clifton, J. 2016. "Explaining Trump: widespread government corruption." Pew Research Center website.

Cloud, J., and J. Morse. 2001. "Home sweet school." *Time,* August 27, pp. 47-54.

Clouston, S. A.P., et al. 2015. "Educational inequalities in health behaviors." *Journal of Health and Social Behavior* 56:323-40.

Cohen, A. 2004. "The supreme struggle." *New York Times,* January 18.

Cohen, C. 2003. "Winks, nods, disguises—and racial preference." *Commentary* 116:34-39.

Cohen, J. E. 1997. *Presidential Responsiveness and Public Policy-Making.* Ann Arbor: University of Michigan Press.

Cohen, L. E., and M. Felson. 1979. "Social change and crime rate trends." *American Sociological Review* 44 (August):588-607.

Cohen, P. N., and M. L. Huffman. 2003. "Occupational segregation and the devaluation of women's work across U.S. labor markets." *Social Forces* 81:881-908.

Cohen, R. A., M. E. Martinez, and E. P. Zammitti. 2016. "Health insurance coverage." National Center for Health Statistics website.

Cohen, S. 1984. "Cocaine Anonymous." *Drug Abuse and Alcoholism Newsletter* 13 (3).

Coker, T. R., et al. 2009. "Perceived racial/ethnic discrimination among fifth-grade students and its association with mental health." *American Journal of Public Health* 99:878-84.

Colborn, T., D. Dumanoski, and J. Peterson Myers. 1997. *Our Stolen Future.* New York: Plume.

Cole, C. V. 1995. "Sexual abuse of middle school students." *School Counselor* 42 (January):239-45.

Coleman, M. G. 2003. "Job skill and black male wage discrimination." *Social Science Quarterly* 84:892-906.

——. 2004. "Racial discrimination in the workplace." *Industrial Relations* 43:660-89.

Coleman-Jensen, A., et al. 2016. "Household food security in the United States in 2015." U.S. Department of Agriculture website.

Coles, J., et al. 2015. "Childhood sexual abuse and its association with adult physical and mental health." *Journal of Interpersonal Violence* 3:1929-44.

Collins, J. L., and V. Mayer. 2010. *Both Hands Tied: Welfare Reform and the Race to the Bottom in the Low-Wage Labor Market.* Chicago: University of Chicago Press.

Collins, M. D., and J. H. Frey. 1992. "Drunken driving and informal social control: The case of peer intervention." *Deviant Behavior* 13 (January–March):73-87.

Collins, R. L., et al. 2016. "Alcohol advertising exposure among middle school-age youth." *Journal of Studies on Alcohol and Drugs* 77: 384-92.

Collins, S. D. 2004. "Dissuading state support of terrorism." *Studies in Conflict and Terrorism* 27:1-18.

Collins, W., et al. 2007. "The physical science behind climate change." *Scientific American,* August, pp. 64-73.

Collom, E. 2005. "The ins and outs of homeschooling." *Education and Urban Society* 37:307-335.

Commager, H. S., ed. 1945. *The Pocket History of the Second World War.* New York: Pocket Books.

Committee for the Compilation of Materials on Damage Caused by the Atomic Bombs in Hiroshima and Nagasaki. 1981. *The Physical, Medical, and Social Effects of the Atomic Bombings,* trans. Eisei Ishikawa and David L. Swain. New York: Basic Books.

Commoner, B. 1971. *The Closing Circle.* New York: Alfred A. Knopf.

Condon, G. E. 2005. "Bush says spying is needed to guard U.S." *San Diego Union-Tribune,* December 20.

Condron, D. J., and V. J. Roscigno. 2003. "Disparities within: Spending inequality and achievement in an urban school district." *Sociology of Education* 76:18-36.

Conger, R. D., F. O. Lorenz, G. H. Elder Jr., J. N. Melby, R. L. Simons, and K. J. Conger. 1991. "A process model of family economic pressure and early adolescent alcohol use." *Journal of Early Adolescence* 11 (November): 430-49.

Connor, P. 2016a. "About six-in-ten Syrians are now displaced from their homes." Pew Research Center website.

Connor, P. 2016b. "Nearly 1 in 100 worldwide are now displaced from their homes." Pew Research Center website.

Connors, G. J., J. S. Tonigan, and W. R. Miller. 2001. "A longitudinal model of intake symptomatology, AA participation, and outcome." *Journal of Studies on Alcohol* 62:817-25.

Coohey, C. 2004. "Battered mothers who physically abuse their children." *Journal of Interpersonal Violence* 19:943-52.

Cook, T. E. 1998. *Governing with the News: The News Media as a Political Institution.* Chicago: University of Chicago Press.

Coolbaugh, K., and C. J. Hansel. 2000. "The comprehensive strategy: Lessons learned from pilot sites." *Juvenile Justice Bulletin.* Washington, DC: Government Printing Office.

Copeland, W. E., et al. 2013. "Adult psychiatric outcomes of bullying and being bullied by peers in childhood and adolescence." *JAMA Psychiatry* 70:419-26.

Corliss, H. L., C. S. Goodenow, L. Nichols, and S. B. Austin. 2011. "High burden of homelessness among sexual-minority adolescents." *American Journal of Public Health* 101: 1683–89.

Corrigan, P. 2004. "How stigma interferes with mental health care." *American Psychologist* 59:614–25.

Corso, P. S., V. J. Edwards, X. Fang, and J. A. Mercy. 2008. "Health-related quality of life among adults who experienced maltreatment during childhood." *American Journal of Public Health* 98:1094–1100.

Costa, J. 2013. "What's the cost of a seat in Congress?" MapLight website.

Costello, D. M., L. C. Dierker, B. L. Jones, and J. S. Rose. 2008. "Trajectories of smoking from adolescence to early adulthood and their psychosocial risk factors." *Health Psychology* 27:811–18.

Costello, R. M. 2006. "Long-term mortality from alcoholism." *Journal of Studies on Alcohol* 67:694–99.

Cotter, D. A., J. M. Hermsen, S. Ovadia, and R. Vanneman. 2001. "The glass ceiling effect." *Social Forces* 80:655–82.

Couch, K. A., and R. Fairlie. 2010. "Last hired, first fired? Black-white unemployment and the business cycle." *Demography* 47:227–47.

Council on Contemporary Families. 2003. "U.S. husbands first, U.S. government last in support for working wives." *Work and Family Newsbrief*, June, p. 4.

Coverdill, J .E., C. A. Lopez, and M. A. Petrie. 2011. "Race, ethnicity and the quality of life in America, 1972–2008." *Social Forces* 89:783–805.

Coyle, J. 2004. "Fox News' use of 'fair and balanced' challenged legally." *The America's Intelligence Wire,* July 20.

Cozzarelli, C., A. V. Wilkinson, and M. J. Tagler. 2001. "Attitudes toward the poor and attributions for poverty." *Journal of Social Issues* 57:207–27.

Craig, C. L., R. C. Brownson, S. E. Cragg, and A. L. Dunn. 2002. "Exploring the effect of the environment on physical activity." *American Journal of Preventive Medicine* 23:36–43.

Crandall, B. 2006. *Gender and Religion.* Charleston, SC: BookSurge.

Crary, D. 2016. "Survey doubles estimate of transgender adults." *San Diego Union-Tribune*, July 1.

Crawford, J. A. 2014. "DSM-IV alcohol dependence and marital dissolution." *Journal of Studies on Alcohol and Drugs* 75:520–29.

Crawford, T., and M. Naditch. 1970. "Relative deprivation, powerlessness, and militancy: The psychology of social protest." *Psychiatry* 33 (May):208–23.

Crofford, L. J. 2007. "Violence, stress, and somatic syndromes." *Trauma, Violence, & Abuse* 8:299–313.

Croghan, I. T., et al. 2006. "Is smoking related to body image satisfaction, stress, and self-esteem in young adults?" *American Journal of Health Behavior* 30:322–33.

Cronin, T. E., and M. A. Genovese. 1998. *The Paradoxes of the American Presidency.* New York: Oxford University Press.

Crosnoe, R. 2006. "The connection between academic failure and adolescent drinking in secondary school." *Sociology of Education* 79:44–60.

Crowne, S. S., et al. 2011. "Concurrent and long-term impact of intimate partner violence on employment stability." *Journal of Interpersonal Violence* 26:1282–1304.

Crusto, C. A., et al. 2010. "Posttraumatic stress among young urban children exposed to family violence and other potentially traumatic events." *Journal of Traumatic Stress* 23:716–24.

Cullen, H. 2016. "Think it's hot? Just wait." *The New York Times*, Aug. 21.

Cummings, P., D. C. Grossman, F. P. Rivara, and T. D. Koepsell. 1997. "State gun safe storage laws and child mortality due to firearms." *Journal of the American Medical Association* 278 (October 1):1084–86.

Cunradi, C. B., R. Caetano, and J. Schafer. 2002. "Religious affiliation, denominational homogamy, and intimate partner violence among U.S. couples." *Journal for the Scientific Study of Religion* 41:139–51.

Curtis, K., and B. C. Wilding. 2007. *Is It in Us?* New York: Body Burden Work Group and Commonweal Biomonitoring Resource Center.

Cussen, M., and W. Block. 2000. "Legalize drugs now!" *American Journal of Economics and Sociology* 59:525–36.

Dales, R., et al. 2004. "Air pollution and sudden infant death syndrome." *Pediatrics* 113:628–31.

Dalgard, O. S., et al. 2009. "Job demands, job control, and mental health in an 110-year follow-up study." *Work & Stress* 23:284–96.

Dalla, R. L. 2000. "Exposing the 'Pretty Woman' myth: A qualitative examination of the lives of female streetwalking prostitutes." *Journal of Sex Research* 37:333–43.

———. 2001. "Et tu Brute? A qualitative analysis of streetwalking prostitutes' interpersonal support networks." *Journal of Family Issues* 22:1066–85.

Daneback, K., A. Cooper, and S. Manisson. 2005. "An Internet study of cybersex participants." *Archives of Sexual Behavior* 34:321–28.

D'Augelli, A. R., and A. H. Grossman. 2001. "Disclosure of sexual orientation, victimization, and mental health among lesbian, gay, and bisexual older adults." *Journal of Interpersonal Violence* 16:1008–28.

D'Augelli, A. R., A. H. Grossman, and M. T. Starks. 2006. "Childhood gender atypicality, victimization, and PTSD among lesbian, gay, and bisexual youth." *Journal of Interpersonal Violence* 21:1462–82.

Davenport, C. 1995. "Assessing the military's influence on political repression." *Journal of Political and Military Sociology* 23 (Summer):119–44.

Davidson, R. C., and E. L. Lewis. 1997. "Affirmative action and other special consideration admissions at the University of California, Davis, School of Medicine." *Journal of the American Medical Association* 278 (October 8):1153–58.

Davies, J. C. 1962. "Toward a theory of revolution." *American Sociological Review* 27 (February):5–19.

Davies, S., and N. Guppy. 1997. "Fields of study, college selectivity, and student inequalities in higher education." *Social Forces* 75 (June):1417–38.

Davies, S., and J. Tanner. 2003. "The long arm of the law." *The Sociological Quarterly* 44:385–404.

Davis, A. 2016. "In U.S., concern about crime climbs To 15-year high." Gallup Poll website.

Davis, A. J., et al. 1995. "Home care for the urban chronically ill elderly in the People's Republic of China." *International Journal of Aging and Human Development* 41 (4):345–58.

Davis, D. W. 2007. *Negative Liberty: Public Opinion and the Terrorist Attacks on America.* New York: Russell Sage Foundation.

Davis, D. W., and B. D. Silver. 2004. "Civil liberties vs. security: Public opinion in the context of the terrorist attacks on America." *American Journal of Political Science* 48:28–46.

Davis, J. J., V. J. Roscigno, and G. Wilson. 2016. "American Indian poverty in the contemporary United States." *Sociological Forum* 31:5–28.

Davis, K. C., J. Norris, W. H. George, J. Martell, and J. R. Heiman. 2006. "Men's likelihood of sexual aggression." *Aggressive Behavior* 32:581–89.

Davis, N. J. 1993. *Prostitution: An International Handbooki on Trends, Problems, and Policies.* Westport, CT: Greenwood.

Davison, T. E., and M. P. McCabe. 2005. "Relationships between men's and women's body image and their psychological, social, and sexual functioning." *Sex Roles* 52:463–75.

Dawood, K., R. C. Pillard, C. Horvath, W. Revelle, and J. M. Bailey. 2000. "Familial aspects of male homosexuality." *Archives of Sexual Behavior* 29:155–64.

Day, A. 1991. "Morality, war: Do they mix?" *Los Angeles Times,* January 15.

Death Penalty Information Center. 2016. "Facts about the death penalty." Death Penalty Information Center website.

DeBell, M. 2008. "Children living without their fathers." *Social Indicators* 87:427–43.

Degenhardt, L., C. Day, E. Conroy, and S. Gilmour. 2006. "Examining links between cocaine use and street-based sex work in New South Wales, Australia." *Journal of Sex Research* 43:107–14.

Dehaven-Smith, L. 2011. "Myth and reality of whistleblower protections." *Public Integrity* 13:207–20.

Dekeseredy, W. S., and A. HallSanchez. 2016. "Adult pornography and violence against women in the heartland." *Violence Against Women*, published online.

Del Castillo, D. 2001. "Pakistan's Islamic colleges provide the Taliban's spiritual fire." *Chronicle of Higher Education* 48:A19–21.

Del Rosso, J. 2014. "The toxicity of torture." *Social Forces* 93:383–404.

Della Giusta, M., M. L. Di Tommaso, I. Shima, and S. Strom. 2007. "What money buys: Clients of street sex workers in the US." *Memorandum,* No. 10/2006. Department of Economics, University of Oslo.

DellaVigna, S., and E. Kaplan. 2006. "The Fox news effect: Media bias and voting." NBER Working Paper No. 12169. NBER website.

Demarest, J., and R. Allen. 2000. "Body image: Gender, ethnic, and age differences." *Journal of Social Psychology* 140:465–72.

Demerouti, E., S. Geurts, A. Bakker, and M. Euwema. 2004. "The impact of shiftwork on work-home conflict, job attitudes, and health." *Ergonomics* 47:987–1002.

De Micheli, D., and M. L. Formigoni. 2002. "Are reasons for the first use of drugs and family circumstances predictors of future use patterns?" *Addictive Behaviors* 27:87–100.

DeMuth, S., and D. Steffensmeier. 2004. "The impact of gender and race-ethnicity in the pretrial release process." *Social Problems* 51:222–42.

DeNavas-Walt, C., R. W. Cleveland, and M. I. Roemer. 2001. "Money income in the United States: 2000." *Current Population Reports.* Washington, DC: Government Printing Office.

DeNavas-Walt, C., and B. D. Proctor. 2015. *Income and poverty in the United States: 2014.* U.S. Census Bureau website.

DeParle, J. 2009. "Welfare aid isn't growing as economy drops off." *The New York Times,* Feb.2.

Dentler, R. A., and P. Cutright. 1965. "Social effects of nuclear war." In *The New Sociology,* ed. I. L. Horowitz, pp. 409–26. New York: Oxford University Press.

Department of Defense. 2016. "DOD releases 2014 annual report on suicide." DOD website.

Desilver, D. 2014. "America unions membership declines as public support fluctuates." Pew Research Center website.

DeSilver, D. 2015. "How Americans are—and aren't—making ecofriendly lifestyle changes." Pew Research Center website.

Desilver, D. 2016. "More older Americans are working, and working more, than they used to." Pew Research Center website.

Desmond, M., and R. T. Kimbro. 2015. "Eviction's fallout: housing, hardship, and health." *Social Forces* 94: 295–324.

DeStafano, L., and D. Colasanto. 1990. "Unlike 1975, today most Americans think men have it better." *Gallup Poll Monthly,* February, 293.

de Tocqueville, A. 1955. *The Old Regime and the French Revolution.* New York: Anchor Books.

Deutsch, C. H. 1990. "Saying no to the 'mommy track.'" *New York Times,* January 28.

Dew, M. A., et al. 2001. "Prevalence and risk of depression and anxiety-related disorders during the first three years after heart transplantation." *Psychosomatics* 42:300-13.

Dey, J. G., and C. Hill. 2007. *Behind the Pay Gap.* Washington, DC: AAUW Educational Foundation.

Dickens, W. T., and J. R. Flynn. 2006. "Black Americans reduce the racial IQ gap." *Psychological Science* 17:913-20.

Diekman, A. B., and S. K. Murnen. 2004. "Learning to be little women and little men: The inequitable gender equality of nonsexist children's literature." *Sex Roles* 50:373-85.

Diem, C., and J. M. Pizarro. 2010. "Social structure and family homicides." *Journal of Family Violence* 25:521-32.

Diener, E., M. Diener, and C. Diener. 1995. "Factors predicting the subjective well-being of nations." *Journal of Personality and Social Psychology* 69:851-64.

DiMaio, V. J. 2000. "Homicidal asphyxia." *American Journal of Forensic and Medical Pathology* 21 (March):1-4.

Distefan, J. M., J. P. Pierce, and E. A. Gilpin. 2004. "Do favorite movie stars influence adolescent smoking initiation?" *American Journal of Public Health* 94:1239-44.

Dittmar, H., E. Halliwell, and S. Ive. 2006. "Does Barbie make girls want to be thin? The effect of experimental exposure to images of dolls on the body image of 5- to 8-year-old girls." *Developmental Psychology* 42:283-92.

Dixon, J., C. Gordon, and T. Khomusi. 1995. "Sexual symmetry in psychiatric diagnosis." *Social Problems* 42 (August):429-49.

Dixon, K. A., and C. E. Van Horn. 2003. "The disposable worker: Living in a job-loss economy." *Heldrich Work Trends Survey* 6, no. 2.

Doan, L., A. Loehr, and L.R. Miller. 2014. "Formal rights and informal privileges for same-sex couples." *American Sociological Review* 79: 1172-95.

Dobbin, F., and E. L. Kelly. 2007. "How to stop harassment: Professional construction of legal compliance in organizations." *American Journal of Sociology* 112: 1203-43.

Dohrenwend, B. P., et al. 2006. "The psychological risks of Vietnam for U.S. veterans." *Science* 313:979-82.

Dokqupil, T. 2012. "Is the onslaught making us crazy?" *Newsweek,* July 16.

Domhoff, G. W. 1990. *The Power Elite and the State: How Policy Is Made in America.* New York: Aldine de Gruyter.

Domina, T., and K. Koch. 2002. "Convenience and frequency of recycling." *Environment and Behavior* 34:216-38.

Donchin, Y., et al. 1995. "A look into the nature and causes of human errors in the intensive care unit." *Critical Care Medicine* 23 (February):294-300.

Donnerstein, E. 1980. "Pornography and violence against women: Experimental studies." *Annals of the New York Academy of Sciences* 347:227-88.

Donnerstein, E., and D. Linz. 1984. "Sexual violence in the media: A warning." *Psychology Today* (January):14-15.

Donohue, L. K. 2008. *The Cost of Counterterrorism: Power, Politics, and Liberty.* Cambridge, UK: Cambridge University Press.

Doodson, L.J., and A.P.C. Davies. 2014. "Different challenges, different well-being." *Journal of Divorce & Remarriage* 55:49-63.

Dooley, D., K. A. Ham-Rowbottom, and J. Prause. 2001. "Underemployment and depression." *Journal of Health and Social Behavior* 41:421-36.

Doran, K., and J. Price. 2014. "Pornography and marriage." *Journal of Family and Economic Issues* 35:489-98.

Dordick, G. A. 2002. "Recovering from homelessness: Determining the 'quality of sobriety' in a transitional housing program." *Qualitative Sociology* 25:7-32.

Dorius, C. J., S. J. Bahr, J. P. Hoffman, and E. L. Harmon. 2004. "Parenting practices as moderators of the relationship between peers and adolescent marijuana use." *Journal of Marriage and Family* 66:163-78.

Dover, E. D. 1998. *The Presidential Election of 1996: Clinton's Incumbency and Television.* Westport, CT: Praeger.

Downey, L., and B. Hawkins. 2008. "Race, income, and environmental inequality in the United States." *Sociological Perspectives* 51:759-81.

Doyle, R. 2002. "Bad things happen." *Scientific American,* June, p. 26.

Drew, D., and D. Weaver. 2006. "Voter learning in the 2004 presidential election." *Journalism and Mass Communication Quarterly* 83:25-42.

Drucker, P. F. 1968. *The Age of Discontinuity.* New York: Harper and Row.

Drug Enforcement Administration. 2002. "Flunitrazepam (Rohypnol)." DEA website.

Duke, A. A., et al. 2011. "Alcohol dose and aggression." *Journal of Studies on Alcohol and Drugs* 72:34-43.

Duncan, G. J., and K. Magnuson. 2011. "The long reach of early childhood poverty." *Pathways,* Winter, pp. 22-27.

Dunifon, R., A. Kalil, and A. Bajracharya. 2005. "Maternal working conditions and child well-being in welfare-leaving families." *Developmental Psychology* 41:851-59.

Dunifon, R.E., and L. Kowaleski-Jones. 2002. "Who's in the house?" *Child Development* 73:1249-64.

Dunn, J., J. Golding, L. Davies, and T. G. O'Connor. 2000. "Distribution of accidents, injuries, and illnesses by family type." *Pediatrics* 106:68-72.

Durán, M., M. Moya, and J. L. Magias. 2011. "It's his right, it's her duty: Benevolent sexism and the justification of traditional sexual roles." *Journal of Sex Research* 48:470-78.

DuRant, R. H., et al. 2008. "Party behaviors and characteristics and serial drunkenness among college students." *Journal of Studies on Alcohol and Drugs* 69:91-99.

Durkheim, E. 1933. *The Division of Labor in Society,* trans. George Simpson. New York: Free Press.

Durose, M. R., et al. 2005. *Family Violence Statistics.* Washington, DC: Government Printing Office.

Durose, M. R., E. L. Smith, and P. A. Langan. 2007. "Contacts between police and the public, 2005." *Bureau of Justice Statistics Special Report,* April.

Dutton, D. G., E. O. Boyanowsky, and M. H. Bond. 2005. "Extreme mass homicide: From military massacre to genocide." *Aggression and Violent Behavior* 10:437–73.

Dutton, M. A., S. Kaltman, L. A. Goodman, K. Weinfurt, and N. Vankos. 2005. "Patterns of intimate partner violence." *Violence and Victims* 20:483–97.

Duwe, G. 2015. "The benefits of keeping idle hands busy." *Crime and Delinquency* 61:559–86.

Dye, T. R. 1995. *Who's Running America?* Englewood Cliffs, NJ: Prentice-Hall.

Eaker, E. D., L. M. Sullivan, M. Kelly-Hayes, R. B. D'Agostino, and E. J. Benjamin. 2004. "Anger and hostility predict the development of atrial fibrillation in men in the Framingham Offspring Study." *Circulation* 109:1267–71.

Earls, C. M., and H. David. 1989. "A psychological study of male prostitution." *Archives of Sexual Behavior* 18 (5):401–20.

Eddings, J. 1995. "A persistent stealth racism is poisoning black-white relations." *U.S. News and World Report,* October 23.

Edelhertz, H. 1983. "White-collar and professional crime." *American Behavioral Scientist* 27 (October–November):109–28.

Edelstein, M. E. 1988. *Contaminated Communities: The Social and Psychological Impacts of Residential Toxic Exposure.* Boulder, CO: Westview Press.

Editorial Projects in Education Research Center. 2006. "State policies on standards-based education over the past decade found to have a positive relationship with gains in student achievement." Education Week website.

Education Week. 1997. "Quality Counts: A Report Card on the Condition of Public Education in the 50 States." Education Week website.

——. 2000. *Quality Counts 2000: Who Should Teach?* Education Week website.

——. 2003. "To close the gap, quality counts." Educational Week website.

Education Week Research Center. 2016. "2016 education rankings put states, nation to the test." EWRC website.

Edwards, G. C., III, and B. D. Wood. 1999. "Who influences whom? The president, Congress, and the media." *American Political Science Review* 93 (June):327–44.

Eggen, D. 2012. "Lobbying dips sharply in 2011." *Washington Post,* January 26.

Egley, A., J.C. Howell, and M. Harris. 2014. "Highlights of the 2012 national youth gang survey." Office of Juvenile Justice and Delinquency Prevention website.

Ehrenhalt, A. 1997. "Big numbers that haunt the government." *Governing Magazine,* January, pp. 7–12.

Ehrenreich, B. 1999. "Nickel-and-dimed: On (not) getting by in America." *Harper's Magazine,* January, pp. 37–52.

Eichenwald, K. 2002. "White-collar defense stance: The criminal-less crime." *New York Times,* March 3.

Eisen, S. V., et al. 2012. "Mental and physical health status and alcohol and drug use following return from deployment to Iraq or Afghanistan." *American Journal of Public Health* 102:566–73.

Eisikovitz, Z. C., J. L. Edleson, E. Guttmann, and M. Sela-Amit. 1991. "Cognitive styles and socialized attitudes of men who batter." *Family Relations* 40 (January):72–77.

Eisler, P., and M. Kelley. 2006. "Public wary of links with lobbyists." *USA Today,* October 18.

Eitle, D., S. J. D'Alessio, and L. Stolzenberg. 2006. "Economic segregation, race, and homicide." *Social Science Quarterly* 87:638–57.

El-Bassel, N., N. Guterman, D. Bargal, and K.-H. Su. 1998. "Main and buffering effects of emotional support on job- and health-related strains." *Employee Assistance Quarterly* 13 (3):1–18.

Eliason, M. J., S. L. Dibble, and P. A. Robertson. 2011. "Lesbian, gay, bisexual, and transgender (LGBT) physicians' experiences in the workplace." *Journal of Homosexuality* 58:1355–71.

Ellis, B. J., et al. 2003. "Does father absence place daughters at special risk for early sexual activity and teenage pregnancy?" *Child Development* 74:801–21.

Ellison, C. G., J. P. Bartkowski, and K. L. Anderson. 1999. "Are there religious variations in domestic violence?" *Journal of Family Issues* 20 (January):87–113.

Ellison, C. G., and D. A. Powers. 1994. "The contact hypothesis and racial attitudes among black Americans." *Social Science Quarterly* 75 (June):385–400.

Elms, A. C. 1972. *Social Psychology and Social Relevance.* Boston: Little, Brown.

Emerson, M. O., G. Yancey, and K. J. Chai. 2001. "Does race matter in residential segregation?" *American Sociological Review* 66:922–35.

Emery, M. 2006. *The Future of Schools: How Communities and Staff Can Transform Their School Districts.* New York: Rowman & Littlefield.

Engardio, P. 2006. "Outsourcing: Job killer or innovation boost?" *Business Week Online,* November 9.

Engel, J. 1989. *Addicted: Kids Talking about Drugs in Their Own Words.* New York: Tom Doherty.

Engelman, R. 2009. "Fertility falls, population rises, future uncertain." In *Vital Signs, 2009,* ed. L. Starke, pp. 83–85. Washington, DC: Worldwatch Institute.

Entwisle, D. R., and K. L. Alexander. 1992. "Summer setback: Race, poverty, school composition, and mathematics achievement in the first two years of school." *American Sociological Review* 57 (February):72–84.

Environmental Protection Agency. 2013. "The national rivers and streams assessment." EPA website.

Environmental Protection Agency. 2015. "Air quality guide for ozone." EPA website.

Epstein, C. F. 2007. "Great divides: The cultural, cognitive, and social bases of the global subordination of women." *American Sociological Review* 72:1–22.

Epstein, D. J. 2003. "Secret ingredients." *Scientific American,* August, pp. 22–23.

Epstein, J. F., and J. C. Groerer. 1997. "Heroin abuse in the United States." *OAS Working Paper.* Rockville, MD: SAMHSA.

Epstein, P. R. 2000. "Is global warming harmful to health?" *Scientific American,* August, pp. 50–57.

Equal Employment Opportunity Commission. 2013. "Summary of state and local goverment full-time employment." EEOC website.

Ericson, M., and F. Hossain. 2003. "In perspective: America's conflicts." *New York Times,* April 20.

Erlanger, S. 1999. "The guesses that turned out wrong." *New York Times,* March 28.

Essed, P. 1991. *Understanding Everyday Racism: An Interdisciplinary Theory.* Newbury Park, CA: Sage.

Esses, V. M., P. M. Brochu, and K. R. Dickson. 2011. *Analyses of Social Issues and Public Policy.* Online journal.

Etzion, D. 2003. "Annual vacation: Duration of relief from job stressors and burnout." *Anxiety, Stress, and Coping* 16:213–26.

Evans, G. W. 2004. "The environment of childhood poverty." *American Psychologist* 59:77–92.

Evans, G. W., J. Brooks-Gunn, and P. K. Klebanov. 2011. "Stressing out the poor." *Pathways,* Winter, pp. 16–21.

Evans, M.D.R., J. Kelley, and J. Sikora. 2014. "Scholarly culture and academic performance in 42 nations." *Social Forces* 92:1573–1605.

Evans, N., A. Farkas, E. Gilpin, C. Berry, and J. P. Pierce. 1995. "Influence of tobacco marketing and exposure to smokers on adolescent susceptibility to smoking." *Journal of the National Cancer Institute* 87 (October):l538–45.

Evans-Campbell, T., T. Lindhorst, B. Huang, and K. L. Walters. 2006. "Interpersonal violence in the lives of urban American Indian and Alaska Native women." *American Journal of Public Health* 96:1416–22.

Even-Chen, M. S., and H. Itzhaky. 2007. "Exposure to terrorism and violent behavior among adolescents in Israel." *Journal of Community Psychology* 35:43–55.

Ewan, C., E. Lowy, and J. Reid. 1991. "Falling out of culture: The effects of repetition strain injury on sufferers' roles and identity." *Sociology of Health and Illness* 13 (June): 168–92.

Fagan, A. A. 2003. "Short- and long-term effects of adolescent violent victimization experienced within the family and community." *Violence and Victims* 18:445–59.

——. 2005. "The relationship between adolescent physical abuse and criminal offending." *Journal of Family Violence* 20:279–90.

Fagin, D. 2008. "China's children of smoke." *Scientific American,* August, pp. 72–79.

——, and M. Lavelle. 1999. *Toxic Deception: How the Chemical Industry Manipulates Science, Bends the Law, and Endangers Your Health.* Monroe, ME: Common Courage Press.

Fallis, R. K., and S. Opotow. 2003. "Are students failing in school or are schools failing students?" *Journal of Social Issues* 59:103–20.

Falsani, C. 1996. "Churches, clergy split on capital punishment." *Chicago Tribune,* May 24.

Fang, X., and P. S. Corso. 2008. "Gender differences in the connections between violence experienced as a child and perpetration of intimate partner violence in young adulthood." *Journal of Family Violence* 23:303–13.

Farkas, G. 2004. "The black-white test score gap." *Contexts* 3:12–19.

Farley, J. E., and G. D. Squires. 2005. "Fences and neighbors: Segregation in 21st-century America." *Contexts* 4:33–39.

Farley, M., et al. 2011. "Comparing sex buyers with men who don't buy sex." Paper presented at Psychologists for Social Responsibility annual meeting, July 15.

Farley, R. 2011. "The waning of American apartheid?" *Contexts* 10:36–43.

Farr, K. 2009. "Extreme war rape in today's civil-war-torn states." *Gender Issues* 26:1–41.

Fausto-Sterling, A. 1992. *Myths of Gender: Biological Theories about Women and Men.* New York: Basic Books.

Fearon, J., and D. Laitin. 2002. "A world at war." *Harper's Magazine,* March, p. 84.

Feder, B. J. 1991. "In the clutches of the superfund mess." *New York Times,* June 16.

Federal Bureau of Investigation. 2002. *Crime in the United States: 2002.* FBI website.

——. 2009b. "Move over Mafia: The new face of organized crime." FBI website.

——. 2010. "Smishing and vishing and other cyber scams to watch out for this holiday." FBI website.

——. 2011. "Domestic terrorism: Focus on militia extremism." FBI website.

——. 2015a. "Crime in the United States, 2014." FBI website.

——. 2015b. "Latest hate crime statistics available. FBI website.

Federal Election Commission. 2016. "Pac Count–1974 to present." FEC website.

Federal Interagency Forum on Child and Family Statistics. 2015. *America's Children.* Washington, DC: Government Printing Office.

Feeney, J. A. 2000. "Implications of attachment style for patterns of health and illness." *Child: Care, Health, and Development* 26:277–88.

Feld, L., and N. Wilcox. 2008. *Netroots Rising: How a Citizen Army of Bloggers and Online Activists Is Changing American Politics.* Westport, CT: Praeger.

Fell, J.C., et al. 2016. "Assessing the impact of twenty underage drinking laws." *Journal of Studies on Alcohol and Drugs* 71:249–60.

Felland, L. E., et al. 2003. "The resilience of the health care safety net, 1996–2001." *Health Services Research* 38:489–502.

Felson, R. B., and S. F. Messner. 2000. "The control motive in intimate partner violence." *Social Psychology Quarterly* 63:86–94.

Ferber, A. L. 2000. "Racial warriors and the weekend warriors: The construction of masculinity in mythopoetic and white supremacist discourse." *Men and Masculinities* 3:30–56.

Ferguson, C. J., and R. D. Hartley. 2009. "The pleasure is momentary . . . the expense damnable?: The influence of pornography on rape and sexual assault." *Aggression and Violent Behavior* 14:323–29.

Ferguson, M. 2011. "You cannot leave it at the office: Spillover and crossover of coworker incivility." *Journal of Organizational Behavior* 33:571–88.

Fergusson, D. M., L. J. Horwood, and E. M. Rider. 2005. "Partner violence and mental health outcomes in a New Zealand birth cohort." *Journal of Marriage and the Family* 67:1103–19.

Fernandez-Mateo, I. 2009. "Cumulative gender disadvantage in contract employment." *American Journal of Sociology* 114:871–923.

Ferraro, K., and J. M. Johnson. 1983. "How women experience battering: The process of victimization." *Social Problems* 30 (3):325–39.

Ferraro, K. F., and J. A. Kelley-Moore. 2003. "Cumulative disadvantage and health: Long-term consequences of obesity?" *American Sociological Review* 68:707–29.

Ferraro, K. F., M. H. Schafer, and L. R. Wilkinson. 2016. "Childhood disadvantage and health problems in middle and later life." *American Sociological Review* 81:107–33.

Ferraro, K. J. 1989. "Policing woman battering." *Social Problems* 36 (February):61–74.

Ferriss, A. L. 2000. "The quality of life among U.S. states." *Social Indicators Research* 49 (January):1–23.

Fiedler, M. E. 2010. *Breaking Through the Stained Glass Ceiling.* New York: Seabury Books.

Field, K. 2004. "Fighting trafficking in the United States." *CQ Researcher* 14:284–85.

Fiel, J.E. 2013. "Decomposing school resegregation." *American Sociological Review* 78:828–48.

Fierro, I., C. Morales, and F. J. Alvarez. 2011. "Alcohol use, illicit drug use, and road rage." *Journal of Studies on Alcohol and Drugs* 72:185–93.

Figlio, D., and C. Hart. 2011. "Does competition improve public schools?" *Education Next* 11:74–80.

Fine, G. A. 2000. "Games and truths: Learning to construct social problems in high school debate." *Sociological Quarterly* 41 (Winter):103–23.

——. 2006. "The chaining of social problems: Solutions and unintended consequences in the age of betrayal." *Social Problems* 53:3–17.

Finkelhor, D., H. Hammer, and A. J. Sedlak. 2008. "Sexually assaulted children: National estimates and characteristics." *NISMART,* August, U.S. Department of Justice.

Finkelhor, D., H. Turner, R. Ormrod, S. Hamby, and K. Kracke. 2009. "Children's exposure to violence." *Juvenile Justice Bulletin,* October.

Finn, J. D., S. B. Gerber, C. M. Achilles, and J. Boyd-Zaharias. 2001. "The enduring effects of small classes." *Teachers College Record* 103:145–83.

Fiscella, K., P. Franks, and C. M. Clancy. 1998. "Skepticism toward medical care and health care utilization." *Medical Care* 36 (February):180–89.

Fischer, M., and B. Geiger. 1996. "Resocializing young offenders in the kibbutz." *International Journal of Offender Therapy and Comparative Criminology* 40 (1):44–53.

Fischer, M. J., and D. S. Massey. 2007. "The effects of affirmative action in higher education." *Social Science Research* 38:531–49.

Fish, J. M. 1995. "Mixed blood." *Psychology Today,* November–December, pp. 55–61.

Fisher, D. E., and M. J. Fisher. 2001. "N: The nitrogen bomb." *Discover,* April, pp. 50–57.

Fitzgerald, M. M., et al. 2005. "Perceptions of parenting versus parent-child interactions among incest survivors." *Child Abuse and Neglect* 29:661–81.

Fitzgerald, S. R., J. A. Haythornthwaite, S. Suchday, and C. K. Ewart. 2003. "Anger in young black and white workers." *Journal of Behavioral Medicine* 26:283–96.

Flavin, C. 1987. "Reassessing nuclear power." In *State of the World 1987,* ed. L. R. Brown, pp. 57–80. New York: W. W. Norton.

——. 2005. "Preface." In *State of the World 2005,* ed. L. Starke, pp. xix–xxi. New York: W. W. Norton.

Flavin, C., and S. Dunn. 1999. "Reinventing the energy system." In *State of the World 1999,* ed. L. R. Brown et al., pp. 22–40. New York: W. W. Norton.

Flavin, C., and R. Engelman. 2009. "The perfect storm." In *State of the World 2009: Into a Warming World,* ed. L. Starke, pp. 5–12. New York: W. W. Norton.

Flavin, P., A. C. Pacek, and B. Radcliff. 2010. "Labor unions and life satisfaction." *Social Indicators Research* 98: 435–49.

——. 2014. ""Assessing the impact of the size and scope of government on human well-being." *Social Forces* 92:1241–58.

Flavin, P., and G. Shufeldt. 2016. "Labor union membership and life satisfaction in the United States." *Labor Studies Journal* 41:171–84.

Flegal, K. M., B. I. Graubard, D. F. Williamson, and M. H. Gail. 2005. "Excess deaths associated with underweight, overweight, and obesity." *Journal of the American Medical Association* 293:1861–67.

Fleury, R. E., C. M. Sullivan, D. I. Bybee, and W. S. Davidson II. 1998. " 'Why don't they just call the cops?' Reasons for differential police contact among women with abusive partners." *Violence and Victims* 13 (Winter):333–46.

Flewelling, R. L., and K. E. Bauman. 1990. "Family structure as a predictor of initial substance use and sexual intercourse in early adolescence." *Journal of Marriage and the Family* 52 (February):171–81.

Flisher, A. J., et al. 1997. "Psychosocial characteristics of physically abused children and adolescents." *Journal of the American Academy of Child and Adolescent Psychiatry* 36 (1):123–31.

Flores, E., et al. 2008. "Perceived discrimination, perceived stress, and mental and physical health among Mexican-origin adults." *Hispanic Journal of Behavioral Science* 30:401–24.

Flynn, C. A., and W. E. Brown. 1991. "The effects of a mandatory alcohol education program on college student problem drinkers." *Journal of Alcohol and Drug Education* 37 (1):15–24.

Flynn, G. 2003. "The reverse-discrimination trap." *Workforce* 82:106–7.

Foerstel, H. N. 2001. *From Watergate to Monicagate.* Westport, CT: Greenwood.

Fogarty, B .J., et al. 2015. "News attention to voter fraud in the 2008 and 2012 US elections." Research & Politics website.

Fokir, M. A. 2011. "Violence against women survey: 2011." United Nations website.

Folke O., S. Hirano, and J. M. Snyder. 2011. "Patronage and elections in U.S. States." *American Political Science Review* 105:567–85.

Fonow, M. M., L. Richardson, and V. A. Wemmerus. 1992. "Feminist rape education: Does it work?" *Gender and Society* 6 (March):108–21.

Ford, E. S., G. Zhao, J. Tsai, and C. Li. 2011. "Low-risk lifestyle behaviors and all-cause mortality." *American Journal of Public Health* 101:1922–29.

Ford, J. A., and R. D. Schroeder. 2009. "Academic strain and non-medical use of prescription stimulants among college students." *Deviant Behavior* 30:26–53.

Ford, M. E., and J. A. Linney. 1995. "Comparative analysis of juvenile sexual offenders, violent nonsexual offenders, and status offenders." *Journal of Interpersonal Violence* 10 (March):56–70.

Forma, P. 2009. "Work, family and intentions to withdraw from the workplace." *International Journal of Social Welfare* 18:183–92.

Forrest, W. 2014. "Cohabitation, relationship quality, and desistance from crime." *Journal of Marriage and Family* 76:539–56.

Forum on Child and Family Statistics. 2016. *America's Children in Brief: Key National Indicators of Well-Being, 2016.* Washington, DC: Government Printing Office.

Foubert J. D., and A. J. Bridges. 2016. "Predicting bystander efficacy and willingness to Intervene in college men and women." *Violence Against Women*, published online.

Fox, S., and M. Duggan. 2013. "The diagnosis difference." Pew Research Center website.

Fragoso, Z. L., et al. 2016. "Burnout and engagement." *Workplace Health and Safety*, June 9.

France, M. 2004. "Close the lawyer loophole: Their ability to reduce legal liability for executives is fueling white-collar crime." *BusinessWeek,* February 2, p. 70.

Francia, P. L., and P. S. Hernson. 2003. "The impact of public finance laws on fundraising in state legislative elections." *American Politics Research* 31:520–39.

Francis, B., and C. Skelton. 2005. *Reassessing Gender and Achievement.* London: Routledge & Kegan Paul.

Francoeur, R. T. 1991. *Becoming a Sexual Person.* 2nd ed. New York: Macmillan.

Frank, K. 2003. " 'Just trying to relax': Masculinity, masculinizing practices, and strip club regulars." *Journal of Sex Research* 40:61–75.

——. 2005. "Exploring the motivations and fantasies of strip club customers in relation to legal regulations." *Archives of Sexual Behavior* 34:487–504.

Frederick, B. 2008. "Constituency population and representation in the U.S. House." *American Politics Research* 36:358–81.

Frederico, C. M. 2006. "Ideology and the affective structure of whites' racial perceptions." *Public Opinion Quarterly* 70:327–53.

Freudenberg, N., J. Daniels, M. Crum, T. Perkins, and B. E. Richie. 2005. "Coming home from jail." *American Journal of Public Health* 95:1725–36.

Freudenburg, W. 2009. "Polluters' shell game." *Worldwatch* 22:17–21.

Freund, K., R. Watson, and D. Rienzo. 1989. "Heterosexuality, homosexuality, and erotic age preference." *Journal of Sex Research* 26 (1):107–17.

Frey, R. S., and A. Al-Roumi. 1999. "Political democracy and the physical quality of life." *Social Indicators Research* 47 (May):73–97.

Frieden, T. R., et al. 2005. "Adult tobacco use levels after intensive tobacco control measures." *American Journal of Public Health* 95:1016–23.

Friedenberg, E. Z. 1972. "The revolt against democracy." In *The Prospect of Youth,* ed. T. J. Cottle, pp. 147–56. Boston: Little, Brown.

Friedland, D. S., and R. H. Price. 2003. "Underemployment: Consequences for the health and well-being of workers." *American Journal of Community Psychology* 32:33–45.

Friedman, M. S., et al. 2011. "A meta-analysis of disparities in childhood sexual abuse, parental physical abuse, and peer victimization among sexual minority and sexual nonminority individuals." *American Journal of Public Health* 101:1481–94.

Friedman, S. 2002. "9/11 boosts focus on interruption risks." *National Underwriter Property and Casualty– Risk and Benefits Management* 106:17.

Friese, B., et al. 2011. "Drinking behavior and sources of alcohol." *Journal of Studies on Alcohol and Drugs* 72:53–60.

Frisco, M. L., and K. Williams. 2003. "Perceived housework equity, marital happiness, and divorce in dual-earner households." *Journal of Family Issues* 24:51–73.

Fritz, G. K. 2003. "Inhalant abuse among children and adolescents." *The Brown University Child and Adolescent Behavior Letter* 19:8.

Frone, M. R. 2006. "Prevalence and distribution of alcohol use and impairment in the workplace." *Journal of Studies on Alcohol* 67:147–56.

Fry, R. 2007. *The Changing Racial and Ethnic Composition of U.S. Public Schools.* Washington, DC: Pew Hispanic Center.

Fulcher, M., E. L. Sutfin, and C. J. Patterson. 2008. "Individual differences in gender development." *Sex Roles* 58:330–41.

Fuller, G. E. 2011. "US can blame itself for anger in the Middle East and start making peace." *Christian Science Monitor,* February 4.

Fullerton, A .S., and K. F. Anderson. 2013. "The role of job insecurity in explanations of racial health inequalities." *Sociological Forum* 28:308–25.

Furnas, J. C. 1965. *The Life and Times of the Late Demon Rum.* New York: Capricorn.

Furstenberg, F. F., Jr., T. D. Cook, J. Eccles, G. H. Elder Jr., and A. Sameroff. 1999. *Managing to Make It: Urban Families and Adolescent Success.* Chicago: University of Chicago Press.

Gabriel, R. A. 1987. *No More Heroes: Madness and Psychiatry in War.* New York: Farrar, Straus, and Giroux.

Gage, A. J. 2016. "Exposure to spousal violence in the family, attitudes and dating violence perpetration among high school students in Port-au-Prince." *Journal of Interpersonal Violence* 31:2445–74.

Galdi, S., A. Maass, and M. Cadinu. 2014. "Objectifying media: their effect on gender role norms and sexual harassment of women." *Psychology of Women Quarterly* 38:398–413.

Galea, S., et al. 2002. "Psychological sequelae of the September 11 terrorist attacks in New York City." *New England Journal of Medicine* 346:982–87.

Gallagher, K. P. 2005. "International trade and air pollution." *Journal of Environmental Management* 77:99–103.

Galliano, G., L. M. Noble, L. A. Travis, and C. Puechl. 1993. "Victim reactions during rape/sexual assault." *Journal of Interpersonal Violence* 8 (March):109–14.

Gallinsky, E., et al. 2005. *Overwork in America.* New York: Families and Work Institute.

Gan, W. Q., et al. 2016. "Exposure to loud noise, bilateral high-frequency hearing loss and coronary heart disease." *Occupational and Environmental Medicine* 73:34–41.

Garcia, M. 2002. "War-stripped, barren Afghan environment will take years to recover." Knight Ridder/Tribune News Service, February 11. Knight Ridder/Tribune website.

Gardner, G. 2006. "Deforestation continues." In *Vital Signs: 2006-2007,* ed. L. Starke, pp. 102–103. New York: W. W. Norton.

Gardner, G., E. Assadourian, and R. Sarin. 2004. "The state of consumption today." In *State of the World 2004,* ed. L. Starke, pp. 3–23. New York: W. W. Norton.

Gardner, G., and B. Halweil. 2000. *Underfed and Overfed: The Global Epidemic of Malnutrition.* Washington, DC: Worldwatch Institute.

Garson, B. 1975. *All the Livelong Day: The Meaning and Demeaning of Routine Work.* New York: Penguin.

Gastil, J., and J. P. Dillard. 1999. "Increasing political sophistication through public deliberation." *Political Communication* 16 (1):3–23.

Gauderman, W. J., et al. 2007. "Effect of exposure to traffic on lung development from 10 to 18 years of age." *The Lancet* 369:571–77.

Gavaler, J. S. 1991. "Effects of alcohol on female endocrine function." *Alcohol Health and Research World* 15 (12): 104–109.

Gawande, A. 2009. "The cost conundrum." *The New Yorker,* June 1, pp. 36–44.

Gegax, T. T., and L. Clemetson. 1998. "The abortion wars come home." *Newsweek,* November 9.

Gellhorn, M. 1959. *The Face of War.* New York: Simon and Schuster.

Gelsema, T. I., et al. 2006. "A longitudinal study of job stress in the nursing profession." *Journal of Nursing Management* 14:289–99.

Gennetian, L. A., L. M. Lopoo, and A. S. London. 2008. "Maternal work hours and adolescents' school outcomes among low-income families in four urban counties." *Demography* 45:31–53.

Gentile, D. A., S. Coyne, and D. A. Walsh. 2011. "Media violence, physical aggression, and relational aggression in school age children." *Aggressive Behavior* 37:193–206.

Genuis, S. J. 2008. "Fielding a current idea: Exploring the public health impact of electromagnetic radiation." *Public Health* 122:113-24.

Gerber, A. S., D. P. Green, and C. W. Larimer. 2008. "Social pressure and voter turnout." *American Political Science Review* 102:33-48.

Gerber, A. S., D. P. Green, and R. Shachar. 2003. "Voting may be habit-forming." *American Journal of Political Science* 47:540-50.

Geronimus, A. T., J. Bound, and C. G. Colen. 2011. "Excess black mortality in the United States and in selected black and white high-poverty areas, 1980-2000." *American Journal of Public Health* 101:720-29.

Gershon, R. R. M., B. Barocas, A. N. Canton, X. Li, and D. Vlahov. 2009. "Mental, physical, and behavioral outcomes associated with perceived work stress in police officers." *Criminal Justice and Behavior* 36:275-89.

Ghosh, J. K. C., M. Wilhelm, and B. Ritz. 2013. "Effects of residential Indoor air quality and household ventilation on preterm birth and term low birth weight in Los Angeles County, California." *American Journal of Public Health* 103:686-94.

Gibbons, F. X., et al. 2014. "Effects of perceived racial discrimination on health status and health behavior." *Health Psychology* 33:11-19.

Ghosh, J. K. C., M. Wilhelm, and B. Ritz. 2013. "Effects of residential Indoor air quality and household ventilation on preterm birth and term low birth weight in Los Angeles County, California." *American Journal of Public Health* 103:686-94.

Gibbons, F. X., et al. 2014. "Effects of perceived racial discrimination on health status and health behavior." *Health Psychology* 33:11-19.

Gibbs, D. A., S. L. Martin, L. L. Kupper, and R. E. Johnson. 2007. "Child maltreatment in enlisted soldiers' families during combat-related deployments." *Journal of the American Medical Association* 298:528-35.

Gibson, J. W. 1994. *Warrior Dreams: Violence and Manhood in Post-Vietnam America.* New York: Hill and Wang.

Gill, D. A., J. S. Picou, and L.A. Ritchie. 2012. "The *Exxon Valdez* and BP oil spills: A comparison of initial social and psychological impacts." *American Behavioral Scientist* 56:3-23.

Gillen, M., E. Lefkowitz, and C. Shearer. 2006. "Does body image play a role in risky sexual behavior and attitudes?" *Journal of Youth and Adolescence* 35:230-42.

Gilligan, J. 2001. "The last mental hospital." *Psychiatric Quarterly* 72:45-61.

Giusta, M. D., M. L. Di Tommaso, I. Shima, and S. Strom. 2009. "What money buys: Clients of street sex workers in the U.S." *Applied Economics* 41:2261-77.

Glantz, S. A., K. W. Kacirk, and C. McCulloch. 2004. "Back to the future: Smoking in the movies in 2002 compared with 1950 levels." *American Journal of Public Health* 94:261-63.

Glosser, G., et al. 2000. "Psychiatric aspects of temporal lobe epilepsy before and after anterior temporal lobectomy." *Journal of Neurological and Neurosurgical Psychiatry* 68 (1):53-8.

Goeders, N. E. 2003. "The impact of stress on addiction." *European Neuropsychopharmacology* 13:435-41.

Gohm, C. L., S. Oishi, J. Darlington, and E. Diener. 1998. "Culture, parental conflict, parental marital status, and the subjective well-being of young adults." *Journal of Marriage and the Family* 60 (May):319-34.

Goldberg, W. A., J. Prause, R. Lucas-Thompson, and A. Himsel. 2008. "Maternal employment and children's achievement in context." *Psychological Bulletin* 134:77-108.

Golden, D. 2006. *The Price of Admission: How America's Ruling Class Buys Its Way into Elite Colleges—and Who Gets Left Outside the Gates.* New York: Crown.

Goldman, N., et al. 2004. "Sex differentials in biological risk factors for chronic disease." *Journal of Women's Health* 13:393-403.

Goldsmith, M. 2004. "Resurrecting RICO: Removing immunity for white-collar crime." *Harvard Journal on Legislation* 41:281-317.

Golge, Z. B., M. F. Yavuz, S. Muderrisoglu, and M. S. Yavuz. 2003. "Turkish university students' attitudes toward rape." *Sex Roles* 49:653-61.

Gomez, O. L., and G. Carrasquilla. 1999. "Factors associated with unjustified Caesarean section in four hospitals in Cali, Colombia." *International Journal of Quality Health Care* 11 (October):385-89.

Gonzalez-Barrera, A. 2015. "More Mexicans leaving than coming to the U.S." Pew Research Center website.

Gordon, J. 2002. "Cool war: Economic sanctions as a weapon of mass destruction." *Harper's Magazine,* November, pp. 43-49.

Gorman, C. 1992. "Danger overhead." *Time,* October 26, p. 70.

Gorman, E. H., and J. A. Kmec. 2009. "Hierarchical rank and women's organizational mobility." *American Journal of Sociology* 114:1428-74.

Gottman, J., et al. 2003. "Correlates of gay and lesbian couples' relationship satisfaction and relationship dissolution." *Journal of Homosexuality* 45:23-44.

Gould, J. B. 2002. "Playing with fire: The civil liberties implications of September 11th." *PAR* 62:74-79.

Gove, W. R., and M P. Geerken. 1977. "The effect of children and employment on the mental health of married men and women." *Social Forces* 56:66-76.

Goyette, K. 2008. "College for some to college for all: Social background, occupational expectations, and educational expectations over time." *Social Science Research* 37:461-84.

Grabe, S., and J. S. Hyde. 2006. "Ethnicity and body dissatisfaction among women in the United States." *Psychological Bulletin* 132:622-40.

Graefe, D. R., and D. T. Lichter. 2007. "When unwed mothers marry." *Journal of Family Issues* 28:595-622.

Graham, H. D., and T. R. Gurr, eds. 1969. *The History of Violence in America.* New York: Bantam.

Graham, K., D. W. Osgood, S. Wells, and T. Stockwell. 2006. "To what extent is intoxication associated with aggression in bars?" *Journal of Studies on Alcohol* 67:382-90.

Grant, B. F., et al. 2004. "The 12-month prevalence and trends in DSM-IV alcohol abuse and dependence." *Drug and Alcohol Dependence* 74:223-34.

Gray, G. C., et al. 2002. "Self-reported symptoms and medical conditions among 11,868 Gulf War-era veterans." *American Journal of Epidemiology* 155:1033-44.

Gray, M., and J. Tudball. 2003. "Family-friendly work practices." *Journal of Industrial Relations* 45:269-91.

Green, K. M., E. E. Doherty, K. A. Zebrak, and M. E. Ensminger. 2011. "Association between adolescent drinking and adult violence." *Journal of Studies on Alcohol and Drugs* 72:701-10.

Green, J. M., and A. R. King. 2009. "Domestic violence and parental divorce as predictors of best friendship qualities among college students." *Journal of Divorce & Remarriage* 50:100-18.

Greenberg, E. S., and L. Grunberg. 1995. "Work alienation and problem alcohol behavior." *Journal of Health and Social Behavior* 36 (March):83-102.

Greenfeld, L. A. 1998. *Alcohol and Crime.* Washington, DC: Government Printing Office.

Greenwood, J. L. 2012. "Parent-child relationships in the context of mid- to late-life parental divorce." *Journal of Divorce & Remarriage* 53:1-17.

Greitemeyer, T. 2009. "Effects of songs with prosocial lyrics on prosocial thoughts, affect, and behavior." *Journal of Experimental Social Psychology* 45:186-90.

Greitemeyer, T., and S. Osswald. 2010. "Effects of prosocial video games on prosocial behavior." *Journal of Personality and Social Psychology* 98:211-21.

Grekin, E. R., K. J. Sher, and J. L. Krull. 2007. "College spring break and alcohol use." *Journal of Studies on Alcohol and Drugs* 68:681-88.

Grewal, K., S. Gravely-Witte, D. E. Stewart, and S. L. Grace. 2011. "A simultaneous test of the relationship between identified psychosocial risk factors and recurrent events in coronary artery disease patients." *Anxiety Stress and Coping* 24:463-75.

Grieco, E. M., and R. C. Cassidy. 2001. "Overview of race and Hispanic origin." U.S. Census Bureau website.

Griffin, K. W., J. G. Rabkin, R. H. Remien, and J. B. W. Williams. 1998. "Disease severity, physical limitations, and depression in HIV-infected men." *Journal of Psychosomatic Research* 44 (February):219-27.

Grimmett, R. F. 2006. "Conventional arms transfers to developing nations, 1998-2005." *CRS Report for Congress,* October 23.

Grineski, S., B. Bolin, and C. Boone. 2007. "Criteria air pollution and marginalized populations." *Social Science Quarterly* 88:535-54.

Griswold, D. 2010. "Global markets keep U.S. economy afloat." Cato @ Liberty website.

Grodsky, E., and D. Pager. 2001. "The structure of disadvantage: Individual and occupational determinants of the black-white wage gap." *American Sociological Review* 66:542-67.

Grogan, S., and H. Richards. 2002. "Body image: Focus groups with boys and men." *Men and Masculinities* 4:219-32.

Grogan-Kaylor, A., and M. D. Otis. 2003. "Effect of childhood maltreatment on adult criminality." *Child Maltreatment* 8:129-37.

Grogger, J., and L. A. Karoly. 2005. *Welfare Reform: Effects of a Decade of Change.* Cambridge, MA: Harvard University Press.

Gross, D., A. Sambrook, and L. Fogg. 1999. "Behavior problems among young children in low-income urban day care centers." *Research in Nursing Health* 22 (February):15-25.

Gross, J. 1998. "In quest for the perfect look, more girls choose the scalpel." *New York Times,* November 29.

Grossman, D., and S. Shulman. 1990. "Down in the dumps." *Discover* (April):36-41.

Grosswald, B. 2003. "Shift work and negative work-to-family spillover." *Journal of Sociology and Social Welfare* 30:30-42.

Grov, C., B. J. Gillespie, T. Royce, and J. Lever. 2011. "Perceived consequences of casual online sexual activities on heterosexual relationships." *Archives of Sexual Behavior* 40:429-39.

Grubb, A. R., and J. Harrower. 2009. "Understanding attribution of blame in cases of rape." *Journal of Sexual Aggression* 15:63-81.

Grubb, W. N., and M. Lazerson. 2004. *The Education Gospel: The Economic Power of Schooling.* Cambridge, MA: Harvard University Press.

Grunberg, L., R. Anderson-Connolly, and E. S. Greenberg. 2000. "Surviving layoffs." *Work and Occupations* 27 (February):7-31.

Gryparis, A., et al. 2004. "Acute effects of ozone on mortality from the 'Air Pollution and Health: A European Approach' project." *American Journal of Respiratory and Critical Care Medicine.* [e-published ahead of print date]. AJRCCM website.

Grzywacz, J. G., D. M. Almeida, S. D. Neupert, and S. L. Ettner. 2004. "Socioeconomic status and health: A micro-level analysis of exposure and vulnerability to daily stressors." *Journal of Health and Social Behavior* 45:1-16.

Guinart, M., and M. Grau. 2014. "Qualitative analysis of the short-term and long-term impact of family breakdown on children." *Journal of Divorce & Remarriage* 55:408-22.

Gunn, R. A., et al. 1995. "Syphilis in San Diego County 1983–1992: Crack cocaine, prostitution, and the limitations of partner notification." *Sexually Transmitted Diseases* 22 (1):60–6.

Guo, J., J. D. Hawkins, K. G. Hill, and R. D. Abbott. 2001. "Childhood and adolescent predictors of alcohol abuse and dependence in young adulthood." *Journal of Studies on Alcohol* 62:754–62.

Gurr, T. R. 1969. "A comparative study of civil strife." In *The History of Violence in America,* ed. H. D. Graham and T. R. Gurr, pp. 572–632. New York: Bantam.

Gussler-Burkhardt, N. L., and P. R. Giancola. 2005. "A further examination of gender differences in alcohol-related aggression." *Journal of Studies on Alcohol* 66:413–22.

Gutierrez-Lobos, K. 2000. "The gender gap in depression reconsidered." *Social Psychiatry and Psychiatric Epidemiology* 35:202–10.

Guzzo, K. B., and S. R. Hayford. 2014. "Fertility and the stability of co-habiting unions." *Journal of Family Issues* 35:547–76.

Haber, J. R., et al. 2010. "Effect of paternal alcohol and drug dependence on offspring conduct disorder." *Journal of Studies on Alcohol and Drugs* 71:652–63.

Hacker, J. S., and P. Pierson. 2010. *Winner-Take-All Politics: How Washington Made the Rich Richer—and Turned Its Back on the Middle Class.* New York: Simon and Schuster.

Haddad, S. 2003. "Islam and attitudes toward U.S. policy in the Middle East." *Studies in Conflict and Terrorism* 26:135–54.

Hagan, J., and H. Foster. 2001. "Youth violence and the end of adolescence." *American Sociological Review* 66:874–99.

Hagerman, E. 1990. "California's drive to mass transit." *World Watch* (September–October):7–8.

Haines, M. M., S. L. Brentnall, S. A. Stansfeld, and E. Klineberg. 2003. "Qualitative responses of children to environmental noise." *Noise Health* 5:19–30.

Hair, E. C., et al. 2009. "Parent marital quality and the parent-adolescent relationship: Effects on adolescent and young adult health outcomes." *Marriage & Family Review* 45:218–48.

Hakim, D. 2008. "Net providers to block sites with child sex." *New York Times,* June 10.

Hald, G. M., N. M. Malamuth, and C Yuen. 2010. "Pornography and attitudes supporting violence against women." *Aggressive Behavior* 36:14–20.

Haley, R. W., A. M. Maddrey, and H. K. Gershenfeld. 2002. "Severely reduced functional status in veterans fitting a case definition of Gulf War syndrome." *American Journal of Public Health* 92:46–47.

Hall, J. H., W. Fals-Stewart, and F. D. Fincham. 2008. "Risky sexual behavior among married alcoholic men." *Journal of Family Psychology* 22:287–92.

Hallman, W. K., and A. Wandersman. 1992. "Attribution of responsibility and individual and collective coping with environmental threats." *Journal of Social Issues* 48 (4):101–18.

Halpern-Felsher, B. L., and S. G. Millstein. 2002. "The effects of terrorism on teens' perceptions of dying." *Journal of Adolescent Health* 30:308–11.

Halvorsen, A., V. E. Lee, and F. H. Andrade. 2009. "A mixed-method study of teachers' attitudes about teaching in urban and low-income schools." *Urban Education* 44:181–224.

Hamberger, L. K., and S. E. Larsen. 2015. "Men and women's experience of intimate partner violence." *Journal of Family Violence* 30:699–717.

Hamby, S., D. Finkelhor, H. Turner, and R. Ormrod. 2011. "Children's exposure to intimate partner violence and other family violence." *Juvenile Justice Bulletin*, October.

Hammarstrom, A. 1994. "Health consequences of youth unemployment." *Social Science and Medicine* 38 (March):699–709.

Han, W., D. P. Miller, and J. Waldfogel. 2010. "Parental work schedules and adolescent risky behaviors." *Developmental Psychology* 46:1245–67.

Hanna-Attisha, M., et al. 2016. "Elevated blood lead levels in children associated with the Flint drinking water crisis." *American Journal of Public Health* 106:283–90.

Hannon, L., and J. Defronzo. 1998. "The truly disadvantaged, public assistance, and crime." *Social Problems* 45:383–92.

Hansell, S., and H. R. White. 1991. "Adolescent drug use, psychological distress, and physical symptoms." *Journal of Health and Social Behavior* 32 (September):288–301.

Hansen, J. 2004. "Defusing the global warming time bomb." *Scientific American,* March, pp. 68–77.

Hanson, S. L. 1994. "Lost talent: Unrealized educational aspirations and expectations among U.S. youths." *Sociology of Education* 67 (July):159–83.

Hanson, T. L. 1999. "Does parental conflict explain why divorce is negatively associated with child welfare?" *Social Forces* 77 (June):1283–316.

Hao, L., and S. Pong. 2008. "The role of school in the upward mobility of disadvantaged immigrants' children." *The Annals of the American Academy of Political and Social Science* 620:62–89.

Hardesty, P. H., and K. M. Kirby. 1995. "Relation between family religiousness and drug use within adolescent peer groups." *Journal of Social Behavior and Personality* 10 (1):421–30.

Hardin, G. 1971. "The tragedy of the commons." In *Man and the Environment,* ed. W. Jackson, pp. 243–54. Dubuque, IA: Wm. C. Brown.

Harford, T. C., H. Wechsler, and B. O. Muthen. 2003. "Alcohol-related aggression and drinking at off-campus parties and bars." *Journal of Studies on Alcohol* 64:704–11.

Harford, T. C., H. Wechsler, and M. Seibring. 2002. "Attendance and alcohol use at parties and bars in college." *Journal of Studies on Alcohol* 63:726–33.

Harlow, C. W. 2005. "Hate crime reported by victims and police." *Bureau of Justice Statistics Special Report.* Washington, DC: Government Printing Office.

Harmless, A. 1990. "Developmental impact of combat exposure: Comparison of adolescent and adult Vietnam veterans." *Smith College Studies in Social Work* 60 (March):185-95.

Harrell, E. 2005. "Violence by gang members, 1993-2003." Bureau of Justice Statistics Crime Data Brief, June.

——. 2011. *Workplace Violence, 1993-2009.* Washington, DC: Department of Justice.

——. 2015. "Victims of identity theft, 2014." Bureau of Justice Statistics website.

Harrell, E., and L. Langton. 2014. "Household poverty and nonfatal violent victimization, 2008-2012." Bureau of Justice Statistics website.

Harriger, J. A., R. M. Calogero, D. C. Witherington, and J. E. Smith. 2010. "Body size stereotyping and internalization of the thin ideal in preschool girls." *Sex Roles* 63:609-20.

Harrington, M. 1962. *The Other America.* Baltimore: Penguin.

Harrison, B. 1994. *Lean and Mean: The Changing Landscape of Corporate Power in the Age of Flexibility.* New York: Basic Books.

Harrison, P. J., I. P. Everall, and J. Catalan. 1994. "Is homosexual behavior hard-wired? Sexual orientation and brain structure." *Psychological Medicine* 24 (November):811-16.

Harry, J. 1989. "Parental physical abuse and sexual orientation in males." *Archives of Sexual Behavior* 18 (June):251-61.

Hart, H. 1957. "Acceleration in social change." In *Technology and Social Change,* ed. F. R. Allen et al., pp. 27-55. New York: Appleton-Century-Crofts.

Hartley, C. C. 1998. "How incest offenders overcome internal inhibitions through the use of cognitions and cognitive distortions." *Journal of Interpersonal Violence* 13 (February):25-39.

Hashemian, F., et al. 2006. "Anxiety, depression, and posttraumatic stress in Iranian survivors of chemical warfare." *Journal of the American Medical Association* 296:560-66.

Hassan, N. 2001. "An arsenal of believers: Talking to the 'human bombs.'" *The New Yorker,* November 19, pp. 36-42.

Hatton, E. 2011. *The Temp Economy: From Kelly Girls to Permatemps in Postwar America.* Philadelphia, PA: Temple University Press.

Hatzenbuchler, M. L., K. M. Keyes, and D. S. Hasin. 2009. "State-level policies and psychiatric morbidity in lesbian, gay, and bisexual populations." *American Journal of Public Health* 99:2275-81.

Hauke, A., J. Flintrop, E. Brun, and R. Rugulies. 2011. "The impact of work-related psychosocial stressors on the onset of musculoskeletal disorders in specific body regions." *Work & Stress* 25:243-56.

Hawdon, J. E. 2001. "The role of presidential rhetoric in the creation of a moral panic." *Deviant Behavior* 22:419-45.

Hawkins, D. 1996. "Homeschool battles." *U.S. News and World Report,* February 12, pp. 28-29.

Hay, C., and R. Meldrum. 2010. "Bullying victimization and adolescent self-harm." *Journal of Youth and Adolescence* 39:446-59.

Hayman, P. M., and D. J. Scaturo. 1993. "Psychological debriefing of returning military personnel: A protocol for post-combat intervention." *Journal of Social Behavior and Personality* 8 (5):117-30.

Haynie, D. L. 2002. "Friendship networks and delinquency." *Journal of Quantitative Criminology* 15:99-134.

Haywood, M. D., E. M. Crimmins, T. P. Miles, and Y. Yang. 2000. "The significance of socioeconomic status in explaining the racial gap in chronic health conditions." *American Sociological Review* 65:910-30.

Headey, B., R. Muffels, and M. Wooden. 2008. "Money does not buy happiness: Or does it?" *Social Indicators Research* 87:65-82.

Heaney, C. A., B. A. Israel, and J. S. House. 1994. "Chronic job insecurity among automobile workers: Effects on job satisfaction and health." *Social Science and Medicine* 38 (May):1431-37.

Heaton, R. B. 2002. "Factors contributing to increasing marital instability in the United States." *Journal of Family Issues* 23:392-409.

Heilig, J. V.;, and J. J. Holme. 2013. "Nearly 50 years post-Jim Crow." *Education and Urban Society* 45: 609-32.

Heilman, M. E. 2001. "Description and prescription: How gender stereotypes prevent women's ascent up the organizational ladder." *Journal of Social Issues* 57:657-74.

Heim, N. 1981. "Sexual behavior of castrated sex offenders." *Archives of Sexual Behavior* 10 (1):11-19.

Helfand, I. 1999. "Moving the world back from nuclear brink." *San Diego Union-Tribune,* October 18.

Henig, D. 2012. "Iron in the soil: Living with military waste in Bosnia-Herzegovina." *Anthropology Today* 28:21-23.

Henry, W. A., III. 1994. "Pride and prejudice." *Time,* June 17, pp. 54-59.

Herek, G. M. 2009. "Hate crimes and stigma-related experiences among sexual minority adults in the United States." *Journal of Interpersonal Violence* 24:54-74.

Hernandez, D. J. 2011. "Double jeopardy: How third-grade reading skills and poverty influence high school graduation." Research report, Annie E. Casey Foundation.

Herne, M. A., M. L. Bartholomew, and R.L. Weahkee. 2014. "Suicide mortality among American Indians and Alaska Natives, 1999-2009." *American Journal of Public Health* 104:336-42.

Herrenkohl, T.I., et al. 2013. "Developmental impacts of child abuse and neglect related to adult mental health, substance use, and physical health." *Journal of Family Violence* 28:191-99.

Herring, C. 2002. "Is job discrimination dead?" *Contexts* 1:13-18.

Herrnstein, R. J., and C. Murray. 1994. *The Bell Curve: Intelligence and Class Structure in American Life.* New York: Free Press.

Herron, J., and M. W. Smith. 2012. "The disaster of Hurricane Katrina: Malfeasance, official deviance, and the failure to serve and protect a community." *International Journal of Interdisciplinary Social Sciences* 6:1833–82.

Hersey, J. 1946. *Hiroshima.* New York: Alfred A. Knopf.

Hesse-Biber, S. 1996. *Am I Thin Enough Yet? The Cult of Thinness and the Commercialization of Identity.* New York: Oxford University Press.

Hetherington, E. M. 1993. "An overview of the Virginia longitudinal study of divorce and remarriage with a focus on early adolescence." *Journal of Family Psychology* 7:39–56.

Hetherington, M. J. 1999. "The effect of political trust on the presidential vote, 1968–96." *American Political Science Review* 93 (June):311–23.

Heymann, J. 2000. "What happens during and after school: Conditions faced by working parents living in poverty and their school-aged children." *Journal of Children and Poverty* 6:5–20.

Hicks, M. H. 2006. "The prevalence and characteristics of intimate partner violence in a community study of Chinese American women." *Journal of Interpersonal Violence* 21:1249–69.

Hicks, W. D., et al. 2015. "A principle or a strategy? Voter identification laws and partisan competition in the American States." *Political Research Quarterly* 68:18–33.

Higgins, J. A., and I. Browne. 2008. "Sexual needs, control, and refusal." *Journal of Sex Research* 45:233–45.

Higham, A., et al. 2016. "Electronic cigarette exposure triggers neutrophil inflammatory responses." *Respiratory Research* 17:56.

Hightower, J. M. 2008. *Diagnosis Mercury: Money, Politics and Poison.* Washington, DC: Island Press.

Hill, E. J., A. J. Hawkins, V. Maartinson, and M. Ferris. 2003. "Studying 'working fathers.'" *Fathering* 1:239–62.

Hill, E. J., V. Martinson, and M. Ferris. 2004. "New-concept part-time employment as a work-family adaptive strategy for women professionals with small children." *Family Relations* 53:282–92.

Hilton, J. M., and K. Kopera-Frye. 2006. "Loss and depression in cohabiting and noncohabiting custodial single parents." *The Family Journal* 14:28–40.

Hing, B. O. 1998. "Don't give me your tired, your poor: Conflicted immigrant stories and welfare reform." *Harvard Civil Rights–Civil Liberties Law Review* 33 (1):159–82.

Hingson, R., T. Heeren, R. Zakoes, M. Winter, and H. Wechsler. 2003. "Age at first intoxication, heavy drinking, driving after drinking, and risk of unintentional injury among U.S. college students." *Journal of Studies on Alcohol* 64:23–31.

Hingson, R. W., T. Heeren, and E. M. Edwards. 2008. "Age at drinking onset, alcohol dependence, and their relation to drug use and dependence, driving under the influence of drugs, and motor-vehicle crash involvement because of drugs." *Journal of Studies on Alcohol and Drugs* 69:192–201.

Hinze, S. W. 2004. " 'Am I being over-sensitive?' Women's experience of sexual harassment during medical training." *Health* 8:101–27.

Hipp, J. R. 2011. "Violent crime, mobility decisions, and neighborhood racial/ethnic transition." *Social Problems* 58:410–32.

Hipp, J. R., D. J. Bauer, P. J. Curran, and K. A. Bollen. 2004. "Crimes of opportunity or crimes of emotion? Testing two explanations of seasonal change in crime." *Social Forces* 82:1333–72.

Hira, R. 2009. "U.S. workers in a global job market." *Issues in Science and Technology* 25:53–58.

Hirschman, C., and E. Mogford. 2009. "Immigration and the American industrial revolution from 1880 to 1920." *Social Science Research* 38:897–920.

Hirschman, R. S., H. Leventhal, and K. Glynn. 1984. "The development of smoking behavior: Conceptualization and supportive cross-sectional survey data." *Journal of Applied Social Psychology* 14 (May–June):184–206.

Hobfoll, S. E., D. Canetti-Nisim, and R. J. Johnson. 2006. "Exposure to terrorism, stress-related mental health symptoms, and defensive coping among Jews and Arabs in Israel." *Journal of Consulting and Clinical Psychology* 74:207–18.

Hobson-Horton, L. D., and L. Owens. 2004. "From freshman to graduate: Recruiting and retaining minority students." *Journal of Hispanic Higher Education* 3:86–107.

Hochschild, J. L., and N. Scovronick. 2003. *The American Dream and the Public Schools.* New York: Oxford University Press.

Hochstetler, A., et al. 2014. "The criminal victimization-depression sequela." *Crime and Delinquency* 60:785–806.

Hoeffel, E. M., et al. 2012. "The Asian Population: 2010." *2010 Census Briefs.* U.S. Census Bureau website.

Hoefer, R., and C. Curry. 2012. "Food security and social protection in the United States." *Journal of Policy Practice* 11:59–76.

Hoffmann, J. P., and S. J. Bahr. 2014. "Parenting style, religiosity, peer alcohol use, and adolescent heavy drinking." *Journal of Studies on Alcohol and Drugs* 75:222–27.

Hofstadter, R., and M. Wallace, eds. 1970. *American Violence.* New York: Vintage.

Hogan, M. J., M. A. Long, P. B. Stretesky, and M. J. Lynch. 2006. "Campaign contributions, post-war reconstruction contracts, and state crime." *Deviant Behavior* 27:269–97.

Hoge, C. W., A. Terhakopian, C. A. Castro, S. C. Messer, and C. C. Engel. 2007. "Association of posttraumatic stress disorder with somatic symptoms, health care visits, and absenteeism among Iraq war veterans." *American Journal of Psychiatry* 164:150–53.

Hogg, R. S., et al. 2008. "Years of life lost to prison." *Harm Reduction Journal* 5:4–8.

Hokayem, C., and M. L. Heggeness. 2014. "Living in near poverty in the United States: 1966–2012." U.S. Census Bureau website.

Holahan, C. J., R. H. Moos, C. K. Holahan, R. C. Cronkite, and P. K. Randall. 2001. "Drinking to cope: Emotional distress and alcohol use and abuse." *Journal of Studies on Alcohol* 62:190–98.

Holcomb, D. R., L. C. Holcomb, K. A. Sondag, and N. Williams. 1991. "Attitudes about date rape: Gender differences among college students." *College Student Journal* 25 (December):434–39.

Holford, T. R., et al. 2014. "Tobacco control and the reduction in smoking-related premature deaths in the United States, 1964–2012." *Journal of the American Medical Association* 311:164–71.

Hollingworth, W., et al. 2006. "Prevention of deaths from harmful drinking in the United States." *Journal of Studies on Alcohol* 67:300–308.

Holmes, E. K., H. A. Jones-Sanpei, and R. D. Day. 2009. "Adolescent outcome measures in the NLSY97 family process data set." *Marriage & Family Review* 45:374–91.

Holmes, T. H., and M. Masuda. 1974. "Life change and illness susceptibility." In *Stressful Life Events,* ed. B. S. Dohrenwend and B. P. Dohrenwend, pp. 45–72. New York: John Wiley & Sons.

Holt, T. J., and A. M. Bossler. 2009. "Examining the applicability of lifestyle-routine activities theory for cybercrime victimization." *Deviant Behavior* 30:1–25.

Holtfreter, K., M. D. Reisig, and T. C. Pratt. 2008. "Low self-control, routine activities, and fraud victimization." *Criminology* 46:189–220.

Hong, J., and M. M. Seltzer. 1995. "The psychological consequences of multiple roles." *Journal of Health and Social Behavior* 36 (December):386–98.

Hood, E. 2005. "Investigating indoor air." *Environmental Health Perspectives* 113:158.

Hood, M. V., Q. Kidd, and I. L. Morris. 2015. "Tea leaves and southern politics." *Social Science Quarterly* 96: 923–40.

Hopcroft, R. L., and D. B. Bradley. 2007. "The sex difference in depression across 29 countries." *Social Forces* 85:1483–1507.

Horos, C. V. 1974. *Rape.* New Canaan, CT: Tobey.

Horowitz, J. M. 1999. "Bad news on formaldehyde." *Time,* January 18, p. 94.

Horowitz, M. C. 2016. "Public opinion and the politics of the killer robots debate." Research & Politics website.

Horwitz, A. V., and L. Davies. 1994. "Are emotional distress and alcohol problems differential outcomes to stress? An exploratory test." *Social Science Quarterly* 75 (September):607–21.

Hossler, D., J. Schmit, and N. Vesper. 1999. *Going to College: How Social, Economic, and Educational Factors Influence the Decisions Students Make.* Baltimore, MD: Johns Hopkins University Press.

Houle, J.N. 2014. "Disparities in debt." *Sociology of Education* 87: 53–69.

House, J. S. 2002. "Understanding social factors and inequalities in health." *Journal of Health and Social Behavior* 43:125–42.

Howard, M. O., et al. 2010. "Inhalant use, inhalant-use disorders, and antisocial behavior." *Journal of Studies on Alcohol and Drugs* 71:201–9.

Howard, S. 2014. "Bhopal's legacy." BMJ, December 11.

Hoyt, T., A. M. Wray, and J. K. Rielage. 2014. "Preliminary investigation of the roles of military background and posttraumatic stress symptoms in frequency and recidivism of intimate partner violence perpetration among court-referred men." *Journal of Interpersonal Violence* 29: 1094–1110.

Hu, M., M. Davies, and D. B. Kandel. 2006. "Epidemiology and correlates of daily smoking and nicotine dependence among young adults in the United States." *American Journal of Public Health* 96:299–308.

Huang, C., et al. 2015. "Children's exposure to intimate partner violence and early delinquency." *Journal of Family Violence* 30:953–65.

Hubka, D., W. Hovdestad, and L. Tommyr. 2009. "Child maltreatment in Disney animated feature films: 1937–2006." *The Social Science Journal* 46:427–41.

Huesmann, L. R., J. Moise-Titus, C. Podolski, and L. D. Eron. 2003. "Longitudinal relations between children's exposure to TV violence and their aggressive and violent behavior in adulthood: 1977–1992." *Developmental Psychology* 39:201–21.

Hughes, A. 2004. "Researchers study 'sick' buildings." *Civil Engineering,* May 4, p. 33.

Humes, K. R., N. A. Jones, and R. R. Ramirez. 2011. *Overview of Race and Hispanic Origin: 2010.* U.S. Census Bureau website.

Hummer, R. A., et al. 1999. "Race/ethnicity, nativity, and infant mortality in the United States." *Social Forces* 77 (March):1082–118.

Hummer, T. A. 2015. "Media violence effects on brain development." *American Behavioral Scientist* 54: 1709–1806.

Hunter, C. D., et al. 2016. "The roles of shared racial fate and a sense of belonging with African Americans in black immigrants' race-related stress and depression." *Journal of Black Psychology.* Published online.

Hussey, J. M., J. J. Chang, and J. B. Kotch. 2006. "Child maltreatment in the United States." *Pediatrics* 118:933–42.

Hutchinson, P. 1962. *The Christian Century Reader.* New York: Association Press.

Hyde, J. S. 2005. "The gender similarities hypothesis." *American Psychologist* 60:581–92.

Hyde, J. S., and J. DeLamater. 2007. *Understanding Human Sexuality.* New York: McGraw-Hill.

Hynes, H. P. 2011. "The invisible casualty of war." *Peace Review* 23:387–95.

Iceland, J., and R. Wilkes. 2006. "Does socioeconomic status matter? Race, class, and residential segregation." *Social Problems* 53:248–73.

ICF International. 2010. "Communities in Schools national evaluation." ICF International website.

Ickovics, J. R., and J. Rodin. 1992. "Women and AIDS in the United States: Epidemiology, natural history, and mediating mechanisms." *Health Psychology* 11 (1):1–16.

Ilg, R., and E. Theodossiou. 2012. "Job search of the unemployed by duration of unemployment." *Monthly Labor Review,* March, pp. 41–49.

Ingersoll, S., and D. LeBoeuf. 1997. "Reaching out to youth out of the educational mainstream." *Juvenile Justice Bulletin* (February).

Ingmar-Paul, K., and K. Moser. 2006. "Incongruence as an explanation for the negative mental health effects of unemployment." *Journal of Occupational and Organizational Psychology* 79:595–621.

Institute on Taxation and Economic Policy. 2015. *Who Pays? A Distributional Analysis of the Tax System in All 50 States.* ITEP website.

Isaac, R. J., and V. C. Armat. 1990. *Madness in the Streets: How Psychiatry and the Law Abandoned the Mentally Ill.* New York: Free Press.

Isaacs, J. B. 2012. "Starting school at a disadvantage." Research report, Center on Children and Families at Brookings.

Ising, H., H. Lange-Asschenfeldt, H. J. Moriske, J. Born, and M. Eilts. 2004. "Low frequency noise and stress." *Noise Health* 6:21–28.

Ivanov, V.K., et al. 2012. "Leukemia incidence in the Russian cohort of Chernobyl emergency workers." *Radiation and Environmental Biophysics* 51:143–49.

Jackson, P. B., and S. Mustillo. 2001. "I am woman: The impact of social identities on African American women's mental health." *Women's Health* 32:33–59.

Jacobe, D. 2008. "Food prices a hardship for 64% of low-income Americans; One in five of those making less than $30,000 a year call the situation 'severe.'" *Gallup Poll News Service,* April 24.

Jacobs, D., and J. T. Carmichael. 2002. "The political sociology of the death penalty." *American Sociological Review* 67:109–31.

Jacobs, D., and L. Myers. 2014. "Union strength, neoliberalism, and inequality." *American Sociological Review* 79:752–74.

Jacobs, D., Z. Qian, J. T. Carmichael, and S. L. Kent. 2007. "Who survives on death row? An individual and contextual analysis." *American Sociological Review* 72:610–32.

Jacobs, L. A. 2001. "What makes a terrorist?" *State Government News* 44:10–14.

Jacobs, N., and D. Harvey. 2005. "Do parents make a difference to children's academic achievement? Differences between parents of higher and lower achieving students." *Educational Studies* 31:431–48.

Jacobsen, P. B., et al. 2002. "Predictors of posttraumatic stress disorder symptomatology following bone marrow transplantation for cancer." *Journal of Consulting and Clinical Psychology* 70:235–40.

Jacobson, I. G., et al. 2008. "Alcohol use and alcohol-related problems before and after military combat deployment." *Journal of the American Medical Association* 300:663–75.

James, D. J., and L. E. Glaze. 2006. "Mental health problems of prison and jail inmates." *Bureau of Justice Statistics Special Report,* September.

Jamieson, A., H. B. Shin, and Jennifer Day. 2002. *Voting and Registration in the Election of November 2000.* Washington, DC: Government Printing Office.

Jaret, C. 1991. "Recent structural change and US urban ethnic minorities." *Journal of Urban Affairs* 13 (3):307–36.

Järvinen, M., and G. Miller. 2010. "Methadone maintenance as last resort." *Sociological Forum* 25:804–23.

Jarvis, K. L., E. E. Gordon, and R. W. Novaco. 2005. "Psychological distress of children and mothers in domestic violence emergency shelters." *Journal of Family Violence* 20:389–402.

Jasinski, J. L., J. K. Wesely, J. D. Wright, and E. E. Mustaine. 2010. *Hard Lives, Mean Streets: Violence in the Lives of Homeless Women.* Boston: Northeastern University Press.

Jehle, J. M. 2005. *Criminal Justice in Germany.* Berlin: Federal Ministry of Justice.

Jena, A. B., A. R. Olenski, and D. M. Blumenthal. 2016. "Sex differences in physician salary in US public medical schools." *Journal of the American Medical Association.* JAMA website.

Jessor, R., F. M. Costa, P. M. Krueger, and M. S. Turbin. 2006. "A developmental study of heavy episodic drinking among college students." *Journal of Studies on Alcohol* 67:86–94.

Jeynes, W. H. 2006. "The impact of parental remarriage on children." *Marriage & Family Review* 40:75–102.

Jiang, L., and T. M. Probst. 2016. "The moderating effect of trust in management on consequences of job insecurity." *Economics and Industrial Democracy,* July 6.

Jimerson, S., B. Egeland, L. A. Stroufe, and B. Carlson. 2000. "A prospective longitudinal study of high school dropouts." *Journal of School Psychology* 38:525–49.

Jin, R. L., C. P. Shah, and T. J. Svoboda. 1995. "The impact of unemployment on health." *Canadian Medical Association Journal* 153 (September 1):529–40.

Jiobu, R. M., and T. J. Curry. 2001. "Lack of confidence in the federal government and the ownership of firearms." *Social Science Quarterly* 82:77–88.

Johnson, B. R., S. J. Jang, D. B. Larson, and S. De Li. 2001. "Does adolescent religious commitment matter?" *Journal of Research in Crime and Delinquency* 38:22–44.

Johnson, C. 2004. *The Sorrows of Empire: Militarism, Secrecy, and the End of the Republic.* New York: Metropolitan Books.

Johnson, C. K. 2005. "Obesity goes from no. 2 killer to no. 7." *San Diego Union-Tribune,* April 20.

Johnson, D. 2014. "7 common myths about people on welfare." Everyday Feminism website.

Johnson, D. P., and J. Friedman. 1993. "Social versus physiological motives in the drug careers of methadone clinic clients." *Deviant Behavior* 14 (January–March):23–42.

Johnson, I. M. 2007. "Victims' perceptions of police response to domestic violence incidents." *Journal of Criminal Justice* 35:498–510.

Johnson, J. G., P. Cohen, E. M. Smailes, S. Kasen, and J. S. Brook. 2002. "Television viewing and aggressive behavior during adolescence and adulthood." *Science* 295:2468–71.

Johnson, N. J., P. D. Sorlie, and E. Backlund. 1999. "The impact of specific occupation on mortality in the U.S. national longitudinal mortality study." *Demography* 36 (August):355–67.

Johnson, P. R., and J. Indvik. 1994. "Workplace violence." *Public Personnel Management* 23 (Winter):515–23.

Johnson, R. A., and D. R. Gerstein. 1998. "Initiation of use of alcohol, cigarettes, marijuana, cocaine, and other substances in U.S. birth cohorts since 1919." *American Journal of Public Health* 88 (January):27–33.

Johnson, R. C., and R. F. Schoeni. 2011. "Early-life origins of adult disease." *American Journal of Public Health* 202:2317–24.

Johnson, S.M., and E. O'Connor. 2002. *The Gay Baby Boom.* New York: New York University Press.

Johnston, D. D., and D. H. Swanson. 2003. "Invisible mothers: A content analysis of motherhood ideologies and myths in magazines." *Sex Roles* 48:21–33.

Jones, B. 2016. "Americans' views of immigrants marked by widening partisan, generational divides." Pew Research Center website.

Jones, J. M. 2016. "Americans' identification as 'environmentalists' down to 42%." Gallup Poll website.

Jones, M. T. 2010. "Mediated exhibitionism: The naked body in performance and virtual space." *Sexuality & Culture* 14:253–69.

Jones, S., and D. Myhill. 2004. "Seeing things differently: Teachers' constructions of under-achievement." *Gender and Education* 16:531–46.

Jones-Webb, R., et al. 2016. "Effects of economic disruptions on alcohol use and problems." *Journal of Studies on Alcohol and Drugs* 77:261–71.

Jorgenson, A. K. 2006. "Global warming and the neglected greenhouse gas." *Social Forces* 84:1779–98.

Kabir, Z., G. N. Connolly, L. Clancy, H. K. Koh, and S. Capewell. 2008. "Coronary heart disease deaths and decreased smoking prevalence in Massachusetts, 1993–2003." *American Journal of Public Health* 98: 1468–69.

Kahlenberg, S. G., and M. M. Hein. 2010. "Progression on Nickelodeon? Gender-role stereotypes in toy commercials." *Sex Roles* 62:830–47.

Kahn, J. R., J. Garcia-Manglano, and S. M. Bianchi. 2014. "The Motherhood penalty at midlife." *Journal of Marriage and Family* 76:56–72.

Kalleberg, A. L. 2009. "Precarious work, insecure workers: Employment relations in transition." *American Sociological Review* 74:1–22.

Kalmijn, M., and P. J. De Graaf. 2012. "Life course changes of children and well-being of parents." *Journal of Marriage and Family* 74:269–80.

Kalmuss, D. 2004. "Nonvolitional sex and sexual health." *Archives of Sexual Behavior* 33:197–209.

Kane, E. W. 1995. "Education and beliefs about gender inequality." *Social Problems* 42 (February):74–89.

Kang, S. Y., S. Magura, and J. L. Shapiro. 1994. "Correlates of cocaine/crack use among inner-city incarcerated adolescents." *American Journal of Drug and Alcohol Abuse* 20 (4):413–29.

Kaplan, R. M., and R. G. Kronick. 2006. "Marital status and longevity in the United States population." *Journal of Epidemiology and Community Health* 60:760–65.

Kar, B. R., S. L. Rao, and B. A. Chandramouli. 2008. "Cognitive development in children with chronic protein energy malnutrition." *Behavioral and Brain Functions* 4:31.

Karamoskos, P. 2015. "Drone warfare." *Medicine, Conflict and Survival* 31:125–27.

Karg, R.S., et al. 2014. "Past year mental disorders among adults in the United States." SAMHSA website.

Karlson, K.B. 2015. "Expectations on track?" *Social Forces* 94:115–41.

Karney, B.R., and T.E. Trail. 2016. "Associations between prior deployments and marital satisfaction among army couples." *Journal of Marriage and Family.* Published online.

Kass, S. J., S. J. Vodanovich, and J. Y. Khosravi. 2011. "Applying the job characteristics model to the college education experience." *Journal of the Scholarship of Teaching and Learning* 11:56–68.

Katz, J. 1988. *Seductions of Crime: Moral and Sensual Attractions of Doing Evil.* New York: Basic Books.

Keller, P. S., et al. 2011. "Parent problem drinking, marital aggression, and child emotional insecurity." *Journal of Studies on Alcohol and Drugs* 72:711–22.

Keller, U., and K. H. Tillman. 2008. "Post-secondary educational attainment of immigrant and native youth." *Social Forces* 87:121–52.

Kelloway, E. K., and B. H. Gottlieb. 1998. "The effect of alternative work arrangements on women's well-being." *Womens Health* 4:1–18.

Kelly, J. F., M. E. Pagano, R. L. Stout, and S. M. Johnson. 2011. "Influence of religiosity on 12-step participation and treatment response among substance-dependent adolescents." *Journal of Studies on Alcohol and Drugs* 72:1000–1011.

Kelly, P. 2008. *Lydia's Open Door: Inside Mexico's Most Modern Brothel.* Berkeley, CA: University of California Press.

Kena, G., et al. 2016. "The condition of education 2016." National Center for Education Statistics website.

Kendler, K. S., L. M. Thornton, and C. A. Prescott. 2001. "Gender differences in the rates of exposure to stressful life events and sensitivity to their depressogenic effects." *American Journal of Psychiatry* 158:587–93.

Kennedy, L. W., and S. W. Baron. 1993. "Routine activities and a subculture of violence: A study of violence on the street." *Journal of Research in Crime and Delinquency* 30 (February):88–112.

Kenworthy, L. 1999. "Do social-welfare policies reduce poverty? A cross-national assessment." *Social Forces* 77 (March):1119–39.

Kerley, K. R., and H. Copes. 2004. "The effects of criminal justice contact on employment stability for white-collar and street-level offenders." *International Journal of Offender Therapy and Comparative Criminology* 48:65–84.

Kernsmith, P. D., and R. M. Kernsmith. 2009. "Female pornography use and sexual coercion perpetration." *Deviant Behavior* 30:589–610.

Kerrissey, J. 2015. "Collective labor rights and income inequality." *American Sociological Review* 80: 626–53.

Keyes, C. L. M., and E. J. Simoes. 2012. "To flourish or not: Positive mental health and all-cause mortality." *American Journal of Public Health* 102:2164–72.

Khatchadourian, R. 2016. "The unseen." *The New Yorker,* June 20.

Khattak, S., et al. 1999. "Pregnancy outcome following gestational exposure to organic solvents." *Journal of the American Medical Association* 281 (March 24–31):1106–9.

Khawaja, M., and R. R. Habib. 2007. "Husbands' involvement in housework and women's psychosocial health." *American Journal of Public Health* 97:860–66.

Kheifets, L., A. A. Afifi, and R. Shimkhada. 2006. "Public health impact of extremely low-frequency electromagnetic fields." *Environmental Health Perspectives* 114:1532–37.

Kilgore, E.A., et al. 2014. "Making it harder to smoke and easier to quit." *American Journal of Public Health* 104:65–8.

Kilmer, J. R., et al. 2006. "Misperceptions of college student marijuana use." *Journal of Studies on Alcohol* 67:277–81.

Kilpatrick, D. G., et al. 2000. "Risk factors for adolescent substance abuse and dependence." *Journal of Consulting and Clinical Psychology* 68:19–30.

Kim, H. S. 2011. "Consequences of parental divorce for child development." *American Sociological Review* 76:487–511.

Kim, H., and H. Kim. 2005. "Incestuous experience among Korean adolescents." *Public Health Nursing* 22:472–82.

Kim, J., and K. A. Gray. 2008. "Leave or stay? Battered women's decision after intimate partner violence." *Journal of Interpersonal Violence* 23:1465–82.

Kim, J., S. Park, and C. R. Emery. 2009. "The incidence and impact of family violence on mental health among South Korean women." *Journal of Family Violence* 24:193–202.

Kim, R., K. K. Nakamura, G. Fong, R. Cabarloc, B. Jung, and S. Lee. 1992. "Asian immigrant women garment workers in Los Angeles." *Amerasia Journal* 18 (1):69–82.

King, D. Y. 1998a. "Qualifications of Indonesia's civil servants: How appropriate to the dynamic environment?" *Journal of Political and Military Sociology* 26 (Summer):23–38.

———. 1998b. "Reforming basic education and the struggle for decentralized educational administration in Indonesia." *Journal of Political and Military Sociology* 26 (Summer):83–95.

King, K. B., and H. T. Reis. 2012. "Marriage and long-term survival after coronary artery bypass grafting." *Health Psychology* 31:55–62.

Kingston, D. A., P. Fedoroff, P. Firestone, S. Curry, and J. M. Bradford. 2008. "Pornography use and sexual aggression." *Aggressive Behavior* 34:341–51.

Kinnier, R. T., A. T. Metha, J. L. Okey, and J. M. Keim. 1994. "Adolescent substance abuse and psychological health." *Journal of Alcohol and Drug Education* 40 (Fall):51–56.

Kirby, J. A. 1996. "Big Apple excises X-rated rot." *Chicago Tribune,* April 19.

Kirby, J. B., and T. Kaneda. 2005. "Neighborhood socioeconomic disadvantage and access to health care." *Journal of Health and Social Behavior* 46:15–31.

Kirsh, S. J., and P. V. Olczak. 2002. "The effects of extremely violent comic books on social information processing." *Journal of Interpersonal Violence* 17:1160–78.

Klein, E. J., H. J. Davies, and M. A. Hicks. 2001. "Child pornography: The criminal-justice system response." National Center for Missing and Exploited Children website.

Kliewer, S. 2004. "Allowing spirituality into the healing process." *Journal of Family Practice* 53:616–24.

Kline, M., J. R. Johnston, and J. M. Tschann. 1991. "The long shadow of marital conflict: A model of children's post-divorce adjustment." *Journal of Marriage and the Family* 53 (February):297–309.

Klug, B. J., and P. T. Whitfield. 2002. *Widening the Circle: Culturally Relevant Pedagogy for American Indian Children.* New York: Routledge/Falmer.

Knee, J. A. 2004. "Is that really legal?" *New York Times,* May 2.

Knoke, D., and Y. Ishio. 1998. "The gender gap in company job training." *Work and Occupations* 25 (May):141–67.

Knudsen, H. K., P. M. Roman, J. A. Johnson, and L. J. Ducharme. 2005. "A changed America? The effects of September 11th on depressive symptoms and alcohol consumption." *Journal of Health and Social Behavior* 46:260-73.

Koenig, E. 2015. "Job satisfaction, focus on research steady." Quirk's Media website.

Koenig, L. B., and G. E. Vaillant. 2009. "A prospective study of church attendance and health over the lifespan." *Health Psychology* 28:117-24.

Koepke, L., J. Hare, and P. B. Moran. 1992. "Relationship quality in a sample of lesbian couples with children and child-free lesbian couples." *Family Relations* 41:224-29.

Koerner, S. S., M. Korn, R. P. Dennison, and S. Witthoft. 2011. "Future money-related worries among adolescents after divorce." *Journal of Adolescent Research* 26: 299-317.

Kogevinas, M., et al. 1998. "Respiratory symptoms, lung function and use of health services among unemployed young adults in Spain." *European Respiratory Journal* 11 (June):1363-68.

Kohut, A. 2015. "Despite of lower crime rates, support for gun rights increases." Pew Research Center website.

Kolbert, E. 2006. "Untransformed." *The New Yorker,* September 25, pp. 64-65.

Komarovsky, M. 1940. *The Unemployed Man and His Family.* New York: Dryden Press.

Konstantopoulos, S. 2009. "What is the impact of class size on student learning?" *Teachers College Record.* TCR website.

Kopecki, D. 2006. "On the hunt for fraud." *Business Week,* October 11, p. 11.

Koretz, G. 1997. "The downside of downsizing." *BusinessWeek,* April 28.

Koss, M. P., and J. A. Gaines. 1993. "The prediction of sexual aggression by alcohol use, athletic participation, and fraternity affiliation." *Journal of Interpersonal Violence* 8 (March):94-108.

Kotch, J. B., et al. 2008. "Importance of early neglect for childhood aggression." *Pediatrics* 121:725-31.

Kouwe, Z. 2009. "2 money managers held in new Wall St. fraud case." *New York Times,* February 26.

Kowalski, B. R., and R. J. Lundman. 2007. "Vehicle stops by police for driving while black." *Journal of Criminal Justice* 35:165-81.

Kozaryn, L. D. 2002. "Bush says Saddam Hussein 'must be stopped.'" U.S. Department of Defense website.

Kozol, J. 1992. *Savage Inequalities: Children in America's Schools.* New York: Crown.

Kramer, L. A., and E. C. Berg. 2003. "A survival analysis of timing of entry into prostitution." *Sociological Inquiry* 73:511-28.

Kramer, R. 1999. "Weaving the public into public administration." *Public Administration Review* 59 (January-February):89-92.

Krassas, N. R., J. M. Blauwkamp, and P. Wesselink. 2001. "Boxing Helena and corseting Eunice: Sexual rhetoric in *Cosmopolitan* and *Playboy* magazines." *Sex Roles* 44:751-71.

Kreager, D. A. 2008. "Guarded borders: Adolescent interracial romance and peer trouble at school." *Social Forces* 87:887-910.

Kreeger, K. Y. 2002. "Deciphering how the sexes think." *Scientist,* January 21, pp. 28-33.

Kristiansen, S., and M. Ramli. 2006. "Buying an income: The market for civil service positions in Indonesia." *Contemporary Southeast Asia* 28:207-33.

Kristof, K. 2011. "10 most outrageous ways government wastes your money." CBS News website, December 20.

Krogstad, J. M. 2015. "114th Congress is most diverse ever." Pew Research Center website.

——. 2016. "Roughly half of hispanics have experienced discrimination." Pew Research Center website.

Krogstad, J. M., and K. Parker. 2014. "Public is sharply divided in views of Americans in poverty." Pew Research Center website.

Krogstad, J. M., and J. S. Passel. 2015. "5 Facts about illegal immigration in the U.S." Pew Research Center website.

Krugman, P. 2006. "Broken promises." *New York Times,* August 28.

Krumei-Mancuso, E. 2016. "Sex work and mental health." *Archives of Sexual Behavior*, published online.

Kruttschnitt, C., J. D. McLeod, and M. Dornfeld. 1994. "The economic environment of child abuse." *Social Problems* 41 (May):299-315.

Krysan, M. 2008. "Does race matter in the search for housing?" *Social Science Research* 37:581-603.

Kryzanek, M. J. 1999. *Angry, Bored, Confused: A Citizen Handbook of American Politics.* Boulder, CO: Westview Press.

Kuchment, A. 2016. "Drilling for earthquakes." *Scientific American*, July.

Kucsera, J. V., G. Siegel-Hawley, and G. Orfield. 2015. "Are we segregated and satisfied?" *Urban Education* 50:535-71.

Kuhr, S., and J. M. Hauer. 2001. "The threat of biological terrorism in the new millennium." *American Behavioral Scientist* 44:1032-41.

Kulbarsh, P. 2015. "Police suicide statistics." Officer.com website.

Kulik, L. 2011. "Developments in spousal power relations: Are we moving toward equality?" *Marriage & Family Review* 47:419-35.

Kull, S., C. Ramsay, and E. Lewis. 2003. "Misperceptions, the media, and the Iraq war." *Political Science Quarterly* 118:569-98.

Kuo, F. E., and W. C. Sullivan. 2001. "Environment and crime in the inner city." *Environment and Behavior* 33:343-67.

Kuo, L. 2002. *Prostitution Policy: Revolutionizing Practice through a Gendered Perspective.* New York: New York University Press.

Kuo, M. 2000. "Asia's dirty secret." *Harvard International Review* 22:42-45.

Kuperberg, A. 2014. "Age at coresidence, premarital cohabitation, and marriage dissolution." *Journal of Marriage and Family* 76:352-69.

Kuttner, R. 1998. "Must good HMOs go bad?" *New England Journal of Medicine* 338 (May 21):16-22.

——. 2005. "Generous to a fault?" *San Diego Union-Tribune,* January 6.

Kwate, N. O. A., and I. H. Meyer. 2009. "Association between residential exposure to outdoor alcohol advertising and problem drinking among African American women in New York City." *American Journal of Public Health* 99: 228-30.

Lacayo, R. 2003. "The war comes back home." *Time,* May 12, pp. 30-34.

Lacey, M. 2005. "Beyond the bullets and blades." *New York Times,* March 20.

LaCroix, A. Z., et al. 1991. "Smoking and mortality among older men and women in three communities." *New England Journal of Medicine* 324 (June 6):1619-25.

Ladwig, K. H., B. Marten-Mittag, B. Formanek, and G. Dammann. 2000. "Gender differences of symptom reporting and medical health care utilization in the German population." *European Journal of Epidemiology* 16:511-18.

Laffaye, C., C. Kennedy, and M. B. Stein. 2003. "Post-traumatic stress disorder and health-related quality of life in female victims of intimate partner violence." *Violence and Victims* 18:227-38.

LaGrow, S., et al. 2011. "Determinants of the overall quality of life of older persons who have difficulty seeing." *Journal of Visual Impairment & Blindness* 105:720-30.

Lai, T., et al. 2016. "Ambient air pollution and risk of tuberculosis." *Occupational and Environmental Medicine* 73:56-61.

Lamb, H. R. 1998. "Deinstitutionalization at the beginning of the new millennium." *Harvard Review of Psychiatry* 6 (May-June):1-10.

Landberg, J., and T. Norstrom. 2011. "Alcohol and homicide in Russia and the United States." *Journal of Studies on Alcohol and Drugs* 72:723-30.

Landen, M., et al. 2014. "Alcohol–attributable mortality among American Indians and Alaska Natives in the United States, 1999-2009." *American Journal of Public Health* 104:343-49.

Landolt, M. A., et al. 2004. "Gender nonconformity, childhood rejection, and adult attachment: A study of gay men." *Archives of Sexual Behavior* 33:117-28.

Landrigan, C. P., et al. 2010. "Temporal trends in rates of patient harm resulting from medical care." *New England Journal of Medicine* 363:2124-34.

Lanford, D., and J. Quadagno. 2016. "Implementing Obamacare." *Sociological Perspectives* 59:619-39.

Langhinrichsen-Rohling, J., D. A. Lamis, and P. S. Malone. 2011. "Sexual attraction status and adolescent suicide proneness." *Journal of Homosexuality* 58:52-82.

Langstrom, N., and M. C. Seto. 2006. "Exhibitionistic and voyeuristic behavior in a Swedish national population survey." *Archives of Sexual Behavior* 11:23-35.

Lanier, C. A. 2001. "Rape-accepting attitudes." *Violence against Women* 7:876-85.

Lantz, P. M., et al. 1998. "Socioeconomic factors, health behaviors, and mortality." *Journal of the American Medical Association* 279 (June 3):1703-8.

Larcinese, V., L. Rizzo, and C. Testa. 2006. "Allocating the U.S. federal budget to the states." *Journal of Politics* 68:447-56.

Lareau, A. 2003. *Unequal Childhoods: Class, Race, and Family Life.* Berkeley: University of California Press.

Larsen, C. D., J. G. Sandberg, J. M. Harper, and R. Bean. 2011. "The effects of childhood abuse on relationship quality." *Family Relations* 60:435-45.

Lauer, J. C., and R. H. Lauer. 1986. *'Til Death Do Us Part: How Couples Stay Together.* New York: Haworth.

Lauer, R. H. 1974. "Rate of change and stress: A test of the 'future shock' thesis." *Social Forces* 52:510-16.

——. 1976. "Defining social problems: Public opinion and textbook practice." *Social Problems* 24 (October): 122-30.

——. 1991. *Perspectives on Social Change.* 4th ed. Boston: Allyn and Bacon.

Lauer, R. H., and J. C. Lauer. 1983. *The Spirit and the Flesh: Sex in Utopian Communities.* Netuchen, NJ: Scarecrow.

——. 1988. *Watersheds: Mastering Life's Unpredictable Crises.* New York: Little, Brown.

——. 1999. *Becoming Family: How to Build a Stepfamily That Really Works.* Minneapolis, MN: Augsburg.

——. 2018. *Marriage and Family: The Quest for Intimacy.* 8th ed. New York: McGraw-Hill.

Laumann, E. O., R. T. Michael, J. H. Gagnon, and S. Michaels. 1994. *The Social Organization of Sexuality.* Chicago: University of Chicago Press.

Lauster, N., and A. Easterbrook. 2011. "No room for new families?" *Social Problems* 58:389-409.

Lauzen, M. M., and D. M. Dozier. 2005. "Maintaining the double standard: Portrayals of age and gender in popular films." *Sex Roles* 52:437-46.

Law, W. 1906. *A Serious Call to a Devout and Holy Life.* New York: E. P. Dutton.

Lawyer, S. R., K. J. Ruggiero, H. S. Resnick, D. G. Kilpatrick, and B. E. Saunders. 2006. "Mental health correlates of the victim-perpetrator relationship among interpersonally victimized adolescents." *Journal of Interpersonal Violence* 21:1333–53.

Leary, W. E. 1996. "No evidence power lines a threat." *San Diego Union-Tribune,* November 1.

Leatherdale, S. T., P. W. McDonald, R. Cameron, and K. S. Brown. 2005. "A multilevel analysis examining the relationship between social influences for smoking and smoking onset." *American Journal of Health Behavior* 29:520–30.

Lebeque, B. 1991. "Paraphilias in U.S. pornography titles: 'Pornography made me do it' (Ted Bundy)." *Bulletin of the American Academy of Psychiatry and Law* 19 (1):43–48.

Lebov, J. F., et al. 2016. "Pesticide use and risk of end-stage renal disease among licensed pesticide applicators in the Agricultural Health Study." *Occupational and Environmental Medicine* 73:3–12.

Lee, B. A., C. R. Farrell, and B. G. Link. 2004. "Revisiting the contact hypothesis: The case of public exposure to homelessness." *American Sociological Review* 69:40–63.

Lee, B. A., and M. J. Greif. 2008. "Homelessness and hunger." *Journal of Health and Social Behavior* 49:3–19.

Lee, D. J., S. J. Niemcryk, C. D. Jenkins, and R. M. Rose. 1989. "Type A, amicability and injury: A prospective study of air traffic controllers." *Journal of Psychosomatic Research* 33 (2):177–86.

Lee, G. R., and J. R. Bulanda. 2005. "Change and consistency in the relation of marital status to personal happiness." *Marriage and Family Review* 38:69–84.

Lee, M. R., and G. C. Ousey. 2001. "Size matters: Examining the link between small manufacturing socioeconomic deprivation and crime rates in nonmetropolitan communities." *Sociological Quarterly* 42:581–602.

Lee, V. E., and D. Burkam. 2002. *Inequality at the Starting Gate: Social Background Differences in Achievement as Children Begin School.* Washington, DC: Economic Policy Institute.

Lehman, W. E. K., D. J. Farabee, M. L. Holcom, and D. D. Simpson. 1995. "Prediction of substance use in the workplace: Unique contributions of personal background and work environment variables." *Journal of Drug Issues* 25 (2):253–74.

Lehmann, J. B., C. U. Lehmann, and P. J. Kelly. 1998. "Development and health care needs of lesbians." *Journal of Women's Health* 7 (April):379–88.

Leidholdt, D., and J. G. Raymond. 1990. *The Sexual Liberals and the Attack of Feminism.* New York: Pergamon.

Leighninger, M. 2011. "Citizenship and governance in a wild, wired world." *National Civic Review,* Summer, pp. 20–30.

Lemieux, S. R., and E. S. Byers. 2008. "The sexual well-being of women who have experienced child sexual abuse." *Psychology of Women Quarterly* 32:126–44.

Lemke, S., P. L. Brennan, K. K. Schutte, and R. H. Moos. 2007. "Upward pressures on drinking." *Journal of Studies on Alcohol and Drugs* 68:437–45.

Lemonick, M. D. 1996. "What's wrong with our sperm?" *Time,* March 18, pp. 78–79.

Lenski, G. E. 1966. *Power and Privilege.* New York: McGraw-Hill.

Leshner, A. I. 1998. "Addiction is a brain disease—and it matters." *National Institute of Justice Journal* (October):2–6.

Leslie, M. 2003. "Acid rain collection." *Science* 301:899.

Leveille, S. G., C. C. Wee, and L. I. Iezzoni. 2005. "Trends in obesity and arthritis among baby boomers and their predecessors, 1971–2002." *American Journal of Public Health* 95:1607–13.

Leventhal, A. M., et al. 2015. "Association of electronic cigarette use with initiation of combustible tobacco product smoking in early adolescence." *Journal of the American Medical Association* 314:700–7.

Levi, M. 1998. "A state of trust." In *Trust and Governance,* ed. V. Braithwaite and M. Levi, pp. 77–98. New York: Russell Sage Foundation.

Levin, H. 2006. "Worker democracy and worker productivity." *Social Justice Research* 19:109–21.

Levy, C. J. 1999. "More power was supposed to grease these skids." *New York Times,* June 27.

Levy, D. T., et al. 2016. "The application of a decision-theoretic model to estimate the public health impact of vaporized nicotine product initiation in the United States." *Nicotine and Tobacco Research*, published online.

Levy, J. A., C. P. Gallmeier, and W. W. Wiebel. 1995. "The outreach assisted peer-support model for controlling drug dependency." *Journal of Drug Issues* 25 (3):507–29.

Lewis, J. L., and E. Kim. 2008. "A desire to learn: African-American children's positive attitudes toward learning within school cultures of low expectations." *Teachers College Record* 110:1304–29.

Lewis, M. A., et al. 2011. "They drink how much and where? Normative perceptions by drinking contexts and their association to college students' alcohol consumption." *Journal of Studies on Alcohol and Drugs* 72:844–53.

Lewis, R. 2002. "Race and the clinic: Good science?" *Scientist* 16 (February 18):16.

Lewis, V. A., M. O. Emerson, and S. L. Klineberg. 2011. "Who we'll live with: Neighborhood racial composition preferences of whites, blacks and Latinos." *Social Forces* 89:1385–1408.

Lichter, S. R., L. S. Lichter, D. R. Amundson, and J. M. Fowler. 1987. "The truth about Pravda: How the Soviets see the United States." *Public Opinion* (March–April):12–13.

Lieberman, B. 2004. "Rising CO_2 levels threaten oceans, scientists say." *San Diego Union-Tribune,* July 16.

Light, P. C. 1999. *The True Size of Government.* Washington, DC: Brookings Institution Press.

Lii, J. H. 1995. "Week in sweatshop reveals grim conspiracy of the poor." *New York Times,* March 12.

Lindberg, S. M., J. S. Hyde, J. L. Petersen, and M. C. Linn. 2010. "New trends in gender and mathematics performance." *Psychological Bulletin* 136:1123–35.

Ling, D. C., W. C. W. Wong, E. A. Holroyd, and S. A. Gray. 2007. "Silent killers of the night: An exploration of psychological health and suicidality among female street sex workers." *Journal of Sex and Marital Therapy* 33:281–99.

Lipari, R. N., and B. Jean-Francois. 2016. *A day in the life of college students aged 18 to 22: substance use facts.* Substance Abuse and Mental Health Services Administration. Rockville, MD.

Lippert, A. M. 2016. "Stuck in unhealthy places." *Journal of Health and Social Behavior* 57:1–21.

Liptak, A., N. A. Lewis, and B. Weiser. 2002. "After Sept. 11, a legal battle on the limits of civil liberty." *New York Times,* August 4.

Liskow, B. I., et al. 2000. "Mortality in male alcoholics after ten to fourteen years." *Journal of Studies on Alcohol* 61:853–61.

Litrownik, A. J., R. Newton, W. M. Hunter, D. English, and M. D. Everson. 2003. "Exposure to family violence in young at-risk children." *Journal of Family Violence* 18:59–73.

Litvinov, A. 2015. "'These kids are just pawns': The rising toll of inequitable school funding." *NEA Today,* July 20.

Liu, L. 2006. "Quality of life as a social representation in China." *Social Indicators Research* 75:217–40.

Liu, X., and H. B. Kaplan. 1996. "Gender-related differences in circumstances surrounding initiation and escalation of alcohol and other substance use/abuse." *Deviant Behavior* 17 (1):71–106.

Livingston, D. W. 1998. *The Education-Jobs Gap: Underemployment or Economic Democracy.* Boulder, CO: Westview Press.

Lleras, C. 2008. "Employment, work conditions, and the home environment in single-mother families." *Journal of Family Issues* 29:1268–97.

Locke, B. D., and J. R. Mahalik. 2005. "Examining masculinity norms, problem drinking, and athletic involvement as predictors of sexual aggression in college men." *Journal of Counseling Psychology* 52:279–83.

Locke, M. 1996. "Suicide, natural causes: How most inmates die on death rows." *Chicago Tribune,* March 6.

Lockhart, L. L., B. W. White, V. Causby, and A. Isaac. 1994. "Letting out the secret: Violence in lesbian relationships." *Journal of Interpersonal Violence* 9 (December):469–92.

Loeber, R., and D. P. Farrington. 1998. *Serious and Violent Juvenile Offenders: Risk Factors and Successful Interventions.* Newbury Park, CA: Sage.

Loftus, J. 2001. "America's liberalization in attitudes toward homosexuality, 1973 to 1999." *American Sociological Review* 66:762–82.

Logan, T. D. 2010. "Personal characteristics, sexual behaviors, and male sex work." *American Sociological Review* 75: 679–704.

London, A. S., E. Allen, and J. M. Wilmoth. 2013. "Veteran status, extramarital sex, and divorce." *Journal of Family Issues* 34:1452–73.

Long, C. 2013. "Are we failing gifted students?" *NEA Today,* September 18.

Long, S. H., and M. S. Marquis. 1999. "Geographic variation in physician visits for uninsured children: The role of the safety net." *Journal of the American Medical Association* 281 (June 2):2035–41.

Longres, J. F. 1991. "An ecological study of parents of adjudicated female teenage prostitutes." *Journal of Social Service Research* 14 (1–2):113–27.

Lopata, H. Z. 1984. "Social construction of social problems over time." *Social Problems* 31 (February):249–72.

Lopez, G. 2015. "Gun violence In America." VOX website.

Lopez, V. 2008. "Understanding adolescent property crime using a delinquent events perspective." *Deviant Behavior* 29:581–610.

Lorentzen, E., H. Nilsen, and B. Traeen. 2008. "Will it never end? The narratives of incest victims on the termination of sexual abuse." *The Journal of Sex Research* 45:164–74.

Lorenz, F. O., K. A. Wickrama, R. D. Conger, and G. H. Elder Jr. 2006. "The short-term and decade-long effects of divorce on women's midlife health." *Journal of Health and Social Behavior* 47:111–25.

Loring, M., and B. Powell. 1988. "Gender, race, and DSM-III: A study of the objectivity of psychiatric diagnostic behavior." *Journal of Health and Social Behavior* 29 (March):1–22.

Louie, M. C. 1992. "After sewing, laundry, cleaning and cooking, I have no breath left to sing." *Amerasia Journal* 18 (1):1–26.

Loury, G. C. 2005. "Racial stigma and its consequences." *Focus* 24:1–6.

Loveless, T. 1999. "Will tracking reform promote social equity?" *Educational Leadership* 56 (April):28–32.

Lovell, D. 2008. "Patterns of disturbed behavior in a supermax population." *Criminal Justice and Behavior* 35:985–1004.

Lowe, M. E. 2009. "Gay, lesbian, and queer theologies." *Dialog: A Journal of Theology* 48:49–61.

Lowi, T. J., and J. Romance. 1998. *A Republic of Parties? Debating the Two-Party System.* Lanham, MD: Rowman and Littlefield.

Loxton, D., M. Schofield, and R. Hussain. 2006. "Psychological health in midlife among women who have ever lived with a violent partner or spouse." *Journal of Interpersonal Violence* 21:1092–1107.

Lu, L., and X. Wang. 2008. "Drug addiction in China." *Journal of the New York Academy of Sciences* 1141:304–17.

Lucas, J. L., and R. B. Heady. 2002. "Flextime commuters and their driver stress, feelings of time urgency, and commute satisfaction." *Journal of Business and Psychology* 16:565-71.

Lundwall, R. A. 2002. "Parents' perceptions of the impact of their chronic illness or disability on their functioning as parents and on their relationships with their children." *The Family Journal* 10:300-7.

Lung, F. W., T. J. Lin, Y. C. Lu, and B. C. Shu. 2004. "Personal characteristics of adolescent prostitutes and rearing attitudes of their parents." *Psychiatry Research* 125:285-91.

Luo, F., et al. 2011. "Impact of business cycles on U.S. suicide rates, 1928-2007." *American Journal of Public Health* 101:1139-46.

Lutfey, K. E., et al. 2010. "Physician cognitive processing as a source of diagnostic and treatment disparities in coronary heart disease." *Journal of Health and Social Behavior* 51:16-29.

Lynn, M., et al. 2011. "Examining teachers' beliefs about African American male students in a low-performing high school in an African American school district." *Teachers College Record.* TCR website.

Lyons, L. 2004. "$10 million question: To work or not to work?" Gallup Poll website.

McBroom, J. R. 1992. "Alcohol and drug use by third, fourth, and fifth graders in a town of 20,000." *Sociology and Social Research* 76 (April):156-60.

McCabe, J., K. L. Brewster, and K. H. Tillman. 2011. "Patterns and correlates of same-sex sexual activity among U.S. teenagers and young adults." *Perspectives on Sexual and Reproductive Health* 43:142-50.

McCabe, S. E., et al. 2011. "Gender in twentieth-century children's books." *Gender & Society* 25:197-226.

McCaffery, J. M., G. D. Papandonatos, C. Stanton, E. E. Lloyd-Richardson, and R. Niaura. 2008. "Depressive symptoms and cigarette smoking in twins from the National Longitudinal Study of Adolescent Health." *Health Psychology* 27:207-15.

McCall, L. 2001. "Sources of racial wage inequality in metropolitan labor markets." *American Sociological Review* 66:520-41.

McCallum, C., and S. McLaren. 2011. "Sense of belonging and depressive symptoms among GLB adolescents." *Journal of Homosexuality* 58:83-96.

McCarthy, B. 2014. "Sex work: a comparative study." *Archives of Sexual Behavior* 43:1379-90.

McCarthy, J. 2016. "One in eight U.S. adults say they smoke marijuana." Pew Research Center website.

McCarthy, M. 2016. "U.S. spent more on mental illness than on any other conditions in 2013." *BMJ* 353:2895.

McClam, E. 2005. "Role in tax scam admitted by KPMG." *San Diego Union-Tribune,* August 30.

McCleese, C. S., and L. T. Eby. 2006. "Reactions to job content plateaus." *Career Development Quarterly* 55:64-76.

McConaghy, N., et al. 2006. "Fraternal birth order and ratio of heterosexual/homosexual feelings in women and men." *Journal of Homosexuality* 51:161-74.

McConkey, D. 2001. "Whither Hunter's culture war? Shifts in evangelical morality, 1988-1998." *Sociology of Religion* 61:149-74.

McCormick, C. M., and S. F. Witelson. 1994. "Functional cerebral asymmetry and sexual orientation in men and women." *Behavioral Neuroscience* 108 (June):525-31.

McDevitt, J., J. Balboni, L. Garcia, and J. Gu. 2001. "Consequences for victims: A comparison of bias- and non-bias-motivated assaults." *American Behavioral Scientist* 45:697-713.

MacDonald, M., and D. Nierenberg. 2003. "Linking population, women, and biodiversity." In *State of the World 2003,* ed. L. Starke, pp. 38-61. New York: W. W. Norton.

McDonald, R., E. N. Jouriles, M. J. Briggs-Gowan, D. Rosenfield, and A. S. Carter. 2007. "Violence toward a family member, angry adult conflict, and child adjustment difficulties." *Journal of Family Psychology* 21:176-84.

McDonald, R., et al. 2006. "Estimating the number of American children living in partner-violent families." *Journal of Family Psychology* 20:137-42.

McDonough, P., and P. Berglund. 2003. "Histories of poverty and self-rated health trajectories." *Journal of Health and Social Behavior* 44:198-214.

McDowall, D., C. Loftin, and B. Wiersema. 2000. "The impact of youth curfew laws on juvenile crime rates." *Crime and Delinquency* 46 (January):76-91.

MacEachern, D. 1990. *Save the Planet: 750 Ways You Can Help Clean Up the Earth.* New York: Dell.

McFarlane, J., P. Willson, A. Malecha, and D. Lemmey. 2000. "Intimate partner violence." *Journal of Interpersonal Violence* 15 (February):158-69.

McFarlin, S. K., W. Fals-Stewart, D. A. Major, and E. M. Justice. 2001. "Alcohol use and workplace aggression." *Journal of Substance Abuse* 13:303-21.

MacFie, C. C., S. V. Baudouin, and P. B. Messer. 2016. "An integrative review of drug errors in critical care." *Journal of the Intensive Care Society* 17:63-72.

McGarva, A. R., M. Ramsey, and S. A. Shear. 2006. "Effects of driver cell-phone use on driver aggression." *Journal of Social Psychology* 140:133-46.

McGinn, A. P. 1999. "Charting a new course for oceans." In *State of the World 1999,* ed. L. R. Brown et al., pp. 78-95. New York: W. W. Norton.

———. 2000. *Why Poison Ourselves?* Washington, DC: Worldwatch Institute.

———. 2002. "Reducing our toxic burden." In *State of the World 2002,* ed. L. Starke, pp. 75-100. New York: W. W. Norton.

McIntyre, R. S., M. Gardner, R. J. Wilkins, and R. Phillips. 2011. *Corporate Taxpayers & Corporate Tax Dodgers:*

2008-10. Washington, DC: Citizens for Tax Justice and the Institute on Taxation and Economic Policy.

McKee, M., and V. Shkolnikov. 2001. "Understanding the toll of premature death among men in Eastern Europe." *British Medical Journal* 323:1051-55.

McKellar, J., E. Stewart, and K. Humphreys. 2003. "Alcoholics Anonymous involvement and positive alcohol-related outcomes." *Journal of Consulting and Clinical Psychology* 71:302-8.

McKeown, A., and G. Gardner. 2009. *Climate Change Reference Guide.* Washington, DC: Worldwatch Institute.

McLaughlin, D. K., and C. S. Stokes. 2002. "Income inequality and mortality in U.S. counties." *American Journal of Public Health* 92:99-104.

McLaughlin, H. l., C. Uggen, and A. Blackstone. 2012. "Sexual harassment, workplace authority, and the paradox of power." *American Sociological Review* 77:625-47.

McLaughlin, K. A., et al. 2012. "Socioeconomic status and adolescent mental disorders." *American Journal of Public Health* 102:1742-50.

MacLean, A. 2010. "The things they carry: Combat, disability, and unemployment among U.S. men." *American Sociological Review* 75:563-85.

McMahon, S. 2007. "Understanding community-specific rape myths." *Affilia: Journal of Women and Social Work* 22:357-70.

McMenamin, B., and J. Novack. 1999. "The white-collar gestapo." *Forbes,* December 1, pp. 82-91.

McMullin, D., R. J. Wirth, and J. W. White. 2007. "The impact of sexual victimization on personality." *Sex Roles* 56: 403-14.

McQuaid, J. R., et al. 2000. "Correlates of life stress in an alcohol treatment sample." *Addictive Behaviors* 25 (January-February):131-37.

McWilliams, J. M., E. Meara, A. M. Zaslavsky, and J. Z. Ayanian. 2007. "Health of previously uninsured adults after acquiring Medicare coverage." *Journal of the American Medical Association* 298:2886-94.

Mack, J. E., and J. Z. Rubin. 1991. "Is this any way to wage peace?" *Los Angeles Times,* January 31.

Mackenbach, J. P., et al. 2008. "Socioeconomic inequalities in health in 22 European countries." *New England Journal of Medicine* 358:2468-81.

Magee, C. S. P. 2003. "Third-party candidates and the 2000 presidential election." *Social Science Quarterly* 84: 574-95.

Mager, J., and J. G. Helgeson. 2011. "Fifty years of advertising images." *Sex Roles* 64:238-52.

Magnuson, K., and L. M. Berger. 2009. "Family structure states and transitions." *Journal of Marriage and Family* 71: 575-91.

Mahtesian, C. 1999. "So much politics, so little time." *Governing,* August, pp. 22-26.

Major, V. S., K. J. Klein, and M. G. Ehrhart. 2002. "Work time, work interference with family, and psychological distress." *Journal of Applied Psychology* 87:427-36.

Makarios, M., B. Steiner, and L. F. Travis. 2010. "Examining the predictors of recidivism among men and women released from prison in Ohio." *Criminal Justice and Behavior* 37:1377-91.

Makarios, Steiner, and Travis. 2010. "Examining the predictors of recidivism among men and women released from prison in Ohio." *Criminal Justice and Behavior* 37:1377-91.

Makary, M. A., and M. Daniel. 2016. "Medical error—the third leading cause of death in the U.S." *BMJ* 353:21-39.

Makela, K., et al. 1996. *Alcoholics Anonymous as a Mutual-Help Movement: A Study in Eight Societies.* Madison: University of Wisconsin Press.

Males, M. 2010. "Traffic crash victimizations of children and teenagers by drinking drivers age 21 and older." *Journal of Studies on Alcohol and Drugs* 71:351-56.

Malhotra, N., and C. Raso. 2007. "Racial representation and U.S. Senate apportionment." *Social Science Quarterly* 88:1038-48.

Malik, N., and S. Malik. 2016. "Relationship of life events and psychiatric symptoms among adolescents." *Pakistan Journal of Medical Research* 55:44.

Malik, S., et al. 2008. "Maternal smoking and congenital heart defects." *Pediatrics* 121:810-16.

Mancini, C., A. Reckdenwald, and E. Beauregard. 2012. "Pornographic exposure over the life course and the severity of sexual offenses." *Journal of Criminal Justice* 40:21-30.

Mandel, H., and M. Semyonov. 2006. "A welfare state paradox: State interventions and women's employment opportunities in 22 countries." *American Journal of Sociology* 111: 1910-49.

Manderscheid, R. W. 2009. "Promoting universal coverage." *Behavioral Healthcare* 29:32.

Maniam, S. 2016. "Sharp differences over who is hurt, helped by their race." Pew Research Center website.

Maniglio, R. 2013. "Child sexual abuse in the etiology of anxiety disorders." *Trauma, Violence, and Abuse* 14: 96-112.

Mann, R. E., and C. R. Hollin. 2007. "Sexual offenders' explanation for their offending." *Journal of Sexual Aggression* 13:3-9.

Mann, R. E., R. F. Zaleman, R. G. Smart, B. R. Rush, and H. Suurvali. 2006. "Alcohol consumption, alcoholics anonymous membership, and suicide mortality rates, Ontario, 1968-1991." *Journal of Studies on Alcohol* 67:445-53.

Manning, W. D., and J. A. Cohen. 2012. "Premarital cohabitation and marital dissolution: An examination of recent marriages." *Journal of Marriage and Family* 74:377-87.

Mansour, S. A. 2004. "Pesticide exposure—Egyptian scene." *Toxicology* 198:91-115.

Marano, H. E. 1996. "Why they stay." *Psychology Today,* May-June, pp. 57-78.

Marano, H. E., and E. Strand. 2003. "Points of departure." *Psychology Today,* July/August, pp. 48–49.

Maratea, R. 2008. "The e-rise and fall of social problems: The blogosphere as a public arena." *Social Problems* 55:139–60.

Margolis, J., R. Estrella, J. Goode, J. J. Holme, and K. Nao. 2008. *Stuck in the Shallow End: Education, Race, and Computing.* Cambridge, MA: MIT Press.

Markey, C., and P. Markey. 2005. "Relations between body image and dieting behaviors." *Sex Roles* 53:519–30.

Markham, D. 2003. "Attitudes towards patients with a diagnosis of 'borderline personality disorder.'" *Journal of Mental Health* 12:595–612.

Markowitz, F. E. 2003. "Socioeconomic disadvantage and violence." *Aggression and Violent Behavior* 8:145–54.

Marks, A. 2006. "Prosecutions drop for U.S. white-collar crime." *Christian Science Monitor,* August 31.

Markward, M. J. 1997. "The impact of domestic violence on children." *Families in Society* 78 (January–February):66–71.

Marsch, L. A. 1998. "The efficacy of methadone maintenance interventions in reducing illicit opiate use, HIV risk behavior and criminality." *Addiction* 93 (April):515–32.

Marshall, W. L., and H. Moulden. 2001. "Hostility toward women and victim empathy in rapists." *Sexual Abuse* 13:249–55.

Martell, R. F., C. Parker, and C. G. Emrich. 1998. "Sex stereotyping in the executive suite." *Journal of Social Behavior and Personality* 13 (1):127–38.

Martin, C. S., P. R. Clifford, and R. L. Clapper. 1992. "Patterns and predictors of simultaneous and concurrent use of alcohol, tobacco, marijuana, and hallucinogens in first-year college students." *Journal of Substance Abuse* 4 (3):319–26.

Martin, E. K., C. T. Taft, and P. A. Resick. 2007. "A review of marital rape." *Aggression and Violent Behavior* 12:329–47.

Martin, J. K., and P. M. Roman. 1996. "Job satisfaction, job reward characteristics, and employees' problem drinking behaviors." *Work and Occupations* 23 (February):4–25.

Martin, P. S. 2003. "Voting's rewards: Voter turnout, attentive publics, and congressional allocation of federal money." *American Journal of Political Science* 47:110–27.

Marullo, S. 1987. "The functions and dysfunctions of preparations for fighting nuclear war." *Sociological Focus* 20 (April):135–53.

Marx, S. 2006. *Revealing the Invisible: Confronting Passive Racism in Teacher Education.* New York: Routledge.

Masarik, A.S., et al. 2016. "Couple resilience to economic pressure over time and across generations." *Journal of Marriage and Family* 78:326–45.

Mason, W. A. 2001. "Self-esteem and delinquency revisited (again)." *Journal of Youth and Adolescence* 30:83–102.

Massoglia, M. 2008. "Incarceration as exposure." *Journal of Health and Social Behavior* 49:56–71.

Matthew, E. M. 2011. "Effort optimism in the classroom." *Sociology of Education* 84:225–45.

Mathews, D. 2006. "The Rescue Foundation." *New Internationalist* 390:33.

Matthews, S. K., and R. Agnew. 2008. "Extending deterrence theory." *Journal of Research in Crime and Delinquency* 45:91–118.

Matthies, E., R. Hoger, and R. Guski. 2000. "Living on polluted soil." *Environment and Behavior* 32:270–86.

Maume, D. I. 2008. "Gender differences in providing urgent childcare among dual-earner parents." *Social Forces* 87:273–97.

Maume, D. I., R. A. Sebastian, and A. R. Bardo. 2010. "Gender, work-family responsibilities, and sleep." *Gender & Society* 224:746–68.

May, P. A. 1991. "Fetal alcohol effects among North American Indians." *Alcohol Health and Research World* 15 (3):239–48.

Mayall, A., and D. E. Russell. 1993. "Racism in pornography." *Feminism and Psychology* 3 (2):275–81.

Mayer, E. A., M. Craske, and B. D. Naliboff. 2001. "Depression, anxiety, and the gastrointestinal system." *Journal of Clinical Psychiatry* 61:28–36.

Mayer, J. 2005. "High stakes." *The New Yorker,* September 19, pp. 37–38.

Mazerolle, L., C. Kadleck, and J. Roehl. 2004. "Differential police control at drug-dealing places." *Security Journal* 17:61–69.

Meadows, R. J., and K. L. Anklin. 2002. "Study of the criminal motivations of sentenced jail inmates." In *Visions for Change: Crime and Justice in the Twenty-First Century,* 3rd ed., ed. R. Muraskin and A. R. Roberts, pp. 287–302. New York: Prentice-Hall.

Meckler, L. 1998. "Blacks in America get sick more than whites, die sooner." *San Diego Union-Tribune,* November 27.

Medler, A. 2002. "The maturing politics of education choice." *Teachers College Record* 104:173–95.

Mehio Sibai, A., N. Shaar Sameer, and S. el Yassir. 2000. "Impairments, disabilities and needs assessment among non-fatal war injuries in South Lebanon, Grapes of Wrath, 1996." *Journal of Epidemiology and Community Health* 54 (January):35–39.

Melançon, C., and M. Gagné. 2011. "Father's and mother's psychological violence and adolescent behavioral adjustment." *Journal of Interpersonal Violence* 26:991–1011.

Menard, K. S., A. H. Phung, M. F. Ghebrial, and L. Martin. 2003. "Gender differences in sexual harassment and coercion in college students." *Journal of Interpersonal Violence* 18:1222–39.

Mendell, M. J., et al. 2006. "Indicators of moisture and ventilation system contamination in U.S. office buildings as risk factors for respiratory and mucous membrane symptoms." *Journal of Occupational & Environmental Hygiene* 3:225–33.

Mendez, E. 2011. "U.S. job satisfaction struggles to recover to 2008 levels." Gallup Poll website.

Mendoza, M., and C. Sullivan. 2006. "Uncle Sam struggling to collect on fines." *San Diego Union-Tribune,* March 19.

Merton, R. K. 1957. *Social Theory and Social Structure.* New York: Free Press.

Mesch, G. S. 2000. "Women's fear of crime." *Violence and Victims* 15:323–36.

Meurer, J. R., H. Yang, C. E. Guse, M. C. Scanlon, and P. M. Layde. 2006. "Medical injuries among hospitalized children." *Quality and Safety in Health Care* 15:202–7.

Meyer, I. H. 2003. "Prejudice, social stress, and mental health in lesbian, gay, and bisexual populations." *Psychological Bulletin* 129:674–97.

Meyer, L. B. 2003. "Economic globalization and women's status in the labor market." *Sociological Quarterly* 44:351–83.

Meyers, C. 1988. *Discovering Eve: Ancient Israelite Women in Context.* New York: Oxford University Press.

Michalos, A. C., B. D. Zumbo, and A. Hubley. 2000. "Health and the quality of life." *Social Indicators Research* 51:245–86.

Michelson, M. R. 2003. "Getting out the Latino vote: How door-to-door canvassing influences voter turnout in rural central California." *Political Behavior* 25:247–63.

Mickelson, R. A. 1990. "The attitude-achievement paradox among black adolescents." *Sociology of Education* 63 (January):44–61.

——. 2001. "Subverting Swann: Tracking as second generation segregation in Charlotte, North Carolina." *American Educational Research Journal* 38:215–52.

——. 2015. "The cumulative disadvantages of first- and second-generation segregation for middle school achievement." *American Educational Research Journal* 52:657–92.

Miech, R. A., et al. 2016. *Monitoring the Future National Survey Results on Drug Use.* Ann Arbor: Institute for Social Research.

Milburn, M. A., R. Mather, and S. D. Conrad. 2000. "The effects of viewing R-rated movie scenes that objectify women on perceptions of date rape." *Sex Roles* 43: 645–64.

Milkie, M. A., K. M. Nomaguchi, and K. E. Denny. 2015. "Does the amount of time mothers spend with children or adolescents matter?" *Journal of Marriage and Family* 77:355–72.

Military Education. 2016. "The true cost of military equipment spending." Military Education website.

Miller, A. B., T. To, D. A. Agnew, C. Wall, and L. M. Green. 1996. "Leukemia following occupational exposure to 60-Hz electric and magnetic fields among Ontario electric utility workers." *American Journal of Epidemiology* 144 (July 15):150–60.

Miller, J. 2001. *One of the Guys: Girls, Gangs, and Gender.* New York: Oxford University Press.

Miller, J., and D. Jayasundara. 2001. "Prostitution, the sex industry, and sex tourism." In *Sourcebook on Violence against Women,* ed. C. M. Renzetti, J. L. Edleson, and R. K. Bergen, pp. 459–80. Thousand Oaks, CA: Sage.

Miller, K. A., et al. 2007. "Long-term exposure to air pollution and incidence of cardiovascular events in women." *New England Journal of Medicine* 356:447–58.

Miller, L. M. 2011. "Physical abuse in a college setting." *Journal of Family Violence* 16:71–80.

Miller, L. R., and E. A. Grollman. 2015. "The social costs of gender nonconformity for transgender adults." *Sociological Forum* 30:809–31.

Miller, M. C. 2005. *Fooled Again.* New York: Basic Books.

Miller, T. R., D. T. Levy, R. S. Spicer, and D. M. Taylor. 2006. "Societal costs of underage drinking." *Journal of Studies on Alcohol* 67:519–28.

Miller, W. R., and P. L. Wilbourne. 2002. "Mesa Grande: A methodological analysis of clinical trials of treatments for alcohol use disorders." *Addiction* 97:265–77.

Miller-Day, M. 2008. "Talking to youth about drugs: What do late adolescents say about parental strategies?" *Family Relations* 57:1–12.

Mills, C. W. 1956. *The Power Elite.* New York: Oxford University Press.

——. 1959. *The Sociological Imagination.* New York: Oxford University Press.

Milrod, C., and M. A. Monto. 2012. "The hobbyist and the girlfriend experience." *Deviant Behavior* 33: 792–810.

Minino, A. M., and B. L. Smith. 2001. "Deaths: Preliminary data for 2000." *National Vital Statistics Reports,* October 9.

Mintz, E. 1998. "Members' diligence in casting ballots climbs to a 45-year high." *Congressional Quarterly Weekly Report,* January 3, p. 24.

Mirowsky, J., and C. E. Ross. 1995. "Sex differences in distress: Real or artifact?" *American Sociological Review* 60 (June):449–68.

Mirowsky, J., and C. E. Ross. 2015. "Education, health, and the default American lifestyle." *Journal of Health and Social Behavior* 56:297–306.

Mitchell, C. M., J. Beals, and N. R. Whitesell. 2008. "Alcohol use among American Indian high school youths from adolescence and young adulthood." *Journal of Studies on Alcohol and Drugs* 69:666–75.

Mitchell, R. S. 1969. *The Homosexual and the Law.* New York: Arco.

Mitka, M. 2014. "Firearm-related hospitalizations: 20 US children, teens daily." *Journal of the American Medical Association* 311:664.

Miyake, Y., et al. 2010. "Brain activation during the perception of distorted body images in eating disorders." *Psychiatry Research: Neuroimaging* 181:183–92.

Moen, P., D. Dempster-McClain, and R. M. Williams Jr. 1992. "Successful aging: A life-course perspective on women's multiple roles and health." *American Journal of Sociology* 97 (May):1612–38.

Moen, P., and Y. Yu. 2000. "Effective work/life strategies." *Social Problems* 47:291–326.

Mohai, P., and R. Saha. 2007. "Racial inequality in the distribution of hazardous waste: A national-level reassessment." *Social Problems* 54:343–70.

Mohler-Kuo, M., G. W. Dowdall, M. P. Koss, and H. Wechsler. 2004. "Correlates of rape while intoxicated in a national sample of college students." *Journal of Studies on Alcohol* 65:37–45.

Mokdad, A. H., J. S. Marks, D. F. Stroup, and J. L. Gerberding. 2004. "Actual causes of death in the United States, 2000." *Journal of the American Medical Association* 291:1238–45.

Molitor, F., and K. W. Hirsch. 1994. "Children's toleration of real-life aggression after exposure to media violence." *Child Study Journal* 24 (3):191–207.

Mollica, R.F., et al. 1994. "The effect of trauma and confinement on functional health and mental health status of Cambodians living in Thailand-Cambodia border camps. *Journal of the American Medical Association* 270:581–86.

Monastersky, R. 1999. "China's air pollution chokes crop growth." *Science News,* March 27, Science News website.

Monk-Turner, E., et al. 2010. "The portrayal of racial minorities on prime time television." *Studies in Popular Culture* 32:101–14.

Monroe, L. M., et al. 2005. "The experience of sexual assault." *Journal of Interpersonal Violence* 20:767–76.

Montemurro, B., C. Bloom, and K. Madell. 2003. "Ladies night out: A typology of women patrons of a male strip club." *Deviant Behavior* 24:333–52.

Monto, M. A. 2001. "Prostitution and fellatio." *Journal of Sex Research* 38:140–45.

——. 2004. "Female prostitution, customers, and violence." *Violence against Women* 10:160–88.

Monto, M. A., and N. McRee. 2005. "A comparison of the male customers of female street prostitutes with national samples of men." *International Journal of Offender Therapy and Comparative Criminology* 49:505–29.

Moore, A. A., et al. 2005. "Longitudinal patterns and predictors of alcohol consumption in the United States." *American Journal of Public Health* 95:458–65.

Moore, P. 1999. "New evidence links air pollution with lung cancer." *Lancet* 353 (February 27):729.

Moore, T. H. M., et al. 2007. "Cannabis use and risk of psychotic or affective mental health outcomes." *The Lancet* 370:319–28.

Moore, T. S. 2010. "The local of racial disadvantage in the labor market." *American Journal of Sociology* 116:909–42.

Moos, R. H., and B. S. Moos. 2004. "Long-term influence of duration and frequency of participation in Alcoholics Anonymous on individuals with alcohol use disorders." *Journal of Consulting and Clinical Psychology* 72:81–90.

Morain, D. 1990. "Complex, costly cleanups may snarl base closings." *Los Angeles Times,* June 19.

Morales, L. 2011. "Near record-low confidence in U.S. public schools." Gallup poll website.

Moran, C. 2002. "Federally mandated school choice has few takers locally." *San Diego Union-Tribune,* September 3.

Morgan, R. E. 2014. "Nonfatal domestic violence, 2003–2012." Bureau of Justice Statistics website.

Morin, R. 2011. "For many injured veterans, a lifetime of consequences." Pew Research Center website.

Morin, R., and R. Kochhar. 2010. "Lost income, lost friends—and loss of self-respect." Pew Research Center website.

Moritsugu, K. 2001. "U.S. economy struggles to bear brunt of terrorism's costs." Knight Ridder/Tribune News Service. Knight Ridder/Tribune website.

Morland, L. A., et al. 2008. "Intimate partner violence and miscarriage." *Journal of Interpersonal Violence* 23:652–69.

Morreale, A. 2015. "Hiding in plain sight: the spiraling cost of white- collar crime." *Comprehensive Financial Investigative Solution,* CFIS website.

Morrell, S. L., R. J. Taylor, and C. B. Kerr. 1998. "Unemployment and young people's health." *Medical Journal of Australia* 168 (March 2):236–40.

Morris, E. W. 2005. "'Tuck in that shirt!' Race, class, gender, and discipline in an urban school." *Sociological Perspectives* 48:25–48.

Morrongiello, B. A., and K. Hogg. 2004. "Mothers' reactions to children misbehaving in ways that can lead to injury." *Sex Roles* 50:103–18.

Morton, H. 2004. "Identity thieves." S*tate Legislatures* 30:30–41.

Moses, T. 2009. "Self-labeling and its effects among adolescents diagnosed with mental disorders." *Social Science & Medicine* 68:570–78.

Mosher, D. L., and R. D. Anderson. 1986. "Macho personality, sexual aggression, and reactions to guided imagery of realistic rape." *Journal of Research in Personality* 20 (March):77–94.

Mossakowski, K. N. 2009. "The influence of past unemployment duration on symptoms of depression among young women and men in the United States." *American Journal of Public Health* 99:1826–32.

Motivans, M. 2003. "Money laundering offenders, 1994–2001." *Bureau of Justice Statistics Special Report.* Washington, DC: Government Printing Office.

Mouawad, J. 2008. "The big thirst." *New York Times,* April 20.

Moulder, J. E., K. R. Foster, L. S. Erdreich, and J. P. McNamee. 2005. "Mobile phones, mobile phone base stations and cancer." *International Journal of Radiation Biology* 81: 189-203.

Moyer, M., "How much is left?" *Scientific American,* September, pp. 74-82.

Muench, U., et al. 2015. "Salary differences between male and female nurses in the United States." *Journal of the American Medical Association* 313:1265-67.

Mukamal, K. J., and E. B. Rimm. 2001. "Alcohol's effects on the risk for coronary heart disease." *Alcohol Research and Health* 25:255-61.

Mukherjee, S., S. K. Das, K. Vaidyanathan, and D. M. Vasudevan. 2008. "Consequences of alcohol consumption on neurotransmitters." *Current Neurovascular Research* 5:266-72.

Muldoon, O. T., and K. Wilson. 2001. "Ideological commitment, experience of conflict and adjustment in Northern Irish adolescents." *Medicine, Conflict, and Survival* 17:112-24.

Mulford, C., and P. C. Giordano. 2008. "Teen dating violence." *NIJ Journal, Issue* 261:34-40.

Mulia, N., Y. Ye, S. E. Zemore, and T. K. Greenfield. 2008. "Social disadvantage, stress, and alcohol use among black, Hispanic, and white Americans." *Journal of Studies on Alcohol and Drugs* 69:824-33.

Mulkey, L. M., R. L. Crain, and A. J. C. Harringon. 1992. "One-parent households and achievement: Economic and behavioral explanations of a small effect." *Sociology of Education* 65 (January):48-65.

Mullins, L. C., K. P. Brackett, D. W. Bogle, and D. Pruett. 2004. "The impact of religious homogeneity on the rate of divorce in the United States." *Sociological Inquiry* 74: 338-54.

Mumen, S. K., et al. 2016. "Boys act and girls appear." *Sex Roles* 74: 78-91.

Mumford, E. A., and B. G. Taylor. 2014. "National survey on teen relationships and intimate violence." *NORC* website.

Mumola, C. 2005. "Suicide and homicide in state prisons and local jails." *Bureau of Justice Statistics Special Report,* August.

Munsch, C. L. 2016. "Flexible work, flexible penalties." *Social Forces* 94:1567-91.

Murbeth, S., M. Rousarova, H. Scherb, and E. Lengfelder. 2004. "Thyroid cancer has increased in the adult populations of countries moderately affected by Chernobyl fallout." *Medical Science Monitor* 10:300-6.

Murdaugh, C., S. Hunt, R. Sowell, and I. Santana. 2004. "Domestic violence in Hispanics in the southeastern United States." *Journal of Family Violence* 19:107-15.

Murray, J. P. 2008. "Media violence." *American Behavioral Scientist* 51:1212-30.

Murthy, R. S. 2014. "Mental health of survivors of 1984 Bhopal disaster." *India Psychiatry Journal* 23:86-93.

Murty, K. S., J. B. Roebuck, and G. R. Armstrong. 1994. "The black community's reactions to the 1992 Los Angeles riot." *Deviant Behavior* 15:85-104.

Musser, G., and S. Nemecek. 2000. "A new kind of war." *Scientific American,* June, p. 47.

Mustanski, B., R. Andrews, and J. A. Puckett. 2016. "The effects of cumulative victimization on mental health among lesbian, gay, bisexual, and transgender adolescents and young adults." *American Journal of Public Health* 106:527-33.

Mustanski, B. S., M. L. Chivers, and J. M. Bailey. 2002. "A critical review of recent biological research on human sexual orientation." *Annual Review of Sex Research* 13:89-140.

Myhill, D., and S. Jones. 2006. "'She doesn't shout at no girls': Pupils' perceptions of gender equity in the classroom." *Cambridge Journal of Education* 36:99-113.

Myrdal, G. 1944. *An American Dilemma.* New York: Harper and Bros.

Nader, R. 1990. "Corporate state is on a roll." *Los Angeles Times,* March 5.

Najman, J. M., et al. 2010. "Family poverty over the early life course and recurrent adolescent and young adult anxiety and depression." *American Journal of Public Health* 200:1719-23.

Napoli, M. 1998. "Hormone-disrupting chemicals." *HealthFacts,* November, p. 1.

National Academy of Sciences. 2009. "Smoking bans reduce the risk of heart attacks associated with secondhand smoke." NAS website.

National Alliance to End Homelessness. 2016. "The state of homelessness in America. NAEH website.

National Center for Education Statistics. 2016. "Charter school enrollment." NCES website.

National Center for Health Statistics. 2000. "Puerto Ricans' health fares worse than other U.S. Hispanics." Press release. NCHS website.

——. 2016. *Health, United States, 2015.* Hyattsville, MD: National Center for Health Statistics.

National Center on Addiction and Substance Abuse at Columbia University. 1998. *Back to School 1998: The CASA National Survey of American Attitudes on Substance Abuse.* Washington, DC: National Center on Addiction and Substance Abuse.

National Coalition for the Homeless. 2000. *Welfare to What II?* Washington, DC: NCH.

——. 2006. "A dream denied: The criminalization of homelessness in U.S. cities." NCFH website.

——. 2009. "Who is homeless?" NCH website.

——. 2016. "No safe street." NCH website.

National Institute of Justice. 1996a. "Alternative sanctions in Germany: An overview of Germany's sentencing practices." *Research Preview,* February.

——. 1996b. "The cycle of violence revisited." *Research Preview,* February.

National Institute on Alcohol Abuse and Alcoholism. 2001. *Alcohol: Getting the Facts.* Bethesda, MD: NIAAA.

National Institute on Drug Abuse. 1998. "Marijuana: Facts for teens." NIDA website.

——. 2004. "Preventing drug use among children and adolescents." NIDA website.

——. 2005. "NIDA infofacts: Methamphetamine." NIDA website.

——. 2014. "Adolescents and young adults." NIDA website.

National Marriage Project. 2012. "The state of our unions." National Marriage Project website.

National Study of Charter Schools. 2000. "The state of charter schools 2000." National Study of Charter Schools website.

National Survey on Drug Use and Health. 2004. "Religious beliefs and substance use among youths." *The NSDUH Report,* January 30.

Needle, R., et al. 2008. "Sex, drugs, and HIV." *Social Science and Medicine* 67:1447-55.

Nelson, D. E., et al. 2013. "Alcohol-attributable cancer deaths and years of potential life lost in the United States." *American Journal of Public Health* 103:641-8.

Neria, Y., et al. 2000. "Posttraumatic residues of captivity." *Journal of Clinical Psychiatry* 61 (January):39-46.

Neria, Y., L. DioGrande, and B. G. Adams. 2011. "Posttraumatic stress disorder following the September 11, 2001, terrorist attacks." *American Psychologist* 66: 429-46.

Ness, E. 2003. "Federal government's program in attacking the problem of prostitution." *Federal Probation* 67:10-12.

Ness, R. B., et al. 1999. "Cocaine and tobacco use and the risk of spontaneous abortion." *New England Journal of Medicine* 340 (February 4):333-39.

Netemeyer, R. G., J. C. Andrews, and S. Burton. 2005. "Effects of antismoking advertising-based beliefs on adult smokers' consideration of quitting." *American Journal of Public Health* 95:1062-66.

Netter, W. J. 2003. "Curing the unique health identifier." *Jurimetrics* 43:165-86.

Newman, B. S. 2007. "College students' attitudes about lesbians." *Journal of Homosexuality* 52:249-65.

Newman, K., C. Fox, D. Harding, J. Mehta, and W. Roth. 2004. *Rampage: The Social Roots of School Shootings.* New York: Basic Books.

Newman, K. S., and R. L. O'Brien. 2011. "Taxing the poor: How some states make poverty worse." *Pathways,* Summer, pp. 22-26.

Newman, R. J. 1998. "A U.S. victory, at a cost of $5.5 trillion." *U.S. News and World Report,* July 13.

Newport, F. 2011. "Despite negativity, Americans mixed on ideal role of government." *Gallup Poll Archives.* Gallup Poll website.

Newton, J. 1998. "White guys: Hegemonic masculinities." *Feminist Studies* 24:11-20.

Nguyen-Louie, T. T., et al. 2015. "Effects of emerging alcohol and marijuana use behaviors on adolescents' neuropsychological functioning over four years." *Journal of Studies on Alcohol and Drugs* 76:738-48.

Nicaise, V., G. Cogerino, J. E. Bois, and A. J. Amorose. 2006. "Students' perceptions of teacher feedback and physical competence in physical education classes." *Journal of Teaching in Physical Education* 25:36-57.

Nieves, E. 1999. "For patrons of prostitutes, remedial instruction." *New York Times,* March 18.

Nijhof, G. 1995. "Parkinson's disease as a problem of shame in public appearance." *Sociology of Health and Illness* 17 (March):193-205.

Nixon, A. E., et al. 2011. "Can work make you sick? A meta-analysis of the relationships between job stressors and physical symptoms." *Work & Stress* 25:1-22.

Nixon, K., L. Tutty, P. Downe, K. Gorkoff, and J. Ursel. 2002. "The everyday occurrence: Violence in the lives of girls exploited through prostitution." *Violence against Women* 8:1016-43.

Noble, K. G., M. J. Farah, and B. D. McCandliss. 2006. "Socioeconomic background modulates cognition-achievement relationships in reading." *Cognitive Development* 21:349-68.

Nolan, S. A., J. P. Buckner, C. H. Marzabadi, and V. J. Kuck. 2008. "Training and mentoring of chemists." *Sex Roles* 58:235-50.

Noonan, M. C., and M. E. Corcoran. 2004. "The mommy track and partnership: Temporary delay or dead end?" *The Annals of the American Academy of Political and Social Science* 596:130-50.

Noonan, M. C., M. E. Corcoran, and P. M. Courant. 2005. "Pay differences among the highly trained." *Social Forces* 84:831-51.

Nooyens, A. C. J., B. M. van Gelder, and W. M. M. Verschuren. 2008. "Smoking and cognitive decline among middle-aged men and women." *American Journal of Public Health* 98:2244-50.

Nord, M., and H. Hopwood. 2008. "A comparison of household food security in Canada and the United States." *Economic Research Report No. (ERR-67).* U.S. Department of Agriculture.

Norman, J. 2015. "In U.S., support for Tea Party drops to new low." Gallup Poll website.

Norman, J. 2016. "Americans' confidence in institutions stays low." Gallup Poll website.

Norton-Hawk, M. A. 2002. "Lifecourse of prostitution." *Women, Girls, and Criminal Justice* 3:1-9.

——. 2004. "Comparison of pimp- and non-pimp-controlled women." *Violence against Women* 10:189-94.

Nunley, J. M., et al. 2016. "The effects of unemployment and underemployment on employment opportunities." *ILR Review*, June 22.

Oakes, J. 2005. *Keeping Track: How Schools Structure Inequality.* 2nd ed. New Haven, CT: Yale University Press.

Obach, B. K. 2002. "Labor-environmental relations." *Social Science Quarterly* 83:82-100.

Obot, I. S., F. A. Wagner, and J. C. Anthony. 2001. "Early onset and recent drug use among children of parents with alcohol problems." *Drug and Alcohol Dependence* 65:1-8.

O'Brien, R. M., J. Stockard, and L. Isaacson. 1999. "The enduring effects of cohort characteristics on age-specific homicide rates, 1960-1995." *American Journal of Sociology* 104 (January):1061-95.

Occupational Safety and Health Administration. 1996. "Information about OSHA." OSHA website.

——. 2002. "Occupational injury and illness incidence rates per 100 full-time workers." OSHA website.

O'Connor, P. 2014. "Attitudes toward poverty show dramatic change." *Wall Street Journal*, June 20.

O'Connor, R. E., R. J. Bord, B. Yarnal, and N. Wiefek. 2002. "Who wants to reduce greenhouse gas emissions?" *Social Science Quarterly* 83:1-17.

Office of Juvenile Justice and Delinquency Prevention. 2006. "Teen dating violence awareness and prevention week." *OJJDP's E-Mail Information Resource.*

Office of Management and Budget. 2016. "Budget of the U.S. Government." OMB website.

Office of National Drug Control Policy. 2003a. *Cocaine.* Washington, DC: Government Printing Office.

——. 2003b. *What Americans Need to Know about Marijuana.* Washington, DC: Government Printing Office.

——. 2008. *Teen Marijuana Use Worsens Depression.* Washington, DC: Government Printing Office.

——. 2011. "2011 national drug control strategy." ONDCP website.

Ogden, C. L., et al. 2016. "Trends in obesity prevalence among children and adolescents in the United States, 1988-1994 through 2013-2014." *Journal of the American Medical Association* 315:2292-99.

Ohshige, K., et al. 2000. "Cross-sectional study on risk factors of HIV among female commercial sex workers in Cambodia." *Epidemiology of Infections* 124 (February):143-52.

Okagaki, L., and P. A. Frensch. 1998. "Parenting and children's school achievement." *American Educational Research Journal* 35 (Spring):123-44.

Okechukwu, C. A., et al. 2012. "Household food insufficiency, financial strain, work-family spillover, and depressive symptoms in the working class." *American Journal of Public Health* 102:126-33.

O'Keefe, M. 1994. "Linking marital violence, mother-child/father-child aggression, and child behavior problems." *Journal of Family Violence* 9 (March):63-78.

Olds, D. L., C. R. Henderson Jr., and R. Tatelbaum. 1994. "Prevention of intellectual impairment in children of women who smoke during pregnancy." *Pediatrics* 93 (February):228-33.

Ong, P. M. 1991. "Race and post-displacement earnings among high-tech workers." *Industrial Relations* 30 (Fall):456-68.

Opp, R. D. 2002. "Enhancing program completion rates among two-year college students of color." *Community College Journal of Research and Practice* 26:147-63.

Orchowski, L. M., C. A. Gidycz, and H. Raffle. 2008. "Evaluation of a sexual assault risk reduction and self-defense program." *Psychology of Women Quarterly* 32:204-18.

Orfield, G., and C. Lee. 2005. *Why Segregation Matters: Poverty and Educational Inequality.* Cambridge: The Civil Rights Project at Harvard University.

Osawa, H., and M. Hayashi. 2009. "Status of the indoor air chemical pollution in Japanese houses based on the nationwide field survey from 2000 to 2005." *Building and Environment* 44:1330-36.

Osberg, L., and T. Smeeding. 2006. "'Fair' inequality? Attitudes toward pay differentials." *American Sociological Review* 71:450-73.

Osborne, C., and L. M. Berger. 2009. "Parental substance abuse and child well-being." *Journal of Family Issues* 30:341-70.

Osmond, D. H., L. M. Pollack, J. P. Paul, and J. A. Catania. 2007. "Changes in prevalence of HIV infection and sexual risk behavior in men who have sex with men in San Francisco." *American Journal of Public Health* 97:1677-83.

Ott, J. C. 2011. "Government and happiness in 130 nations." *Social Indicators Research* 102:3-22.

Ouweneel, P. 2002. "Social security and well-being of the unemployed in 42 nations." *Journal of Happiness Studies* 3:167-92.

Overpeck, M. D., R. A. Brenner, A. C. Trumble, L. B. Trifiletti, and H. W. Berendes. 1998. "Risk factors for infant homicide in the United States." *New England Journal of Medicine* 339 (October 22):1211-12.

Oxman, T. E., D. H. Freeman Jr., and E. D. Manheimer. 1995. "Lack of social participation or religious strength and comfort as risk factors for death after cardiac surgery in the elderly." *Psychosomatic Medicine* 57 (January–February):5-15.

Pagani, L., et al. 2009. "Risk factor models for adolescent verbal and physical aggression toward fathers." *Journal of Family Violence* 24:173-82.

Pager, D. 2003. "The mark of a criminal record." *American Journal of Sociology* 108:937-75.

Paige, S. 1998. "Babylon rides high-tech wave." *Insight on the News,* September 28.

Pais, J., K. Crowder, and L. Downey. 2014. "Unequal trajectories: Racial and class differences in residential exposure to industrial hazard." *Social Forces* 92:1189-215.

Palumbo, T. 2010. "Dynamics of economic well-being: Spells of unemployment, 2004-2007." *Household Economic Studies.* U.S. Census Bureau website.

Palzkill, B., and A. Fisher. 1990. "Between gymshoes and high-heels: The development of a lesbian identity and existence in top class sport." *International Review for the Sociology of Sport* 25 (3):221-34.

Panuzio, J., et al. 2007. "Relationship abuse and victims' posttraumatic stress disorder symptoms." *Journal of Family Violence* 22:177-85.

Pape, R. 2005. *Dying to Win: The Strategic Logic of Suicide Terrorism.* New York: Random House.

Parent, M., M. Rousseau, P. Boffetta, A. Cohen, and J. Siemiatycki. 2007. "Exposure to diesel and gasoline engine emissions and the risk of lung cancer." *American Journal of Epidemiology* 165:53-62.

Park, A. 2008. "America's health checkup." *Time,* December 1, pp. 41-51.

Park, B. Y., et al. 2016. "Is internet pornography causing sexual dysfunctions?" *Behavioral Science* 6:17-27.

Park, C. L., S. Armeli, and H. Tennen. 2004. "The daily stress and coping process and alcohol use among college students." *Journal of Studies on Alcohol* 65:126-35.

Parker, F. 1975. "What's right with American education." In *Myth and Reality,* 2nd ed., ed. G. Smith and C. R. Kniker, pp. 29-36. Boston: Allyn and Bacon.

Parker, K. F., and A. Reckdenwald. 2008. "Concentrated disadvantage, traditional male role models, and African-American juvenile violence." *Criminology* 46:711-35.

Parker, R. E. 1994. *Flesh Peddlers and Warm Bodies: The Temporary Help Industry and Its Workers.* New Brunswick, NJ: Rutgers University Press.

Parker, T., et al. 2010. "Beyond the prison bubble." *NIJ Journal* 268:31-36.

Parker-Pope, T. 2008. "Love, sex and the changing landscape of infidelity." *New York Times,* October 27.

Parks, M. 1991. "Cherynobyl." *Los Angeles Times,* April 23.

Paschall, M. J., M. Bersamin, and R. L. Flewelling. 2005. "Racial/ethnic differences in the association between college attendance and heavy alcohol use." *Journal of Studies on Alcohol* 66:266-74.

Pasley, K., J. Kerpelman, and D. E. Guilbert. 2001. "Gendered conflict, identity disruption, and marital instability." *Journal of Social and Personal Relationships* 18:5-27.

Passel, J. S., and D. Cohn. 2008. "Undocumented immigration now trails legal inflow, reversing decade-long trend." Pew Research Center website.

———. 2010. "Unauthorized immigrant population." Pew Research Center website.

Paternoster, R., and P. Mazerolle. 1994. "General strain theory and delinquency: A replication and extension." *Journal of Research in Crime and Delinquency* 31 (August):235-63.

Patterson, J., and P. Kim. 1991. *The Day America Told the Truth.* New York: Prentice-Hall.

Paul, P. 2004. "The porn factor." *Time,* January 19.

Pavalko, E. K., K. N. Mossakowski, and V. J. Hamilton. 2003. "Does perceived discrimination affect health? Longitudinal relationships between work discrimination and women's physical and emotional health." *Journal of Health and Social Behavior* 44:18-33.

Pavkov, T. W., et al. 2010. "Tribal youth victimization and delinquency." *Cultural Diversity and Ethnic Minority Psychology* 16:123-34.

Pawel, D. J., and J. S. Puskin. 2004. "The U.S. Environmental Protection Agency's assessment of risks from indoor radon." *Health Physics* 87:68-74.

Pear, R. 2009. "Health care reform." *New York Times,* May 28.

Pearce, L. D., and D. L. Haynie. 2004. "Intergenerational religious dynamics and adolescent delinquency." *Social Forces* 82:1553-72.

Peaslee, A. L. 1969. "Education's role in development." *Economic Development and Cultural Change* 17:293-318.

Pedersen, E. R., and J. W. LaBrie. 2008. "Normative misperceptions of drinking among college students." *Journal of Studies on Alcohol and Drugs* 69:406-11.

Peek, C. W., G. D. Lowe, and L. S. Williams. 1991. "Gender and God's word: Another look at religious fundamentalism and sexism." *Social Forces* 68 (June):1205-21.

Peguero, A. A. 2011. "Violence, schools, and dropping out." *Journal of Interpersonal Violence* 26:3753-72.

Peleg-Oren, N., and M. Sherer. 2001. "Cancer patients and their spouses." *Journal of Health Psychology* 6:329-38.

Peleman, R. A. 2004. "New and re-emerging infectious diseases." *Current Opinion in Anaesthesiology* 17:265-70.

Pellegrini, L. C., and R. Rodriguez-Monguio. 2013. "Unemployment, medicaid provisions, the mental health industry, and suicide." *The Social Science Journal* 50: 482-90.

Peretti, P. O., and A. di Vitorrio. 1993. "Effect of loss of father through divorce on personality of the preschool child." *Social Behavior and Personality* 21:33-38.

Peri, G. 2011. "The impact of immigration on native poverty through labor market competition." *NBER Working Paper No. 17570.* National Bureau of Economic Research website.

Perina, K. 2002. "Covenant marriage: A new marital contract." *Psychology Today,* March-April, p. 18.

Perl, R. F. 2006. "International terrorism: Threat, policy, and response." *CRS Report for Congress,* August 16.

Perlini, A. H., and T. L. Boychuk. 2006. "Social influence, desirability and relationship investment." *Social Behavior and Personality* 34:593-602.

Perlo-Freeman, S., and C. Solmirano. 2014. "Trends in world military expenditure, 2013." Stockholm International Peace Research Institute website.

Perry, B. 2011. "The labeling paradox." *Journal of Health and Social Behavior* 52:460-77.

Perry, S. W. 2004. *American Indians and Crime.* Washington, DC: Bureau of Justice Statistics.

Perry, S. L. 2016. "Does viewing pornography reduce marital quality over time?" *Archives of Sexual Behavior,* published online.

Perry-Jenkins, M., R. L. Repetti, and A. C. Crouter. 2000. "Work and family in the 1990s." *Journal of Marriage and the Family* 62:981-98.

Peterson, R., et al. 2015. "Identifying homelessness among veterans using VA administrative data." *PLoS One,* July 14. PLoS One website.

Petoskey, E. L., K. R. Van Stelle, and J. A. De Jong. 1998. "Family variables in substance-misusing male adolescents." *American Journal of Drug and Alcohol Abuse* 24 (1):61-84.

Petrill, S. A., A. Pike, T. Price, and R. Plomin. 2004. "Chaos in the home and socioeconomic status are associated with cognitive development in early childhood." *Intelligence* 32:445-60.

Petry, N. M., and B. Martin. 2002. "Low-cost contingency management for treating cocaine- and opioid-abusing methadone patients." *Journal of Consulting and Clinical Psychology* 70:398-405.

Petterson, S. M., and A. B. Albers. 2001. "Effects of poverty and maternal depression on early child development." *Child Development* 72:1794-813.

Pettit, B., and B. Western. 2004. "Mass imprisonment and the life course: Race and class inequality in U.S. incarceration." *American Sociological Review* 69:151-69.

Peugh, J., and S. Belenko. 2001. "Alcohol, drugs, and sexual function." *Journal of Psychoactive Drugs* 33:223-32.

Pew Center on the States. 2008. "Grading the states 2008." Pew Center on the States website.

Pew Research Center. 2003. "The 2004 political landscape." Pew Research Center website.

———. 2006. "Are we happy yet?" Pew Research Center website.

———. 2007. "Blacks see growing values gap between poor and middle class." Pew Research Center website.

Pew Research Center. 2013."Educational attainment by Latino origin group, 2013." Pew Research Center website.

Pew Research Center. 2016. "State of the news media." Pew Research Center website.

Pew Research Center for the People & the Press 2009. "Economy, jobs trump all other policy priorities in 2009." Pew Research Center for the People & the Press website.

Pfaff, D., ed. 2002. *Hormones, Brain and Behavior.* San Diego, CA: Academic.

Pfeffer, F. T., and F. R. Hertel. 2015. "How has educational expansion shaped mobility trends in the United States?" *Social Forces* 94:143-80.

Pfefferbaum, B., et al. 2001. "Traumatic grief in a convenience sample of victims seeking support services after a terrorist incident." *Annals of Clinical Psychiatry* 13:19-24.

———. 2002. "Exposure and peritraumatic response as predictors of posttraumatic stress in children following the 1995 Oklahoma City bombing." *Journal of Urban Health* 79:354-63.

Phelan, J. C., E. J. Bromet, and B. G. Link. 1998. "Psychiatric illness and family stigma." *Schizophrenia Bulletin* 24 (1): 115-26.

Phillips, D. P., G. E. C. Barker, and M. M. Eguchi. 2008. "A steep increase in domestic fatal medication errors with use of alcohol and/or street drugs." *Archives of Internal Medicine* 168:1561-66.

Phillips, D. P., T. E. Ruth, and L. M. Wagner. 1993. "Psychology and survival." *The Lancet* 342 (November 6):1142-45.

Phillips, J. A. 2006. "The relationship between age structure and homicide rates in the United States, 1970 to 1999." *Journal of Research in Crime and Delinquency* 43: 230-60.

Phillips-Howard, P. A., et al. 2010. "Wellbeing, alcohol use and sexual activity in young teenagers." *Substance Abuse Treatment, Prevention, and Policy* 5:27-34.

Physicians for Human Rights. 2002. "War-related sexual violence in Sierra Leone." Physicians for Human Rights website.

Pierce, J. 2002. "Poll: 8 of 10 want Internet obscenity laws enforced." *American Center for Law and Justice Newsletter,* March 18.

Pierce, J. P., et al. 1998. "Tobacco industry promotion of cigarettes and adolescent smoking." *Journal of the American Medical Association* 279 (February 18):511-15.

Pilippo, S., L. Mustaniemi, H. Lenko, R. Aine, and J. Maenpaa. 1999. "Surgery for ovarian masses during childhood and adolescence." *Journal of Pediatric and Adolescent Gynecology* 12 (November):223-27.

Pine, J. C., B. D. Marx, and A. Lakshmanan. 2002. "An examination of accidental-release scenarios from chemical-processing sites: The relation of race to distance." *Social Science Quarterly* 83:317-31.

Pinheiro, P. S. 2006. *World Report on Violence Against Children.* Geneva, Switzerland: United Nations.

Pinkerton, J. P. 2003. "A grand compromise." *Atlantic Monthly,* January/February, pp. 115-16.

Pinkleton, B. E., Y. Fujioka, and E. W. Austin. 2000. "The role of interpretation processes and parental discussion in the media's effects on adolescents' use of alcohol." *Pediatrics* 105:343-49.

Piper, B. J., et al. 2016. "Use and misuse of opioids in Maine." *Journal of Studies on Alcohol and Drugs.* 77: 556-65.

Piquero, N. L., S. G. Tibbetts, and M. B. Blankenship. 2006. "Examining the role of differential association and techniques of neutralization in explaining corporate crime." *Deviant Behavior* 26:159-88.

Pitcavage, M. 2001. "Camouflage and conspiracy: The militia movement." *American Behavioral Scientist* 44:957-81.

Pittman, L. D., and P. L. Chase-Lansdale. 2001. "African American adolescent girls in impoverished communities." *Journal of Research on Adolescence* 11:199-224.

Plane, D. L., and J. Gershtenson. 2004. "Candidates' ideological locations, abstention, and turnout in U.S. midterm Senate elections." *Political Behavior* 26:69-93.

Planty, M., et al. 2016. "Female victims of sexual violence, 1994-2010." Bureau of Justice Statistics website.

Platt, A. 1969. *The Child Savers: The Invention of Delinquency.* Chicago: University of Chicago Press.

Pochagina, O. 2006. "The sex business as a social phenomenon in contemporary China." *Far Eastern Affairs* 34:118-34.

Pollack, H. A. 2001. "Sudden infant death syndrome, maternal smoking during pregnancy, and the cost-effectiveness of smoking cessation intervention." *American Journal of Public Health* 91:432-36.

Pollard, C. A., H. J. Pollard, and K. J. Corn. 1989. "Panic onset and major events in the lives of agoraphobics: A test of contiguity." *Journal of Abnormal Psychology* 98 (August):318-21.

Polling report. 2016. The Polling Report website.

Pollock, J. M., J. L. Mullings, and B. M. Crouch. 2006. "Violent women." *Journal of Interpersonal Violence* 21:485-502.

Polman, H., B. O. de Castro, and M. A. G. van Aken. 2008. "Experimental study of the differential effects of playing versus watching violent video games on children's aggressive behavior." *Aggressive Behavior* 34:256-64.

Pool, R. 1993. "Evidence for homosexuality gene." *Science* 261 (July 16):291-92.

Popenoe, D., and B. D. Whitehead. 1999. *Should We Live Together?* Rutgers, NJ: National Marriage Project.

Portegies, P., and N. R. Rosenberg. 1998. "AIDS dementia complex." *CNS Drugs* 9 (January):31-40.

Porter, E. 2015. "Education gap between rich and poor is growing wider." *The New York Times,* September 22.

Porter, J., and L. M. Williams. 2011. "Intimate violence among underrepresented groups on a college campus." *Journal of Interpersonal Violence* 26:210-24.

Porter, M. E., and S. Stern. 2016. "Social progress index, 2016." Social Progress Index website.

Posner, R. A. 2001. "Security versus civil liberties." *Atlantic Monthly,* December, pp. 46-47.

Potterat, J. J., et al. 2004. "Mortality in a long-term open cohort of prostitute women." *American Journal of Epidemiology* 159:778-85.

Potterat, J. J., D. E. Woodhouse, J. B. Muth, and S. Q. Muth. 1990. "Estimating the prevalence and career longevity of prostitute women." *Journal of Sex Research* 27 (May): 233-43.

Poulsen, F. O., D. M. Busby, and A. M. Galovan. 2013. "Pornography use associated with couple outcomes." *Journal of Sex Research* 50:72-83.

Pratt, T. C., and J. Maahs. 1999. "Are private prisons more cost-effective than public prisons?" *Crime and Delinquency* 45 (July):358-71.

Presser, H. B. 2004. "The economy that never sleeps." *Contexts* 3:42-49.

Preston, S. H., and A. Stokes. 2011. "Contribution of obesity to international differences in life expectancy." *American Journal of Public Health* 101:2137-43.

Price, J., et al. 2016. "How much more xxx is Generation X consuming?" *Journal of Sex Research* 53:12-20.

Prince, D. A. 1986. "A psychological profile of prostitutes in California and Nevada." Unpublished PhD dissertation, United States International University, San Diego, CA.

Pringle, P. 1997. "Remembering while building for the future." *San Diego Union-Tribune,* April 27.

Prior, M. 2006. "The incumbent in the living room." *Journal of Politics* 68:657-63.

Proctor, B. D., J. L. Semega, and M. A. Kollar. 2016. "Income and poverty in the United States: 2015." U.S. Census Bureau website.

Proulx, R. J., and L. Jimerson. 1998. "Business as usual? Not in Vermont." *School Business Affairs* 64 (April):9-14.

Purdy, M. 2008. "Personal tragedies illuminate the consequences of war." *Nieman Reports* 62:68-69.

Qato, D. M., et al. 2008. "Use of prescription and over-the-counter medications and dietary supplements among older adults in the United States." *Journal of the American Medical Association* 300:2867-78.

Qouta, S., R. Punamäki, T. Miller, and E. El-Sarraj. 2007. "Does war beget child aggression?" *Aggressive Behavior* 34:231-44.

Quillian, L. 1995. "Population, perceived threat, and prejudice in Europe." *American Sociological Review* 60:586-611.

——. 2014. "Does segregation create winners and losers?" *Social Problems* 61:402-26.

Quinn, D. M. 2015. "Kindergarten black-white test score gaps." *Sociology of Education* 88: 120-39.

Rahim, H. F. A., et al. 2009. "Maternal and child health in the occupied Palestinian territory." *The Lancet* 373:967-77.

Rahn, W. M., and T. J. Rudolph. 2005. "A tale of political trust in American cities." *Public Opinion Quarterly* 69:530-60.

Raine, A., P. Brennan, and S. A. Mednick. 1994. "Birth complications combined with early maternal rejection at age 1 year predispose to violent crime at age 18 years." *Archives of General Psychiatry* 51 (December):984-88.

Rainwater, L. 1967. "Crisis of the city: Poverty and deprivation." *Washington University Magazine* (Spring):17-21.

Raloff, J. 1999. "Formaldehyde: Some surprises at home." *Science News,* January 9, p. 22.

Rand, M. R. 2008. "Criminal victimization, 2007." *Bureau of Justice Statistics Bulletin.* Washington, DC: Government Printing Office.

Ranson, G. 2001. "Men at work: Change—or no change?— in the era of the 'new father.'" *Men and Masculinities* 4:3-26.

Raphael, J., and D. L. Shapiro. 2004. "Violence in indoor and outdoor prostitution venues." *Violence against Women* 10:126-39.

Ratnesar, R. 2002. "Revenge: Arafat—and why the rage keeps burning." *Time,* April 8.

Räty, H. 2006. "What comes after compulsory education?" *Educational Studies* 32:1-16.

Rauscher, K. J., C. W. Runyan, M. D. Schulman, and J. M. Bowling. 2008. "U.S. child labor violations in the retail and service industries." *American Journal of Public Health* 98:1693-99.

Ray, B. D. 2013. "Homeschooling associated with beneficial learning and societal outcomes but educators do not promote it." *Peabody Journal of Education* 88:324-41.

Ream, R. K., and R. W. Rumberger. 2008. "Student engagement, peer social capital, and school dropout among Mexican American and non-Latino white students." *Sociology of Education* 81:109-39.

Reardon, S. F. 2012. "Brown fades: the end of court-ordered school desegregation and the resegregation of American public schools." *Journal of Policy Analysis and Management* 31: 876-904.

Rehm, J. 2011. "The risks associated with alcohol use and alcoholism." *Alcohol Research and Health* 34:135-43.

Rehnquist, W. H. 1998. *All the Laws but One: Civil Liberties in Wartime.* New York: Alfred A. Knopf.

Reid, J., P. Macchetto, and S. Foster. 1999. *No Safe Haven: Children of Substance-Abusing Parents.* Washington, DC: National Center on Addiction and Substance Abuse.

Reilly, D. M. 1984. "Family therapy with adolescent drug abusers and their families: Defying gravity and achieving escape velocity." *Journal of Drug Issues* 14 (Spring):381-91.

Reine, I., M. Novo, and A. Hammarstrom. 2004. "Does the association between ill health and unemployment differ between young people and adults?" *Public Health* 118:337-45.

Reinhardt, J. M., P. Meadows, and J. M. Gillette. 1952. *Social Problems and Social Policy.* New York: American Book.

Reinherz, H. A., R. M. Giaconia, A. M. Hauf, M. S. Wasserman, and A. D. Paradis. 2000. "General and specific childhood risk factors for depression and drug disorders by early adulthood." *Journal of the American Academy of Child Adolescent Psychiatry* 39 (February):223-31.

Reitzel-Jaffe, D., and D. A. Wolfe. 2001. "Predictors of relationship abuse among young men." *Journal of Interpersonal Violence* 16:99-115.

Remery, C., A. van Doorne-Huiskes, and J. Schippers. 2003. "Family-friendly policies in the Netherlands." *Personnel Review* 32:456-73.

Renner, M. 1991. "Military victory, ecological defeat." *World Watch* (July–August):27-34.

——. 1993a. *Critical Juncture: The Future of Peacekeeping.* Washington, DC: Worldwatch Institute.

——. 1993b. "Preparing for peace." In *State of the World 1993,* ed. L. Brown, pp. 139-57. New York: W. W. Norton.

——. 1997. *Small Arms, Big Impact.* Washington, DC: Worldwatch Institute.

——. 1999. "Ending violent conflict." In *State of the World 1999,* ed. L. R. Brown et al., pp. 151-68. New York: W. W. Norton.

——. 2002. "Breaking the link between resources and repression." In *State of the World 2002,* ed. L. Starke, pp. 149-73. New York: W. W. Norton.

——. 2006. "Vehicle production continues to expand." In *Vital Signs: 2006-2007,* ed. L. Starke, pp. 64-65. New York: W. W. Norton.

Resmovits, J. 2013. "Teacher survey shows record low job satisfaction in 2012." *Huffington Post,* February 21.

Revkin, A. C. 2001. "EPA ties tiniest soot particles to early deaths." *New York Times,* April 21.

Reynal-Querol, M. 2002. "Ethnicity, political systems, and civil wars." *Journal of Conflict Resolution* 46:29-54.

Reynolds, J. 2004. "When too much is not enough: Actual and preferred work hours in the United States and Abroad." *Sociological Forum* 19:89-120.

Ricchiardi, S. 1998. "Double vision." *American Journalism Review* 20 (3):30-36.

Rice, R. W., M. R. Frone, and D. B. McFarlin. 1992. "Work-nonwork conflict and the perceived quality of life." *Journal of Organizational Behavior* 13 (March):155-68.

Rich, N. 2010. "For whom the cell tolls." *Harper's Magazine,* May, pp. 44-53.

Richards, M., M. J. Jarvis, N. Thompson, and M. E. J. Wadsworth. 2003. "Cigarette smoking and cognitive decline in midlife." *American Journal of Public Health* 93:994-98.

Richardson, J. W. 2002. "Poor, powerless and poisoned." *Journal of Children and Poverty* 8:141-57.

Richey, W. 2012. "In voter ID case, South Carolina fights back against Obama administration." *Christian Science Monitor,* February 8.

Richman, J. A., L. Cloninger, and K. M. Rospenda. 2008. "Macrolevel stressors, terrorism, and mental health outcomes." *American Journal of Public Health* 98:323-29.

Richtel, M. 2007. "For pornographers, Internet's virtues turn to vices." *New York Times,* June 2.

Rieder, M., and I. Choonara. 2012. "Armed conflict and child health." *Archives of Disease in Childhood* 97:59-62.

Rieger, G., J. A. W. Linsenmeier, L. Gygax, and J. M. Bailey. 2008. "Sexual orientation and childhood gender nonconformity." *Developmental Psychology* 44:46-58.

Rifkin, R. 2014a. "Public faith in Congress falls again, hits historic low." Gallup Poll website.

Rifkin, R. 2014b. "In U.S. support for daily prayer in schools dips slightly." Gallup Poll website.

Rifkin, R. 2015. "In U.S., healthcare insecurity at record low." Gallup Poll website.

Rigg, K. K., and G. E. Ibanez. 2010. "Motivations for non-medical prescription drug use." *Journal of Substance Abuse Treatment* 39:236–47.

Riggle, E. D. B., S. S. Rostosky, and S. G. Horne. 2010. "Psychological distress, well-being, and well-being in same-sex couple relationships." *Journal of Family Psychology* 24:82–6.

Rinfret-Raynor, M., A. Riou, S. Cantin, C. Drouin, and M. Dube. 2004. "A survey on violence against female partners in Quebec, Canada." *Violence against Women* 10:709–28.

Rivara, F. P., et al. 1997. "Alcohol and illicit drug abuse and the risk of violent death in the home." *Journal of the American Medical Association* 278 (August 20):569–75.

Roane, K. R. 1998. "Prostitutes on wane in New York streets but take to Internet." *New York Times,* February 23.

Robelen, E. W. 2006. "NAEP reanalysis finds lag in charter school scores." *Education Week.* Education Week website.

Robelen, E. 2013. "Global-achievement study casts U.S. scores in better light." *Education Week,* January 15.

Roberts, A.I., et al. 2013. "Perinatal air pollution exposures and autism spectrum disorder in the Children of Nurses' Health Study II participants." *Environmental Health Perspectives* 121:746–54.

Roberts, D. F., L. Henriksen, and P. G. Christenson. 1999. *Substance Use in Popular Movies and Music.* Washington, DC: Government Printing Office.

Roberts, J. T. 1993. "Psychosocial effects of workplace hazardous exposures: Theoretical synthesis and preliminary findings." *Social Problems* 40 (February):74–89.

Robinson, T. N., M. L. Wilde, L. C. Navracruz, K. F. Haydel, and A. Varady. 2001. "Effects of reducing children's television and video game use on aggressive behavior." *Archives of Pediatric and Adolescent Medicine* 155:17–23.

Robison, K. K., E. M. Crenshaw, and J. C. Jenkins. 2006. "Ideologies of violence: The social origins of Islamist and leftist transnational terrorism." *Social Forces* 84:2009–26.

Rodgers, H. R., Jr., and C. S. Bullock. 1972. *Law and Social Change.* New York: McGraw-Hill.

Rodgers, J. E. 1994. "Addiction—A whole new view." *Psychology Today,* September–October, pp. 32–39.

Rodriguez, E. 2001. "Keeping the unemployed healthy." *American Journal of Public Health* 91:1403–11.

Roeber, J., et al. 2007. "Types of alcoholic beverages usually consumed by students in 9th–12th grades—Four states, 2005." *Morbidity and Mortality Weekly Report* 56:737–40.

Rogers-Dillon, R. 1995. "The dynamics of welfare stigma." *Qualitative Sociology* 18 (4):439–56.

Rogge, R. D., and T. N. Bradbury. 1999. "Till violence does us part." *Journal of Consulting and Clinical Psychology* 67 (June):340–51.

Roisman, G. I., E. Clausell, A. Holland, K. Fortuna, and C. Elieff. 2008. "Adult romantic relationships as contexts of human development." *Developmental Psychology* 44: 91–101.

Rojek, J., R. Rosenfeld, and S. Decker. 2012. "Policing race." *Criminology* 50:993–1024.

Rolland, J. S. 1987. "Chronic illness and the life cycle: A conceptual framework." *Family Process* 26 (2):203–21.

Romo, H. D. 1999. "Tracking programs derail minority and disadvantaged students' success." *Community College Journal* 69 (January):12–17.

Röndahl, G., S. Innala, and M. Carlsson. 2007. "To hide or not to hide, that is the question! Lesbians and gay men describe experiences from nursing work environment." *Journal of Homosexuality* 52:211–33.

Roodman, D. M. 1999. "Building a sustainable society." In *State of the World 1999,* ed. L. R. Brown et al., pp. 169–88. New York: W. W. Norton.

Roosevelt, M. 2004. "The tragedy of Tar Creek." *Time,* April 26, pp. 42–47.

Rorabaugh, W. J. 1979. *The Alcoholic Republic: An American Tradition.* New York: Oxford University Press.

Roscigno, V. J., D. L. Karafin, and G. Tester. 2009. "The complexities and processes of racial housing discrimination." *Social Problems* 56:49–69.

Roscigno, V. J., D. Tomaskovic-Devey, and M. Crowley. 2006. "Education and the inequalities of place." *Social Forces* 84:2121–45.

Rose, K. M., et al. 2004. "Women's employment status and mortality." *Journal of Women's Health* 13:1108–18.

Rosen, J. 2000. "Talk is cheap—Campaign finance reform meets the Internet." *New Republic,* February 14, pp. 20–24.

Rosen, K. H., and S. M. Stith. 1995. "Women terminating abusive dating relationships." *Journal of Social and Personal Relationships* 12 (February):155–60.

Rosenbaum, J. E., S. J. Popkin, J. E. Kaufman, and J. Rusin. 1991. "Social integration of low-income black adults in middle-class white suburbs." *Social Problems* 38 (November):448–61.

Rosenberg, D. 2002. "Stem cells: Slow progress." *Newsweek,* August 12.

Rosenblum, J. D. 1995. *Copper Crucible: How the Arizona Miners' Strike of 1983 Recast Labor-Management Relations in America.* Ithaca, NY: ILR Press.

Rosenfeld, R. 2002. "Crime decline in context." *Contexts* 1:25–34.

Rosenfeld, S. 2007. "Turning back the clock on voting rights." *Social Policy* 38:52–66.

Rosenfield, S. 1997. "Labeling mental illness: The effects of received services and perceived stigma on life satisfaction." *American Sociological Review* 62 (August): 660–72.

Rosenman, R. H. 1990. "Type A behavior pattern: A personal overview." *Journal of Social Behavior and Personality* 5 (1):1–24.

Rosenthal, J. 2006. "Precisely false vs. approximately right." *New York Times,* August 27.

Rosenthal, M. N., A. M. Smidt, and J. J. Freyd. 2016. "Still second class." *Psychology of Women Quarterly* 40:364–77.

Rosenthal, R., and L. Jacobson. 1968. "Self-fulfilling prophecies in the classroom: Teachers' expectations as unintended determinants of pupils' intellectual competence." In *Social Class, Race, and Psychological Development,* ed. M. Deutsch, I. Katz, and A. R. Jensen, pp. 219–53. New York: Holt, Rinehart, and Winston.

Roskes, E., R. Feldman, S. Arrington, and M. Leisher. 1999. "A model program for the treatment of mentally ill offenders in the community." *Community Mental Health Journal* 35:461–72.

Rosoff, S. M., H. N. Pontell, and R. H. Tillman. 2002. *Profit without Honor: White-Collar Crime and the Looting of America.* 2nd ed. New York: Prentice-Hall.

Ross, M. W. 2005. "Typing, doing, and being: Sexuality and the Internet." *Journal of Sex Research* 42:342–52.

Ross, S. L., and M. A. Turner. 2005. "Housing discrimination in metropolitan America." *Social Problems* 52:152–80.

Rossi, J. A., et al. 2016. "Ergonomics and beyond." *Human Factors* 58: 777–95.

Roston, E., and J. F. O. McAllister. 2004. "Humiliation in an Iraqi jail." *Time,* May 10, p. 20.

Roth, J. A., and C. S. Koper. 1999. *Impacts of the 1994 Assault Weapons Ban: 1994–96.* Washington, DC: National Institute of Justice.

Roth, L. M. 2003. "Selling women short: Gender differences in compensation on Wall Street." *Social Forces* 82:783–802.

Rothman, E. F., et al. 2011. "Drinking style and dating violence in a sample of urban, alcohol-using youth." *Journal of Studies on Alcohol and Drugs* 72:555–66.

Roy, A. 2003. "Distal risk factors for suicidal behavior in alcoholics." *Journal of Affective Disorders* 77:267–71.

Ruback, R. B., J. N. Shaffer, and V. A. Clark. 2011. "Easy access to firearms: Juveniles' risks for violence offending and violent victimization." *Journal of Interpersonal Violence* 26:2111–38.

Rubin, A. J. 2009. "Iraqi surveys start to unveil the mental scars of war, especially among women." *New York Times,* March 8.

Rugh, J. S., and D. S. Massey. 2010. "Racial segregation and the American foreclosure crisis." *American Sociological Review* 75:629–51.

Ruo, B., et al. 2003. "Depressive symptoms and health-related quality of life." *Journal of the American Medical Association* 290:215–21.

Russell, D. E. H. 1982. *Rape in Marriage.* New York: Macmillan.

———. 1986. *The Secret Trauma: Incest in the Lives of Girls and Women.* New York: Basic Books.

Ryan, C. L., and K. Bauman. 2016. "Educational attainment in the United States: 2015." U.S. Census Bureau website.

Ryan, W. 1971. *Blaming the Victim.* New York: Pantheon Books.

Sabin, J. A., R. G. Riskind, and B. A. Nosek. 2015. "Health care providers' implicit and explicit attitudes toward lesbian women and Gay Men." *American Journal of Public Health* 105:1831–41.

Sabin, M., R. L. Cardozo, L. Nackerud, R. Kaiser, and L. Varese. 2003. "Factors associated with poor mental health among Guatemalan refugees living in Mexico 20 years after civil conflict." *Journal of the American Medical Association* 290:635.

Sacco, V. F. 2003. "Black hand outrage: A constructionist analysis of an urban crime wave." *Deviant Behavior* 24:53–77.

Sacks, J. J., T. R. Simon, A. E. Crosby, G. Shelley, and M. P. Thompson. 2001. "Attitudinal acceptance of intimate partner violence among U.S. adults." *Violence and Victims* 16:115–26.

Salam, M. T., Y. F. Li, B. Langholz, and F. D. Gilliland. 2004. "Early-life environmental risk factors for asthma." *Environmental Health Perspectives* 112:760–65.

Salfati, C. G., A. R. James, and L. Ferguson. 2008. "Prostitute homicides." *Journal of Interpersonal Violence* 23:505–43.

Samaan, R. A. 2000. "The influences of race, ethnicity, and poverty on the mental health of children." *Journal of Health Care for the Poor and Underserved* 11 (February):100–10.

Samet, J. M., et al. 2000. "Fine particulate air pollution and mortality in 20 U.S. cities, 1987–1994." *New England Journal of Medicine* 343:1742–49.

Sampat, P. 2000. *Deep Trouble: The Hidden Threat of Groundwater Pollution.* Washington, DC: Worldwatch Institute.

Sampson, R. J. 2008. "Rethinking crime and immigration." *Contexts* 7:28–33.

Sampson, R. J., S. W. Raudenbush, and F. Earls. 1997. "Neighborhoods and violent crime: A multilevel study." *Science* 277 (August 15):918–24.

Sampson, R. J., P. Sharkey, and S. W. Raudenbush. 2008. "Durable effects of concentrated disadvantage on verbal ability among African-American children." *Proceedings of the National Academy of Sciences USA* 105:845–52.

Samuels, C. A. 2012. "Oregon community schools model shows staying power." *Education Week*, March 13. Education Week website.

Sanchez-Jankowski, M. 1991. *Islands in the Street: Gangs and American Urban Society.* Berkeley: University of California.

Sandelowski, M., C. Lambe, and J. Barroso. 2004. "Stigma in HIV-positive women." *Journal of Nursing Scholarship* 36:122–28.

Sandstrom, A. 2016. "Women relatively rare in top positions of religious leadership." Pew Research Center website.

San Francisco Bureau. 2001. "New program hits racist property deeds." *Sun Reporter,* May 24, p. 3.

Sang, B., J. Warshow, and A. J. Smith, eds. 1991. *Lesbians at Midlife: The Creative Transition.* San Francisco: Spinsters.

Saphores, J. M., H. Nixon, O. A. Ogunseitan, and A. A. Shapiro. 2006. "Household willingness to recycle electronic waste." *Environment and Behavior* 38:183–208.

Saporito, S., and D. Sohoni. 2006. "Coloring outside the lines: Racial segregation in public schools and their attendance boundaries." *Sociology of Education* 79:81–105.

Sarafino, E. P., M. E. Paterson, and E. L. Murphy. 1998. "Age and impacts of triggers in childhood asthma." *Journal of Asthma* 35 (2):213–17.

Sargent, J. D., T. A. Wills, M. Stoolmiller, J. Gibson, and F. X. Gibbons. 2006. "Alcohol use in motion pictures and its relation with early-onset teen drinking." *Journal of Studies on Alcohol* 67:54–65.

Sawin, J. L. 2004. "Making better energy choices." In *State of the World 2004,* ed. L. Starke, pp. 24–45. New York: W. W. Norton.

Sawin, J. L., and W. R. Moomaw. 2009. "An enduring energy future." In *State of the World,* ed. L. Starke, pp. 130–50. New York: W. W. Norton.

Scarpa, A. 2003. "Community violence exposure in young adults." *Trauma, Violence, and Abuse* 4:210–27.

Schachter, S., and J. E. Singer. 1962. "Cognitive, social, and psychological determinants of emotional state." *Psychological Review* 69 (September):379–99.

Schapiro, M. 2007. "Toxic inaction." *Harper's Magazine,* October, pp. 78–83.

Scharber, H. 2014. "Does 'out of work' get into the womb?" *Journal of Health and Social Behavior* 55:266–82.

Scheff, T. 1966. *Being Mentally Ill.* Chicago: Aldine.

Scher, R. K. 1997. *The Modern Political Campaign.* New York: M. E. Sharpe.

Schieman, S., and G. Plickert. 2008. "How knowledge is power: Education and the sense of control." *Social Forces* 87:153–83.

Schlosser, E. 1997. "The business of pornography." *U.S. News and World Report,* February 10.

Schmidley, D. 2003. The *Foreign-Born Population in the United States: March 2002.* Washington, DC: Government Printing Office.

Schmitt, D. P., A. Realo, M. Voracek, and J. Allik. 2008. "Why can't a man be more like a woman? Sex differences in big five personality traits across 55 cultures." *Journal of Personality and Social Psychology* 94:168–82.

Schnake, M. E., S. C. Bushardt, and C. Spottswood. 1984. "Internal work motivation and intrinsic job satisfaction: The effects of goal clarity, goal difficulty, participation in goal setting, and task complexity." *Group and Organization Studies* 9 (June):201–19.

Schneider, D., K. Harknett, and S. McLanahan. 2016. "Intimate partner violence in the Great Recession." *Demography* 3:471–505.

Schneider, J. P. 2003. "The impact of compulsive cybersex behaviours on the family." *Sexual and Relationship Therapy* 18:329–54.

Schnittker, J. 2007. "Working more and feeling better: Women's health, employment, and family life, 1974–2004." *American Sociological Review* 72:221–38.

Schnurr, P. P., A. Spiro III, and A. H. Paris. 2000. "Physician-diagnosed medical disorders in relation to PTSD symptoms in older male military veterans." *Health Psychology* 19 (January):91–97.

Schofer, E., and J. W. Meyer. 2005. "The worldwide expansion of higher education in the twentieth century." *American Sociological Review* 70:898–920.

Schonfeld, A. M., S. N. Mattson, and E. P. Riley. 2005. "Moral maturity and delinquency after prenatal alcohol exposure." *Journal of Studies on Alcohol* 66:545–54.

Schott, L., and L. Pavetti 2012. "Many states cutting TANF benefits harshly despite high unemployment and unprecedented need." Center on Budget and Policy Priorities website.

Schramm, D. G., et al. 2013. "Economic costs and policy implications associated with divorce." *Journal of Divorce & Remarriage* 54:1–24.

Schuckit, M. A., T. L. Smith, and J. Kalmijn. 2013. "Relationships among independent major depressions, alcohol use, and other substance use and related problems over 30 Years in 397 families." *Journal of Studies on Alcohol and Drugs* 74:271–79.

Schutz, D. 2007. "Essay review: Pay your money and take your 'school choice.'" *Teachers College Record.* TCR website.

Schwartz, J. 2004. "Air pollution and children's health." *Pediatrics* 113:1037–43.

———. 2006. "A scarred region mends, with help from many friends." *New York Times,* November 13.

Scott, D. 1999. "Equal opportunity, unequal results." *Environment and Behavior* 31 (March):267–90.

Scott, J. 1990a. "Job-related illness called America's invisible killer." *Los Angeles Times,* August 31.

———. 1990b. "Parents' smoking linked to children's lung cancer." *Los Angeles Times,* September 6.

Scott, J., and D. Leonhardt. 2005. "Class in America: Shadowy lines that still divide." *New York Times,* May 15.

Scott, M. S., and C. F. Delgado. 2005. "Identifying cognitively gifted minority students in preschool." *Gifted Child Quarterly* 49:199.

Scott, W. A., R. Scott, and M. McCabe. 1991. "Family relationships and children's personality: A cross-cultural, cross-source comparison." *British Journal of Social Psychology* 30 (March):1–20.

Scully, D., and J. Marolla. 1984. "Convicted rapists' vocabulary of motive: Excuses and justifications." *Social Problems* 31 (5):530–45.

Seal, K. H., et al. 2009. "Trends and risk factors for mental health diagnoses among Iraq and Afghanistan veterans using Department of Veterans Affairs health care, 2002–2008." *American Journal of Public Health* 99: 1651–58.

Seccombe, K., K. B. Walters, and D. James. 1999. "'Welfare mothers' welcome reform, urge compassion." *Family Relations* 48 (April):197–206.

Seeman, M., A. Z. Seeman, and A. Budros. 1988. "Powerlessness, work, and community: A longitudinal study of alienation and alcohol use." *Journal of Health and Social Behavior* 29 (September):185–98.

Selke, W. L., and H. E. Pepinsky. 1982. "The politics of police reporting in Indianapolis, 1948–1978." *Law and Human Behavior* 6 (3–4):327–42.

Semple, S. J., T. L. Patterson, and I. Grant. 2002. "Gender differences in the sexual risk practices of HIV1 heterosexual men and women." *AIDS and Behavior* 6:45–54.

Senanayake, S. N., and M. J. Ferson. 2004. "Detention for tuberculosis: Public health and the law." *Medical Journal of Australia* 180:573–76.

Sengupta, S. 2008. "Decades later, toxic sludge torments Bhopal." *New York Times,* July 7.

Senn, C. Y., and H. L. Radtke. 1990. "Women's evaluations of and affective reactions to mainstream violent pornography, nonviolent pornography, and erotica." *Violence and Victims* 5 (3):143–55.

Sennett, R., and J. Cobb. 1972. *The Hidden Injuries of Class.* New York: Vintage Books.

Settles, I. H., L. M. Cortina, J. Malley, and A. J. Stewart. 2006. "The climate for women in academic science." *Psychology of Women Quarterly* 30:47–58.

Shackelford, T. K., and J. Mouzos. 2005. "Partner killing by men in cohabiting and marital relationships." *Journal of Interpersonal Violence* 20:1310–24.

Shah, N. 2011. "Academic gains vary widely for charter networks." *Education Week.* Education Week website.

Shane, S., and M. Mazzetti. 2009. "In adopting harsh tactics, no look at past use." *New York Times,* April 22.

——. 1994. "The crab bucket syndrome." *New York Times,* June 19.

——. 1996. "Where we stand." *New York Times,* March 24.

Shannon, K., V. Bright, K. Gibson, and M. W. Tyndall. 2007. "Sexual and drug-related vulnerabilities for HIV infection among women engaged in survival sex work in Vancouver, Canada." *Canadian Journal of Public Health* 98:465–69.

Shapiro, J. R., and A. M. Williams. 2012. "The role of stereotype threats in undermining girls' and women's performance and interest in STEM fields." *Sex Roles* 66:175–83.

Shaw, B. A., N. Agahi, and N. Krause. 2011. "Are changes in financial strain associated with changes in alcohol use and smoking among older adults?" *Journal of Studies on Alcohol and Drugs* 72:917–25.

Shawn, H. 2011. "Responding to the cyber threat." FBI website.

Shearer, E. 2016. "Candidates' Social media outpaces their websites and emails as an online campaign news source." Pew Research Center website.

Sheehan, M. J., and M. W. Watson. 2008. "Reciprocal influences between maternal discipline techniques and aggression in children and adolescents." *Aggressive Behavior* 34:245–55.

Shehan, C. L., M. A. Burg, and C. A. Rexroat. 1986. "Depression and the social dimensions of the full-time housewife role." *Sociological Quarterly* 27:403–21.

Sheinberg, M., and P. Fraenkel. 2001. *The Relational Trauma of Incest.* New York: Guilford Press.

Shelton, B. A., and D. John. 1999. "Who does what and how much do they do? Gender and total work time." *Sociological Focus* 32:287–302.

Shemyakina, O. N., and A. C. Plagnol. 2013. "Subjective well-being and armed conflict." *Social Indicators Research* 113:1129–52.

Shen, Y., J. Arkes, and T. V. Williams. 2012. "Effects of Iraq/Afghanistan deployments on major depression and substance use disorder." *American Journal of Public Health* 102:S80–S87.

Sher, G. 2003. "On the decriminalization of drugs." *Criminal Justice Ethics* 22:12–15.

Sherman, A. M., and E. L. Zurbriggen. 2014. "Boys can be anything." *Sex Roles* 70:195–208.

Sherman, L. W., et al. 1998. *Preventing Crime: What Works, What Doesn't, What's Promising.* Washington, DC: Government Printing Office.

Shierholz, H. 2013. "Lagging minimum wage is one reason why Americans' wages have fallen behind productivity." Economic Policy Institute website.

Shih, J. H., and N. K. Eberhart. 2010. "Gender differences in the associations between interpersonal behaviors and stress generation." *Journal of Social and Clinical Psychology* 29:243–55.

Shipler, D. K. 2004. *The Working Poor: Invisible in America.* New York: Alfred K. Knopf.

Shojania, K. G., E. C. Burton, K. M. McDonald, and L. Goldman. 2003. "Changes in rates of autopsy-detected diagnostic errors over time." *Journal of the American Medical Association* 289:2849–56.

Shorey, R. C., G. L. Stuart, and T. L. Cornelius. 2011. "Dating violence and substance use in college students." *Aggression & Violent Behavior* 16:541–50.

Short, K. 2014. "The supplemental poverty measure: 2013." U.S. Census Bureau website.

Shrader-Frechette, K. 2005. "Radiobiology and gray science: Flaws in landmark new radiation protections." *Science and Engineering Ethics* 11:167–69.

Shukla, K., and M. Wiesner. 2016. "Relations of delinquency to direct and indirect violence exposure among economically disadvantaged, ethnic-minority midadolescents." *Crime and Delinquency* 62:423-55.

Sicotte, D., and S. Swanson. 2007. "Whose risk in Philadelphia? Proximity to unequally hazardous industrial facilities." *Social Science Quarterly* 88:515-34.

Siddika, N., et al. 2016. "Prenatal ambient air pollution exposure and the risk of stillbirth." *Occupational and Environmental Medicine* 73:573-81.

Siegel, M., C. S. Ross, and C. King. 2013. "The relationship between gun ownership and firearm homicide rates in the United States, 1981-2010." *American Journal of Public Health* 103: 2098-105.

Siegel, M., and E. F. Rothman. 2016. "Firearm ownership and suicide rates among US men and women, 1981-2013." *American Journal of Public Health*, published online.

Siegrist, J. 1995. "Emotions and health in occupational life." *Patient Education and Counseling* 25 (July):227-36.

Signorielli, N. 1989. "Television and conceptions about sex roles: Maintaining conventionality and the status quo." *Sex Roles* 21 (September):341-60.

Silberg, J., M. Rutter, B. D'Onofrio, and L. Eaves. 2003. "Genetic and environmental risk factors in adolescent substance use." *Journal of Child Psychology and Psychiatry and Allied Disciplines* 44:664-76.

Simcha-Fagan, O., J. C. Gersten, and T. S. Langner. 1986. "Early precursors and concurrent correlates of patterns of illicit drug use in adolescents." *Journal of Drug Issues* 16 (Winter):7-28.

Simon, H. B. 2006. "Old bugs learn some new tricks." *Newsweek,* December 11.

Simon, T., J. Mercy, and C. Perkins. 2001. *Injuries from Violent Crime, 1992-98.* Washington, DC: Government Printing Office.

Simon, T., et al. 2001. "Attitudinal acceptance of intimate partner violence among U.S. adults." *Violence and Victims* 16:115-26.

Simone, A., and B. H. Kleiner. 2004. "Practical guide to work-place reduction." *Management Research News* 27:125-32.

Simons, D. A., S. K. Wurtele, and R. L. Durham. 2008. "Developmental experiences of child sexual abusers and rapists." *Child Abuse and Neglect* 32:549-60.

Simons, R. L., and L. B. Whitbeck. 1991. "Sexual abuse as a precursor to prostitution and victimization among adolescent and adult homeless women." *Journal of Family Issues* 12 (September):361-79.

Simons-Morton, B., et al. 2016. "The effect of residence, school status, work status, and social influence of alcohol use among emerging adults." *Journal of Studies on Alcohol and Drugs* 77:121-32

Simpson, G. E., and M. Yinger. 1965. *Racial and Cultural Minorities.* New York: Harper and Row.

Singer, L. T., et al. 2002. "Cognitive and motor outcomes of cocaine-exposed infants." *Journal of the American Medical Association* 287:1952-60.

Sintov, N. D., et al. 2009. "Predictors of illicit substance dependence among individuals with alcohol dependence." *Journal of Studies on Alcohol and Drugs* 70:269-78.

Siordia, C. 2014. "Married once, twice, and three or more times." *Journal of Divorce & Remarriage* 55:206-15.

Sirgy, M. J., D. Efraty, P. Siegel, and D. J. Lee. 2001. "A new measure of quality of work life (QWL) based on need satisfaction and spillover theories." *Social Indicators Research* 55:241-302.

Skanberg, A., and E. Ohrstrom. 2002. "Adverse health effects in relation to urban residential soundscapes." *Journal of Sound and Vibration* 250:151-55.

Skinner, K. B., S. J. Bahr, D. R. Crane, and V. R. A. Call. 2002. "Cohabitation, marriage, and remarriage." *Journal of Family Issues* 23:74-90.

Skocpol., T., and V. Williamson. 2012. *The Tea Party and the Remaking of Republican Conservatism.* Oxford, UK: Oxford University Press.

Slesnick, N., et al. 2010. "Prevalence of intimate partner violence reported by homeless youth in Columbus, Ohio." *Journal of Interpersonal Violence* 25:1579-93.

Slevin, P., and S. F. Kovaleski. 2000. "Outside Palm Beach, complaints growing." *Washington Post,* November 11.

Sloan, M. 2006. "Election shows corruption still matters." *San Diego Union-Tribune,* December 6.

Slominski, L., A. Sameroff, K. Rosenblum, and T. Kasser. 2011. "Longitudinal pathways between maternal mental health in infancy and offspring romantic relationships in adulthood." *Social Development* 20:762-82.

Smart, R. G. 1991. "Crack cocaine use: A review of prevalence and adverse effects." *American Journal of Drug and Alcohol Abuse* 17 (March):13-26.

Smith, A. 2011. "The Internet and political news sources." Pew Research Center website.

Smith, C. A., L., J. Elwyn, T. O. Ireland, and T. P. Thornberry. 2010. "Impact of adolescent exposure to intimate partner violence on substance use in early adulthood." *Journal of Studies on Alcohol and Drugs* 71:219-30.

Smith, D. 2006. "Offshoring: Political myths and economic reality." *The World Economy* 29:249-56.

Smith, H. P., and R. J. Kaminski. 2011. "Self-injurious behaviors in state prisons." *Criminal Justice and Behavior* 38:26-41.

Smith, P. D., P. C. Rivers, and K. J. Stahl. 1992. "Family cohesion and conflict as predictors of drinking patterns: Beyond demographics and alcohol expectancies." *Family Dynamics of Addiction Quarterly* 2 (2):61-69.

Smith, R. A. 2005. "Do the determinants of promotion differ for white men versus women and minorities?" *American Behavioral Scientist* 9:1157-81.

Smith, S. J., D. C. Zanotti, A. M. Axelton, and D. A. Saucier. 2011. "Individuals' beliefs about the etiology of same-sex sexual orientation." *Journal of Homosexuality* 58:1110-31.

Smith, T. W. 2011. "Public attitudes toward homosexuality." National Opinion Research Center website.

Smith, T. W., and J. Son. 2015. "Trends in gun ownership in the United States, 1972-2014." NORC website.

Smolowe, J. 1995. "Enemies of the state." *Time,* May 8, pp. 58-69.

Snapp, S. D., et al. 2015. "Messy, butch, and queer: LBGTQ youth and the school-to-prison pipeline." *Journal of Adolescent Research* 30:57-82.

Snow, D. L., et al. 2006. "The role of coping and problem drinking in men's abuse of female partners." *Violence and Victims* 21:267-85.

Snyder, H. N., and M. Sickmund. 1999. *Juvenile Offenders and Victims: 1999 National Report.* Washington, DC: Office of Juvenile Justice and Delinquency Prevention.

——. 2006. *Juvenile Offenders and Victims: 2006 National Report.* Washington, DC: National Center for Juvenile Justice.

Sobel, E., et al. 1995. "Occupations with exposure to electromagnetic fields: A possible risk factor for Alzheimer's disease." *American Journal of Epidemiology* 142 (September 1):515-24.

Socall, D. W., and T. Holtgraves. 1992. "Attitudes toward the mentally ill: The effects of label and beliefs." *Sociological Quarterly* (3):435-45.

Solomon, Z., R. Dekel, and G. Zerach. 2008. "The relationships between posttraumatic stress symptom clusters and marital intimacy among war veterans." *Journal of Family Psychology* 22:659-66.

Solomon, Z., D. Shimrit, G. Zerach, and D. Horesh. 2011. "Marital adjustment, parental functioning, and emotional sharing in war veterans." *Journal of Family Issues* 32:127-47.

Solowij, N., et al. 2002. "Cognitive functioning of long-term heavy cannabis users seeking treatment." *Journal of the American Medical Association* 287:1123-31.

Somers, M. R., and F. Block. 2005. "From poverty to perversity: Ideas, markets, and institutions over 200 years of welfare debate." *American Sociological Review* 70:260-87.

Sommers, B.D., et al. 2016. "Changes in utilization and health among low income adults after Medicaid expansion or expanded private insurance." *JAMA Internal Medicine* Published online.

Sorenson, J., R. Wrinkle, V. Brewer, and J. Marquart. 1999. "Capital punishment and deterrence: Examining the effect of executions on murder in Texas." *Crime and Delinquency* 45 (October):481-93.

Soria, K. M., and S .Linder. 2014. "Parental divorce and first-year college students' persistence and academic achievement." *Journal of Divorce & Remarriage* 55:103-16.

Sorokin, P. A. 1942. *The Crisis of Our Age.* New York: E. P. Dutton.

South, S. J. 2001. "Time-dependent effects of wives' employment on marital dissolution." *American Sociological Review* 66:226-45.

Southwell, P. L. 2008. "The effect of political alienation on voter turnout, 1964-2000." *Journal of Political and Military Sociology* 36:131-45.

Spano, R., C. Rivera, and J. M. Bolland. 2010. "Are chronic exposure to violence and chronic violent behavior closely related to developmental processes during adolescence?" *Criminal Justice and Behavior* 37:1160-79.

Sparks, S. D. 2010. "Raising expectations is aim of new effort." *Education Week* 30:16-17.

Specter, M. 1996. "10 years later, through fear, Chernobyl still kills in Belarus." *New York Times,* March 31.

Spector, P. E. 2002. "Employee control and occupational stress." *Current Directions in Psychological Science* 11:133-36.

Spence, N. J., D. E. Adkins, and M. E. Dupre. 2011. "Racial differences in depression trajectories among older women." *Journal of Health and Social Behavior* 52:444-59.

Spergen, I. A., and G. D. Curry. 1990. "Strategies and perceived agency effectiveness in dealing with the young gang problem." In *Gangs in America,* ed. C. R. Huff. Newbury Park, CA: Sage.

Spilerman, S., and T. Lunde. 1991. "Features of educational attainment and job promotion prospects." *American Journal of Sociology* 97 (November):689-720.

Spivak, A. L., and S. F. Sharp. 2008. "Inmate recidivism as a measure of private prison performance." *Crime & Delinquency* 54:482-508.

Spix, C., et al. 1998. "Short-term effects of air pollution on hospital admissions of respiratory diseases in Europe." *Archives of Environmental Health* 53 (January-February):54-64.

Sprang, G. 1999. "Post-disaster stress following the Oklahoma City bombing." *Journal of Interpersonal Violence* 14 (February):169-83.

St. George-Hyslop, P. H. 2000. "Piecing together Alzheimer's." *Scientific American,* December, pp. 76-83.

St. Jean, Y., and J. R. Feagin. 1998. *Double Burden: Black Women and Everyday Racism.* Armonk, NY: M. E. Sharpe.

Stack, S. 1990. "Execution publicity and homicide in South Carolina: A research note." *Sociological Quarterly* 31 (4):599-611.

Stack, S., and J. Scourfield. 2015. "Recency of divorce, depression, and suicide risk." *Journal of Family Issues* 36:695-715.

Stack, S., I. Wasserman, and R. Kern. 2004. "Adult social bonds and use of Internet pornography." *Social Science Quarterly* 85:75-88.

Stafford, L. 2016. "Marital sanctity, relationship maintenance, and marital quality." *Journal of Family Issues* 37:119-31.

Stanley, M., I. Floyd, and M. Hill. 2016. "TANF cash benefits have fallen by more than 20 percent in most states and continue to erode." Center on Budget and Policy Priorities website.

Stanley, S. M., S. W. Whitton, and H. J. Markham. 2004. "Maybe I do: Interpersonal commitment and premarital or nonmarital cohabitation." *Journal of Family Issues* 25:496–519.

Stansfeld, S. A., et al. 2009. "Aircraft and road traffic noise exposure and children's mental health." *Journal of Environmental Psychology* 29:203-207.

Stansfeld, S. A., and M. P. Matheson. 2003. "Noise pollution: Non-auditory effects on health." *British Medical Bulletin* 68:243-57.

Stanton, A. H., and M. S. Schwartz. 1961. "The mental hospital and the patient." In *Complex Organizations*, ed. A. Etzioni, pp. 234-42. New York: Holt, Rinehart and Winston.

Stauber, S., et al. 2012. "A comparison of psychosocial risk factors between 3 groups of cardiovascular disease patients referred for outpatient cardiac rehabilitation." *Journal of Cardiopulmonary Rehabilitation and Prevention.* PubMed website.

Steelman, L. C., and B. Powell. 1991. "Sponsoring the next generation: Parental willingness to pay for higher education." *American Journal of Sociology* 96 (May):1505-29.

Stein, B. D., et al. 2004. "A national longitudinal study of the psychological consequences of the September 11, 2001, terrorist attacks." *Psychiatry* 67:105-17.

Stein, M. B., et al. 2004. "Relationship of sexual assault history to somatic symptoms and health anxiety in women." *General Hospital Psychiatry* 26:178-83.

Steinberg, L., B. B. Brown, and S. M. Dornbusch. 1997. *Beyond the Classroom: Why School Reform Has Failed and What Parents Need to Do.* New York: Touchstone.

Stephens-Davidowitz, S. 2013. "How many American men are gay?" *The New York Times*, Dec. 8.

Stepler, R. 2016. "Hispanic, black parents see college degree as key for children's success." Pew Research Center website.

Sternberg, R. J., E. L. Grigorenko, and K. K. Kidd. 2005. "Intelligence, race, and genetics." *American Psychologist* 60:46-59.

Stevens, D. J. 1994. "Predatory rapists and victim selection techniques." *Social Science Journal* 31 (4):421-33.

Stevens, M. L. 2001. *Kingdom of Children: Culture and Controversy in the Homeschooling Movement.* Princeton, NJ: Princeton University Press.

Stewart, D. N., and D. M. Szymanski. 2012. "Young adult women's reports of their male romantic partner's pornography use as a correlate of their self-esteem, relationship quality, and sexual satisfaction." *Sex Roles* 67:257-71.

Stewart, M., et al. 2016. "Respiratory health inequities experienced by low-income children and parents." *Journal of Poverty* 20:278-95.

Stewart, E. A., and R. L. Simons. 2009. *The Code of the Street and African-American Adolescent Violence.* National Institute of Justice website.

Stewart, W. F., J. A. Ricci, E. Chee, S. R. Hahn, and D. Morganstein. 2003. "Cost of lost productive work time among U.S. workers with depression." *Journal of the American Medical Association* 289:3135-44.

Stewart, W. F., J. A. Ricci, E. Chee, D. Morganstein, and R. Lupton. 2003. "Lost productive time and cost due to common pain conditions in the U.S. workforce." *Journal of the American Medical Association* 290:2443-54.

Stice, E., and S. K. Bearman. 2001. "Body-image and eating disturbances prospectively predict increases in depressive symptoms in adolescent girls." *Developmental Psychology* 37:597-607.

Stiles, B. L., X. Liu, and H. B. Kaplan. 2000. "Relative deprivation and deviant adaptations." *Journal of Research in Crime and Delinquency* 37 (February):64-90.

Stine, S. M. 1998. "Opiate dependence and current treatments." In *New Treatments for Chemical Addictions,* ed. E. F. McCance-Katz, pp. 75-111. Washington, DC: American Psychiatric Association.

Stires, L. K. 1991. "The Gulf 'war' as a sanctioned massacre." *Contemporary Social Psychology* 15 (December):139-43.

Stirling, K., and T. Aldrich. 2008. "Child support: Who bears the burden." *Family Relations* 57:376-89.

Stith, S. M., et al. 2000. "The intergenerational transmission of spouse abuse." *Journal of Marriage and Family* 62:640-54.

Stix, G. 2006. "A climate repair manual." *Scientific American,* September, pp. 46-49.

Stockholm International Peace Research Institute. 2016. SIPRI Yearbook, 2016. Stockholm International Peace Research Institute website.

Stokes, B. 2014. "Which countries don't like America and which do." Pew Research Center website.

Stokes, B. 2015. "Americans agree on trade: Good for the country, but not great for jobs." Pew Research Center website.

Stolberg, S. G., et al. 2016. "New front line in culture war: the bathroom." *The New York Times*, May 22.

Stoll, B. M., G. L. Arriaut, D. K. Fromme, and J. A. Felker-Thayer. 2005. "Adolescents in stepfamilies." *Journal of Divorce & Remarriage* 44:177-89.

Stone, P. H. 2006. *Heist: Superlobbyist Jack Abramoff, His Republican Allies, and the Buying of Washington.* New York: Farrar, Straus & Giroux.

Story, L. B., and R. Repetti. 2006. "Daily occupational stressors and marital behavior." *Journal of Family Psychology* 20:680-89.

Stotzer, R. L. 2014. "Law enforcement and criminal justice personnel interactions with transgender people in the United States." *Journal of Aggression and Violent Behavior* 9:263-77.

Stratigos, A. J., and A. D. Katsambas. 2003. "Medical and cutaneous disorders associated with homelessness." *Skinned* 2:168-72.

Straus, M. A. 2001. "New evidence for the benefits of never spanking." *Society* 38:52-60.

Straus, M. A., D. B. Sugarman, and J. Giles-Sims. 1997. "Spanking by parents and subsequent antisocial behavior of children." *Archives of Pediatrics and Adolescent Medicine* 151 (August):761-67.

Strecher, V. J., M. W. Kreuter, and S. C. Kobrin. 1995. "Do cigarette smokers have unrealistic perceptions of their heart attack, cancer, and stroke risks?" *Journal of Behavioral Medicine* 18 (February):45-54.

Street, A. E., J. L. Gradus, J. Stafford, and K. Kelly. 2007. "Gender differences in experiences of sexual harassment." *Journal of Consulting and Clinical Psychology* 75:464-74.

Streissguth, A. P. 1992. "Fetal alcohol syndrome: Early and long-term consequences." In *Problems of Drug Dependence 1991,* ed. L. Harris. Rockville, MD: National Institute on Drug Abuse.

Stringhini, S., et al. 2010. "Association of socioeconomic position with health behaviors and mortality." *Journal of the American Medical Association* 303:1159-66.

Stroebel, S. S., et al. 2012. "Father-daughter incest." *Journal of Child Sexual Abuse* 21:176-99.

Strohschein, L. 2005a. "Household income histories and child mental health trajectories." *Journal of Health and Social Behavior* 46:359-75.

——. 2005b. "Parental divorce and child mental health trajectories." *Journal of Marriage and Family* 67:1286-1300.

Strossen, N. 1995. "The perils of pornophobia." *Humanist,* May-June, pp. 5-7.

Stuart, G. L., T. M. Moore, S. E. Ramsey, and C. W. Kahler. 2003. "Relationship aggression and substance use among women court-referred to domestic violence intervention programs." *Addictive Behaviors* 28:1603-10.

——. 2004. "Hazardous drinking and relationship violence perpetration and victimization in women arrested for domestic violence." *Journal of Studies on Alcohol* 65:46-53.

Substance Abuse and Mental Health Services Administration. 2015. "Behavioral Health Barometer: United States, 2015." SAMHSA website.

Sturm, J. J., K. Yeatts, and D. Loomis. 2004. "Effects of tobacco smoke exposure on asthma prevalence and medical care use in North Carolina middle school children." *American Journal of Public Health* 94:308-13.

Sullivan, D. A. 2001. *Cosmetic Surgery: The Cutting Edge of Commercial Medicine in America.* New Brunswick, NJ: Rutgers University Press.

Sultan, D. H. 2009. "Landmines and recovery in Sudan's Nuba Mountains." *Africa Today* 55:45-61.

Sum, A., and I. Khatiwada. 2010. "The Nation's underemployed in the 'Great Recession' of 2007=09." *Monthly Labor Review,* November, pp. 3-15.

Sun, C., A. Bridges, R. Wosnitzer, E. Scharrer, and R. Liberman. 2008. "A comparison of male and female directors in popular pornography." *Psychology of Women Quarterly* 32:312-25.

Sun, Y., and Y. Li. 2011. "Effects of family structure type and stability on children's academic performance trajectories." *Journal of Marriage and Family* 73:541-56.

Sung, H., et al. 2005. "Major state tobacco tax increase, the master settlement agreement, and cigarette consumption." *American Journal of Public Health* 95:1030-35.

Surowiecki, J. 2013. "The pay is too damn low." *The New Yorker,* August 12 & 19.

Surratt, H. L., J. A. Inciardi, S. P. Kurtz, and M. C. Kiley. 2004. "Sex work and drug use in a subculture of violence." *Crime and Delinquency* 50:43-59.

Sutfin, E. L., et al. 2015. "The Impact of Trying Electronic Cigarettes on Cigarette Smoking by College Students." *American Journal of Public Health* 105:e-83-e89.

Sutherland, E. H. 1968. "White collar criminality." In *Radical Perspectives on Social Problems,* ed. Frank Lindenfeld, pp. 149-60. New York: Macmillan.

Sutherland, E. H., and D. R. Cressey. 1955. *Principles of Criminology.* 5th ed. Philadelphia: J. B. Lippincott.

Swaab, D. F., and M. A. Hofman. 1990. "An enlarged suprachiasmatic nucleus in homosexual men." *Brain Research* 537 (1-2):141-48.

Swan, S. H. 2006. "Does our environment affect our fertility?" *Seminars in Reproductive Medicine* 24:142-46.

Swanson, J. W., et al. 2002. "The social-environmental context of violent behavior in persons treated for severe mental illness." *American Journal of Public Health* 92:1523-31.

Swedler, D. I., et al. 2015. "Firearm Prevalence and Homicides of Law Enforcement Officers in the United States." *American Journal of Public Health* 105:2042-48.

Swers, M. L. 2002. *The Difference Women Make: The Policy Impact of Women in Congress.* Chicago, IL: University of Chicago Press.

Swift, A. 2015. "Most Americans Continue to Say Death Penalty Morally OK." Gallup Poll website.

Symanski, R. 1974. "Prostitution in Nevada." *Annals of the Association of American Geographers* 64 (September):357-77.

Symmes, P. 2012. "Hunted in Alabama." *Newsweek,* February 13, pp. 26-27.

Sypnowich, C. 2000. "The culture of citizenship." *Politics and Society* 28:531-55.

Taft, C. T., et al. 2006. "Examining the correlates of psychological aggression among a community sample of couples." *Journal of Family Psychology* 20:581-88.

Taft, P., and P. Ross. 1969. "American labor violence: Its causes, character, and outcome." In *The History of Violence in*

America, ed. H. D. Graham and T. R. Gurr, pp. 281–395. New York: Bantam.

Talbot, M. 2003. "Catch and Release." *Atlantic Monthly,* January/February, pp. 97–100.

Talukdar, D. 2008. "Cost of being poor: Retail price and consumer price search differences across inner-city and suburban neighborhoods." *Journal of Consumer Research* 35: 457–71.

Tamborini, C.R., C. Kim, and A. Sakamoto. 2015. "Education and lifetime earnings in the United States." *Demography* 52:1383–1407.

Tanner, J. C. 2006. "XXX adult content: Coming to a phone near you?" *America's Network,* June, pp. 26–32.

Tarabah, A., et al. 2015. "Exposure to violence and children's desensitization attitudes in Lebanon." *Journal of Interpersonal Violence.* Published online.

Tax Policy Center. 2011. "The tax policy briefing book." Tax Policy website.

Taylor, M. J., A. S. Barusch, and M. B. Vogel-Ferguson. 2006. "Heterogeneity at the bottom: TANF closure and long-term welfare recipients." *Journal of Human Behavior in the Social Environment* 13:1–14.

Taylor, P., and C. Cooper. 2008. "'It was absolute hell': Inside the private prison." *Capital & Class* 96:3–30.

Taywaditep, K. J. 2001. "Marginalization among the marginalized: Gay men's anti-effeminacy attitudes." *Journal of Homosexuality* 42:1–28.

Teasdale, B., and M. S. Bradley-Engen. 2010. "Adolescent same-sex attraction and mental health." *Journal of Homosexuality* 57:287–309.

Technology for a Quieter America. Washington, D.C.: The National Academies Press.

Teicher, M. H. 2002. "Scars that won't heal: The neurobiology of child abuse." *Scientific American,* March, pp. 68–75.

Teig, S., and J. E. Susskind. 2008. "Truck driver or nurse? The impact of gender roles and occupational status on children's occupational preferences." *Sex Roles* 58:848–63.

Tempier, R., et al. 2006. "Psychological distress among female spouses of male at-risk drinkers." *Alcohol* 40:41–49.

Tennesen, M. 2010. "Sour Showers." *Scientific American,* September, p. 23.

Terkel, S. 1972. *Working.* New York: Avon Books.

Terry-McElrath, Y. M., P. M. O'Malley, and L. D. Johnston. 2008. "Saying no to marijuana: Why American youth report quitting or abstaining." *Journal of Studies on Alcohol and Drugs* 69:796–805.

———. 2014. "Alcohol and Marijuana Use Patterns Associated With Unsafe Driving Among U.S. High School Seniors." *Journal of Studies on Alcohol and Drugs* 75:378–89.

Testa, M., and J. H. Hoffman. 2012. "Naturally occurring changes in women's drinking from high school to college and implications for sexual victimization." *Journal of Studies on Alcohol and Drugs* 73:26–33.

Thabet, A. A., and P. Vostanis. 2000. "Posttraumatic stress disorder reactions in children of war." *Child Abuse and Neglect* 24 (February):291–98.

Thompson, M. 2008. "America's medicated army." *Time,* June 16, pp. 38–42.

Thompson, M. P., J. B. Kingree, and S. Desai. 2004. "Gender differences in long-term health consequences of physical abuse of children." *American Journal of Public Health* 94:599–604.

Thomson, E., and U. Colella. 1992. "Cohabitation and marital stability: Quality or commitment?" *Journal of Marriage and the Family* 54 (May):259–68.

Thomson, E., T. L. Hanson, and S. S. McLanahan. 1994. "Family structure and child well-being: Economic resources vs. parental behaviors." *Social Forces* 73:221–42.

Thoreau, H. D. 1968. *Walden and the Essay on Civil Disobedience.* New York: Lancer.

Thornberry, T. P., D. Huizinga, and R. Loeber. 2004. "The causes and correlates studies." *Juvenile Justice* 9:3–19.

Thorne, P. S., et al. 2001. "Indoor environmental quality in six commercial office buildings in the Midwest United States." *Applied Occupational and Environmental Hygiene* 16:1065–77.

Thottam, J. 2004. "When execs go." *Time,* April 26, pp. 40–41.

Throop, D. R. 1997. "What are men's issues?" World Wide Web Virtual Library: Men's Page website.

Thrupp, L. A. 1991. "Sterilization of workers from pesticide exposure: The causes and consequences of DBCP-induced damage in Costa Rica and beyond." *International Journal of Health Services* 21 (4):731–57.

Thuen, F., et al. 2015. "Growing up with one or both parents." *Journal of Divorce & Remarriage* 56:451–74.

Tickell, C. 1992. "The quality of life: What quality? Whose life?" *Environmental Values* 1 (Spring):65–76.

Tierney, J. 1998. "Calling all noisebusters." *New York Times Magazine,* February 22, p. 24.

Tiet, Q., et al. 2001. "Relationship between specific adverse life events and psychiatric disorders." *Journal of Abnormal Child Psychology* 29:153–64.

Tilesik, A. 2011. "Pride and prejudice: Employment discrimination against openly gay men in the United States." *American Journal of Sociology* 117:586–626.

Ting, Y. 1997. "Determinants of job satisfaction of federal government employees." *Public Personnel Management* 26 (Fall):313–34.

Tjaden, P., and N. Thoennes. 2006. "Extent, nature, and consequences of rape victimization: Findings from the national violence against women study." NIJ website.

Tolbert, C. J., J. A. Grummel, and D. A. Smith. 2001. "The effects of ballot initiatives on voter turnout in the American states." *American Politics Research* 29:625-48.

Tomaskovic-Devey, D., and V. J. Roscigno. 1996. "Racial economic subordination and white gain in the U.S. South." *American Sociological Review* 61 (August):565-89.

Tomaskovic-Devey, D., et al. 2006. "Documenting desegregation: Segregation in American workplaces by race, ethnicity, and sex, 1966-2003." *American Sociological Review* 71:565-88.

Toner, R., and S. G. Stolberg. 2002. "Decade after health care crisis, soaring costs bring new strains." *New York Times,* August 11.

Torpy, J. M., and R. M. Glass. 2006. "Anorexia nervosa." *Journal of the American Medical Association* 295:2684.

Torrey, E. F. 1994. "Violent behavior by individuals with serious mental illness." *Hospital and Community Psychiatry* 45 (July):653-62.

Tower, R. B., and M. Krasner. 2006. "Marital closeness, autonomy, mastery, and depressive symptoms in a U.S. Internet sample." *Personal Relationships* 13:429.

Traeen, B., T. S. Nilsen, and H. Stigum. 2006. "Use of pornography in traditional media and on the Internet in Norway." *Journal of Sex Research* 43:245-54.

Tran, A. G. T. T., R. M. Lee, and D. J. Burgess. 2010. "Perceived discrimination and substance use in Hispanic/Latino, African-born black, and Southeast Asian immigrants." *Cultural Diversity and Ethnic Minority Psychology* 16:226-36.

Treas, J., and D. Giesen. 2000. "Sexual infidelity among married and cohabiting Americans." *Journal of Marriage and the Family* 62 (February):48-60.

Treas, J., T. van der Lippe, and T. C. Tai. 2011. "The happy homemaker? Married women's well-being in cross-national perspective." *Social Forces* 90:111-32.

Tregea, W., and M. Larmour. 2009. *The Prisoners' World: Portraits of Convicts Caught in the Incarceration Binge.* New York: Lexington Books.

Troisi, A., A. Pasini, M. Saracco, and G. Spalletta. 1998. "Psychiatric symptoms in male cannabis users not using other illicit drugs." *Addiction* 93 (April):487-92.

Tronko, M., et al. 2012. "Thyroid cancer in Ukraine after the Chernobyl accident." *Journal of Radiological Protection* 32:65-70.

Truman, J. L., and L. Langton. 2015. "Criminal Victimization, 2014." Bureau of Justice Statistics website.

Tsang, M. C., R. W. Rumberger, and H. M. Levin. 1991. "The impact of surplus schooling on worker productivity." *Industrial Relations* 30 (Spring):209-28.

Tu, H. T., and J. D. Reschovsky. 2002. "Assessment of medical care by enrollees in for-profit and nonprofit health maintenance organizations." *New England Journal of Medicine* 346:1288-93.

Tucker, J., and C. Lowell. 2015. "National snapshot: Poverty among women & families." National Women's Law Center website.

Turner, H. A., and K. Kopiec. 2006. "Exposure to interparental conflict and psychological disorder among young adults." *Journal of Family Issues* 27:131-58.

Turner, R. J., and D. A. Lloyd. 1999. "The stress process and the social distribution of depression." *Journal of Health and Social Behavior* 40 (December):374-404.

Turnipseed, D. 1992. "Anxiety and perceptions of the work environment." *Journal of Social Behavior and Personality* 7 (3):375-94.

Tuxill, J. 1999. *Nature's Cornucopia.* Washington, DC: Worldwatch Institute.

Twenge, J. M. 2000. "The age of anxiety? Birth cohort change in anxiety and neuroticism, 1952-1993." *Journal of Personality and Social Psychology* 79:1007-21.

Twenge, J. M., R. A. Sherman, and B.E. Wells. 2016. "Changes in American adults' reported same-sex sexual experiences and attitudes, 1973-2014." *Archives of Sexual Behavior* 45:1713.

Tyack, D. 2003. *Seeking Common Ground: Public Schools in a Diverse Society.* Cambridge: Harvard University Press.

Tyler, K. A., and K. A. Johnson. 2006. "Trading sex: Voluntary or coerced?" *Journal of Sex Research* 43:208-16.

Uchitelle, L. 1996. "More downsized workers are returning as rentals." *New York Times,* December 8.

Uchitelle, L., and N. R. Kleinfield. 1996. "On the battlefields of business, millions of casualties." *New York Times,* March 3.

Uecker, J. E. 2012. "Marriage and mental health among young adults." *Journal of Health and Social Behavior* 53:67-83.

Uggen, C. 2000. "Work as a turning point in the life course of criminals." *American Sociological Review* 67:529-46.

——, and A. Blackstone. 2004. "Sexual harassment as a gendered expression of power." *American Sociological Review* 69:64-92.

Ullman, S. E. 1998. "Does offender violence escalate when rape victims fight back?" *Journal of Interpersonal Violence* 13 (April):179-92.

Ullman, S. E., and H. H. Filipas. 2001. "Correlates of formal and informal support seeking in sexual assault victims." *Journal of Interpersonal Violence* 16:1028-47.

Ungar, S. 1992. "The rise and (relative) decline of global warming as a social problem." *Sociological Quarterly* 33 (4):483-501.

United Nations. 2015. "The world's women." United Nations website.

United Nations Environment Programme. 2016. "Urban air pollution." UNEP website.

United Nations General Assembly. 2006. "Report of the special representative of the Secretary-General for children and armed conflict." United Nations website.

Unnever, J. D., and F. T. Cullen. 2007. "The racial divide in support for the death penalty: Does white racism matter?" *Social Forces* 85:1281-1301.

Unsworth, M. E. 1999. "Freedom of information: Its ebb and flow." *American Libraries,* June-July, pp. 82-86.

U.S. Bureau of Economic Analysis. 2016. "U.S. international trade in goods and services." BEA website.

U.S. Census Bureau. 1975. *Historical Statistics of the United States, Colonial Times to 1970.* Washington, DC: Government Printing Office.

———. 2007. *Statistical Abstract of the United States.* Washington, DC: Government Printing Office.

———. 2013. "Wealth and asset ownership." U.S. Census Bureau website.

———. 2015. "American Indian and Alaska Native heritage month." U.S. Census Bureau website.

U.S. Department of Health and Human Services. 1995. "Preliminary estimates from the 1994 national household survey on drug abuse." *Advance Report Number 10* (September).

U.S. Department of Health and Human Services. 2006. *The Health Consequences of Involuntary Exposure to Tobacco Smoke.* Washington, DC: Government Printing Office.

U.S. Department of Justice. 1992. *Drugs, Crime, and the Justice System.* Washington, DC: Government Printing Office.

———. 2006. *Compendium of Federal Justice Statistics, 2004.* Washington, DC: Government Printing Office.

U.S. Department of Labor. 2000. *Futurework: Trends and Challenges for Work in the 21st Century.* Department of Labor website.

U.S. Department of State. 2016. "Country reports on terrorism." U.S. Department of State website.

U.S. Department of Transportation. 2015. "Highway statistics 2014." DOT website.

U.S. Energy Information Administration. 2016a. "International energy outlook." EIA website.

U.S. Energy Information Administration. 2016b. "Total energy." EIA website.

U.S. Fish & Wildlife Service. 2016. "Listed species summary." Environmental Conservation Online System website.

U.S. Forest Service. 2016. "Forest service research and development performance and accountability report." USFS website.

U.S. Geological Survey. 2016. "Mineral commodity summaries 2016." USGS website.

U.S. Government Accountability Office. 2016. "K-12 education." GAO website.

U.S. Public Health Service. 1995. *Healthy People 2000.* Washington DC: Government Printing Office.

U.S. Riot Commission. 1968. *Report of the National Advisory Commission on Civil Disorders.* New York: Bantam.

University of Georgia. 2007. "Violence costs nation $70 billion annually, study finds." *Science Daily.* Science Daily website.

Usdansky, M. L. 2009. "A weak embrace: Popular and scholarly depictions of single-parent families, 1900-1998." *Journal of Marriage and Family* 71:209-25.

———, R. A. Gordon, X. Wang, and A. Gluzman. 2011. "Depression risk among mothers of young children." *Journal of Family and Economic Issues* 32:1-12.

Usher, A., and N. Kober. 2011. "Keeping informed about school vouchers." Center on Education Policy Report.

Vaaler, C. E., C. G. Ellison, and D. A. Powers. 2009. "Religious influences on the risk of marital dissolution." *Journal of Marriage and Family* 71: 917-34.

Vaisey, S. 2006. "Education and its discontents: Overqualification in America, 1972-2002." *Social Forces* 85:835-64.

Valera, E. M., and H. Berenbaum. 2003. "Brain injury in battered women." *Journal of Consulting and Clinical Psychology* 71:797-804.

Valera, R. J., R. G. Sawyer, and G. R. Schiraldi. 2001. "Perceived health needs of inner-city street prostitutes." *American Journal of Health Behavior* 25:50-59.

Van Deerlin, L. 2003. "Abandoning the bill of rights." *San Diego Union-Tribune,* June 11.

VanDenburg, W. M., and P. J. Harmelink. 2008. "Accounting implications of the subprime meltdown." *The CPA Journal* 78:24-27.

Vandepitte, J., et al. 2006. "Estimates of the number of female sex workers in different regions of the world." *Sexually Transmitted Infections* 82:8-25.

Vandervalk, I., E. Spruijt, M. De Goede, W. Meeus, and C. Maas. 2004. "Marital status, marital process, and parental resources in predicting adolescents' emotional adjustment." *Journal of Family Issues* 25:291-317.

Vanheusden, K., et al. 2008. "Patterns of association between alcohol consumption and internalizing and externalizing problems in young adults." *Journal of Studies on Alcohol and Drugs* 69:49-57.

van Hook, M. P., E. Gjermeni, and E. Haxhiymeri. 2006. "Sexual trafficking of women." *International Social Work* 49:29-40.

Van Koppen, P. J., and R. W. J. Jansen. 1999. "The time to rob: Variations in time of number of commercial robberies." *Journal of Research in Crime and Delinquency* 36 (February):7-29.

Vaughan, K. K., and G. T. Fouts. 2003. "Changes in television and magazine exposure and eating disorder symptomatology." *Sex Roles* 49:313-20.

Vazsonyi, A. T., L. M. Belliston, and D. J. Flannery. 2004. "Evaluation of a school-based universal violence prevention program." *Youth Violence and Juvenile Justice* 2:185-206.

Vedantam, S., A. Epstine, and B. Geiger. 1997. "Tobacco firm says smoking is addictive." *San Diego Union-Tribune,* March 21.

Ventegodt, S., et al. 2005. "Global quality of life (QOL), health and ability are primarily determined by our consciousness." *Social Indicators Research* 71:87–122.

Verger, P., et al. 2004. "The psychological impact of terrorism." *American Journal of Psychiatry* 161:1384–89.

Villaveces, A., et al. 2000. "Effect of a ban on carrying firearms on homicide rates in two Colombian cities." *Journal of the American Medical Association* 283 (March 1):1205–09.

Vinokur, A., and M. L. Selzer. 1975. "Desirable versus undesirable life events: Their relationship to stress and mental distress." *Journal of Personality and Social Psychology* 32 (August):329–39.

Vizcaya, D., et al. 2015. "Cleaning products and short-term respiratory effects among female cleaners with asthma." *Occupational and Environmental Medicine* 72:757–63.

Vlahov, D., S. Galea, J. Ahern, H. Resnick, and D. Kilpatrick. 2004. "Sustained increased consumption of cigarettes, alcohol, and marijuana among Manhattan residents after September 11, 2001." *American Journal of Public Health* 94:253–54.

Volscho, T. W., and N. J. Kelly. 2012. "The rise of the super-rich." *American Sociological Review* 77:679–99.

Vora, E. A., and J. A. Vora. 2002. "Undoing racism in America." *Journal of Black Studies* 32:389–404.

Voydanoff, P. 2004. "The effects of work demands and resources on work-to-family conflict and facilitation." *Journal of Marriage and Family* 66:398–412.

Wade, T. J., and D. J. Pevalin. 2004. "Marital transitions and mental health." *Journal of Health and Social Behavior* 45:155–70.

Wagner, M. B. 1990. *God's Schools: Choice and Compromise in American Society.* New Brunswick, NJ: Rutgers University.

Wagstaff, M. C., and B. E. Wilson. 1988. "The evaluation of litter behavior modification in a river environment." *Journal of Environmental Education* 20 (Fall):39–44.

Wahl, O. F. 2003. "News media portrayal of mental illness." *American Behavioral Scientist* 46:1594–1600.

Wainwright, J. L., and C. J. Patterson. 2006. "Delinquency, victimization, and substance use among adolescents with female same-sex parents." *Journal of Family Psychology* 20:526–30.

———. 2008. "Peer relations among adolescents with female same-sex parents." *Developmental Psychology* 44:117–26.

Waite, L. J., and K. Joyner. 2001. "Emotional satisfaction and physical pleasure in sexual unions." *Journal of Marriage and the Family* 63:247–64.

Waldman, J. D., and H. L. Smith. 2012. "Strategic planning to reduce medical errors." *Journal of Medical Practice Management* 27:230–36.

Walker, R., L. Shannon, and T. K. Logan. 2011. "Sleep loss and partner violence victimization." *Journal of Interpersonal Violence* 26:2004–24.

Wallace, J. M., et al. 2007. "Religiosity and adolescent substance use: The role of individual and contextual influences." *Social Problems* 54:308–27.

Wallis, C. 2004. "Hidden scars of battle." *Time,* July 12, p. 35.

———. 2011. "Performing gender: A content analysis of gender display in music videos." *Sex Roles* 64:160–72.

Walt, S. M. 2005. *Taming American Power: The Global Response to U.S. Primacy.* New York: W. W. Norton.

Wang, P. S., O. Demler, and R. C. Kessler. 2002. "Adequacy of treatment for serious mental illness in the United States." *American Journal of Public Health* 92:92–98.

Wang, P. S., et al. 2005. "Twelve-month use of mental health services in the United States." *Archives of General Psychiatry* 62:629–40.

Warner, L. A., H. R. White, and V. Johnson. 2007. "Alcohol initiation experiences and family history of alcoholism as predictors of problem-drinking trajectories." *Journal of Studies on Alcohol and Drugs* 68:56–65.

Wasley, P. 2009. "Strains in the safety net." *Chronicle of Philanthropy* 21:10.

Wasserman, J. A., and J. M. Clair. 2010. *At Home on the Street: People, Poverty and a Hidden Culture of Homelessness.* Boulder, CO: Lynne Rienner.

Watt, T. T. 2002. "Marital and cohabiting relationships of adult children of alcoholics." *Journal of Family Issues* 23:246–65.

Wauterickx, N., A. Gouwy, and P. Bracke. 2006. "Parental divorce and depression." *Journal of Divorce & Remarriage* 45:43–68.

Webb, J. T. 2000. "Mis-diagnosis and dual diagnosis of gifted children." Paper presented at the Annual Conference of the American Psychological Association.

Weber, L. 2016. "An entirely curable disease is a top 10 killer around the world." *Huffington Post,* October 13.

Weeks, G. B., and J. R. Weeks. 2010. *Invisible Forces: Latin American Migration to the United States and Its Effects on the South.* Albuquerque, NM: University of New Mexico Press.

Weinberg, A., and L. Weinberg, eds. 1963. *Instead of Violence.* New York: Grossman.

Weinstein, A., and M. Lejoyeux. 2010. "Internet addiction or excessive Internet use." *American Journal of Drug and Alcohol Abuse* 36:277–83.

Weisbrot, M. 2000. "Globalism for dummies." *Harper's Magazine,* May, pp. 15–19.

Weisburd, D., E. Groff, and N. Morris. 2011. "Hot spots of juvenile crime: Findings from Seattle." *Juvenile Justice Bulletin.* OJJDP website.

Weisburd, D., and L. G. Mazerolle. 2000. "Crime and disorder in drug hot spots." *Police Quarterly* 3:331–49.

Weiser, D. A., et al. 2015. "Family background and propensity to engage in infidelity." *Journal of Family Issues.* Published online.

Weismantle, M. 2001. "Reasons people do not work." *Current Population Reports.* Washington, DC: Government Printing Office.

Weiss, H. E., and L. W. Reid. 2005. "Low-quality employment concentration and crime." *Sociological Perspectives* 48:213-32.

Weisz, M. G., and C. M. Earls. 1995. "The effects of exposure to filmed sexual violence on attitudes toward rape." *Journal of Interpersonal Violence* 10 (March):71-84.

Weitzer, R. 2007. "Prostitution: Facts and fictions." *Contexts* 6 (Fall):28-33.

——. 2010. "Sex work: Paradigms and policies." In *Sex for Sale: Prostitution, Pornography, and the Sex Industry,* ed. R. J. Weitzer, pp. 1-46. New York: Routledge.

——. 2012. *Legalizing Prostitution: From Illicit Vice to Lawful Business.* New York: New York University Press.

Weitzer, R., and S. A. Tuch. 2004. "Race and perceptions of police misconduct." *Social Problems* 51:305-25.

Weitzman, E. R., and I. Kawachi. 2000. "Giving means receiving: The protective effect of social capital on binge drinking on college campuses." *American Journal of Public Health* 90:1936-39.

Welch, C. E. 2016. "Every Student Succeeds Act (ESSA)." *Parenting for High Potential* 5:2-5.

Welch, K., and A. A. Payne. 2010. "Racial threat and punitive school discipline." *Social Problems* 57:25-48.

Wellenius, G.A., et al. 2012. "Ambient air pollution and the risk of acute ischemic stroke." *Archives of Internal Medicine* 172: 229-34.

Wells, S., et al. 2014. "Linking Masculinity to Negative Drinking Consequences." *Journal of Studies on Alcohol and Drugs* 75:510-19.

Welsh, W. N. 2002. "Court-ordered reform of jails." In *Visions for Change: Crime and Justice in the Twenty-first Century,* 3rd ed., ed. R. Muraskin and A. R. Roberts, pp. 390-407. New York: Prentice-Hall.

Wen, M. 2008. "Family structure and children's health and behavior." *Journal of Family Issues* 29:1492-1519.

West, J., et al. 2010. "Head Start children go to kindergarten." ACF-OPRE Report. Administration for Children & Families website.

West, S., and G. Mottola. 2016. "A population on the brink: American renters, emergency savings, and financial fragility." *Poverty & Public Policy* 8:56-71.

Westerhoff, N. 2009. "Why do men buy sex?" *Scientific American Mind* 20:70-75.

Western, B., M. Kleykamp, and J. Rosenfeld. 2006. "Did falling wages and employment increase U.S. imprisonment?" *Social Forces* 84:2291-2311.

Western, B., and J. Rosenfeld. 2011. "Unions, norms and the rise in U.S. wage inequality." *American Sociological Review* 76:513-37.

Westervelt, S. D., and K. J. Cook. 2008. "Coping with innocence after death row." *Contexts* 7:32-37.

Whatley, M. A. 2005. "The effect of participant sex, victim dress, and traditional attitudes on causal judgments for marital rape victims." *Journal of Family Violence* 20:191-200.

Wheaton, B., and P. Clarke. 2003. "Space meets time: Integrating temporal and contextual influences on mental health in early adulthood." *American Sociological Review* 68:680-706.

Wheaton, D. 2016. "Prisons get higher funding boost than schools." *San Diego Union-Tribune,* July 31.

Wheeler, D. L. 1994. "An ominous legacy of the atomic age." *Chronicle of Higher Education,* January 12.

Whisman, M. A. 2006. "Childhood trauma and marital outcomes in adulthood." *Personal Relationships* 13:375.

Whisman, M. A., L. A. Uebelacker, and M. L. Bruce. 2006. "Longitudinal association between marital dissatisfaction and alcohol use disorders in a community sample." *Journal of Family Psychology* 20:164-67.

Whitaker, D. J., T. Haileyesus, M. Swahn, and L. S. Saltzman. 2007. "Differences in frequency of violence and reported injury between relationships with reciprocal and nonreciprocal intimate partner violence." *American Journal of Public Health* 97:941-47.

Whitam, F. L., and R. M. Mathy. 1991. "Childhood crossgender behavior of homosexual females in Brazil, Peru, the Philippines, and the United States." *Archives of Sexual Behavior* 20 (April):151-70.

White, G. F., J. Katz, and K. E. Scarborough. 1992. "The impact of professional football games upon violent assaults on women." *Violence and Victims* 7 (2):157-71.

White, H. R., N. Jarrett, E. Y. Valencia, R. Loeber, and E. Wei. 2007. "Stages and sequences of initiation and regular substance use in a longitudinal cohort of black and white male adolescents." *Journal of Studies on Alcohol and Drugs* 68:173-81.

White, L. K., and A. Booth. 1985. "Stepchildren in remarriages." *American Sociological Review* 50 (October): 689-98.

White, R. K. 1966. "Misperception and the Vietnam war." *Journal of Social Issues* 22 (July):1-19.

Whitehead, B. D., and D. Popenoe. 2001. *The State of Our Unions: The Social Health of Marriage in America.* National Marriage Project website.

Whitlock, E. P., M. R. Polen, C. A. Green, T. Orleans, and J. Klein. 2004. "Behavioral counseling interventions in primary care to reduce risky/harmful alcohol use by adults." *Annals of Internal Medicine* 140:557-68.

Whitton, S. W., G. K. Rhoades, S. M. Stanley, and H. J. Markman. 2008. "Effects of parental divorce on marital commitment and confidence." *Journal of Family Psychology* 22:789-93.

Whooley, M. A. 2006. "Depression and cardiovascular disease." *Journal of the American Medical Association* 295:2874-81.

Whoriskey, P. 2011. "Wealth-gap divide: Lawmakers, constituents." *San Diego Union-Tribune*, December 27.

Wickrama, K., et al. 1995. "Role identity, role satisfaction, and perceived physical health." *Social Psychology Quarterly* 58:270–83.

Wickrama, K. A. S., R. D. Conger, F. O. Lorenz, and T. Jung. 2008. "Family antecedents and consequences of trajectories of depressive symptoms from adolescence to young adulthood." *Journal of Health and Social Behavior* 49:468–83.

Wiener, L., et al. 2016. Impact of care-giving for a child with cancer on parental health behaviors, relationship quality, and spiritual faith." *Journal of Pediatric Oncology Nursing* 33:378–98.

Wild, T. C. 2002. "Personal drinking and sociocultural drinking norms." *Journal of Studies on Alcohol* 63:469–75.

Wilens, T. E., et al. 2002. "A family study of the high-risk children of opioid- and alcohol-dependent parents." *American Journal on Addictions* 11:41–51.

Wilensky, H. L. 1967. *Organizational Intelligence.* New York: Basic Books.

Willems, J. L. 2002. "7 Mustard gas: Signs, symptoms and treatment." *Journal of Toxicology: Clinical Toxicology* 40:250–51.

Williams, C. L. 1995. *Still a Man's World: Men Who Do "Women's Work."* Berkeley and Los Angeles: University of California Press.

Williams, D. T., J. E. Cheadle, and B. J. Goosby. 2015. "Hard times and heart break." *Journal of Family Issues* 36:924–50.

Williams, D. R., H. W. Neighbors, and J. S. Jackson. 2003. "Racial/ethnic discrimination and health." *American Journal of Public Health* 93:200–208.

Williams, J. 2004. "Facts that should change the world." *New Statesman,* May 10, p. 21.

Williams, K., and A. Dunne-Bryant. 2006. "Divorce and adult psychological well-being." *Journal of Marriage and Family* 68:1178–96.

Williams, R., and R. Nesiba. 2005. "The changing face of inequality in home mortgage lending." *Social Problems* 52:181–208.

Williams, T., and W. Kornblum. 1985. *Growing Up Poor.* Lexington, MA: DC Heath.

Williamson, C., and T. Cluse-Tolar. 2002. "Pimp-controlled prostitution." *Violence against Women* 8:1074–92.

Willis, B. M., and B. S. Levy. 2003. "Child prostitution increasing." *Southern Medical Journal* 96:69.

Willoughby, B. J., and D. M. Busby. 2016. "In the eye of the beholder." *Journal of Sex Research* 53:678–88.

Willoughby, T., P. J. C. Adachi, and M. Good. 2012. "A longitudinal study of the association between violent video game play and aggression among adolescents." *Developmental Psychology* 48:1044–57.

Wills, T. A., et al. 2007. "Movie exposure to smoking cues and adolescent smoking onset." *Health Psychology* 26:769–76.

Wilper, A. P., et al. 2009a. "The health and health care of US prisoners." *American Journal of Public Health* 99:666–72.

———. 2009b. "Health insurance and mortality in US adults." *American Journal of Public Health* 99:2289–95.

Wilson, E. O. 2000. *Sociobiology: The New Synthesis.* Cambridge, MA: Harvard University Press.

Wilson, G. 2005. "Race and job dismissal." *American Behavioral Scientist* 48:1182–99.

Wilson, G. C. 2002. "Truth be told, they do lie." *National Journal,* March 2, p. 636.

Wilson, M.M. 2014. "Hate crime victimization, 2004–2012." Bureau of Justice Statistics website.

Winick, C., and P. M. Kinsie. 1971. *The Lively Commerce.* Chicago: Quadrangle.

Wiseman, J. P. 1991. *The Other Half: Wives of Alcoholics and Their Social-Psychological Situation.* New York: Aldine de Gruyter.

Witt, H. 2004. "9 years after Oklahoma City blast, militias remain shadowy groups in U.S." Knight Ridder/Tribune News Service, April 18.

Witt, S. D. 1997. "Parental influence on children's socialization to gender roles." *Adolescence* 32 (Summer):253–59.

Wolfe, S. E., et al. 2016. "Routine cell activity and exposure to sext messages." *Crime and Delinquency* 62:614–44.

Wolfinger, N. H. 1998. "The effects of parental divorce on adult tobacco and alcohol consumption." *Journal of Health and Social Behavior* 39 (September):254–69.

———. 2005. *Understanding the Divorce Cycle: The Children of Divorce in Their Own Marriages.* New York: Cambridge University Press.

Wolfner, G. D., and R. J. Gelles. 1993. "A profile of violence toward children." *Child Abuse and Neglect* 17 (March):197–212.

Womack, S. R., et al. 2016. "Bidirectional associations between cannabis use and depressive symptoms from adolescence through early adulthood among at-risk young men." *Journal of Studies on Alcohol and Drugs* 77: 287–97.

Wong, W. C. W., E. A. Holroyd, A. Gray, and D. C. Ling. 2006. "Female street sex workers in Hong Kong." *Journal of Women's Health* 15:390–99.

Wood, D. 2004. "Defense spending a threat to world economic stability." *San Diego Union-Tribune,* January 19.

Wood, P. B., and J. P. Bartkowski. 2004. "Attribution style and public policy attitudes toward gay rights." *Social Science Quarterly* 85:58–74.

Woods, K. C., N. T. Buchanan, and I. H. Settles. 2009. "Sexual harassment across the color line." *Cultural Diversity and Ethnic Minority Psychology* 15:67–76.

Woods, N. F., and F. M. Lewis. 1995. "Women with chronic illness: Their views of their families' adaptation." *Nursing Journal* 16 (March–April):135–48.

Woolf, S. H., and L.Y. Aron. 2013. "The US disadvantage relative to other high-income countries." *Journal of the American Medical Association* 309:771–72.

Worden, A. P., and B. E. Carlson. 2005. "Attitudes and beliefs about domestic violence." *Journal of Interpersonal Violence* 20:1219–43.

Work and Family Newsbrief. 2003. "Telework found to reduce conflict: Those who work from home at least two to three days a week report having lower levels of work-family conflict than those who don't." *Work and Family Newsbrief*, p. 3.

Worklife Report. 2003. "Vacation advantage for European workers." *Worklife Report* 14:12–13.

World Bank. 2014. "Economic monitoring report to the ad hoc liaison committee." World Bank website.

World Economic Forum. 2015. "The global gender gap report." World Economic Forum website.

World Health Organization. 2007. "Climate and health." WHO website.

——. 2014. *Global Status Report on Alcohol and Health.* WHO website.

——. 2016a. "Ambient air pollution: A global assessment of exposure and burden of disease." WHO website.

——. 2016b. "HIV/AIDS." WHO website.

Wren, C. S. 1997. "Ex-addicts find methadone more elusive than heroin." *New York Times,* February 2.

Wright, E. R., D. E. Wright, B. L. Perry, and C. E. Foote-Ardah. 2007. "Stigma and the sexual isolation of people with serious mental illness." *Social Problems* 54:78–98.

Wright, H. I., J. S. Gavaler, and D. Van Thiel. 1991. "Effects of alcohol on the male reproductive system." *Alcohol Health and Research World* 15 (12):110–14.

Wright, P. J., R. H. Fortinsky, K. E. Covinsky, P. A. Anderson, and C. S. Landefeld. 2000. "Delivery of preventive services to older black patients using neighborhood health centers." *Journal of the American Geriatric Society* 48 (February):124–30.

Wrushen, B. R., and W. H. Sherman. 2008. "Women secondary school principals." *International Journal of Qualitative Studies in Education* 21:457–69.

Wu, E. Y., et al. 2014. "Paternal hostility and maternal hostility in European American and African American families." *Journal of Marriage and Family* 76:638–51.

Wu, Z., and C. M. Schimmele. 2005. "Food insufficiency and depression." *Sociological Perspectives* 48:481–504.

Wurdinger, S. D. 2005. *Using Experiential Learning in the Classroom.* New York: Rowman and Littlefield.

Wysocki, D., and C. Childers. 2011. "'Let my fingers do the talking'; Sexting and infidelity in cyberspace." *Sexuality & Culture* 15:217–39.

Xu, J. 2008. "Sibship size and educational achievement." *Comparative Education* 52:413–36.

Xu, Y., M. L. Fiedler, and K. H. Flaming. 2005. "Discovering the impact of community policing." *Journal of Research in Crime and Delinquency* 42:147–86.

Xue, Y., M. A. Zimmerman, and R. Cunningham. 2009. "Relationship between alcohol use and violent behavior among urban African American youths from adolescence to emerging adulthood." *American Journal of Public Health* 99:2041–48.

Yao, M. Z., C. Mahood, and D. Linz. 2010. "Sexual priming, gender stereotyping, and likelihood to sexually harass." *Sex Roles* 62:77–88.

Yardley, J. 2002. "The 10 percent solution." *New York Times,* April 14.

Yarrow, A. L. 2009. "State of mind: America's teaching corps is made up of three groups with distinct attitudes about their profession." *Education Week*, October 19. Education Week website.

Yates, J. 2006. "Unions and employee ownership." *Industrial Relations* 45:709–33.

Ybarra, M. L., et al. 2008. "Linkages between Internet and other media violence with seriously violent behavior by youth." *Pediatrics* 122:929–37.

Yip, P. S., and J. Thorburn. 2004. "Marital status and the risk of suicide." *Psychological Reports* 94:401–7.

Yoder, J. D., and L. L. Berendsen. 2001. "Outsider within the firehouse." *Psychology of Women* 25:27–36.

Young, C. 2012. "Losing a job: The nonpecuniary cost of unemployment in the United States." *Social Forces* 91:609–34.

Young, M. L. 1998. "A plethora of paradoxes." *USA Today,* March, p. 15.

Young-Wolff, K. C., K. S. Kendler, and C. A. Prescott. 2012. "Interactive effects of childhood maltreatment and recent stressful life events on alcohol consumption in adulthood." *Journal of Studies on Alcohol and Drugs* 73:559–69.

Youth, H. 2003. "Watching birds disappear." In *State of the World 2003,* ed. L. Starke, pp. 14–37. New York: W. W. Norton.

Yu, T. 2006. "Challenging the politics of the 'model minority' stereotype." *Equity and Excellence in Education* 39: 325–33.

Yuan, A. S. V. 2016. "Father-child relationships and nonresident fathers' psychological distress." *Journal of Family Issues* 37:603–21.

Yuen, W. W., et al. 2016. "Psychological health and HIV transmission among female sex workers." *AIDS Care* 7:816–24.

Yung, K. 2004. "Job stresses starting to take toll." *San Diego Union-Tribune,* May 24.

Zapotosky, M., and C. Harlan. 2016. "Justice Dept. to end use of private prisons." *The San Diego Union Tribune,* August 19.

Zautra, A. J., M. A. Okun, S. E. Robinson, and D. Lee. 1989. "Life stress and lymphocyte alterations among patients with rheumatoid arthritis." *Health Psychology* 8 (1):1–14.

Zehr, M. A. 2011. "Capacity issue looms for vouchers." *Education Week*, June. Education Week website.

Zhai, F., J. Brooks-Gunn, and J. Waldfogel. 2011. "Head Start and urban children's school readiness." *Developmental Psychology* 47:134–52.

Zhang, A., L. Musu-Gillette, and B.A. Oudekerk. 2016. "Indicators of school crime and safety 2015." Bureau of Justice Statistics website.

Zhang, L., W. W. Smith, and W. C. McDowell. 2009. "Examining digital piracy." *Information Resources Management Journal* 22:24–44.

Zheng, T. 2009. *Red Lights: The Lives of Sex Workers in Postsocialist China*. Minneapolis: University of Minnesota Press.

Zimmerman, T. S., S. A. Haddock, and C. R. McGeorge. 2001. "Mars and Venus: Unequal planets." *Journal of Marital and Family Therapy* 27:55–68.

Zimring, F. E. 2011. "How New York beat crime." *Scientific American*, August, pp. 75–79.

Zlotnick, C., D. M. Johnson, and R. Kohn. 2006. "Intimate partner violence and long-term psychosocial functioning in a national sample of American women." *Journal of Interpersonal Violence* 21:262–75.

Zweigenhaft, R. L., and G. W. Domhoff. 2006. *Diversity in the Power Elite: How It Happened, Why It Matters*. Lanham, MD: Rowman and Littlefield.

Zych, I., R. Ortega-Ruiz, and R. Del Rey. 2015. "Systematic review of theoretical studies on bullying and cyberbullying." *Journal of Aggression and Violent Behavior* 23:1–21.

Page numbers in italics refer to figures or tables. Page numbers in bold refer to running glossary terms.

Military technology, 424
Militias, 110, 275
Minimum wage, 182, 188
Ministry of Education and Culture (MOEC), 283
Ministry of Home Affairs (MOHA), 283
Ministry of Religious Affairs (MORA), 283
Minorities. *See* Ethnicity; Race problem
Minority perspectives, 249, 252-253
Minors in need of care, 80
Miscellaneous chemicals, 453
Misperception, international, 440-441
Misplaced concreteness, fallacy of, **17**-18
Model minority, 252
"Mommy Track", 212
Mood disorders, 390
Moral self-image, 440
Morbidity, **399**
Morphine, *49*
Morphine derivatives, *49*
Mothers Against Drunk Drivers (MADD), 47, 266
Motor consequences, 126
Motor skills, 298
Motor vehicle theft, 76, 86, 96
Multiple decision-making centers, 178
Multiple-level factors, 12
Murder, 75, 86, 96, 99, 116
Mustard gas, *402*, 424
Mutual influence, 8, 12
Myths, 210
    about homosexuality, 216-217
    about illness, 406
    of inferiority, 244-245
    about rape, 18-19, 127-130
    of success around corner, 244
    of unauthorized immigration, 233-234

Nagasaki, 424
National Alliance to End Homelessness, 167
National Center for Health Statistics, 385
National Coalition for Homeless (2006),
    172-173
National Crime Victimization Survey, 82
National Health and Social Life Survey, 213
National Issues Forum (NIF), 288
National Labor Relations Board (NLRB), 263, 311
National Organization for Women (NOW), 210,
    265
National Rifle Association (NRA), 118, 265
"National security", 418
National Sickle Cell Anemia Control Act (1972),
    398
National surveys, 391
National Voter Registration Act, 269
National White Collar Crime Center, 77
Nature bats last, 471
Nazi, concentration camps, 428
Negative sanctions, 218-219
Negligence, crimes of, 76
"Netroots", 282-283
Neuroses, 389
Neurosis, **390**
Neurotoxins, 462
New Deal, 264
New Zealand, intimate partner violence in, 109
Nicotine, *50. See also* Tobacco
Nicotine-dependent individuals, 58
Nitric acid, 448
Nitrogen dioxide, 450, 455
No Child Left Behind Act (2002), 345
No open discussion of sex, 146
"No tolerance" rule, 68
Noise pollution, 401, 455, 460, 464

Non sequitur, fallacy of, **21**, 21-22, 113, 271-272,
    326, 368, 373, 396
Non-Hispanic whites, 166, 238, 249
Nonintervention, 376
Nonnegligent manslaughter, 75
Nonverbal interaction, 184
Normative sexual behavior, 220
Norms, **8**
    and alcohol use, 43-44
    and crime, 90-91
    about divorce, 368
    and drug use, 59
    female, 203-204
    and prostitution, 145, 146
    and rape, 127, 131
    sexual, 219-220
    and sexual deviance, 138-139
    and violence, 122, 113-114, 368
North American Task Force on Prostitution, 149
Norway, pornography in, 151
Not-in-my-backyard (NIMBY), 472
Nuclear bombs, 424, 425-426
Nuclear family, **352**
Nuclear power, 461-462
Nurturing, 196

"Obamacare", 408
Obesity, 411
Obscenity, **150**, 150-156
    contributing factors of, 154-155
    definition of, 150
    extent of, 151-152
    online, 139-140, 151
    and private action, 156
    and public policy, 156
    and quality of life, 152-154
Occupational carcinogens, 401, *402*, 463, 469
Occupational Safety and Health Administration
    (OSHA), 313, 316
Occupational sex segregation in developing
    countries, 202-203, *203*
Occupational structure, 297
Occupations distribution, *298*
Ociocultural factor, 216
Offenders, family background, 94
Official records, 82
    problems with, 83-84
    statistical analysis of, 25-28
Oil spills, 453, 464
Oklahoma City bombing (1995), 109-110,
    111-112
Oklahoma study, 100
Oneida community, 374
Open marriages, 353
Opioids, *49*
Oppression, 194
Oral sex, 140, *141,* 146
Order, government securing, 264, 266, 275
Organ transplants, 393
Organic chemicals, 452
Organic mental disorders, 390
Organic sewage, 452
Organizational context of work, 310-311
Organizational democracy, 317
Organized crime, 76, *79*, 79-80
"Outreach-assisted peer support" program, 67
Outsourcing, 296, 308-309
Outsourcing process, 296
Overfertilization of water from excess nutrients,
    452
Overgeneralization, 15-16
Oxycodone HCl, *49*

Ozone layer, 451, 464

Palestinians, 419, 424, 429, 437
Parallel traditional breadwinner role of males, 203
Paralyzing fear, 130
Paranoid disorders, 390
Paraphilia, **151**
Parental behavior, 68
Parental hostility, 367
Part-time work, 309
Participant observation, **29**, 30
Participatory management, 317
Patriot Act (2001), 433, 434
Patronage, **272**
Patterns of family life, 183-184
Payoff, 332-333
Peace Builders, 122
Pedophiles, **151**
Peer pressure, 59
Peer support, 67
People homosexual, 214
    biological explanations, 214
    sociocultural explanations, 214-216
Perceived happiness, 170
Period of work, 300
Persian Gulf War, 431
"Person of authority", 124
Personal attack, fallacy of, 18, 222, 244, 277, 279,
    300, 338, 373, 378, 406, 440
Personal problems, **4**
    social problems *vs.*, 4-7
Personal Responsibility and Work Opportunity
    Reconciliation Act (1996), 275
Personality disorders, 390
Pesticide DDT, 454
Pesticides, **454**, 464
"Phishing", 76
Photosynthesis, **465**
Physical abuse, 126, 143-144
Physical costs of crime, 88
Physical health, 400
    alcohol use and, 39-40
    contributing factors of, 397-406
    crime and, 88
    divorce and, 363
    drug use and, 55-56
    environmental problems and, 460-462
    ethnicity and, 242
    gender inequality and, 204-205
    homelessness and, 168, 175
    overview of, 385-389
    poverty and, 242, 175-176
    prostitution and, 149, 142-144
    and quality of life, 392-399
    rape and, 124-126
    unemployment and, 306-307, *307*
    of veterans, 424
    violence and, 110-111, 365
    war and, 421-425
    work and, 303-306, 463
Physical illness, 385
    AIDS, **387-389**
    pattern in American society, 404
Physical punishment, norm of, 113
Physical reactions, 125
Physical threat, 462-464
Physical trauma, 125-126
Physical violence, 362
Pica, **401**
Pimp, **143**, 143-144, 147
Placebo, **52**
Planned obsolescence, 469-470